The Correspondence of Henry Oldenburg

Volume VIII
1671-1672

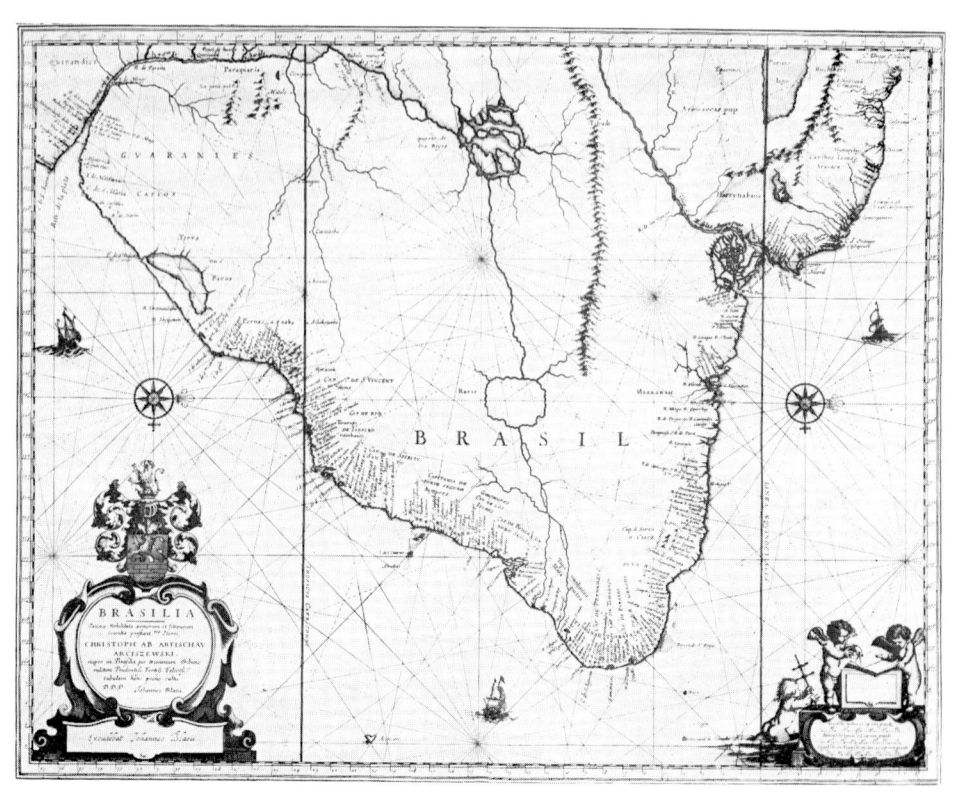

Map of Brazil
From Joan Blaeu, Atlas maior, sive cosmographis Blauiana
(Amsterdam, 1662), Vol. XII
See Letter 1780a

The
Correspondence
of
Henry Oldenburg

Edited and Translated by
A. RUPERT HALL & MARIE BOAS HALL

Volume VIII
1671-1672

The University of Wisconsin Press

Madison, Milwaukee, and London 1971

Published 1971
The University of Wisconsin Press
Box 1379, Madison, Wisconsin 53701
The University of Wisconsin Press, Ltd.
27-29 Whitfield Street, London, W. 1
Copyright © 1971
The Regents of the University of Wisconsin
All rights reserved
First Printing
Printed in the Netherlands
Koninklijke Drukkerij G. J. Thieme N.V., Nijmegen
ISBN 0-299-05950-2; LC 65-11201

Contents

List of Plates, xiii
Preface, xv
List of Abbreviated Titles, xvii
Introduction, xix

THE CORRESPONDENCE

1683	Hevelius to Oldenburg, 21 April 1671	3
1683a	Summary of Tables	8
1684	Willughby to Oldenburg, 21 April 1671	9
1685	Oldenburg to Leibniz, 24 April 1671	10
1686	Selbie to Oldenburg, 28 April 1671	13
1687	Oldenburg to Sluse, 28 April 1671	15
1688	Leibniz to Oldenburg, 29 April 1671	22
1689	Werden to Oldenburg, 29 April 1671	30
1690	Oldenburg to Willughby, 29 April 1671	32
1691	Helmfeld to Oldenburg, 3 May 1671	33
1692	Wallis to Oldenburg, 9 May 1671	36
1693	Oldenburg to Wallis, 9 May 1671	36
1694	Kisner to Oldenburg, 12 May 1671	36
1695	Dodington to Oldenburg, 12 May 1671	42
1696	Lister to Oldenburg, 28 April and 13 May 1671	43
1697	Flamsteed to Oldenburg, 13 May 1671	45
1698	Sylvius to Oldenburg, 13 May 1671	48
1699	Wallis to Oldenburg, 13 May 1671	50
1700	Beale to Oldenburg, 13 May 1671	52
1701	Oldenburg to Willughby, 16 May 1671	56
1702	Oldenburg to Flamsteed, 20 May 1671	57
1703	Lister to Oldenburg, 22 May 1671	57
1704	Oldenburg to Selbie, 24 May 1671	60

1705	Malpighi to Oldenburg, 24 May 1671	60
1706	Dodington to Oldenburg, 25 May 1671	62
1707	Oldenburg to Lister, 27 May 1671	63
1708	Flamsteed to Oldenburg, 29 May 1671	65
1709	Oldenburg to Hevelius, 29 May 1671	67
1710	Oldenburg to Kirkby, 29 May 1671	69
1711	Lister to Oldenburg, 30 May 1671	69
1712	Lister to Oldenburg, 31 May 1671	71
1713	Wallis to Oldenburg, 2 June 1671	72
1714	Bell to Oldenburg, 3 June 1671	74
1715	Oldenburg to Ray, 3 June 1671	75
1716	Leibniz to Oldenburg, 8 June 1671	76
1717	Sylvius to Oldenburg, 8 June 1671	83
1718	Hevelius to Oldenburg, 9 June 1671	85
1719	Wallis to Oldenburg, 10 June 1671	88
1720	Oldenburg to Lister, 10 June 1671	89
1721	Leibniz to Oldenburg, 10 June 1671	91
1722	Beale to Oldenburg, c. 12 June 1671	92
1723	Oldenburg to Hevelius, 12 June 1671	97
1724	Oldenburg to Leibniz, 12 June 1671	99
1725	Oldenburg to Dodington, 12 June 1671	105
1726	Lister to Oldenburg, 14 June 1671	105
1727	Sachs to Oldenburg, 16 June 1671	107
1728	Beale to Oldenburg, c. 16 June 1671	111
1729	De Graaf to Oldenburg, 19 June 1671	114
1730	Oldenburg to Beale, 20 June 1671	116
1731	Oldenburg to Lister, 24 June 1671	116
1732	Werden to Oldenburg, 24 June 1671	117
1733	Beale to Oldenburg, 24 June 1671	119
1734	Oldenburg to Beale, 27 June 1671	126
1735	Oldenburg to Bernard, 27 June 1671	126
1736	Wallis to Oldenburg, 27 June 1671	128
1737	Oldenburg to Beale, 1 July 1671	132
1738	Ray to Oldenburg, 3 July 1671	132
1739	Fermat to Oldenburg, 4 July 1671	134
1740	Flamsteed to Oldenburg, 4 July 1671	136
1741	Lister to Oldenburg, 5 July 1671	137
1742	Oldenburg to Sylvius, 5 July 1671	138
1743	Beale to Oldenburg, 8 July 1671	139

1744	Pardies to Oldenburg, 8 July 1671	143
1745	Sluse to Oldenburg, 8 July 1671	145
1745a	Contents of the *Antoniana Margarita*	151
1746	Willughby to Oldenburg, 10 July 1671	153
1747	Hill to Oldenburg, 13 July 1671	155
1748	Oldenburg to Lister, 13 July 1671	156
1749	Oldenburg to Willlughby, 13 July 1671	158
1750	Páll Björnsson to Oldenburg, 13 July 1671	158
1751	Lister to Oldenburg, 17 July 1671	163
1752	Oldenburg to Huygens, 22 July 1671	167
1753	Oldenburg to Werden, 24 July 1671	172
1754	Oldenburg to Kisner, 24 July 1671	172
1755	Vogel to Oldenburg, 25 July 1671	173
1756	Oldenburg to Beale, 25 July 1671	176
1757	Oldenburg to Lister, 27 July 1671	176
1758	Oldenburg to Willughby, 27 July 1671	178
1759	Oldenburg to Wallis, 1 August 1671	179
1760	Flamsteed to Oldenburg, 1 August 1671	179
1761	Wallis to Oldenburg, 4 August 1671	181
1762	Oldenburg to Leibniz, 5 August 1671	182
1763	Oldenburg to Wallis, 5 August 1671	184
1764	Beale to Oldenburg, 6 August 1671	186
1765	Oldenburg to Fermat, 7 August 1671	190
1766	Oldenburg to Flamsteed, 8 August 1671	190
1767	Oldenburg to Pardies, 10 August 1671	191
1768	Oldenburg to Wallis, 10 August 1671	193
1769	Cassini to Oldenburg, 10 August 1671	193
1770	Wallis to Oldenburg, 10 August 1671	195
1771	Vogel to Oldenburg, 11 August 1671	198
1772	Wallis to Oldenburg, 13 August 1671	202
1773	Oldenburg to Wallis, 15 August 1671	204
1774	Sylvius to Oldenburg, 15 August 1671	205
1775	Wallis to Oldenburg, 16 August 1671	205
1776	Flamsteed to Oldenburg, 23 August 1671	207
1777	Willughby to Oldenburg, 24 August 1671	209
1778	Lister to Oldenburg, 25 August 1671	212
1779	Oldenburg to Cassini, 26 August 1671	216
1780	Oldenburg to Hill, ?30 August 1671	220
1780a	Inquiries for Brazil	220

1781	Oldenburg to Ray, 31 August 1671	251
1782	Oldenburg to Willughby, 31 August 1671	252
1783	Oldenburg to Vogel, 1 September 1671	252
1784	Beale to Oldenburg, 2 September 1671	253
1785	Oldenburg to Lister, 4 September 1671	257
1786	Ray to Oldenburg, 12 September 1671	258
1787	Lister to Oldenburg, 13 September 1671	263
1788	Oldenburg to Beale, 14 September 1671	265
1789	Winthrop to Oldenburg, September 1671?	265
1790	Kirkby to Oldenburg, 16 September 1671	268
1791	Flamsteed to Oldenburg, late September 1671	268
1792	Hevelius to Oldenburg, 27 September 1671	271
1792a	Astronomical Observations	275
1793	Oldenburg to Leibniz, 28 September 1671	277
1794	Pardies to Oldenburg, 10 October 1671	281
1795	Oldenburg to Ray, 11 October 1671	286
1796	Oldenburg to Willughby, 11 October 1671	288
1797	Oldenburg to Lister, 12 October 1671	289
1798	Oldenburg to Huygens, 14 October 1671	291
1799	Leibniz to Oldenburg, 15 October 1671	292
1800	Lister to Oldenburg, 16 October 1671	300
1801	Oldenburg to De Graaf, 16 October 1671	303
1802	Becher to Oldenburg, 16 October 1671	303
1803	W. Winthrop to Oldenburg, 17 October 1671	305
1804	Oldenburg to Lister, 21 October 1671	306
1805	Malpighi to Oldenburg, 22 October 1671	308
1806	Thevenot to Oldenburg, 28 October 1671	310
1807	Huygens to Oldenburg, 28 October 1671	313
1808	Lister to Oldenburg, 28 October 1671	317
1809	Sachs to Oldenburg, 29 October 1671	321
1810	Le Bourgeois to Oldenburg, 31 October 1671	325
1811	Vogel to Oldenburg, 1 November 1671	330
1811a	Sivers' Observations	335
1812	Oldenburg to Borelli, 2 November 1671	337
1813	Oldenburg to Wallis, 4 November 1671	339
1814	Oldenburg to Lister, 4 November 1671	339
1815	Wallis to Oldenburg, 6 November 1671	341
1816	Tenison to Oldenburg, 7 November 1671	344
1817	Oldenburg to Hevelius, 9 November 1671	349

1818	Oldenburg to Wallis, 11 November 1671	354
1819	Lister to Oldenburg, 11 November 1671	354
1820	Oldenburg to Le Bourgeois, 11 November 1671	355
1821	Oldenburg to Vogel, 14 November 1671	356
1822	Oldenburg to Dodington, 14 November 1671	358
1823	Helmfeld to Oldenburg, 15 November 1671	359
1824	Flamsteed to Oldenburg, 15 November 1671	361
1825	Oldenburg to Lister, 18 November 1671	364
1826	Flamsteed to Oldenburg, 21 November 1671	365
1827	Oldenburg to Sluse, 21 November 1671	368
1828	Wallis to Oldenburg, 23 November 1671	372
1829	Hjärne to Oldenburg, 23 November 1671	373
1830	Vernon to Oldenburg, 23 November 1671	383
1831	Oldenburg to Flamsteed, 25 November 1671	387
1832	Oldenburg to Wallis, 26 November 1671	387
1833	Wallis to Oldenburg, 27 November 1671	387
1834	Winthrop to Oldenburg, 28 November 1671	389
1835	Flamsteed to Oldenburg, 2 December 1671	390
1836	Oldenburg to Vernon, 4 December 1671	392
1837	Oldenburg to Wallis, 5 December 1671	393
1838	Kirkby to Oldenburg, 9 December 1671	393
1839	Witsen to Oldenburg, 10 December 1671	396
1840	Oldenburg to Vernon, 11 December 1671	397
1841	Oldenburg to Flamsteed, 12 December 1671	398
1842	Oldenburg to Malpighi, 14 December 1671	398
1843	Sluse to Oldenburg, 17 December 1671	401
1844	Oldenburg to Pardies, 18 December 1671	412
1845	Oldenburg to Sachs, 22 December 1671	417
1846	Fermat to Oldenburg, 22 December 1671	420
1847	Oldenburg to Dodington, 22 December 1671	422
1848	Cassini to Oldenburg, 22 December 1671	423
1849	Flamsteed to Oldenburg, 23 December 1671	427
1850	Oldenburg to Lister, 23 December 1671	428
1851	Oldenburg to Tenison, 23 December 1671	430
1852	Oldenburg to Vogel, 26 December 1671	430
1853	Vernon to Oldenburg, 27 December 1671	431
1854	Vernon to Oldenburg, 30 December 1671	431
1854a	Cassini's Discovery of Japet	439
1855	Oldenburg to Wallis, 30 December 1671	443

1856	Oldenburg to Huygens, 1 January 1671/2	443
1857	Oldenburg to Newton, 2 January 1671/2	447
1858	Hannemann to Oldenburg, 3 January 1671/2	448
1859	Pardies to Oldenburg, 3 January 1671/2	451
1860	Dodington to Oldenburg, 5 January 1671/2	461
1861	Newton to Oldenburg, 6 January 1671/2	461
1862	Oldenburg to Wallis, 9 January 1671/2	462
1863	Lister to Oldenburg, 10 January 1671/2	462
1864	Oldenburg to Kirkby, 12 January 1671/2	466
1865	Wallis to Oldenburg, 14 January 1671/2	466
1866	Oldenburg to Huygens, 15 January 1671/2	468
1866a	Newton's Telescope	470
1867	Oldenburg to Ott, 15 January 1671/2	474
1868	Oldenburg to Cassini, 15 January 1671/2	475
1869	Oldenburg to Wallis, 16 January 1671/2	478
1870	Vernon to Oldenburg, 17 January 1671/2	478
1871	Newton to Oldenburg, 18 January 1671/2	482
1872	Wallis to Oldenburg, 18 January 1671/2	482
1873	Wallis to Oldenburg, 18 January 1671/2	484
1874	Oldenburg to Dodington, 18 January 1671/2	490
1875	Oldenburg to Malpighi, 18 January 1671/2	491
1876	Dodington to Oldenburg, 19 January 1671/2	493
1876a	Cornelio to Dodington, 9 January 1671/2	494
1877	Vernon to Oldenburg, 20 January 1671/2	497
1878	Oldenburg to Newton, 20 January 1671/2	502
1879	Malpighi to Oldenburg, 22 January 1671/2	503
1880	Oldenburg to Lister, 24 January 1671/2	505
1881	Oldenburg to Fermat, 25 January 1671/2	506
1882	Oldenburg to Newton, 27 January 1671/2	508
1883	Newton to Oldenburg, 29 January 1671/2	509
1884	Oldenburg to Pardies, 29 January 1671/2	509
1885	Vogel to Oldenburg, 31 January 1671/2	512
1886	Huygens to Oldenburg, 3 February 1671/2	517
1887	Bernard to Oldenburg, 4 February 1671/2	523
1888	Flamsteed to Oldenburg, 5 February 1671/2	524
1889	Wallis to Oldenburg, 5 February 1671/2	527
1890	Oldenburg to Bernard, 6 February 1671/2	527
1891	Newton to Oldenburg, 6 February 1671/2	528
1892	Oldenburg to Newton 8 February 1671/2	528

1893	Oldenburg to Cornelio, 9 February 1671/2	529
1894	Oldenburg to Dodington, 9 February 1671/2	532
1895	Flamsteed to Oldenburg, 10 February 1671/2	532
1896	Newton to Oldenburg, 10 February 1671/2	533
1897	Oldenburg to Lister, 10 February 1671/2	534
1898	Kirkby to Oldenburg, 10 February 1671/2	535
1899	Oldenburg to Huygens, 12 February 1671/2	536
1900	Oldenburg to Toinard, 15 February 1671/2	538
1901	Oldenburg to Flamsteed, 16 February 1671/2	541
1902	Dodington to Oldenburg, 16 February 1671/2	541
1903	Oldenburg to Newton, 17 or 19 February 1671/2	543
1904	Newton to Oldenburg, 20 February 1671/2	544
1905	Hill to Oldenburg, 20 February 1671/2	544
1906	Collins to Oldenburg, *c.* 20 February 1671/2	545
1907	Oldenburg to Bartholin, 22 February 1671/2	548
1908	Oldenburg to Malpighi, 22 February 1671/2	551
1909	Oldenburg to Dodington, 23 February 1671/2	555
1910	Lister to Oldenburg, 24 February 1671/2	555
1911	Cornelio to Oldenburg, 24 February 1671/2	558
1911a	Cornelio to Dodington, 24 February 1671/2	561
1912	Oldenburg to Dodington, 26 February 1671/2	565
1913	Oldenburg to Lister, 27 February 1671/2	566
1914	Vernon to Oldenburg, 27 February 1671/2	567
1915	Hevelius to Oldenburg, 28 February 1671/2	568
1916	Oldenburg to Sluse, 4 March 1671/2	571
1917	Malpighi to Oldenburg, 5 March 1671/2	577
1918	Flamsteed to Oldenburg, 8 March 1671/2	580
1919	Dodington to Oldenburg, 8 March 1671/2	582
1920	Oldenburg to Huygens, 11 March 1671/2	584
1921	Grew to Oldenburg, 12 March 1671/2	586
1922	Oldenburg to Newton, 16 March 1671/2	590
1923	Newton to Oldenburg, 16 March 1671/2	591
1924	Oldenburg to Hevelius, 18 March 1671/2	591
1925	Oldenburg to Winthrop, 18 March 1671/2	594
1926	Oldenburg to Kirkby, 18 March 1671/2	596
1927	Mauritius to Oldenburg, 19 March 1671/2	596
1927a	The Comet of March 1671/2	600
1928	Newton to Oldenburg, 19 March 1671/2	604
1929	Lister to Oldenburg, 19 March 1671/2	604

1930	Dodington to Oldenburg, 21 March 1671/2	606
1931	De Graaf to Oldenburg, 21 March 1671/2	610
1932	Mauritius to Oldenburg, 22 March 1671/2	612
1933	Oldenburg to Newton, 23 March 1671/2	612
1934	Oldenburg to Vogel, 23 March 1671/2	613
1935	Oldenburg to Sivers, 23 March 1671/2	614
1936	Malpighi to Oldenburg, 26 March 1672	614
1937	Newton to Oldenburg, 26 March 1672	617
1938	Swammerdam to Oldenburg, 26 March 1672	617
1939	Oldenburg to Newton, *c.* 26 March 1672	619
1940	Charas to Oldenburg, 28 March 1672	619
1941	Newton to Oldenburg, 30 March 1672	626
1942	Pardies to Oldenburg, 30 March 1672	626
1943	Charas to Oldenburg, 30 March 1672	629
1944	Huygens to Oldenburg, 30 March 1672	635

Index, 639

List of Plates

Map of Brazil
frontispiece

following page 276

PLATE I
Portrait of Sylvius

PLATE II
Picard's Quadrant

Preface

With this volume we reach the beginning of the dramatic period of Isaac Newton's first contacts with the Royal Society, contacts highly fruitful for the development of optics. Since Newton's letters and Oldenburg's replies have been so recently printed in *The Correspondence of Isaac Newton* we have not thought it necessary to reprint them in their entirety here. Instead we have, while giving them their proper numbers in the sequence of Oldenburg's correspondence, merely given short summaries, with editorial comment. We have in all cases indicated where they may be found printed, and from what source; occasionally, where Oldenburg's memorandum only survives, we have printed this in full, since the editors of Newton's correspondence did not customarily assign letter numbers to such memoranda.

We have, as always, continued to retain idiosyncracies of spelling and style. In the case of the most egregious eccentric in this respect—John Flamsteed—we have a number of contemporary emendations by Oldenburg, who frequently supplied words unconsciously omitted by Flamsteed as he wrote in haste. We have generally included these in square brackets.

We have to thank the Babson Institute of Wellesley, Massachusetts, for permission to print Letter 1924, and for supplying a photostat of the original. We are most grateful to the owner of the manuscripts of Letters 1807 and 1846 for similar courtesy.

With our eighth volume we find ourselves no less indebted than before to the many friends and colleagues who have so kindly and patiently answered our interminable questions and lightened our ignorance.

We wish especially to thank Mrs. Gunnel Ingham, Dr. John B. Blake of the National Library of Medicine, Bethesda, Maryland, Mr. E. J. Freeman of the Wellcome Historical Library, London, and Docent Wolfram Kock of the Medicinhistoriska Museet, Stockholm, all of whom helped us on medical matters; Dr. A. L. Peck of Christ's College, Cambridge, Dr. Helen Wallis and Miss Sarah Jeacock of the British Museum Map

Room, Dr. W. P. Stearn of the British Museum for Natural History, Professor Koenraad W. Smart of University College, London, Viscount Parker, Mr. Albert Van Helden, and Mrs. A. L. Davis. We are once again indebted to our patient secretary, Mrs. K. H. Fraser. And as always, we gratefully acknowledge our greatest debt, that to the President and Council of the Royal Society and to their Librarian, Mr. I. Kaye, and his assistants; notably the Council has generously provided grants financing assistance in the transcription of letters for subsequent volumes.

A. RUPERT HALL
MARIE BOAS HALL

Imperial College
April 1970

Abbreviated Titles

Adelmann
Howard B. Adelmann, *Marcello Malpighi and the Evolution of Embryology*. 5 vols. Ithaca, N.Y., 1966.

Baily
Francis Baily, *An Account of the Revd. John Flamsteed*. London, 1835.

Birch, *Boyle*
Thomas Birch (ed.), *The Life and Works of the Honourable Robert Boyle*, 2nd ed. 6 vols. London, 1772.

Birch, *History*
Thomas Birch, *The History of the Royal Society*. 4 vols. London, 1756–57.

B.M.
British Museum.

BN
Bibliothèque Nationale, Paris (Lat. = Fonds Latin; Fr. = Fonds Français; N.a.L. = Nouvelles acquisitions Latines; N.a.f. = Nouvelles acquisitions françaises).

Bologna
Biblioteca Universitaria di Bologna.

Boncompagni
Bullettino de Bibliografia et di Storia delle Scienze Matematiche e Fisiche, pubblicato di B. Boncompagni, Vol. XVII. Rome, 1884.

CUL MS. Add.
Cambridge University Library, Additional Manuscript.

Denis, *Mémoires*
Jean Denis (ed.), *Mémoires concernant les Arts & les Sciences*. Paris, 1672.

Gerhardt
C. J. Gerhardt (ed.), *Der Briefwechsel von Gottfried Wilhelm Leibniz mit Mathematikern*, I. Berlin, 1899.

Grew, *Musaeum*
Nehemiah Grew, *Musaeum Regalis Societatis. Or A Catalogue & Description of the Natural and Artificial Rarities belonging to the Royal Society and preserved at Gresham College*. London, 1681.

Hannover MSS.
Leibniz Briefe 695 in the Königliche Bibliothek, Hannover, Germany.

Leiden
The Library at the Rijksuniversiteit, Leiden.

MHS (1878)
Massachusetts Historical Society, *Proceedings*, XVI (1878).

Newton, *Correspondence*
H. W. Turnbull *et al.* (eds.), *The Correspondence of Isaac Newton*. Cambridge, 1959——.

Observatoire
Volumes VI to XII of the bound correspondence of Hevelius, preserved in the library of the Observatoire de Paris. These letters are numbered, not foliated.

Œuvres Complètes
Christiaan Huygens, *Œuvres Complètes*. The Hague, 1888–1950.

Opera omnia
Marcello Malpighi, *Opera omnia*. 2 vols. London, 1686.

Phil. Trans.
Henry Oldenburg (ed.,) *Philosophical Transactions: giving some Accompt of the present Undertakings, Studies and Labours of the Ingenious in many considerable parts of the World*. London and Oxford, 1665–77.

Rigaud
[Stephen Jordan Rigaud], *Correspondence of Scientific Men of the Seventeenth Century ... in the Collection of ... the Earl of Macclesfield*. 2 vols. Oxford, 1851.

Turnbull, *Gregory*
H. W. Turnbull, *James Gregory Tercentenary Memorial Volume*. London, 1939.

Winthrop Papers
Papers of the Winthrop family, preserved by the Massachusetts Historical Society, Boston, Mass.

Introduction

The letters in this volume were written in the period of eleven months from April 1671 to March 1672; its close coincides with the outbreak of the Third Dutch War, an event inevitably disruptive to the flow of Oldenburg's correspondence. Of the 261 letters printed here only a small proportion are nonscientific and very few are medical. Natural history becomes one of the dominant themes, represented in the frequent correspondence of Martin Lister and Francis Willughby, in the few letters from John Ray, in the "Inquiries for Brazil," in the account of Iceland, and at a higher level in the letters and communications of Malpighi. There are even reflections of the Royal Society's former keen interest in agriculture. New figures of importance emerge—here are not only Lister, De Graaf, and Malpighi, but Grew and Swammerdam. Microscopy was becoming a specialized science, no longer a magnified entomology as it had largely been even in Hooke's *Micrographia*, and the first fruits of its specialization appear in discoveries sent to the Royal Society, whose importance as a central distributing agency for scientific news was universally recognized, and whose approval was eagerly sought.

Another major interest is astronomy. There are many letters from Flamsteed, whose observing equipment was steadily improving (partly through the kindness of his patrons the Towneleys and that of Jonas Moore) and whose expertise and devotion steadily increased: to the former Oldenburg contributed by the loan of books. Hevelius' activity as a correspondent was less than in previous years, for he was engaged in completing his splendid *Machina Coelestis*. We hear of the Abbé Picard's visit to northern cities on his way to Tycho Brahe's observatory of Uraniborg. His colleague Cassini also appears many times, now the dominant figure in observational astronomy. Huygens was quiet, hardly even yet (it seems) fully recovered from his grave illness; yet, if he long ignored Sluse's rather overextended preoccupation with Alhazen's Problem, when he takes it up it is clear that his powers are undiminished. Among the many astronomical events of these months were further opportunities for the confirmation of Huygens' theory of Saturn's ring, when its plane again passed through the Earth. After some ten or eleven years considerable sunspots were observed once more (this is, of course, the normal period of variations in such solar activity), and studied with attention by Cassini, Picard, Vogel and Sivers in Hamburg, and others. Late in 1671, Cassini discovered a second satellite of Saturn. Then, at the beginning of 1672, a new comet was seen, to be made the occasion of a special pamphlet by Hevelius and the subject of notices sent to Oldenburg from several parts of Europe. In all the activity hinted at here it must be said the English, excepting Flamsteed, played only a small part; through ill luck or negligence they missed most of the excitement. Hence the *Philosophical Transactions* at this time contain an unusually high proportion of material originating abroad.

Equally it would be true to remark that the *Transactions* contributed largely to foreign journals. None of these companions was in a markedly thriving condition. The *Giornale de' Letterati* did not expire, as rumor reported, but its life hung upon Paris and London. The *Journal des Sçavans* was intermittent and feeble, but Jean Denis brought fresh life to French learned journalism with the publication of his *Mémoires concernant les Arts et les Sciences* (often dealing with the same material as the *Journal des Sçavans*) and *Conférences sur les Sciences*. At least these consisted of more than threadbare book reviews. In Germany the *Miscellanea curiosa* had its difficulties, though these seem to have arisen rather from lack of organization than lack of material; yet the material was highly specialized, and far from modern in its character. The death of P. J. Sachs was to break a connection that might have produced more fruit. All these comparisons prove the point that the *Philosophical Transactions* was Europe's preeminent scientific journal; everyone wanted it—preferably a private copy sent direct by post —everyone was gratified to see his own contribution printed in it. The reason for Oldenburg's success as an editor is obvious: he had an immense intelligence network, and was unremitting in its repair and extension. He also had a keen eye for what was important and scientifically interesting, and the epistolary nature of so many of the communications gave them a freshness and urgency often lacking in other journals of the day. And by reviewing books without rancor he established a position of authority which made the *Philosophical Transactions* seem nonpartisan and even Olympian. Not that controversy was totally lacking—Wallis continued to answer in the *Philosophical Transactions* the ill-advised mathematical pretensions of the aged Hobbes, who perhaps indiscreetly presented his work to the Royal Society. But editorially Oldenburg sensibly remained aloof, and often avoided publishing the more acrimonious pages in the controversy.

The names of many new correspondents appear in this volume, though few became regular writers of letters. Oldenburg's fame as Secretary of the Royal Society and the diffusion of the *Philosophical Transactions* (especially with the progress of their translation into Latin, much as Oldenburg had disliked that enterprise) brought him a number of unsolicited letters. Some of the new writers were, like Erich Mauritius and Nicolas Toinard, men whose distinction as scholars has dimly survived to the present day, but who were really outside the new intellectual movements. Others, like the great Swedish intellectual and public figure Urban Hjärne or the obscure French traveler Esaie Le Bourgeois testify in their letters to the attraction exercised by London and the Royal Society upon all who made the literary tour of Europe; the latter's reaction to English society is a more poignant picture than any known to us of a Frenchman's distress in England. (Years before, in his diary of travel, Christiaan Huygens had similarly compared London and Paris to the former's disadvantage.)

The preponderance of these new names is northern: some no doubt came in through Oldenburg's contact with the Academia Curiosorum. Leibniz too brought in some other Germans, notably Johannes Ott, a writer on optics. John Werden at last established a line of communication with Sweden, and gave news of Olaus Rudbeck. Nearer at home and more interesting was Jan Swammerdam, known for some years as an entomologist, but now appearing as an authority on human anatomy; in 1672 he, Theodor Kerckring, and Oldenburg's regular correspondent Regnier De Graaf were all promoting discoveries (or rather pseudodiscoveries) purporting to prove that mammals reproduce by means of eggs. Swammerdam's personal relation to the Royal Society seems to have been effected by Nicolaas Witsen, author of a large and splendid book on ships, who was very probably personally acquainted with Oldenburg.

After Swammerdam the most scientifically notable of the new foreign correspondents was Father Pardies, S.J., whose name is well known to all students of Newton as the most courteous of the critics of Newton's first optical paper—indeed, the only one who ever confessed that Newton had satisfied his objections. In this volume something more of this acute but kindly mathematician appears, and of the beginning of a promising correspondence that was cut short by Pardies's premature death, leaving his big work on mechanics incomplete. Otherwise communications from

Frenchmen in this volume are of slight importance, and the rôle played by Vernon in substituting for them was the more crucial. Vernon not only kept in touch with Huygens and Cassini; he followed all the activity of the Paris Observatory, stimulated Cassini into sending firsthand reports of his chief observations to London, and supplied an elaborate English summary of Picard's *Mesure de la Terre*.

In his attempts to secure information from the more exotic parts of the world Oldenburg met with some promise of success. The merchant Thomas Hill (probably a younger brother of Abraham Hill, a member of the Original Council of the Royal Society who was to be Treasurer from 1679 to 1700), living in Lisbon, was cordial in attempts to secure answers to questions about the natural history of Brazil from the Jesuits there. The inquiries compiled by Oldenburg in Letter 1780a, as well as many other casual allusions, remind us how dependent European science still was for its knowledge of the flora, fauna, diseases, and ethnology of the tropics on the very small number of competent naturalists who had visited those regions, often many decades earlier. This particular exchange will continue in the future.

At last, moreover, Oldenburg received letters from Tommaso Cornelio, whose reputation as the most intelligent and learned naturalist south of Rome had impressed him long before. Cornelio gave a typical (but not wholly welcome) counterblast to superstition. He was a close friend of Malpighi's, but Dodington at Venice—soon, unfortunately, to be recalled to London—was better placed for serving as a postal intermediary. As for Malpighi himself, though little enough of a personal nature emerges in this volume other than his deep sense of loyalty and obligation towards the Royal Society, this was the period in which two of his greatest works were sent to London: his first study of the anatomy of plants (sent without illustrative figures, and therefore held back from publication by Oldenburg) and his earliest series of observations on the developing chick, which were immediately given to the printer, the Royal Society particularly charging Oldenburg to see that the engraving of the figures was effected in the most accurate way; thanks to modern techniques and the devotion of Howard B. Adelmann these may now be examined in faithful facsimile.

It is a curious fruit of Malpighi's sense of obligation that he was able to obtain from a printer in Bologna what were, presumably, proof copies of some early papers by Cassini, written before he left that city, and send them to London where now (in the British Museum Library) they remain as possibly unique examples of material that was never openly published.

Another young English scientist first appearing here, one whose name must invariably be linked with Malpighi's, is Nehemiah Grew, whose first book on plant anatomy appeared at the end of 1671. Although Oldenburg seems sometimes to have been overzealous in knocking the heads of experts together in order to make the sparks fly—in a way that could produce results, as with Huygens' final and highly elegant solution of Alhazen's Problem (Letter 1944)—in this instance he was equally anxious not to discourage Malpighi nor to offend the English enthusiasts (Grew and Lister) by setting up a foreign rival against them. In fact, of course, the investigations of Grew and Malpighi were not only totally independent but just about as disparate as they could well be. One can only suppose that Oldenburg's initial extreme vagueness about the English botanist and the hesitation in his despatch of a copy of *The Anatomy of Vegetables Begun* sprang from an excess of tact. Perhaps he already knew that Malpighi was by no means of an insensitive or phlegmatic temper.

Among the new correspondents in this volume Isaac Newton's name is inevitably outstanding. Oldenburg had known of his mathematical abilities for several years. It almost seems as though he was content to leave Newton's genius to the care of Barrow and Collins so long as he understood it to be exclusively directed to pure mathematics and mathematical optics, but as soon as he knew that Newton had made an important discovery in practical optics Oldenburg became eager to pursue a correspondence with him directly and while giving notice of his discovery abroad at the same time protect his priority. (There could be no more obvious refutation of the charge sometimes levied against Oldenburg's conduct of the Society's correspondence, that he clandestinely imparted English discoveries for foreigners to claim as their own.) However, Oldenburg apparently had no direct part in the bringing of Newton's reflecting telescope to London, nor in his election to the Royal Society, which was proposed by Seth Ward.

As we point out in notes later, the story behind this submission of the new telescope to inspection by the Royal Society is irretrievably lost. There is good reason to suppose that Newton abandoned his "glassworks" and constructed his first reflector in 1669. No one knew of this at the time. In the summer or autumn of 1671 (neither the time nor the motives of his action are known) Newton made a second instrument, a little larger than the first, and this obviously he showed to his friends in Cambridge, possibly to Barrow, certainly to Thomas Gale, Professor of Greek and like Newton a Fellow of Trinity College. It was perhaps Gale who was responsible for spreading the news abroad. The intriguing possibility exists that interest in Newton's invention was strongly stimulated by Letter 1799 from Leibniz, which reached Oldenburg at about the critical point in time—that is, before 16 November 1671. In it Leibniz wrote of his "universal lenses" and catadioptrical telescope, where a curved mirror is plainly hinted at. Although there is no record that this letter was read at a meeting of the Royal Society (despite evidence that Oldenburg intended to do just this), it is hard to believe he would have suppressed all mention of this optical news when (as so many letters in this volume prove) there was a good deal of interest in optics in England following on the publication of Barrow's *Lectiones opticae*. If Leibniz's words came to anyone who knew of Newton's telescope they would be certain to draw attention to its existence, and from that knowledge to the suggestion of actually examining it in London was only a small step. At any rate, news of Newton's success was getting about by mid-December, and during the holiday while the Royal Society was in recess—so urgent did the matter seem—the reflecting telescope was tried out at Whitehall and elsewhere.

That it was not immediately brought to perfection has always been a problem on which the letters in this volume shed some further light; after all, through the labors of Hadley, Short, Herschel, and Parsons the speculum-metal reflector became in the eighteenth century and later one of the great instruments of astronomical discovery. Why was it neglected for a couple of generations immediately following Newton's miniature success? It may be that at this time (before the ultimate limits of the long refractor had yet been reached) the theoretical advantages of reflection were not conspicuous, while Newton's own instrument, marvel that it was, was too small and crude for actual use (Newton himself always observed with refracting telescopes). The slightly halfhearted attempts of the Royal Society to have instruments constructed of a useful size failed, just as James Gregory's attempts of a similar kind had failed in London ten years before. It was predicted that the alloy would turn out to be too soft and irregular to take a good figure, and so it proved. The loss of light in reflection was overestimated, in relation to the technical advantages of the reflecting instrument that permit it to receive a relatively larger aperture. If these technical advantages had been so overwhelmingly obvious that some Huygens or Burattini had devoted as much labor to the perfection of mirrors as they willingly gave to the improvement of lenses, surely the reflector would soon have surpassed the refractor in practice as well as in theory.

As usual in these later years there is little enough of Oldenburg himself in the following pages. Just before this volume opens (at the beginning of the seventh year of the *Philosophical Transactions* with no. 69) he had published a *Preface* which may contain a genuine personal view of the criticism to which the Royal Society had been subjected, and of which little more was to be heard. Oldenburg's response was directed to scholarly critics, such as may have flourished in the University of Oxford (compare Letters 1865 and 1872), not touching at all on the virulent attacks of Stubbe. To disparage the "New Philosophy" as an innovation, wrote Oldenburg, is an error, since "'tis so old as to have been the Discipline in Paradise," is confirmed by the example of the sages of the East, and justified by the atomism of the Greeks themselves. Can it possibly be wrong in modern atomists to have purged "the Old Atoms of Greece from the Heathenish Errors of Greece"? Nor have the modern philosophers neglected antiquities. Lambecius and Salmasius have already been praised in the *Transactions*, and if only others would study ancient authors "to give us an accurate Accompt of the Temple of Belus, the Gardens of Semiramis, the Bridge over the Euphrates, the Walls and Towers in Babylon and Ninive, and the Obeliskes and other Wonders of the Assyrian Monarchy ... " and much else besides, he would do as good service for learning as John Greaves did with his *Pyramidographia*. In actual study of the visible remains of the ancient world the moderns have not been negligent either, Oldenburg alleged, citing the works of recent travelers and geographers. In general, old knowledge restored is as good as new, or better: "For we are well assured, that Old Wisdom is much to be preferr'd before newer notions environ'd with endless controversies; though at the same time we use the freedom of *trying* all, that we may retain what's true and good."

In the following year (no. 81) Oldenburg returned to the same theme, quoting St. Jerome upon whose lines concerning the [imagined] distant travels of Apollonios "whether he were a magician, as the vulgar said, or a philosopher as the Pythagoreans relate," Oldenburg commented, "we may easily apprehend, what a relish this good Father had for the reputation of Philosophy. And if any do wax pale at the growth of it, they seem to shew thereby, how little they have either of the intelligent Piety of this Holy man, or of Civility of the Gentile Philosophers." It is true, he went on, that as operative philosophy began to tread on the heels of triumphant philology "emergent adventures and great successes were encountred by dangerous oppositions and strong obstructions"; Galileo and others suffered for their celestial discoveries, Sir Walter Raleigh was falsely accused of atheism because of his love of chemistry and other arts, while Gilbert and Harvey were deemed extravagant. But the wiser, mild counsels of Bacon and Peiresc had smoothed the path for science, and the virtues of philosophy prevailed once more in Europe so that their fame reaches even to the Moghuls, as Bernier relates. So sound philosophers may "retain an internal satisfaction among themselves ... each to other sufficient Theaters." If this was hardly denunciation of the narrow, well-trodden path of Scholasticism and praise of the unfettered spirit such as Oldenburg voiced sometimes to his private correspondents, it was not an unfair nor an undignified pronouncement.

Preeminent amoung the English promoters of the true and the good was Robert Boyle, still Oldenburg's best patron though scarcely more than a venerated author in the following pages. One odd document of this time records the close personal relation continuing between the two men:

> A. 1671 in summer I deliver'd to Mr Boyl for ye press ye Latin of ye tracts of Cosmical qualities, Cosmical Suspicions etc.
> Thesame year Dec. 2. I deliver'd to yesame ye Latin version of his 3. Tracts, Of ye Saltnes of ye Sea, ye Intestin Motion, Respiration.
> Received in summer 1671 from Mr Boyle . . . . . 3 lb.
> Febr. 20. 1671/72 received from yesame . . . . . 5 lb
> One parcel of these papers made 13 sheets, wch was reckoned but for 12. wch made 6 lb.
> The other made as many sheets, wch maketh 6 lb more, so yt there rests 4[1]

It is clear that Oldenburg was still engaged in translating Boyle's English prose into Latin, that he was paid by Boyle for this at the rate of ten shillings for each printed sheet, and that in a period of some six months he had earned £12, no mean sum in relation to Oldenburg's total income. He may well have done other literary work of the same sort, besides publishing the *Philosophical Transactions*, of which no evidence remains.

One point should perhaps be made now about Oldenburg's relation to his correspondents that might have been made before. It is easy to observe that Oldenburg often relates to them the interest their communications have awakened in the Society and the profuse thanks they were felt to deserve. These compliments are (to modern taste) sometimes fulsome and may seem meretricious. Any reader turning to the slightly bleak pages of

[1] Royal Society MS. Boyle Letters, III, no. 41. The final number, though correct, may have been altered. The paper is in Oldenburg's hand.

Thomas Birch's *History of the Royal Society*—as we so often do ourselves—will fail to discover such compliments. But they do, in fact, exist in the original Journal Book, recording proceedings at the meeting, from which Birch made his extracts. Quoting from Volume IV, for example:

> 16 November 1671. It was ordered also that the discoverer [Martin Lister] should be thanked from the Society for his generous communications, and his letter, accompanying the same, dated at York November 11. 1671, enter'd.

Compare Letter 1825. And again:

> 1 February 1671/2. [Minute relating to Letter 1849 from Flamsteed] The Author to be thanked, and the letter to be registered. Ordered also that the letters of Mr Vernon [Letters 1854, 1870, 1878] be entred in the Letter-Book, and to thank the Author for them.

If it was reasonable for Birch to omit these compliments and details from his printed compilation, as it obviously was, it would have been equally improper of Oldenburg not to pass them on to his correspondents who took so much trouble on the Society's behalf.

Other more puzzling examples of omission may be discovered complicating the minutiae of the Society's historical record. There are in some instances still extant the Original Minutes—Oldenburg's own rough draft from which the clerk prepared the entry in the Journal Book. In the Original Minutes for 30 November 1671 the following item appears:

> Swammerdami icon[ismus] de uteri ovario, et justelli narratio de experimentis circa eandem rem faciendis a Pecqueto.

That is to say: "Swammerdam's picture of the ovary of the uterus, and Justel's account of the experiments about the same subject to be made by Pecquet." This is a most interesting record, found neither in the Journal Book nor, therefore, in Birch's *History*. It appears from it that Swammerdam's first anatomical plate, dedicated to Nicholas Tulp (see Letter 1938, note 2), was received by the Royal Society, presumably from Justel; we know no more of the incident, Justel's letter is lost, and therefore we could not assign it a place in our series. Indeed, since the entry was not thought worthy of the Journal Book, it is even possible that there is some mistake, though not easy to imagine what it might be. If true, it is merely one more instance, among so many others, of how the presentation of a discovery or theory or printed work to the Royal Society was almost essential to scientific recognition in the early 1670s.

The Correspondence

1683
Hevelius to Oldenburg

21 April 1671

From the original in Royal Society MS. H 2, no. 25
Partly printed in *Phil. Trans.*, no. 73 (17 July 1671), 2197–98

Illustri Viro
Domino Henrico Oldenburgio
Illustrissimae Regiae Societatis Secretario
J. Hevelius Salutem

Literas meas die 4 Martij datas,[1] spero Te bene accepisse, ac etiam desiderio meo, imprimis Illustrissimo et Excellentissimo domino Regni Mareschalli, ratione illius Mycroscopij elaborandi satisfecisse; et ut ut

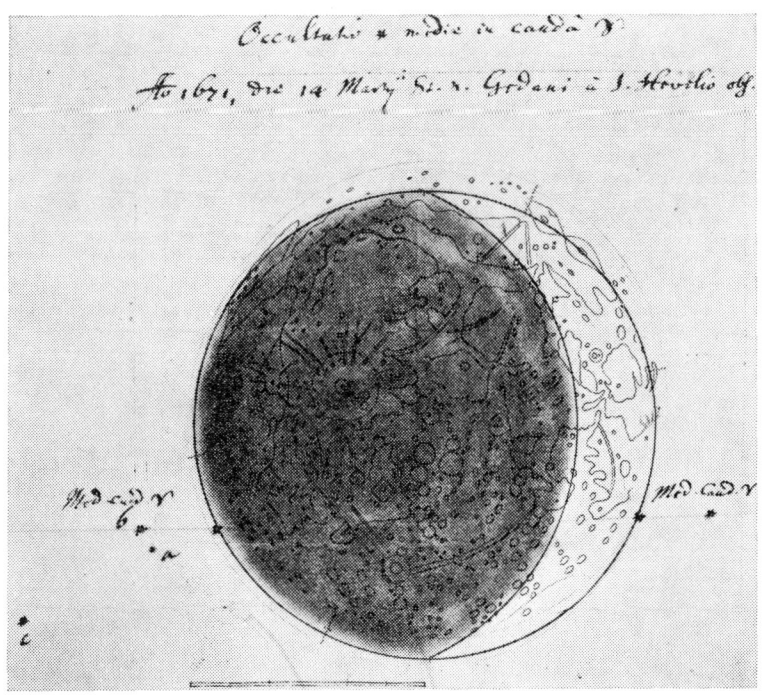

nullum adhuc responsum obtinuerim, minime tamen dubito, quin illud prima occasione mihi transmittas. Pecuniam si qua indigeas, dominus Courbeij Mercator noster per amicum Londini Tibi numerari curabit; prout iam sine dubio intellexisti.² Libros illos cum Ephemeridibus Eruditorum hucusque editis ne etiam obliviscaris (si nondum factum est) transmittere, multis nominibus me Tibi magis magisque obstringes, inprimis si adjicias instrumentum illud, pro mensurandis stellarum diametris, et minoribus distantijs capiendis, a Clarissimo domino Hoockio (quem officiose salutes rogo) promissum.³ Hac vice, ne literae meae prorsus nudae appareant, en Vobis unam atque alteram observationem bene notabilem, quas inter caeteras plurimas nuper habui: cum certus sim Illustrissimae Regiae Societati eas fere haud usque adeo ingratas. Prior est Occultatio duarum Stellularum in Cauda ♈ : *a* Stellula est minutissima globo hactenus nondum adscripta, super mediam in cauda ♈ ; *b* vero est ipsa media in Cauda ♈,⁴ ambae fuerunt a Luna Corniculata tectae, prout ex adiuncto schemate, et observatione ipsa patet [*see figure, p. 3*].⁵ Secunda observatio circa Spicam ♍ per-

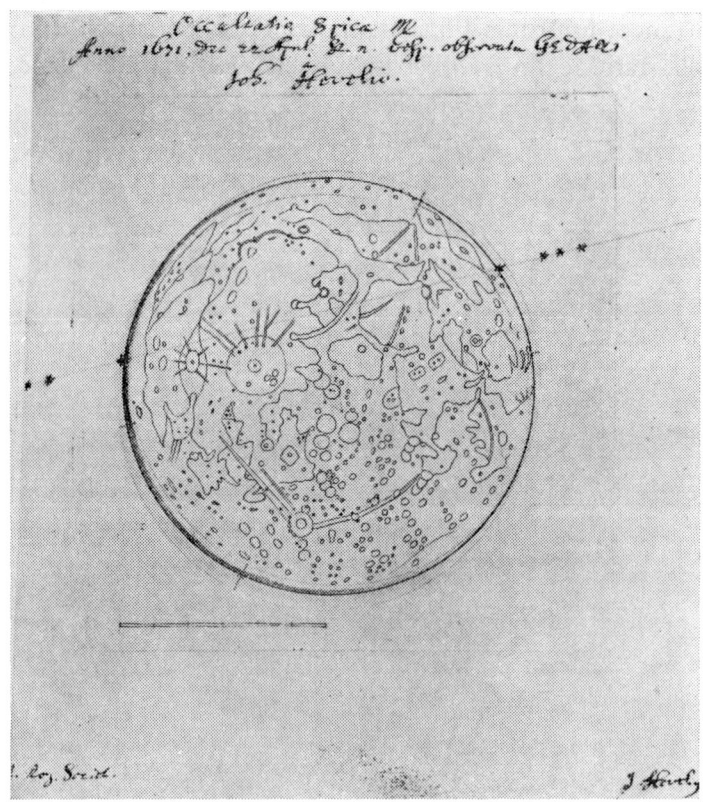

quam notabilis est, eo praeprimis attento, quod Tabulae Rudolphinae hic Gedani nullam occultationem prorsus permittant, et nihilominus Luna plena propemodum, stellam dictam ad 10 fere minuta occultaverit. Quam observationem cum caelo admodum sereno, et ex voto Tubo longissimo impetraverim, volui et hanc Vobis cum eius Schemate communicare. Non dubito quin eandem a Vobis vel alijs peractam mihi pariter non denegetis. De reliquo mearum etiam partium esse duxi Vobis quantocyus significare, me nudius tertius die videlicet 29 Aprilis st. no. novam illam stellam sub capite Cygni, ad viam lacteam, quam anno praeterito a Mense Iunio et Iulio, 14 Octobr. usque conspexi, denuo observasse, et quidem eodem ipso loco, quo tum subsistebat, magnitudine mihi nunc aliquanto major apparet.[6] Quippe excedit Rostrum Cygni et illum in ancone inferioris alae Cygni aequatur fere Pectori Cygni, nisi quod lumino paullo obtusiori et rubicundiori modo luceat.[7] Qua die vero primum rursus illuxerit, affirmare quidem adeo certo non possum. Nam cum fere in ea fuerim opinione, illam vel nunquam, ut plerumque factum est, vel adeo cito non redituram, ad illum locum haud saepius oculos direxi, non fieri potuit, cum hac hyeme, nocturno tempore, circa et infra horizontem Caput Cygni perpetuo haeserit;[8] certus tamen sum ad Mensem decemb., Januar. imo Febr. haud extitisse conspicuum. Nam post 14 Octobr. quo videri desijt, memini me eam saepius quaesivisse eo in loco, sed nusquam apparuisse. Idcirco quantum colligere datur, vix ante initium Martij, imo procul omni dubio adhuc tardius iterum prodijt. Quid Vobis hac de re innotuit, an aliquis eam citius viderit, et qua magnitudine, volupe erit intelligere.[9] Pridie eam a reliquis quibusdam Fixis dimensus sum: distat a Cauda Cygni 20° 55′ 20″, ab ancone alae superioris Cygni 17° 47′ 50″, a Capite vero Serpentarij 39° 19′ 40″, sic ut eodem plane loco adhuc persistat, ubi antea fuerit.[10] De reliquo mihi penitus persuadeo, cum semel, et quidem adeo brevi tempore redierit; illam saepius fore invisibilem, rursusque conspicuam cum incremento et decremento, adinstar illius in collo Ceti.[11] Proinde operae pretium erit cum Philosophiae Peripateticae plurimum intersit scire, an dentur eiusmodi evidenter alterationes in ipso aethere plures? ut imposterum diligentius ad eam attendamus: num aliqua certa hypothesis de eius occasu et ortu, item decremento et incremento comminisci a nobis possit? et an singulis annis, ut illa in Collo Ceti sub adspectum veniat? an certo anni et omni tempori pari ratione? an vero cum retardatione, an anticipatione aliqua certa? et denique an semper aequali magnitudine, simili colore et lumine prodeat, ac permaneat? Ego auxiliante Deo meam operam hac in parte promitto; reliqui Uraniae Cultores quin idem faciant nullus plane dubito. Plura, cum ad binas meas a Vobis responsum, tum desideratum Mycroscopium, librosque promissos obtinuero, quarum rerum ut quantocyus particeps reddar, Te etiam atque etiam rogatum volui. Vale feliciter et quam officiose saluta totam Illustrissimam Regiam nostram Societatem. Dabam Gedani Anno 1671, die 1 Maij st n.

TRANSLATION

J. Hevelius greets the illustrious Mr. Henry Oldenburg, Secretary of the very illustrious Royal Society

I hope that you have safely received my letter of 4 March [N.S.][1] and also have been able to satisfy my desire to have a microscope made for the very illustrious and excellent King's Marshall, and although I have received no word of reply I am sure you will send it me by the first opportunity. If you need money for it, our factor Mr. Courbey will arrange to have it paid to you by a friend in London, as I don't doubt you have gathered already.[2] You will oblige me still more on many counts if you will not forget to send me those books, together with the *Philosophical Transactions* published up to now, especially if you will add that instrument for measuring the diameters of the stars and other small distances promised me by Mr. Hooke (whom I beg you to greet dutifully in my name).[3] On the present occasion, that my letter may not seem wholly barren, here are for you one or two observations well worth noting which I made recently; for I am sure they will be not unwelcome to the Royal Society. The first is an occultation of two starlets in the tail of Aries; the starlet *a* is a very minute one, marked on no globe, about the middle of the tail of Aries; *b* is the central star of the tail.[4] Both were covered by the crescent moon as is shown in the annexed sketch and the observation itself.[5]

<p align="center">Occultation of a star in the middle of the tail of Aries,
observed at Danzig by J. Hevelius, 14 March 1671 N.S.
[<i>For the figure, see page 3</i>]</p>

The second observation is a very remarkable one about Spica Virginis, and is particularly noteworthy because the *Rudolphine Tables* allow absolutely no occultation here at Danzig, and yet all the same the moon, almost full, covered the said star for almost ten minutes. As I carried out this observation in a very clear sky and with a telescope as long as could be desired, I wished to communicate it with its sketch to you. No doubt you will not deny me the same thing as

<p align="center">Occultation of Spica Virginis,
observed at Danzig by Joh. Hevelius, 22 April 1671 N.S.,
in the evening
[<i>For the figure, see page 4</i>]</p>

made by yourselves or others. For the rest, I thought I should let you know as soon as possible that I have again observed the day before yesterday, that is 29 April, N.S., that new star below the head of Cygnus towards the Milky Way which I watched last year from the months of June and July up to the fourteenth of October, almost in the very same place that it occupied then, but appearing to me a little greater in magnitude.[6] Indeed it exceeds the star in the beak of Cygnus and that in the bend of the lower wing, being almost equal to the star in the breast except that it now shines with a duller and ruddier light.[7] As to the day when it first shone, I can say nothing definite. For as I was almost convinced that it would either never return, as is often the case, or not return so quickly, I did not often turn my eyes in that direction; it could not be done, as during this winter the head of Cygnus remained constantly about and below the horizon;[8] yet I am certain that it was not to be observed in the months of December, January, or even February. For after 14 October [N.S.] when I ceased to see it, I remember that I quite often sought for it in that place, without its ever appearing anywhere. For that reason one may gather that it scarcely appeared again before the beginning of March, and one might confidently say later than that. It would be agreeable to know what you have observed of this, and whether anyone saw it earlier, and of what magnitude.[9] On the previous day I measured its distance from the rest of the fixed stars: its distance from the tail of Cygnus is 20° 55′ 20″, from the bend of the upper wing of Cygnus 17° 47′ 50″, from the head of Serpentarius 39° 19′ 40″, so that obviously it still remains in the place where it was before.[10] For the rest, I am quite convinced that as it has returned once and after so short a time-interval, it will often be invisible and visible once more, with an increase and decrease like that of the star in the neck of Cetus.[11] Hence it will be worth while (for it is very important to the Peripatetic philosophy to know whether there are many obvious alterations of this kind in the ether itself) for us to pay careful attention to it in the future: can we devise any firm hypothesis concerning its rising and setting, and its waxing and waning? And will it return to sight in particular years, like that in the neck of Cetus? And in a manner constant for all time with respect to the year? Or with a fixed retardation or anticipation? And lastly will it always appear of the same color and constant magnitude? With God's help I promise my share in this task, and I have no doubt that other lovers of astronomy will do theirs. [I will write] more, when I have received an answer from yourself, as well as the microscope I desired; all of which I beg you again and again to let me have as soon as possible. Farewell, with all good wishes, and greet the whole of our Royal Society very dutifully in my name. Danzig, 1 May 1671, N.S.

NOTES

1 Vol. VII, Letter 1637 of 22 February.
2 Ten pounds had been paid to Oldenburg by Kirkby; see Vol. VII, Letter 1664.

3 For this stellar micrometer, see Vol. V, pp. 187, 355.
4 As Oldenburg pointed out when reading Hevelius' letter to the Royal Society on 11 May 1671, this and the following occultation had been predicted by Flamsteed in *Phil. Trans.*, no. 66 (12 December 1670), 2030, sent to Hevelius with Letter 1599 (Vol. VII). The star b is δ Arietis, a is probably no. 53 in Flamsteed's catalogue.
5 The original figure is now in Royal Society Letter Book IV, p. 295, whence we have reproduced it. Hevelius gave the details of the observations in an enclosure, Letter 1683a.
6 See Vol. VII, Letters 1509 and 1536.
7 The stars are β, ε, and γ Cygni, of magnitudes three, two and a half, and two.
8 The head of Cygnus is only slightly north of the Tropic of Cancer.
9 Oldenburg was to follow the extract of this letter in *Phil. Trans.*, no. 73 (17 July 1671) with an English quotation from the *Journal des Sçavans* of 22 June 1671 [N.S.], where an account was given of observations upon this variable star made by Anthelme Voituret (its first discoverer; see Vol. VII, Letter 1474) and Jean Picard.
10 Unfortunately, Hevelius had not given these distances before, so comparison is impossible. The stars are α and β Cygni and (probably) β Draconis.
11 That is, Mira Ceti, first observed as a new star by Fabricius in 1596, a long-period variable star.

1683a

Summary of Tables

Enclosure with Letter 1683
From the original in Royal Society MS. H 2, no. 25

Occultatio duarum stellarum in Cauda Arietis Gedani, Anno 1671 die 14 Martij st. n. observata a Johanni Hevelio

. . . .

Occultatio Spicae Verginis Anno 1671 die 22 Aprilis st. n. vesperi observata Johanni Hevelio

. . . .

TRANSLATION

An occultation [by the Moon] of two stars in the tail of Aries observed at Danzig by Johannes Hevelius on 14 March 1671, N.S.

[The occultation began at 8h. 10′, and ended at 10h. 0′.]

An occultation of Spica Virginis [by the Moon] on 22 April 1671, N.S., in the evening, observed by Johannes Hevelius.

[The occultation began at 10h. 45′ and ended at 11h. 55′ 30″. Spica occulted at 117° from the Moon's vertical point, and emerged at 23° from the same.]

NOTE

It seemed sufficient here to summarize the important data given by Hevelius in tabular form. As with other observations of this period, Hevelius himself published a full account of both in *Machina coelestis*, Vol. II (Danzig, 1679), pp. 550, 558–59, and figure *KK*.

1684
Willughby to Oldenburg
21 April 1671

From the original in Royal Society MS. W 3, no. 43

Middleton
Aprill 21th

Sr

Yours of Aprill 18th iust now came to my hands: but that you speake of, of Ap. 4th[1] I never received.

Wee are much beholden to mr Lister For his ingenuous agreement with us in our experiments and to your selfe for your kind communicating of it.[2] the Word, bleed, is to bee repeated out of the Former part of the Period you transcribed: if you thinke the sence not clear enough insert it as you please.

Wee must adde further to prevent all mistakes, that in a verie sharp Frost the bleeding is stopped till the weather begins to change: but in a moderate Frost though it stops in the night, yet in the day time if the sun shines out, the Trees will bleed though the Frost continue. Wee doe not find anie thing contrarie in the pages you referre us to, to what wee now assert. there wee say, that cold did not promote but rather hinder bleeding, which wee find holds true if the cold be without Frost. since my last wee have made tryall upon Wallnut and Sycamore as to the Transmitting of water, and Find, that the water runs thorough both; but nothing so fast as thorough Birch.

I am Sr
your Faithfull servant
Francis Willughby

I hope you will pardon my great Hast beeing loth to loose the very first opportunitie of answering what you desired.

ADDRESS

For Mr Henry
Oldenburg Secretary
to the Royall Society
at his house in the
palmell / London

POSTMARK AP 24

NOTES

Reply to Letter 1681 in Vol. VII.
1 Letter 1667 (Vol. VII).
2 See Letter 1656 (Vol. VII).

1685
Oldenburg to Leibniz
24 April 1671

From the original in Hannover MSS., f. 7
Printed in Gerhardt, p. 55

Nobilissimo et Amplissimo Viro
Domino Gothofredo Gulielmo Leibnitzio, J.U.D.
et Consiliario Moguntino dignissimo
Henr. Oldenburg Salutem

Paucis abhinc diebus[1] per Tabellionem ordinarium de plurimis rebus Philosophicis, nec non de Hypothesi tua Physica ad Te scripsi; inprimis vero ursi, ut partem ejus secundam de Abstractis Motus regulis[2] quantocius, ad majorem totius rei lucem, huc transmittas. Spero, literas illas rite Tibi fuisse traditas. Iam quod scribam aliud non suppetit, nisi ut significem, me per Bibliopolam nostratem Martinum, et per Schultzium Hamburgensem, ad Zunnerum Francofurtensem libros a Te desideratos, quos quidem eorum concessu potui, transmisisse, nempe

	lib. sterl.	shil.	d.
Phil. Transact. annorum 68, 69, 70	1 -	0 -	0
Lexicon Bluntij[3]	0 -	4 -	6
Boylius de Rarefactione Aeris[4]	0 -	0 -	6
Boilius Tractatus aliquot de qual. Cosmicis etc.[5]	0 -	1 -	8
Glanvils Plus Ultra[6]	0 -	1 -	6
Mercur. librarius[7]	0 -	1 -	6
Summ.	1 -	10 -	8[8]

Persuasissimum habeo, Te Curaturum, ut Zunnerus Schultzio de precio satisfaciat, ut Schultzius deinde possit satisfacere Martino; absque quo si fuerit, difficilis erit imposterum Martinus noster in consimili occasione. Vale, et a Tui observatissimo plurimum salve.

Dabam Londini d. 24. April 1671.

Deinceps Schultzius Amplitudini Tuae suppeditabit omnes hujusmodi libros, in Anglia impressos: Noster enim Martinus cum eo rem habet.

ADDRESS
Nobilissimo et Consultissimo Viro
Domino Gothofredo Guilielmo Leibnitz
J.U.D. et consiliario Moguntiaco
Maintz

TRANSLATION

Henry Oldenburg greets the very noble and excellent Mr. Gottfried Wilhelm Leibniz, LL.D., most worthy Councilor at Mainz

I wrote to you a few days ago[1] by the ordinary post about a number of philosophical matters, as well as your *Hypothesis physica nova*. In particular I urged you to send here as soon as possible the second part on the abstract laws of motion,[2] to clarify the whole further. I hope that letter was safely delivered to you. I have nothing else to communicate to you now, except to let you know that I sent you the books you wanted by our bookseller Martin and by Schulz at Hamburg to Zunner at Frankfurt, that is, so far as I could get hold of them:

	£	s	d
Philosophical Transactions for 1668, 1669, 1670	1	0	0
Blunt's Lexicon[3]		4	6
Boyle on the rarefraction of air[4]			6
Boyle's Tracts on Cosmical Qualities[5]		1	8
Glanvill's *Plus Ultra*[6]		1	6
Mercurius Librarius[7]		1	6
Total	1	10	8[8]

I am fully confident that you will arrange for Zunner to satisfy Schulz as regards the price, and then Schulz can satisfy Martin; if this is not done our Mr. Martin will make difficulties the next time. Farewell, and accept all good wishes from your most devoted. London, 24 April 1671.

From now on Schulz will supply your excellency with all of the books printed in England, for our Mr. Martin has an arrangement with him.

ADDRESS
To the very noble and wise
Mr. Gottfried Wilhelm Leibniz LL.D.
Councillor at Mainz,
    Mainz

NOTES

1 Vol. VII, Letter 1676.
2 See Vol. VII, Letter 1644, note 12.
3 Thomas Blount, *Glossographia, or a dictionary interpreting all such hard words . . . as are now used in our refined English tongue* (London, 1656; 3rd ed., 1670).
4 Robert Boyle, *Tractatus . . . ubi mira aeris (etiam citra calorem) rarefactio detecta* (etc.) . . . (London, 1670, 1671).
5 A Latin version of *Cosmicall Qualities* was published at Amsterdam and Hamburg in 1671; see Vol. VII *passim*.
6 Joseph Glanvill, *Plus Ultra* (London, 1668).
7 *Mercurius Librarius, or, a Catalogue of Books Printed and Published* . . . appeared for each term of the year and listed books published in London.
8 Properly, £1.9.8.

1686
Selbie to Oldenburg
28 April 1671
From the original in Royal Society MS. S 1, no. 111

Durham Apr. ye 28th 1671

Honored Sr

Amongst many felicities their is noe one more gratefull, then a Correspondence with soe generous and free a Temper as I apprehend you to bee, and under yt sence shall accompt it noe smal obligation that you will please to accept of any thinge my poore Indeavours may Contribute. Judgeing a Communication to bee the only medium to Improve and prosper, Especially to one of soe sublime and mature a genious as I presume Inhabitts your worthie selfe, And in order there too, as an Earnest of a groweing Respect doe freelie answeere your desires[1] in Imparting the volatile Salt of Tartar wch is performed by draweing of Zwelfer's acetum 3 or 4 times from Sal Tartarij[2] provided your acetum bee good and come of with as much force as when poured on, Butt in Case you finde itt Infeebled next time poure on fresh, and in Conclusion you will at least have 2 parts of the Salt of Tarter Ellevated like flakes of Sylver to the middle of your glass Bodie, wich beeing Exposed to any aire resolves into a pleasant green Liquor, Butt being Kept drie Remaines in the bodie of a glorious Salt: This process being facile enough, A wide doore is opned to the attayneing of the spiritum salis Tartarij wch if noble Helmontt may bee credited is the Apex Medici:[3] As to the Tincture of Corral if you please to give me an Effectuall Menstruum I shall accept itt thankfully, haveing tryed severall, wch I make bold to premise least you should Recommend any thinge of the same nature, vizd Lee Febures 2 menstruums spiritum salis, spiritum mellis[4] together with Bas Valentines process[5] and Severall others, none of wch Ever answered my Expectations: Sr. as to my paraliticall patient, To satisfie you farther & more particularly as to ye Symptomes thus, his distemper haith been upon him aboute 4 yeares his Age about 30, a dull phlegmatique melancholly splenetick Constitution, his Stomach good, Rests well, noe depravation neither off sence nor motion, Butt only an Imbecillitie in his left legg, wth Tensions & slight Contractures from his right shoulder downe to his breast, goes wth a Staffe in one hand & a smal assistance of ones hand to support the other side, Butt the most direfull Symptome is a dull Stupefactive habitt in the bowells, never goeing to Stoole wthout artificiall helps wth a great weakness in the Explusive faculty & spincture[6] Muscle ariseing from a Consent of the Spina dorsi[7] upon these nerves as an Effect of his paralitick dissaffection. Now Sr: by this hynt togeither wth reference to my former paper I hope you will be Inabled to give me your possitive advise, how perhaps ye Kinges Bath may bee in this Case From your observance of persons haveing mad Tryall thereof Thoe your mentioning Mr Boyles declineing of the Bath doth in some measure discourage us, yett his Case I suppose did much differ being Complicated and his Palsey an accedent, but ariseing from other distempers. However wee should Rejoyce to Knowe the generall Methodd for his Recovery: Butt worthie Sr I am now ashamed for this prolixity, being senseable of your weightie affaires, only I hope your Candour will pass by this Trouble & grant a pardon as alsoe to vouchsafe 2 or 3 Lines unto him that subscribes Sr:

Your Reall Freind and Sarvant
R Se

Sr Itt is much against my nature to urge, for a speedie answere butt bee assured itt will bee much longed for nothing beeing more welcome.

ADDRESS
 For
His worthy Freinde
 Henry Oldenburg
  Esqe at his house
   in the pell mell
    these present
     London

NOTES

For this correspondent, see Vol. VII, Letters 1575 and 1660.
1 Compare Letter 1660 (Vol. VII, p. 532); by implication, a letter from Oldenburg (or a message in the lost Letter 1679 to Nelson) is missing here.
2 "acid ... salt of tartar"; for Johann Zwelfer, see Letter 1660, note 13. Here Oldenburg has written in the margin of the letter: "if the solution of salt of Tartar be filtred after every time yt the liqr is pourd upon it, it will be much purified. What uses he hath put it to, as 'tis a menstruum."
3 "spirit of salt of tartar ... climax of medicine." For Van Helmont's pronouncements

on the utility of volatile salt of tartar, see *De Febribus*, XV, §25, and XVII, §13 *ad. fin.*, and *Scholarum humoristarum passiva deceptio*, I, §89. However, the expression *apex medici* does not occur in any of these passages.

4 "two solvents, spirit of salt and spirit of honey." Nicholas Lefevre published *Traicté de la Chymie* (Paris, 1660) Englished as *A Compleat Body of Chymistry* (London, 1670).

5 Probably Selbie had read one of the collected English versions of "Basil Valentine," including the *Twelve Keys* and lesser works (London, 1656, 1658).

6 sphincter.

7 That is, "descent of the backbone."

1687
Oldenburg to Sluse
28 April 1671

From the copy in Royal Society MS. O 2, no. 50

Per Illustri et Reverendo admodum Viro
Domino Renato Francisco Slusio Canonico Leodiensi &c
Henr. Oldenburg S.P.D.

Cum fas non putem, Virum Ecclesiasticis juxta et Politicis curis districtum praeproperis responsionibus urgere, visum fuit nostram de acceptis tuis novissimis, nono Martij datis, significationem nonnihil sufflaminare. Erant illae gratissimae, ut nunquam non sunt tuae, agnoscimusque Dominus Collinsius, et Ego una cum allis beneficium illud, quo tuam Æquationum limites designandi methodum indicasti, quoque pro eximio tua candore, alias illas de Problematibus opticis methodos te communicaturum polliceris. Domino Hugenio Parisios (quod brevi futurum) reverso, omni dubio procul intelliges, pergratum ipsi fore, tua de argumento illo cogitata perspicere.[1]

Te jam vidisse autumem Diophanti Alexandrini opera, nuper Tolosae, parario Domini Fermati filio recusa, atque dicti Fermati Observationibus, nec non doctrinae Analyticae Invento novo, ex varijs ejusdem epistolis, Jacobi Billij cura collecto, locupletata.[2] Quanti sit inventum illud, quod dicitur, novum, tuum erit tuique similium, penitius dispicere.

Marchettum de solidorum resistentia jam vidimus:[3] non tamen ideo de generosa tua eundem ad nos curandi promptitudine Tibi obstricti sumus. At necdum Laloveram tuumque ipsius de Mesolabo Tractatum, quem Te

Amstelodamum, huc porro curandum misisse scripseras,⁴ accepimus nulli tamen dubitantes, Mercatorem Damium solita fide eos sibi traditos huc transmissurum, nec non precium debitum, jussi nostro, cuivis a Te designato Bibliopolae Batavo promptissime soluturum. Certe libri, qui in Italia, et remotiori Germaniae parte imprimuntur, tarde admodum in Angliam veniunt: Proinde tanto magis Tibi devinciemur, si, re ferente, de singulis bonae notae libris Mathematicis et Physicis, inibi editis, et Leodium vel in viciniam transvectis, exemplar unum ad me curare volueris; Vel libris nostratibus vel aere, prout Tibi placuerit beneficium illud mente gratissima compensare annitemur. Intelleximus, Gottignij Dioptricam,⁵ nec non Mengolij Musicam⁶ in Italia prodijsse, quos libros avide exspectamus.

Gomezium Pereiram quod attinet, recte omnino ais, ejus sententiam de Brutorum anima, et mentis humanae immortalitate, cum Cartesij dogmatibus coincidere.⁷ Invenitur liber ille in bibliotheca Bodlejana Oxonij, deque eo Amicus quidam meus⁸ qui eum rogatu meo perlustraverat, haec non ita pridem perscripsit.

"Statuit Author ille, Bruta non percipere, et crebro sensationem eorum Magnetismi Phaenomenis illustrat; vultque, varios illos in Brutis motus, quos nos amorem vel, odium interpretamur, nil nisi varias nervorum in crebro concussiones et effectiones esse, quae objectorum sensibilium indolem et operationem consequantur. Ait insuper, si quis vel conceptum notitiamve simplicassimam, qualis est, nosse herum, Brutis concesserit, ei omnino fatendum, etiam Rationem universaliumque cognitionem iisdem inesse."

Hactenus Amicus meus Oxoniensis; qui librum illum perquam subtiliter scriptum existimat adeoque salivam mihi movit, bibliopolarum nostratium officinas perscrutandi, dispiciendique, num exemplar ejus reperire queam. Est Launaeus quidam Parisiensis, Philosophicae Democritianae Hyperaspistes acerrimus, qui nuper in dissertatione sua de Philosophia in genere, cap. 4. p. 29. Edit. Gallicae, ait, se aliquando Cartesij furta propalaturum, ostensurumque, eum nil praestitisse aliud, quam quod Epicuri pallium inverterit, illudque pro novo venditaverit. Ipsissima ejus verba; si ea forte malueris, haec sunt.

"Le systeme cartesien est nouveau en verité par quantité de suppositions chimeriques, qu'il a introduites, mais il n'est pas nouveau quant aux principes, ny à la pluspart des conclusions; ainsi que nous le ferons voir, quand nous decouvrirons un jour ses larcins, et prouverons qu'il n'a fait que retourner le manteau d'Epicure, pour faire croire qu'il s'en avoit un neuf."9

Editus hic nuper fuit libellus cujusdam Butleri de Tempore Nativitatis et Passionis Christi, in quo Author doctissimum Seneschallum refellere conatur.10 Ut verum dicam, liber hic ob commenta quaedam Astrologica, in Christianam religionem injuria, prohibitus est: qualis qualis tamen fuerit, eum brevi si velis, ad Te transmittemus, longe praestantiori Doctoris Wallisii Tractatu, tertia nempe et ultima Mechanices ipsius parte sociandi.11 Prodiere hic etiam non ita pridem libelli sequentes: 1 Boylius de Origine Formarum et Qualitatum; idemque de Mira Aeris rarefactione; uterque in sermonem Latinum versus in 12º. 2. Gulielmi Hoelli Epitome Historiae universalis12 in 12º. Audio, a Willisio nostro in usum publicum parari Tractatum de Anima et Morbis Capitis:13 Et a Gualtero Needhamo, librum de Saliva, aliumque de Animalibus sub terra degentibus.14

Inquisivi, ut jusseras, an chymici nostrates sciant purum Antimonij regulum, et ad argenti splendorem adductum, sine ulla additione in verum sublimatum, vulgari vel argenteo simile, sublimare? Responsum accepi negativum, postquam plures eosque pro peritioribus habitos, sciscitatus fueram. Aiunt, siquis artem illam noverit, facile ei fore, AEs ita dealbere, ut argentum aemuletur &c.

Scriptum illud Barrovianum de jacobi Gregorij Problemate antehac Tibi communicatum, observationibus quisbusdam, a dicto Gregorio concinnatis, auctum fuit, quas Tibi impertiri non gravabimur,15 Ait ille,

"In primo Clarissimi Domini Barrovij Problemate $HMDO = \frac{DE^2}{2}$, etiam posito, rectam THO eandem esse cum curva KXL in secundo Problemate; nescio, an ex hoc capite ulla possit dari secundi Problematis solutio. Vereor, plenam tertij Problematis solutionem a secundo non dependere: si enim EZF fuerit recta, rectae AD parallela, ex secundo Problemate (quod in hoc casu idem est cum primo) integre soluto, datur tantummodo (sicut ego percipio) una tertij Problematis solutio, nempe $VADB$ Rectangulum, cujus latus $VA = EA$, vel DF: si vero infinitae non dentur, sicut dubito in omnibus hisce, datur saltem altera, nimirum $VADB$ [semicirculus], cujus radius est aequalis ipsi AE vel DF. Subtilissima sunt et acerrima Ingenij specimina, quae subjungit Vir Doctissimus. Existimo Theoremata illa non solum maximas quantitates, sed etiam, minimas quandoque determinare.

Ex. gr. (in primo Theoremate) si Cycloformis potestatis m, centro D, diametro DA (si ita loqui liceat) descripta per punctum L, tota intra curvam BLA cadat; erit DG^m et GL^m absolute minimum; si vero dicta Cycloformis alibi occurrat curvae BLA, dantur plura minima. Si Cycloformis tota extra curvam BLA cadat; erit DG^m & GL^m absolute maximum; si alibi occurat, dantur plura maxima. Idem etiam dicimus in secundo Theoremate; si supponatur, BLA extendi in rectam, et super eadem in punctis suis respectivis ordinatas [LG] perpendiculariter erigi; item Centro B, Diametro BLA, per punctum G Cycloformem describi: quae hic censemus, tertio et quarto Theoremati applicamus, ponendo Hyperboliformem Potestatibus debitam loco Cycloformis; In hoc solo est discrimen, quod (cum Hyperboliformis sit figura interminabilis) in figura terminata BDA non detur absolute minimum; si fuerit TG semper ad GL, sicut determinata R, ad aliam ex Puncto G ipsi AD perpendiculariter erectam, et ex hisce alijs descripta figura, vel illi analoga, ponatur loco Cycloformis, eandem adhuc quinto applicando: Denique si super AD ex punctis G erigantur Perpendiculares, quarum quadrata aequentur spatij semper respectivi $ADGL$ duplo, et figura ex his conflata ponatur vice cycloformis, dicta quoque sexto applicantur."

Vale Vir Illustrissime, meque Virtutis et Doctrinae Tuae cultorem studiossimum amare perge. Dab. Londoni April 28. MDCLXXI

TRANSLATION

Henry Oldenburg sends many greetings to the very illustrious and reverend Mr. René François de Sluse, Canon of Liège, &c.

As I think it improper to compel a man busy with both clerical and civil affairs to make hasty replies, I thought fit to swell a little my notice of the receipt of your recent letter dated 9 March [N.S.]. It was very welcome, as your letters always are; Mr. Collins and I, with others, acknowledge your kindness in hinting at your method of designating the limits of equations, as also your openness in promising to communicate at another time those methods for dealing with problems in optics. When Mr. Huygens has returned to Paris (which will be in the near future) you will no doubt learn that he will be very glad to see your thoughts on that question.[1]

I think you will already have seen the works of Diophantos of Alexandria recently printed at Toulouse by the agency of Mr. Fermat's son, enriched by the said Fermat's comments and by a newly discovered theory of analysis extracted from various of his letters by the diligence of Jacques de Billy.[2] How significant that method called *new* is, will be for yourself and others like you to consider more thoroughly.

We have already seen Marchetti on the resistance of solid bodies but we are no less obliged to you for your kindness in sending it to us so promptly.[3] But we have not yet received the La Loubère and your treatise on *Mesolabum*, which, you write, you sent to Amsterdam to be sent on here;[4] yet we do not doubt that the merchant Dames will, with his usual reliability, send them on here when they have been delivered to him, and will pay the proper price as we have ordered him to do, very promptly, to whatever Dutch bookseller you may have designated. Certainly books printed in Italy and the more distant parts of Germany arrive very tardily in England; hence we will be under the greater obligation to you, if, things being as they are, you will arrange to have a single copy [sent] me of each of the notable books in mathematics and physics published there and brought to Liège or its vicinity. We will endeavor to recompense you cheerfully either with our books or with money, as you shall choose. We have heard that the dioptrics of Gottignies[5] and the *Musica* of Mengoli have appeared in Italy,[6] and we look forward eagerly to these books.

As for Gomez Pereyra you say justly that his opinion concerning the souls of animals and the immortality of the human mind chimes with the doctrine of Descartes.[7] That book may be found in the Bodleian Library at Oxford, and a certain friend of mine[8] who looked through it at my request wrote as follows about it not long ago:

"That author lays it down that animals do not perceive and that sensation in their brains belongs to the phenomena of magnetism; and he supposes that those different emotions in animals which we qualify as love or dislike are nothing but varied states and vibrations of the nerves in the brain brought about by the characteristics and actions of physical bodies. He further maintains that if anyone should allow to an animal even the most elementary concept or notion, such as knowing its master, he must fully concede that they have reason and knowledge of universals."

So far my Oxford friend, who thinks that the book is written in a most subtle manner and makes me eager to search through and examine our booksellers' shops to see if I can find a copy of it. De Launay is a Parisian, a most skilful defender of the Democritean philosophy, who has recently written in his *Dissertation on Philosophy in general* (Chapter 4, p. 29, of the French edition) that he will at some time disclose Descartes's plagiary and will prove that he had done nothing but turn Epicurus's cloak inside out and sell it as a new garment. These are his very own words, in case you would prefer them:

"The Cartesian system is indeed new in the multitude of the chimerical suppositions its author has introduced, but as to its principles it is not new, nor as to the majority of its conclusions; as we shall make manifest one day when we shall reveal his plagiaries and prove that he has done nothing but turn Epicurus's cloak inside out, to make believe he has a new one."[9]

There was recently published here a little book by one Butler on the dates of the Nativity and Passion of Christ, in which the author endeavors to refute the very learned Seneschal.[10] To tell the truth, because of some astrological remarks harmful to the Christian religion the book has been banned here; such as it was, however, we will soon if you wish send it to you as a companion to something far superior, Dr. Wallis's treatise forming the third and final part of his *Mechanics*.[11] The following books appeared here not long ago: (1) Boyle, *De origine formarum et qualitatum*, and the same, *De mira aeris rarefactione*, both translated into Latin, in 12mo; (2) William Howell, *Epitome Historiae Universalis*, in 12mo.[12] I hear that our Willis has prepared for publication a treatise on the soul, and diseases of the head;[13] and Walter Needham a book on saliva and another on animals living beneath the Earth's surface.[14]

As you instructed me, I have asked whether our chemists know the pure regulus of antimony, brought to the brightness of silver and subliming by itself without any addition as a true sublimate, like the common or silvery sublimate? I have received a negative response after I had made enquiries of many, and those reckoned to be the most skilful. They say that if anyone masters that art it will be easy for him so to whiten copper that it rivals silver.

That paper of Barrow's on James Gregory's problem that was formerly imparted to you has now been augmented by some observations concocted by Gregory, which we are happy to impart to you.[15] He writes:

"In the first of the famous Mr. Barrow's problems $HMDO = \dfrac{DE^2}{2}$, and it is also postulated that the straight line THO is the same as the curve KXL in the second problem; I cannot tell whether any solution to the second problem may be derived under this head. I fear that a complete solution of the third problem does not depend on that of the second; for if EZF were a straight line parallel to AD, when the second problem is completely solved (it becomes in this case identical with the first), there is given so far as I can see only a single solution of the third, that is to say $VADB$ is a rectangle whose side $VA = EA = DF$; and if there be not an infinite number, as I fear there may be in all these cases, there are at any rate other ones, such as when [the semicircle] $VADB$ has a radius equal to AE or DF. These specimens of the learned man's intellect are most keen and ingenious. I believe that that theorem may determine not only maximum values but minima also on occasions.

For example, in the first theorem, if a cycloform of degree m is described with center D, diameter DA (if one may so term it), through the point L, so that the whole may fall within the curve BLA, DG^m and GL^m will be absolutely minimum. But if the cycloform curve meets the curve BLA anywhere else, there are several minima. If the whole cycloform falls outside the curve BLA, DG^m

and GL^m are absolute maxima; if however the cycloform meets the curve BLA elsewhere, there are several maxima. We say the same of the second theorem: if it be supposed that BLA be extended as a straight line, and that ordinates [LG] are erected upon it perpendicularly at their appropriate points, and if further a cycloform is described through the point G with center B and diameter BLA. Our reasoning here we apply to the third and fourth theorem, employing a hyperboliform of due degrees in place of the cycloform; only there is this distinction, that as the hyperboliform is an unlimited figure there can be no absolute minimum in the limited figure BDA. If TG were always in the same ratio to GL as the fixed quantity R to another erected normally to AD from the point G, and from these others a figure be described, this or one analogous to it may be employed in place of the cycloform, applying that to the fifth [proposition]. Lastly, if perpendiculars be erected upon AD from the points G, the squares of which are respectively equal always to twice $ADGL$, and the figure composed of these be employed in place of the cycloform, they may be applied to the aforesaid sixth proposition."

Farewell, most illustrious Sir, and continue to love me as a most zealous admirer of your virtue and learning. London, 28 April 1671.

NOTES

Reply to Letter 1643.
1 Huygens left The Hague on 2 June 1671, arriving in Paris towards the end of the month.
2 Samuel de Fermat, ed., *Diophanti Alexandrini Arithmeticorum libri sex* . . . (Toulouse, 1670). Jacques de Billy, S.J. (1602–79) was a teacher of mathematics at Dijon, where he died.
3 Alessandro Marchetti, *De resistentia solidorum* (Florence, 1669).
4 See Vol. VII, Letter 1548, the postscript, and Letter 1507, note 8. La Loubère's book was *De cycloide* (Toulouse, 1660).
5 For this non-book, see Vol. VII, Letter 1602, note 3.
6 Pietro Mengoli, *Speculazioni di musica* (Bologna, 1670).
7 See Vol. VII, Letter 1548 and note 11.
8 Probably this was Wallis, who executed many similar commissions for Oldenburg, and who is known to have seen Sluse's letter when he last visited London. We have not found this account of the book elsewhere.
9 Gilles de Launay, *Dissertation de la philosophie en général* (Paris, 1668); the quotation from chap. 4 is on p. 74 of the second edition, *Introduction a la philosophie* (Paris, 1675).
10 See Vol. VII, Letter 1590, notes 37 and 38.
11 See Vol. VII, Letter 1506, note 5.
12 Presumably his *Elementa historiae* (London, 1671).
13 *De anima brutorum . . . exercitationes duae: prior physiologica, altera pathologica* (Oxford, 1672) does, in fact, deal with the pathology of the brain, or "head." See *Phil. Trans.*, no. 83 (20 May 1672), 4071–73.
14 We could not find such a book; compare Letter 1649, note 6.

15 The following extract is from James Gregory's letter to John Collins of 15 February 1671 (see Turnbull, *Gregory*, pp. 171–72). We have inserted in brackets a word or two from Gregory's own copy. For a mathematical explanation, see *ibid.*, pp. 173–76. It is in this letter that Gregory demonstrates his knowledge of Taylor's Theorem (1715). He replies to Barrow's paper sent him by Collins (sse Vol. VII, Letter 1590, note 7). The figures may be found in Vol. VII, pp. 363–66.

1688
Leibniz to Oldenburg
29 April 1671

From the copy in Royal Society Letter Book IV, 285–89
Printed in Gerhardt, pp. 55–59

Vir Amplissime,

Quoniam his nundinis Francofurtensibus nihil a vobis accepi, vereri incipio, ne, quas ego literas prolixas satis per Cursorem publicum ad Te, cum parte Schediasmatis mei novi destinaveram, perierint.[1] Schediasma ipsum, Illustri Societati Regiae, ut vides, inscriptum est; autore, per Te potissimum, veniam a consessu tantorum Virorum sibi pollicente. Adjunxi aliud, quod Academiae Regiae Parisinae inscripsi; summa utrique huc redit: Theoria motus Abstracti, invictas propemodum Compositionis continui difficultates explicat, Geometriam indivisibilium, et Arithmeticam infinitorum confirmat; ostendit nihil esse sine partibus in rerum natura; infinitus actu cujuscunque continui partes esse; doctrinam de angulis esse de quantitatibus inextensorum; Motum esse Motu fortiorem, ergo et comatum conatu: conatum autem esse motum per punctum in instanti; punctum ergo puncto majus esse. Si corpus premat corpus, conari, ac proinde incipere in ejus loco esse; ergo incipere uniri, seu penetrare; terminos igitur esse eosdem; ergo corpora se prementia cohaerere; conatus diversos, inter se per minima mixtos, producere novi generis motus; nullam esse conhaesionem quiescentis; omnem potentiam esse a celeritate; omne corpus esse mentem instantaneam, mentem servare conatum amisso motu, corpus non servare: sed mentem ab agendo desistere non posse, mentem propagare seipsam sine nova creatione; multaque Theoremata admiranda a me demonstrabuntur, non minore claritate Geometrica, quam quae de punctis et conatibus ratiocinari licet: nam quod in corporibus praestant spatia et motus, id in mentibus puncta et conatus. Caeterum hoc loco explicui omnis generis figurarum et motuum originem ex meris rectis; ipsa lentium elaborandarum fundamenta; corporum absolute consideratorum inter se concurrentium eventa saepe paradoxa, quia a Phaenomenis dissentanea; nam alia plane est magnitudo, figura, motus corporis apparens, alia vera. Cum igitur eventa motus apparentis, differant a regulis veri, sed insensibilis, seu non apparentis, cogitandum fuit [de] ratione conciliandi, seu de quibusdam motibus veris insensibilibus, qui hos sensibiles saepe tam paradoxos producerent. Id quamdiu omnes naturae sinus nondum excussimus, praestari non nisi per Hypothesin potest, quae quanto clarior, simplicior, brevior, concinnior, phaenomenis, quae hactenus novimus potissimis difficillimisque solvendis sufficientior, tanto veritati propior habenda est. Hypothesis autem mea in summa huc redit: suppono, Solem simul gyrare circa suum centrum, et radiare extra se; ita radiatione apprehendet, gyratione circumaget totum quem vocant magnum orbem suum, ex aethere, et globis in eo disseminatis, planetis nimirum et tellure, constantem. Cur autem globi illi ab aethere diversi distinctique? quia separato motu circa proprium centrum suum circumferuntur; atque in specie terra nostra, dum gyratione sua particulari opponit se aetheri, circa solis centrum cum ipso gyrato, efficit ut ex duobus his motibus solis radiantis aetherem moventis recto, et telluris obnitentis circulari velut in officina vitriaria, simplicissimo artificialium genere, bullae quaedam seu vasa subtilia fiant, velut fundamenta specierum, et corporum particularium. Reliqua pars aetheris, quae libera mansit, gyrabitur cum luce circa Tellurem motu, ut conjicere licet, fortissimo; tellurem enim secum abripere non potest, quin illa separatum sibi motum retineat. His statim tum vim Elasticam, tum Gravitatem efficit: Vim Elasticam, quia si quid crassi consistentisque aetheri occurrat, quod in tantam subtilitatem divisum non est, quanta est aetheris gyrantis, id motui aetheris obsistit, quia ab eo abripi eadem celeritate non potest: necesse est ergo, vel disjiciatur in similem aethereae tenuitatem, motui aptam, vel dejiciatur in locum ubi motus tam fortis, ac proinde tanta tenuitate opus non est; id est, prope centrum: a disjectione Vis Elastica, a dejectione, Gravitas: Ab his duabus pleraque corporum phaenomena. Nam omnes reactiones, fermentationes solutionesque et praecipitationes ferme reduci possunt ad reactionem, quae est inter acidum et alcali, haec vero pendet a Vi Elastica. Est enim Alcali instar sclopeti ventanei aere onerati; quorum ex vitro constantium acervi, si violenter ad rupturam usque commisceantur, quis ejaculante uno, altero sorbente, exoriturus sit tumultus, facile cogitatu est: idem proportione, tumultu non nisi effectibus suis sensibili, in reactionibus omnibus contingere cogitemus. His positis omnia de principiorum Chemicorum numero litigia cessandi, etiam methodi medendi stabiliendae initi aliquando ratio poterit; contraria enim contrariis substantia, similibus gradu, curanda sunt: Alcalia scilicet per acida, et contra, sed subtilitate proportionata; unde specificae medicamentorum vires. Haec satis, opinor, harmonica, aliis non paucis congruentiis confirmantur. Quid enim memorabilius, quam rationem directionis magneticae ad polos manifestissimam hinc reddi posse, quod hactenus, quantum scio, nemo praestitit. Nam librata, et potissimum magnetica, si se quomodocunque, vel directe, vel oblique in longitudinem, seu inter orientem occidentemque collocarent, torrenti aetheris ab Oriente in Occidentem moti se opponerent; quod ne fiat, collocant se tandem post multas variationes in latitudinem, inter meridiem et septentrionem, seu versus polos; quibus positis fortasse ad declinationis magneticae causam aliquando perveniri potest. Ex eodem principio aetheris circulati, motus marium, et ventorum, leges Refractionis et Reflexionis, pendulorum synchronismos multaque alia naturae phaenomena deduxi, quanta vix ex hypothesi tam simplice quisquam. Quae alia his connexa in re naturali, mechanica et civili molior, alias fusius dicam. Nunc, Vir Amplissime, Te vehementer rogo, ut efficias, hoc quicquid est hominis ignoti et peregrini, et multis aliis morosioribus studiis ultra solitum distracti, a tantis viris, quantis inscriptum est, boni saltem consuli.

Non nisi exemplum [unum] mitto, quia mittendi ratio alia, quam per cursorem ordinarium non fuit. Valde vellem igitur, ut quia tam exiguum est, apud vos pro commodiore distributione recuderetur, aut fortasse Transactionibus, si quidem commode fieri potest, ad aliarum Epistolarum dissertationumque instar, annecteretur;[2] quod vero potissimum peto, hoc est, ut judicia, monita, animadversiones, supplementa, emendationes, stricturas, egregiorum virorum scripto scilicet, et tanti videtur, ab unoquoque, pro re nata, comprehensas mihi resciscere liceat:[3] Inprimis oro, ut Wardi, Boilaei, Wrenni, Wallisii, Wilkensii, Willisii, Loweri, Collinsii, Mercatoris, Hookii, aliorum magnorum Virorum sententiae ad me Tuo beneficio perveniant; poterit fortasse rudior adhuc doctrina poliri exactius, et sicubi maxime laborare videbitur, demonstrationum robore firmius emuniri. Caeterum Doctissimi Wilkinsii Characterem Universalem beneficio Amplissimi Viri Guilielmi Curtii[4] nuper legi; Tabulae perplacent: vellem res, quae describi nisi pictura non possunt, ut sunt varia animalium, plantarum, instrumentorum genera, figuris adjectis exhibuisset. Utinam esset qui in Latinum traduceret, quanquam nemo posset rectius Autore; Dummodo rerum non aliter declarabilium figurae, nonnullarumque vocum ignotiorum explicationes adjicerentur.

Quaesivi literis nuperis, verane sint, quae in itinerario narrat Monconisius de pulvere tam mirandae compositionis, ut integras naves destruere possit, quem habeat Drebelii gener Küflerus; item quid de ejus fornace pisterio; de registro, se sponte sua ad debitum caloris gradum demittente; de aquae marinae distillatione ibidem asseruntur.[5] Quaesivi etiam, quis eventus fuerit praedictionis circa Declinationes Magneticas, autore, ni fallor, Bondio, quam in vestris Transactionibus legi.[6] Quid judicetis de Experimento Magnetico P. Grandamici, qui ait, Terrellam polo impositam et ita in subere libratam, certum quendam Meridianum, ubique locorum polo, seu Meridiano loci sine declinatione ulla obverter:[7] Item, an veram putetis inclinationem magneticam Gilberti et Kircheri, qua acus elevationem poli monstret.[8] Haec duo, illud inprimis, valde nosse vellem, ad Hypotheses meas Magneticas perficiendas; neminique rectius quam Vobis explorata puto. Nihilne novi circa Tubos Opticos inventum? an cum fructa perfecta Machina Wrenniana pro vitris Sectionum Conicarum?[9] Ottius quidam, natione Helvetius, juvenis doctus, ait machinam facilem sectionibus conicis exhibendis se reperisse, cujus meminit in dissertatione sua de Visu.[10] Scribitur mihi, in Helvetia, Tiguri, ni fallor, Stollium quendam, virum eruditum, sudorem scintillantem nonnunquam (certo anni tempore, de quo specialiora expecto) indusio excutere.[10a] Similes extant observationes apud Borellum, et alios. Becherus, Medicus Germanus,[11] asserit, invenisse se rationem ex solo limo communi, adhibito saepeque abstracto et cohobato[12] oleo lini, faciendi ferrum artificiale, per omnia simile naturali, nullo prius ferri in limo vel lino vestigio. De Wernero, inventi Hydraulici Autore, diu est quod nihil audivi; expecto responsum Augusta.[13] Vale faveque Cultori Tuarum Virtutum

Gottfredo Guliel. Leibnitio
J.U.D. et Consil. Moguntino

Francofurti 29. Aprilis
st. vet. 1671.

TRANSLATION

Most excellent Sir,

Since I received nothing from you at this time of the Frankfurt Fair, I begin to fear that the pretty stout letter I sent you by the public post, together with a part of my *New Theory*, must have perished.[1] That *Theory* is itself, as you see, dedicated to the Royal Society, the author begging to be excused for this by that assembly of great men, especially through your means. I have added the other one which I dedicated to the Académie Royale [des Sciences] in Paris. The gist of both may be thus expressed: the theory of abstract motion explains the hitherto unresolved difficulties of continuous composition, confirms the geometry of indivisibles and arithmetic of infinitesimals; it shows that there is nothing in the realm of nature without parts; that the parts of any continuum are in fact infinite; that the theory of angles is that of the quantities of unextended bodies; that motion is stronger than motion, and endeavor stronger than endeavor—however, endeavor is instantaneous motion through a point, and so a point may be greater than a point. If a body presses upon another body it endeavors, and therefore commences to be, in its place; and therefore to be united with it or to penetrate into it; therefore their boundaries become identical, and accordingly bodies pressed together cohere; different *conatus* [endeavors] mixed one with another by the least particles produce motions of a new kind; there is no cohesion arising from rest; all power [or force] is the product of velocity; every body is an instantaneous mind; the mind maintains the *conatus* after the motion has been dissipated, but the body does not maintain it; but the mind cannot be abandoned by the agent, the mind propagates itself without new creation; and many admirable theorems will be demonstrated by myself with a geometrical clarity no less than that with which it is possible to reason about points and endeavors; for what space and motion are to bodies, so point and endeavor are to minds. Moreover I have in this place explained the generation of every kind of shape and motion from perfectly straight lines, the very foundation of lens-grinding; the phenomena, frequently paradoxical, of bodies in the absolute sense colliding, because these are discrepant from experiments; for the one clearly deals with the magnitude, shape, and motion of the apparent body, the other with the true body. Since, therefore, the phenomena of the motion of the apparent body differ from the rules of the true body, or that which is imperceptible or non-apparent, it was necessary to think of a way of reconciling [them], or of certain true, imperceptible motions which might be the cause of these perceptible ones that are often so paradoxical. So long as we have not plumbed all Nature's secrets, we can only suggest this in the form of an hypothesis, which may be supposed to be the closer to the truth in proportion as it is the more clear, simple, brief, elegant and adequate for solving phenomena which we have hitherto known to be extremely important and difficult. The gist of my hypothesis, however, is as follows: I suppose that the Sun rotates about its center and at the same time radiates, so that by this radiation it may seize upon the whole of its great orb, as they call it, consisting of the ether and the globes scattered in it (that is to say, the planets and the Earth), and spin them around by its own gyration. But why are these globes to be distinguished from the ether? Because they are borne each with a separate motion about its own center, and notably our Earth, while with its own particular rotation it opposes itself to the ether that is revolved round the center of the Sun with itself, creates as it were the bases of the species [of things] and of particular bodies from these two motions, that of the radiating Sun moving the ether in a straight line and that of the Earth thrusting against [the ether] in a circle—just as in glassworks with a very simple kind of knack they make certain very delicate globes or vessels. The rest of the ether, remaining free, will spin around the Earth with light, having a motion that is, one may suppose, extremely powerful, for it cannot drag the Earth along with itself because the Earth retains its separate motion. This immediately gives rise to both elasticity and gravity: the elastic force [of the air], because if something of a certain thickness and consistency meets with the ether, and is not divided with such a degree of subtlety as the spinning ether is, it resists the ether, because this cannot drag it along at the same speed; accordingly, it must either be thrust upwards into ether of a like thinness, appropriate to [its] motion, or thrust downwards to a place where the motion is so strong that such a great subtlety is not required, that is, towards the center; from the upward thrust arises the elastic force, from the downward thrust gravity. And from these two many of the phenomena of bodies [arise]. For all reactions, fermentations, solutions, and precipitations can confidently be reduced to the reaction between acid and alkali, and this depends upon the elastic force. For the alkali is like a charged air gun; if heaps of these made of glass be mingled together to the point of rupture, it is easy to see that with one shooting off and another absorbing a din arises. We may reason that the same, in proportion, happens in all reactions with a perceptible noise having its own effects. With these principles postulated, a theory can at some time be opened up whereby all disputes concerning the number of chemical principles may be terminated and the method of healing may be established; for contrary substances are to be dealt with by contraries of like degree, alkalis by acids and vice versa, but delicately balanced, whence arise the virtues of specific medicines. These principles (which are pretty harmonious, in my view) are confirmed by several others consonant to them. For what can be more noteworthy, than the fact that they yield a most manifest theory of the magnetic compass, which no one so far as I know has furnished before? For suspended bodies, magnetic ones particularly, if they are placed in any way whatever either directly or obliquely as to longitude (that is, on an east-west line), expose themselves to movement by the etherial torrent from East to West; that this may not happen they set themselves in a north-south line after many variations in latitude, that is, towards the poles. When this has been agreed perhaps it will be possible to discover the cause of magnetic declination. From this same principle of an etherial circulation the motions of the winds and oceans, the laws of reflection and refraction, the isochronism of pendulums and many other phenomena of nature have been deduced by myself, more than any one else has been able to derive from such a simple hypothesis. What other matters I have been engaged upon in natural philosophy, mechanics, and politics related to these ideas I may report elsewhere at greater length. For the present, excellent Sir, I eagerly beseech you to dispose those distinguished men (to whom it is dedicated) to think well of this production by an unknown wanderer much preoccupied with other less agreeable studies.

I send you only [one] copy because there was no way of sending to you other than by the ordinary post. Accordingly, I very much hope that as it is so slight it may be reprinted by yourselves for a more convenient circulation, or perhaps annexed to the *Transactions* if that may conveniently be done, as other letters and essays have been.[2] What I particularly beg is that it may be possible for me to ascertain the opinions, comments, remarks, addenda, corrigenda, and criticisms of those distinguished men upon that paper as each may think it worthwhile according to circumstances.[3] Especially I beg that the opinions of Ward, Boyle, Wren, Wallis, Wilkins, Willis, Lower, Collins, Mercator, Hooke, and other leading figures among you may reach me through your good offices; perhaps it will be possible for this rather crude theory to be given greater refinement, and secured more firmly by strength of demonstration where it shall seem to labor. Moreover I recently read the learned Wilkins's *Universal Character* by the favor of that worthy man William Curtius;[4] the tables pleased me very much, but I could wish that things that are not be described without illustrations such as the various kinds of animals, plants, and tools had been shown with figures. I wish that there were someone who would translate it into Latin, although no one could do that better than the author; so long as things are not made clearer by figures, explanations of a few more difficult terms should have been added.

In a recent letter I asked whether it is true, as Monconys writes in his *Travels*, that Drebbel's relative Küffler has a powder of such an astonishing composition that it will destroy whole ships; also as regards his baking oven, and the "register" (control) spontaneously adjusting itself to the proper degree of heat; also the distillation of seawater claimed in the same place.[5] I also asked the result of the prediction about magnetic declinations made, I think, by one Bond of which I read in your *Transactions*.[6] What do you think of the magnetic experiment of Fr. Grandami, who says that a terrella placed on its pole and so floated on a cork on a certain meridian, will at any place turn to the pole or meridian of the place without any declination?[7] Further, do you think that magnetic inclination of Gilbert and Kircher, by which the needle shows the altitude of the pole, is true?[8] I very much wish that these two things, the former especially, were definitely confirmed, for the improvement of hypotheses of magnetism. I think no one can test them better than yourselves. Is nothing new invented in the way of optical tubes? And is Wren's machine perfected, with profit, in order to make lenses of conic section?[9] A certain Ott, a learned young Swiss, says he has discovered a simple mechanical device for displaying the conic sections, which he mentions in his dissertation on vision.[10] I hear from Switzerland, from Zurich, unless I am mistaken, that a certain Stoll, a learned man, shakes out sparkling drops of sweat from his undergarment (at a certain time of year, of which I await details).¹⁰ᵃ There are observations of a similar sort in Borelli and others. Becher, a German medical man,¹¹ asserts that he has discovered a way of making an artificial iron solely from common lime, employing linseed oil that has been many times drawn and cohobated,¹² this iron being in all respects similar to natural iron though there was none at first in the lime or the linseed. It is a long time since I heard anything of Werner, the hydraulic inventor; but I await a reply from Augsburg.¹³ Farewell and think well of this admirer of your virtues

Gottfried Wilhelm Leibniz
LL.D. and Councilor at Mainz

Frankfurt, 29 April 1671, O.S.

NOTES

1 Letter 1644 in Vol. VII, acknowledged by Oldenburg in Vol. VII, Letter 1676.
2 See Vol. VII, Letter 1644, note 15.
3 See Vol. VII, Letter 1673 and Letter 1676, note 1.
4 For this English Resident in Germany, who was a correspondent, see Vol. III, p. 511, note 6.
5 This is not quite what Leibniz wrote before about Küffler in Letter 1644 (Vol. VII, p. 490). Balthazar de Monconys (1611–65; see Vol. II, p. 64, note 1) made his visit to Cornelius Drebbel's son-in-law J. S. Küffler on 2 June 1663; see Charles Henry, *Les Voyages de Balthasar de Monconys: documents pour l'histoire de la Science* (Paris, 1887), pp. 52–54.
6 See Vol. V, p. 95, note 1.
7 See Vol. VII, Letter 1644, note 3.
8 In *De magnete*, bk. V (London, 1600) William Gilbert argued that magnetic "declination" (dip) is proportional to latitude. Athanasius Kircher wrote several works on magnetism, the most important being *Magnes, sive de arte magnetica* (Rome, 1641).
9 See Vol. VI, *passim*.
10 See Johannes Ott, *Cogitationes physico-mechanicae de natura visionis* (Heidelberg, 1670), noticed in *Phil. Trans.*, no. 71 (22 May 1671), 2163–65; and for the author, Letter 1867 below.
10a Possibly sparks of frictional electricity.
11 That is, Johann Joachim Becher, who has many times figured in this correspondence. The allusion is to his *Experimentum chymicum novum* (Frankfurt, 1671); see *Phil. Trans.*, no. 74 (14 August 1671), 2234.
12 To draw is to extract the essence by a solvent; to cohobate, to reflux distill.
13 See Vol. VII, Letter 1506, note 9.

1689
John Werden to Oldenburg
29 April 1671
From the original in Royal Society MS. W 3, no. 49

Stockholme 29th Aprill Old Stile 1671

Sr

Mr. Rudbeckius hath not yet declared any thing further of his long since proposed Invention for raysing of Water. His Bridge at Upsall I have seene;[1] as allsoe his Modelles for one Ship (or rather yacht) to sayle against the Wind in smooth Waters; & for another of a Different mold from the Ordinary to be ballasted by a Counterpoyse of Water. These three I am promised to have Draughts of, which I will not fayle to send Coppyes of either to you or my Ld. Sandwich.[2]

My sealed Weatherglass (which I had from Mr. ———[3] at Gresham Colledge) conteynes in the whole Shanke or Tube, betweene the two Bowles 26¼ Inches; & the marke ☉ is 19. Inches below ye upper bowle (or 7¼ above the lower) Now by this Glasse ye Weather in Stockholme, was Coldest on Wednesday 8. Febry. last old stile at 9. in ye morneing, the wind at N.N.W. & the Spirit at 4⅝ Inches below ☉, the Skye being very cleere & dry sunshine. At this present Saturday 29th Aprill 1671 Old Stile; at 3. afternoone ye Weather very cleere, & dry & warme sunshine, ye wind little, at E, ye spirit is allmost at 6. Inches above ☉ soe suddaine an Alteration we have allready. This last winter is here sayd to have beene very mild (yet our first shipping came not up to Stockholme, by reason of ye Ice, till ye 15th Aprill instant) & I thinke I have heard the like of England; but howsoever if any Other Glasse in England have been observed about the same tyme, one may (grossly) guess at the Proportion of heate & Cold; betweene London & Stockholme; whose Latitude is not more yn 58°–45′ though most of the Maps make it more.[4] My Glasse is placed in a North roome, where there is noe fire at all made, & where ye sun comes not, till very late in ye Evening; & I have kept a very exact account of it ever since October last 1670.

I would very fayne know what further improvement hath beene made, about reduceing Pocket Watches to the same Exactnesse as Pendulums; My Pendulum (of about 40. Inches long, bought of Mr. Jones at the Temple.)⁵ I find agrees very neerly to ye Sun, by allowance of the Differences in ye Table of Æquations.⁶ But it hath an Inconvenience, by haveing ye Lesser weight placed thus ◯ (which is) yt I must allwayes give it a whole turne or the Case gives it not roome to move; whereas it should have been placed thus. ◯ Horizontally, by which I might turne it as much or as little as needs.⁷ But being in hast I tooke the Pendulum such as it was, which neverthelesse is a very good one.

I have Num. 60. & all before it of the Philos. Transactions & I pray You let some servant bring Number 61.⁸ & all forwards as they shall from tyme to tyme be Extant, (except my Father⁹ have got ym for me allready, which upon Enquiry may easily be knowne) to my Fathers Lodgeings in St. James's, & there he will be payd for ym. allsoe I want ye Table or Index from Number 23. to Numr. 32. both included. If you will Command me any thing, leave your Letter either at my father's Lodgeing in St. James's, or with Mr. Cooke at Mr. Secy. Trevor's Office in Whitehall.¹⁰

I have wrote long since to my father to send me Mr. Boyles bookes of Cold; & when they come (if anie thing be of such easy practise therein as yt it doe encourage me) I will endeavour to informe my selfe as particularly as may be on yt subject; for though Rudbeckius commonly resides at Upsall; & Mr. Stiernhielme is now growne very old & (Ime told) not very communicable, besides yt he is much absent allsoe; there want not others yt are very ingenious, to improve any good hints, you will send to Sr

your very humble servaunt
Jo Werden

Mr Oldenburg

NOTES

The writer of this letter, John Werden or Worden (1640–1716) was called to the bar in 1660, and in 1664 was appointed a Baron of the Exchequer for Cheshire. He was Secretary to the Embassy in Spain and Portugal under the Earl of Sandwich, and in 1669 was sent to Sir William Temple in Holland with secret instructions from the King. In July 1670 he was sent to Sweden as Envoy Extraordinary (see Vol. VII, Letter 1496). He was raised to the rank of baronet in 1672 and acted as secretary to the Duke of York whose cause, however, he deserted after James's accession to the Crown by going over to William III in 1688.

1 Compare Vol. VII, Letter 1496, p. 96.
2 Edward Montagu, first Earl of Sandwich (1625–72), Pepys's patron, with whom Werden was connected as noted above.

3 Blank in original; presumably either Robert Hooke or the operator, Richard Shortgrave. The instrument was an alcohol thermometer. The mark probably indicated the freezing point of water. If we assume that the lower bulb was of about two inches external diameter, the bore about one-tenth inch, and the tube was calibrated according to Hooke's system, then 1°H would occupy about one inch on the tube. Possibly the tube was marked with such intervals, which Werden supposed to be metric inches. If so, since 1°H = 4.3°F approximately, the January temperature would be about 14°F and the April one about 56°F, which seems reasonable (compare Louise D. Patterson, "The Royal Society's Standard Thermometer, 1663–1709," *Isis*, 44, 1958, 51–64).
4 The latitude of Stockholm is in fact 59°23'.
5 Henry Jones (*c*. 1642–95), of the Inner Temple Gate (or Lane) was admitted to the Clockmakers' Company in 1663, and became its Master in 1691–92. He was one of the most skilled makers of the day.
6 That is, making allowance for the difference between mean time and apparent solar time—the equation of time.
7 Huygens invented the idea of adjusting the effective length of a pendulum by having the main bob fixed, at roughly the correct length, with a small bob movable above it on a screwed portion of the rod. Evidently Werden's small bob was a disk, the rod passing diametrically through it. Putting the rod through the center of the disk would not have solved his problem unless the disk was made longer and of less radius.
8 Dated 18 July 1670, but (as always) actually on sale a week or so later.
9 Robert Werden (d. 1690) was a royalist officer often in difficulties with the Puritans. After the Restoration he served in the Duke of York's guards and his household, reaching the rank of lieutenant-general.
10 Sir John Trevor (1626–72), a former M.P. and diplomat, was knighted and appointed Secretary of State in 1668.

1690

Oldenburg to Willughby

29 April 1671

From the memorandum in Royal Society MS. W 3, no. 43

Rec. Apr. 24. 71.
Answ. Apr. 29. by carrier, and sent ye stick wth ye Insect-seed had from M. Henshaw.[1] Thanked him for ye Experiments of transmitting water through trees.

NOTES

This was written on the envelope of Willughby's Letter 1684 of 21 April. As Oldenburg's later Letter 1701 of 16 May makes plain, this letter in fact did not leave London until two weeks after its date of writing.

1 Nathaniel Henshaw M.D. (1628–73), had on 30 March "produced a small twig surrounded in part with circles of the eggs of an insect," which was given to Oldenburg to be sent to Willughby.

1691
Helmfeld to Oldenburg
3 May 1671
From the original in Royal Society MS. H 3, no. 3

Nobilissime Domine, Amice plurimum Colende

Vereor ne desideres officium meum; quod Tibi pro nostra et meritorum multorum et studiorum parium conjunctione deesse non debet: sed tamen vereor ne literarum officium a me requiras, quas Tibi et jam pridem et saepe mississem, nisi quotidie discessum hujus amici expectans et Tuae et ejus voluntati satisfacere maluissem. Nobilis ille est Moschus germanicis tamen parentibus natus qui illum juvenem in studia in Germaniam miserunt ubi brevi tempori eos Medicina et physicis profectus fecit, ut Jenae laurea Doctorali cum applausu coronatus fuerit.[1] Peracto ergo hoc studiorum cursu Italiam Galliamque bene perlustravit, et cum nunc ipsi mens sedeat adire quoque Angliam, nolui ejus petito deesse, et Tibi illum ceu summo Musarum fautori et patrono amice recommendare. Vir sane egregiae indolis est, commendatae eruditionis, et de quo non dubium est quin aliquando in Russia collecturus sit, quae florentissimae vestrae societati illustrandae erunt. Caeterum, si bene ominor, accuratiorem istam succi illius in Suecia reperti,[2] jamdudum Tibi promissam jure desideratis descriptionem, verum est fateor promissi Tibi, nec dum mihi licuit promissis stare non mea, quod nefas esset sed aliorum certe culpa. Tametsi enim non summe in omnia incubuerim qui mihi possem beneficio amicorum qui ibi degunt certissimam ejus et copiosissimam acquirere relationem frustra est quod conatus sum, nescio an ipsorum negligentia aut rei contempta quod mirer. Tu interim Vir Nobilissime bene haec interpretaveris et promptam meam potius voluntatem quam ejus effectum respicies; persuadendo Tibi quam certissime me, in patriam dante Deo reducem quantum quidem potuero effectis traditurum quae sincere Tibi promissi, quaeque in rem Tuam adeoque totius Societatis incrementum esse videbuntur. Praeter haec nihil habeo quod hac vice ulterius scribam, nisi quod amice Tibi significatum velim discedere ex hoc loco animum mississe et lustratis reliquis quibusdam eminentioris notae Galliae locis Hispanicam meditari. Si placet quod amice rogo, responso me imposterum dignari, lubeat inscribere literas ut consueristi hactenus; dirigendo eas ad Dominum Eosander[3] Secretarium Regiae Suetici Parisijs agentem, et reddentur istae mihi uticunque locorum fuero. Vale et qui Te semper admiratur fave Tui studiosissimo

Gustavo Helmfeld

Parijs die 13 Maji Anno 1671 [N.S.]

ADDRESS
   A Monsieur
   Monsieur Henry Oldenbourg
      treshumblement
         a
            Londres

TRANSLATION

Most noble Sir, my very dear friend,

I fear you must feel the want of my serivces, in which I should not fail you because of our community of interests and studies; yet I fear you may be expecting a dutiful letter from me, which I should long ago have sent you, and on several occasions, had I not every day awaited the departure of a friend, preferring to satisfy him and you at one stroke. This noble person is a Muscovite, yet is the son of German parents who sent him as a young man to study in Germany, where he soon completed what is required in medicine and physic and received the doctorate at Jena.[1] When he had finished this course of study he did some useful traveling in France and Italy and as he has now set his heart on going to England as well, I could not refuse his request to give him a friendly recommendation to yourself as a chief supporter and patron of the Muses. He is certainly a man of unusual character and commendable learning, and of whom there can be no doubt that in the future he will make such collections in Russia as will adorn your very flourishing Society. Moreover, if I guess correctly, you are longing for that more accurate description of that juice found in Sweden which I faithfully promised you;[2] I confess I really did promise it to you, but it is not my fault that I could not live up to my promises (which would be disgraceful) but the fault of others. For although I did not exploit all my resources by applying to friends living there, in order to acquire a more full and certain relation of it, my endeavor was in vain, because of their incomprehensible neglect or disregard. Meanwhile, noble Sir, you must think cheerfully of this, considering rather the readiness of my goodwill than its results, being assured that most certainly when I have returned home (God willing) I will send you so far as I can in fulfillment of the promises I sincerely made you whatever you desire for your own advantage and that of the Society. Beyond this I have nothing else to write at the present time, except that I have it in mind to leave this place, and am thinking of Spain after visiting some of the more notable places in France. If you shall please to grant my request as a friend to honor me with a reply, please address the letter as you have done hitherto, directing it to Mr. Eosander,[3] Secretary to the King of Sweden, living at Paris, and it will be delivered to me anywhere. Farewell, and be kind to your most zealous admirer,

Gustavus Helmfeld

Paris, 13 May 1671 [N.S.]

ADDRESS
   To Mr. Henry Oldenburg
   very humbly,
   London

NOTES

For this correspondent, see Vol. VII, Letter 1508. His last letter was written on 3 December 1670 (Vol. VII, Letter 1566).
1 His name was Gramann and he was probably the son of Hartman Gramann, a German physician who, after going to Persia with German merchants, settled in Moscow. The younger Gramann delivered this letter on 17 June; on 23 June Oldenburg drew up a series of queries for him to answer upon his return to Moscow. (The draft is in Royal Society Classified Papers, XIX, no. 71.)
2 Possibly the "juice" was amber, but there has been no previous allusion. The whole of this passage is rather strange.
3 See Vol. VII, Letter 1556, note 3.

1692
Wallis to Oldenburg
9 May 1671

Mentioned at the opening of Wallis's succeeding letter, Letter 1699.

1693
Oldenburg to Wallis
9 May 1671

Answered by Wallis in Letter 1699.

1694
Johannes Kisner to Oldenburg
12 May 1671

From the original in Royal Society MS. K, nos. 13 and 14

Nobilissime et Clarissime Domine

Personam nomenque meum Claritati Tuae esse jam incognitum, facile credo; in memoriam autem revocet illud, conversatio, dum anno jam praeterlapso Londini degerem, a mea parte suavissima innita; et literae insuper una cum libro quodam, quae Clarissimo Domino justelio, tum temporis Parisiis degenti, tradendae erant:[1] in quibus Clarissimo justelio a Tua Claritate recommendatus eram, adeo ut respectu hujus recommendationis multis beneficiis gravatus fuerim, hinc necessum habeo ut Clarissimo Domino justelio et recommendationis Authore maximas agam gratias.

Postquam autem ab illo itinere reversus fuerim Francofurtum Patriam meam, petitioni Tuae Londini factae satisfaciendum, promissisque meis standum esse, existimavi, huncque in finem commoda hac occasione Catalogum librorum Cardianum strophen, et disputationem meam Inauguralem misi;[2] D.D. Sylvii praxin conjungere animus erat, verum amici mei occasio non ferebat. illius enim praxeos prima pars edita est Lugd. Batavorum totum autem opus hic Francofurti lucem vidit.[3] Non omnes omnino libri in praesenti continenur Catalogo, quam ob causam me latet. etenim typis excussi sunt praeter praesentes, Kirckringii Commentarius in Currum Triumphalem antimonii Basilii Valentini[4] et ejusdem Anthropogeniae Ichnographia,[5] et Pro veteri Medicina D. Schüyl;[6] Helvetii Diribitorium Medicum;[7] Caroli De la Font de Peste secundum nova principia.[8] de eadem Majore.[9] & de cerebro D. Stenonis latine.[10] Experimenta Digbaeana Medica[11] de solido extra solidum D. Stenonis.[12] Theatrum pharmaceuticum S. Gioseppi Doncelli Neapol.[13] Prodromus omnium fere scientiarum Italice.[14] Montanari del vitro temperato;[15] Cl. D. Foss ex Italia redux Claritati Tuae non incognitus Danus[16] specimen mihi monstravit, ex jam dicto libro depromptum, ni fallor, mediante enim vitro peculiari modo praeparatum omnes liquores ponderabat exactissime et vigesima unius grani parte differentiam liquorum monstrabat; praeterea experimentum Bourrhi de oculis restituendis instituimus, alio tamen modo, succum enim chelidoniae majoris sumsimus, oculos duos dissecuimus, oculis adplicavimus, spatio 24 horarum tum oculos, tum quod mirabile dignum, visionem restituimus.[17] praeterlapsis aliquot septimanis puerum 10 annorum dissecui, inque eo calculum mirabilis structurae in vesica urinaria inveni, (gleich als [*illegible*] ein Worzel)[18] et ureteres maxima magnitudine; phthisicos nonnulles cultello anatomico subjeci, in quibus notatu dignissima observavi. Dominus Doctor Kornman,[19] amicus meus summus alias curiosissima et rarissima possidet; librum enim edet in lucem de tincturis seu essentiis stercorum, quorundam vermium; quos ex quibuslibet floribus vel herbis mediante putrefactione obtinet, qui postmodum eadem herba, vel flore nutriti, stercora ejiciunt, in quibus tinctura herbae, tum color, et vis illius herbae reperitur, ita in momento ex stercoribus collectis, ex vermibus rosas comedentibus tincturam extrahit rubicundissimam, et sic parili modo ex aliis. Insuper alia medicamenta peculiaria, quorum Catalogum alio mittam tempore, obtinet, quae libentissime communicaret, si alia ipsi communicarentur; Caeterum D.D. Joh. Daniel Horstius.[20] D. Eberhardt.[21] D. Schäffer[22] &c. hic chymicis, aliisque scientiis operam navant; et cum Principibus quibusdam aliisque Curiosis literarum commercium exercent.

Si ex praedictis libris, vel aliud quodpiam Claritati Tuae placeret, hic venale quod prostaret, unico solummodo indicet verbo, commoda postmodum occasione per Hollandiam, mittam. Quae nunc Londini exstant curiosa in Societate Regia et alibi imprimis, D.D. Willisii, D. Robert Boyle, (an mortuus an vivus nescio) aliorumque Authorum, scire, desidero & mecum alii novarum rerum naturae et artis cupidissimi; prae caeteris D.D. Ludovicus,[23] qui pulcherrimum de [sale tartaris] volatili tractatum scripsit, ut et Pharmaciam moderno seculo applicandam: Archiater Principi Ernesti Gothaeni. D.D. Wedel.[24] ejusdem Principis Medicus, D.D. Tack.[25] P.P. Giessae, et Archiater Princip. Hassiae. D.D. Rolfincius.[26] D. Schenkius.[27] D. Friderici P. Publici jenenses.[28] D. Schneiderus. P.P. Wittemberg[29] &c.

Responsoriam expecto epistolam a Claritate Tua, quam Domino Wurtzio conterraneo meo, Domino Harell optime notu, vel Tabellioni ordinario tradet;

Nobilissimae Claritatis Tuae observantissimus
Johannes Kisner M.D.

Francofurti 12 Majo 1671.
      raptim

D.D. Sampson[30] praesentes literas tradere non gravetur.

ADDRESS
   Monsieur
  Monsieur Henry
  Oldenburg Secretaire
  de la Societé Royale
    á Londres

TRANSLATION

Very noble and famous Sir,

That my person and name are now unknown to you, worthy Sir, I can easily believe, but the acquaintance begun—on my side with great pleasure—when I stayed in London last year may call them to mind, as also a letter (together with some book or other) which were to be delivered to the celebrated Mr. Justel, then living in Paris; in which letter your excellency recommended me to Mr. Justel.[1] I was overloaded with courtesies as a result of this recommendation, and so it is incumbent upon me to return warm thanks both to Mr. Justel and to the author of the recommendation.

However, after my return to my native Frankfurt from this journey, I thought of satisfying your requests made to me at London and discharging my promises, and with this object I have sent you a catalogue of books, "Cardianastrophe," and my inaugural dissertation.[2] I had intended to add Dr. Sylvius's *Praxis*, but this did not suit my friend's convenience. For although the first part of that *Praxis* was published at Leiden, the whole work has been issued here at Frankfurt.[3] Not all the books are included in the present Catalogue, for a reason unknown to me. For besides these there have been printed Kerckring's *Commentarius in currum triumphalem antimonii Basilii Valentini*[4] and the same author's *Anthropogeniae ichnographia*,[5] and Mr. [F.] Schuyl's *Pro veteri medicina*;[6] Helvetius' *Diribitorium medicum*,[7] Charles de la Font's *De peste* according to new principles.[8] Major on the same.[9] Steno on the brain in Latin.[10] Digby's *Experimenta medica*;[11] Steno's on the solid outside the solid.[12] The *Teatro farmaceutico* of Mr. Giuseppe Donzelli of Naples.[13] The "Sketch of almost every scientific subject" in Italian.[14] Montanari on tempered glass [drops].[15] The good Mr. Foss (a Dane who is not unknown to you)[16] has returned from Italy and showed me a sample extracted from the aforesaid book, if I am not mistaken, for by means of a peculiarly fashioned glass he weighed all fluids most precisely, and revealed the difference of the twentieth part of a grain. We have, besides, begun on Borri's experiment for the restoration of vision, but by another method, for we took the juice of the greater celandine, slashed two eyes, applied [it] to the eyes, and in the space of twenty-four hours restored the eyes and, what is marvellous, their vision.[17] Some weeks ago I dissected a boy ten years old and found in his bladder a calculus of extraordinary structure (just like [*illegible*] a root).[18] I have subjected some consumptives to the scalpel, and observed some noteworthy things. Dr. Kornmann,[19] my great friend, has some very curious and rare things in another place; for he is publishing a book on the dyes, or essences of excrements, among which are those of worms, which he obtains from any flowers or plants through putrefaction. After these worms have fed on the plants or flowers they excrete matter in which the tincture of that plant may be found, both as to color and other virtues. Thus in a moment he extracts from these feces collected from worms feeding on roses a bright red dye, and similarly with others. Moreover he possesses other particular medicines, of which I will send a list at another time, which he will most willingly impart to others, if they will communicate other things to him; further there are here at work on chemistry and other sciences Drs. Johann Daniel Horst,[20] Eberhardt,[21] and Schaeffer[22] who correspond with certain princes and other curious persons.

If any of the aforesaid books, or any other that may be on sale here, should interest you, worthy Sir, you have only to say the word and I will send it to Holland when a convenient opportunity arises. I long to know what matters of curiosity are now stirring with the Royal Society and elsewhere, especially with Dr. Willis, Mr. Boyle (whether he is alive or dead I know not), and other writers; and so besides myself do some other persons, especially Dr. Ludwig,[23] who has written a very fine treatise about the volatile salt of tartar and its application to pharmacy in modern times—he is chief physician to Duke Ernest of Gotha; Dr. Wedel,[24] his other physician; Dr. Tacke,[25] the Public Physician at Giessen and chief medical adviser to the Duke of Hesse; Dr. Rolfinck;[26] Dr. Schenck;[27] Dr. Friderici,[28] Public Physician at Jena; Dr. Schneider,[29] Public Physician at Wittenberg, etc.

I shall look forward to your reply, worthy Sir, to be delivered either by my fellow-citizen, Mr. Wurtz, or by the well-known Mr. Harell, or by the ordinary post, to your very noble excellency's most devoted

Johannes Kisner, M.D.

Frankfurt, 12 May 1671, in haste

Dr. Sampson[30] has kindly taken charge of this letter.

ADDRESS

   Mr. Henry Oldenburg
   Secretary of the Royal Society,
       London

NOTES

All we know of the writer of this letter is contained in it: that he was a graduate in medicine at Jena (there were others of the same family name from that University) and later at Leiden (1670). After leaving Leiden he visited England.

1 We have found no other record of Kisner's visits to London and Paris, nor of the letter to Justel.
2 For this work by Friedrich Hoffman, see, below, Letter 1858, note 2. Two of Kisner's dissertations were printed: one (in philosophy), *De imaginatione ejusque viribus* (Jena, 1665) and a second (in medicine) *De suffocatione hypochondriaca* (Leiden, 1670).
3 On the Leiden printing of Sylvius' *Praxeos medicae idea nova*, see his Letter 731 (Vol. IV, p. 70). This contained Book I only. The Frankfurt edition of 1671 contains three books, Book I having been partially abridged.
4 This was published at Amsterdam in 1671.
5 This also was printed at Amsterdam in 1671.
6 Published at Leiden and Amsterdam in 1670.
7 Jan Frederik Helvetius, *Diribitorium medicum de omnium morborum accidentiumque internorum et externorum definitionibus ac curationibus* (Amsterdam, 1670).
8 *Dissertationes duae medicae de veneno pestilenti* (Amsterdam, 1671).
9 We could not find a plague treatise by an author of this name; it is just possible Kisner meant "a larger one on the same subject."
10 A Latin translation of Steno's *Discours . . . sur l'anatomie du cerveau* (Paris, 1669) by Guido Fanoisius, published at Leiden in 1671.
11 *Experimenta medica, Recueil des remedes et secrets, tirez des Memoires de Monsieur le Chevalier Digby* (Liège, 1671). There was an earlier Paris edition.
12 Kisner has made a mistake in the title, which should be *De solido intra solidum naturaliter contento dissertationis prodromus* (Florence, 1669).
13 First published at Naples in 1661; there were many subsequent editions.
14 We could not trace this compendium.

15 Geminiano Montanari, *Speculazioni fisiche . . . sopra gli effetti di que' vetri temprati . . .* (Bologna, 1671); compare Vol. VII, Letters 1555 and 1619.
16 See Vol. VI, p. 533, note.
17 In G. F. Borri's *Epistolae duae ad Thomam Bartholinum* (Copenhagen, 1669)—see *Phil. Trans.*, no. 64 (10 October 1670), 2081–82—there is an obviously ridiculous claim by Borri that "having cut asunder the Apple of the Eye of divers Animals, and squeezed out the humors . . . he hath restored the sight to those animals . . . and that he had performed this experiment upon many persons . . . ," the remedy consisting of "a certain Water of Celondine, and a Phelgme of Vitriol of Mars [iron sulphate]." One can only hope that Kisner's cruelty was as *gedanken* as Borri's.
18 This is written in German script; the third word is blotted.
19 This physician is previously mentioned in Vol. V, p. 216, but we have discovered nothing about him or this projected book.
20 J. D. Horst (1620–85), successively Professor of Medicine at Marburg and Giessen, was physician to the republic of Frankfurt-am-Main and to the Landgrave of Hesse-Darmstadt.
21 We have not been able to identify this physician.
22 The physician Sebastian Schaeffer (1631–86) of Frankfurt-am-Main settled at Heidelberg and wrote extensively on medicine; however, there was a Wilhelm Ernst Schaeffer actually practising at Frankfurt who wrote on surgery.
23 Daniel Ludwig (1625–80), of Weimar, practised in Wittenberg and Hamburg, and was chief physician to the Duke of Saxe-Gotha. His treatise was published as no. 123 of Vol. II of *Miscellanea Curiosa* (1671). Oldenburg possessed a copy of his *Dissertatio de volatilitate salis tartari*, published at Gotha in 1667.
24 Georg Wolfgang Wedel (1645–1721) had been in this post since 1667; he had a most fluent pen, and published several treatises in Vol. II of *Miscellanea Curiosa*.
25 Johann Tacke (*c.* 1618–75); see Vol. V, p. 217, note 5.
26 Guernerus Rolfinck (1599–1673), a great traveler, taught briefly at Padua (1629) and established himself at Jena.
27 Johann Theodor Schenck (1619–71), received his M.D. at Jena 1645, and was Professor of Medicine there from 1653; he was also physician to the city of Chemnitz.
28 Johann Arnold Friderici (1637–72), M.D. of Jena, and Professor of Medicine there.
29 Probably Conrad Victor Schneider (*c.* 1614–80), Professor of Medicine at Wittenberg, who was physician to the Prince of Anhalt.
30 Presumably this was Henry Sampson (*c.* 1629–1700) of Pembroke Hall, Cambridge, rector of Framlingham in Suffolk, who resigned after the Restoration and turned to medicine. He studied at Padua and proceeded M.D. at Leiden (July, 1668); he was elected an honorary Fellow of the College of Physicians in 1680.

1695
Dodington to Oldenburg
12 May 1671
From the original in Royal Society MS. D 1, no. 22

Venice May 22 1671

Sr

By meanes of a friend at Naples I endeavoured to procure the best History I could get, of ye Bitings and effects of the Tarantula, as you directed. They write me from ye mouth of Dr Cornelio a most eminent man & very curious,[1] as you know in all inquiries into Nature, That the Bitings of Tarantulaes are fabulous, & that there is no such disease, as is reputed: But that that wch is proceedes from ye Heat & drynesse of ye Clymate. The last yeare Dr Cornelio went on purpose into Apuglia to satisfy his Judgment, a man yt seldome takes upon Trust, He saw many Tarantulaes, but found the effects of their bitings to be noething but ye Fancies of ye Credulous vulgar. He sayes there want not several Tracts of this kind, But since all are Fictitious, cui bono?[2]

I will shortly send you dr Cornelios systeme of Philosophy,[3] Sigr Giov. Borellies Book de Lapide.[4] Another Apollonij Pergaei in wch is his Archimede di Maurolyco,[5] And I would allso send you ye Historia naturale de Ferrante Imperiale,[6] in wch there is not one lye, But t'is not to be had for Love or mony. Heere they are now reprinting it; I am Sr ever more

yr affectionate humble servant
J dodington

Mr Oldenbergh

ADDRESS
For Mr Henry Oldenberg Secretary
    to ye Royal Society
        In
            London

NOTES

1 Dr. Tommaso Cornelio of Naples, often mentioned before.
2 "whom do they profit?"

3 Presumably his *Progymnasmata physica* (Venice, 1663).
4 The attribution of this title to Borelli seems to be a mistake.
5 G. B. Borelli published an edition (*Conicorum lib. V. VI. VII*) of Apollonios at Florence in 1661, but this does not include Maurolyco's Archimedes, for which see Vol. VI, p. 423, note 13.
6 Ferrante Imperato, *Dell' Istoria naturale libri XXVIII* (Naples, 1599) was reprinted at Venice in 1672.

1696
Lister to Oldenburg
28 April and 13 May 1671

From the original in Royal Society MS. L 5, no. 30

Yorke Apr. 28. 1671

Sr

Having a suit depending in Chancery, I did verily beleive, it would have brought me up to Towne this Terme wch is at hand: but upon further motions in yt Court, it will not. for this cause I have sent you up by Loft,[1] a small box of some things wch I had got ready for you according to promise & wch I thought to have brought you my selfe. amongst ye rest you will receive ye viviparous Fly:[2] if any part of ym come not whole to your hands, they are soe frequent, yt there is noe pale-side or hedge but does afford ym, soe yt it will be easy to discover ym.

I likewise desire, since I may not yet be soe happy as to kisse your hands in person, yt you will be pleased to make good your favour to me & be assisting to put me up Candidate, as soon as you have an opportunity, yt I may have ye honour to be of your body, if I shall be thought worthy.[3]

I answered your last to me some weeks agoe[4] wherein, though I was still silent of ye plant, wch I said would afford a fixt black, yet I beseech you not to looke upon me, as one yt delights to treasure up secretts. me-thinkes I would have all ye world free & communicative in their notions & inventions, yt soe we might hasten & participate, if possible, even wth posteritie. 'Tis an argument of an disengenious Spirit to be secret, or at least of a weake stock in ym, yt shall seeke to uphold his fame therby. Those secretts too for ye most part, when discovered, proving to be things of noe great value. Indeed first discoveries of phaenomena are agreable surprises & I am wont to suspect ym untill I have made ym over & over again. I hope if I can get leisure to enlarge ye notes I sent you about colours[5] by Autumne & therefore I must desire to peruse ym again. but I tyer you

Sr

          Your most humble servant
            Martin Lister

Sr

This was writ according to ye date but a suddain messenger tooke me away into Craven, whence I returned but yesterday soe yt it was not sent nor ye box mentioned but you will not fail to receive ym ye next opportunity. I shall returne ye Fees if I be accepted.[6] May 13th 1671.

ADDRESS
 These
 For his honoured friend
 Mr Henry Oldenburg
 at his house in ye Palmal
  London

             POSTMARK MA 15

NOTES

1 The carrier from York.
2 See Vol. VII, Letter 1632.
3 Compare Vol. VII, Letter 1601 and its note 6.
4 Vol. VII, Letter 1674 replying to Letter 1669.
5 See Vol. VII, Letter 1634.
6 That is, his dues as a Fellow of the Royal Society.

1697
Flamsteed to Oldenburg
13 May 1671
From the original in Royal Society MS. F 1, no. 68

Derby: May 13 1671

Mr Oldenburge
Sr

The civilities I have on all occasions reaceaved at yr hands, that respect which yu professe to retaine for ye Mathematicall artes, & yr daily endeavors for ye promotion of them engage mee to give yu an account of my laste performances. Wn this day was a sevennight[1] at Night I observed ye moone applieing with her darke side to a starre of ye 4th magnitude whose place is Virgo 9°–53′, latitude 1°–20′ north: at ye stars ingresse under ye moone, ye height of Jupiter was 32°.50′ or 52′ whence I deduce ye hour 9h–16′–30″, & ye star was a little lower then the lowest edge of ye propontis,[2] but how much I dare not assert for my glasse would not receive a whole moone, & ye interposed darke part of her body hindred mee from defineing how much the starre was lower, but very much I am sure it could not be:

The precise emersion I saw not, but ye star when I returned to my glasse was ye breadth of ye Caspian spot[3] distant from the moones limbe & higher then ye supreme part of ye said spot by ye whole lenght [*sic*] of it: then I tooke ye altitude of ye supreme limbe of ye moone 31°–54′ whence I collect ye starr was 31°–45′ & deduce ye hour 10h–24′–36″, & immediately turneing to Jupiter I tooke his height 22°–36′ whence I find ye hour 10h–25′–00″. I dare not affirme that this is altogether an accurate observation, but from ye coherence of it I am induced to beleive it is not faulty; tho it differ at least 10 minutes, if not a quarter of an hour from ye calculation, all thinges being duely considered.[4] I suppose Mr Hooke or some other may have observed it wth yu, whose observations I desire to heare of, that so I may either have mine owne corrected or confirmed:[5] I hope who ever have made any upon the communication of this, will not refuse to impart mee theirs, & I trust yu will please to informe mee of them. I have this weeke likewise tried to find some diurnall appulses but find their will be none to any fixed starrs this yeare observable. I mentioned to yu formerly[6] yt ye moone would passe by Venus on ye 29 of ye next June in ye morneing, but upon better calculation I find that it will be an exceeding wide transit by reason of ye moones great latitude from Venus & ye hieght of ye 90 degree of ye Ecliptick,[7] & not observeable except to those who inhabit ye extreme Northerne, or far Easterne parts of ye Earth. But on ye 20 of September in ye morneing ye Moone passes very neare Jupiter[8] I

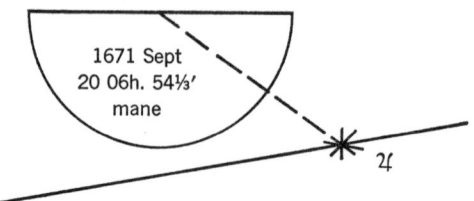

expected yt shee would have covered him but upon frameing my calculation to 18h–54'–22" after ye noone of ye 19th day at London I found:

		°	′	″
The suns place	Aquarius	07	– 01	+ 22
The moones place	Virgo	6	– 21	+ 32
her latitude North		1	– 38	– 49
ye place of Jupiter	Virgo	6	– 40	– 24
his latitude North		0	– 56	– 33
Suns Right Ascension		186	– 26	– 44
Right ascension of time		283	– 35	– 30
Right ascension of ye mid heaven		110	– 02	– 14
The Mid heaven	Cancer	18	– 29	– 35
its declination		22	– 13	– 07
altitude		60	– 41	– 07
The Horoscope	Aquarius	14	– 06	– 24
Midheaven from it		85	– 36	– 47
The Moone from it & Ecliptic		37	– 44	– 50
in a great circle		37	– 46	– 40
Altitude of ye Nonagessime degree		60	– 59	– 00
ye Moones angle orient		63	– 40	– 00
height of ye Moones center		33	– 18	– 00
Azumuth from ye point orient		18	– 58	– 00
parallacticall Angle		34	– 12	– 00
altitude			47	– 30
ye Moones parallax in longitude			39	– 17
latitude			26	– 42

				°	′	″
So ye Moones visible place	...	...	Virgo	7	00	49
Visible North latitude ...	...	...		1	12	07
in consequence of Jupiter	...	...			20	25
with greater latitude	...	...			15	34
theire centers distance ...	...	...			25	40
The Suns true height ...	...	...		6	11	30

The moones semidiameter is 15′–14″: ye Angle of ye moones visible way by ye starre about 6½ de[grees]. Whence I conclude yt by this calculus ye moones limbe will not cover ye starre, but yt Jupiter will stand from it 3⅓ at ye visible conjunction: for illustration of this appearance I have added this scheme of it as usuall. The nearest approach will appeare about sun riseing: I am apt to beleive yt ye latitude of Jupiter will be 1′ 30″ more, or above, then calculated. if so ye approach will be nearer: in Poland & ye easterne & Norherne parts ye moone may cover ye star:

I crave yr pardon Sr for haveing so long deteind yr Hevelius whom I intend now wthin a forthnight to restore:[9] for then I shall have occasion of sendeing somethings to London & shall send it with them: Pray present my respects & services to Mr Hooke if yu see him, & intreat him when his leasure serves to observe how nearely hee can estimate & state ye time of ye Moones semiillumination at ye Quadratures not heedeing whether shee be much elevated or in ye 90 degre,[7] or not, for by something I noted last Quarter in my tube of 13⅓ feet I find it somewhat difficult to determine concerneing ye apparent dichotomy. I would likewise gladly hear what yu may impart concerneing his method of makeing diurnall observations of appulses: I have no more to adde, but that I desire from yu, ye observation of this appulse; of which, I have given yu mine, or any of the praecedent which either by reason of ye indisposition of ye aire, or my body I was prevented from observeing. And to subscribe my selfe, Sr,

Yr obliged servant to command
John Flamsteed

Pray deliver ye enclosed to Mr Collins when yu see him.[10]

ADDRESS
To Henry Oldenburge Esqr
at his house in ye middle
of ye Pell mell neare
   St Jameses Westminster
      these present
         London

POSTMARK MA 15

NOTES

1 Flamsteed has written in the margin "Maii 6 vespere" ("on 6 May in the evening").
2 The Propontis was Hevelius' name (*Selenographia*, Danzig, 1647) for the lunar "sea" named by Riccioli (and still today) the Mare Vaporum.
3 Hevelius' Mare Caspium is the modern Mare Fecunditatis, but it is hard to know what Flamsteed means by the "spot," unless it is the crater Taruntius.
4 This occultation had been predicted by Flamsteed (*Phil. Trans.*, no. 66, 12 December 1670, 2030) as lasting from 9h. 9′37″ to 10h. 14′56″ on 6 May.
5 When this letter was read to the Society on 18 May 1671 "Mr. Hooke was ordered to communicate his observation" to Flamsteed.
6 See Vol. VII, Letter 1636.
7 The moon's position when passing through (or near) the solstitial points.
8 Flamsteed has drawn a small marginal sketch, reproduced below: "Twentieth September 1671, at 6h $54\frac{1}{3}′$ in the morning."
9 That is, the *Selenographia* he had borrowed.
10 His letter to Collins of the same date (Rigaud, II, 115–16) is a shorter version of the present.

1698
Sylvius to Oldenburg
13 May 1671

From the original in Royal Society MS. S 1, no. 97

Vir Amplissime,

Postquam literas meas quavis hora meo amico tradendas adornaveram, en Haga Comitis afferantur mihi a Nobilissimo Barone Libero de Nulant, &c, literae ad Te mittendae,[1] quibus ejusdem Tractatulum, de quo mentionem facit, quemque casu ad manus habebam, si fortassis eo careas, censui jungendum: cumque eodem tempore aliquot Angli domum reversuri Effigiem meam aeri incisam rogarent, arbitratus sum, non futurum Tibi ingratum, si ejus duo exemplaria eadem opera ad Te mitterem,[2] ne illa citius per alium, quam per me in tuas deveneat manus; vicissim tuam, si extet, desiderans & rogans; quo amplius cognoscas, quanti Te merito faciam. Iterum Vale, ac me redama

Totum Tuum
F. De Le Boe, Sylvium

Lugdunum Batavorum 23º Maij 1671. [N.S.]

TRANSLATION

Most worthy Sir,

After I had completed my letter by an appointed time for a friend of mine to carry over, lo and behold there comes a letter brought me from the Freiherr von Nuland at the Hague, to be sent on to you;[1] to which I thought fit to join that little treatise of his that he mentions, which I happened to have at hand, in case by any chance you have it not. And since some Englishmen returning home at the same time have asked for my engraved portrait I judged it would not be unwelcome to you if I send you a couple of copies of the same thing,[2] in case it should reach you quicker by some other means, than straight from myself, at the same time begging you for a copy of yours, should it have been done. By this you may the better know how much I esteem you. Farewell again, and return affection for the affection of him who is

Wholly yours,
F. de le Boe, Sylvius

Leiden, 23 May 1671 [N.S.]

NOTES

Since Oldenburg was Sylvius' only correspondent in London, so far as we know, we assume that this letter was addressed to him.

1 We have found neither the letter from Sylvius—presumably of earlier date—nor that from Franz Wilhelm, Freiherr von Nuland, who is on record as serving in the Spanish army (when he was governor of Cadiz) and in that of Brandenburg. He was a correspondent of Huygens. His book against Descartes, *Elementa physica* (The Hague, 1669) is described by Oldenburg in Vol. VII, Letter 1568.
2 The portrait of Sylvius drawn and engraved by Cornelis van Dalen in 1659 is well known; it is reproduced in his *Opera medica* (Amsterdam, 1679). We here reproduce in Plate I (from Wren's papers) a charcoal and crayon version of the same portrait.

1699
Wallis to Oldenburg
13 May 1671
From the original in Royal Society MS. W 1, no. 120

Oxford. May 13. 1671

Sir

Yours of Tuesday last[1] (if I do not misremember the date) was in part answered before it came by one of mine of ye same date; desiring you to return me ye papers My Lo. Br. last had as soon as you could;[2] wch are not yet come to hand, perhaps they may come by this nights coach. To the experiment His Lop. mentions,[3] I confesse I have sayd nothing in them: & the truth is, it will not be solved by ye same onely principle with ye rest, but hath somewhat singular in it, wch may in time give some light to ye nature of Gravitation: but 'tis rather Physicall than Mathematical, I was not satisfyed what clearly to say in it. Yet since his Lop. thinks it proper that I should say something; I shal do so; & it will be to the same purpose that I have some time spoken (as I remember) in ye Royal Society at Arundel house, (whether any great notice were taken of it or no, I know not:) that whereas heretofore, in ye old Philosophy, Earth &c were thought heavy, & ye Ayr light; it would here seem contrary, & that all actual Gravitation amongst us proceeds from ye Air or Aether's pressure & spring, (which seemes allso to be from somewhat incumbent on it,) without wch these Dull bodies, wch wee call Heavy, would rest in quiet without any actuall gravitation or discension; & be no more apt to move downward, than sidewise; & accordingly, the quicksilver (perfectly freed from Air, & then resting suspended in an inverted Tube to the height of 40, 50, 60, or more inches, much above ye ordinary hight,) being unmolested by ye Airs pressure or spring, (that without, pressing it upward if at all, & there being none in it or above it to presse downward,) rests at quiet in yt position: But if either by a concussion of ye Tube, or by an inward disturbance from ye spring of ye Ayr left within ye Tube or now suffered to enter, it be put into motion, then (in proportion to its quantity of matter, denseness of parts, or what ever yt bee wch is vulgarly or rudely expressed by ye word Weight,) it pursues that motion & will compresse downwards, as it would do sideways in case of a laterall impulse given it: For, not onely downwards, but sidewise allso, the heavyer a body is, the harder it strikes when put in motion. So yt whatever it bee yt wee call Weight in Quicksilver (or ye like) though without such pressure or spring of air it would not begin a motion, yet being put into motion obeys ye Statick laws. And it was this consideration yt made mee, (in ye account I gave you of Monsr. Leibnitzius hypothesis, April.7.1671.)[4] so inclinable to attribute Gravitation to ye Motion or Pressure of ye incumbent Aether. And I think My Lo. Brouncker will not much differ in opinion from mee in this point. But this account of it, though I know not how to give a better, I can but hesitantly deliver, not with a full confidence; being not forward to be positive in new Hypotheses. But if, such as it is, it bee thought proper to bee there published or his Lo. wil vouchsafe to help correct & perfect it, I shall find a place somewhere in those papers to insert it. Yet not omitting that other consideration, of ye little inequalities or asperities even in ye most polite surface, wch cause somewhat of friction or cohaesion or parts whereby motion is more or lesse hindered, (of wch I have oft occasion to speak, as ye cause of Rolling rather then Sliding of a Body moved on ye contiguous surface of another Body;) which may be inough to counterpoise ye action of some very little Ayr wch may (after ye greatest diligence) be yet remaining amongst ye Quicksilver. But in order hereunto, I must desire you, if you can, (out of your Notes or Memory,) to inform mee what day or time this experiment was first exhibited in ye Society then at Gresham College; wch I think was about ye year 1661 or 1662, by Monsr Huygens, but wth ye assistance of ye Ayr-pump, wch hath since by my Lo. Brouncker & Mr. Boyl been done without it.[5] For it will be very convenient (for asserting the Experiment to ye true Authors) to mention ye date of it, & (if it be so) its being Registered in ye Societies Journal.[6] I shal adde no more, but that I am Sr

Your affectionate friend & servant.
John Wallis

I shal be glad to hear of ye reception of this, because of ye inclosed wch is an Original.[7]

ADDRESS
These
For Mr Henry Oldenburg
in the Palmal near St
James's
London

NOTES

1 May 9; the letters referred to here have not survived.
2 See Vol. VII, Letter 1658, note; Wallis's discussion with Lord Brouncker remains mysterious.
3 As appears from what follows, and the entry in Birch, *History*, II, 482, reporting the reading of this letter on 18 May, the experiment was that of the anomalous suspension of mercury at heights above some 30 inches (see Vol. II, pp. 99–101, 123–27).
4 That is, Letter 1673 in Vol. VII.
5 The phenomenon of anomalous suspension was discovered in air-pump experiments made by Huygens, in Holland, in July 1662; the experiment was successfully demonstrated to the Royal Society when Huygens was in London during August 1663. On 7 October Boyle and Brouncker reported getting the same effect without the aid of the air pump.
6 That is, its "Journal Book" or Register.
7 This is not now with the letter.

1700

Beale to Oldenburg

13 May 1671

From *Phil. Trans.*, no. 71 (22 May 1671), 2144–49

Sir,

I am glad, you have my honoured Friend, Mr. Reed's, Advertisements;[1] for he is a person of sure veracity and much experience, and disdains not (for his diversion and recreation) to practise, with his own hands, inoculations and the finer kinds of graftings. And what ever becomes of his expressions for the Descent of Sap, his Instances and Experiments annexed, are very much obliging. You have published my apprehensions as to that point;[2] and no wonder, if the effects, which Mr. Reed mentions, do follow from that correspondence in all parts of the whole Plant, (which is by me acknowledged,) especially, since by the leaves, and all the pores in the branches, and body, the Plant draws a kind sustenance from the Sun, Air and Dews, as by the roots from the succulent soyl. And as the channels (which I may call the Conduits and Strainers) of several Stocks and Cions's do differ, so may some change of the liquor be made by several kinds of

Distillation; as Spirit of Wine is sooner rectified in some kinds of winding Tin-Instruments, than in a plain perpendicular one. And from the forenoted difference of Stocks, and the differing grains of the Roots and Timber, as also from the differing Leaves (if accurately inspected, and considered,) we may in time perhaps discover some particular causes of the differing Sap, Fruit and Blossoms. And it would become the accurateness of this Age, in which so many are expert in Draughts, and in Chalcography, to annex to the figure of Plants, the texture and particular grains of each root, stem, and branch, both for ornament, and to suggest further instructions, whilest we learn their tasts and other qualities.

'Tis about fifteen Years since I published a hint, how to discover by the Colour, Figure, Tenderness, and asperities of the Leaves of young Apple-Plants, and Crabs, first appearing in the Spring, which Plant would yield the more delicate, and which the more austere fruit, and liquor, to several kinds and degrees of delicacy and austerity, fatness[3] and insipidness, and vigour or briskness. And this I think allows a consideration for some efficacy, or sign (at least) of change or operation in the Descent of Sap. But as far as I dare, or did deny the descent of Sap, I meant it in the *vulgar* sense of that expression, viz. the main quantity of Sap, which ascends in the Spring, and is gradually hardened into leaves, blossoms, fruit, timber, in such manner as the Ossification in young Animals is described by Dr. Kerckringius in your last Tract of Num. 70.[4] 'Tis a large quantity of Sap, which is expended on the fruit and growth of some Trees, on Acorns, Wallnuts, Chesnuts; and this returns not to the root in winter, yet consists well with the Sentiment of the Circulation of the Sap, which in some seasons may run the round more swiftly than in other: neither do I discern, that this makes any opposition to Worthy Mr. Reeds intentions.

I have long ago published, and do here again confirm what Mr. Reed remarks, that a dull and insipid Apple is made more gustful by being grafted on the stock of the harshest Crab, and an austere Apple somewhat mitigated on a stock of gentler fruit. And I willingly embrace this occasion to offer my vote, that the Genet-moyles were as well known, and as well spread all over England, as the Red-strake now is. It would be a great ease to the vulgar Husbandman, who (without expenses, curiosity, care, or troubling of grafting,) may by the knotted branches propagate them in ground that deserves not to be called fertile, as they do in the Rye-land, and Gorsty ground[5] in Wales; and the Cider made of the fruit (which when perfectly ripe hath a peculiar fragrancy,) is so delicately agreeable for tender palats, that I was once guilty of giving it publickly the precedence before any Red-strake; and I had frequently the softer sex on my side, till the heat of July did too often alter the case. And there is a Summer-Apple well known to Mr. Reed by the name of French Cornel,[6] early ripe, and very richly full of a most pleasing liquor, which I dare extoll for a most delicious beverage, before the ordinary time for Cider comes in. I do not know, whether by art it can be preserved for durance. 'Tis a small tree, all the branches crisped, and curled, full of knots at every turning, and apt to grow by any branch, that is cut off below the knot. It prospers best in a good mould, better than that of the common fields; yet in the dry Rye-land it bears plentifully every second year, and when one of these trees fails, the next of the same kind may have a full burden; I did not find all of that kind to agree in the year of forbearance.

And because I am fitter and prompter to serve for the benefit of many, than for any curiosity, I crave leave further to advertise, that some soyl which doth hardly bear Apples, does most kindly bear Pears; and there is a great variety of Pears to humor every palate, some early ripe, some long lasting, and for all seasons of the year, some to be rolled,[7] baked or dried, or otherwise to be preserved, which may as well be had from our East-Countries, as from Worcestershire, Herefordshire and Salop; but my chief aim here is for those Pears which yield the richest, wholesomest, and most winy liquor in great adundance, and at good certainty; of which there are many excellent kinds in the confines between Worcester and Hereford from Powick to Bosbury, where the Bareland-pear (mentioned by Mr. Reed) grows in the common arable field; that, and some other pears of uncertain names in Powick do yield a very strong and long lasting liquor. The Horse-pears, as there they call them, the white and the red of several kinds, yield abundance of pleasant liquor. The Ailets great and little, wild and gentle, the Linten pear, Lullam-pear, Squash-pear,[8] have their peculiar excellencies for liquor, and some of them for the largeness of the Tree; yielding constantly some hogsheads of liquor yearly. Where the soil hath not been tryed, and found kindest for Apples, 'tis the surest way to plant Pears alternatively, and where the liquor of Pears is weak, or less lasting, this may be helped by a gentle mixture of Crabs, or of the harshest Apples to humour all palats, and for a help to the Stomach, the mixture being made in the time of grinding the fruit together: and thus, when the better soil is too shallow for Apples, but receives Pears kindly at a greater depth, a hedge-row of Crabs, or wild austere apples, raised on the mounds and ripening in the same season, will, by well ordering it, afford such a perfect remedy, that judicious palats may be deceived, and take it for the best

Cider. I must here give notice, that Sir W.S.[9] recommends the Hamlin-apple of Devon for Cider equal to the best, if not excelling. These disquisitions of the choicest fruits for drink, are modern, and in my memory were scarcely regarded in any part of England that I could hear of. For the best season to transplant, Dr. Lauremberg[10] a person of much experience, and no less learned in the best old Authors, agreeth punctually in all circumstances, and for the like reasons, with the fore-noted worthy Gentleman, that Plants, which cannot well bear the hardship of the Winter, should be transplanted in the Spring; but that such as are able to bear the extremity of a cold winter, should be transplanted in Autumn. In this only he differs, that he saith, Poma, pira, cerasa vulgaria, coryli, oxyocanthi, pruna, &c. facile frigus ferunt, & Autumno transplantari optimo successu solent: and then for the Spring he refers juglandes, persica, abricoca, aliquot cerasorum genus.[11] Lauremb. de Hort. cult. l.1.c. 28. I think, where he wrote and practised, is as cold a Country as England:[12] but the more we are obliged for these latter Experiments, and for the friendly and seasonable caution to decline adventures against the rage of winter. On the sudden I see no good reason, why we should expose any Plants to the hazard of the winters cruelty, since tender plants prosper infallibly by a Vernal transplantation; yet I must tell you, 'tis an old English and a Welsh Proverb concerning Apples, Pears, and the Haw-thorn-quick, Oaks; *Set them at Allhallontide, and* command *them to prosper; set after Candlemas, and* intreat *them to grow*. Mr. Reed's pleasant observation of the prudence and sagacity of Bees, invites me to ask, why we have so few Apiaries in England according to Mr. Mewe's modell, represented in Hartlib's *Common-wealth of Bees*,[13] Pag. 48. &c. which gave him the entertainment at any time to view their Mechanical skil, Chymistry, Industry, Loyalty, and Discipline through the glass-windows of his Hive, and paid him also wax and hony worth twenty nobles yearly at the least. I wish this Royal and Loyal insect had a just and full number of prompt disciples all over England, which would offer no worse sacrifice upon our publick Altars, then Hony and Wax, the good example of Piety, Devotion, Arts and Industry.

NOTES

The date and author are given in the printed heading, p. 2144.
1 This refers to Vol. VII, Letter 1652.
2 Beale's views, together with those of Tonge, had been published in *Phil. Trans.*, no. 43 (11 January 1668/9), 853–62.
3 *Sic* (for "flatness"); see below, Letter 1722.

4 This is mentioned in the review of *Anthropogeniae ichnographia* in *Phil. Trans.*, no. 70 (17 April 1671), 2136–37.
5 "Gorst" is a dialect form of "gorse."
6 This name does not appear in Evelyn's *Pomona* (London, 1664) nor in Parkinson's books.
7 Hard pears were sometimes rolled or bruised to make them seem mellower.
8 These names again do not seem to have been commonly used.
9 Probably Sir William Strode of Devonshire (see Vol. III, p. 309, and p. 311, note 5), the patron of Samuel Colepresse.
10 Peter Villumsen Laurenberg (1585–1639), author of the *Horticultura, libris II comprehensa* (Frankfurt, [1631], 1654) from which Beale proceeds to quote.
11 "The apple, pear, common cherry, hazel, berberis, plum, etc. easily stand the frost and are usually transplanted with great success in the fall . . . walnut, peach, apricot, and a few kinds of cherry."
12 The place was Rostock.
13 In *The Reformed Common-wealth of Bees. Presented in several letters and Observations to Samuel Hartlib, Esqr.* (London, 1655) there is a letter from Hartlib to William Mewe about bees, as well as an account of Christopher Wren's transparent beehive and another new hive invented by Dr. Thomas Browne of Norwich. Beale seems to have attributed Wren's idea to Mewe.

1701

Oldenburg to Willughby

16 May 1671

From the memorandum in Royal Society MS. W 3, no. 43

Writ again May 16. acquainting him, yt ye letter of Apr. 29.[1] went not till May 13. by carrier. Told him of ye improvement of his Experiments wth mercury and Air,[2] and of Paris.[3] and Mor[ison's] books of plants.[4]

NOTES

Second reply to Letter 1684.
1 Letter 1690.
2 For Willughby's experiments on the passage of water through pieces of branch, see Letter 1655 (Vol. VII) and Letter 1684. When similar experiments were made at the meeting of the Royal Society on 4 May, using mercury as the fluid, Willughby's finding that the flow took place more readily from the small end of the branch to the large (inner) end than vice versa was confirmed. The same occurred when air was blown through.

3 On 20 April Hooke had exhibited a method of examining the pores in charcoal with a microscope by filling them with mercury. He proposed that fluid plaster of Paris might serve better, since it would reflect light less glaringly.

4 If we have the name correctly, the allusion is certainly to Robert Morison's *Plantarum umbelliferarum distribution nova* (Oxford, 1672). This was the first earnest or prodromus of Morison's "general and genuine Method, [for] reducing all Vegetables to certain infallible Classes or Heads, by Tables of Affinity or Cognation," forming the first part of *Plantarum historia universalis Oxoniensis*; the second appeared in 1680, and the third was edited after Morison's death in 1683 by Jacob Bobart, the younger. There is an account of the *Distributio* promising its continuation in *Phil. Trans.*, no. 81 (25 March 1672), 4027–28.

1702
Oldenburg to Flamsteed
20 May 1671

Oldenburg has endorsed Flamsteed's Letter 1697 as answered on 20 May; this answer is also recorded in Flamsteed's reply, Letter 1708, as containing the information about appulses which Flamsteed had requested.

1703
Lister to Oldenburg
22 May 1671

From the original in Royal Society MS. L 5, no. 31
Partially printed in *Phil. Trans.*, no. 71 (22 May 1671), 2165–66

Yorke, May 22 1671

Sr

I thanke you for ye care you have of my papers & ye ample satisfaction you have made me for something yt made me looke like a Plagiary, especially considering yt other notes of mine were not long since in question, but I owe ye retrieving of both to your care & obliging pen.[1]

I gave you a short account formerly[2] of certain *Matrices* or Insect-huskes of ye Kermes kind, wch I have some yeares since observed on Plume Trees. This instant May hath afforded me ye same observation & some little improvement of it. 1. I have observed ye same *Patellae*[3] or huskes indifferently on Vine branches, Cherry-laurel, Plume Trees & ye Cherry Tree. ye figure of ye huskes is rounde save where it cleaves to ye branch; for bignesse, somewhat more than ye halfe of a grey pea. These, I say cleave to their branches as ye *Patellae* doe to rockes; for colour they are of a very darke chesnut, extreamly smooth & shining membrane-like. They adhere most commonly to ye underside of a branch or twigg & soe are best secured against ye injuries of weather as too much sun & rain. They are well fastned to ye branches Angle & sometimes many in company. Observe further, yt you will seldome find ym without Vermine as Pismires &c, wch I guesse peirce ym & prey upon ym. Thus much for ye intire *Coccum*.[4]

If you open one of ym, yt is, cutt off dextrously ye top of ye huske wth a rasour, you will find sometimes 5 or more small white maggotts of ye waspe or bee kind, yt is sharpe at both ends: when these are carfully taken out, you will further observe ye remainder of their provision of meal & a partition twixt ym & ye branch, where, what they excerne, is reserved.

Lastly, if, when you have cleared ye huske of maggots, bee meat, & excrements you than rubb ye empty membranes upon white paper, it will freely & copiously tinge ye paper wth a beautifull purple or murrey.[5] At ye date of this none of ye maggotts were yet *in nympha*,[6] soe yt you cannot expect from me, a description of ye Bee or Waspe, they will turne to, when they come to perfection.

I thought good to send you ye Observation, before ye season was over, yt you might ye earlier & in due time communicate it, if you thinke fitting, to ye Curious, who may satisfy ym selves forthwith & verify & improve it. Few Cherry Trees, I suppose, in any place, but will yield ym some of these Berries. However if they shall not be soe fortunat as to light on ym, I shall furnish you by ye Carrier wth ym & other things formerly promised. I am Sir

Your most humble servant
Martin Lister

Since I made this Observation, I begin to doubt of ye truth of what I was informed during my abroad at Montpellier concerning ye insolation of Kermes wormes:[7] indeed, I did my selfe once see ye Kermes Huskes in May upon an Ilex branch & as I remember they were very much like these (perhapps somewhat lesse & rounder) though these matrices must needs be ye worke of a different species of Waspe; but had not than ye curiosity nicely to examine ym. I say I now begin to suspect from ye ressemblance of these two sorts of *Matrices*, yt ye scarlet powder proceeds from ye husk & not from ye dried *sanies*[8] of ye worme, & therefore ye relation I gave you by heare-say ought to be suppressed as false or kept in silence untill it be veryfyed by good authoritie. This jealousie, I say, is suggested to me by ye conformity of ye true Kermes berry & our matrices, yet there is this to make us not wholly to reject it, yt Cochineil is ye whole substance of ye Insect it selfe.

ADDRESS
>These
>For his honoured Friend
>Mr Henry Oldenburg
>at his house in ye Palmal
>>London

POSTMARK MA 24

NOTES

1 See Vol. VII, Letter 1674 *ad fin* and its note 4; the reference is to Oldenburg's reprinting of Letter 1627.
2 Letter 1656 in Vol. VII.
3 Hollow or saucer-shaped, or like an inverted saucer; also applied to the limpet, as a few lines below.
4 A homopterous insect, including those from which cochineal, kermes, and lac are derived.
5 Purple-red or color of the mulberry (Lat. *morum*).
6 Metamorphosed into the immature insect.
7 See Vol. VII, Letter 1645.
8 Body fluid.

1704
Oldenburg to Selbie
24 May 1671

From the memorandum in Royal Society MS. S 1, no. 111

Rec. May 8. 71. Answ. May 24. 1671. Take Juyce of ½ douzen or $\frac{1}{12}$ limones,¹ and having cut off very thin the yellow rinds of about half ye limons employed, put ym into ye strain'd Juyce, and stopping ye glas well, digest ym by ye heat of ye Sun or some equivalent warmth for 8. or 10. days or longer: yn pour off as much clear liquor as you can, and into it put well colour'd corals, not finely beaten, and either in a very gentle heat, or (wch I have found to succeed very well, tho more slowly) in ye cold let ym stand quiet for some days, and ye liquor will be deeply tincted, wch the corals wil cease to be; this Tincture of Coral may be afterwards further elaborated wth spirit of wine, if one pleaseth.

NOTES

Reply to Letter 1686.
1 Presumably the sense of the odd-looking fraction is "1 dozen."

1705
Malpighi to Oldenburg
24 May 1671

From the original in Royal Society Malpighi Letters I, no. 10

Eruditissimo et Praeclarissimo Viro Domino
Henrico Oldemburg Regiae Soc: Angl: Secretario
Marcellus Malpighius S.P.

Novissimis hisce diebus transmisso famigeratissimi Boyli libro sum potitus,¹ huncque Clarissimus Montanarius prae manibus habet, et interim tibi plurimam salutem dicit, et quamprimum quendam circa eandem materiam communicabit. Domini Cassinij, apologia ob auctoris abscentiam nondum luce fruitur;[2] Doctissimus Mengolus ecclesiasticis forte munijs ita occupatur, ut parum phisicis meditationibus vacare valeat. Domini Borelli opus de motionibus a gravitate pendentibus vulgatum, apud nos extat, et Ætnae incendij historiam simul cum Apologia ad P. fabrium e Societate Jesu audio Litteratorum manibus teri.[3] Receptum fasciculum tuta occasione ad Dominum Dodington iam transmisi.

Brevi ad ruris otia me transferam, ut corporis valetudinem aliquo modo firmem; per mensem enim febribus, et acidorum copia vexatus decubui, ita ut veris tempus, studiorum exercitatio valde opportunum, absque linea effugerit.

Dominus Joseph Corcillus[4] Neapolim revertens apud nos est, teque plurimum valere optat, et Domini Cornelij responsorias literas brevi transmissurum spondet. Jun. 3. 71. Bonon.

ADDRESS
Praeclarissimo et Eruditissimo Viro Domino
Enrico Oldemburg Regiae Societatis Angliae Secretario
    Londini

TRANSLATION

Marcello Malpighi sends many greetings to the very famous and learned Mr. Henry Oldenburg, Secretary of the English Royal Society

A few days ago there came into my possession the much discussed volume by Boyle;[1] this the celebrated Montanari has in his hands, and meanwhile he sends you many greetings, and will send you something on the same topic as soon as possible. Because of the author's absence Mr. Cassini's "Apology" has not yet seen the light of day;[2] the highly learned Mengoli is perhaps so busy with ecclesiastical affairs that he has little leisure for thinking about physics. The published work of Mr. Borelli *De motionibus a gravitate pendentibus* we do have here, and I hear that his history of the eruption of Etna together with his "Apologia" to P. Fabri, S.J., are quite common in the hands of the learned.[3] I have already conveyed the package I have received by a secure means to Mr. Dodington.

I shall soon remove myself to leisure in the country, in order to improve my health a bit, for I have been prostrated during one month by fevers, and vexed with excessive acidity, so that this springtime, so suitable for study, has passed away without a line [written].

Mr. Giuseppe Corcilli is with us on his way back to Naples,[4] and wishes you all good health, hoping soon to return you Mr. Cornelio's letter in response. 3 June 1671. Bologna.

ADDRESS

To the very famous and learned
Mr. Henry Oldenburg, Secretary
to the English Royal Society,
London

NOTES

Reply to Letter 1654 (Vol. VII).
1 The *Tractatus ubi mira aeris rarefactio detecta* (London, 1670, 1671).
2 As previously noted, Cassini's "Apologia" on behalf of Montanari was never published; compare Letter 1917, note 4.
3 On these writings, see Vol. VII, Letter 1470, note 3.
4 See Letter 1596 in Vol. VII.

1706

Dodington to Oldenburg

25 May 1671

From the original in Royal Society MS. D 1, no. 23

Venice June 5th 1671 [N.S.]

Honoured Sr

I have rec'd yrs March 15 and having perused Mr Boyles last acctt of experiments in matter of ayre,[1] I have delivered the Book unto Sigr Travagino, a most excellent man without doubt, but so vexed with law suites, & diverted by trade and Interest, that I think his greatest thoughts now are how to grow rich.

The inclosed from Sigr Malpighi[2] came to me just now. And on so good an occasion I would not withold the adjoyned Giornale de letterati.[3]

This is all at present from Sr

Yr most humble servant
Jo: dodington

Mr Oldenbergh

NOTES

Reply to Letter 1653 (Vol. VII).
1 See the previous letter, note 1.
2 Letter 1705.
3 Possibly the issue for 29 May 1671.

1707

Oldenburg to Lister

27 May 1671

From the original in Bodleian Library MS. Lister 34, f. 23

Sir,

Since you are so generous and obliging as to be constant in yr philosophical communications, ye R. Society is resolv'd to continue their acknowledgements for yesame, before whom I could not but read what you imparted in yr last of May 22nd,[1] as before yt, I gave ym a touch of yr candour and franknesse, wch you so handsomely declar'd in a former of yrs of April 28.[2] upon the occasion of yr yet concealing ye name of ye Plant, wch affords ye English fixt black.[3] Yr Insect-husks of ye Kermes-kind gave occasion to ye Company to discourse of the various excrescencies of Plants, conceived by some to arise from Flyes or other Insects casting their seed upon Plants, wch sending up and affording vegetable Juyce to ye place thus infected, doe breed an intumescence there, wch becomes a matrix for ye seed to grow into a living creature of ye kind, that had spit there, wch insect being come to maturity eats its way out of ye excrescence or matrix, and flyeth away; whence ye holes in ym.

We have of late made divers Experiments concerning the Texture of Trees, not only by transmitting water, but also Quicksilver through pieces of branches;[4] and have found, yt both those substances passe through ym, yet so, yt from the Lesser end they passe more easily to ye bigger end; than vice versa. Thesame we have tried wth blowing Air through pieces of wood, having on one end been wetted wth spitle, wth the like successe.

Sr, when I proposed you Candidate, wch was last Thursday was sennight, (viz. May 18th), it was received wth a general liking: And I am confident, yt as soon as there is a competent number for Election (our meetings being actually somewhat thin about this time of ye year,) you will be chosen in wth as general a consent.

You mention in yrs of April 28. yt I should not faile to receive some curiosities from you by ye next opportunity. Nothing as yet is come to hand of yt nature; wch I say not, to importune you, but only to advertise you in reference to ye Carrier; wch kind of people is sometimes carelesse of such smal things. For the rest, I pray to remaine assured of my being sincerely Sir

Yr faithfull servt
Oldenburg

London
May 27. 1671.

ADDRESS
    To his honor'd friend
    Martyn Lister Esquire
    At his house wthout Mickel-
    gate-barre   at
            Yorke

NOTES

Reply to Letter 1703.
1 Letter 1703 was read to the Society on 25 May 1671.
2 In Letter 1696; there is no record that this was read to the Society.
3 Letter 1674 (Vol. VII) was read to the Society on 20 April 1671.
4 See Letter 1701.

1708
Flamsteed to Oldenburg
29 May 1671
From the original in Royal Society MS. F 1, no. 69

Derby Maij 29 1671

Mr Oldenburge:
Sir

Herewith I returne yu ye Hevelius[1] whom I thinke I have thoroughly perused & whom tho I can not altogeather approve I find it impossible not to commend: his schemes are neate but if I bee not deceived I see some things otherwise in ye moone then hee presents them; which I suppose is onely caused by ye difference of our glasses; for I find, yt a small tube, I have, represents ye spots more clearly visible tho not so distinct, nor so many of ye small ones, as my large tube does: in which ye large darker parts of ye moone such as ye Pontus Euxinus, &c, appeare of a far fainter color then in ye small tube: his connexion of his phases is altogeather inartificiall,[2] for tho hee confesse frequently ye sections of ye light & shade to be Ellipticall,[3] yet hee describes them allwayes under circles, which can not but much distort ye genuine face of [ye] moone: However I must allwaies acknowledge ye favors yu have cumulated on mee in ye lending this Author & ye civill returnes of yr letters in ye last of which May 20[4] yu have gratified mee wth ye observations of some of those appulses I have calculated, but had not opportunity to awaite my selfe: Mr Hookes observation of yt of May ye 6, each thinge considered, differs not 2 minutes in time from mine.[5] I could wish hee had noted, as Hevelius uses, ye spots under which ye star emergd, which I cannot suppose him so negligent as not to have done, but rather not to have communicated to yu. In ye observation of Mons: Hevelius of ye moones appulse to ye star in cauda Arietis,[6] ye places, of ye transit are wanteing, to wit, under what spotts ye star incedes, which if it be noticed in his to yu, I hope yr next to Mee will let me understand.

I am glad I have his observation of ye appulse to Spica:[7] I hope yu have given him notice of my praeadmonitions of ye lunar appearance. I very much desire to have ye times of some appearance observed both at London and Dantzick yt I may ye better rectifie my selfe of ye difference of our meridians from yt of Dantzick. I hope ye occultation of Saturne was observed wth yu,[8] For the aire with us was cleare yt night, but my selfe being from home, at ye funeralls of some relations had neither conveniency to waite nor observe it: With my cordiall acknowledgements & thankes for all yr favors I rest in hast

yr obliged servant
John Flamsteed

ADDRESS

To Henry Oldenburge Esqr
at his house in ye middle of
ye Pellmel in st Jameses
    Westminster these present
        London

NOTES

1 Oldenburg's copy of *Selenographia*, borrowed some months earlier.
2 Ill contrived.
3 The terminator.
4 Letter 1702.
5 Flamsteed had predicted (*Phil. Trans.*, no. 66, 12 December 1670, 2030) an occultation by the moon of a fourth magnitude star in Virgo; reminded by Oldenburg on 4 May 1671 (Birch, *History*, II, 479), Hooke observed this on the sixth and reported on the eleventh that the obscuration had begun at 9.23 P.M. instead of 9.09½ P.M. as predicted by Flamsteed, but had lasted about as long as he had foretold.
6 "in the tail of Aries." Hevelius described this observation in Letter 1683, read to the Society by Oldenburg on 11 May.
7 This is in the same letter.
8 The Moon's passage over Saturn was predicted by Flamsteed for the night of 21 May; on the twenty-fifth Hooke confessed he had "missed of that observation."

1709
Oldenburg to Hevelius
29 May 1671

From the original in Observatoire XI, no. 35

Illustrissime Domine Heveli,

Mitto jam, ut nuper per tabelionum promiseram,[1] Microscopium illud quod desiderasti: Spero illud omnibus, qui rite tractare noverunt, perplaciturum. Sunt ibi quinque lentes objectivae, capsulae superiori inclusae,[2] quae, ut Tu probe nosti, pro diversitate objectorum, majorum minorumve, sunt adhibendae. Adjunxi libros nonnullos Mathematicos et Physicos, quos omnes Te cum voluptate lecturum crediderim.

	(lib.) Sterl.	sol.	
Microscopium constat libris sterl	10 -	0 -	0.
Transactiones Anni 1670	0 -	7 -	0.
Wallisii duo Tomi de motu	0 -	$15\frac{1}{2}$ -	0.
Barrovii Opticae et Geom. lectiones	0 -	9 -	0.
Boylius de Formarum origine, et de Aeris rarefactione mira	0 -	3 -	0.
Pro capsula et bajulo	0 -	2 -	0.
Summa	11 -	$16\frac{1}{2}$ -	0.

Accepi 10 libras Sterling a mercatore Samuele Lee reliquum ex libris tuis, antehac in usum tuum venditis, impendi; semperque, quavis occasione data, pro viribus testatum faciam, me esse

Amplitudinis Tuae Observantissimum,
H. Oldenburg

Raptim Londini d. 29. Maji 1671

Literae inclusae ut Domino Kirkby rite tradantur, impense rogo.[3]

TRANSLATION

Most illustrious Mr. Hevelius

As I recently promised you by the ordinary post,[1] I now send you the microscope you wanted. I hope all good judges will find it satisfactory. There are five objective lenses with it, enclosed in the upper compartment,[2] which are, as you know very well, to be employed according to the greater or less size of the object. I have added some books on mathematics and physics all of which I believe you will read with pleasure:

	£	s	d
The microscope comes to	10	0	0
Transactions for 1670		7	0
Wallis's two volumes on motion		15½	0
Barrow's Optical and Geometrical Lectures		9	0
Boyle on the *Origin of Forms*, and on the *Rarefaction of the Air*		3	0
For the box, and the porter		2	0
Total	11	16½	0

I have received ten pounds sterling from the merchant Samuel Lee, and have charged the remainder to your books, formerly sold for your benefit; and will always, when opportunity serves, prove myself to be, your excellency's most devoted

H. Oldenburg

London, 29 May 1671, in haste

I beg that the enclosed letter may be safely delivered to Mr. Kirkby.[3]

NOTES

1 See Vol. VII, Letter 1680.
2 Microscopes of this period often had a screw-on dust cap over the eyepiece, of wood, made as a little box having a screw-on lid; objectives not in use were stored in this little box.
3 Letter 1710, now lost.

1710

Oldenburg to Kirkby

29 May 1671

Mentioned in Kirkby's Letter 1838 of 9 December 1671; it was enclosed in Letter 1709.

1711

Lister to Oldenburg

30 May 1671

From the original in Royal Society MS. L 5, no. 32
Partially printed in *Phil. Trans.*, no. 72 (19 June 1671), 2176–77

Yorke. May 30. 1671

Sr,

You may be pleased to annex a late Observation to ye last I sent you:[1] both being cheifly concerning ye improvement of colours & from ye Insect-kind.

There is a Cimex[2] of ye largest size, of a red colour, spotted black & wch is to be found very frequently & plentifully at least in its season upon Henbain: I therefore in my private Notes have formerly intitled it "*Cimex ruber maculis nigris distinctus super folia Hyoscyami frequens.*"[3] This Insect in all probabilitie does feed upon this plant (on wch only we have yet observed it) if not upon ye leaves by striking its Trunk (ye note of distinction of this kind of Insect from ye rest of ye Beetle kinds) into ym, & sucking thence much of its subsistence, like as other sorts of *Cimices* will upon ye body of Man, etc, yet upon ye unctuous & greasy matter, wth wch ye leaves seem to ye touch to abound. It is further observable, yt yt horrid & strong smell wth wch ye leaves of this plant does affect our nostrills, is very much qualifyed in this Insect & in some measure aromatick & agreeable & therefore we may expect, yt yt dreadful Narcosis soe eminently in this plant, may likewise be usefully tempered in this Insect wch we refer to Tryal.

About the latter end of May, & sooner, you may find adhering to ye upper side of ye leaves of this plant, certain oblong orange-coloured Eggs, wch are ye Eggs of this Insect. Note 1. yt these Eggs, yet in ye belly of ye Females, are white, & are soe somtime after they are layed; but as ye yong ones groe neer ye time of their being hatched, they acquire a deeper colour & are hatched Cimices & not in the disguise of Wormes. 2. as to ye colour these riper eggs yeild, if they be crushed upon white paper, they staine it of ym selves (without any addition of salts) wth as lively a Vermilion or *couleur de feu*,[4] as any thing I know in Nature Cochneil scarce excepted when assisted wth oil of Vitriol. whether this be not precisely soe I refer to ye Tryal & judgment of ye Curious. I have sent you a couple of ye Cimices ymselves, though you scarce find a Henbain-plant without ym.

I add concerning ye Purple Huskes, whereof I gave you an account in my last, yt I have found ym since on rose Tree twiggs alsoe & yt very darke coloured ones yeilding an exquisite Murrey: soe yt I conclude yt ye Tree they may be found on, scarce contributs any thing to ye colour or vertue of the Huskes, but they are ye sole worke & product of ye Mother Insect indifferently choosing a Twigg of any Tree in order to ye convenient placing & hyving her eggs. I am Sr

Your most humble servant
Martin Lister

on Munday last[5] I delivered to Loft himselfe a little box for you: I shall be glad to learne it comes safe to your hands. he hath changed his Inn & now lodges at ye Beare in Basinghall street.

I am affraid ye *patellas Kermiformes* will be sriveled dryed & decayed before you receive ym. they seemed to srinke very much yt little time I kept ym by me: but I make noe doubt you may be stored in any neighbouring orchard. pardon my impatience.

ADDRESS
    These
For His honoured friend
    Mr Henry Oldenburg
  at his house in ye Palmal
      London

POSTMARK IV 2

NOTES

1 Letter 1703.
2 Properly a bedbug; Lister evidently uses the word in the sense of "parasite."
3 "A red cimex distinguished by black spots, common upon the leaves of henbane."
4 "fire color."
5 Probably meaning 22 May, the date of Letter 1703.

1712
Lister to Oldenburg
31 May 1671

From the original in Royal Society MS. L 5, no. 33

May 31.71.

Sr

I received yours of 27 of May this Morning. I am very much pleased wth ye successe of your Expts in order to ye discovery of ye Texture of Vegetables. I may send you one of these dayes a rude notion of mine, wch perhapps may give some little light to ye matter.

You will find yt ye *Patellae Kermi-formes* I sent you[1] are noe more ye excrescencies of ye plant they adhaer to, than I believe ye true Kermes will be found to be upon nice & needfull examination: but are ye real & sole worke of Insect Animals, wholly independent either for nourishment or production from ye Vegetable.

As concerning ye Question of truly Vegetable Excrescencies whether ye Wormes to be found in ym are according to F Redi ye genuine off spring of ye Vegetable Soule, or as some of ye honourable Assemble doe well thinke, yt they are produced by accident as blistring & envenoming ye respective plants, I have long since, upon ye publishing of yt Number of ye Transactions, wherin you give us an account of F. Redi's booke,[2] writ my mind at large to Mr Wray, who I make noe doubt will, upon your request, send you ye discourse:[3] wch, I say was writ before I saw ye booke it selfe: but since yt I have seen & perused it & have had some part of an other summers leisure I have something more to add in confirmation of my former thought, wch you may command, when I shall understand, yt ye first discourse is come to your hands.

be pleased to alter ye Title of ye 8 spider & make it Araneus viridis, cauda nigris punctis superne notata, ipso ano croceo.[4]

I am obliged to you for ye good opinion, ye R.S. has of me, who am of my selfe but a hasty well wisher & a true Labourer to my power & leisure. Again Yours.

NOTES

Reply to Letter 1707.
1 See Letter 1703.
2 Francesco Redi's *Esperienze intorno alle generazione degl'insetti* (Florence, 1668) was reviewed in *Phil. Trans.*, no. 57 (25 March 1670), 1175–76.
3 See Ray's reply to Letter 1715 from Oldenburg, Letter 1738. Lister's original "discourse" seems now to be lost, but see below Letter 1751.
4 See Vol. VII, Letter 1589a, where the eighth spider is so decribed; what Lister originally wrote cannot now be determined.

1713
Wallis to Oldenburg
2 June 1671

From the original in Royal Society MS. W 1, no. 121
Printed, with some changes, in *Phil. Trans.*, no. 74 (14 August 1671), 2231

Oxoniae. Junij. 2. 1671.

Clarissime Vir,

Accepi nuperrime, a te transmissam, D. Leibnitzij *Theoriam Motus Abstracti*:[1] de qua judicium meum expetis. Duo autem sunt quae suadeant ne illud praestem. Alterum; quod res invidiosa videatur de aliorum scriptis censuram agere: Alterum; quod occupatissimo tempore huc advenerit, quo aegre tempus obtinuerim semel atque iterum attentius legendi, nedum omnia pensiculatius expendendi. Quoniam vero tu id expetis, haec pauca dicam. Multa scilicet mihi contenta, ego plane approbo, ut subtiliter et solide dicta; quaeque Virum curiosum et cogitabundum indicant. Si pauca sint quibus non statim assentiar, ignoscet spero Vir humanissimus.

Et speciatim, fateor mihi nondum satisfactum esse, ut, primis saltem cogitationibus, statim assentiar, Cohaesionem omnem ex continuo celerique sed inobservabili particularum motu fieri, (quod ille Theoriae motus concreti fundamentum ponit;) uti nec pridem, cum, ante aliquot annos, similem quietis et cohaesionis causam assignaverit Nelius noster.[2] Quid olim aliquando fiet, post rem accuratius perpensam, nec dicere possum nec praevidere. Interim ego ἀπέχω, nec quicquam in aliorum praejudicium pronuntio; quin liberum quique sit eam quam rationi magis consentaneam judicaverit sententiam amplecti. Vale.

Tuus
Johannes Wallis

I desire, when you send mee my Lords sense of my letter you shewed him,[3] that you will not forget to send mee word when first that experiment was made amongst us, & how, & whether in ye Society at Gresham College.

ADDRESS
    These
For Mr Henry Oldenburg
in the Palmal neer St
James's
    London

TRANSLATION

Oxford, 2 June 1671

Very famous Sir,

I recently received Mr. Leibniz's *Theoria motus abstracti*,[1] sent by yourself, of which you seek my opinion. Two considerations persuade me not to offer it to you. The one is, that it may seem invidious to criticize the writings of others; the other is, that it came at this most busy season, when I have barely had time to read it over a couple of times pretty carefully and not to weigh it thoughtfully. However, as you ask for it, I will say thus much briefly. I entirely approve of much that is contained in it, as soundly and cleverly expressed, indicating a curious and reflective author. If there are a few points which I cannot accept immediately, I hope this kindly man will pardon me. And particularly I confess that I am not yet satisfied that I can at once agree, at least upon my initial reflections, that all cohesion is caused by a swift but unobservable and continuous motion of particles (which he takes to be the basis of the sound theory of motion), just as not long since (but a few years ago) our countryman [William] Neile assigned a similar cause to rest and cohesion.² What conclusion I may come to, when I have reflected on it more thoroughly, I cannot yet say or foresee. Meanwhile I keep silent and pronounce no opinion prejudicial to others, so that everyone may freely adopt whatever view shall seem to his judgment most agreeable to reason. Farewell.

Yours
John Wallis

. . . .

NOTES

1 We do not have the letter Oldenburg wrote to Wallis. The *Theoria* had been given to Hooke for consideration; on 25 May Hooke gave a disappointing account and the Society ordered that the work be sent to Wallis.
2 For Neile's writings on mechanics, see Vols. V and VI *passim*.
3 See Letter 1699 and its note 3.

1714
Phineas Bell to Oldenburg
3 June 1671

From the original in Royal Society MS. B 2, no. 11

Freind I had nott [time to]¹ see thee againe at my being at London since my Comeing home [I have] bene makeing parte inquiry as to the Manner of the husbandry as to Corne of this part of yorkeshire And findes it very various both by reason the soyle of the Land differs some being Clay some Mixt others more sandy some gravelly Land others very stony, I doe not finde thatt they alter any thing at all In there ploughes though the Land do differ And againe they vary according to the genious of the Husbandman butt as to Ardures of ploweing Quantity of seede and lastly In time of soweing some being for earely some for layte soweing, I mett wth one Husbandman who told mee that on 2 parcells of Land both alike he sowd wheate on the one And Rye on the other thatt the wheate did take more of the strength of the soyle Away then the Rye by much And the Rye Land did yearely afforde a much better barley Croppe after the Rye then after the wheate And this was his observation many yeares, the

Reason thatt he gave thatt the Rye caryed nothing els with It on its straw butt the bare stalke butt lett all fall noe [*sic*] Rotte on the grounde And soe helped It butt thatt wheate did carry wth It much more Leaves or Hawme² as he Called It And soe Required a stronger Land, I was Inquireing after it further of Another Husbandman thatt I doe accounte as skilfull as any in those parts hee did assure me the Cleare Contrary thatt Rye take more of his Land then wheat how to reconcile It I doe nott know onely the one Land is Clay the other a Mixt Land If in any thing I can serve thee or the society pray Lett mee know by the bearer or by the post is thy Frend

Phinehas Bell

June the 3d ♄³ 1671
          um

ADDRESS
For Henry Oldenbrough
    In the Pell Mell
        London

NOTES

We have not been able to identify the writer of this letter.
1 The paper was torn by breaking the seal.
2 Haulm.
3 Saturday.

1715
Oldenburg to Ray

3 June 1671

From the memorandum in Royal Society MS. L 5, no. 32

Writ to Mr Wray jun. 3. 71. according to ye import of this letter.

NOTE

This is written on the envelope of Lister's Letter 1711 of 30 May 1671. Obviously Oldenburg asked Ray to send him the "discourse" Lister had described; Ray replied on 3 July.

1719
Leibniz to Oldenburg
8 June 1671
From the copy in Royal Society Letter Book IV, 322-26
Printed in Gerhardt, pp. 59-62

Non dubito quin postremae meae literae, quibus residuum Hypotheseos meae, tum et festinata de abstracta motus theoria cogitata, ad Te recte pervenerint:[1] Ex iis licebit, opinor, perspicere indolem sententiae meae, quanquam poliendae ejus perficiendaeque curam non abjecerim; neque enim adeo difficile erit, ubi otium suppetet, editis ineditisque meis amicorumque cogitatis experimentisque illustrare sententiam, ad explicanda omnia latissime patentem. Certe nihil est Experimentorum publice notorum, quae non ei, notabili harmoniae simplicissimae claritate, conciliare sperem. Omnes omnium gentium temporumque philosophi de Spiritu quodam Universali, seu Anima mundi disseruere, unde vita rebus ratione carentibus et motus: ne Aristotelis quidem loca desunt; at qui Spiritus ejus motum, causamque motus et effecta mechanice exposuerit, notus est mihi nemo. Magno me beneficio affeceris, Vir Amplissime, si egregiorum apud vos Virorum, quibus abundatis, tum judicia mihi perscripseris, tum favorem notitiamque conciliaveris; non eorum tantum, qui naturae novam lucem infundunt, sed et qui circa Theologiam naturalem et moralia aliquid praeclari moliuntur. Licetne aliqua Experimentorum Relationumque per communicationem nancisci, quae in Historia Societatis enumerantur, praesertim si quid vicissim aperiri communicarive possit? Si qua judicia de Schediasmate meo insinuata sunt Illustri Societati, ea, rogo, ut mihi qualia sunt, etiam cum Autorum nominibus, si licet, integra descripta mittas: reprehensiones enim, modo aculei absint, non aegre fero. De Machinae Wernerianae successu haec comperi; in fodinis Schwazensibus Bavariae ditionis hactenus frustra fuisse, sive ipsius artificii vitio, sive, ut solet, obstrectatorum malitia, aut fortasse sumptuum mora, qui, ut cogitatu facile est, ad talia in magno opere prosequenda non exigui requiruntur: Autorem ergo ad extremum, facta redeundi afferendorumque necessariorum spe, domum abiisse, nondum rediisse.

Sed nondum ideo res tota mihi damnanda videtur, qui scio, quot mali genii bonis se conatibus opponant. Ego, ut certiora tandem nanciscar, ad

Wernerum ipsum, curante Amico, cui familiaris est, scripsi. Responsum habebitis, ubi ego nactus fuero.

Grandamici experimentum Magneticum, de quo antehac loquebar,[2] hoc est: Magnes Sphaericus raticulae subereae, vel alteri vasculo aquis innatanti imponatur, ea ratione, ut polus ejus *b* Borealis, hoc est, ille qui sibi relictus borealem coeli plagam, sive verius, telluris polum; Australis autem *a*

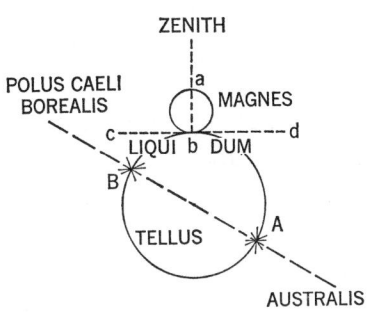

respiciat zenith. Hoc enim modo constitus magnes, post aliquot hinc inde reciprocationes, in liquido *cd* horizonti parallelo, disponet quasdam suas partes constanter in Austrum, et oppositas in Boream sine ulla declinatione. Quare, si in terrella, sic consistente ope lineae meridianae accurate repertae per aliquod e problematibus Astronomicis, designetur in superficie Terrellae Meridianus circulus, erit is universalis pro omnibus terrae locis, citra usitatam illam declinationem Magneticam, tantopere variam et inconstantem. Haec ille. Valde desidero, nosse rei veritatem ad Theorias meas magneticas perficiendas, et experimentum ipsum tale est, ut mereatur a diligentissimis observatoribus excuti. Quo facto, si quid mihi certi perscripseris, magno me beneficio affeceris. Kircherus,[3] Zucchius,[4] Scottus[5] approbant; sed scis, alios testes domesticis accedere debere: si verum est, sequetur, causam declinationis agere in solum Magnetis polum, cui si sic vacillandi libertas adimatur, declinationem cessaturam; de quo fateor esse cur dubitem. Licetne nosse, quid rei sit mirabilis ille pulvis Keilfferi, Drebelii generi, cujus meminit Monconisius in itinerario, qui totas naves destruere possit; Meminere ejus etiam Ephemerides Gallicae, in judicio de Monconisio.[6] Verumne quod ibi narratur, experimentum sumptum esse coram Cromwello? Continuaturne Atlas Anglicanus?[7] Ignosce Te Quaestionibus obtundenti. Unum est praeterea, quo, post tot beneficia, fortiore etiam, si id fieri potest, modo, Vir Amplissime, me Tibi obstringes. Comperi, apud vos olim prodiisse librum quendam Anglicum *Gabrielis Plate* de rebus subterraneis,[8] inque eo narrari processum quendam eliciendi Salem ex Antimonio, qui sit quidem infructuosus ob paucitatem, et sumptuum magnitudinem, evincat tamen veritatem transmutationis. Hunc processum ex illo libro, quem audio apud vos esse sic satis vulgarem, mihi verbotenus describi valde desidero, eaque in re curanda benevolentiam tuam invoco. Experimentum a Bechero, Medico Germano, descriptum, faciendi ferrum ex rebus non-metallicis, imo nec mineralibus, nescio an ad vos pervenerit: memini ejus, ni fallor, nuper;[9] id ita habet, si limus, unde lateres coquuntur et furni parantur, ad aerem siccatus, ut cribrari possit, oleo lini ita perfundatur, ut globuli inde formari possint, pro colli retortae capacitate;[10] idque eum in finem, ne facta distillatione ob exemptionem capitis mortui, retorta frangi debeat, deinde ut ignis parvos globulos vehementius quam totam massam penetret: Repleatur globulis retorta, et per gradus ex aperto igne distilletur augendo sub finem ignem fortiter. Prodibit oleum simile illi, quod vulgo vocant, Philosophorum.[11] Finita distillatione globuli nigrescentes contundantur et cribentur, in patinam ponantur, et superfusa aqua communi moveantur; turbidum per inclinationem gradatim effundatur; limpeda nova addatur; idque tam diu, donec effusa aqua clare decurrat, et in fundo patinae grave nigrum sedimentum maneat. Hoc siccatum chartae imponatur; adhibitus magnes pulvisculum terreum extrahet, qui repetita extractione copiosus colligetur, ex quo ferrum fiet in omnibus probis optimum. Haec Becherus, qui putat ex reactione quadam inter limum et oleum lini fieri ferrum. Quod concedendum erit, si verum est, sine oleo ferrum extrahi non posse: Imo, alio olei limive genere adhibito, alia metalla oriri; sed sunt, qui putant, esse tantum latentis in limo ferri extractionem, cum etiam Sendivogius[12] alicubi asserat, in omni terra plurimum Martis latere. Sed Vos rectius arbitrabimini. Experimentum ipsum verum est, et coram Eminentissimo Electore Moguntino nuperrime sumtum, qui incomparabili judicio et maxima harum rerum experientia, decora in Reip. administratione elucentia, velut distinguit. Unum restat, quod non possum, quin ubi significem: Est mihi amicus, in re metallurgica egregie versatus; is rationem invenit et in praxin deduxit chalybem ex ferro in quantitate cum magno fructu parandi. Sed cum talia ita comparata sint, ut fructus eorum ab iis demum, quibus fundus est rem tentandi in magno, authoritasque et notitia securitasque consumptionis, sentiatur; Statuit vendere inventum suum iis qui rectius queant uti, quales vos judicat: nec si contrahetur, quicquam petet antequam sumptibus suis assertionem suam apud vos verificaverit. Res est consideratur digna: Nec hic vulgare aliquid, ac tritum suspicere.

Si quid nonnunquam apud vos notabile incidit, quod scire liceat, Transactionibusque non inseratur, ejus me significatione subinde mire beatis. Quod restat, vale; quam primum literis me tuis recrea, Illustri Societati commenda, faveque Vir Amplissime

> Cultori Virtutum Tuarum
> *Gottfredo Guilielmo Leibnitio*
> J.U.D. et Consil. Mog.

Moguntiae 8/18 Junii 1671.

TRANSLATION

I have no doubt that my last letter reached you safely,[1] in which I sent you the rest of my hypothesis and also some hasty reflections on the abstract theory of motion. From that you can, I think, follow the drift of my thought, although I gave no trouble to polishing and perfecting its expression, and when leisure permits it will not be difficult to illustrate my thought from my published and unpublished papers and from the ideas and experiments of my friends, opening everything up for a fuller explanation. Certainly there is nothing among published experiments which cannot, as I hope, be made agreeable to it, with a remarkable clarity of simple harmony. All philosophers of every race and time have discoursed of a certain universal Spirit or Soul of the Universe giving life and motion to things lacking both; nor are such passages lacking in Aristotle. But no one known to me has explained mechanically the motion, and the cause and effects of motion, of his Spirit. You will do me a great service, worthy Sir, if you will write to me the conclusions of the outstanding men among you, of whom you have so many, and will also promote their good opinion and esteem; I do not refer only to those who seek to throw a new light upon Nature, but to those also who strive for something worthwhile in natural theology and moral science. Is it permissible to obtain some knowledge of the experiments and relations mentioned in the *History* of the Society, especially if something may be revealed or communicated in exchange? If some judgments of my theoretical proposals are to be introduced to the illustrious Society, I beg you to send me a full description of them, whatever they may be, together with the authors' names, for I will not take criticism badly, if it lack bitterness. I have learned this about the success of Werner's machine: up to now, in the Swabian mines of Bavaria, its power has proved a fraud, whether because of some defect in the device itself, or the ill will (common enough) of its detractors, or perhaps the long continuance of the outgoings, which it is easy to imagine must necessarily be very large in a great work of this kind. Accordingly the inventor has gone home, having lost hope of fulfilling his promises, and has not yet returned.

But to myself, knowing how many ill-wishers oppose good endeavors, the thing does not yet seem altogether worthy of condemnation. To get better information I have written to Werner himself, through a friend who is his intimate acquaintance. You shall have the reply, as soon as I do.

Grandami's magnetical experiment, of which I wrote before,[2] is this: A spherical magnet is placed on a little cork raft or other vessel floating on water in such a way that its north pole b (that is, the pole which left to itself [turns to] the northern direction of the sky or more accurately the Earth's northern pole) [is turned downwards]; its south pole a points to the zenith [*see the figure on page 77*]. With the magnet thus positioned it will after a few oscillations in the horizontal [surface of] the fluid cd arrange some parts of itself constantly to the South, and the opposite ones to the North without any [magnetic] declination. For which reason if a meridian circle be drawn on the terrella (employing an accurate meridian line obtained by astronomical techniques), when it is thus disposed, it will serve as a universal meridian anywhere on Earth, without any of that customary magnetic declination that is so variable and inconstant. So far he. I very much desire to know the truth of this business in order to perfect my theoriers of magnetism, and the experiment is such that it deserves to be carried out by careful observers. If that is done, and you will write me something definite about it, you will do me a useful service. Kircher,[3] Zucchi,[4] and Schott[5] confirm it; but you are aware that other testimony should support that of servants. If it is true, it follows that the cause of the declination lies in the magnetic pole solely, so that the declination would cease if this freedom to move about could be taken from it; and it is in this respect that I feel doubts. Is it permissible to know what sort of stuff that remarkable powder is of Küffler's, Drebbel's relative, mentioned by Monconys in his *Travels*, which can destroy whole ships; the same is mentioned again in the *Journal des Sçavans* in a review of Monconys.[6] Is it true, as it is there related, that a trial was made in Cromwell's presence? Is the English *Atlas* being continued?[7] Forgive me for bludgeoning you with questions. There is one more favor, after so many others, and if you could perform this for me you would render my obligations to you still greater, if that is possible, worthy Sir. I had heard that there was formerly published in your part of the world a certain book, in English, by Gabriel Plattes,[8] dealing with subterranean matters, and that in it there is described some process or other for extracting a salt from antimony, which even though it may be unfruitful because of the poverty [of the yield] and the great costliness [of the operation], makes the truth of transmutation quite clear. I am very anxious to have this process described to me word for word out of that book, which I hear was quite commonplace among you, and I invoke your kindness in obtaining this for me. I do not know whether the experiment described by Becher, a German physician, of making iron from nonmetallic and even nonmineral substances, has reached you yet; I think I mentioned it recently.[9] He maintains that if the earth out of which bricks are baked and furnaces are made is air-dried till it can be sieved, and is moistened with linseed oil, then it can be shaped into balls, of such a size as will pass through the neck of a retort.[10] The object of this procedure is to avoid having to break the retort to extract the *caput mortuum* when the distillation is completed, and so that the fire may penetrate these little balls more thoroughly than a whole mass. The retort is filled with these balls and the distillation effected by degrees on an open fire, increasing the heat greatly towards the end. An oil is given off similar to that commonly called the Oil of the Philosophers.[11] When the distillation is finished the blackened balls are crushed and sieved, placed in a dish, and stirred up with some water; the turbid fluid is poured off by tilting the dish gradually and clear, fresh water added. This is continued until the water poured off remains clear and a heavy black sediment remains at the bottom of the dish. When this has been dried it is placed on paper and a magnet applied to it will attract an earthy dust, which may be accumulated by repeated magnetic attraction. From this an iron may be made satisfying every test. So says Becher, who thinks that the iron is formed by some reaction between the earthy matter and the linseed oil. Which must be accepted, if it is true that the iron cannot be extracted without the oil, and the more so, if when another oil or earth is employed, another metal is produced. But there are those who think that there is only an extraction of iron hidden in the earthy matter, as Sendivogius[12] somewhere declared that there is much iron in all earth. But you will be the arbiters. The experiment itself is a real one, lately performed before the Most Eminent Elector of Mainz, who is just as distinguished for his incomparable judgment and vast experience in such things, as for gracious excellence in statecraft. There is one more thing I really must put to you: There is a friend of mine who is remarkably skilled in metallurgy; he has invented a way of making steel from iron in quantitiy, and put it into practice with success. But as that sort of thing is here so regarded, that the usefulness of it is only in the last place evident to those who have the means, authority, and position for testing the thing on the large scale, he has decided to sell his invention to those who can make a proper use of it, such as he judges the English to be; and if an agreement may be reached he seeks nothing at all until his assertions have been verified by yourselves at his expense. The matter is worthy of consideration, and nothing commonplace or ordinary is to be feared.

If there is anything noteworthy going on among you that may be known but is not inserted in the *Transactions*, you will please me very much by sending me word at once. For the rest, farewell; refresh me as soon as possible with a letter, commend me to the Illustrious Society, and, worthy Sir, think well of this admirer of your virtues

Gottfried Wilhelm Leibniz
L.L.D. and Councilor at Mainz

Mainz, 8/18 June 1671

NOTES

Reply to Letter 1676 (Vol. VII).
1 Letter 1688.
2 See Letter 1644 (Vol. VII) and Letter 1688, p. 28, above.
3 Probably Athanasius Kircher's *Magnes sive de arte magnetica* (Rome, 1641), but Kircher wrote several other works on magnetism.
4 Niccolo Zucchi, *Nova de machinis philosophia* (Rome, 1649).
5 Gaspar Schott, *Magiae universalis naturae et artis* (Würzburg, 1657–59).
6 See Letter 1688, note 5. The notice of the relevant part of Monconys's book is in the *Journal des Sçavans* for 10 May 1665 [N.S.], where, however, the name of Küffler does not appear.
7 No work at this time bore the title *English Atlas* (though this title was used by Moses Pitt for an unfinished project he began to publish at Oxford in 1680). Probably Leibniz referred to the projected world atlas of John Ogilby (1600–76), who had set up a printing press in London after the Fire and was appointed Royal Cosmographer. Of the five projected volumes, *Africa* had appeared in 1670 and *America* in 1671; *Asia* was to follow in 1673, and Part I of *Britannia* in 1675.
8 Gabriel Plattes, *A Discovery of Subterraneall Treasure* (London, 1639, 1653, 1679). In chapter 9 Plattes described how to make gold from a "regulus" compounded of iron and antimony [oxide], treated with mercury sublimate, distilled and mixed with silver amalgam—but in such small quantity as to be uneconomic.
9 See Letter 1688, *ad fin.*
10 As the syntax of the Latin is so fragmented, we have modified the English for the sake of continuity.
11 According to Jean Beguin (*Tyrocinium Chymicum*, Paris, 1610) this oil was made by heating bits of broken brick, or pebbles, plunging them red-hot into old olive oil, and distilling the result several times.
12 Michael Sendivogius (possibly 1556–1636), Polish chemist and alchemist, author of the influential *Novum Lumen Chymicum* (earliest edition probably Paris, 1608).

1717
Sylvius to Oldenburg
8 June 1671

From the original in Royal Society MS. S 1, no. 100

Amplissimo, Doctissimoque Viro
D. Henrico Oldenburgh,
Societati Regiae Anglicanae
a Secretis
Salutem et observantia
Franciscus De Le Boe, Sylvius

Postquam, Te judice, licet mihi per Te Vestro Regi Augustissimo, ac Vestrae Societati Regiae Illustrissimae Donariolum meum offerre,[1] praeter notata exemplaria quinque, totidem addidi Medicis Vestris, quibus conatus meos trutinari licebit, tribuenda, et inprimis Clarissimo D. Entio,[2] cum quo aliquando per literas communicavi. Literarum ad Regem Sacratissimum scriptarum formulam his addo, ut, si aliquid contineant, quod ipsarum traditionem impediat, apud Te serventur. Ignosce homini cunctis bene cupienti et precanti, sed in solemnibus minus versato ideoque ope ac opera tua indigenti.

Tradentur haec Tibi per D. Jacobum Rufine[3] Londinensem, quem egregie doctum promovi nuperrime solemniter in Medicinae Doctorem. Utinam idem cum multis alijs mea informatione usis praxin exerceat quibusvis aegris faelicissimam! Optime Vale, Vir optime, ac me Virtutum tuarum amantissimum amare perge. Dabam Lugduni Batavorum, XIV Cal. Quint. MDCLXXI. Stylo Gregoriano.

P.S. Quod pene mihi exciderat, sex Orationculae meae de Affectus nostri Epidemii Causis[4] nuper editae invenies hinc exemplaria, Societati vestrae Regiae itidem offerenda. Iterum Vale.

ADDRESS

Amplissimo, et Doctissimo Viro,
Domino Henrico Oldenburg,
Societati Regiae Anglicanae a Secretis
Londinum.

TRANSLATION

Franciscus de le Boe Sylvius [sends] his greetings and respects to the very worthy and learned Mr. Henry Oldenburg, Secretary of the English Royal Society

After offering my little gift to your most august king and to your very illustrious Royal Society through yourself,[1] and subject to your judgment, besides the [previously] noted five copies I have added as many more to be bestowed upon your physicians who may be proper to consider my endeavors, and especially the famous Mr. Ent,[2] with whom I have formerly had contact by letters. I add to these the form of my letter to his most sacred Majesty so that if it contains anything that might impede its delivery, it may remain with you. Pardon this in a man desiring and seeking good in all, but little experienced in formalities and so needing your aid and labor.

These things will be delivered to you by Mr. James Rufine of London,[3] a remarkably learned man on whom I recently conferred with all solemnity the degree of Doctor of Medicine. May he practise on every kind of patient with great success, along with many others who have received my teaching! Farewell, best of men, and continue to love me as a great admirer of your virtues. Leiden, 18 June 1671, N.S.

P.S. It almost slipped my memory that you will find here six copies of my little speech about the causes of our epidemic affliction,[4] also to be offered to your Royal Society. Farewell again.

ADDRESS
> To the very worthy and learned
> Mr Henry Oldenburg,
> Secretary of the English Royal Society,
> London.

NOTES

1 Compare Letter 1698. On 30 June Oldenburg brought to the Society's meeting *nine* copies of Sylvius' *Praxeos medicae idea nova* (Leiden, 1671), which were distributed to the President, the repository, the two Secretaries and five Fellows, together with the six orations. (The tenth of course went to Charles II.)
2 Sir George Ent (1604–89), M.D., knighted in 1665 after the king had heard his lecture at the College of Physicians.
3 See Vol. VI, p. 62, note 7. Rufine proceeded M.D. on 4 May 1671, his thesis being "De passione coeliaca."
4 *Oratio de affectus epidemii, A 1669 Leidam depopulantis, causis naturalibus* (Leiden, 1670).

1718
Hevelius to Oldenburg
9 June 1671

From the original in Royal Society MS. H 2, no. 26
Partially printed in *Phil. Trans.*, no. 78 (18 December 1671), 3027

Illustri Viro
Domino Henrico Oldenburgio
Illustrissimae Regiae Societatis Secretario
J. Hevelius Salutem

Nisi denuo rarissimum quoddam phaenomenum mihi feliciter observare obtigisset, quod Vobis quantocyus communicandum esse existimaverim, profecto prius responsum Tuum ad meas 1 Maij datas expectassem;[1] quem tamen brevi, cum rebus iam saepius a me expetetis, nec non Mycroscopii pro Illustrissimo domino Mareschallo me a Te obtenturum spero. Nuper die Lunae 1 Junij st. n. rursus Saturnum a Luna tectum mihi ex

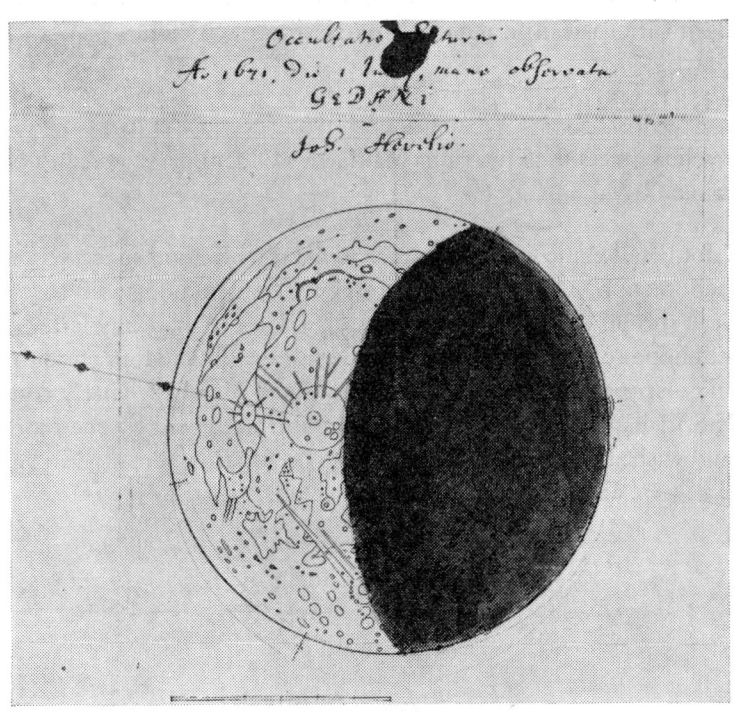

voto annotare obtigit: Initium Occultationis accidit hora matutina hic Dantisci 3 38′ 27″, circa Montem Germanicianum.² Linea itineraria, quantum ex solo ingressu haud obscure colligere licuit, transijt per M. Aetnam, centrum fere Lunae, per M. Horminium, M. Herculis, et superiorem partem Maris Caspij.³ Erat spectaculum multo iucundissimum, Sole orienti, Saturnum occultari, ac Tubo 20 pedum appulsum distincte admodum animadvertere; facies tamen Saturni genuina eiusque annuli eo tubo, eoque tempori haud satis accurate, ob crepusculum, solemque Horizonti adeo vicinum apparuit: hinc etiam Saturni exitum, ut ut omnem admoverim lapidem neutiquam deprehendere mihi licuit, praesertim cum sol ad duodecim propemodum [sic] gradibus iam elevaretur. Nihilominus merito nobis gratulamur, quod hanc rarissimam occultationem Saturni nobis observare obtigerit. Ego, quantum memini, bis tantum, si huius anni observationem excipias, intra 41 annos, Saturnum a Luna tectum vidi: anno nimirum 1630, die 19 Junij vespere hora 11 fere, cum in Freto Danico, circa Insulam Huennam versarer: rursus anno 1661, die 3 August. hic Dantisci hora 7 58′ 20″ vespere. Nam etsi tales occultationes saepius contingant, non tamen semper serenitas Coeli affulget, ut eas observare possimus, nec momentum Coniunctionis in nostro perpetuo accidit horizonte. Dabam Gedani Anno 1671, die 19 Junij st. n. Vale feliciter, et saluta quam officiosissime totam Illustrissimam Societatem.⁴

TRANSLATION

J. Hevelius greets the illustrious Mr. Henry Oldenburg, Secretary of the most illustrious Royal Society

If it had not befallen me to observe recently and with good success a certain very rare phenomenon, which I thought ought to be communicated to you as soon as possible, I should certainly have waited first for a reply to my letter of 1 May;¹ which I still hope to obtain shortly with the things I have often enough asked for and the microscope for our very illustrious Lord Marshall. Lately (on Monday, 1 June, N.S.) I happened again to observe Saturn covered by the moon, as well as one could wish; the commencement of the occultation here at Danzig occurred at 3h 38′ 27″ A.M., about the Mons Germanicianus.²

Occultation of Saturn,
observed at Danzig by
Joh. Hevelius, 1 June 1671,
in the morning.

[*For the figure, see page 85*]

The line of passage, so far as I could determine it doubtfully because of the sun's rising, passed through Mount Etna, near the center of the moon, Mount Horminius, Mount Hercules, and the upper part of the Caspian Sea.³ It was a most delightful spectacle, with the sun rising and Saturn about to be occulted, to observe the appulse most distinctly with my twenty-foot telescope. Yet the true appearance of Saturn and his ring appeared with that tube and at that time only pretty inaccurately, because of the twilight and the sun's being so near the horizon. Hence too I was not at all able to detect the emergence of Saturn, though I strove to do so, especially as the sun was risen almost to twelve degrees [above the horizon] already. Nevertheless we were duly thankful that it had befallen us to observe this very rare occultation of Saturn. So far as I recall I have only twice in forty-one years (excepting the observation of this year) seen Saturn hidden by the moon, that is to say in the year 1630, about 11 o'clock on 19 June, as I was going about the island of Hven in the Danish Sound; and again in 1661, here at Danzig, at 7h 58′ 20″ P.M. on 3 August. For although such occultations happen often enough the sky is not always brilliantly clear so that we can observe them, nor does the instant of conjunction always occur above our horizon. Danzig, 19 June 1671, N.S. Farewell, and greet the whole most illustrious Society very dutifully.⁴

NOTES

1 Letter 1683. Oldenburg had replied in Letter 1709. This letter was read to the Society on 2 November 1671.
2 This imaginary feature of the lunar landscape is placed by Hevelius at about lunar lat. $+15°$, long. $-65°$. Hevelius' vision of the moon in this region was very imperfect —it was delineated in the 1640s—and Grimaldi's, published by Riccioli in 1651 in his *Almagestum novum*, is much superior.
3 These features are respectively the crater Copernicus, Grimaldi's "Theon Senior" (lat. $0°$, long. $+20°$), Grimaldi's "Beda" (lat. $-5°$, long. $+35°$), and the Mare Foecunditatis.
4 Hevelius as usual enclosed a detailed table of the observation (see also *Machina coelestis*, II, Danzig, 1679, p. 564).

1719
Wallis to Oldenburg
10 June 1671
From the original in Royal Society MS. W 1, no. 112

Oxford June 10. 1671

Sir,

I thank you for your intimation of readynesse to do my son the kindness I desired.[1] If hee came too late, or that otherwise there were no opportunity: we must be content. I have since the time of that solemnity heard nothing from him of what passed.[2] The inclosed paper I had written presently after I sent my letter to the same effect[3] & before I received your Answere. I had sooner sent it, but that I have been in continual expectation of receiving my Lords sense upon it;[4] & an account of matter of fact how & when that experiment began & had its progresse with ye Royal Society or ye members of it: that so I might accordingly have altered the narrative in ye beginning of it, before I had sent it. I desire you will furnish mee with ye history of fact; in wch none can better inform you (I think) than my Lord himself; & return mee ye paper as soon as you can. For ye presse stays for Copy, having not inough to finish ye sheet now in hand. And what I have now sent them (two or three leaves) will but just help out out sheet; & this paper is next to follow.[5] I have no more at present, but that I am Sr

Your affectionate friend to [serve you]
John Wallis

ADDRESS
These
For Mr Henry Oldenburg,
in the Palmal near St James's
London

NOTES

1 John Wallis, the younger (b. 1651). The letter to which this is a reply is lost.
2 Probably Wallis wished Oldenburg to arrange for his son to witness the solemnity, which was (no doubt) the installation of the King of Sweden and the Duke of Saxony

(both by proxy), together with the Duke of Albemarle, as Knights of the Garter at Windsor on 29 May 1671. (Ashmole officiated as Windsor Herald.)
3 Presumably Letter 1699. The enclosure mentioned is no longer preserved.
4 Compare the postscript to Letter 1713.
5 The experiment is described in *Mechanica, sive de motu pars tertia* (London, 1671), ch. XIV, prop. XIII, Scholium (John Wallis, *Opera mathematica*, Oxford, 1695, I, 1050–51). It is very near the end of the work.

1720
Oldenburg to Lister
10 June 1671

From the original in Bodleian Library MS. Lister 34, f. 25

London June 10. 1671

Sir,

Yr Letter, and yr present (I mean, the litle philosophical box, sent by Luft) are both come well to hand, and were produced on Thursday last¹ before the R. Society, who upon hearing ye one, and viewing the other, commanded the Curator to put all into their repository wth care, and order'd me to see yr letter entred in their Letterbook as also to return you new acknowledgements in their name.² Some of ye Company were excited hereafter to observe that kind of viviparous flyes, and those *Cimices* feeding upon Henbain and the *patellae kermi-formes*, wth the rest. You did not mention, of what tree those branches were, on wch those particular *patellae*, sent by you, adhered. The Society will be very glad to see yr notion concerning the texture of Vegetables. There is now a young Student yt is publishing the Anatomy of Vegetables from the Seed to ye Seed, wch is commended to be a curious and ingenious piece.³ Time will show more what it is.

At our last meeting (wch was but thin, and not numerous enough for an election) there were exhibited to the Society some curious Observations touching Glow-worms, wch I cannot but impart to you, for yr thoughts and remarkes thereon.⁴ They were these;

May 27. 71. Between 11. and 12. at night the Observer, having put a Glow-worm into a smal thin box, such as pills are usually put in, saw her shine through ye box very clearly on one side, ye box shutt, putting white paper into the box, and ye worm into ye paper, it shin'd through the paper and box both.

May 28. In ye morning about 8. a clock, she seem'd dead, and holding her in a very dark place, he could perceive very litle light, and yt only when she was turn'd upon her back, and by consequence put into some litle voluntary motion, wch happily ye darkness of ye place would not let me observe. After Sun-set yt night, she walked briskly up and down in her box, shining as clearly as ye night before, and *yt*, when there was so much day-light that I could read in Sylvius wthout a candle.

May 29. In ye 'morning she seem'd dead again, at night recover'd herself, and shined as well as ever through ye box, and opening ye box, and holding a large candle in his hand, ye light of it did not sensibly diminish yt of ye Glow-worm.

May 30. About 10. a clock at night, he set the box wth ye Worm in it in his bed-chamber about 4. yards from his bed-side in a window, where he perceived it shine through ye box for almost an hour; he then falling asleep, at his awakening found it shining, and observ'd it in plain day-light for about ½ hour, and then wholly ceasing. Looking immediatly upon his watch, it was near 4. a clock in the morn. of May 31.

May 31. The worm shin'd pretty clearly in his kitchen, a very lightsome room, at 5. a clock in ye evening, at wch time ye sun shined gloriously into ye same room. And looking about 11. a clock at night into his box, ye worm shin'd litle, having contracted her body into a bending posture; ye light scarce so big as a great pins head; upon touching of her, shee extended herself, walked in her box, and at first extent, shineth as glorious as ever. He adds, 1. yt he never saw her shine wthout some sensible motion either in her body or legs. 2. In her clearest shining, she extends her body a third part beyond its usual length. 3. To the observers thinking, she emitted a sensibly heat in her clearer shining.

So far he. I have made it my request to Mr Wray to give me view of yr discourse about ye question of truly Vegetable Excrescencies.[5] When I shall have received his answer you will hear again from Sir

Yr very humble and
faithf. servt
Oldenburg

ADDRESS

For his much honor'd friend,
Martyn Lister Esquire
at his house wthout Mickelgate-barr at
        York.

NOTES

Reply to letter 1711.
1 June 8, 1671.
2 The contents of the box seem not to have survived, but the letter itself was duly copied into Letter Book IV, 309.
3 Nehemiah Grew's *The Anatomy of Vegetables begun* (London, 1671) had been licensed by the Council on 11 May 1671; it was reviewed in *Phil. Trans.*, no. 78 (18 December 1671), 3037–43. Grew was born in 1641.
4 These were in the form of a letter dated 31 May 1671 from John Templer to Walter Needham and were printed in *Phil. Trans.*, no. 72 (19 June 1671), 2177–78. John Templer (d. 1678) was a Cambridge graduate who was intruded Rector of Braybrooke (Northhamptonshire) in 1659, but conformed in 1662 and retained his position.
5 In Letter 1715.

1721
Leibniz to Oldenburg
10 June 1671

This is mentioned in Oldenburg's reply, Letter 1793.

1722
Beale to Oldenburg
c. 12 June 1671

From the original in B.M. MS. Add. 4294, ff. 29–30, 33

Deare bror

I could not write to yu by Sat post,[1] though I was concernd to acknowledge yr favours, by last carrier. I have adventurd, as yu directed, to Dr Chamb.[2] If yt succeedes, I shall endeavour to serve him more industriously. I could then write but rashly, & too hastily. And my last to yu was a burden, for wch yu had neede to call in his ayde, together wth ye ayde of others; soe I told him.

And in my next designe, I shall againe [be] at some speciall wayes of inciteing, & engageing ye ayde of ye learnedest forreigners to adorne ye R Institution, & yr following Tracts wth ye most usefull, & ye most splendid Antiquityes; wch wilbe so remote, as to carry ye allurement of *Noveltyes*, & highly to advance our Moderne Philosophy. And I was glad to see, yt in yr *last of 71*, yu had found ye right clue to considerable Antiquityes.[3] Though yu have no Coll[ege] nor revenue, Yet *these Jesuites* have store of all things; And, if yu can learne, howe to plough in ye fields of Philosophy, wth their Flameing bulls, (or to use a more holy style) their heyfer) by a right ordering of *that utensile*, yu may do more, than by ten Universityes. Yet retaine this hint in yr bosome, for ye world is a malicious interpreter; (I have discoursd of it more than once to Mr. Boyle, & to others of chiefe note in ye RS. & we did not differ in our iudgements.) Wn my next designe is open, yu will see manifold reasons for it. Meanewhile *remarke* whence yu had yr *last informations*, & sollicite fervently for more of ye like. Never had we a better or clearer accompt of ye *Euripus*.[4] A thousd times repeated, & as on purpose to beget wonder, but not a line of accuratenes, till nowe. Wt sayes Dr Wallis to this, & to Rohaults sentiment, yt *ye flux & refluxe of ye Sea depends from ye pressure of ye Moone* in ye manner as he represents it *n 70*. p. *2140*.[5] The Remainders in Egypt, of wch yu have given us two pregnant touches,[6] are esteemed by many of ye most learned, more considerable, than ye most famous monuments in Rome or Greece; & deserve to be more punctually researched. Tis about 5 yeares, since we had intelligence, yt three iudicious persons were set out thence to enquire ye Inland affayres (for Art, commodityes, commerce,

Trade) of Affrica, & Asia. Are not these notes from ye same men? And, wt is yt Relation of a Voyage made into *Mauritania* in Affric, by ye Sieur Rowland Freius, by ye French Kings Order 1666 Englished & sold at ye white heart little Britaine, price 1s 6d?[7] Freius was an Artiste.

From Oxford I heare, yt ye Sheldonian presses are most nobly engaged. 1. Josephus[8] 2. The Antiquity, Origin, &, history of Oxon.[9] 3. The *Marmora Arundeliana*, wth greate improvements, engraven in brasse as they are nowe placed.[10] They have found among ye stones sent by my Lord Howard one inscription of ancienter date than any taken notice of by Mr Selden.[11] I pray yu take notice of this in yr next. And then yu may adde, That Gassendus styles it The Golden booke of ye learned Selden de Arundeleanis Marmoribus, &c.[12] And affirmes yt they were first bought by ye famous Cl. Fab. Lord of Peireskey, & afterwds lost by his Factor Samson. See Gass: in vita Peiresc. lib. 4. neere ye beginning pag. 33. English.[13] And here we may complaine yt those elaborate collections, costely reserches of Ld Peiresc, so rich of Inscriptions, discoveryes of Antiquityes & usefull philosophy, lye buried in Manuscripts & Lumber, a Worke so worthy ye Light, & worthy ye powerfull Command of ye French Kg, yt bountifull Patron to so many learned Universityes.

4thly, The Sheldonian presse is publishing a specimen of Learned Dr Morisons Herbal as a prodrome to his great worke.[14]

5 The Catalogue of ye Bodleian Library printed in folio wth greate care.[15]

6 They are now seriously deliberating about printing there all ye old Mathematicians, & ye best of ye later; wch wilbe a vast undertakeing. And in all these They serve ye ends of ye RS. But trust not to this, till yu have it better confirmed.

Yu may remembr yt some yeares agoe, I made all ye noise I could to yu, & for Dr Wallis, to promote such a worke, but accordg to *Dr Pells Idea of Mathem* wch would have savd much of ye vast charges, & time, wch is precious.[16]

Then Dr Wallis had his hands full. Perhaps he may nowe or in ye season, be at more leysure, if he hath recovered his health, for wch I pray heartily. Mr Glanvil hath my book of *yt Idea*. How is it, yt in his laste answer to Stub pag 13 he referres to his *Answere to Dr Casaubon*.[17] Of wch we heare nothing abroade. Perhaps he is disswaded from medling any more wth *Vindications*.

I pray yu correct in mine n. 71. pag. 2145 line 18 flatnes for fatnes. p. 2146 l. 9 trouble for troubling.[18] & above all p. 2148. l. 16. after I thincke, *Suedeland*. for thus it should be. I thinke Suedeland, where he wrote

& practised, is as could a Countrey, as England &c. Tis materiall. He wrote *Rostochij ex hortulo nostro domestico*.[19] Anno 1631. And practised there & in ye lowe Countreyes. I do not reguard ye printers mistake in ye same line l. c1. 28 for l.1.c.28.

Yu forgot p. 2153[20] In ye head to Sylvius Boe, to refer to vol. 3. no. 40. p. 811.[21] Where yu give an accompt of Sylvius, but (as I guesse cursorily) He nowe alterd his methode first intended, besides ye compleating ye Tract.

If yu have a minde to name Dr Morisons Prodrome above mentioned: remember yt yu gave accompt of his Praeludia Botanica Vol. 4. n. 46. p. 934.

If you meete wth any considerable French, yu may enquire, whether any care hath beene taken to publish his 82 Volumnes of most elaborate Manscripts.[22] I knowe not whethr they are abroade. But were left in ye hands of his kinsman (I thinke his Nephew) ye Baron of Rians. Most of them are ye Concernement of France & othr Monarchs & Provinces.

But all ye learned are concernd for his 24th Volum of Ancient & moderne Inscriptions in 2 Volume.

And for his 36 vol of Mathem. & Astron.

And his 37 vol of Poems Latine & French, Pasquels, devices.

And Vol 41. Learned letters. & Vol 43 Weights & measures.

And Vol. 45. Moneyes & ye busines of Moneyes.

And there are proper for ye Virtuosi Vol 52. Gardens & fruites.

Vol 53. Wonders in Nature. curious Inventions, Curiosityes.

Vol 55. Medals Arabian, Saxon British. Inventoryes of Cabinets. &c. some of these last were embeseled. Are they yet recovered, to encourage chalcography & informe for Antiquityes.

Vol 60 more epistles of learned men & Observ Math

I should have named sooner Vol. 5. Antiquityes, Calendars, Opticall glasses.

On ye Eyes & Sight of Men & beasts.

And Vol 6 Inscriptions, Subscriptions, Eulogyes, Epitaphs.

Vol 8 Voyages.

Vol. 16. Statues, Seales, ye Tripod, Pourtraites &c.

And many other very considerables. This is part of wt I reserve for yr Parisian correspondent. But not to imbroyle him till yu have his answere to ye last motion relating to Borellus[23] &c &c

This I send now because ye chiefe of French nobles are so thicke about yu in London.

Sr you see yt yr last preface was as seasonable, as if it had beene propheticall.[24] It may be a gag for Envy, & a spur for ye Industrious, & perhaps I may do yu service yt way, before this Vol be finished.

But I should not give yu all this trouble this busy time.

yr most affect servant
V.V.[25]

Sr I wrote to Dr Chamberlaine, yt by ye only superscription of these two letters yu would find me out. I shall advise of easeing yu of ye trouble hereafter.

Antonio Le Grand hath done his parte.[26]

But I doubt his demonstrations nor yt of Des Cartes will satisfy Atheists.

ADDRESS
For my honoured friend
Henry Oldenburg Esqr
At his house in Pell Mell
Westminster

Post is paid 3d

NOTES

Oldenburg has endorsed this letter as received on 14 June 1671.

1 Presumably Saturday, 10 June, is meant.
2 For Edward Chamberlayne, see Vol. VI, p. 363, note 2. In 1671 he published at London *An Academy or College wherein young Ladies and Gentleman may at a very Moderate Expence be Educated...* We know nothing of his business with Beale, whose earlier letters are lost.
3 In *Phil. Trans.*, no. 71 (22 May 1671), 2151–53 was published "A narrative of some Observations lately made by certain Missionaries in the Upper Egypt," by F. Brothais who is not identified. Beale seems to have taken him to be a Jesuit; in any case this account is followed by (pp. 2153–55) an "Extract of a French Letter, written by F. Jacques Paul Babin, a Jesuit, to F. Ignatius Bardy [Pardies] of the same Company... and lately communicated by the Learned Jesuit Bertet to a Friend of his in London; concerning the Flux of the Euripus." The friend was presumably Collins.
4 See note 3, above; Euripus is the narrow channel between the western coast of Greece and the island of Eubbea (Euboea), which has strange tides.
5 *Phil. Trans.*, no. 70 (17 April 1671), 2138–41, contains a review of Jacques Rohault, *Traité de Physique* (Paris, 1671).
6 Besides Père Brothais's letter, *Phil. Trans.*, no. 71, contains a review (pp. 2160–62) of *Relatione dello Stato presente dell' Egypto* by Johann Michael Wansleben (Paris, 1670).
7 Roland Frejus, *Relation d'un Voyage fait dans la Mauritanie en 1666* (Paris, 1670), was printed in English as *The Relation of a Voyage made into Mauritania...* (London, 1671). Beale had been reading a bookseller's catalogue.

8 Beale seems to have been wrong about this, unless the edition published between 1687 and 1700 was already under way.
9 Presumably Anthony à Wood's great work, *The History & Antiquities of the Colleges and Halls of the University of Oxford*, not published in this form until the eighteenth century; a Latin translation, *Historia et Antiquitates Oxoniensis*, was published at Oxford in 1674.
10 *Marmora Oxoniensis, ex Arundellianus Seldenianis aliisque conflata* (Oxford, 1676).
11 See John Selden, *Marmora Arundelliana* (London, 1628). Henry Howard of Norfolk (1628–84), now Baron Howard, had sent the Arundel marbles to Oxford in 1667.
12 "on the Arundel marbles."
13 Pierre Gassendi, *The Mirrour of true Nobility and Gentility, being the life of... Peiresk* (London, 1657). Nicolas Claude Fabri de Peiresc (1580–1637) was a Provençal antiquarian, scholar, amateur scientist, and patron of learning, as well as Councillor of the Parlement of Aix. In science he was, like his friend Gassendi, particularly interested in astronomy, and was one of the first Frenchmen to have a telescope constructed to permit him to see for himself Galileo's celestial discoveries. He maintained an enormous correspondence on scientific, antiquarian, and artistic subjects, much of which was published in the nineteenth century (e.g. seven volumes by Philippe Tamizey de Larroque, *Collection de Documents inédits sur l'histoire de France*, 2e série, Paris, 1888–98, which includes correspondence with Galileo and Mersenne).
14 See Letter 1701, note 4.
15 Thomas Hyde, *Catalogus impressorum librorum Bibliothecae Bodlejanae* (Oxford, 1674).
16 John Pell, *An Idea of Mathematicks* was first published in John Dury, *The Reformed Librarie-keeper* (London, 1650), though written (for Samuel Hartlib) about 1634.
17 *A Further Discovery of M. Stubbe in a brief reply to his last pamphlet against Jos. Glanvill* (London, 1671). Glanvill does in fact briefly deal with the criticisms advanced by Meric Casaubon (see *A Letter... to Peter du Moulin... concerning natural experimental philosophie, and some books lately sent out about it*, Cambridge, 1669) in *A Praefatory Answer to Mr. Henry Stubbe* (London, 1671), pp. 93–95.
18 These corrections to the printed version of Letter 1700 were published by Oldenburg in the next issue, that is *Phil. Trans.*, no. 72 (19 June 1671), 2190, except for the insertion of "Suedeland," for which see Letter 1733.
19 "from our household garden at Rostock."
20 Actually, p. 2159 in no. 71 (the account of Sylvius' *Praxeos medicae*).
21 This was the earlier account of Book I only, in 1668.
22 Beale is as usual supremely inconsequential: in defiance of logic, not Morison but Peiresc is meant. At Peiresc's death his possessions and manuscripts passed to the family of his younger brother, who also inherited the seigneurie of Rians, originally acquired by their uncle, Claude Fabri de Callas. Peiresc's nephew (also Claude) does not seem to have been much interested in his uncle's manuscripts, which have since become scattered. Some are in the Bibliothèque Méjanes in Aix, some in the Bibliothèque Inguimbertine in Carpentras, some in the Bibliothèque Nationale in Paris. Beale's information about the subjects in which Peiresc was interested seems quite accurate.
23 Probably Pierre Borel; see Vol. I, p. 232.
24 Oldenburg wrote a lengthy preface to Vol. VI of the *Transactions* (published at the commencement of no. 69, dated 25 March 1671), in which he quoted Cowley and defended the "new philosophy" against the charge that it despised antiquity and ancient learning.
25 See Vol. VII, Letter 1603, note.

26 Presumably this refers to Antoine Le Grand's *Philosophia veterum e mente Renati Descartes, more scholastico breviter digesta* (London, 1671), reviewed in *Phil. Trans.*, no. 70 (17 April 1671), 2137-38.

1723
Oldenburg to Hevelius
12 June 1671
From the original in Observatoire X, no. 104

Londini d. 12. jun. 1671

Vir Illustris,

Ante paucos dies, curante mercatore Cock, ad Te per mare expedivi insigne Microscopium una cum libris illis, quos ante hac a me rogaveras. Gratae omnino fuerunt Regiae Societati Observationes tuae, in epistola tua, 1. Maji [N.S.] scripta, commemoratae. Tempus pluvium et nebulosum in causa fuere, quod hic loci nec Occultatio stellarum in cauda ♈ 4 Martij, nec illa Spicae ♍, 12 Aprilis, observatae fuerunt. Non nisi illam animadvertimus, quae 6. Maji contigit Luna, post occasum solis, Borealem trium sub ventre ♍ cooperiente, quae observatio satis congruit cum calculo, quem Flamstedius Noster in praemonitione sua iniverat.[1] At piget omnino, fugisse nos conjunctionem Saturni cum Luna, 21. Maji celebratam:[2] Spes interim nos fovet, Caelum Tibi magis quam Nobis indulsisse. Praeter reliquas illas Eclipses stellares, ab eodem Flamstedio praedictas, et Tibi antehac communicatas, notat idem in epistola sua nuper ad me rure scripta, 20. Sept. 1671 mane Solis ortum, Lunam proxime transituram ♃, non vero cooperituram.[3]

Puto, Clarissimum Bulialdum Observationem Eclipseos Spicae Virginis ad Tabulas Philolaicas et Rudolphinas exegisse, Tibique differentiam significasse.[4]

Non dubitamus, quin summa cura porro sis observaturus novam stellam circa rostrum Cygni, nec non Saturni phases, hac aestate sine ansis, juxta Systema Hugenianum, conspiciendi. Nescio, quo fato accidit, Dominum Hookium necdum quicquam de Stella Cygni, nec de Saturno, ansis manco, observasse. Intelligo, Parisienses Astronomos, praeeunte Cassino,

Observationibus coelestibus nunc demum, extructa jam Observatoria specula, gnaviter incu[m]bituros. Nil quicquam ipsis deest, quo minus institutum Philosophicum feliciter promoveant, munificentia Regia quosvis in eam rem sumptus necessarios liberaliter suppeditante. Vale, Vir Optime, et plurimum salve a Tui

Observantissimo,
H. Oldenburg

TRANSLATION

Illustrious Sir,

A few days ago I sent to you by sea, in charge of the merchant Cock, a very good microscope together with those books which you had formerly asked me for. Your observations recorded in your letter of 1 May [N.S.] were very welcome to the Royal Society. The wet and cloudy weather furnished the reason why neither the occultation of the little stars in the tail of Aries on 4 March, nor that of Spica Virginis on 12 April, were observed here. We only took note of that on 6 May when, after sunset, the Moon covered the northernmost of three stars under the belly of Virgo, which observation agreed pretty well with the calculation which our fellow-countryman Flamsteed put out in his advance notice.[1] But it is quite distressing that the occurrence of the conjunction of Saturn with the Moon on 21 May escaped us;[2] meanwhile, we hope that the heavens were more kindly towards you. Besides the other stellar eclipses predicted by the above-named Flamsteed and communicated to you already, he remarks in a recent letter to me written from the country that on 20 September 1671, in the morning after sunrise, the Moon will pass close to Jupiter without actually covering the planet.[3]

I think that the famous Boulliaud has compared the observation of the eclipse of Spica Virginis with the Philolaic and Rudolphine Tables, and has imparted the difference to you.[4]

We have no doubt that you will continue to observe the new star near the beak of Cygnus and the phases of Saturn with the greatest care; the latter is to be seen this summer without anses, according to Huygens' theory. I cannot tell what accidents of fate have so far prevented Mr. Hooke observing anything of the star in Cygnus or of Saturn without his anses. I understand that under the leadership of Cassini the Parisian astronomers have at last fallen seriously to work upon celestial observations, the Observatory's telescopes having been erected. They lack nothing for the successful pursuit of scientific goals, since the royal bounty has generously furnished all the finance needed for that purpose. Farewell, best of men, with very many good wishes for your health from

Your most devoted,
H. Oldenburg

NOTES

Reply to Letter 1683.
1 See Letter 1708 and its note 5.
2 See Letter 1708, note 8.
3 See Letter 1697.
4 On 15 June Oldenburg had produced "a Latin paper" from Boulliaud about this occultation, comparing his own calculation with Hevelius' observation. This was entered in Register Book IV, 120 as "Mons Bullialdus his Calculation of the places of the Sun and Moon on April 22. 1671. &c. From the Philolaick Tables."

1724
Oldenburg to Leibniz
12 June 1671

From the original in Hannover MSS., ff. 9–10
Printed in Gerhardt, pp. 62–66

Amplissimo et Consultissimo Viro
Domino Gothof. Guilielmo Leibnitio J.U.D. et Consil. Moguntino
Henr. Oldenburg Sal.

Exhibita, prout jusseras, Regiae Societati Hypothesi tua Physica, nec non Motus Abstracti Theoria, mox Illa, more suo, utrumque libellum, diversis vicibus, nonnullis e caetu suo Mathematicis et Physicis evolvendum atque examinandum commendavit.¹ Factum hic, quod fieri assolet in ferenda de rebus extra Mathematicam evidentiam positis sententia: In diversas quippe opiniones Philosophi illi abiere. Interim, qui favere sensis tuis omnium maxime videbatur, erat Clarissimus Wallisius, Geometriae Professor Savilianus Oxonii; cujus mentem, si placet, paucis, et quidem primo de Hypothesi ipsa, sic accipe;²

"Legi semel atque iterum Dn. Leibnitii Hypothesin novam, de qua opinionem meam petitis. Authorem quod spectat, utut de nomine (quod memini) mihi ignotum prius, aestimare tamen debeo, ut qui, in loco magno inter magna negotia positus, vacare tamen potest liberae Philosophiae, et rerum causis investigandis, quique ad multa respexisse videtur. Opus quod attinet, multa inibi reperio summa cum ratione dicta, et quibus Ego plane assentior, ut quae sint sensis meis consona. Talia sunt, *debere Physicum ad Mechanicas rationes, quam fieri potest, omnia accommodare* §15. *Nihil seipsum, ex abstractis Motus rationibus, in lineam priorem restituere, etiam sublato impedimento, nisi accedat nova vis,* §23.³ *Omnia corpora sensibilia, saltem dura, esse Elastica; Atque, ab Elatere oriri Reflexionem,* §22.⁴ (Quae meis de Motu Hypothesibus, *Transactionibus Philosophicis* jam antehac insertis omnino congruunt, quaeque in Mechanicis seu de Motu tractatu fusius prosequor capp. 11. et 12.)⁵ Item, *Attoli gravia non metu vacui, sed propter Atmosphaerae aequilibrium,* §25. *Levitatem vero per accidens tantum sequi ex Gravitate* (gravioribus minus gravia sursum pellentibus) §24. *Irruptionem Aeris (sed et Aquae* etc.) *in vas exhaustum ob Aeris Gravitatem et Elaterem fieri,* §26. Item, *Exhausti atque Distenti* (ut loquitur) *Effectus; unde Fermentationes, Deflagrationes et Displosionum omne genus,) nempe, displodente altero; quod alterum absorbet,* (seu admittit potius,) §27. 39. 40. Nam et haec etiam ab Elatere fiunt, vel in Contento, vel in Continente, vel Utroque; illic, explicante se quod nimis fuerat impressum; hic, contrahente se quod nimis fuerat distentum: quippe utrovis modo, nedum utroque fiet irruptio vel explosio, dummodo locus sit, quo sine impedimento recipi possit quod ejiciendum erit. Suntque haec plane consona traditis nostris Mechan. c. 14. Sed et illud, *Gravitatem in inferioribus oriri ex Motu* (vel pressu) *superioris aetheris,* §13. 16. magna saltem verisimilitudine dicitur: quamquam enim Gravitatis causa (ut et Elateris) tam sit in abscondito, ut mihi nondum usquequaque satisfactum sit quid in ea re statuam, Naturae tamen phaenomena Pulsione quam Tractatione felicius utplurimum explicantur. Aliaque multa sunt, quae repetitu non est opus, quae magna verisimilitudine, si non et certitudine, dicta judico; quaeque per se satis consistunt independenter ab aliis; neque enim ita inter se sunt connexa omnia, ut uno vacillante caetera simul ruant. De tota vero Hypothesi ne quid statim pronuntiem, id saltem facit, quod non sim pronus Ego (in rebus saltem pure Physicis, non Mathematicis) assensum novis Traditis adhibere, donec vel Eruditorum sententiis in utramque partem ventilatis, quid statuendum sit rectius constet, vel ipsa sui evidentia (quod in Veris hypothesibus non raro fit) veritas eluceat. Fundamentum Hypotheseos novae petit ex *Abstracta sua motus Theoria* (quam necdum vidi, ut nec hujus Tractatus posteriora, quae passim citantur), nempe, *Quod nulla sit cohaesio quiescentis, sed omnis consistentia seu cohaesio oriatur a Motu,* §7. 12. 34. (quod cum Guilielmi Neilii nostri placitis coincidit). Contra vero, Honoratissimus Boylius *Consistentiam in particularum quiete, et Fluiditatem in earundem continuo motu,* collocat. Alii, ad *varias Atomorum figuras, hamatas et varie implicitas,* rem referunt. Neque Ego is sum, qui in tanta sententiarum varietate me velim arbitrum interponere. Sed tempori res permittenda est et Doctorum in utramque partem rationibus. Quippe, idem fere obtinet in novis Hypothesibus atque in Pendulorum Oscillationibus, ubi, post crebras hinc inde factas reciprocationes, tandem in perpendiculo fit quies. Id vidimus in *Hypothesi Copernicana*, quae utut fuerit Veteribus cognita, tamdiu tamen jacuit sepulta ut pro nova haberetur: Et quamvis optima esset suffulta ratione, non tamen statim obtinuit, sed a variis fuit variis modis impetita, et acriter disputata, donec tandem rationibus authoritati praevalentibus ita jam universim admittitur, ut vix quispiam harum rerum gnarus de ea dubitet, nisi quibus Cardinalium decretum praejudicio est: Et quanquam Tycho novam illius loco substituerit, quae illi aequipolleret, ea tamen tot onerata est incommodis, ut existimandus videatur potius ad frangendam invidiam id fecisse (quoniam Telluris motus ita Vulgi opinionibus horribilis videbatur) quam quod Copernici Hypothesin ex animo repudiaverit. Idem dicendum de *Circulatione Sanguinis Harveana*; quae utut optime stabilita fuerit et oculorum αὐτοψία comprobata, disceptata tamen fuit inter Londinenses Medicos viginti plus minus annis, antequam in publicum prodiret; et ab aliis postea. Quae tamen deinceps post maturam rei pensitationem (quod tempori dandum erat) ab omnibus ut indubitata recipitur. Sic Galilaei Hypothesis (ob Antlias, aquam non ultra certam altitudinem attrahentes, primum excogitata) quam Torricellius in graviori liquido adeoque magis tractabili promovit, *Æquilibrium Atmosphaerae* pro Veterum Fuga Vacui substituens, non nisi post diutinas hinc inde disputationes cum apud Viros Doctos locum obtinuit, quem jam habet. Idem de *Jolivii nostri Vasis Lymphaticis*, ante multos annos Londinensibus Medicis ab illo indicatis atque ab iisdem admissis et approbatis dicendum erit: Quae tamen ita rationi consona reperta sunt et oculari inspectioni manifesta, ut tandem longo post tempore inter alios aliquot acriter disputatum sit, quis eorum primus Inventor fuerit. Idemque in hoc negotio, aliisque novis Hypothesibus exspectandum, quae nec oculi inspectione nec certa demonstratione probari possunt, ut, si veris retionibus fundatae sint, tandem, quamvis non nisi post velitationes utrimque factas, in libere philosophantium animis locum obtinebunt, interea pendulae mansurae."

Secundo, idem Wallisius de *Theoria Motus Abstracti* haec alio tempore multo parcius respondet;[6]

"Accepi transmissam Dn. Leibnitii Theoriam Motus Abstracti; de qua etiam judicium meum expectatis: Duo autem sunt quae suadeant, ne illud praestem. Alterum, quod res invidiosa videatur de aliorum scriptis censuram agere: Alterum, quod occupatissimo tempore huc advenerit, quo aegre tempus obtinuerim semel atque iterum attentius legendi, nedum omnia pensiculatius expendendi. Quoniam vero id petitis, haec pauca dicam. Multa scilicet inibi contenta, Ego plane approbo, ut subtiliter et solide dicta, quaeque virum curiosum et cogitabundum indicant. Si paucae sint quibus non statim assentiar, ignoscet, spero, vir humanissimus. Et speciatim, fateor, mihi nondum satisfactum esse, ut, primis saltem cogitationibus, statim assentiar, Cohaesionem omnem ex continuo celerique sed inobservabili particularum motu fieri (quod ille Theoriae Motus Concreti fundamentum ponit;) uti nec pridem mihi fiebat satis, cum, ante aliquot annos, similem quietis et Cohaesionis causam assignaverit Nelius noster. Quid olim aliquando fiet, post rem accuratius perpensam, nec dicere possum, nec praevidere. Interim Ego ἀπέχω, nec quicquam in aliorum praejudicium pronuntio; quin liberum cuique sit, eam quam rationi magis consentaneam judicaverit sententiam amplecti."

Hucusque Wallisius noster, qui forte rem totam a Te propositam, concesso ampliori otio, penitius excutiet. *Neilius* ille, quem indigitat, vir adhuc juvenis, e Societate Regia, aetate juxta ac ingenio florenti satis nuper concessit. Is anno 1667. sua de Principiis et Natura Motus Cogitata primum Doctissimo Wallisio et mihi, deinceps vero ipsi Societati Regiae exhibuerat, prout in ejusdem Archivis consignata reperiuntur.[7] Supponebat ille, Nullum quiescens habere resistentiam ad Motum; et, duo corpora sibi invicem occurentia, ambo in concursus instanti a Motu desinere. Nullam ipse Mundo admittebat Reflexionem, statuens, nullam materiae particulam posse retroagi quin prius moveri desineret; si vero denuo moveatur, a novo id impulsu oriri, etc.

Caeterum, Vir Amplissime, morem gessi desiderio tuo, et pro commodiori distributione Scriptum tuum hic recudendum tradidi.[8] Hoc sane pacto, Doctorum quorumvis nostratium sententias longe lateque explorabit, ab iisque forsan, ubi Tu necdum clare cernis, ampliorem aliquam lucem faenerabitur. Tu interim valeas feliciter et scientias Philosophicas pro virili augere pergas. Dabam Londini d. 12. Junij 1671.

P.S. Jam ante aliquot septimanas transmittendos ad Te curavi libros, quos petieras. Martinus noster Bibliopola Londinensis, commendavit eos Schultzio Hamburgensi; hic Zunnero Francofurtano. Tu operam dabis, si placet, ut quantocius resciscam, postquam tum illi libri, tum haec literae ad manus tuas pervenerint; meminerisque inscriptionis solitae, nempe
    A Monsieur
     Monsr Grubendol à Londres.

Nil praeterea, nisi ut literae tuae rite curentur vel Amstelodamum vel Antverpiam; inde enim tuto ad nos transferentur.

Si quid Parisienses de tua Hypothesi et Motus Theoria consuerint, id nobis a Te communicatum iri omnino confidimus.

TRANSLATION

Henry Oldenburg greets the very worthy and wise Mr. Gottfried Wilhelm Leibniz, LL.D., Councilor at Mainz

Just as you instructed me, I showed your *Hypothesis physica nova*, together with the *Theoria motus abstracti*, to the Royal Society, and at once the Society (as its custom is) commended both books, on different occasions, to certain mathematicians and natural philosophers to be read and considered.[1] What was done on this occasion was what is usually done when judgments have to be reported about matters lying outside the rigor of mathematics; for indeed those philosophers diverge into a variety of opinions. Meanwhile, he who seemed most of all to favor your views was the famous Wallis, Savilian Professor of Geometry at Oxford, whose opinion you may have here in these few words, if you please, dealing first with the *Hypothesis* itself:[2]

[*The next few paragraphs are taken from Letter 1673 (Vol. VII); the translation may be found on pp. 562–64.*]

Secondly, the same Wallis has on another occasion replied more succinctly about the *Theoria motus abstracti*:[6]

[*This passage is taken from Letter 1713, above; the English may be found on pp. 73–74.*]

So far our Mr. Wallis, who may perhaps examine everything you have put forward more thoroughly, given more leisure. That *Neile*, of whom he speaks, while still a young man, a Fellow of the Royal Society in the prime of his age and mental vigor, was carried off not long ago. In the year 1667 he showed his reflections on the principles and nature of motion first to the very learned Wallis and myself and then to the Royal Society itself, just as they may be found lodged in the Society's archives.[7] He supposed that no resting body has a repugnancy to motion, and that when two bodies strike each other, both lose their motion at the moment of impact. He allowed no rebounding in the universe, postulating that no particle of matter could rebound unless first it had ceased to move; if in fact it does begin to move again, this must come from a fresh impulse, etc.

Moreover, worthy Sir, in order to fulfil your desire and for the more convenient distribution of your writings I have sent them to be reprinted here.[8] When that has been done, they will seek out the opinions of our men of learning far and wide and perhaps will borrow some light from them where you so far have seen but darkly. Meanwhile, may you continue in good health and contentment, pursuing the philosophical sciences with all your might. London, 12 June 1671.

P.S. I made arrangements some weeks ago for the books you want to be sent to you. Our Mr. Martin, the London bookseller, entrusted them to Schulz at Hamburg, and he to Zunner at Frankfurt. Please give yourself the trouble to let me know as soon as possible after those books and this letter have come to your hands. You will have recalled the usual address, namely

A Monsieur

Monsr Grubendol à Londres

Nothing more, except your letters may properly be directed via Amsterdam or Antwerp, for thence they will be safely passed on to us.

If the Parisians have formed any opinion of your *Hypothesis* and *Theory of Motion*, we are fully confident that you will communicate it to us.

NOTES

Reply to Letter 1688.
1 The *Hypothesis*, exhibited to the Society on 23 March 1670/1, was commended to Boyle, Wallis, Wren, and Hooke; the *Theoria* was entrusted to Hooke and Wallis (18 and 25 May).
2 See Letter 1673 (Vol. VII, pp. 559–65).
3 Wallis wrote "22."
4 Wallis wrote "21."
5 Wallis wrote "13."
6 See above, Letter 1713.
7 For the discussion in March 1667 of Neile's "hypothesis in philosophy" by Oldenburg and Wallis, see Vol. III, pp. 373, 374, note 2. (The later letters are in Vols. III and IV.)
8 This edition by John Martin (London, 1671) of the two tracts together is noticed in *Phil. Trans.*, no. 73 (17 July 1671), 2213–14.

1725
Oldenburg to Dodington
12 June 1671
From the memorandum in Royal Society MS. D 1, no. 21

Answ. jun. 12. 1671.
Non retinui copiam.¹

NOTES

Reply to Letter 1670 (Vol. VII).
1 "I kept no copy."

1726
Lister to Oldenburg
14 June 1671
From the original in Royal Society MS. L 5, no. 34
Partly printed in *Phil. Trans.*, no. 73 (17 July 1671), 2196–97

Yorke June 14th 1671

Sr

June 10th I found several of ye *Patellae Kermiformes* hatched in a Box, where I had purposely put ym. They prove a sort, as I guessed by ye figure of ye Worme, of Bees, but certainly ye least, yt I ever yet saw of yt Tribe; as not exceeding in their whole bulke ye halfe of a Pismire. They are very compact & thick for their bignesse: of a coale black colour They seeme to want neither stings, nor ye Three balls in a triangle in their forehead, wch yet are things to be referred to ye testimonie of a Microscope. That wch is very remarkable to ye naked Eye, is a white or straw colour large & round Spott on ye back: of their 4 Wings ye upper paire are shaded or darke spotted, ye undermost paire are cleer. We may entitle ym according to our coustome Apiculae nigrae macula super humeros subflavescente insignitae, e patellis sive favis membranaceis, veri Kermes similibus, suaque itidem purpura tingentibus, cerasi aut rosae aliarumve arborum virgis adtextis, exclusae.[1]

This of ye purple Huskes & ye other Historie of Scarlet-staining Eggs I present you as parralells of our English store to Kermes & Cocheneil, I meane additaments to encrease ye number of agreable tinging Materials & not Medicaments, unlesse wary & safe Tryal shall discover to us if they have any medicinal qualities, as use & coustume has made us beleive ye Exotick have in a high degree.

Yours of June 10th came safe to my hands.

One of ye huskes I sent you adhered to a Rose Tree twigg & ye other to a Cherry tree. But a rose bush since has afforded me some scores of these Patelles, many of wch are hatched in ye Box I put ym. It is to be further observed yt those yt looke ye blackest, yeilde ye deepest & best purple 2. yt as ye Bees come to maturitie, ye dye seemes to be spent & ye Huskes grow dry. 3. That ye yong ones make theyr way out at several small holes, wheras ye tru Kermes husk seemes to be peirced but in one place.[2]

I thanke you for ye Observation about ye shining of a Gloworme. It was never my good fortune, since I had ye Curiositie to examine things, to light upon any one Gloworme, save, yt I tooke one flying ith aire in St Johns walke in Cambridge, some 4 or 5 yeares agoe; & doe still keep it by me as a great raritie. its Wings were sheathed like a beetle etc. of its shining I made noe observation, save yt its light, wch it gave under a Glasse, where I kept it, was very green & faint. it was a sullen & sluggish animal. Mr. Skippon one of your society hath since assured me, yt he hath taken up these *Cicindelae volantes*[3] (if I well remember) in Kent. Aldrovandus[4] will have wings only a distinction of sex, not species.

I am glad of ye news of ye publishing of yt Curious peice about ye Anatomy of Vegetables:[5] my notes are yet in some disorder & my selfe at this present very much out of health. I desire you to excuse this scrible. I am

Your most humble servant
Martin Lister

ADDRESS
>   These
> For his honoured friend
> Mr. Oldenburg
> at his house in ye
> Palmal
>   at
>   London

NOTES

Reply to Letter 1720.
1 "Small black bees marked with a pale yellowish spot on the shoulders issuing from husks or papery cells, like the true Kermes [insect] and likewise staining purple, adhering to the twigs of cherry or rose or other trees."
2 Lister corrected this last sentence in his letter of 16 October; see Letter 1800, p. 302.
3 "flying glowworms."
4 Ulyssi Aldrovandi, *De animalibus insectis libri septem* (Bologna, 1602).
5 See Letter 1720, note 3.

1727
Sachs to Oldenburg
16 June 1671

From the copy in Royal Society Letter Book IV, 316–18

Amplissimo Viro
Domino Henrico Oldenburgio Soc. Reg. Illust. Secro
Phil. Jac. Sachs à Lewenheimb, Ph. et M.D.; Physicus
et Reip. Vratislavensis Ordin. et Acad. Curiosorum,
Salutem et officia

Pergimus nunc pro virili ad edendum alterum Ephemeridum Germanicanum Annum,[1] pro quo exornando plurimi eruditi Medici sua Symbola liberaliter contulerunt, inter quos nominare possum Dn. D. Bernhardi à Berniz[2] Reg. Maj. Poloniae Archiatrum, qui praeter alia descripsi et graphice penicillo depinxit Aquilam Imperialem in Polypodio repraesentatam, Muscum larvatum humana figura: fungum in alveario repertum, egregie uterum cum partibus genitalibus faeminarum representantem; gammarum alatum sive papilionem cancri-formem; gammarum Vegetabilem in Betae radice; varias Orchidum species, calculum faeminae e vesica exsectum, qui mentitur membrum virile cum scroto: omitto alia curiosa Medica Pratica, quae hinc inde varij Exercitatissimi practici communicarunt; speroque indies majori alacritate et studio plures accessuros, si DEUS clementissime Halcyonia concesserit, et imminentes undique Christiano Orbi procellas discusserit.

Acerrimus vero noster stimulus erit, si Labores nostros Exteris Nationibus non penitus ingratos futuros intelligamus, et gratissimae fiunt transmissae admonitiones Amicae, quae viam digito quasi monstrant, quomodo ulterius in salebroso hoc itinere procedendum sit, cum ob diversitatem ingeniorum diversae sint sententiae. Cynosyra tamen unica DEI Gloria, Proximi commodum, Veritas et novarum rerum Ingeniosarumque Inventorum propalatio.

Promissae nobis fuerunt per Cardinalem Mediceum Ephemerides Romanae[3] (de Venetis nihil perceperam) quas adhuc expectamus: Nitschius, Prof. in Acad. Giessana, qui Interpres hactenus fuit Ephemerid. Gallican, hisce nundinis pauca saltem folia Anni 1669. et 1670. ex Ephemerid. Gall. edidit Latino idiomate:[4] Gallicum exemplar non vidi, quanquam his nundinis Francofurtens. ea de causa ad Dominum de Justel, Secretarium Regium, et Dominum de Bourdelot, Abbatem, Viros Curiosissimos, Parisios scripserim. Mirarer, si nihil ulterius praeter haec folia integro biennio edidissent, et tam insignis ipsorum fervor tam subito tepuisset.

Itali, Dani, Bohemi, Hungari alijque Exteri Medici, et Helvetij, Observationes quasdam Medicas communicarunt Practicas, forte etiam ab Excellentissimis Medicis Anglicis, apud quos nostro seculo Medicina videtur Principatum quendam sibi vendicare, eadem liberalitas Tuo patrocinio exspectari possit, cum tam ipsa Praxi exercitatissima quam investigatione causa morbificae ingeniosissima, et non raro dissectione cadaverum morbo peremptorum perspicacissima, communicandis observationibus quibusdam insignem faciem toti Reipublicae Medicae praeferre possint.

Lubet praeterea sententiam tuam exquirere, num scilicet ad coercendas Incendiorum flammas violentiores, non possit Aqua aliqua mistura impregnari, quae per tubulos simul igni violenter infusa fortius, quam communi modo flammas coerceret. Solent equidem instrumenta ista cuprea cum pregrandibus tubulis fabrefacta, et maxima vi impulsa impulsu suo una cum aqua, ignis contraria, flammas extinguere; sed forte ars humana adhuc majus excogitare possit compendium. Videmus Lac equidem maximopere flammas cohibere, quia simplex aqua a flamma resolvitur in vapores, vapores sursum elevati ignem non petunt; contra Lac sua glutinositate se affigit rei accensae, ac intra poros ignem videtur suffocare; sed cum tanta Lactis non suppetat copia, siquid analogi excogitari possit, quod non purum pingue sit, ne flammam simul alat, forte res videtur non parvi momenti.

Excell. D. Willis in Tract. suis eruditissimis mentionem facit cujusdam preparationis ut martem, oculos cancri, corall. &c. absque menstro corrosivo possit disponere,[5] ut vires suas in quemvis liquorem deponant et in eo solvantur: quem praeparandi modum si sub fide silentij revelare vellet, sane conarer egregio aliquo remedio Chymico eandem gratiam recompensare; notus mihi Spiritus aliquis volatilis, qui liquori maxime approbato junctus, in morbis convulsivis egregiam exhibuit operam, quam libenter communicarem, pariter non omnibus revelandum. Vale interim, Vir Amplissime, ulterius conatibus nostri Collegij, et mihi favere perge. Vratislaviae, 16 Junii 1671.

TRANSLATION

Philipp Jacob Sachs von Lewenheimb, Ph.D., M.D., Physician in Ordinary to the Principality of Wroclaw and Member of the Investigators' Academy, sends his greetings and respects to the very worthy Mr. Henry Oldenburg, Secretary of the Illustrious Royal Society

We are now pushing on with all our strength towards the publication of another year of the German journal,[1] for the perfection of which many learned physicians have generously given their contributions, among whom I may mention Doctor Bernard von Berniz, chief physician to the king of Poland,[2] who (among other things) has described and with a lively pencil depicted the imperial eagle represented in a fern, a moss bewitched into a human form, a fungus found in a beehive, imitating in a very remarkable way the womb and other female reproductive organs, a winged lobster or crablike butterfly, a vegetable lobster in a beet, various species of orchids, a stone dissected from a woman's bladder resembling the male organ and scrotum; I make no mention of other curiosities of medical practice which other very experienced practitioners have communicated from time to time and I hope that from day to day there will be further additions, through increasing eagerness and zeal, if God will of his great mercy vouchsafe us peaceful times and dissipate the storms that threaten Christendom from all sides.

Our stimulus will be extremely keen, if we understand that our labors are not altogether unwelcome to foreigners, and any friendly advice sent to us will be very welcome which may serve to guide us in proceeding further along this rugged road, since different minds form different opinions. But our unique aim is the Glory of God, the welfare of our fellow men, truth, and the promulgation of the new and ingenious works of innovators.

We were promised the journal of Rome[3] by Cardinal de' Medici (I had as yet seen nothing from Venice), but we still await it; Nitzsche, the professor at the University of Giessen who has up to now translated the *Journal des Sçavans*,[4] has made available in Latin at least a few sheets from that *Journal* for 1669 and 1670 at the [last book] fair. I have not seen a copy of it in French, although at the Frankfurt Fair I did write on that account to Mr. Justel, [one of the] King's secretaries, and Mr. de Bourdelot, an abbé, at Paris; both are very inquisitive men. I shall be surprised if they have published no more than these few sheets in two whole years, and if their warm fervor should have cooled so suddenly.

Italians, Danes, Bohemians, Hungarians, Swiss, and other foreign medical men share some practical observations in medicine with us, and perhaps the same generosity may be expected from the very excellent English physicians, among whom in this century medicine seems to claim a certain preeminence, through your intercession, since they can improve the whole shape of medicine remarkably by communicating some observations appertaining to both their most skilful practice and their very ingenious investigation of the causes of disease, and not infrequently their highly perceptive dissections of the bodies of those carried off by disease.

Further, I wish to know your opinion, whether water could not have some mixture dissolved in it for putting out the flames of fires when these are pretty violent, so that when pumped on the fire through pipes it would put out the flames more effectively than the ordinary method does. Those copper devices are usually constructed with very large pipes and when worked with great vigour their force against the fire, together with the water, extinguishes the flames. Yet perhaps human art can formulate a still greater resource. For we see that milk restrains flames most of all, because plain water disperses into vapors and these vapors flying up no longer seek the fire, whereas milk on the other hand, being glutinous, holds the burning matter to itself and the fire seems to be stifled within its pores. But as milk is not available in sufficient quantity, if something analogous could be thought of that is not merely fatty (lest it too should feed the flame), perhaps it would seem of no small importance.

The excellent Mr. Willis in his very learned treatises mentions about a certain preparation that it so disposes iron, crab's-eyes, coral, etc., without being a corrosive solvent, that they transfer their effectiveness to any fluid and are dissolved in it;[5] if he would reveal the way of making this preparation under pledge of secrecy I would certainly try to compensate him with some notable chemical remedy for this favor. There is a certain volatile spirit known to me which when combined with a highly regarded fluid does wonders in convulsive diseases, which I would gladly communicate, though likewise not to all eyes. Meanwhile, farewell worthy Sir, and continue to think well of the endeavors of our College, and of myself. Wroclaw, 16 June 1671.

NOTES

1 This was the second volume of the *Miscellanea curiosa medico-physica* of the Academia Naturae Curiosorum, published at Jena in 1671.
2 The only fact about the physician and botanist Martin Bernard von Berniz that can be added to the text is that he was the author of *Catalogus plantarum... quo anno 1651 in hortis regiis Varsoviae et circa eamdem in locis silvaticis, praetensibus* [etc.]... *nascuntur* (Danzig, 1652).
3 The *Giornale de' Letterati*.
4 Fridericus Nitzsche (1645–1702), M.A. Leipzig, 1664, was at this time Professor of Mathematics at Giessen University. He published Latin versions of the first five volumes of the *Journal des Sçavans* (1665–1670). Later he became an authority on law.
5 See Thomas Willis, *Of Fermentation* (London, 1659), Ch. IX *ad fin* (*Remaining Medical Works*, London, 1681, p. 35). Willis calls it "a preparation, whereby without any Corrosive, or Acid Liquor, by the mediation only of a gentle heat, the body of Iron is opened" so that it becomes soluble in water, etc.

1728

Beale to Oldenburg

c. 16 June 1671

From the quotation in Bodleian Library MS. Smith 45, ff. 65–67

It is our blot, yt ye Ld Bacons Novum Organum, and some of his other Essays in philosophy, were never yet rendred into English, as it is ad[uced] in Latin in one fair volum at Frankford.¹ Never was it so much as methodized or analys'd, yt I can hear of; neither his method in N. organum explicated or punctually exemplified; or his Errors (wch are there in affr[ont] to Gilbert, and later discoveries) so much as excused or noted in a marginal remark. Of this I complain'd formerly to Honorable M. Boyle, who had [once] an intention to doe something in it, if God had been pleas'd to preserve his health. Mr Theoph. Gale² should be advis'd for the honor of ye English, to begin wth Ld Bacon, who was born A. 1560.³ died 1626. aetat 66; before the other moderns of fame. Peyreskius was born A. 1580.

died A. 1637. Aetat 57. Des-Cartes born 1596 died 1650. Aetat 54. who retired to his philosophy whole 25. years, wch is a[lmost] 20 years more than Ld Bacons leisure for ye Body of his philosophy, and for particulars. 'Tis remarquable, yt Gilbert by his Loadstone guess'd at ye Terrestrial rotation, before Galilaeus made his Telescopical discoveries; his Nuncius[4] being first publish't A. 1610. Keplers Dioptrice wth his vote for Galilaeus[5] about a year after; and Gassendus his Inst. Astronom. 1647.[6] All these, together wth Harvy and others, should be recommended to Mr Gale, and the Epistles of Des-Cartes[7] will give him much light; so also will his abettors, de La Roure,[8] Papin,[9] Regius,[10] Lipstorpius.[11] But Mr Gales best taske will be to methodize and give ye substance of Mr Boyle's works; That Gentlemans writings and discoveries affording copious Topicks for very splendid and instructive results. For Example, if his 30th Experiment in ye Continuat[ion] of Exper. Philosophy,[12] concerning ye Gravity of any Cylinder of ye Atmosphere, were drawn out ready calculated from an inch to a mile, in 3. colums; the first, when the Baroscope is at 28. inches, wch seldom is so light in England, and only in extream stormes and tempests; and 2dly, when 'tis at 29, wch is more ordinary, and 3dly, when at 30, wch is wth us in England very frequent; The Observation would seem very strange, and almost incredible to ym yt have not taken notice of it, as it is by him demonstrated. And all along in his writings may find abundance of extraordinarys, never so conspicuously cleared before, nor any writings, old or new, yt I know, so pregnant of alluring inferences.

I shall here add, what seems unfinish't in Ld Bacons preliminary methods, and wch perhaps will hardly be well done but by some very industrious person, who hath carefully perused all his remaines, Latin, and English; and one, yt is so happy as to obtain ye advice and assistance of some of ye chief modern philosophers yet alive:

1. The six parts premised to his Nov. Organum, under the head, of *Distributio operis*,[13] are not to this day sufficiently exemplified, though himself doth in the following Tracts referr to some of those heads as in some manner absolv'd.

2. Lib. 2. Nov. Org. aph. 10. he distributes further than I can find any where exemplified.[14]

3. L. 2. Nov. org. aph. 21. he propounds 9. parts for his Nov. Org; and of these I find but two, viz. The first, *De praerogativis Instantiarum*, and ye 8th, *De Paracevis ad Inquisitionem*, handled, explicated, or exemplifyd.[15]

And this being done, as to Ld Bacon, it would be a very acceptable and usefull worke, and suitable to what Mr Gale hath already performed, if he would reduce the modern discoveries into such order, as would best illustrate and compleat Bacons N. Organum, and his other methods, as far as they deserve to be consider'd.

NOTES

Oldenburg had received this letter from Beale by 27 June, when he quoted it in Letter 1735; his immediately previous letter from Beale was of the twenty-fourth (Letter 1733), and it is obvious that the present one was earlier still. It was probably acknowledged in Letter 1730, and so (we suppose) written about the sixteenth, following a few days after Letter 1722. The right-hand margin of one page has been concealed in binding.

1 Francis Bacon, *Opera omnia* (Frankfurt, 1665).
2 Theophilus Gale (1628–78), a Fellow of Magdalen College, Oxford, before the Restoration, spent some time at Caen with Lord Wharton, returning to England in 1665 and living as a dissenting minister. He was author of *A Discourse touching the Original of Human Literature* (Oxford, 1669, 1671), deriving it from the Hebrews, reviewed in *Phil. Trans.*, no. 74 (14 August 1671), 2231–32.
3 Actually, 22 January 1560/61.
4 Galileo's *Sidereus nuncius*.
5 Kepler's *Dioptrice* (Augsburg, 1611) contained before the main text an account of Galileo's letters describing the progress of his astronomical discoveries with the telescope since the publication of the *Sidereus nuncius* in the spring of 1610. All these works were included in the London, 1653, edition of the book mentioned in the next note.
6 Pierre Gassendi, *Institutio astronomica juxta hypotheseis tam veterum quam Copernici et Tychonis* (Paris, 1647).
7 See Vol. VII, Letter 1672, note 10.
8 Jacques du Roure, author of a *Philosophie tirée des anciens et des nouveaux auteurs* (Paris, 1654); this Cartesian writer was mentioned by Oldenburg in Vol. I, p. 215 (where the note should be amended).
9 Nicolas Papin, *Considérations sur le traité "Des passions de l'âme de Descartes"* (Paris, 1652).
10 Henri le Roy (1598–1679), a physician and philosopher who taught at Utrecht, was one of the first major exponents of Cartesianism; he published *Fundamenta physices* (Amsterdam, 1646), with a second, enlarged edition (*Philosophia naturalis*, Amsterdam, 1654).
11 Daniel Lipstorp (1631–84), mathematician and jurist, published *Specimina philosophiae cartesianae quibus accedit ejusdem authoris Copernicus redivius* at Leiden in 1653.
12 That is, *A Continuation of New Experiments Physico-Mechanical, touching the Spring and Weight of the Air* (Oxford, 1669); see Birch, *Boyle*, III, 236–38, and also Vol. VI, Letters 1285, 1285a, and 1286.
13 "Plan of the Work."
14 Here Bacon states the necessity for a "Natural and Experimental History" of nature as the basis of the "Tables and Arrangements of Instances, in such a method and order that the understanding may be able to deal with them," with induction as "the very key of interpretation."
15 "Of Prerogative instances... Of Preparations for Investigation"; Beale is quite correct.

1729
De Graaf to Oldenburg
19 June 1671
From the original in Royal Society MS. G. no. 8

Clarissimo Praestantissimoque Viro
D. Henrico Oldenburgio
R. De Graaf S.

Praeterito die iovis cum nauta, qui singulis septimanis Rotterodamo Londinum proficiscitur, ad Te misi tractatum meum de succo Pancreatico recenter editum, in cuius calce epistolam de Partibus Genitalibus mulierum reperies,[1] quae omnia ut hilari fronte excipias et benigne interpreteris obnixe rogo.

Caeterum gavisus sum quod tandem aliquando disputationem nostram de Testium structura eousque adegerim, ut Clarissimus D. Clarkius rem totam ad ulteriorem per observationes et experimenta elucidationem remittat. ea quae de motu seminis commemoras, unius figurae ad te missae fabrica solvuntur, quemadmodum Clarissimo illi viro ostendam si amice mecum contentionis serram reciprocare desideret. Nimis profecto discretus mihi videtur Clarissimus D. Clarkius quam ut propter unum verbum, nullo iniuriandi animo e calamo prolapsum, totum litterarum nostrarum commercium abrumperet; quandoquidem luculenter viderit, quod ego toties illius verba, quae iuvenilis ardoris impetu in deteriorem partem flecti potuissent, [*paper torn*] animo preterire maluerim. idem et Tu doctissime Oldenburgii satis superque animadvertere potuisses cum nunquam ad verba aliquantulum acerbiori stilo hinc inde in litteris tuis inserta nisi suavissimis terminis responderim. vale et C.D. Clarkium meis verbis officiose saluta

Vester humilli famulus
R De [*Graaf*][2]

raptim delphis
29 Junii 1671 [N.S.]

ADDRESS
  A Monsieur
    Monsieur Grubendol
      A Londres

TRANSLATION

R. De Graaf greets the very famous and distinguished Mr. Henry Oldenburg

I sent you last Thursday by a sailor who goes from Rotterdam to London each week my recently published treatise on the pancreatic juice, at the tail end of which you will find a letter concerning the female reproductive organs;[1] I earnestly beseech you to receive all this favorably and judge it kindly.

For the rest, I am delighted that I have at last so far prevailed in our former dispute about the structure of the testes that the famous Mr. Clarke postpones the whole issue to be further elucidated by experiments and observations. The points you note about the motion of the semen are resolved by the construction of the single figure sent to you, as I shall demonstrate to that celebrated person if he should desire to continue his friendly altercation with me. For it seems to me that the famous Mr. Clarke is surely too sensible a person to break off our whole correspondence because of a single word let fall from the pen without any thought of insult, since he will have seen perfectly clearly that I have many times preferred to pass calmly over the words of that man, which could be given an ill interpretation in the hastiness of youthful ardor. And you too, learned Oldenburg, could have noticed more than sufficiently, that I never replied to those words of sharper tone introduced here and there into your letters save in the most gentle terms. Farewell, and greet the famous Mr. Clarke most dutifully with my own words

Your humble servant,
R. De [Graaf][2]

Delft, in haste, 29 June 1671

ADDRESS
To Mr. Grubendol
London

NOTES

Reply to Letter 1497 in Vol. VII, of which the text is lost. It appears that Timothy Clarke took offence at De Graaf's tone in Letter 1472 (Vol. VII), though why he should have done so is not obvious.

1 *De succo pancreatico* (Leiden, 1671), an enlarged version of *De succi pancreatici natura et usu* (Leiden, 1664); the letter "De partibus genitalibus mulierum" is addressed to Lucas Schacht, Professor of Physic at Leiden. It was to be developed in De Graaf's book of similar title of 1672; see *Phil. Trans.*, no. 79 (22 January 1671/2), 3066–68.
2 The signature has been cut away.

1730
Oldenburg to Beale
20 June 1671

Mentioned in Beale's reply, Letter 1733, and on the endorsement of Letter 1722.

1731
Oldenburg to Lister
24 June 1671
From the original in Bodleian Library MS. Lister 34, f. 27

London June 24. 71.

Sir,

As I cannot Justly forbear to produce yr communications before ye Society from time to time, so yt Illustrious Company never failes to injoyn me to return you their hearty thanks, wch you are now to receive particularly for yr letter of june 14th, and ye remarkable contents thereof;[1] wch I intend, God permitting, to insert in the Transactions of july, as I have done the first part in those of this month, now ready to come abroad; where I have also publish't yr well-considered Inquiries and Table of Spiders;[2] this being a proper season for ye Curious to make observations upon yt subject.

My late intelligence from Paris informs me, yt now in a few weeks there will come abroad their Royal Academies first Book of Plants, together wth Cuts and short Descriptions, as also wth a Discourse concerning the quantity of Salts, Spirits, Oyles etc. wch the severall plants doe afford.[3]

I have not yet received from Mr Wray yr discourse about Vegetable Excrescensies, wch you gave me leave in yrs of May 31th.[4] to desire the loan of. Doubting of ye delivery of my letter,[5] I may shortly send him a duplicate, to goe sure. Now I can say no more in great haste, than yt I am constantly Sir

Yr faithf. servt
Oldenburg

ADDRESS
To his honor'd friend
  Martyn Lister Esquire
    at his house wthout Mickel-
    gate barr
      at
        York

NOTES

Reply to Letter 1726.
1 It was read to the Society on 22 June 1671.
2 Letters 1589 and 1589a in Vol. VII.
3 We have not recovered any Parisian correspondence for this period. Oldenburg's information was overoptimistic. As noted before, Nicolas Robert and Abraham Bosse had been painting and engraving plants for some years, and Claude Perrault was eager to prepare a sumptuous herbal; but Denis Dodart, progenitor of the *Mémoires pour servir à l'histoire des plantes*, was not appointed to the Académie until 1673, and the book appeared only in 1676 (with thirty-nine plates, and the chemical studies of Duclos and Bourdelin).
4 Letter 1712.
5 Letter 1715 (a memorandum only).

1732
Werden to Oldenburg
24 June 1671

From the original in Royal Society MS. W 3, no. 50

Stockholme. Saturday
24. June. 1671.

Sr

I have perused with greate satisfaction the New Treatise of Mr. Boyle (about ye Aire) yt you have sent me, & shall speedily send it according to yr directions to Mr. Rudbeckius in hopes your Repeated Civilityes to him may make him hereafter more dilligent in his Returnes yn hitherto, For as yet I have not beene able to obtaine the Coppyes promised me; though allsoe undertaken for by His brother in Law (One Lohrman,[1] a Student of Physicke & esteemed a Good Proficient in makeing of Opticke Glasses) wherefore wn I have wayted a Convenient tyme for his acknowledgement of the receipt of this new Treatise, if the sd Coppyes come not yn I will send such a draught of his Bridge as I tooke my selfe in passing; & such a One as I remember of the yacht to goe agst ye wind but as for ye Other to be conterpoysed with Water I have quite forgotten it.

As for his Engine to rayse water, I much doubt yt there is noe such thing, for upon frequent Enquiryes of Mr. Lohrman (who is genlly. privy to all Mr. Rudbeck's Practises) He seemes to hint, yt there have some new difficultyes intervened in ye Practicability of yt. Experiment, which perhaps is the reason Mr. Rudbeckius takes noe more notice of it.

I have with much pleasure begun to reade Mr. Boyles Treatise of Cold, & to the end of the 6th Title (for I am gotten noe further) I find Mr. Boyles informations agreable to those of most men's here; whether as to the Effects of Cold on Humane bodyes or their Thawing by rubbing ym wth snow: but Doctor Durier (or Du Rieds) who was in France, & is here this Kings Physitian,[2] tells me yt a more effectual Remedy yn snow, as he hath tryed upon himselfe & others, is to Mash or Chew Pease, & yn cover over ye frozen Part, whether Nose Cheekes or Eares, wth ym. for wch purpose in Winter he carries allwayes pease in his pockett.

You will oblige me to let me heare of you sometymes, & particularly of such practicall Improvements in Mechanickes as shall occur to you.

I have Number. 68. of the Phylosophicall Transactions, & all before it, except only Number. 66 which by some mistake (of the Stationer I thinke) hath not beene sent me amongst the last parcell; wherefore if My father hath not allready prevented you, please to let Numb. 66 be sent to St. James'es & the other Numbers after 68. vizt. 69. 70. &c. as they shall be extant.

I am Sr.

> Your very humble Servaunt
> Jo. Werden

Mr. Oldenburg

[P.S.] Yesterday at 3. in ye Afternoone, ye Spiritt in my sealed Weatherglasse was up at $7\frac{7}{8}$ Inches above $\odot$ yt is $12\frac{1}{2}$. Inches higher yn. it was at lowest in Febry last wch makes me ye apter to beleeve wt. divers have assurd me, vizt yt the heat here (during the small tyme it lasts) is greater yn in Spayne.

ADDRESS
   For Henry Oldenburgh Esqr.
   Secretary to the Royall Society.
   at his house in ye Palmal
   neere St. James'es
         London

NOTES

   This letter was not received until 16 November 1671. Werden last wrote Letter 1689; Oldenburg's reply to it, sent with Boyle's *Tractatus... ubi mira aeris... rarefactio detecta* (London, 1670), has not survived.
  1 Gustavus Lohrman took an M.D. degree at Upsala in 1664 and at Leiden in 1666. He was later a professor at Upsala.
  2 Grégoire-François Du Rietz (1607–82) came of an old Flemish family and after taking his M.D. at Salamanca became physician to Louis XIII; in 1642 he went to Sweden, serving Queen Christina and Charles X Gustavus. With other medical men he founded a medical college in Stockholm in 1663.

1733
Beale to Oldenburg
24 June 1671

From the original in B.M. Sloane MS. 4280, ff. 35r–36v, 38

D Br

Yrs of Jun. 20 is full of highly considerables. But I heare nothing of a large letter I venturd for Dr Ch[amberlayne] in Hatton G[arden]. I was so full of business, yt I forgote date to yu.[1]

I wrote to Oxford, mentioning *Gale*,[2] but I am not strong enough to engage him nor do knowe any way of particular adresse.

Borellus[3] is, in my iudgement, much too weake, & not to be compared wth Gassend. I am glad yu have made better choice, & I hope yu will not forget to call *for a good* answere from time to time. And yet upon ye double hint yu give me, yt ye Bigots, and Sorbonists are apt to censure ye Cartesians, I am consulting for a seasonable occasion, Howe as well for yr selfe, as publisher of these Tracts, as for ye RS, yu may once for all declare,

That neyther yu, nor ye RS, are engaged, or addicted eyther to ye Cartesian, or to ye Epicurean Philosophy, or to any body of phil. or systeme, wch hovers in Generals, or adventures further in any notional way, then may be supported by a sufficient share of faythfull & severe experiments. Neyther are yu, or ye RS at all concerned for ye defence of all writers, wch are in those tracts abreviated; Not, though they may be members of ye RS, yr busines being chiefely to excite or whet on ye disquision; & to admitt ingenuous men to a free hearing, & fayre conference among ye Learned. *Nullius in Verba*.

Sr this I propose to prevent a blot, if any censure should come fourth; & allso more freshly to mind us of our owne worke: & to recomend to all ye Judicious, ye prudence of yr Engagement.

Sr Did not I foretell yu, wt was to be expected from Dr H M.[4] His confidence is as strong as Enthusiasme; & yet yu see wt he does. As if he had a mind to drawe a suspicion, or (at leaste) to rayse ye style of Infamy agst ye RS & candid Experiment, as to be so Magicall as to call in ye ayde of Spirits & Angells. If Honble Mr Boyles health will beare it, He owes him a chastisement; as he promiseth in his *Contin of New Exp*, page 173 in ye Margine,[5] And then under one He may refell[6] *Hon Fab*,[7] & others, who have made a noyse; but some are not worthy to be named, or taken notice of: Neyther should they have had my consent to have beene mentioned in yr Tracts. For I see they knowe not ye true use of reasone, but fill up all wth confidence. For yr condescending to mention such men (I am loathe to name them) yu may have neede of ye above mentioned Apology, wch may stand in ye way to do better service for ye RS in a time of neede.

And yet yu may note Howe far greate wits can swerve from Reasone, & greate Mathematicians carry all their Mathematics about them, to blind arte, & sophisticate reasone, especially wn prepossessed wth a pretence to Religion, as Ricciolus[8] & Fabri doe (whom I doe not name contemptuously) & generally all ye Jesuites to justify ye Censure of Galileus, & Campanella,[9] some drawe all ye Mathematicall lines in a hurry, others whirle all ye heavens, & all ye world about our eares in a trice. But wt makes our Mosaicall countreyman, The Anonymous in yr Tract 60 pag 1083 to be so positive for notions quite worne out, as if he had newely waked out of a long sleepe, & had not heard wt ye learned hath beene doing this long time.[10]

Yu say yu can get wt correspondence yu please wth those de SJ. 1. I will shew yu ye greate importance 2. The peculiar use to be made of them. 1. They have a secrete & effective influence & powerfull negotiation by all trades, & Merchandises, by all Arts & languages, in all imaginable guises & disguises, all over ye world, by sea & land, That (to say truth) They are like Spirits good or bad, invisible & irresistible. Marke this Calculation.

1536

Theyr order was instituted or first designed about ye yeares 1540.[11]

At first they were but 11 or 12, & after confind to 60.[12] About 70 yeares after, Anno 1608, (as Ribadmira calculates it)[13] they were growne to be 10581 in number, & they had 293 Colleges (besides 123 houses) & out of their Colleges they could then rayse two Millions of Crownes yearely. Sr by this yu may iudge, wt a vaste growth they may have in ye last 70 yeares. 2. Such safe use yu may make of them, as Gassendus lib. 5. pag. 85 affirmes Peireskius to have done,[14] by addresses (sometimes of Compasse) to ye Generall of ye Soc, if he be fit for it, to engage some to oblige Mankind in rectifying ye Longitudes, in collecting Historyes, in their severall places, of ye rarityes of nature, & ye Wonders of Art newe & old, in finding ye severall declinations, & variations of ye Magneticall compasse, & in all such things as cannot well be done or made significant for yr importance, wthout an universall information.

Flamsted's Observ[ations] in yr n. 55, & 66,[15] are a present for such of them [the Jesuits], & others yt are able, & at leysure to examine it, & it will adorne yr Tracts, if yu attend to ye issue, & to a further accompt of ye rocke of salt ibidem n. 66.[16] & to all such other informations, as yu have recorded at any time. To wt yu say, yt ye J[esuits] begin to plough wth yr heifer, I can easily believe yt there is scarse a P[rivy] Councell or Junto in ye world, in wch they do not agitate, at least like Husbands, but yu may easily avoyde ye danger, by adhering closely to yr principles of declining controversyes in Rel[igion], or reflecting on it. And wn all is done, They are to be suspected in pointe of candour, & severe truth, till yr example & strict examination can render them cautious. And yr surest aide must be from ye Jes of France, who are men free from ye Inquisition, & more truely Catholic, than ye Bigots of Sp. Who are as narrowe & Ignorant in their large dominions, as N England for Robinson.[17] And yet there is a hot faction betweene ye Dominicans & some other orders, & ye J[esuits]. And from a good hand I had it, yt yr greate house of H[oward] of N[orfolk] are not favourites wth ye J[esuits]. This in yr bosome, & for yr directions.

I knowe not, whether yr Parisian Corresp[ondent] be Prot[estant], or Roman, but by him yu may enquire Wt Peireskij, or Gassendi are nowe in France, Jes or noble. Wt Kirchner & Cardinal Vertuosi in Rome &c. I was once sollicitous, yt one of ye RS would collect ye severall arguments for ye

Terrestriall motion, such as may be made by ye Telescope from ye grossenes of ye planets, changeablenesse & obscurity of some fixed stars, ye distance of some, the Cometicall motions in Auzout & Hevel, the Earthquakes in Travagini ye Venetian n. 60;[18] but now I should forbeare it, to avoyd ye malice of ye J[esuits] for a time. But I note wth wt candor Gassend lib. 4 pag. 78 makes Peiresk applaud ye successe, That our Gilbert by ye Magnet should so happily concurre wth ye Telescopicall discoveryes of Galileus for ye System of ye World &c. And for his affections to Galilaeus & his bounty of 500 crowns to Campanella. Gass. l. 5. p. 111 &c English.

Yu say yu will mind some stationers to do good things towards ye restauration. For ye reasons yu have recited, yu must take heede of being seene or noted a zelote for Des Cart. And, though my opinion be nothing, yet I conceive Hugenius in ye right n. 65 pag. 2007.[19] And I should preferre Wilhelmus there & much rather *de Lana* n 69. (who pretends as a Baconian to Experiments, especially, if his flowry viols prove true;)[20] & Rohault n. 70 who seemes to be full of neate conceipts,[21] & ye Florentine & Germaine Experiments, to be renderd into English,[22] [rather] then ye Anonymus of Locall motion,[23] & such adventures, as will fayle of truth in ye severe discussion. For, though every free Essay deducts from ye tyranny of Aris-[totle], yet sober Truth alone is yr busines, & will crowne yu in ye end wth Victory. If Cartes his owne writings were in good English, it would invite ye Gentry to ye study of Geometry & shewe howe our language serves for Philosophicall disquisitions; & yt these moderne adventures, wn exposed in ye naked dress of our domestic tongue, have some better savour, then ye old unintelligible principles. So far I yield, & in yt sense I applaud Antonio Le Grands succintnes, & accuratenes, if it were purveyd into as proper English, as it is in Latine.[24] I guesse it to be done by Mr Hornex but I have no grounde at all for my guesse.[25]

Our proper & fundamentall Worke, if it were possible, were to set[?] right Ld Bacons methode in his N. Organ[um]. But of this I have given yu too much in my former.[26] Only here I will adde, yt yu neede not endeavour to engage Mr Gale expresseley & by name for ye RS. Let him do yr worke & begin wth Bacon as ye first, & surest of moderne & find his best reste, & retreate in Mr. Boyle. And then let him use his prudence to decline ye Envy, & malice of Stubs. Perhaps he will receive it better if ye busines alone, & as for English reputation in Bacon, Gilbert &c, be fayrely represented. And I will say againe, yt no worke can better inspire him, than Gass[endi] in Peyr[esc] if from thence he tasts Bacon, Mr Boyle &c

I do not conceive, yt ye J[esuits] or Sorbon. are seriously jealous for Transubtantiation: for I have seene it soe attemperd by newe modelling, in severall of their acutest, yt tis quite another matter, than wn ye negative was capitall in our Q Marys dayes. But there are in Rome & in England, some, yt feare ye impartiall discussions of cleare, & emancipated Reasone; &, Though they talk high for Transubstantion [sic], for *this*, or for *that*, they may thinke of other matters.

I thinke I have replyed to all points of yr laste. Did yu not receive 6 or 7 rules from me, relating to Caske. I have found ye paper for best & speediest seasoning of Timber if it be of concernment.

The Bodleian Catalogue is a good Example I wish all ye Libraryes in ye world were at least so published.27

I long to knowe, whether Dr Ch[amberlayne] received my long & rude letter.

For ye reason yu urge, yu may omit Suedeland wthout erratum. He was in ye power of Suedeland, perhaps not in ye very same climate.

Some of these hints are only for yr *reserved*. Yu may have thousands of ye J[esuits] to serve yu: yu cannot serve them for their fireworks: This is yr prerogative & yu may use other considerable *Orders in ye Ro*[man church] & there ye greate H[oward] of N[orfolk] can assiste yu. I heare of no J[esuit] very fond for Cartes. Yu are free, they are all enslavd to run false. If yu turne to ye Tracts recited, yu will more clearly understand my briefe hints.

Yr *V. V.*

We [must—*paper torn*] set on ye work direct & select wth iudgement, & correct errours. tis no matter, w[ho] hath ye luck or leysure to bear ye burdens: They carry the mud, lime & stone: yu are ye Architects; & thus yr Enemyes may serve yu, And Oxon will gaine yu credite abroad, by their Sheldonian [*paper torn*]nes,28 if yu give due notice, wt they are doing. Yu may carry all meerly by conduct, & happy correspondence.

Yr Barometer,29 & Dr Wrens Engine to draw in perspective Num. 45. or only those tracts, in wch these instruments are described are presents for a Jes. of note. by then they may serve yu, they cannot hurt yu. Ut mam nostri.30 They are yr curious scales & would engage them, & set them on worke. Think often on these things.

Wt is Dr Barrow doing in Camb[ridge]. I pray yu hath no man made obiections agst cosen Reedes advertisements.31 I pray be tender there; for yu knowe, yt he is oblieging & hath done us many kindnesses. Will WW give us ye rest of N[ovum] Or[ganum].³² I hope yr Tracts wilbe fit & ready for ye commencement & Acts of Camb[ridge] & Ox[ford].

Jun. 24.71. Perhaps I may set this hasty stuffe in better order & more to ye maine point. Keep this safe.

ADDRESS
    For my much honored friend
        Henry Oldenburg Esqr
           at his house in Pell Mell
                Westminster

                                      post is paid 3d.

NOTES

1 See Letter 1722 (which is without date), p. 92.
2 See Letter 1728, note 2.
3 Presumably the meaning is, "Borel does not defend the new philosophy as forcefully as Gassendi," and the reference is to Pierre Borel, *Vitae Renati Cartesii, summi philosophi compendium* (Paris, 1656), translated as *A Summary or Compendium of the Life of the most Famous Philosopher Renatus Descartes* (London, 1670).
4 Henry More (1614–87), the Cambridge Platonist; the allusion is to his *Antidote against Atheisme* in *A Collection of Several Philosophical Writings*, 2nd ed., folio (London, 1662), Bk II, Ch. II, as Boyle says in his note (see below).
5 In the *Continuation of New Experiments Physico-Mechanical*, see Birch, *Boyle*, III, 274–75; here Boyle argues that the cohering of two flat polished surfaces demonstrates the pressure of the atmosphere, despite the objections of a "very learned writer ["H.M." in note, to which] an answer may in due place... be returned." The answer appeared in *Tracts... containing New Experiments, touching the Relation betwixt Flame and Air* (London, 1672).
6 Refute.
7 Honoré Fabri.
8 Giovanni Battista Riccioli (1598–1671).
9 Tommaso Campanella (1568–1639), a Dominican, was imprisoned for twenty-eight years after 1599 and tortured seven times on the charge of conspiring to free Naples from Spanish rule—a charge possibly fabricated because of Campanella's opposition to authority. He was a follower of Telesio and a critic of Aristotle. The last five years of his life were spent in Paris.
10 The anonymous book (by Samuel Gott) *The Divine History of Genesis of the World explicated and illustrated* (London, 1670), is given a page and a half in *Phil. Trans.*, no. 60 (20 June 1670), 1083–84; the author opposed the mechanical philosophy and sought to create a complete account of the world from the words of Genesis.
11 Beale first wrote "1540," then "1536" above that date. In fact, in 1536 Ignatius Loyola went to Rome with nine companions to dedicate their service to the Pope; in 1540 Paul III approved the rules drawn up for the Order.
12 This early limitation was removed by Julius III, Paul's successor.
13 Properly, Pedro Ribadeneira, S.J. (1527–1611), who was a hagiographer of his Order; his life of Loyola was published in 1572.

14 This is the book mentioned in Letter 1722, note 13.
15 That is, Flamsteed's predictions for 1670 and 1671.
16 See Vol. VII, Letters 1544 and 1562, printed in *Phil. Trans.*, no. 66.
17 Probably this is a rather strange allusion to John Robinson (1575–1625), a Norfolk clergyman who went with the religious separatists to Holland; he was pastor to the group who emigrated in the *Mayflower*, but died before fulfilling his intention to join them at Plymouth.
18 There is a review of Francisco Travagino's *Super observationibus a se factis tempore ultimorum terrae-motuum...physica disquisitio* (Leiden, 1669), in *Phil, Trans.*, no. 60 (20 June 1670), 1084–85.
19 In *Phil. Trans.*, no. 65 (14 November 1670), pp. 2007–9, there is an account of Franz Wilhelm, Freiherr von Nuland's *Elementa physica* (The Hague, 1669), to which was prefaced a similarly anti-Cartesian letter from Huygens to the author (mentioned on p. 2008), reprinted in *Œuvres Complètes*, VI, 420-21.
20 This (*Phil. Trans.*, no. 69, 25 March 1671, 2114-16) is a notice of Francisco Lana's *Prodromo...all' Arte Maestra* (Brescia, 1670), in which is a Helmontian taradiddle about generating flowers and fruits in a glass vessel from an oily liquor in which picked flowers were steeped.
21 For this book, see Letter 1722, note 5.
22 The *Saggi* of the *Accademia del Cimento* and the *Miscellanea Curiosa*.
23 *A Discourse of Local Motion, by A. M. Englisht out of French* (London, 1670), described in *Phil. Trans.*, no. 65, 2010–12; the translation was by Oldenburg; the original is *Discours du mouvement local* (Paris, 1670), also published anonymously, but actually by Father Ignace-Gaston Pardies.
24 The book mentioned in Letter 1722, note 26, was not so far as we know translated into English.
25 Anthony Horneck (1641–97) became F.R.S. in January 1668/9. Of German origin, he became chaplain at Queen's College, Oxford, and a popular writer and preacher.
26 See Letter 1728.
27 See Letter 1722, note 15.
28 Paper torn; this presumably refers to the activities of the Sheldonian Press.
29 Hooke's wheel-barometer is described in no. 13 (4 June 1666), 218–19, and Boyle's "statical baroscope" in no. 14 (2 July 1666), 231–39.
30 Possibly "Ut materiam nostri," that is, "As (providing) material for us."
31 Beale alludes to Letter 1652 (Vol. VII) from Richard Reed, which had been printed in the *Philosophical Transactions*, and upon which he himself commented in Letter 1700.
32 We have not been able to guess at the identity of "WW" or, therefore, to explain what is meant.

1734
Oldenburg to Beale
27 June 1671

This is mentioned in an endorsement by Oldenburg upon Letter 1733, and again in Beale's reply, Letter 1743.

1735
Oldenburg to Bernard
27 June 1671
From the original in Bodleian Library MS. Smith 45, ff. 65–67

Sir,

I take this opportunity to acknowledge the favour of yr last in May,[1] and wthall to recommend to your humanity ye bearer hereof Monsr Graman,[2] a Doctor of Physick, born in Moscow, though not of Moscovian Parents, and sent young into Germany to study, where he made such progress, yt he was promoted to ye degree of Doctor of Physic, in wch profession he is like to be engaged in the service of the Great Czar of Moscovy, after his return from his travels through Germany, Italy, France, England and Holland. He was permitted to be present at one of our Society's meetings, and is now going to acquaint himself wth the Learn'd at Oxford, and among ym wth yrself, and some of ye chief Physitians there, as also wth yr Library, and ye state of ye whole University; I have assured him of yr affability, and readines to oblige strangers; being confident, you will rather exceed than come short of my ingagements to him upon that account; especially since this person is like to prove a good correspondent to us in ye communication of natural things from Moscovy, Cazan, Siberia etc.

But this is not all I have to say to you on this occasion; I hear, you have wth you Mr Gale, ye Learn'd Author of ye *Court of ye Gentiles*,[3] wherein is attempted the Derivation of all Philology and Philosophy from the Jewish Church. An Intelligent friend of mine,⁴ living in the Country, and aiming much at ye honor of ye English nation in ye matter of advancing sciences and arts, wisheth very much yt something might be undertaken by yt worthy Author, I mean, Mr Gale, whereby it might be made publick, how much the world is obliged to ye Noble Lord of Verulam, Gilbert, Harvy, and the Honorable Mr Boyle (among others,) to Experimental and Usefull Philosophy especially since the famous Peyreskius and Gassendus could hold to commend the Ld Bacon, by name, upon that account as may be seen in that excellent Description of Peireskius his Life by Gassendus, than wch, in my opinion, nothing is more apt to inspire such a writer as Is desired upon this subject; for as much as it doth all along endear the present engagement both for the restauration of ye Ancient, and ye advancement of Arts and Knowledge in the modern way.

But ye above mentioned Anonymous freind recommends wthall ye Englishing of L. Bacon, as a fundamental work, the setting right his method in his N. Organum; concerning wch I shall here give you his owne words, viz.⁵

[*The quotation that follows has been printed above as Letter 1728.*]

So far my well-wishing friend. If you, Sir, could so [?] insinuate it to Mr Gale, either yrself, or by yr acquaintance yt have an interest in him, as to make it effectual, it might prove a considerable service for ye promotion of Learning, and the glory of England. If you will oblige me wth giving me yr thoughts hereupon by ye return of this bearer; and excuse my prolixity.

I cannot conclude wthout expressing my sollicitude for my Couzen Wroth;⁶ but will hope, yt by yr next you will give me cause to alleviate my anxiety for him. My hearty service to [him].

Dr Pell is considering, as I hear, *Fermats his Doctrinae Analyticae Inventum Novum*;⁷ and we are generally thoughtfull how to procure Patronage and Encouragement for ye design of reprinting ye Ancient Mathematicians.⁸ MyLd of Sarum declared, yt, when he should find the business put into a way, and see what others did, he would not be backward to contribute.

I intreat you, Sir, yt you would a little peruse and consider *Marchettis* Book de *Resistentia Solidorum*, and let me know yr thoughts of it. I suppose, Dr Wallis hath one of ym, if you have none. I doubt not, but you have seen

Borelli de Motionibus naturalibus, a gravitate pendentibus: for wch, many declare a good esteem, among whom is Sir

> Yr faithful friend and servt
> Oldenburg

London june 27. 1671.

NOTES

1 This letter has not been found.
2 No doubt this is the young physician mentioned in Letter 1691. His visit to the Royal Society is otherwise unrecorded.
3 See Letter 1728, note 2.
4 John Beale; compare Letters 1728 and 1733.
5 This quotation (Letter 1728) is from a lost original of Beale's.
6 Sir John Wroth (if this was he) died in this present year.
7 Published by Jacques de Billy in the Toulouse *Diophantus*; in a letter to Gregory of late 1671 Collins remarks that this *Inventum novum* "as it is delivered by Billy, hath not so much Lustre as with reason might have been expected, if it had come immediately from the hands of its learned author Fermat" (Turnbull, *Gregory*, p. 199).
8 Compare Letter 1722, p. 93. In fact Barrow, Halley, and others did much work of this kind.

1736
Wallis to Oldenburg
27 June 1671

From the original in Royal Society MS. W 1, no. 123

Oxford, June 27. 1671.

Sir,

On Saturday June 24, I had a sight of Mr. *Hobs's Rosetum*, (he should have called it Fimetum.)¹ It comes forth with its Keeper (that it might do no hurt) For ye Animadversions printed with it (from I know not what hand) are a sufficient Confutation of it.² On Munday, that is, yesterday, I had leisure to peruse so much as may serve to confute ye whole. For his Construction of ye first Probleme or Proposition, (on which the rest depend,) is False; & with it, ye rest therefore come to nought.

To cut a line in extreme and mean proportion, was taught by *Euclide* & demonstrated; *prop.* 30. *lib.* 6. with whom all Geometers hitherto have agreed. The result of which amounts to thus much, That if ye line to be so cut be $1R$, the greater segment thereof will be $\frac{\sqrt{5}-1}{2} R$; And, consequently, ye lesser $\frac{3-\sqrt{5}}{2} R$ wch multiplied or drawn into ye whole $1R$, produceth $\frac{3-\sqrt{5}}{2} R^2$, equal to ye square of ye Greater segment.[3] But Mr Hobs gives us here another construction; according to which, ye greater segment should be $\frac{\sqrt{5}-2\sqrt{3}}{2} R$. But whether you will rather trust *Euclide's* geometry or Mr *Hobs's*, I leave to your judgement. If you will trust neither; then try Mr *Hobs's*, as we have done *Euclide's*. To cut a line *in extreme & meane proportion*, is, so to cut it as that, ye *Rectangle of ye whole & ye lesser segment* be equal to ye *Square of ye greater*. Now Mr *Hobs's* greater segment being $\frac{\sqrt{5}-2\sqrt{3}}{2} R$, ye lesse must be $\frac{2-\sqrt{5}-2\sqrt{3}}{2} R$ that so both together may be equal to ye whole $1R$. Which lesser segment drawn into ye whole, produceth $\frac{2-\sqrt{5}-2\sqrt{3}}{2} R^2$. Wch should be equal to ye square of ye greater segment, but is not. For the square of $\frac{\sqrt{5}-2\sqrt{3}}{2} R$ is $\frac{5-2\sqrt{3}}{4} R^2$.[3a] But, in *Euclide's* case, ye Rectangle was equal to ye square, as it ought to be. This perhaps with Mr *Hobs* (who's Arithmetick & Geometry cannot agree,) will not pass for a demonstrative confutation of his construction, (nor do I care whether it will or not;) with others, it will.

The falts in Mr *Hobs's* construction & (pretended) demonstration of it, (beside a great many little ones) are at lest these three great ones.

First, in his Construction, in stead of *Describatur centro D quadrans DAC secans FE et GH in K et X*.[4] He might as well have sayd, *sumatur ubivis in IG puncto X*;[5] (For so his whole demonstration following will just as well agree, as now it doth, without altering one word or letter;) or, *ubivis in IG utcunque in utramque partem producta*;[6] (For then he need onely in like manner produce *EA*; or, in stead of *secans AE*, say, *secans AE saltem productam*[7] *pag.* 2. *lin.* 17.) So that, *X* being taken arbitraryly, his *EX* (which he will have to be ye greater segment) may be of what length hee please; & his demonstration for it, stand just as now it doth. As any who will take ye pains to apply *verbatim* his Demonstration to this Construction will presently discern.

Next, in his Demonstration, having shewed, yt *the two right angles mXI, IXl* are equal to ye five angles *mXF, FXy, yXZ, ZXE, EXl, taken altogether pag. 2. lin. 18. 19*; (without proving, or so much as saying, whether they be or be not all equal to each other;) He then (silently supposing them to be all equal) goes to prove from hence, that *the angles ZEX, ZXE, are equal*, because *otherwise the sayd two right angles were not so divided* (quinquifariam) *into five equal parts, pag. 3, lin. 4, 5.* The truth is; ye first, third, & fifth of those angles are equal each to other; & ye second & fourth equal (not to any of ye other three, but) each to other; But, whether one of these two, be equal, lesse, or greater than one of these three, his Demonstration shows not, nor doth so much as attempt it; though on this depend the whole strength of his argument.

The third is, *pag. 3. lin 17, 18.* where; Because *the angles yXz, Xyr are equal*; & *the angles yXr, yrX, equal*; *and ye angles yXz, zEX, equal*: he infers, *that ye angles zXE, zEX are allso equal.* Which doth not follow from thence. Yet the want of this, destroys his demonstration.

If all this be not inough; His second Proposition confutes his first. For, by his second, *As EF to FC*, that is, as 2 to $\sqrt{5}-1$; so is, *the greater segment AB*, to ye *lesser BG*; & consequently, *the whole AG, to ye greater segment AB*: As Euclide's construction would have it; not, as Mr *Hobs prop. 1.* makes it, as 2 to $\sqrt{5}-2\sqrt{3}$.

His first Proposition thus failing, it will not be necessary for ye confuting of his book, to trouble you with what faults are in ye rest. For that failing, all that depends upon it must needs fall with it. But if you desire more; I refer you to ye Latin Paper.[8]

What in ye end of his book is intended against mee,[9] (beside some childish trifling with words, & indeavouring to pervert ye sense of them,) amounts mostly to this, That *he doth not like Algebra; he doth not understand Symbols; hee likes not ye doctrine of Indivisibles; nor ye doctrine of Infinities*; (nor do I care whether hee do or do not:) and ye whole is so weak & frothy, that it neither needs nor is worth answering; But I may safely trust ye Reader with it; who if he do but confer what Mr Hobs says, with ye places to which it doth refer, will easyly see its emptynesse without my help. I am Sr

Yours to serve you
John Wallis

June 27. 1671

Sir,

I send you this, as that wch you may, if it be not quite to late, publish in this months transactions: & refer ye Latine paper to wch this refers (wch I shall send you very suddenly) to ye next. If it be quite too late to insert it, you may at lest intimate yt you have it, but want room for it.[10] The Post is going, so yt I can say no more but that I am

Yours &c
John Wallis

ADDRESS

For Mr Henry Oldenburg,
in the Palmal near St James's
London

NOTES

1 Thomas Hobbes *Rosetum geometricum, cum censura brevi doctrinae Wallisianae de motu* (London, 1671) is noticed in *Phil. Trans.*, no. 72 (19 June 1671), 2185–86. *Rosetum* means rose garden; *fimetum*, a dunghill.
2 We cannot explain this, or say what the "Animadversions" are, as they are not part of the *Rosetum*, nor normally bound with it.
3 That is, if a is such that $a = (1-a)^2$, then $a = \dfrac{3-\sqrt{5}}{2}$.
3a In this case Wallis's arithmetic is as bad as Hobbes's.
4 "Let the quadrant DAC be described with center D cutting FE and GH in K and X."
5 "Let the point X be taken anywhere in IG."
6 "anywhere in IG produced in either direction."
7 "at least cutting AE produced."
8 The Latin version of this letter—which is an even more elaborate confutation of Hobbes—is dated 16 July; it was printed in *Phil. Trans.*, no. 73 (17 July 1671), 2202–9. Of this there is a draft in Bodleian Library MS. Savile 104, ff. 3–5.
9 That is, Hobbes's criticisms of the first two parts of *Mechanica, sive de motu*.
10 In fact Oldenburg said nothing till he published the Latin version next month; to this he added a note saying that the "short of this Answer" was intended for the June issue, but could not be included, so Wallis decided to enlarge it.

1737
Oldenburg to Beale
1 July 1671

This is mentioned in Beale's reply, Letter 1743.

1738
Ray to Oldenburg
3 July 1671

From the original in Royal Society MS. R 1, no. 13
Printed in *Phil. Trans.*, no. 74 (14 August 1671), 2219–20

Middleton July 3

Sr

Had I not been absent from this place when your Letter came hither you had not so long expected an answer. As to the particulars therein contained, I remember well that Mr Lister did a good while since write me his opinion concerning vegetable excrescencies and the insects therein bred or harboured; But the Lr conteining that discourse I have not a[t] present by me: it being sent away in a bundle of other letters & papers into Essex. I have therefore written to him to desire him to take the pains himself to send you his thoughts upon that subject. Whether there be any spontaneous or anomalous generation of animals, as hath been the constant opinion of Naturallists heretofore, I think there is good reason to question. It seems to me at present most probable that there is no such thing; but that even all insects are the naturall issue of parents of the same species with themselves. F. Redi hath gone a good way in proving this, having cleared the point concerning generation *ex materia putrida*.[1] But still there remain two great difficulties. The first is to give an account of the production of insects bred in the by-fruits & excrescensies of Vegetables, wch Redi doubts not to ascribe to the Vegetative soul of the plant wch yields those excrescencies, but for this I referre you to Mr Lister. the second to give an account of the generation of insects bred in the bodies of other animals. I hope shortly to be able to give you an account of the generation of some of those insects, which have been thought to be spontaneous, & wch seem as unlikely as any to be after the ordinary & usuall way.

Of such an insect as you mention feeding upon Ranunculs, which when dried yields a musky sent I have no knowledge. I can at present call to mind but two sorts of insects that I have seen, wch smell of musk. The one is the common Capricornus or Goatchafer,[2] wch is mentioned by all naturallists that write of insects, & wch smells so strong of that perfume, that you may sent it at a good distance as it flies by or sits near you: the other is a small sort of Bee, which in the South & East parts of England is frequently to be met withall in gardens among flowers in Spring-time. I remember they were very plentifull in Sir Edw. Dukes[3] Tulip-Garden, when the tulips flowred. Sr Edward is now dead, his house was not far from Saxmundham in Suffolk; the name of the parish I have forgot. I have by me the description & anatomy of a porpesse (wch fish I happily met withall at W. Chester)[4] being with my Lord-bishop of that place) in which there are some particulars that I find not in the descriptions of Rondeletius[5] or others, wch if you please I shall send you. Now give me leave to take notice to you of a mistake or two in the Philosoph. Transactions wch concern me, the one is N.68. p.2064 within 3 lines of the bottome, where after Cichory flowers is omitted but also Larkspurre, Borage.[6] for as it stands now it is not Grammaticall sence. I know not whether this was my omission or yours. the other is N.70. p. 2134. l.7.[7] Where *Fungus* is put instead of *muscus*; but these errata I esteem not so materiall as to need correcting. This is all at present I have to trouble you with. I rest

Your very humble servant
John Ray

I am this day beginning a voyage into into the North & shall not return hither this moneth or five weeks.[8]

ADDRESS
> These
for Mr Henry Oldenburgh
secretary to the Royall
Society at his house in the
> Pell-mell
> London

NOTES

Reply to Letter 1715.
1 In his *Esperienze intorno alle generazione degl' Insetti* (Florence, 1668); "from putrid matter."
2 That is, a capricorn beetle.
3 Sir Edward Duke (*c*. 1604–71) of Benhall, a parish and seat a mile and a half from Saxmundham, Suffolk, had been knighted in 1641, shortly after his election as M.P. for Orford, and was created baronet in 1661.
4 This was done in April 1669; apparently the porpoise was bought and dissected by Willughby. "W[est] Chester" signifies simply Chester. For the account, see Ray's letter of 12 September 1671 (Letter 1786).
5 Guillaume Rondelet, *De piscibus marinis* (Lyons, 1554–55).
6 The reference is to the printed version of Letter 1593 (Vol. VII). The fault was in the printing.
7 Ray alludes to the printed version of Letter 1634 (Vol. VII, p. 461). The mistake was Lister's.
8 Ray went on a tour to Settle (Yorkshire), Berwick-on-Tweed, and Brignall with the botanist Thomas Willisel.

1739
Fermat to Oldenburg
4 July 1671
From the original in Royal Society MS. F 1, no. 50

A Toulouse le 14me Juillet [N.S.]

Monsieur

J'ai eu desia l'honneur de vous remercier treshumblement, comme ie le fais encore, de l'ouvrage que vous aves eu la bonté de m'envoier,[1] Il est rempli de plusieurs experiences tres curieuses et il est tout a faict digne de Monsieur Boyle, il paroistroit beaucoup plus beau si le traducteur eut pris un peu plus de soin a bien expliquer les pensées de l'autheur, ie ne doubte pas qu'il ne soit plus agreable en sa langue naturelle, Je me persuade que vous aurès iettè les yeux sur le nouveau Diophante,[2] et il me tarde bien de sçavoir vostre sentiment, et celui de vos amis sur ce suiect, plusieurs personnes de grand capacité ont fort estimé les observations, et ont trouvè aussi fort a leur gré cet Inventum Analyticae qui est au commencement, Il y avoit quelques fautes d'impression qui ont estè corrigées, Mr Justel vous en envoiera un exemplaire avec l'Errata, J'espere que vous me fairès le faveur de le garder pour l'amour de moi, et que si vous avès faict quelque descouverte depuis peu dans vos conferences, vous m'en apprendères des nouvelles, Je suis avec respect Monsieur

Vostre tres humble et\
tres obeissant serviteur\
Fermat

ADDRESS
  Monsieur
  Monsieur Oldenbourg
    a Londres

TRANSLATION

Toulouse, 14 July [N.S.]

Sir,

I have already had the honor of thanking you very humbly, as I do again, for the book you have been so good as to send me.[1] It is filled with many very curious experiments and is entirely worthy of Mr. Boyle; it would seem much finer if the translator had taken a little more care to explain thoroughly the author's ideas. I do not doubt that it is much pleasanter in its original language. I am certain that you will have cast your eyes over the new Diophantos;[2] I am very anxious to learn your opinion and that of your friends on this subject. Many very able people have esteemed the observations very highly and have also found that *Inventum analyticae* at the beginning very much to their taste. There were several printing errors which have been corrected; Mr. Justel will send you a copy with the errata. I hope you will do me the favor of keeping it for my sake, and that if you have made any discoveries recently at your meetings you will send me news of them. I am, Sir, with respect

Your very humble and obedient servant,\
Fermat

ADDRESS
  Mr. Oldenburg
  London

NOTES

Oldenburg has endorsed this "Rec. le 30 juill. 71," which establishes the year.
1 This was presumably either the *Tractatus de cosmicis rerum qualitatibus* (Amsterdam, 1671) or the *Tractatus ubi mira aeris... rarefactio detector* (London, 1670, 1671).
2 The work mentioned in Letter 1687, note 2. It is not certain when Oldenburg received his copy, although the book was known in London by May, and probably April; for the copy sent to him from Paris was entrusted to "Lord Aylesbury's man, ...but the fellow sold the book by the way and spent the money" (Collins to Gregory, 25 March 1671; Rigaud, II, 218).

1740
Flamsteed to Oldenburg
4 July 1671

From the original in Royal Society MS. F 1, no. 71

Derby: July 4 1671

Sr

Not haveing heard any thing from yu since I returnd yr Hevelius[1] I have desired my kinsman[2] to waite on you wth this to enquire if yu have reaceaved it & to desire yr excuse for that I returned not ye enclosed[3] & to beg yr pardon for yt I retaine two generall schemes one for ye full moones another for ye generall phases which were destined to accompany ye volume loose. hee mentions that any numbers of them may be bought I desire if ye may be had wth yu, yt yu will please to informe mee, or how I may produce some, which may be very beneficiall to mee in observations: if yu heare any thinge from Hevelius when his Machina[4] or observations will come forth or any thinge worth seeing will come forth or is come to yr hands yu may by [writing] gratifie mee much in it if yu please to informe me by ye returne of my kinsmans who will safely convey yours to

Yr obliged friend & servt
John Flamsteed

I have sent a small tracte De inaequalitate dierum naturalium[5] to Mr Collins of which & what else yu desire to know my kinsman can informe yu:

ADDRESS
To Henry Oldenburge
Esqe at his house in the
middle of ye pell-mell
in St James'es Westminster
these present

NOTES

1 See Letter 1708.
2 His cousin, Thomas Wilson (to whom he wrote on the previous day).
3 Perhaps something from *Selenographia*; nothing is now with this letter.
4 His *Machina coelestis*, of which Part I appeared in 1673.
5 On 3 May 1671 Flamsteed had written to Collins (Rigaud, II, 113): "I have by me a sheet or two, which I wrote some five years agone De aequatione temporis astronomica, which I have last summer made Latin, and would gladly it might see the light." See also his earlier letter to Collins of 24 January 1669/70 and his autobiography, both in Baily, pp. 22–23, 107. He presented a copy to Sir Jonas Moore in 1672, and subsequently bought it back at the sale of Moore's library.

1741

Lister to Oldenburg

5 July 1671

From the original in Royal Society MS. L 5, no. 35

Yorke July 5. 1671

Sr

I cannot absolutely promise my selfe, yt Mr Wray thought ye Letter, wherein I gave him an account of my opinion concerning Vegetable Excrescensies, worth ye preserving: yet if it be lost, I shall endeavour to give you satisfaction by writing my thoughts again on yt subject.[1] but at present I am much indisposed.

The discovery of our English Kermes, has very much pleased some of ye curious in these parts: who resolve upon Tryalls of it ye next season. I know not whether I advertised you, yt ye deep purple or violet wth wch ye inside of ye huskes are lined, is much spent if ye Huskes be not taken, whilst ye Bees are in *Vermiculo*[2] & ye blackest huskes are richest in colour. Yesterday in very good company we compared our English *purple Kermes*, wth ye *scarlet Kermes* or Graines of ye Shopps, & found ym in every point to agree save in ye colour or their juices & particularly (finding in some parcells of ye Shopps many yet sticking to little Twiggs of ye Ilex) we confidently affirme yt those as well as ours are only contiguous to ye Ilex branches & are not *excrescencies* of ye Tree, much lesse *fruit* or *berries*, by wch abusive names they have been too long known; but yt they are ye artifice & sole worke of ye mother Bee in order to ye more convenient hiving & nourishment of her young. I am Sr

Your most humble servant
Martin Lister

ADDRESS
These
For his much honoured friend
Mr Henry Oldenburg
at his house in ye Palmal
London

NOTES

Reply to Letter 1731.
1 See below, Letter 1751.
2 "in worm."

1742
Oldenburg to Sylvius
5 July 1671

Mentioned in Sylvius' Letter 2065 of 17 September 1672 (Vol. IX) as having been received by him on 12 August 1671.

1743
Beale to Oldenburg
8 July 1671
From the original in B.M. MS. Add. 4294, ff. 31-32

Jul. 8. 71.

Deare bror

After I have acknowledged ye favour of yr last & very excellent Tract,[1] I must deplore my owne unfortunatenes, yt I never received yr letter of Tuesd was sevenight,[2] wch yu say *had many particulars*. I was in great want of yr instructions in many particular; & now, since yu have taken ye paines, for me to be disappointed, tis a double dammage. By yr hints I see, yt yu received my laste;[3] In wch ye growth of ye J[esuits] is calculated. And can yu doubt, yt by this time they are lesse than a hundred thousand, & have a thousand Colleges, & best share of gold & silver in both ye Indyes. They are sd to double their numbers & wealth, every seaven yeares.

I have longd for Honble Mr. Bs booke[4] this long time. This sets us all at worke afresh, & for ever. And it came in a lucky day, a time of need. I pray yu send me word in yr next, How he hath his health. Yu note how Lord Hollis hath redeemd our nation from a blot; in wch yu may see, wt ill-bred & dishonest beasts some of our Lawyers & Countrey Justices are.[5] Mr Lyster is very accurate, & does yu good service;[6] & Sylvius addresseth fayrely.[7] But have yu a Venetian Journall, & such raretyes from it?[8] Thus one of yr prefaces (Vol. 4) becomes a Prophecy.[9] And ye Torrecellian Experiment runs on. And yet no man hath tryed ye expence of spirits odorate & inodorous, in all seasons of sun moon &c. in glasses, by curious scales in vegetables, animals, every thing. This may shewe greater wonders, than Sanctorius could imagine.[10] The glowormes have enlightned me, & yet all is as I expected.[11]

John Seller, & all such as assiste Merchants, Comerce, & navigation do deserve Encouragement, & ye best information yt can be obtained from time to time.[12] They say Sr T Al hath done like a sot, Sprag like a man.[13] Tis a fortnight, since we in this countrey had expresse letters from a persone of greate credite in Madrid, yt ye Jamaicans have rifled *Panama*, the booty or prize a vast treasury.[14] If true, yu may guesse, yt ye J[amaicans] have ye clue to passe & repasse through ye J[amaican] Labyrinth by ye charmes of Medea.[15] I hope yu will excite Lana to prosecute Experiments.

We had no thunder last Sat. onely a small sprinkle of raine about 11 of yt morning. Extreame heate ye Friday before, & much Lightning in ye night. The baroscope very lowe, but I tooke not punctuall notice how lowe. No thunder, & but very gentle raine, & seldome, & small showers hitherto.

We want philosophers in Tangier, Jamaica & other parts of ye Weste. I thinke I gave yu notice, yt a Minister (once an able Lecturer in Cornehill London) came not long ago to my house from Tangier. He gave me ye list of all ye Intelligent there, but could commend none there for any literary capacityes. Nowe I minde yu, yt in December, Dr Palmer, Archd of Northampton,[16] proposed a correspondence to be setled at Tangier, Aberdene, Edinburg, Catnes, London, for observation of ye Moones Altitude on ye same dayes; to ye end yt by takeing a Chord of 17, 20, or 25 degrees, instead of ye semidiameter of ye Earth, to subtend ye paralactic Angle, the distance of ye moon may be solidly demonstrated.

The like correspondence wth Smyrna, Aleppa, Bantam & far in ye East, And wth Bermudas, Barbados, Jamaica in ye West for correcting our Maps by ye ecclipses of ye moon at least (sayeth he,) ye beginning or ending. Could this have beene then done, yu had by this time rous'd up ye Astronomers & Geographers to correct or ascertaine their Tables, & Charts. Nowe yr Correspondence is well increased towards Germany, Venice, Rome, & I mervayle ye Jes[uits] do not praeoccupate yt honor. Yu can be sure of Mr Flamsteds assistance. Is Dr Palmer yet liveing, & friendly?

It would encrease ye value of yr Tracts, if yu could get breefe & punctuall answeres to yr printed Quaeryes *from Greeneland* & other places of like concernment in Naturalls.[17] I hope yu are all revived by Mr Boyles last & very copious instructions. I pray yu, How is he, for his health? This request I double upon you.

A Jamaican of a good family told me this weeke, yt he met Stub at Wells,[18] who sd He was of ye R.S.[19] pertinaciously faceing it downe, & adding, yt he was like to be undone for opposing ye Soc. Surely they be birds of a feather. For I caught this Gent in more falsityes then one. He hath travayld much, & is a stout brandy-man.

It is true yt ye French King wn he affrighted us & all our neighbours, was suddenly enforced by ye plague to disband, & fayld of his mighty worke at Dunkirk.[20] I heare yt Is. Vossius is busy amongst ye MS in St

James Library.²¹ Can he do any thing for ye R.S. Wt a losse is there of ye MS in ye Escuriall.²² We see yt no marbles nor rocks of stone buildings can secure from ye Fire of Gods wrath. We & they & all ye World have summons to thinke of an Universal Conflagration, wch wn it comes, wilbe surpriseing. God strengthen our fayth, & give us grace to amend our lives. Wch is ye surest way to be inrolld in ye incombusticall booke of Eternity. All happines to yu & yr deare Lady.

yr most aff. s.
V.V.

Sr We need not presse more for ye perfecting of No[vum] Org[anum] since Mr B[oyle] hath now published ye only true & effectuall Organum Philosophicum.²³ There is no other Logic to assiste Inventions & Artificiall Accomodations.

Does ye Venetian Journal come foorth weekely or monethly.²⁴ Are they strong enough in Sweden & Denmarke for a Journall.²⁵ They would thinke of it in Leyden or Amsterdam, if they were not so much enthralld to their God Mammon. Wt thinke yu of Portugall? In Spaine ye Monckes are too dull, & ye Nobles illiterate. Yu cannot loose glory by ye concurrence & aide of others. For yu have allready cut out worke enough for all ye world some ages to come & more yu prepare dayley; & this stifles ye Peripatetic, who does already hum very dully, like an humble bee in a pitcher. Sr Minde ye forreigners of this, yt they may see yu do not envy but excite their diligence. And minde them all to adhere closely to Experiment & Matter of Fact. Not to make too much haste to notions, nor too long nor too boldly to insiste on them. Otherwise we shall do little better than ye Schoolemen. Who rayse hot animostityes, & endlesse contentions about uselesse Scepticismes. Lord Bacon's Anticipations & Scala Intellectus will growe & be founded most naturally upon ye dayly advancement of Experiments.²⁶

Who is this Christoph Sandius who gives us Nucleum eccles Hist.²⁷ Is he Dutch or English; They say ye Ingenuous & learned do every where rise up to him. But I am too heavy upon yu.

Yr last next before this of Jul. 1. was of Jun. 20. My last a reply to it.²⁸

NOTES

Reply to Letter 1737.
1 *Phil. Trans.*, no. 72, dated 19 June 1671.
2 That is, 27 June.

3 Letter 1733.
4 *Some Considerations Touching the Usefulnesse of Experimental Naturall Philosophy... The Second Tome* (Oxford, 1671), which was reviewed in *Phil. Trans.*, no. 72 (19 June 1671), 2179–81.
5 *A True Relation of the Unjust Accusation of certain French Gentlemen*, published by Denzil, Lord Holles (London, 1671), is a description of Holles' quarrel with Chief Justice Keeling as a result of an attempt to prevent a miscarriage of justice.
6 Letter 1589 (Vol. VII) with Letter 1589a and Letter 1711 were published in this number.
7 Nothing by or about Sylvius is printed in this number; Oldenburg must have written Beale the substance of Sylvius's Letter 1717.
8 This refers to two extracts from the *Giornale de' Letterati* of 15 March 1671 [N.S.] also printed in *Phil. Trans.*, no. 72, pp. 2167–69 and 2169–70. The second, by Carlo Rinaldini, is about freezing water *in vacuo* compared with freezing water in air.
9 In this preface, printed in *Phil. Trans.*, no. 45 (25 March 1669), 898, Oldenburg instanced the existence of the *Journal des Sçavans* and the *Giornale de' Letterati* as signs that "all Civil Nations, who have a Gust for useful knowledge, will, in good time... become so many mutual Ayds to each other: And this will hopefully redound to the General good of Mankind."
10 In *Ars de medicina statica* (Venice, 1614), Santorio endeavored to measure body losses by exhalation.
11 See Letter 1720 and its note 4.
12 John Seller, hydrographer, publisher, and book- and mapseller, published two works at London in 1671: *The English Pilot* and *The Sea Atlas*.
13 Sir Thomas Allin (1612–85) had twice been sent in command of the Mediterranean fleet to reduce the menace of the Barbary pirates; he was recalled in November 1670, and in April 1671 appointed Comptroller of the Navy. He was succeeded as commander by Sir Edward Spragge (d. 1673), who destroyed the Barbary fleet at anchor in Bugia Bay in May 1671—an action which ultimately produced peace.
14 This refers to the well-planned buccaneering raid (under commission from the Council of Jamaica) by Captain Henry Morgan (1635?–88) and his men in January 1670/1.
15 Perhaps Ariadne's thread would seem more appropriate, but it was Medea who put to sleep the dragon guarding the golden fleece.
16 See Vol. IV, pp. 4 and 35.
17 The "Inquiries for Greenland" were printed in *Phil. Trans.*, no. 29 (11 November 1667), 554–55. For the account returned from Iceland, see Letter 1750.
18 Henry Stubbe made the voyage to Jamaica with a view to practising medicine there; an account by him was published in *Phil. Trans.*, no. 27 (23 September 1667), 494–509, continued in no. 36 (15 June 1668), 699–709.
19 Stubbe was never F.R.S. It is possible that Beale meant to write: "was enemy of ye R.S."
20 This is very obscure, but it may be worthwhile to recall that Vauban executed great engineering works at Dunkirk, whereby it was made the main base for French privateers like Jean Bart.
21 Isaac Vossius (1618–89), son of Gerard John Vossius, had been F.R.S. since 1664; he was a scholar, but with an interest in scientific and technical matters. He came to reside in England in 1670, and was appointed Canon of Windsor in 1673.
22 In 1671 there occurred at the Escorial a disastrous fire said to have destroyed 4,000 manuscripts as well as many printed books.
23 "philosophical instrument."

24 The *Giornale de' Letterati* appeared monthly.
25 In fact, Thomas Bartholin was collecting at this time material for his *Acta medica et philosophica A. 1671 et 1672*, published at Copenhagen in 1673 and continued in subsequent years.
26 The "Ladder of the Intellect" is the title of the intended fourth part of the *Great Instauration*, and "The Forerunners; or Anticipations of the New Philosophy" that of the fifth part. Neither was completed by Bacon.
27 The title is *Nucleus historiae ecclesiasticae* (Amsterdam, 1668). The author, Christopher Sandius (Christophe von den Sand), was born at Königsberg in 1644 and died in Holland in 1680. He was a radical theologian.
28 Letter 1733.

1744
Ignace-Gaston Pardies to Oldenburg
8 July 1671

From the original in Royal Society MS. P 1, no. 73

Monsieur

Quoy que je n'aye pas l'honneur d'estre connu de vous, je ne puis neanmoins m'ampescher de vous escrire pour vous temoigner de ma part quelque sorte de la reconnoissance que tous ceux qui aiment les lettres vous doivent. On m'a fait voir depuis quelque temps une partie de vos journaux, et je suis ravi d'y trouver des remarques si belles et si judicieuses dont vous les avez remplis. comme j'ay une passion extraordinaire pour les sciences, j'ay aussi un respect et une consideration extraordinaire pour les personnes qui travaillent à les perfectionner d'où vous pouvez voir Monsieur que j'ay pour vous toute l'estime imaginable puis que je suis persuadé de vostre capacité, et que je voys le soin que vous prennez de faire fleurir les belles sciences. J'ay encore un autre sujet de vous témoigner ma reconnoisance, parce qu'on m'a dit que vous aviez pris la peine de traduire un *discours du mouvement local*, dont je suis l'autheur: certainement je n'eusse pas cru que de si petites choses comme celles qui viennent de moy pussent avoir trouvé assez de faveur auprés de personnes si intelligentes: c'est assurément un excés de vostre bonté Monsieur, et du desir que vous avez de faire valloir jusques aux moindres choses qui pourroient servir à éclaircir quelque verité. On fit imprimer dernierement quelques remarques que j'avois faites sur une lettre de M Descartes[1] que je vous envoye par un jeune homme nommé M. Buthler, qui pourra vous dire combien grande est l'estime que jay pour vous.[2] J'espere aussi de vous pouvoir envoyer au premier jour une petite Geometrie[3] que j'ay fait avec quelque soin. Cependant je vous seray tres obligé si vous voulez souffrir que je vous témoigne de temps en temps mon respect, et que dans cette lettre, Je vous assure que je suis Monsieur

Vostre tres-humble et
tres-obeissant serviteur
Pardies
de la Companie de Jesus

A Paris 18. Juillet 1671 [N.S.]

ADDRESS
  A Monsieur
  Monsieur Oldenburg
    A Londres

TRANSLATION

Sir,

Although I do not have the honor of being known to you, I nevertheless cannot forbear to write to you, to testify for my part to some extent the gratitude which the whole learned world owes to you. I was recently shown a portion of your journal and I was delighted to find there such fine, judicious comments as those with which you have filled it. As I have an extraordinary inclination towards the sciences, so I have also an extraordinary respect and regard for people who work to improve them; from whence, Sir, you can see that I have all possible esteem for you, since I am convinced of your capabilities and since I see the care you take to make sound science flourish. There is another subject on which I must testify my gratitude to you, because I have been told that you have taken the trouble to translate a *Discours du mouvement local*, of which I am the author. Certainly I could never have believed that such trivial things as those which I produce could have found so much favor among such intelligent people: this is surely an excess of kindness on your part, Sir, and of the desire you have to give value to even the least of the things which can possibly serve to illuminate some truth. Recently some remarks which I made on a letter of Mr. Descartes have been printed;[1] this I send you by a young man named Mr. Butler, who will be able to tell you how great is my esteem for you.[2] I hope also to be able to send you very soon a little *Geome-*

try[3] which I have written with some care. Meanwhile, I would be very much obliged to you if you would permit me from time to time to testify my respect to you, and in this letter I assure you that I am, Sir,

> Your very humble and obedient servant,
> *Pardies, S.J.*

Paris, 18 July 1671 [N.S.]

ADDRESS
  To Mr. Oldenburg
  London

NOTES

Ignace-Gaston Pardies (1636–73) was born in Pau; his father was a councillor of the Parlement. He entered the Society of Jesus in 1652 and after training taught at the Jesuit College of Louis-le-Grand (or Clermont) in Paris. At this time he had already published several works in science; his *Discours du mouvement local* (Paris, 1670) was well known to Oldenburg: see Letter 1733, note 23.

1 *Remarques sur une Lettre de M. Descartes touchant la Lumiere*. The British Museum copy is without title page, although there is as a frontispiece a vignette of a robed female figure prostrate on the ground while a skeleton with scythe and trident sails overhead on a cloud. Pardies's "remarks" are preceded by a long extract from Descartes's letter.
2 We have not been able to identify him.
3 *Elements de Geometrie* (Paris, 1671).

1745
Sluse to Oldenburg
8 July 1671

From the original in Royal Society MS. S 1, no. 68
Printed in Boncompagni, pp. 656–59

Nobilissimo et Clarissimo Viro
Domino Henrico Oldenburg Societatis Regiae Secretario
Renatus Franciscus Slusius Salutem

Quanquam nihil Te dignum habeam, Vir Clarissime, et religio mihi sit inutili scriptione tempora tua morari, pudet tamen debere me tamdiu responsum humanissimis tuis 28 Aprilis datis, quibus, ut soles, me mirum in modum obligasti: Expectavi sane, si quid id ad excusationem facit, Clarissimi Hugenii literas quas sperare me jusseras; sed hactenus frustra; sive quod Parisios nondum sit reversus, seu potius quod ad εὑρημάτων nostrorum mediocritatem non attendat, quippe cui meliora domi nascuntur.¹

Diophantum Tolosae recusum, quae Typographorum nostrorum ἀφιλοκαλία est, nondum obtinere licuit. Sed ante aliquot dies huc allatus est P. Billij Diophantus redivivus,² in quo Problemata plurima subtili artificio soluta reperi, non tamen methodum illam certissimam, quam polliceri videbatur libri titulus. Nisi forte ex Analysi, qua utitur, illam colligi velit Vir doctissimus, ratus cum Seneca, longum esse iter per praecepta, breve et efficax per exempla.³

Gomezium Pereiram quod attinet, ille inter libros veteres et situ deformes hic a me repertus est, quem quia non vidisse te scribis, Elenchum operis, qualis ab ipso auctore prefixus est, ad Te mittendum censui, ut intelligas quam prope ad Cartesii sententiam accedat. dignus sane videtur Auctor cuius ingenium in meliora tempora incideret. Launaeum, Philosophiae Democriticae Hyperaspisten agnoscere mihi licuit vel ex ipsis diariis Amstelodamensibus, in quibus illius cum Rohaltio, satis acrem de rebus Philosophicis concertationem nuper legi.⁴ Huius Physica Parisiis gallice edita est, in qua, ut obiter pervolvendo animadverti, Cartesium κατὰ πόδα sectatur.⁵ De Gottignii Dioptrica,⁶ Mengolii Musica,⁷ aliisve libris in Italia editis nondum hic quidquam audivimus. Ex Germania allata est nuper Aldrovandi dendrologia, edente Montalbano in fol:,⁸ Jani Gunterii de Jure manium liber φιλολογικός.⁹

Rolfincii Chymia Genevae recusa.¹⁰ et quae maxime videre gavisus sum Acta tua Philosophica Anni 1669, versa a Johan Sterpino et Francofurti impressa.¹¹ Horum siquid desideres, magnopere me obligabis si a me voles accipere.

Vidimus etiam Basilii Valentini currum Antimonii cum Kerchringii notis;¹² Francisci Redii libellum de Insectis;¹³ Silvij ideam novam medicinae; Nobilissimi Boylii tractatus aliquot simul editos de Cosmicis rerum qualitatibus, in quibus se semper sibi similem praestat Vir Magnus. Sed cum haec omnia vel Amstelodami vel Parisiis edita sint, existimo jamdudum ad te pervenisse: sed si quid fortasse desit, quaeso ut verbulo indicare velis, et continuo transmittam.

Plurimum humanitati tuae debeo, quod id, de quo scripseram, a Chymicis vestratibus exquirere volueris. Hoc certe a me praestitum esse, fidem faciet αὐτοψία, adiunxi enim aliquid stibii μετεωριζομένου huiusmodi, sed leviter contusum, ut facilius se compingi pateretur.¹⁴ Neque tamen ad conciliandum Veneri candorem ad has cogitationes adductus sum, sed ut experirer, num hac via, ad arcana, quae Basilius iactat, facilius perveniri posse. Coeterum cum modo nihil melius occurrat, patere quaeso ut de transactionibus tuis Philosophicis paullisper tecum agam. In responsione D. Wittie ad hydrologiam chymicam, quam exhibes n. 51, narratur auctoritate Doctoris Heer nostratis, aquam Spadanam si transferatur nihil a communibus aquis discrepare, et in singulis lagenis aquae vitrum (quod pars poculi media existimatur) decedere.[15] Verum, quod pace viri doctissimi dictum sit, nec vitrum pars lagenae dimidia apud nos existimatur, immo nec fortasse duodecima. Veritati non congruit, aliquid aquis Spadanis transportatione decedere. Scripserat id quidem in prima Spadacrenes suae editione Dr. Heer,[16] Auctoritate Frambesarii[17] deceptus; sed proprio experimento id falsum esse postmodum deprehendit. Ex quatuor enim Spadanis fontibus, tres absque iactura transferri se patiuntur. Savenirius autem, quem spiritu maxime turgere existimant, et de quo Frambesarius hanc fabellam vulgarat, transfertur quoque incolumis, nisi quod lagenas prae caeteris disrumpere existimetur; sed non tam certo successu, quin aliis id causis adscribi possit. Vide, si placet, eiusdem Spadacrenes editionem Amstelodamensem[18] Anni 1645. pag. 48 et sequenti.

Ut paginam impleam, occasione eorum quae de vi electrica scripsisti,[19] narrabo tibi quid ante aliquot annos mihi acciderit. Solveram nitrum purissimum in aqua communi, ob nescio quod experimentum; cui cum satisfecissem, phialam vitream probe obturatam posueram in fenestra, ubi per aliquot septimanas haesit. Cum autem postmodum phiala uti vellem, solutionem in scutellam terream effudi, ac in mensa deposui, in qua alia scutella similis, luto ex contusis, ut solet, lateribus praeparato, plena, ac trium quatuorve palmorum intervalla remota erat. Post dies aliquot cubiculum, in quo haec posueram, ingressus, cum in scutella nihil aquae reperissem, a famulo effusam existimavi, sed illo negante, et se nequidem cubiculum ingressum asserente, suspicatus id quod erat, observavi nitrum, penetrata scutella, a parte exteriori effloruisse, quod decussum rursus in eadem scutella cum aqua solvi. Verum non multo post evolvit, ut prius, vix ullo relicto sui vestigio. Elapsis demum aliquot diebus, coelo sereno, quod antea pluvium fuerat, cum nihil minus cogitarem, lutum illud pene siccum candidis spiculis horrens, et quasi pruina coopertum animadverti, quam nitrum esse mox deprehendi.

Experimentum repetere hactenus mihi non contigit, et an tentanti successurum sit, ignoro; hoc tantum affirmare possum, rem ita accidisse, prout narravi. Sed iam satis ineptiarum.

Vale itaque, Vir Nobilissime, meque inter cultores tuos porro numerare perge. Dabam Leodii die 18 Julii Gregor: MDCLXXI.

Spero iam ad te pervenisse Libros quod misi. Domino enim Dames traditos fuisse mihi fidem fecit ille cui commiseram.

TRANSLATION

René François Sluse greets the very noble and famous Mr. Henry Oldenburg, Secretary of the Royal Society

Although I have nothing worthy of you, famous Sir, and I scruple to waste your time with useless scribbles, still I ought to feel shame for delaying so long a reply to your very kind letter of 28 April by which, as usual, you obliged me very much indeed. If I may offer some excuse, it is that I had expected the letter from the celebrated Huygens which you instructed me to hope for, but as yet in vain, either because he is not yet returned to Paris or rather because he pays no heed to the mediocrity of our discoveries since finer ones are furnished him at home.[1]

I have not yet succeeded in obtaining the Diophantus printed at Toulouse because our booksellers have no taste for excellence. But a few days ago the *Diophantus redivivus* of Fr. de Billy was brought here,[2] in which I find very many problems resolved by a most subtle artifice rather than by any sound method such as the book's title seems to promise. Unless perhaps that very learned author wishes us to deduce it from the analysis he has used, in accord with Seneca's principle: "Tedious is instruction by precept, quick and easy learning by example."[3]

As for Gomez Pereyra, I found him here among the ancient books spoiled by mold, and as you write that you have not seen it I decided to send you the list of contents just as the author prefaced it to the book so that you might learn how closely he approaches Descartes's views. It seems that the author's mind was surely worthy of falling on better times. I was able to classify de Launay as a defender of the philosophy of Democritos from the Amsterdam journals, in which I recently read of his pretty bitter controversy with Rohault about philosophical matters.[4] The *Physics* of the latter is published in French at Paris,[5] in which I noticed as I looked it through that Rohault is a faithful follower of Descartes at every point. We have heard nothing at all here as yet of the *Dioptrics* of Gottignies or the *Music* of Mengoli,[7] or other books published in Italy. Aldrovandi's *Dendrologia* was recently brought to us from Germany as edited in a folio volume by [Ovidio] Montalbani;[8] Jacobus Gutherius, *De jure manium*.[9]

Rolfinck's *Chemistry* is published at Geneva.[10] And what I am most delighted to see, your *Philosophical Transactions* for the year 1669 translated by John Sterpin and printed at Frankfurt.[11] If you wish for any of these you will oblige me very much by accepting them from my hands.

We have also seen Basil Valentine's *Triumphal Chariot of Antimony* with Kerckring's notes,[12] Francisco Redi's little book on insects;[13] Sylvius' [*Praxeos*] *Medicae idea nova*; the very noble Boyle's little group of treatises published together on the cosmical qualities of things, in which that great man shows himself as he always is. But as all these things have also been published either at Amsterdam or at Paris, I think that they will have reached you already; but if any one of them is by any chance lacking, I beg you to say the word and I will send it you at once.

I am much indebted to you for your kindness in consenting to ask your chemists about the matters of which I wrote to you. This much I can certainly vouch for, since seeing is believing, that I added something of this sort of antimony sublimate, but lightly bruised, so that it would allow itself to be compacted more easily.[14] And I was not led to these ideas by trying to make copper brilliantly reflective, but by seeking to discover whether it was possible along these lines to attain more easily to the arcana which Basil discusses. For the rest, as no better topic occurs to me, allow me please to go over your *Philosophical Transactions* with you for a little while. In Mr. Wittie's *Answer* to the *Hydrologia chymica*, which you give in no. 51, it is related on the authority of our countryman Dr. Heer that if the water of Spa is carried away it in no way differs from ordinary water, and that from each bottle a glassful (supposed to be half a pint) disappears.[15] But to speak the truth *pace* that very learned man, a glassful is not reckoned as half a bottle here, nor perhaps even one-twelfth. It is not true that anything is lost from the Spa waters when they are taken away. Dr. Heer wrote as much in the first edition of his *Spadacrene*,[16] being deceived by the authority of Frambesarius,[17] but he afterwards learned his mistake through his own trial. For of the four fountains at Spa, three permit their water to be taken away without any diminution; however, the Sauvenière spring (which they take to be most inflated with spirit) can also be carried away in safety although Frambesarius spread this fable about it, except that it is thought more liable to break bottles than the others are. Yet this does not happen so regularly as to be ascribable to no other causes. Consult, please, the Amsterdam,[18] 1645, edition of the same *Spadacrene*, p. 48 *et seq.*

In order to fill up the page, *apropos* of your remarks on the electric force,[19] I will tell you what happened to me a few years ago. I had dissolved some very pure niter in common water for some experiment or other, and when I had done this, after stopping up the glass phial carefully, I put it in the window where it remained for a few weeks. However, when I wanted to make use of that phial again later I poured the solution into an earthenware saucer and placed it on a table, on which at a distance of fifteen or twenty inches was another similar saucer full of a lute made from crushed bricks in the usual way. After a few days I went into the closet in which I had put these things and finding no water left in the saucer I concluded that it had been thrown away by the servant, but he denying this and assuring me he had never entered that closet and suspecting what the cause was, I observed that the niter, having penetrated the saucer, had effloresced on its outside. Having brushed this off I dissolved it again in the same saucer with water. Not long after the same happened as before, hardly any remains being left. Finally, after a few days lapse, with the weather clear which previously had been rainy, as I was giving no thought to the matter at all, I noticed that the lute was quite dry and bristling with shiny needles as though coated with rime, which I soon inferred was niter.

It has not hitherto happened to me to repeat that experiment and I do not know whether, if tried, it would succeed; this only I can assure you, that the facts were as I have just related them. But now enough of such absurdities.

So farewell, most noble Sir, and continue to count me among your admirers. Liège, 18 July 1671, N.S.

I hope that the books I sent have already reached you. For he to whom I entrusted them assured me that they were delivered to Mr. Dames.

NOTES

Reply to Letter 1687.
1 See Letter 1687, note 1. No letter from Huygens to Sluse at this time is extant.
2 Jacques de Billy, *Diophanti redivivi pars prior... pars posterior* (Lyons, 1670), a book based on the work of Bachet and Pierre de Fermat.
3 Seneca, *Ep. ad Lucilium*, Ep. VI, sec. 5.
4 See Letter 1687, note 9. Sluse here refers to the *Hollantze Mercurius* for May 1671, pp. 66–67 of the edition published at Haarlem. De Launay was an atomist, Rohault of course a Cartesian. The newspaper recounts from Paris a dispute between the two at a gathering of philosophers in de Launay's house "in the suburb of St. Germain" (the date is not stated; such meetings had taken place since 1656), when "the disputing parties would have come to the point of pulling each other's hair out if the Duc de Liancourt, du Perez, Desmarez, and other excellent persons had not held them back. So that the question was not pursued further, which caused the company to start laughing and making jokes..."; our translation.
5 See Letter 1722, note 5.
6 See Vol. VII, Letter 1602, note 3.
7 See Letter 1687, note 6.
8 Ulyssi Aldrovandi, *Dendrologiae... libri duo... Ovidius Montalbanus... opus colligit* (Bologna, 1668).
9 Sluse was mistaken in the exact form of the name of this author, Jacques Gouthieres; the book was published at Paris in 1615.
10 Werner Rolfinck, *Chimia in artis formam redacta* (Jena, 1661; reprinted at Geneva, 1671).
11 See Letter 1638 and later in Vol. VII.
12 See Letter 1694, note 4.
13 See Letter 1712, note 2.
14 This sentence is difficult to understand in the absence of further explanation.
15 See *Phil. Trans.*, no. 51 (20 September 1669), 1039 and (dealing with the same issue) Letter 1301 and its note 4 (Vol. VI, pp. 275–79). We have rendered *poculum* (cup) here by "pint," which was the word Oldenburg had used. William Simpson's *Hydrologia chymica* (London, 1669) provoked a rebuttal in the same year from Robert Wittie, entitled *Pyrologia mimica*.

16 This first edition of Henricus ab Heer's *Spadacrene. Hoc est fons spadanus...* appeared at Liège in 1614.
17 Nicholas Abraham de Framboisière; see Vol. VI, p. 279, note 4.
18 Correctly, Leiden.
19 See Oldenburg's preface to the fourth volume (no. 45, dated 25 March 1669), where he talks, on pp. 895-96, of "Electricity" and "Magnetismes" in connection with the "attraction" of substances, virtues, etc., through the air.

1745a
Contents of the *Antoniana Margarita*

Enclosure with Letter 1745
From the original in Royal Society MS. S 1, no. 68

Elenchus Operis

Bruta sensu carere ostenditur col. 1a et seq. ac per universum hoc opus.

Qualiter intuitive et abstractive noscamus.

Sensibilia communia, non proprie per se sensibilia nominanda, sed per accidens.

Non esse sensum communem organicam facultatem probatur, et Galeni et Avicennae nonnullae sententiae notantur.

Qualiter opinatum sit huc usque operationes intellectus in nobis fieri, et huius improbatio.

Quid universale sit, et nonnulli errores, qui de eo opinabantur, explicantur.

An ens et essentia differant realiter an non, explicatur, et commentator quidam libelli B. Thomae reprehenditur.

Quid continuum, contiguum, sit, exprimitur, multo aliterque quam hucusque intelligebatur.

De principiis rerum naturalium, praecipue de prima materia agitur, ei ipsam non esse, ut Aristoteles opinatus est, evidenter probatur.

De ignea sphaera ac de isto infimo igne, nonnulla tractantur contra aliquorum opinionem.

Quis sit productor animarum vegetativarum, et earum quae sensitivae appellantur, ubi Aristoteles esplicatur, et nonnullae eiusdem sententiae notantur.

Quantitatem, figuram, et relationes ac alia quae nonnulli doctissimi viri opinati sunt distincta esse a rebus quantiter aliis denominatis, non posse distingui, probatur.

Duae methodi quibus cognoscenda sunt, quae accidentia realiter differant a substantia, et quae non, proponuntur.

Quo distinguantur formae eductae de potentia materiae a non eductis.

Paraphrasis in 3 de Anima cum Authoris commenticulis.

Solutiones argumentorum opinantium intellectiones et sensationes esse accidentia realiter distincta ab anima intelligente et sentiente.

De Immortalitate Animae.

TRANSLATION

The Contents of the Work

That animals lack feeling is shown in col. 1a *et seq.* and throughout the whole of this work.

How we know things intuitively and abstractly.

Things known to the common sense are not properly to be called sensible, but only accidentally.

It is proved that the common sense is not an organic faculty and some opinions of Galen and Avicenna are commented on.

How the workings of the mind within ourselves have hitherto been thought to be performed, and the disproof of this [account].

What may exist universally; and some errors in reasoning about this explained.

Whether *being* and *essence* are in reality different or not is explained, and the commentator on a certain passage in the Blessed Thomas is reproved.

What it is to be continuous or contiguous is explained in a very different way from that which has been understood hitherto.

On the principles of natural things and especially of the first matter, and it is very clearly proved that it is not as Aristotle believed.

Some points contrary to the usual views concerning the sphere of fire and the lower region of fire are discussed.

Who is the creator of vegetable souls, and of those called sensitive, where Aristotle is explained and some of his opinions receive comment.

It is proved that quantity, shape, and relationship and other things that some learned men have thought to be distinct from other things denominated quantitatively cannot be so distinguished.

Two methods are propounded by which it may be known which accidents do really differ from substances, and which do not.

In which forms deriving from the potentiality of matter are distinguished from those not so derived.

A paraphrase of the third book of *De anima* with a slight commentary by the author.

The resolution of the arguments of those who believe that thoughts and sensations are accidents really distinct from the soul that thinks and senses.

On the immortality of the soul.

1746
Willughby to Oldenburg
10 July 1671

From the original in Royal Society MS. W 3, no. 44
Partly printed in *Phil. Trans.*, no. 74 (14 August 1671), 2221

Middleton July 10th

Sr

I have at last received your letter and your little stick with the Egges which are not yet Hatched but all care shall bee taken about them.[1]

The Cartrages that I got at Astrop neare a twelvemonth agoe,[2] doe now allmost every day afford mee a bee and I can Heare them Knawing out their way before I see them so that there is nothing irregular in the way of breeding of those bees. but wee may challenge all the Atheists in the world to contrive it better than god and nature has. Having shut up their young ones in those Cells with sufficient provision they all before Winter, as well the uppermost as lowermost, come to their Full growth or are turned into Nymphas in which condition they are designed to ly all Winter as the most of insects doe the next summer those must necessarily bee First excited out of their torpor and changed into Flyars by the externall heat and air that ly next it. if anie bee laid so late that they have not time enough to come to the state of Nymphas before Winter, they will most certainly die and then it is noe losse nor inconvenience though their Cells bee perforated.

the scolopendra spoke of by the Lipsick Philosophers in your Transactions P. 2082 n. 31[3] is that which is [by] our Bruerus described to Muffet: see the latter part of the chapter in Muffet de Julis Pag: 202.[4] I saw it in the cloisters of Trinitie Colledge in Cambridge 12 or 13 years agoe, it shall goe Hard but I will send you some shortly. I earnestly desire you to sollicit Mr Lister For an account of the breeding of his musca icneumones.[5] his letter to Mr Wray which I saw,[6] you are not likely to have, or at least not a great while. I had an opportunitie to have discovered it to the royall Societie the last time I was there but I was resolved it should come From nobody but himselfe, it is so very ingenious and true that I would faine it were known and when you send mee word you have it from Mr Lister I will send you a great manie observations both of my own and Mr Wrays to confirme it. I am Sir

Your Faithfull servant
Francis Willughby

If you can convenientlie without much trouble to you I desire the Favour of you to send mee some of the butterflys of Silkwormes or at least to observe whither the Antennae or Hornes bee Feathered on both sides ⇐⇐⇐ and whither the Antennae of the males bee the same with those of the Females.

ADDRESS
   For Mr Henry
   Oldenburg Secretary
   to the royall
   Society at his house
   in the pellmell
       London

POSTMARK JY 12

NOTES

1 The letter referred to, presumably later than Letter 1701, has not been found.
2 See Vol. VII, Letters 1493 and 1518.
3 See *Phil. Trans.*, no. 68 (20 February 1670/71), 2082, the thirty-first of the observations reported by Oldenburg from the *Miscellanea curiosa*, Vol. I, dealing with the light emitted by a luminous centipede (modern order Geophilomorpha).
4 See Thomas Mouffet, *Insectorum sive minimorum animalium theatrum* (London, 1634), p. 202 (Ch. VIII), where the author writes (translating): "Our countryman Brewer [Bruerus], a skilful and diligent explorer of nature, relates that he has himself seen scolopendrae shining in the dark..." Oldenburg misunderstood Willughby's meaning and printed in *Phil. Trans.* "is that which is our *Bruchus*, described by Muffet..." (a bruchus is a beetle of the weevil kind, not a millipede or centipede). We do not know who Brewer was. Oldenburg published a correction in *Phil. Trans.*, no. 78 (18 December 1671), 3050.

5 "Ichneumon flies," a common group of insects, properly wasps, which are all parasitic on the larvae or pupae of other insects.
6 See Letter 1712 and its note 3.

1747
Thomas Hill to Oldenburg
13 July 1671

From the original in Royal Society MS. H 3, no. 5

Lisbonne ye 23th July 1671 [N.S.]

Worthy Sr

I presume upon our former acquaintance to trouble you wth this addresse wch I am almost forced to. for my great Respects to the R. Society being knowne to several Persons, One has obliged mee to acquaint you That in the Brazeel at the Bahia,[1] Lives a Jesuite, Sonne of [a] Dutch Man, who is a very curious, ingenious & inquisitive Man, and especially desirous to serve the R.S. hee has resided there, many Yeares, and has travelled the Country more than any Man. and is very able to give you satisfaction to ye Inquiryes you please to make, and would follow yr. directions in any observations you would have him make. Hee had himself offerred his Service, but hee was ignorant of the meanes to address his Letters. The Memorial hee sent was accidentally Lost, So that I know not his Name. but hee desired that you would write to him in Latine. the direction may bee left in Blanck, however ye Letter shall bee safely conveyed to him, and his answear Returned. If I had ability, I should offerr my Service to ye Society during my Residence in this Countrey. but I am conscious of my incapacity. Sr. I wish you all ye successe due to the great paines & Study you are engaged in, whereby you oblige the whole World. I kisse yr hands & Rest

Your very humble servant
Tho. Hill

Mr. Henry Oldenburg

ADDRESS
>To Henry Oldenburg Esq.
>Secretary to ye Royal Society
>London

POSTMARK AU 8

NOTES

>The writer of this letter was probably a younger brother of Abraham Hill (1635–1722), Treasurer of the Royal Society. He was an expert musician, and a friend of Pepys until his departure for Portugal as a merchant in 1666; he died in Lisbon in 1675.
>1 Now Salvador, the oldest city and former capital of Brazil.

1748
Oldenburg to Lister
13 July 1671

From the original in Bodleian Library MS. Lister 34, f. 29

Sir,

This is only to thank you for yr last of july 5th and to intreat you to believe, yt I would by no means incommode you when you are indisposed, as I was very sorry to understand you were, by yr last. Only let me desire this favor of you, yt when you find it convenient, you would gratify ye R. Society wth yr thoughts concerning Vegetable Excrescencies, ye account of wch it seems, Mr Wray sent away wth some other letters and papers into Essex, as he signified to me himself by letter, mentioning wthall, yt he had made it his request to you as well as I, to take ye pains of writing yr thoughts again on yt subject.[1] And when you doe this, I beg you would add what you have observed of the *Muscae Ichneumones*:[2] All wch I shall take very particular care to have registred in our Books wth the deserving Author's name, and to enrich ye Transactions wth, by yr permission.

Having inquired of Mr Wray concerning an Insect feeding upon *Ranunculus*, and said to yield a musky sent when dried, I had for answer, he had knowledge of yt particular; but he then call'd to mind two sorts of Insects, he had seen, wch smell of musk: ye one, ye Common Capricornus or Goat-chafer, smelling so strong of yt perfume, yt one may sent it at a good distance as it flyes by or sits near you: ye other is a smal sort of Bee, wch in ye South and East-parts of England is frequently to be met wth in gardens among flowers in the Spring-time.[1]

Mr Willughby, who hath a great respect for you, as well as Mr Wray and many more, writeth yt ye Scolopendra, spoken of by ye German Philosophers in Transact. No. 68. p. 2082. 31. as shining in ye dark, and sparkling when comprest, is yt wch is our *Bruchus* described by Muffet; referring me for it to ye latter part of ye chapt. in Muffet de *Julis* p. 202. and adding, yt he saw it in ye cloisters of Trin. Coll. in Cambridg, 12. or 13. years agoe.[3]

Apprehending I may be tedious to you, I conclude wth assuring yrself, yt I am constantly Sir

Yr faithf. friend and servt
Oldenburg

London July 13. 1671.

ADDRESS

    To his honored friend
    Martyn Lister Esquire
    at his house wthout
    Mickel-gate-barr
        at
            York

NOTES

Reply to Letter 1741.
1 See Letter 1738.
2 See Letter 1746 and its note 4.
3 All this is from Letter 1746.

1749
Oldenburg to Willughby
13 July 1671

From the memorandum in Royal Society MS. W 3, no. 44

rec. july 12. 71. Answ. jul. 13.

NOTE

Reply to Letter 1746. Oldenburg's letter is also mentioned in Willughby's reply to it, Letter 1777.

1750
Páll Björnsson to Oldenburg
13 July 1671

From the copy in Royal Society Letter Book IV, 374–78

Viro amplissimo
Domino Henrico Oldenburg Regiae Societatis Secretario
Salutem

Conabor ad illa proposita τητηρματα[?] paucis atque αὐτοσχεδιαζὶ respondere; plenam atque exactissimam harum rerum historiam primo quoque tempore, si deus vitam indulserit, tibi transmissurus, interea haec pauca accipe.

Aer in Islandia toto anno saluberrimus: Morbis Choliciis, atque Lepra Regio praecipue obnoxia; nulli hic medici; Chirurgi duo, vel ad summum tres; remedijs utimur nullis, nisi emplastris quibusdam, dum vulnera obligantur; omnia divinae curae committimus, inopes medicamentorum.[1] Caeli mutationes lubricae atque incertae; nec unquam ad diversas Anni Tempestates; ita media aestate saepe numero cadunt nives atque grandines, flantque venti vehementissimi, ut nescias, qua hora, inopina furore incipiat tempestas.

Spiritus vini, quem *brendewyn* vocant, oleum quodvis, atque argentum vivum, hac a gelu immuni, ista, inquam, non congelantur. Gelu terram quatuor, ad summum, pedes terram penetrat: Figura nivis varia, ut plurimum ad exemplum vestigij canini; Magnitudinis variae. Grandinis figura sphaerica, maximae magnitudinis, instar globulorum quibus aves, dum virtute pulveris emittuntur, interficimus. Scribam vero haec, si deus volet, exactius: Nulla Corpora equidem, quod sciam, praeservantur apud nos nivis beneficio, nisi pisces recentes, quos, ne tam cito marcescant, nivibus immergimus. Congelata corpora, pene dixerim omnia, tumescunt, mutanturque sapore atque colore.

Meteora nisi ignem lambentem atque Draconem volantem, hic non observavi: saepe hic accidit, utrumque solis latus a duobus (uti videtur) solibus claudi, dilapsis per tres eos soles arcubus duobus. Verum aliquando ista plenius. Nulli stati aut ordinarij venti. Ferrum valde cito ferruginem trahit.

Profunditas maris varia, 80 orgijas, ubi maxima: putei tamen quidam in fundo inventi sine fundo. Quantum salis aqua marina excocta largiatur, ignotum; nullo namque sale gens utitur, paucis admodum exceptis, qui importato sale utuntur. Aqua marina in nocturnis tenebris, sudo caelo, si remis rotatur, veluti igniculis a fornace ascendentibus lucet. De fluentis atque amnibus alias.

Aestus marini ratio prorsus ad motum lunae. Mare tumidum, luna in oriente; atque rursus in occidente Caeli plaga; subsidentia, meridie, atque rursus Borea. Tumor summus sedecim pedes, nisi forte autumno, si mare vehementius solito furere contingat; estque tunc viginti: Gradus fluxus et refluxus aquarum in aequalibus temporum spatijs incerti atque varij; aliquando minores, nunc majores. Plenilunio atque interlunio maximi tumores maris, atque infimae subsidentiae.

Lacus in Islandia innumeri, et paene in altissimis montibus, pleni salmonibus. Fontes innumeri, de petris atque saxis ebullientes. Thermae fere totidem, quarum quaedam adeo calidae, ut horae quadrans Carnis bovinae frusto, quantumlibet magno, ex coquendo satis sit. Ita autem coquitur; Ollae sive lebetes, aqua frigida repleti, super-imponuntur; periculum namque est, ne si ipsum frustum injiciatur in ipsas Thermas adeo ardentes, annihiletur sive ejicietur; mirum tamen, pultem coqui non posse. Harum aqua circa labra Thermarum lapidescit; alias non novi aquas minerales hic locorum.

Montium celsissimorum altitudo quadrans, ni fallor, milliaris germanici;[2] quod qua via geometrica deprehenderim, alias decendum; Tota

Islandia perpetui montes, sive unus mons; litora solum habitantur atque Valles; Montes ignivomi praeter Heclam alij, perpetuis tamen nivibus obducti; quarum rerum integram historiam scribere nunc non vacat; vereor namque, ne Dominus Capitaneus statim mare ingrediatur, Multa atque stupenda eruptionis tempore accidisse dicuntur.

Magnetis declinatio NW. Natura soli argillosa; quibusdam locis tamen ea argilla nullius fere usus; alibi arenosa; cretacea nulla; Agricultura nulla, importatis utimur mercibus, ferro, farre, lino.

Avium genera innumera aestate; hieme Corvi, aquilae, mergi marini, olores; reliqua quo fugiant, ignoro. Animalia domestica oves, boves, equi, canes; quibusdam locis gallinae. Ferae nullae, sola vulpes montes aberrat. Ursi quandoque si glacies Gronlandica appulerit, magno terrore incolarum, qui inermes omnes per Regionem vagantur. Boves faeno, Oves atque equi gramine atque musco marino hiemali tempore vescuntur: de incolis alias. Fodinae lapideae nullae: sulphuris tanta copia, ut navibus quotannis duabus onerarijs sufficiat.

Haec fere sunt quae tam festinanter ad literas Amplitudinae tuae respondere poteram, magnopere orans, qua es humanitate, velis tam luculentae scriptioni suos indulgere naevos, atque adeo jejuna atque inania responsa benigne accipere. quoad exactior atque magis exquisita harum rerum atque aliarum cognatarum explicatio, superius promissa, transmittatur. Vale, vir amplissime, et me virtutibus tuis addictum ama.

Virtutum tuarum studiosissimum
Paulus Biornonius ecclesiae
Seldalinae Minister

Selaaedal. Anno 1671
13 July stylo veteri

P.S. Illud pene neglexeram; Anno scilicet 1642 13 Maiji totum mare quod nostra promontoria alluit, pellucidum fuisse biduo, ut Choncha vel minimus lapillus in fundo, ubi maris altitudo vel 40 fathm., non profundius abesse a navis latere quam tres pedes visa: quod ubi piscatores Islandici animadvertere correpti timore, portus occupant confestim. Hora nona matutina id incepisse. testes sunt homines certi atque frugi bonae vos optici causas inquirite. Alias rara quaedam, atque alterius momenti, si deo visum, scribam.

TRANSLATION

Greetings to the very worthy Mr. Henry Oldenburg, Secretary of the Royal Society

I shall try to answer the proposed desiderata in few and extemporized [phrases]; if God grant me life I will at the first opportunity send you a full and exquisitely accurate narrative of these things; meanwhile accept these few [words].

The air in Iceland is very healthy all through the year. Colics and leprosy are the chief troublesome diseases of this region. There are no physicians here, but two surgeons or three at the most. We use no medicaments except some plasters, when wounds require them. We entrust everything to divine providence, being destitute of medicines.[1] The changes in our skies are capricious and uncertain, not obeying the seasons of the year: so snow and hail often fall at midsummer and the most violent winds blow so that you never know at what unexpected moment the fury of the storm may burst out.

The spirit of wine called brandy, any oils, and quicksilver are here immune from the frost, that is, I mean, they do not solidify. The frost penetrates the earth to a distance of four feet at the most. The shape of snowflakes is various; thus many resemble a dog's pawprint; so is their size diverse also. Hail is spherical, and the size of bird shot used in fowling. If God wills it I will put all this down more exactly. No substances as far as I know are preserved by us with the aid of snow except fresh-caught fish, which are plunged into snow lest they should decay. Frozen substances, I mean almost everything, swell up, changing in both taste and color.

I have observed no meteors here except the flickering fire [aurora?] and "flying dragon." It often happens that (as it seems) the sun is embraced on either side by two mock suns, with two rainbows passing through the three suns. More at length about that another time. There are no fixed or customary winds. Iron very quickly attracts rust.

The depth of the sea is varied, eighty fathoms at the most; yet there are bottomless wells when you try to plumb them. I do not know how much salt boiled seawater yields, for the people here make no use of salt apart from a very few, who use what is imported. In the dark of night when the sky is clear the seawater shines if you splash an oar, just like sparks flying up from a furnace. Of rivers and streams elsewhere.

The tides go wholly by the moon. The tide is at flood when the moon is in the east, and again when it is in the western part of the sky; it is at ebb when the moon is on the meridian and again when the moon is northerly. The highest tide is sixteen feet except perhaps in the fall if the sea happens to be rougher than usual, when it reaches twenty feet. The quantity of the ebb and flow in equal time intervals is varied and uncertain, sometimes less, sometimes more. The spring tides come with the full moon and no moon.

There are innumerable lakes in Iceland and even in the highest mountains they are full of salmon. There are innumerable springs too, gushing out of the stones and rocks. There are almost as many hot springs, some so warm that they will in fifteen minutes boil a piece of beef, however big, till it is done. It is cooked in this way: they place over [the hot spring] cauldrons or pots filled with cold water, for if the piece of meat were put straight into such a terribly hot spring it would be in danger of being destroyed or blown out. Yet it is strange that a porridge cannot be so cooked. The water of these hot springs turns to stone around the brim. I know of no other mineral waters here.

The height of the highest mountains is, if I am not mistaken, a quarter of a German mile;[2] by what geometrical method I learned this is to be related elsewhere. Iceland is everywhere mountainous, or one great mountain, only the shores and valleys being inhabited. There are other volcanic mountains besides Hekla, yet all are covered with snow. I have not leisure now to write a complete account of all these things for I fear that Master Ship Captain may put to sea at any moment. Many astonishing things are said to happen at the time of an eruption.

The magnetic declination is north-west. The nature of the soil is clayey, but in some places the clay is almost useless. Elsewhere it is sandy, nowhere chalky. There is no husbandry. As imported goods we use iron, corn, and flax.

In summer there are numberless kinds of birds; in the winter rooks, eagles, sea ducks, and swans. Where the rest go I don't know. Our domesticated animals are sheep, oxen, horses, dogs, and in some places hens. There are no wild ones except foxes in the mountains. There are bears sometimes if the Greenland ice drifts over, to the great terror of the inhabitants who all go about their business quite unarmed. In the winter time the oxen are fed on hay, the sheep and horses on grass and sea moss; of the inhabitants [I write] elsewhere.

There are no stone quarries; there is such plenty of sulphur as supplies freight for two ships each year.

This is about all that I could in so much haste reply to your letter, worthy Sir, urgently desiring that out of your kindness you will overlook the blemishes of this well-intended paper, and accept cordially so barren and empty a reply. As for the more exact and refined explanation of these and related matters, it shall be sent. Farewell, most worthy Sir, and love me as an admirer of your merits.

Most zealous for your merits,
Páll Björnsson
Minister of the church at Selaardal

Selaardal.[3] 13 July 1671, O.S.

P.S. I almost forgot [to tell you] that in the year 1642 on 13 May the whole ocean washing our promontory was for two days so very transparent that shells and tiny pebbles were seen on the bottom, where the sea was forty fathoms deep, as though no more than three feet down from the boats' sides; when the Icelandic fisherman saw this they took such fright that they made port at once. This began at nine in the morning. As witnesses there are reliable and honest men. Be so good as to look into the optical causes. On another occasion I may write, if God will, of certain rarities and other things of moment.

NOTES

Reply to Letter 1651. It seemed worthwhile to translate this curious document with some care; this version may be compared with Oldenburg's free rendering in *Phil. Trans.*, no. 111 (22 February 1674/5), 238-40. The Greek words in the first sentence are conjectural; the amanuensis obviously copied the original without comprehension, and Oldenburg did not bother to correct his rendering since he did not translate this sentence.
1 It seems difficult to believe that the Icelanders used no folk remedies, so probably Páll meant that there was no learned or "scientific" medicine.
2 This is about 4,400 English feet, approximately the true height of Hekla; but the highest mountain in Iceland is nearly 7,000 feet.
3 Modern Selardu.

1751
Lister to Oldenburg
17 July 1671

From the original in Royal Society MS. L 5, no. 36
Printed in *Phil. Trans.*, no. 75 (18 September 1671), 2254-57

Yorke July 17th 1671

Sir

I understand by yours of ye 13th instant, yt Mr Wray cannot without much trouble retreive ye Letter, wherin I gave him formerly my opinion concerning Vegetable Excrescencies: & yet not wholly to deny you ye satisfaction of what you seem much to desire, I am willing to thinke again upon ye same subject, at least to recollect part of my former thoughts as my memory will serve me.

The occasion than of yt Letter was upon ye account given us by you N.———[1] of ye opinion of ye Italian F. Redj: viz, yt some live plants or their Excrescencies doe truly generate some Insects, To which opinion of F. Redj I told my friend, as I remember, yt I, indeed, had observed yt ye By-fruits of some Vegetables as of ye Oake & Wildrose for example, did grow up togather wth their respective wormes in ym from small beginings to fair & large fruit, some of ym emulating even ye genuine off-spring of ye plant

———et miratur non sua poma.²

And further yt I did beleive ye wormes were furnished wth food in & from ym: but not by any Navil-connexion as yt Author fancies & wch I said to me was unintelligible & yt I should be glad of a notion wch might make out to me such monstrous relation, as halfe animal halfe vegetable, or wch is all one, vegetable vessells inserted into an animal or ye contrary: strange Oeconomie!

That it had never been my good forture (whatever diligence I had used) to discerne Eggs in ye center of Galls, but a Worme constantly, even at ye very first appearance, as near at least as my fortune led me. Yet I would not deny, but yt diligence might one day discover ye egg it selfe, wch I was of ye opinion was affixed to or near ye place by the parent-Insect, where ye Gall rose.

That I ever found ye Wormes in all ye Excrescencies as I had yet met wth, perfectly at libertie: & for ye filaments our author mentions, it was very possible he might be mistaken, it being very hard & a matter not yet treated of in any publick paper, wch & what are ye vessells yt enter into ye Texture of a Vegetable, as of a large Tree for example, much more hard would it be to say this is a Vessel in a small Gall.

That there were many by-fruits of different Figures & shape (though perhapps of a like Texture) upon one & ye same plant, every one of wch did nourish & produce a different race of insects: whence, I told him, I thought might rather be argued, ye diverse workman-shipp of different Insects, than one & ye same principle of Vegetation to be author of several sorts of Animals.

That ye Animals themselves produced of such excrescencies were, for ye kind, of such a Race as were well known to us to be otherwise generated of animal-parents: & therefore it was probable, yt these were so too as well as their Tribe-fellows.

That ye Insect-animals produced of such Excrescencies were male & female; & yt if soe we might argue wth Aristotle (lib. 1. c.1. de Generat. Animal.) yt Nature made not such in vain, & yt if from ye Coit of these animals, wch have their birth from noe animals, animals should be borne, they would either be like their parents & of ye same *species* wth ym; &

if soe, it would necessarily follow (since in ye generation of all other creatures it soe comes to passe) yt their very parents had such origine too: or unlike ym, & if soe (if these alsoe were male & female) of these 2d unlike Off-spring a 3d race of different animals or species would be begott, of ym a 4th & soe in infinitum. And that these Insects wch he & I had observed to be produced of ye Excrescencies of some Vegetables, we had good cause to suspect they were male & female, since some of ym had stings & were tripilious & others not. (Vide Catalog. plant. Cantabridg. ad rosam caninam et alibj.)[3]

These were some at least of ye Arguments, as far as I remember, I used when I formerly writ on this subject to my friend: but since yt Letter, I have perused ye Booke of F. Redj it selfe & doe find yt ye said opinion is barely proposed as a thing not unplausible; but ye proofs therof are reserved, till ye publishing of a curious piece, concerning ye Excrescencies of ye Oake. And therfore I shall be ye lesse earnest in ye refutation of yt Opinion, wch perhapps a more accurate search into nature will in time make ye authour of it himselfe find erroneous.

I presume not to venture to decide this Controversie: my experience in these matters being too insufficient & my leisure & health but little to hasten a convenient stock of particulars & a due examination of ym Yet before I leave this subject, I am willing to run over & present you with a few abbreviated Instances of some of ye several kinds of Vegetable Excrescencies & likewise some unobvious wayes of Insects feeding on plants, & these I shall deliver in confirmation of ye following Propositions

1. That all are not truly Vegetable Excrescencies yt are reputed such. And here we may justly name ye *Purple Kermes* for example, whose history you were pleased to publish. N.N.[4] This, I say, both gives a clear light to the discovery of ye Nature of ye *Scarlet Kermes* (a thing wholly unknown to ye Ancients, as far as we can see by there writings, and noe lesse ignored by ye Moderns, & yet, wch is admirable, in very great esteeme & continued in use for some 1000's of years,) & alsoe is an evident Instance, that some things confidently beleeved Vegetable Excrescencies, are no such matter, but artificial things meerly *contiguous* to ye plant, & which have noe other relation to it, than the *Patella*-shellfish to the Rock it cleaves.[5]

2. Generally, Insect eggs layed upon ye leaves of plants or their respective wormes feeding on them doe not occasion or raise Excrescencies. This truth every body, yt has been ye least curious, is an eye-witness off. Thus for example, ye Eggs of ye common red-butterfly, layed upon ye Nettle are thereon hatched without blistering ye plant into an Excrescence,

& ye stiffe-haired or prickly Caterpillars hatched from them Eggs, feed upon ye leaves without any ill impression, puncture, or prejudice, save that they make clean worke, & eat all before them. I could produce some 100's of Instances, if this were to be doubted of.

3. Some Insect-eggs, laid upon ye leaves or other parts of plants, doe, as soon as hatched, pierce & enter within the plant to feed. To give you a convincing Instance of ye truth of this proposition, take this from my notes.

May 22 I observed on ye back or underside of ye leaves of *Atriplex olida*,[6] certain small milk-white-oblong Eggs, on some leaves 4, on others fewer, or more: These Eggs, were on some plants yet unhatched, but on many of ye same plants, I found ye Egg-shells or skins yet adhering to ye leaves, & ye little maggotts already entred (through I know [not] what invisible holes) within ye two membranes of ye Leafe & feeding on ye inward pulp or substance of ye leafe: in other leaves of yt plant, (he that shall make the observation after me, will find plants enough of this species seased on to vary as I did ye observation in one day) I found those maggotts growne very great & yet ye two membranes, yt is, ye uppermost & undermost skin of ye leafe entire, but raised & hollow like a blather. Note 1. yt those maggotts were of a Conick shape. 2. yt in July they shrunke into Fly-Chrysalises & accordingly came to perfection, etc. To this unobvious way of feeding we thinke we may refer all worme eaten fruits, woods, etc.

4. Wormes feeding or nourished within some of ye parts of some plants doe cause Excrescencies. Thus ye heads or seed vessels of Papaver, Spart. Sylv. Ger. emac.[7] are disfigured for having wormes in ym & grow thrice as bigg as ye not seased ones. This is alsoe plain in ye Excresc. of Pseudo-teucrium[8] & Barbarea[9] etc.

5. The substance of most Vegetable Excrescencies is not ye food of ye Wormes to be found in ym. The instances given in confirmation of ye last proposition doe alsoe confirme this: neither is an Oake aple properly worme eaten, or the Shagged-Galls or Sponges of ye Wild rose, or ye smooth ones on ye leaves of ye same plant, or ye baggs upon ye leaves of ye yellow-dwarfe Willow or ye Elme etc.

This is ye summe of what I have to say at present concerning this subject: being very unwilling to advance further, than my owne private observations will suffer me. Of other matters in your Letter an other time. I am Sir

Yr most humble servant
Martin Lister

ADDRESS
> These
> for his honoured friend
> Mr Henry Oldenburg
> at his house in ye Palmal
> London

POSTMARK JY 19

NOTES

Reply to Letter 1748; this is Lister's revised paper on "vegetable excrescencies."
1 *Phil. Trans.*, no. 57 (25 March 1670), 1175–76.
2 "…and [the tree] is not vain about its own fruit" (Virgil, *Georgics*, ii, 81).
3 That is, Ray's *Catalogus plantarum circa Cantabrigiam nascentium* (Cambridge, 1660); "under 'dog rose' and elsewhere."
4 *Phil. Trans.*, no. 73 (17 July 1671), in which extracts from Letters 1726 and 1741 were printed; Lister here writes in anticipation, of course.
5 The limpet; "cleaves" signifies "adheres to."
6 Wild orach.
7 This is probably the common wild poppy, but we do not understand Lister's name.
8 Probably a form of germander, that is, some plant of the species *chamaedrys* or *teucrium*.
9 Winter rocket or cress.

1752
Oldenburg to Huygens
22 July 1671

From *Œuvres Complètes*, VII, 87–93
Original in the Huygens Collection at Leiden

Monsieur

Ayant sceu de Monsieur vostre Pere que vous estiez de retour à Paris en bonne santé,¹ et une si bonne occasion, comme celle de Monsieur Vernon, s'offrant pour vous saluer et pour vous feliciter de vostre reconvalescence, i'ay cru de ne la devoir pas negliger.² Vous scaurez donc, Monsieur, que tous vos amis icy, dont il y a grand nombre, se rejouissent extremement de ce que vous vous portez si bien que de pouvoir retourner à la philosophie, et se promettent quelque chose extraordinaire de vos estudes renforcez par une vigueur renouvellee de corps et d'esprit. Nous attendons aussi de Messieurs vos colleges plusieurs choses considerables, que l'on nous a fait esperer il y a quelque temps, particulierement la mesure de la terre, l'Anatomie de plusieurs Animaux et la description de quelques Plantes.[3] Vostre Academie, jouissant de toutes les assistances necessaires à executer, fera voir au monde, sans doubte, la force des Esprits Clairvoians, et combien de choses belles et utiles ils peuvent produire.

Quant à la Societé Royale, Elle ne s'assemble point à present, ayant commencé sa vacation qu'elle a accoustumé de faire dans cete saison. Sans cela, Elle persiste à faire des Experiences autant qu'Elle peut. On espere de pouvoir travailler mieux cy-apres. Quelques uns de ses membres ont depuis peu fait imprimer quelques livres nouveaux: Monsieur Boyle, de l'Estrange rarefaction de l'Air &c. Et de l'Utilité de la Philosophie Experimentelle le 2e volume; meditant à present sa response aux objections que Monsieur More a faitez contre quelques unes de ses Experiences;[4] comme aussi un Traité joly et bien philosophique touchant les pierres precieuses.[5] Monsieur Wallis, quoyque malade de la fievre quarte, a achevé la derniere partie de Son Traite de Motu et Mechanice, qui sortira de la presse au premier iour. Monsieur Lower a adjousté a son livre de motu Cordis et Sanguinis, un petit discours de Origine Catharri.[6] Monsieur Willis fait astheur imprimer deux Traitez, l'un de Anima Brutorum, l'autre de Morbis Capitis.[7] Monsieur Mercator quelque chose des logarithmes.[8] De plus, ie ne veux pas vous celer, Monsieur, que i'ay communiqué (ce que ie crois n'avoir pas fait contre vostre gré) la construction du Probleme d'Alhazen (que vous nous envoiatez, il y a quelque temps, imprimée de vostre nouvelle facon) a Monsieur Slusius,[9] qui m'a respondu la dessus bien amplement, et qui semble avoir envie de conferer avec vous sur cete matiere, come vous verrez par la suite.[10] Il dit donc dans sa premiere lettre du 22 novembre 1670 [N.S.];

"Alhazeni problematis constructionem, a Viro Nobilissimo ad vos transmissam ut vidi, protinus eandem esse cum mea suspicabar [...] neque enim (ut hoc obiter addam) quicquam hujusmodi in schedis ejus repertum intellexi."

Jusques icy Monsieur Sluse dans sa 1re lettre; dans l'autre du 9me mars 1671 [N.S.] il dit;[11]

"Quod ad Alhazeni Problema attinet [...] libenter cum ipso communicarem."

Vous voiez, Monsieur, la franchise de ce grand homme; vous en userez selon vostre discretion, et, si vous ne luy escrivez pas vous mesme sur ce sujet,[12] m'instruirez, s'il vous plait, de ce que ie luy respondray là dessus. Je me croiois aucunement obligé de vous faire scavoir tout ce qui s'est passé entre luy et moy en cete matiere; ce qu'ayant fait, vous aurez assez de bonté, de pardonner cete prolixité, puisque i'ay eu assez de patience de transcrire tout cela de ma propre main, ne m'y osant fier à mon copiste.

J'ay mis icy les dernieres Transactions: Monsieur vostre Pere a eu quelques unes des precedentes, que, peut estre, il vous a desia envoyez. Vous prendrez tout en bonne part de Monsieur

      Vostre tres humble et tres obeissant Serviteur
          Oldenburg

Quand on m'escrit par la poste, on continue tousiours cete adresse,
 A Monsieur
Monsieur Grubendol
    à
     Londres.
Rien que cela.

A Londres le 22 juillet 1671.

P.S. Dans les Transactions prochaines on mettra la responce de Monsieur Wallis au livre nouveau de Monsieur Hobbes, dont il est parlé dans celles, qui sont encloses icy.[13]

ADDRESS
 A Monsieur
 Monsieur Christian Hugens de Zulichem,
    a
     Paris

TRANSLATION

Sir,

Having learned from your father that you had returned to Paris in good health,[1] and such a good opportunity as Mr. Vernon's offering himself to let me greet you and congratulate you upon your recovery, I thought I ought not to neglect it.[2]

You must know then, Sir, that all your friends here, who are many, rejoice greatly that your health is now so good as to permit you to return to philosophy and promise themselves that something extraordinary will emerge from your studies, reinforced by a renewed vigor of mind and spirit. We also await many considerable matters from your colleagues, which we have been led to expect for some considerable time, particularly the measurement of the earth, the anatomy of several animals, and the description of certain plants.[3] Your Academy, rejoicing as it does in all things necessary to bring it about, will, without doubt, make the world see the power of clear-sighted minds, as also how many fine and useful things they can produce.

As for the Royal Society, it is not meeting at all at present, having begun the vacation it is in the habit of taking at this time of year. Aside from that, it continues to experiment as much as possible. It is to be hoped that it will work better afterwards. Some of its Fellows have recently published new books: Mr Boyle on the strange rarefaction of air, etc., and *The Usefulness of Experimental Philosophy*, Volume II; he is at present considering his reply to the objections which Mr. More made to some of his experiments,[4] as also a pretty and very philosophical treatise on gems.[5] Mr. Wallis, though sick with a quartan fever, has completed the last part of his treatise *De motu et mechanica*, which will come from the press any day now. Mr. Lower has added to his book *De corde* a little discourse *De origine catharri*.[6] Mr. Willis is publishing at this very moment two treatises, one, *De anima brutorum*, the other, *De morbis capitis*.[7] Mr. Mercator something on logarithms.[8] Further, Sir, I must not conceal from you that I have communicated (I hope not against your wish) the construction of Alhazen's problem (which you sent us some time ago, printed by your new method) to Mr. Sluse,[9] who has replied in a pretty full manner, and he seems to wish to discuss the matter with you as you will see by what follows.[10] He says, then, in his letter of 22 November 1670 [N.S.]:

[*The long quotation which follows is taken from Sluse's Letter 1548; for the translation, see Volume VII, pp. 252–55.*]

So far Mr. Sluse in his first letter; in the other of 9 March 1671 [N.S.] he says:[11]

[*The next paragraph is taken from Sluse's Letter 1643; for the translation, see Volume VII, p. 438*].

You see, Sir, the frankness of this great man; you will treat him according to your discretion and, if you do not write to him yourself on this subject,[12] please instruct me what I should reply to him about it. I thought myself at the least obliged to let you know all that has passed between him and myself in this matter, and having done so, you will be good enough to forgive this prolixity, since I have had the patience to transcribe all this with my own hand, not daring to trust my amanuensis.

I have put with this the latest *Transactions*; your father has had some of the earlier ones and has, perhaps, already sent them to you. You will take everything in good part from, Sir,

Your very humble and obedient servant,
Oldenburg

When anyone writes to me by the post he should always continue to use this address,

A Monsieur
Monsieur Grubendol
à
Londres.

Nothing else.
London, 22 July 1671.

P.S. In the next *Transactions* will be Mr. Wallis's reply to the new book by Mr. Hobbes, which is spoken of in those which are inclosed here.[13]

ADDRESS
   To Mr. Christiaan Huygens of Zulichem,
        Paris

NOTES

1 See Letter 1531 in Vol. VII, and its note 3.
2 According to a letter from Collins to Gregory of 6 May 1671 (Turnbull, *Gregory*, p. 185; Rigaud, II, 221), Vernon had made a visit to London; presumably he returned to Paris in late July.
3 All this has been mentioned before, being the work of Picard (Vol. VI, pp. 433–36), Perrault (Vol. VII, Letter 1648), and Dodart (above, Letter 1731).
4 See Letter 1733.
5 *An Essay about the Origine and Virtues of Gems* (London, 1672.)
6 See Vol. VII, Letter 1487 and note 8.
7 See Letter 1687, note 13.
8 Collins records (Turnbull, *Gregory*, p. 153) Mercator's proposal of some months before to have Moses Pitt publish his table of logarithms and *Cyclomathia*. Apparently nothing emerged.
9 See Vol. VII, Letter 1528 and its note 4.
10 See Vol. VII, Letter 1548: we have abridged the following long quotation, which is from pp. 246–50; for the translation, see pp. 252–55.
11 See Vol. VII, Letter 1643, p. 480, and, for the translation, p. 443.
12 Huygens did not write directly to Sluse, but replied to Oldenburg about this matter on 28 October 1671.
13 In fact Oldenburg refers to Wallis's answer to Hobbes's *Rosetum geometricum* which was to appear in *Phil. Trans.*, no. 73 (17 July 1671); this was presumably not available so early as the twenty-second of the month.

1753
Oldenburg to Werden
24 July 1671

Werden's Letter 1732 of 24 June is endorsed as received on 22 July and answered on 24 July 1671.

1754
Oldenburg to Kisner
24 July 1671

From the memorandum in Royal Society MS. K, no. 13

Acc. d. 18. jul. 71.
resp. d. 24. julii
...5. libros in Catal. nota 10 st. Obtuli commercium, cum Kornmanno et Medicis Franco-furtensibus.

TRANSLATION

Received 18 July, answered on 24 July.
[Asked for] the five books as marked in the catalogue, 10 [shillings?] Offered a correspondence with Kornmann and the Frankfurt physicians.

NOTE

This very rough memorandum for a reply to Letter 1694 is written on a fragment of the envelope, and is nearly illegible.

1755
Vogel to Oldenburg
25 July 1671

From the original in Royal Society MS. F 1, no. 32

Nobilissimo Viro
Henrico Oldenburgio
S.P.D.
Martinus Fogelius

Silui hactenus, Vir Nobilissime, partim propter mutatas aedes, partim propter 3 libellos Docimasticos a me recognitos, quod prima quavis occasione Joannes Blauius Amstelodami excudet. Sunt autem hi; Modestini Faesii cum notis nonnullis D. Jungii;[1] Cyriaci Schreitmanni, ita cum notis Jungii,[2] & Anonymi libellus, omnes Germanico idiomate, quo scripserunt.[3] alia vice addam alias, ut uno volumina omnes de hac arte libelli contineantur, qui aegre hodie inveniuntur.

Jam me accingo conscribendae Introductioni in Historiam Lynceam.[4] Vellem quam maxime Galilei vitae Anglicae impressae compos fieri. Si curare posses, ut Schulzio mittatur, plurimum tibi debebo. Vincentius Viviani, pleraque ista suggessit. Ipse etiam habeo, quod Viviani, nunquam vidit.

Boilei adeo illustris fama est, ut neutri Bibliopolae geminata libelli, de Qualitatibus Cosmicis cum dissertatione de negata Quiete, Editio fraudi esse possit.[5] Schulzius pleraque sua exemplaria jam distraxit.

modo imprimi curat Schefferi memorabilia Gentis Sueticae.[6]

imposterum Boileo inscio nihil tale fiet.[7]

Boilei dissertationem, quam promisisti, nondum accepi.

Volebam Lachmundi de Hildesiae fossilibus[8] & libellum de Cordis mira Inversione per presentem Virum juvenem tibi mittere, sed a Schulzio jam missum intelligo.[9]

Nihilominus Eximii hujus Viri notitiam tibi parare non inutile duxi, partim ut ex ipso Fodinarum Suedicarum, quas curiose lustravit, historiam cognosceres, partim ut quod olim ab ipso observari amplius in Suedia velis, coram eidem exponeres. Nomen ei est Johannis GEZELI. Pater est Episcopus Aboensis.[10] Cum animi dotes ipsum ultro commendent, nolo cum pluribus tibi commendare.

Folium mitto unum ex Ravii Chronologia,[11] quod pridem mittere debui. sed cum aedes, ut dixi, mutaverim, inter schedas meas hactenus latuit. Si integram desideras, ut ejus vanitatem rectius percipias, toto tantum mone. Parat modo idem, qui Praefationem adjecit, Apodixin (si diis placet) temporum restitutorum; satis operose elaboratam. in qua Ravii Chronologiam firmare conatur, Observationibus Astronomicis, quas unicam temporum restituendas normam esse nosti, insuper habitis.

Vale & de Hispanorum Toxico, & Galilaei vita, quaeso, quid sperare habeam, quamprimum significa. Scribebam Hamburgi d. 25 Jul. 1671.

TRANSLATION

Martin Vogel sends many greetings to the very noble Mr. Henry Oldenburg

I have been silent hitherto, noble Sir, partly because I have been moving house and partly because of three little books concerned with docimasy or the art of assaying that I have edited and that Johannes Blaeu of Amsterdam is to print as soon as possible. They are these: by Modestin Fachs with Jung's notes;[1] by Cyriac Schreittmann, also with Jung's notes;[2] and a little anonymous work, all in German as they were written.[3] Another time I will add others, so that a single volume may contain all the pamphlets on this art which today are hard to come by.

I am now pulling myself together to write the introduction to the history of the Lincei.[4] I wish very much to lay hands on the life of Galileo printed in England. If you could manage to send it to Schulz I should be very grateful. Vincenzo Viviani has contributed much towards it. I also have much that Viviani never saw.

Boyle's reputation is so great that the double publication of that little book *De qualitatibus cosmicis* together with *De absoluta quieta* cannot damage either bookseller.[5] Schulz has already distributed many of his copies.

He is now at work printing Scheffer's noteworthy matters concerning the Swedish people.[6]

For the future, nothing of that kind will be done without Boyle's knowledge.[7]

I have not yet received the dissertation by Boyle that you promised me.

I had intended to send you by this young man here Lachmund's *Descriptio fossilium in tractu Hildesheimensi*[8] and a little book on an extraordinary inversion of the heart, but I understand that Schulz has sent them already.[9]

Nevertheless, I have not thought it vain to bring this excellent person to your attention, partly so that you may gather from him an account of the mines in Sweden, which he has examined in detail, and partly so that you may in person explain to him what further observations you wish him to make in Sweden. His name is Johannes Gezelius, his father being Bishop of Åbo.[10] As his own abilities will commend him further, I do not wish to commend him to you in many words.

I send one sheet from Ravius' *Chronologia*,[11] which I should have sent before. But since I have moved house (as I told you), it lay hid among my papers. If you wish for the whole thing, to perceive the depths of his folly, just let me know. The same person who added the preface is now preparing a proof of the restoration of chronology (if the gods permit), pretty elaborately worked out, in which he tries to confirm Ravius' chronology by further astronomical observations, which as you know are the sole criteria by which chronology may be put to rights.

Farewell, and please let me know as soon as possible what I may hope for as regards the Spanish poison and the life of Galileo. Hamburg, 25 July 1671.

NOTES

Reply to Letter 1678 (Vol. VII).
1 *Probier Büchlein* (Leipzig, 1595).
2 *Probierbüchlein* (Frankfurt, 1578).
3 We could not discover that these were ever published in this edition.
4 See Vol. VII, Letter 1668 and note 4, and Letter 1678.
5 This refers to the impending publication of a Latin edition of the *Cosmicall Qualities* (with other tracts) by Richard Davis at Oxford, following upon the three Amsterdam/Hamburg issues by Schulz and his partners. See also Letter 1668 and note 3.
6 Presumably Johann Scheffer (see Vol. III, p. 262, note), *De antiquis verisque regni Sueciae insignibus liber singularis* (Stockholm, 1678).
7 That is, no further unauthorized translation of his writings into Latin; see Letter 1678 (Vol. VII).
8 Friedrich Lachmund, *Admirandorum fossilium quae in tractu Hildesheimensi reperiuntur, descriptio* (Hildesheim, 1669) is reviewed in *Phil. Trans.*, no. 77 (20 November 1671), 3016–17.
9 We have not been able to trace this pamphlet as it was not reviewed in the *Phil. Trans.*
10 Johannes Gezelius, the younger (1647–1718), succeeded his father of the same name (1690) as Bishop of Åbo (now Turku, in southern Finland, west of Helsinki), after holding a cure at Narva. Besides completing his father's commentary on the Bible, he translated the Scriptures into Finnish. He was later a correspondent.
11 Christian Ravius (or Rau, 1603–77), *Dei summi honorem et sacri fontis hebraei gloriam ex eadem, unica vera et infallibilis chronologia biblica* (Kiel, 1670). Ravius' chronology, placing the creation in the year 4140, was rejected by many other scholars as fanciful. We do not know anything about a preface to this work (which is not in the British Museum Library).

1756
Oldenburg to Beale
25 July 1671

This letter was acknowledged by Beale in Letter 1764 of 6 August as received on 3 August.

1757
Oldenburg to Lister
27 July 1671

From the original in Bodleian Library MS. Lister 34, f. 31

Sir

Yr considerable Accompt concerning Vegetable excrescencies, so generously communicated in your last of july 17, I have well received, and doe intend, God permitting, to impart thesame to the R. Society, as soon as they shall open their meetings again, wch are now intermitted, as they are wont to be about this season.[1] I hope, you will permit the publication of this matter, especially since Mr Willughby, who hath formerly seen it, when you wrote it to Mr Wray, giveth it also this Character, that it is so very ingenious and true, yt he would fain it were known;[2] who also adds, that when I shall have sent him word, I have received it from you, (wch I doe by this very post,)[3] he will send me a great many Observations, both of his own and Mr Wrays, to confirm it.

Now, Sir, yt I may not seem altogether ungratefull in my returns, I shall communicate to you an accompt, I lately received from Francford, concerning Tinctures extracted out of ye dung of Insects. It came to me in a Latin letter, as followeth;[4]

"Dn. Doctor Kornman librum edet de Tincturis seu Essentiis Stercorum quorundam Vermium quos ex quibuslibet floribus vel herbis, mediante putrefactione obtinet; qui postmodum eadem herba vel flore nutriti, stercora ejiciunt, in quibus tinctura herbae tum color, et vis illius herbae reperitur; ita in momento e stercoribus, collectis ex vermibus rosas comedentibus, tincturam extrahit rubicundissimam. Sic parili modo ex aliis."

I doubt not, Sir, but you have also been curious this way; and should therefore be glad to be informed of some particular Observations, by you made about it; yt so I may acquaint my friends and correspondents abroad, yt here in England yt matter hath not been left un-considered.

There is another note in thesame Francofordian Letter, (of a different subject,) wch perhaps will not displease you neither. The words are these;[5]

"Experimentum Burrhi, de restituendis Oculis instituimus, alio tamen modo; succum enim Chelidonii majoris sumpsimus, oculos duos dissecuimus, oculis applicavimus; spatio 24. horarum tum oculos, tum (quod miratu dignum) Visionem restituimus."

I am sorry, the Author mentions not the account, upon wch ye Experiment was made. Mean time, I have written to him, and desired to learn yt circumstance, as also the particulars of ye method used in yt Tryal.[6]

Since you are pleased to remit yr answer to the other matters in my former letter[7] to another time, I willingly stay for yr conveniency, and remain

Sir yr faithful servant
Oldenburg

ADDRESS

    To his honored friend
    Martin Lister Esquire
    at his house wthout
    Mickelgate-barr at
          York.

NOTES

Reply to Letter 1751.
1 In fact it was not read, for the Society did not meet again till 2 November after the letter's publication in September.
2 See Letter 1746.
3 See the next letter.
4 See Letter 1694, p. 37; for the translation, see p. 39.
5 See Letter 1694, p. 37; for the translation, p. 39.
6 In Letter 1754, of which only a memorandum survives.
7 Letter 1748.

1758
Oldenburg to Willughby
27 July 1671

From the copies in Royal Society MS. O 2, no. 53 and Letter Book IV, 348–49

An Answer To M. Willughby's Letter of july 10. 1671.

Sr

Next to my hearty thanks for your last of july 10th. I cannot forbeare to let you know, that I have now received the ingenious M. Listers considerable Accompt and opinion concerning vegetable Excrescencyes, [1]and do now claim ye promise, you were in the said letter pleased so generously to make me, of sending us a great many observations both of your owne and M. Wrays, to confirme the same.

When you shall have got some of those shining scolopenders, or Julus's, which you say, you formerly saw in the cloisters of Trinity-Colledge in Cambridge, we shall be very glad to have a sight of some of them. I shall here impart to you an accompt I received the other day out of Germany from a Dr of Physick residing at Francford, concerning Tinctures drawne out of the Dung of Insects; wich I shall do in the same language and words I received it. viz.[2]

"Dn. Dr. Kornman librum edet de Tincturis, seu essentiis stercorum, quorundam vermium, quos ex quibuslibet floribus, vel herbis mediante putrefactione, obtinet. qui postmodum, eadem herba, vel flore nutriti, stercora ejiciunt, in quibus tinctura herbae, tum color, et vis illius herbae reperitur; ita in momento e stercoribus, collectis ex vermibus, rosas comedentibus, tincturam extrahit rubicundissimam. sic parili modo ex alijs."

I am Sir

Your Humble Servant
Oldenburg

London July 27 1671

NOTES

Reply to Letter 1746.
1 See Letter 1751.
2 See Letter 1694, p. 37; a translation of this passage will be found on p. 39.

1759
Oldenburg to Wallis
1 August 1671

As Oldenburg noted in his next letter to Wallis (Letter 1763), he enclosed here a printed paper addressed by Thomas Hobbes to the Royal Society. Wallis received the letter and paper on 3 August (Letter 1761).

For the beginning of Wallis's controversy with Hobbes over the latter's *Rosetum geometricum*, see Letter 1736. Beginning in July 1671, Hobbes printed several rejoinders to Wallis's refutations, three of which, entitled *To the Right Honourable and others, the... Members of the Royal Society* (B.M. shelf mark 740. a. 17/4, 5), were presented to the Society on 2 November 1671, together with a copy of *Rosetum geometricum*. Early in August Wallis began to prepare replies to the first two of these (see Royal Society MS. W 1, no. 124a), and his refutation of all four finally appeared, in English, in *Phil. Trans.*, no. 75 (18 September 1671), 2241–50, and as a separate publication as *An Answer to three papers of Mr. Hobbes, lately published in the months of August and... September* (B.M. shelf mark 740. c. 23 (1).) Hobbes rejoined finally with *Considerations upon the answer of Dr. Wallis to the three papers of Mr. Hobbes* (B.M. shelf mark 740. a. 17/6).

1760
Flamsteed to Oldenburg
1 August 1671

From the original in Royal Society MS. F 1, no. 72

Derby August 1: 1671

Mr Oldenburge

I understand by my kinsman Mr Willson yt hee shewed yu my letter to him & that yu intended mee one back by him but that hee had not ye leasure to call for it. Sr I have desired my freind Mr Sargeant to waite upon yu wth this which desires yu will please to send an answer to my last[1] by him yt I may have yr sentiments concerneing my designe, if yu can not send by him I would gladly receave any thing from yu by ye publick post: Sr I have been lately in Lancashire where I staid one night at Mr Townlys house[2] who hath put some letters of Mr Gascoigne to Mr Crabtree with the answers into my hands.³ I understand yt some of theire papers are in ye hands of Mr Jonas More⁴ of whom, if I knew how I would desire ye like favor I meane to lend them mee for a perusall I have wrote to MrCollins to move him about them & I hope if occasion bee yu will not refuse him yr assistance.⁵ I have wrote to him likewise for Cassini's booke de motibus Circumjovialium which I saw at Townly⁶ & which I hope by yr meanes hee may be informed where to procure me Sr with my thankes alwaies presented for yr favors I subscribe

yr obliged friend & servant
John Flamsteed

ADDRESS
 To Henry Oldenburg Esq
  at his house in the
  Middle of ye Pell mell
  neare St. James'es
  Westminster these
   present

NOTES

1 Letter 1740; we do not know anything of Mr. Sargeant, except that he had been Flamsteed's schoolfellow.
2 Presumably Towneley (the house) is intended, which was the home of Richard Towneley (1629–1707), who is chiefly notable for his interest in observational astronomy and his improvement of William Gascoigne's filar micrometer. In his later autobiographical recollections (Baily, pp. 29–30) Flamsteed recorded that it was in June 1671 that he went to visit *Christopher* Towneley (1604–1674), uncle of Richard, who was not at home. This contemporary record suggests some later lapse of memory.
3 It was certainly Christopher Towneley who had been the friend of Jeremiah Horrox (1617?–41; see Vol. II, p. 165, note 5), William Crabtree (1610–?44; see the same note), and William Gascoigne (1612?–44; see Vol. III, p. 439, note 1), and who had collected the correspondence and papers of these astronomers after their premature deaths. Unfortunately a number of the papers examined by Flamsteed at this time were destroyed by fire not long afterwards.
4 Jonas Moore (1617–79) was another northerner associated with Christopher Towneley. For his possession of Horrox's papers, see Vol. II, p. 164. Moore had been in London as a mathematical teacher since 1649. He was appointed to the Tower as Surveyor of the Ordnance in 1673.
5 Flamsteed's letter to Collins of 1 August 1671 is printed in Rigaud, II, 118–22. His interest in these English astronomers extended back over several months.
6 G. D. Cassini, *Ephemerides mediceorum syderum* (Bologna, 1668; see Vol. V, p. 240); the request is not in any extant letter to Collins.

1761
Wallis to Oldenburg
4 August 1671
From the original in Royal Society MS. W 1, no. 124

To your letter wch I received last night, with Mr. *Hobs's* English paper inclosed, had I not been sick in bed I had presently writt you an Answere. But it is time inough this morning. As to ye first part of his paper, which concerns my *Prop 1. Cap. 5 De Motu*: When he understands it better, he will be of another mind: In the meantime, I am not bound to give him understanding nor is it worth the answering. As for ye Royal Society, whom hee would set on work: I presume, they may find wherein to imploy their time better, than in answering his idle questions. As to ye second part of his paper, which concerns his own *Prop. 5 Roset.* it was answered in this Latine before it was written in English, in my Latine Confutation of his *Rosetum*.[1] As he doth now repeat it in English, his demonstration is peccant in those words (*col. 2 lin. 3, 33, 34,*), *Therefore—the Arc on TV, the Arc on RS, ye Arc on CA, cannot be continually proportional*; (with all that follows:) there being no strength in that inference, whether DC or RS be supposed ye greater; for it may be either notwithstanding his Demonstration. And as to his whole paper; it was very well known by what he had written before, *that Mr Hobs is no Mathematician*; and therefore he might have spared ye pains of publishing this paper further to demonstrate it.

This you may (if you think fit) insert in the transactions for July, onely leaving out ye date.

Yours
Joh. Wallis

Astrop. Aug. 4. 1671.

ADDRESS
   These
   For Mr Henry Oldenburg in
      the Palmal near St James's
         London

NOTES

Reply to Letter 1759.
1 See Letter 1736, note.

1762
Oldenburg to Leibniz
5 August 1671

From the original in Hannover MSS., f. 11
Printed in Gerhardt, pp. 142-43

Amplissime Vir,

Ante paucos dies Studioso cuidam Frankofurtensi, Hamburgum hinc velificaturo, literas ad Te datas commisi, satis, ut puto, prolixas, quas Tibi rite traditas jam esse dubitare nolim.[1] Continent illas, quid philosophorum nostratium nonnulli de Hypothesi tua sentiant, quidque Ego de eadem in Transactionibus philosophicis commemorandum duxerim. Supersunt nonnulla in literis tuis novissime ad me datis, quibus responsum debeo, quod tamen cum paratum necdum habeam, in aliud tempus differre cogor. Interim dimittere harum gerulum nobilissimum[2] haud potui, quin Te salutarem, simul et fidem facerem, me reliqua, quae de me exspectas, quamprimum fieri id poterit, confecturum. Caeterum cum eximius Helmontius,[3] affectu mihi conjunctissimus, propediem ad nos sit reversurus, poteris, si placet, ipsi tuto committere, quaecunque forsan mihi scribenda vel communicanda occurrerint. In novissimo Nundinarum Francofurtensium Catalogo unus alterve liber juridicus occurrit, quorum tituli singulare quid spondere videntur. Sunt ille quidem, Strykii Tractatus de Jure Sensuum,[4] et Gutherii Tractatus de Jure Manium.[5] Siquidem libros hos lectu dignos judicaveris; ut mihi hac occasione transmittas, rogo, operam daturo, ut quibusdam authoribus hinc tibi mittendis beneficium rependam. Vale, et raptim ex nimia festinatione scribenti ignosce

Tibi Addictissimo
H. Oldenburg

Londini d. 5. Augusti 1671.

ADDRESS
   Clarissimo et Amplissimo
   Viro, Domino Gothofredo Guilielmo
   Leibnitio J.U.D. et
   Consiliario Moguntino
         Maintz

TRANSLATION

Worthy Sir,

A few days since I entrusted a pretty full letter (as it seems to me) to a certain student from Frankfurt who was sailing hence bound for Hamburg, and I have no doubt that it has already been safely delivered to you.[1] It contained the thoughts of some of our philosophers concerning your hypothesis and what I thought fit to say about it in the *Philosophical Transactions*. There are some points remaining over from your most recent letter to me upon which I owe you a reply but as I have not yet prepared my answer I must defer them to another occasion. Meanwhile I could hardly dismiss the very noble bearer of these lines[2] without sending you my greetings and at the same time promising you that I will complete the remainder of what you expect from me, as soon as possible. Moreover as the distinguished Van Helmont,[3] who is very closely bound to me by friendship, will soon be returning among us you can, if you please, safely intrust to him whatever it may occur to you to write or communicate to myself. In the most recent catalogue of the Frankfurt Fair there are one or two legal books, whose titles seem to promise something out of the way. They are, a certain Stryk, *De jure sensuum*[4] and Gutherius *Tractatus de Jure Manium*.[5] If you shall judge these books worth reading, I beg you to send them me by this opportunity, and I will endeavor to repay you with some authors sent hence to you. Farewell, and forgive my haste in writing in too great a hurry.

Your most devoted
H. Oldenburg

London 5 August 1671

ADDRESS
To the very famous and worthy Mr. Gottfried Wilhelm Leibniz, LL.D. Councilor at Mainz,
Mainz.

NOTES

1 Letter 1724.
2 His name does not seem to be recorded.
2 Francis Mercury van Helmont; see Letter 1655, note 3 (Vol. VII).
4 Samuel Stryk, *De jure sensuum* (Frankfurt, 1665).
5 See Letter 1745, note 9.

1763
Oldenburg to Wallis
5 August 1671
From the original in Bodleian Library MS. Savile 104, ff. 8–9

Sir,

On Tuesday last, being ye 1st of August, I sent to Oxford for you a Letter,[1] wth an inclosed printed Paper, by M. Hobbes addressed to ye R. Soc. about two propositions, whereof one is deliver'd by you, ye other by him, desiring the Judgement of ye Society concerning ym. I hope, you have received it ere this, and are ready to give us yr thoughts thereupon. Now I thought good to convey to you a copy of the Transactions, wherein yr answer to his Rosetum is printed;[2] wherein I can find but two or three inconsiderable faults of ye presse (marked by me in this printed copy) whereof one is found in ye original written copy, viz. yt of p. 2207. l. 11. where it should be, *p. 49.* instead of *50.* (wch I found by chancing to compare yt quotation wth ye *Rosetum.*) In yesame original there was omitted ye number of ye line quoted in *p. 49*; wch number, I hope, you will find rightly supplied in ye print, where *p. 2207. l. 24.* it is *49. lin. 12.* whereas in the written copy there was no more than, *p. 49. lin.* (wthout ye number of ye line.) I had nobody to read wth me, when I review'd [for ye] presse, wch I was fain to doe twice, and yet could not [get] it done altogether to my mind.

[Mr H]obbes hath sent me another printed Copy of his Rosetum, wherein I find some words blotted out; and some alter'd; wch I found not done in ye first book, I received. I know not, whether you found any such changes, made wth ye pen, in ye Copy, you had of yt Rosetum. As, p. 35. l. 8. for *MC* he hath made it *NC*; p. 46. l. ult. he hath made it *fa* ad *ae*; p. 47 l. 10. he hath made it. *MF* sive *Md.* p. 50. l. 10 he hath made it, Ducta ergo $B\theta$ aequalis erit $\alpha\zeta$;[3] ibid. l. 19. it must be, $\alpha\zeta$; p. 51 l. ult. he hath quite blotted out ye words between *Ck*, and, *aequales*. And again p. 52. l. 1.2. he hath struck out the words between, *aequales erunt*, and, *Quare tres*.[4] Again p. 59. l. 5. it must be, ita *BG* ad *BC*. There is one alteration more p. 62. to yt Consectarium,[5] but I know not what to make of it.

I hear, yt Hobbes sent one of the printed English sheets of his to the king on munday last, and yt ye next day he came himself to his Majty, and there vapour'd of his abilities, and yt Dr. Wallis had no Geometry, but what he got from him. Wch, if true, is so intolerable an impudence, yt he ought to be soundly lash't for it; and I was very sorry, yt none of our Mathematicall Society men, yt know both you and him, were present, to tell him, yt he durst not say such words to yr face. I think, he ought to be perstringed ad vivum[6] and it cannot be too smart, so it be but wth observing yt decorum, wch becoms members of ye R. Society. Sir, you see my freedom; whereupon you may act as shall seem good to yr discretion. I remain.

Yrs

London August 5. 71.

ADDRESS
    To his honor'd friend
    Dr John Wallis, Savilian
    Professor of Geometry, and one
    of his Majies Chaplains
          Oxford

NOTES

The paper is torn in several places causing the loss of some words and particularly the signature.
1 Letter 1759.
2 *Phil. Trans.*, no. 73 (17 July 1671), 2202–9.
3 "Accordingly when $B\theta$ is drawn it will be equal to $\alpha\zeta$..."
4 "they will be equal... For which reason three..."
5 Consequence or corollary.
6 "criticized very severely."

1764
Beale to Oldenburg
6 August 1671
From the original in B.M. MS. Add. 4294, ff. 16–17

Aug. 6. 71
Deare brother,

I was halfe lost, till I received yours of Jul. 25 wch arrived not here, till Aug. 3. So yt it remained wth yu, or in some post-house above a week. And I began to feare yr health; & yu will hardly imagine, how it revivd me to heare of yrs, & Mr Boyles health. & yt yu take care of ye 3 particulars I lately suggested. And yet I heare nothing from Dr Chamb[erlayne], whether he received my large letter, wch was superscribed as yu instructed me, to his Lodgings in Hatton house or garden, Holburne.[1] I hope yu do in yr Councells sometimes debate, & deliberate upon all expedients, *Howe to beare up ye reputation, of ye R.S.*, & to counterpose & antidote ye Universityes, *& London*, & thence England, against ye malignity of ye obstreperous Dunces. It stings me, yt ye lofty pretenders to R[eligion] should abet a vilaine[2] *against* ye RS & his Majesty's everlasting honour. I thinke, I have cause to Feare yt many of ye RS, are allmost discouraged. Their vertue, & resolution is tryed to ye utmost. *Steele* wilbe *steele*, & will not shrinke at ye appearance of *Gold* or *sylver*. Though ye wanton Satyrist hath too much truth on his side.

> Quisque habet nummos, secura naviget, aura,
> Fortunamque suo temperet arbitrio
> Multa loquor; quidvis nummis praestibus, opta,
> Et veniet, clausum possidet arca Jovem.[3]

And some of yu do not want money. Nor greate friends: neyther power, influence, nor personall grandeur. The witty Sir Tho. Overbury, in his characters,[4] sd something to this purpose, yt in *our Universityes*, The Tutors were (in a broad phrase) but paedants their pupills scholeboyes & the old men mopes.

Now all Gods blessings on our mercantile designe towards Japan, & on ye philosophical Comissions thither, & all over ye world.[5]

The Parisian *observatory* cannot do ye greate things in Astronomy wthout correspondents amongst yu, or at greater distances. The Satyrist chides us againe.[6] Ubi est Astronomia? Ubi consultissima Sapientiae via. Quis apud nos venit in templum, et votum fecit, si philosophiae fontem invenisset? Pecuniae cupiditas haec Tropica instituit. Ne quis dubitet pecuniam concupiscere, Jovem quoque peculio exorat. Nolito ergo mirari, si pulcherrimae actes deficiant, quum omnibus Dijs, hominibusque formosior videatur massa auri, quam quicquid Apelles, Phidiasque (Graeculi delirantes) fecerunt. Priscis ante temporibus, cum adhuc nuda placeret virtus, vigebant artes ingenuae; summumque certamen inter homines erat, ne quid profuturum saeculis diu lateret. Itaque harcula[7] omnium plantarum succos Democritus expressit; et ne lapidum virgultorumque vis lateret, aetatem inter Experimenta consumpsit. Eudoxus quidem in cacumine excelsissimi montis consenuit, ut astrorum, caelique motus deprehenderet; et Chrysippus, ut ad Inventionem sufficeret, ter helleboro animum detersit. Ut ad Plastas convertar, Lysippus statuae unius lineamentis inhaerentem inopia exstinxit; et Miron, qui paene hominum animas, ferarumque aere comprehenderat, non invenit haeredem. At nos vino scortisque demersi, ne paratos quidem artes audemus cognoscere, sed accusatores antiquitatis, vitia tantum docemus, et discimus.

Sr This, by a fewe transpositions, is fuller to our purpose, then Dr Sharrocks iudicious citation in his praeface to Honourable Mr Boyles *First Tome of Usefullnes*,[8] & et beares ye Age of 1600 yeares. And it will serve yu for a spur, to drive on some generous spirits to praefer public merite, & future glory, before ye Gods or Idols of Gold, & sylver.

Yu have them, yt by melting downe some of their Idols of Gold, are able to build Observatoryes, & to retaine such, as can manage yr best engines to ascertaine Astronomy in a fewe yeares infinitely beyond all yt is hitherto done by mortalls, from ye beginning of ye world to this day.

I hope all generous spirits, wilbe fervently excited to do ye more in opposition to those degenerated men, by whom The Egyptian Sphynges, Monstra Deum, et latrator Anubis[9] are animated to affront ye greatest merite, & ye highest honour.

1. I thanke God, Mr Evelyns busines[10] & mine doth prosper wonderfully in many places of England. Mr Austen[11] writes to me, yt ye Burgesses of Parliament for ye citty of Oxford Men of greate estates not far from Oxford, are greate planters of Redstrake. Namely Mr Whorwood,[12] whom Mr Austen furnished wth some Thousands (severall thousands are his words) of Redstrakes. & Col. Croke, & allso his brother, ye recorder of Oxford.[13] & many other Kts thereabout, & Gentlemen of Worth. This

(I tell him) is in one of ye eyes of ye Kingdome, & will invite Nobles, Physicians, civilians, & young Gentlemen, to do ye like, wn they are dispersed all abroade, & so to obtaine ye benediction of Ecclesiastics. He sells good cider in his house in Oxford, & is building another house for yt purpose. Yet he complains of Poverty, & would adresse for some reliefe to ye RS. I sent him a small mite, & answered him, yt ye RS had their hands full enough, & thanks little enough from some in Oxford. Who dares do as well for themselves, & us in & about Cambridge, as these do at Oxford. The example of Burgesses & a Recorder is leading & every way effectuall. Cannot Mr Ray rayse some mettald men in his mother University, so much obliged by his elaborate botanics? Trye him in yr next. It will be a meanes to purify their air from ye poison of their neighbouring fens. Orchards & fragrant Evergreens in all their gardens, walkes, avennues & confines, may free them from many plagues, & pestilences. Hoc agitur, ne quid profuturum Academiae et saeculis diutius negligatur.[14] The fruite is food, ye liquor is life spirite & medicine for longevity. The Parliamentmen[15] & Burgesses for Cambridge, are very famous & generous. Doe they do as well in this point, as those of Oxon? For ye reasone I told yu before, yt Camb[ridge] was one of our eyes, & my indulgent mother, (though I have since been obliged to Oxford for peculiar favours above my merits)[16] yt at Mr Hartlib's request, I allowed Roger Daniel, who had once to do wth ye printing presse in Camb[ridge] awell as in London, to publish those slight letters under ye inticeing Title *Herefordshire Orchards a patterne for all England*:[17] And I well remember wt convenient arable fields, a rich vale, & deepe lands, they have about Camb[ridge]. Who can doubt, but yt spacious groves of cider-Orchards, will perfume their vernall Winds,[18] & adorne ye University far beyond Dr Aglionbyes Leyden.[19]

Thus Sr I presse hard upon all my acquaintance, bono tamen publico.[20] And wt good thing hath not prosperd under yr countenance? And more yet would prosper, if some of yr chiefe Members had leysure to do wt they are able to do. Yr chiefe Astronomers, Opt, Mechan. & Physic.[21] Dr Ch Wren, Dr Meret, Mr Hooke &c are full of Businesses, & yet their busines is yr busines. & they do ye workes. wch others can only discourse, or write.

NOTES

1 See Letter 1722 and note 2.
2 Presumably Henry Stubbe.
3 "Whoever has money sails in a fair wind, and directs his fortune at his own pleasure. I have said enough: with money about you, wish for what you like and it will come.

Your safe has Jupiter shut up in it." (Petronius Arbiter, *Satyricon*, trans. Michael Heseltine, Loeb Classical Library, London and New York, 1913, pp. 310, 311.)

4 Sir Thomas Overbury (born 1581, murdered 1613) wrote a poem, *The Wife*, published posthumously in 1614; to the second edition (of the same year) were added twenty-one "characters," more being added to later editions. Only a few were by Overbury.

5 On 14 August Oldenburg prepared "Some Directions and Enquiryes concerning Japan" (Royal Society MS. Classified Papers XIX, no. 72) for the benefit of a certain "M. Peron" and "M. del Boe." At this time the expulsion of foreigners and the persecution of Christianity had already begun in Japan, but foreigners retained a meager base for trade isolated in Nagasaki harbor. Simon Delboe, a merchant (see Vol. V, p. 19, note), and Samuel Baron (as his name properly was) set out about this time in a ship called *The Return* on a trading voyage to Nagasaki, which they certainly reached. Delboe kept a journal, of which a part was published as the second appendix to Engelbert Kaempfer, *The History of Japan*, trans. J. G. Scheuchzer, F.R.S. (London, 1727–28).

6 "Where is astronomy? Where is the most appropriate path to knowledge? Who among us has come to the temple and made an offering, that he might discover the fount of philosophy? Greed for wealth has brought about these changes. Lest any one hesitate about the desire for money, they employ riches in supplicating Jupiter. So don't be surprised if good deeds are wanting when to gods and men alike heaps of gold seem more handsome than the works of those poor deluded Greeks, Apelles and Phidias. Once upon a time when virtue was prized for its own sake the liberal arts flourished and men rivaled each other in ensuring that nothing of benefit to posterity should remain undiscovered. And so Democritus squeezed the juice from every plant and, lest the virtue of any stone or shrub escape him, devoted a whole age to experiments. Eudoxus grew old on top of a very high mountain, trying to understand the motions of the stars and the heavens; and Chrysippus thrice purged his mind with hellebore to make it the more inventive. Now turning to sculpture, Lysippus died of want while dwelling on the form of a single statue, and Myron, who practically captured the souls of men and animals in bronze, found no successor. But we who are sunk in wine and lechery cannot even master the arts we were given, and are traitors to the past because vice is all we can teach or learn." (Petronius Arbiter, *Satyricon*, pp. 172–75; our translation.) Beale has rearranged the lines.

7 This word, plainly written, is meaningless and unnecessary (some texts have *herbarum* for *plantarum*). It is possibly a form of *arcula*: "into a little box."

8 See "The Publisher to the Reader" at the opening of *Some Considerations touching the Usefulnesse of Experimental Naturall Philosophy* (Oxford, 1663; Birch, *Boyle*, II, 1–3), where there is a brief quotation from Petronius. Robert Sharrock (1630–84) was a divine (and D.C.L. Oxford, 1661) much interested in botany; see Vol. I, p. 349, note 5.

9 "Egyptian sphinxes, marvels of the gods, and the Dog Anubis." Anubis was the Egyptian god of the dead, represented as a human figure with the head of a dog or jackal.

10 Silviculture.

11 See Vol. II, p. 330 and p. 331, note 1.

12 Probably Brome Whorwood (1615–84), M.P. for Oxford four times in the years 1661–81, of Holton.

13 Unton Croke, the younger, educated for the law, was active in the Parliamentary Army during the Civil Wars, becoming a colonel only in January 1659/60. Although he welcomed the restoration of the monarchy, he subsequently lived on his estates.

His elder brother Richard (1623–83), also educated as a lawyer and also a supporter of Parliament, was Recorder of Oxford for thirty years, and a Member of Parliament for Oxford for twenty years. He was knighted in 1680/1.

14 "Let this be done, that nothing may be longer neglected for the future of the University and posterity."
15 "Ptmen" in original.
16 Beale was educated at King's College, Cambridge, of which he became a Fellow, but received no formal honors from Oxford.
17 See Vol. I, p. 320, note, and p. 480, note 2.
18 Oldenburg wrote some questions to Newton about cider in 1672, which he answered, and Newton reported at greater length about the establishment of cider orchards near Cambridge in 1676 (see Newton, *Correspondence*, I, 255; II, 93, 110).
19 See the book mentioned in Letter 1603, note 8 (Vol. VII).
20 "but for the public good."
21 Presumably opticians, mechanicians, and physicians.

1765
Oldenburg to Fermat
7 August 1671

Fermat's Letter 1739 of 4 July is endorsed as having been answered on 7 August, eight days after its arrival.

1766
Oldenburg to Flamsteed
8 August 1671

According to Oldenburg's endorsement on Flamsteed's Letter 1760 he replied on this date, three days after receiving it. As Flamsteed's reply (Letter 1776) makes plain, it was sent by the same Mr. Sargeant who brought Flamsteed's letter, and was accompanied by several astronomical papers.

1767
Oldenburg to Pardies
10 August 1671

From the copy in Royal Society MS. O 2, no. 54

To ye Jesuite Pardies

Monsr,

Ayant reconu par l'honneur de la vostre du 18. juillet (qui ne me fut rendue par Monsr. Butler que le 8me de nostre Aoust) vostre passion extraordinaire pour les belles sciences, et vostre bienvueillance particuliere à une personne, qui s'est vouée à pousser de toutes ses forces le progres d'icelles, pour relever de plus en plus la dignité de la nature Humaine, et accroitre les advantages de la vie; Je n'ay pu m'abstenir de vous en tesmoigner par cellecy ma joye et ma reconnoissance. S'il y a dans les journaux, qui se publient icy tous les mois, des remarques, qui ont l'approbation des personnes scavantes et curieuses, il en faut attribuer la plus grande partie à la generosité et doctrine de mes correspondents. Et puisque, Monsieur, ceux de vostre celebre Societé ont l'avantage de faire, par le moien de leur correspondence universelle, quantité de belles et utiles observations sur la Nature et les Arts, je l'estimerois un effet reel de l'ardeur, que vous faitez reluire dans vostre lettre pour l'advancement des belles connoissances, si vous trouviez bon de nous faire part des choses de cette nature là, vous assurant, que je tascheray au possible de vous convaincre de ma gratitude. Je vous suis desia obligé du livre des belles remarques, que vous avez faites sur la lettre de M. des Cartes touchant la Lumiere: Je na'y rien à present pour recompenser vostre liberalité, que la version Angloise de vostre petit traité du Mouvement[1] et l'Hypothese Physique Neuve de Monsr Leibnitius,[2] Conseiller de son Altesse Electorale de Mayence, la quelle fut r'imprimée icy à cause du defaut d'Exemplaires, et la matiere semblant meriter la consideration des curieux par tout. Puisque cet Autheur nous donne ses pensees du mouvement tant abstract que concret (ce qui est le sujet qui entretient presentement les Philosophes d'Europe), on se croit obligé d'examiner tout ce qui se fait sur cette matiere si importante à toute la Philosophie; ce qui me fait juger, Monsieur, que vous serez bien aise de conferer cet escrit avec le vostre, et celuy de Mrs Wallis, Wren et Huges.³ Ce qu'ayant fait vous m'obligerez tres particulierement de m'en dire vostre opinion. Je seray ravi de recevoir la Geometrie de vostre composition, que vous avez eu la bonté de me promettre, et je cheriray toutes les occasions pour vous faire voir que je suis Monsieur

Vostre Treshumble et tres obeissant Serviteur
Oldenburg

A Londres
le 10 Aoust. 1671

TRANSLATION

Sir,

As I was led by the honor of yours of 18 July [N.S.] (only delivered to me by Mr. Butler on our eighth of August) to perceive your extraordinary passion for true science and your particular benevolence towards a person who has devoted all his strength to its progress, in order to elevate further the dignity of human nature, and enrich the comforts of life, I could not abstain from demonstrating to you by this my delight and gratitude. If there appear in the journals published monthly here anything approved by learned and scientific people, this must be ascribed in the greatest part to the generosity and learning of my correspondents. Now, Sir, since the members of your famous Society have the advantage, by the medium of their universal correspondence, of making a large number of fine and useful observations upon nature and the arts, I should regard it as a real effect of the ardor you reveal in your letter for the advancement of true knowledge if you would be so good as to impart to us things of this nature; and I assure you that I shall try as far as possible to convince you of my gratitude. I am already obliged to you for the book of fine comments made by you upon the letter on light of Mr. Descartes. I have at present nothing to send you by way of recompense for your generosity, except the English translation of your little treatise on motion¹ and the *New Physical Hypothesis* of Mr. Leibniz,² Councilor to His Highness, the Elector of Mainz, which was reprinted here because of a shortage of copies, and because the subject seemed to merit consideration by scientists everywhere. Since this author gives us his ideas about both abstract and concrete motion (the subject which at present occupies the philosophers of Europe), we believe it is necessary to examine everything written on this subject, so important for all philosophy; it was this, Sir, that made me judge that you would be very glad to compare this work with yours, and with those of Messieurs Wallis, Wren, and Huygens.³ When you have done this you will very much oblige me if you will tell me your opinion of it. I should be delighted to receive the *Geometry* which you have written, which you were so kind as to promise me, and I will cherish every opportunity to make you aware, Sir, that I am

Your very humble and obedient servant,
Oldenburg

London
10 August 1671

NOTES

Reply to Letter 1744.
1 See Letter 1733, note 23.
2 See Letter 1644, note 15 (Vol. VII).
3 See Vol. V, *passim*.

1768
Oldenburg to Wallis
10 August 1671

This letter was acknowledged by Wallis in Letter 1772.

1769
Cassini to Oldenburg
10 August 1671

From the original in Royal Society MS. C 1, no. 52

Clarissimo Doctissimo Viro
D. Henrico Oldenburg Regiae Societatis
Anglicae Secretario
J. D. Cassinus Salutem

Exemplar mearum aliquot observationum illustrium quarundam macularum solis ad te mitto Vir Clarissime, Astronomis vestris conferendam, ut ad earum restitutionem, si qua futura est, possint ad praescriptum tempus attendere.[1] Hae siquidem hesterna die prope occiduum marginem adhuc visibiles, hodie occasum subiere; post quindecim circiter dies, si tantum habuerint consistentiae, ad ortivum marginem rediturae. His addo observationem Saturni,[2] qui a primo ortu Heliaco anni huius visus rotundus ad diem usque undecimam Augusti; die 14 brachia susceperat quae fiunt indies illustriora, quae tamen iterum hoc anno disparitura censeo. Operae igitur praetium erit ad iteratam hanc disparitionem attendere, ex qua multum luminis Saturni Theoria susciperet.

Profectus est ex Regia Academia nostra D. Picardus Uraniburgum[3] ad observandum ibi Lunarem eclipsim proximi mentis Septembris aliaque ad meridianarum differentiam, Polique altitudinem, quas etiam observationes cum vestris gaudebimus comparare. Me Tibi regiaeque societait vestrae addictissimum profiteor. Vale. Parisijs vigesima augusti 1671 [N.S.]

TRANSLATION

J. D. Cassini greets the very famous and learned Mr. Henry Oldenburg, Secretary of the English Royal Society

I send you a copy of a few of my observations upon some remarkable sunspots, famous Sir, so that you may show it to your astronomers for them to attend to the improvement of the observations at the due time, if there be opportunity.[1] For since these sunspots were still visible yesterday near the western limb [of the sun], and had today passed under that limb, after about fifteen days if they retain their nature so long they should return to the eastern limb. To these I add the observation of Saturn,[2] which I have seen as rounded ever since the first heliacal rising of this year up to the eleventh of August [N.S.]; on the fourteenth it resumed its "arms," and these grow brighter day by day, though I believe that they will disappear again this year. It would accordingly be worthwhile to watch out for this repeated disappearance, from which the theory of Saturn may receive much benefit.

Our Mr. Picard has set out from our Royal Academy for Uraniburg,[3] in order to observe there the lunar eclipse of next September and other things [that are needful for establishing] the difference between the meridians and the height of the Pole, which observations we shall be very happy to combine with your own. I acknowledge myself most devoted to you and to your Royal Society. Farewell. Paris, 20 August 1671 [N.S.]

NOTES

1 On 2 November 1671 Oldenburg read this letter to the Society and produced the printed paper *Nouvelles observations des taches du Soleil faites à l'Académie Royale Les 11.12.13. août 1671* (Paris, 1671), of which he published an English translation in *Phil. Trans.*, no. 75 (18 September 1671), 2250–53.

2 Presumably this does not imply an enclosure; at any rate, none survives. For the printed account of Saturn, see Letter 1807.
3 Uraniburg ("City of the Heavens") was Tycho Brahe's observatory on the island of Hven in the Danish Sound; Jean Picard set out from Paris in July and, passing through Holland, embarked at Amsterdam for Hamburg on 11 August (see also Letter 1771). A scientific account of Picard's journey was published in *Voyage d'Uranibourg* (*Ouvrages de Mathématique de M. Picard*, Amsterdam, 1736, pp. 63–99).

1770
Wallis to Oldenburg
10 August 1671
From the original in Royal Society MS. W 1, no. 126

Oxford. Aug. 10. 1671

Sir,

The insertions mentioned in my last,[1] (which I had not then time, without loosing ye post, to write) I now send you. Had I a copy of the brief answere I sent from Astrop,[2] I would have transcribed it & inserted these in their proper places; but you may do it by these directions. I had once intended in ye first paper to have put in somewhat to ye same purpose; but left it out that it might not bee too long to insert in ye last Transactions had it come time inough. But, for ye next, I think with these it will not be too long. If any thing in it seem too severe, you may either mollify it, or leave it out. As, for *idle questions* you may put *impertinencies*.[3] And, of ye last addition, you may (if it bee thought fit) leave out either one or both clauses: The first of wch respects his sending abroad; ye second, ye words mentioned in your last letter.[4] No more at present but thanks for the Transactions you sent me, & that I am

Your most humble servant
John Wallis

After ye fourth of fift period, ending with these words,—*idle questions*. Adde[5]

He may do as well, ye next time, to ask their Judgement concerning *Euclide's second Postulate*: wherein he requires, *A streight line given*, to be continued (εἰς ἄπειρον)[6] *Infinitely, either way*: Whether, the length of that line so continued one way, be not Infinitely great: Whether, if so continued both ways, it be not yet greater: Whether hereupon there bee a quantity Greater than Infinite: Whether the same given line may not as well (by his 10th Proposition) be continually Bisected, Infinitely: Whether, upon such Bisection Infinitely continued, will not arise a series of Equal parts Infinitely many, (that is, more than any finite number assignable:) Whether, if this line be made ye side of a Triangle, & therein from every point of division be inscribed streight lines parallel to one of the other sides, there will not be a series of lines, infinitely many, in arithmetical proportion, as 1, 2, 3, 4, &c, of wch the Last or Greatest (viz. that other side) is given; (and ye Squares of those, as 1, 4, 9, 16, &c; the Cubes, as 1, 8, 27, 64, &c; and so of other powers:) Whether the Whole Doctrine of Euclide depending on this Postulate, must not therefore be rejected, as not of any use for ye confirming or confuting of any propounded doctrine: rather than Mr Hobs's paralogisms not take place.

As to ye later part, &c.

Next before ye last period, insert[7]

And the thing is Manifest. For DC, DR, DT, being (by construction) in continual proportion, as $1, \sqrt{\tfrac{2}{3}}, \tfrac{2}{3}$: And

DC. CA. Arc on CA extended ÷ ⎫ in the continual proportion of r to q
DR. RS. Arc on RS extended ÷ ⎬ (ye Radius to the Quadrangle Arc:) It
DT. TV. Arc on TV extended ÷ ⎭ is evident that (putting

$r = DC$, and $q = CA$,) the quantities will be these,
$DC = r \times 1$. $CA = q \times 1$. Arc on $CA = q^2/r \times 1$
$DR = r \times \sqrt{\tfrac{2}{3}}$. $RS = q \times \sqrt{\tfrac{2}{3}}$. Arc on $RS = q^2/r \times \sqrt{\tfrac{2}{3}}$;
$DT = r \times \tfrac{2}{3}$. $TV = q \times \tfrac{2}{3}$. Arc on $TV = q^2/r \times \tfrac{2}{3}$

And therefore (q^2/r being ye same in all) the Arcs on TV, on RS, on CA, in continual proportion, (viz: as $\tfrac{2}{3}, \sqrt{\tfrac{2}{3}}, 1$,) whatever bee ye proportion of r to q or to $q\sqrt{\tfrac{2}{3}}$, that is, of DC to CA is RS (greater, lesse, or equal;) notwithstanding Mr *Hobs*'s pretended Demonstration. And Mr *Hobs* needs be (as he is) a very weak Demonstrator who doth not discern it.

Lastly, as to his whole paper, &c.

At the end, adde[8]

: And the more hee Divulgeth it, the more he *proclaimeth or layeth open his folly*. And, if (as, I hear, he sayth) I have no Mathematicks but what I had from him: It seems I have had from him so much that he hath none left for himself. Farewell.

Yours
John Wallis

Query *As to* &c: make a Break, for ye better distinction.

ADDRESS
   For Mr Henry Oldenburg in
   the Palmal near St James
         London

NOTES

1 This seems to be a lost letter, written since Letter 1761. The insertions were to be made in Wallis's replies to Hobbes (see Letter 1759).
2 Letter 1761.
3 Neither of these phrases survived in the printed version.
4 Letter 1763, second paragraph.
5 A reworked version of this passage was printed in *Phil. Trans.*, no. 75 (18 September 1671), 2242.
6 "to infinity."
7 This passage (revised) also appeared in *Phil. Trans.*, no. 75, p. 2244.
8 Oldenburg did not print this passage.

1771
Vogel to Oldenburg
11 August 1671
From the original in Royal Society MS. F 1, no. 33

Viro Doctissimo
D. HENRICO OLDENBURGIO
S.P.D.
Martinus Fogelius

Interea, dum meae a Gezelio, Episcopi Aboensis filio, ad te perferuntur,[1] hoc quicquid est literarum mittere debui, partim ut pro transmissis Ephemeridibus mensis Maji & Novis Philosophicis mecum communicatis gratias maximas agerem, partim ut Clarissimo Picardo obsequerer. Hic scilicet a Rege Galliae mittitur in Daniam, ut Eclipsin Lunae quae mense proximo continget, in Vena, ubi olim Uraniburgum erat, observet eodem tempore, quo Cassinus eandem Parisiis observabit.[2] Cujus rei gratia Instrumenta necessaria, Quadrantem, Horologia pendula, Tubos &c. secum affert. Experietur simul Jovis Satellitum Eclipses a Cassino praedictas, quas hic subjicio, ut Vestri etiam Mathematici eas, ad suorum locorum latitudines, reductas observent. Picardus easdem Hevelio missit, mihique dictavit.[3]

Immersiones Satellitum Jovis in illius Umbram 1671 visibiles Uraniburgi

Septembr.	25 mane		h. 4. 16'	Immersio primi in Umbram Jovis
Octobr.	11 Immersio	2di	h. 4. 26'	
	18 Imm.	1mi	h. 4. 43	
	25 Imm.	1	h. 6. 41	
Nov.	7 Imm.	3	h. 2. 37	
	10 Imm.	2	h. 4. 51	
	12 Imm.	2	h. 4. 18	
	14 Imm.	3	h. 6. 37	
	17	1	h. 6. 49	
	19	1	h. 1. 20	
	&	2di	h. 7. 1	
	26	1mi	h. 3. 10	

Dec.	3	1	h. 5. 8
	8	4ti	h. 0. 10
	Emersio		5. 10
	12 Immers.	1	h. 1. 29
	14	2di	h. 4. 6
	19	1	h. 3. 19
	20	3tii	h. 1. 52
	21	2di	h. 6. 49
	26	1	5. 9
	27	3tii	5. 52

Amplius & hoc monere debui, hac hebdomade nos observasse hic Maculam Solarem, monstratam ab eodem doctissimo Picardo, quam prope Texellam in mari 3/13 Mensis hujus,[4] Tubo 3 ped; primum in medio Solis disco viderat, secutis autem diebus versus limbum occidentalem progressam, circa quem & die 7/17 & die 8/18 vidimus, quotidie scilicet limbo isti propiorem. die 9 eadem adhuc visa. die 10 Caelum non respeximus, quia fere nubilosum fuit. an Siferus viderit, proxime scribam. Vidit Picardus prima vice quasi Scorpii caudam referret, nodis inter se distantibus, qui deinceps coire arctius observati sunt. die 9 erat similtudine seminis Melonis.

Quod Phaenomenon tanto gratius mihi accidit, quanto rarius Macula hactenus in Sole observata fuit. Picardus se a 13 & 14 Octobris anni 1661 nullam vidisse nobis testatus est, neque se ulli observatam a decennio aliquam audivisse.

Gratissimum facies, si Ephemeridibus tuis hanc Observationem inseres, quam Picardus etiam Hevelio hinc significavit, & ut tibi scriberem,[5] non semel petiit.

Est hic Picardus inter Mathematicos Regios Praecipui nominis, auctor libri Mensurae Terrae, quam accuratissime dimensus est.[6] Liber iste in folio maximo, quod vocant, Sumtibus Regiis cum Commentariis Animalium quorundam dissectorum impressus est. Exemplar pro nostra Bibliotheca penes me servo, Senatui offerendum, ubi Picardus Regi Daniae suum Exemplar obtulerit.

Loueri Tractatus de Catarrhi Origine an nunquam in Anglia impressus est? amo potius Anglicos typos quam Belgicos.[7]

Siferus ad Phoranomicam tandem rediit recognoscendam.[8]

Quae de Plantis observavi, adhuc multa egent Experientia.[9]

de Toxico Hispanorum, quaeso, amicos tuos iterum mone. Scripsi ea propter nuper ad Grislejum.[10]

Vale, Vir Nobilissime, & me amare perge. Dabam Hamburgi d. 11. Aug. 1671.

ADDRESS
A Monsr
Monsr Grubendal
  a
    Londres

TRANSLATION

Martin Vogel sends many greetings to the very learned Mr. Henry Oldenburg

While my letter is being carried to you by Gezelius,[1] the son of the Bishop of Åbo, I ought to send you something more not only to thank you very much for the *Transactions* of May that were sent to me and the philosophical news imparted, but in order to oblige the famous Picard. He has been sent hither [or, rather] into Denmark by the French king in order to observe the lunar eclipse that will occur next month from the island of Hven, where formerly Uraniburg stood, at the same time as Cassini observes it at Paris.[2] The instruments necessary for this purpose—a quadrant, pendulum clocks, telescopes, and so on—he brings with him. He will at the same time look out for the eclipses of Jupiter's satellites predicted by Cassini, which I append below so that your mathematicians may observe them too after reducing them to the latitudes of their situations. Picard has sent the same to Hevelius, and dictated them to me:[3]

The immersions of Jupiter's Satellites in his shadow as visible at Uraniburg in 1671

[*For the table, see pages 198–99*]

I ought to advise you further that this week we observed a sunspot here, demonstrated by the same very learned Picard, who had first seen it in the center of the sun's disk at sea, with a three-foot telescope, on the third/thirteenth of this month while off the island of Texel;[4] in the following days it progressed towards the western limb near which we saw it on both the 7/17 and 8/18, each day nearer to the limb. On the ninth it was still visible and on the tenth we did not observe the heavens, because it was pretty cloudy. Whether Sivers saw it I may tell you next time. When Picard saw it the first time it was much like the tail of a scorpion, with separated bulges which afterwards were observed to come together more closely. On the ninth it was like a melon seed.

The occurrence of this phenomenon was the more welcome to me because spots in the sun have been observed infrequently. Picard himself told us he has seen none since 13 and 14 October 1661, and had heard of none observed during the last ten years.

It would be very welcome if you would insert this observation in your *Transactions*, which Picard has already communicated to Hevelius from here, having begged me more than once to write to you.[5]

This Picard is here as the chief figure among the royal mathematicians, and author of the book on the measure of the earth, where it is most exactly surveyed.[6] The book is printed in largest folio size (as they call it), at the king's charges, together with the notes on some dissections of animals. I am holding a copy for our library here in my own possession, to be presented to our Senate just as soon as Picard has offered his copy to the King of Denmark.

Is Lower's treatise on the origin of catarrhs not printed in England yet? I prefer English printing to the Dutch.[7]

Sivers has at last returned to editing the *Phoranomica*.[8]

The things I have observed about plants still demand many experiments.[9]

Please write to your friends again about the Spanish poison. I recently wrote to Grisley about it.[10]

Farewell, most noble Sir, and continue to love me. Hamburg, 11 August 1671.

ADDRESS
  To Mr Grubendol
  London

NOTES

1 Letter 1755.
2 See Letter 1769, note 3.
3 Oldenburg printed these predicted immersions at the end of *Phil. Trans.*, no. 74 (15 August 1671), 2238; Vogel's letter arriving on the twentieth, they were added to the proof.
4 This was the same spot that Cassini had seen (see Letter 1769); Picard gave a full account in his own narrative.
5 In fact Oldenburg mentioned Picard twice, in the August issue (note 3 above) and again in a note to no. 75 (18 September 1671), 2250.
6 See Vol. VI, p. 436, note 2.
7 The Amsterdam edition of Lower's *Dissertatio de origine catharri* has been many times mentioned in Vol. VII (Letter 1487, note 8); Oldenburg drew attention to the separate English publication by John Martin in *Phil. Trans.*, no. 77 (20 November 1671), 3017.
8 See Vol. IV, p. 531.
9 See Vol. VI, Letter 1330.
10 See Vol. VI, pp. 346, 620; for Gabriel Grisley, see Vol. V, p. 432, note.

1772
Wallis to Oldenburg
13 August 1671
From the original in Royal Society MS. W 1, no. 128

Oxford, Aug. 13. 1671

Sir,

To yrs of Aug. 10 (beside thanks for it & for ye receit it,) I have little to reply save what mine by ye last post brought you, wch I suppose by this time is come to hand.¹ If that be not thought clear inough, you may to those insertions adde these yt follow.

In ye first Insertion, after these words, *as 1, 8, 27, 64, &c. and so of other powers*; Adde

(Which is ye proposition at which he cavils:)²

In ye end of yt Insertion, after, *of any doctrine propounded*. Adde³

But if he can (without Latine, Logick, or Mathematicks,) solve These: he need not ask help of ye Royal Society to solve His *Quaere's*.

Or (which wil be harder to solve than all those) Mr *Hobs* may ask himself, who will not allow, that there is any Argument (beside ye Magistrates authority, who commands us to beleeve ye Scripture,) to prove, that *ye World had a beginning*: Whether, in case it had not, there must not have passed an Infinite number of years before Mr *Hobs* was born, (for, if but a finite number, how great so ever, it must have had a beginning so many year before:) Whether, now, there have not passed more years, (that is, more than that Infinite number:) Whether, in that Infinite (or more than Infinite) number of years, there have not been yet a greater number of Days & Hours, (&, of wch the last is given:) Whether, if this be an Absurdity, wee have not (contrary to what Mr *Hobs* would perswade us) an Argument (beside ye authority of Scripture or ye Magistrate) to prove, that ye World had a beginning. And these will be more hard to solve, than all these before, or those of Mr. *Hobs*; Because these *more than Infinite* numbers of Years, Days, & Hours must have *Actually existed*, & been passed allready; whereas it serves *Euclide*, & ye Mathematicians, if their Infinite be but *Imaginable*; with whom it is frequent, upon impossible suppositions, to infer usefull Truthes: (and, by *Infinite*, to mean onely *more than any Finite assignable*;

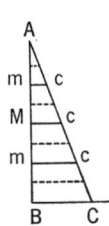
As, If we *suppose* the side of a triangle *AB* to bee bisected in *M*, & each of those Halves again in *m*, & so onwards *Infinitely*; we must withall *suppose* the number of ye parts resulting to be *Infinite*, or more than any assignable *Finite* number: And if we *suppose* further, from every of those Infinite points of division to be drawn as many lines *mc* parallel to ye Base *BC*, these lines must be *supposed*, *Infinitely many*, & these in an Arithmetical progression, as 1, 2, 3, &c., of wch *BC* the *last and greatest is given*. Nor is it necessary that this *Infinite Bisection* be actually performed (or possible so to be:) it is inough, yt if wee *suppose* that, we must *suppose* the other allso. But, in Mr *Hobs's* notion, of ye *Worlds Eternity*, there must have been not onely *supposed*, but *actually existing*, those *Infinites*, and *More than Infinites*.

I am yours &c
John Wallis

ADDRESS

For Mr Henry Oldenburg
Secretary to ye Royall Society
in the Palmal near St James's
London

POSTMARK AU 14

NOTES

1 Letter 1770, received on 11 August.
2 This was not printed.
3 A shorter version of the following long addendum was published in *Phil. Trans.*, no. 75 (18 September 1671), 2243–44; the last sentences (on infinite bisection) were transferred to an earlier point in the paper (p. 2242).

1773
Oldenburg to Wallis
15 August 1671
From the original in Royal Society MS. W 1, no. 130

Sir,

By yr last, wch I received yesterday, me thinks you have pressed yr Adversary home; but I have not yet been able to shew it to MyLd Brouncker, who told me, when I saw him last, that the King had commanded him to take care of getting the printed sheet answer'd in such another sheet, and yt in such a manner, yt every body of common understanding and good sense might be able to apprehend where the error lyeth. This made his Lordip wish very much, yt you, that have already so well satisfaied Mathematicians, would take a litle more pains to satify those also, yt are no Mathematicians, but otherwise intelligent men; and particularly all those Queries about yr Proposition, wch he hath proposed so plausibly, as some doe think: What MyLd shall say after ye view of yr last, you will soon know.

But, I believe, you will be surprised to see this other very bold paper of ye Author,[1] wch came yesterday to my hands, and of wch, I heare, a Copy hath been also by him presented to the king μετὰ πολλῆς φαντασίας.[2] I am very sorry he should give occasion to torment you at such an unseasonable time as this is; though you will soon despatch this also, in the persuasion of Sir

yr. faithf. servt
Oldenb.

Aug. 15. 71.

ADDRESS
To his much honord friend
Dr John Wallis Savillian
Professor of Geometry, and one
of his Majties Chaplains
Oxford

NOTES

Reply to Letter 1772.
1 The second of Hobbes's fly sheets.
2 "with great pomp"; Acts 25:23.

1774
Sylvius to Oldenburg
15 August 1671

Mentioned in Sylvius' Letter 2065 of 17 September 1672 (Vol. IX) as having been written in reply to Oldenburg's letter of 5 July. Both these letters are now lost.

1775
Wallis to Oldenburg
16 August 1671

From the original in Royal Society MS. W 1, no. 129

Mr. Henry Oldenburg

Oxford. Aug. 16. 1671

Sir

I received from you this night, yours of yesterday; in which was a paper of Mr *Hobs*, wherein hee pretends to confute a Theorem which, hee says, hath long time passed for a Truth.

"The Theoreme

"The four sides of a square being divided into any number of equal parts, for example into 10; and streight lines drawn through ye opposite points, which will divide ye square into 100 lesser squares; The received Opinion, and which Dr Wallis commonly useth, is, yt ye root of those 100, namely 10, is ye side of ye whole square."

My Answere.¹

It is not the opinion of *Dr. Wallis* (and Mr *Hobs* knows, it is not; having been oft told the contrary;) and it is so far from being *a received Opinion*, that he doth not know it to be ye Opinion of one Person (unlesse Mr *Hobs*). But hee is of opinion (& so are all Mathematicians, so far as hee knows: that (for instance), the Square do contain 100 *square feet*, the side doth 10 *Long Feet*, (because the *Number* 10 being ye root or side of ye *number 100*; and *Feet in Length* of an *Inch Square*;² the product of ye Rootes, that is *a Foot long, multiplied by 10*; is the Root of the product of ye squares, that is, of *a Foot Square, multiplied by 100*). And so in all other squares. The Root of ye Number of *Squares* in the Plain, is the number of *Lengths* in ye side. And this Mr *Hobs* hath been often told; & particularly in my *Hobbius Heautontimorumenos*³ pag. 142, 143, 144. (&, long before that, in my *Opus Arithmeticum*⁴ pag. 196, 197, 198. and elsewhere,) by

Yours
John Wallis

NOTES

This is written on the envelope of Oldenburg's Letter 1773, to which it is a reply.
1 The printed version of this passage appears in *Phil. Trans.*, no. 75 (18 September 1671), 2245–46.
2 Wallis at first wrote "square Inches" and then changed to "Feet," but here he forgot.
3 See Vol. III, p. 198, note.
4 John Wallis, *Arithmetica infinitorum* (Oxford, 1655).

1776
Flamsteed to Oldenburg
23 August 1671
From the original in Royal Society MS. F 1, no. 73

Derby August 23: 1671

Mr Oldenburge
Sr

I have yours by Mr Sargeant wth ye included paper of Bullialdus for communicateing which and all others, I hold my selfe exceedingly engaged to yu:[1] As for Monsr Bullialdus calculus I find it very rough in collecting ye parallaxes yet by chance to misse not above halfe a minute in each which hee contemnes I suppose as an insensible & therefore tolerable fault, but in my opinion hee ought now to worke his calculations to ye accuracy of seconds since wee may hope to make observations to that exactnesse: I have not had time to calculate the same appearance from ye Caroline tables[2] to ye meridian & height of Dantzick[3] but intend to give it you within a forthnight when I can gaine a safe opportunity to remitte Bullialdus his paper for since ye receit of yours I have beene much retaind from my studies by our businesse & spent my spare hours when gaind in calculating ye next yeares appearances[4] Mr Bullialdus does well to let yu know of ye exactnesse of his numbers when they hit but to informe yu better I can assure yu that in ye Eclipse of 1668 Octob. 25 st. v. supposeing the difference of meridians of Uraniburg & Derby o h 56' his tables erred 23 minutes of time at least; for by a more accurate method of calculation then hee uses, I found the beginning ought to have beene at 11h–24'–23" a.m. ye end 1h–48'–11". wheras I observed ye begining at 11h–00'–30". ye Caroline presenteing then ye begining at 11h–13'–09", whose difference, tho great, is but halfe so much as his. I may adde from my comment on Hevelius, which not intendeing now to publish I shall devest of many thinges to furnish my calculations, yt in ye Eclipse of ye yeare 1661 Martij 20/30 observed by Hevelius at Dantzick ye Caroline numbers, (then which wee hope for much more true) doe erre but little from the appearance, when his, if wee may trust the Hevelian calculation, doe erre allmost intolerably; for The beginning of ye eclipse was

	by observation	Streets tab.	Error +	Bullialdus	Error −
	h ′ ″	h ′ ″		h ′ ″	
	10–13–15	10 15 22	2′–07	9–49–22	23′ 53″
The end	12–27–03	12–29–16	2–13	12–06–59	20–04
the digits	7°.45′	7.53	+8′	8.1	+16′

All these observations you may find in ye Mercurius sub sole of Hevelius[5]

You may further from mee if yu please informe him of that difference of ye heavens from his tables which I thinke hee cannot be ignorant of in ye planet Saturn & request him opinion how it is to be salved by Hevelius observation

	obser.		Caroline	error +	Philolai	error +
	° ′ ″		′ ″	′ ″	° ′ ″	′ ″
Anno 1660 Ap: 25	10 h mm	8°–53′–43″	9–07–08	13–25	9–13–44	20–01
1661 Ap: 7	12		22 –34 –13	22–48–00	13–47	22–55–27	21–14
1661 May 13	10		20 –04 –36	20–20–25	15–49		

I could instance in many particulars but these at present shall suffice till I returne his paper; when I shall shew, how far short his are of our countrimans Mr Steets. As for Mr Wing[6] I cannot thinke him other then ye corrected copy of Bulliald. so desiring yu to excuse this hast I remaine

       Yr obliged friend & servant
        John Flamsteed

I understand Mr Collings dwells now not far from yu pray get mee this delivered to him with ye first convenient opportunity.[7]

ADDRESS
 To Henry Oldenburg Esq
  at his house in the middle
  of ye Pell-mell in St James,
   Westminster these
    present

NOTES

Reply to Letter 1766.
1 It appears from this letter and Flamsteed's next (Letter 1791) that a number of letters written by himself, Boulliaud, and Oldenburg are lost. Flamsteed probably

asked Oldenburg to obtain from Boulliaud (whose *Astronomia Philolaica*, Paris, 1645, he knew very well) precise data for calculating a number of eclipses (whether of the sun or moon is not clear, but presumably the latter); Bouilliaud responded, using the method of his own former work, and Oldenburg sent his paper to Flamsteed. Flamsteed now objects that Boulliaud's values for the parallaxes (probably both sun and moon) are incorrect.

2 See Thomas Streete, *Astronomia Carolina* (London, 1661).
3 For sending to Hevelius.
4 The lunar appulses for 1672 as computed by Flamsteed were printed (in Latin) in *Phil. Trans.*, no. 77 (20 November 1671), 2297–3001.
5 Published at Danzig in 1662.
6 Vincent Wing (1619–69) of Rutland was a "mathematical practitioner" and surveyor who published a number of works on astronomy; Flamsteed means, of course, that they have little independent value.
7 The letter is not otherwise recorded. In the summer or fall of 1671 Collins removed from Bloomsbury Market to Petty France, Westminster, living in the house of his father-in-law, master cook of the Lords' kitchen at the palace.

1777
Willughby to Oldenburg
24 August 1671

From the original in Royal Society MS. W 3, no. 45
Printed in *Phil. Trans.*, no. 76 (22 October 1671), 2279–81

Middleton August 24.

Sir

As I remember, Mr Listers opinion is that the muscae ichneumones lay their eggs in the Bodies of Caterpillars:[1] which I looke upon as very ingenious and true, and must subscribe to it, though I cannot yet absolutely demonstrate it; as I Hoped I should have done before this: which was the reason I did not answer yours of July 13th sooner. These ichneumones have all 4 wings; Antennae like bees; Their Bodies Hanging to their breasts by a slender Ligament as in Wasps, most if not all have stings, and are made of a Maggot that spins herselfe a Theca[2] before shee turnes into a Nympha. There is great variety of them; some breed as Bees doe, laying an Egge which produces a maggot, which they Feed till it comes to its Full growth.

Others as we guesse thrust in their Eggs into plants, the Bodies of living caterpillars, maggots, &c. For it is very surprising to observe that a great Caterpillar instead of beeing changed into a Butterfly according to the usuall course of nature should produce sometimes one; sometimes two or three and sometimes a whole Swarme of ichneumones. I Have observed this anomalous Production in a great manie sorts of Caterpillars both Hairie and Smooth; in severall sorts of maggots, and, which is most strange, in one Water-insect.

When there come manie of these ichneumon maggots out of the bodie of the same Caterpillar they weave all their Thecas togather into one bunch. which is sometimes wound with web about it just like a Bag of Spiders Eggs. but I dare Venture to answer Mr Listers 10th Quaerie[3] pag: 2172 negatively, that none of these Feed upon spiders Eggs. but it is the similitude of those Thecas conglobated together to ye Eggs of Spiders that Has occasioned the coniecture.

One of the greene Caterpillars, common in the Heaths in the North went so farre on to Her naturall change that Shee made Her selfe up into a great Brown Theca allmost of the Shape of a bottle, which was Filled with a swarm of ichneumones.

And I have observed in one or two other sorts that From the very aurelia[4] itselfe Has come an ichneumon. which is very odde that the Caterpillar, stung and impraegnated by the ichneumones, should bee yet so Farre unhurt and unconcerned as to make Her selfe a Theca and to bee turned into an Aurelia.

I have often seen a great ichneumon dragging a Caterpillar in the High way. This year Mr Wray in Companie with another ingenious neighbour, observed one haling a large green Caterpillar much bigger then Her selfe, which after shee had drawn the lenght of a Perch, shee laid down, and then takes out a little Pellet of earth, with which shee had stopped the mouth of a Small Hole like a Worme hole. then shee goes down into it and staying a very little, comes up again and draws ye eruca[5] down with Her into the Hole, and there leaves Her; and afterwards not onely stops but Fills up the Hole, sometimes carriing in little clods, and sometimes scraping Dust with her Feet and throwing it backwards into ye Hole; going down often Herselfe to Ram it close, once or twice shee Flew up into a pine tree which grew iust over Her Hole; perhaps to Fetch Cement. When the Hole was full and even with the superficies of ye ground about it, shee draws two Pine-tree-leaves and lays them near the mouth of ye Hole, and Flyes away; not taking notice that shee came anie more in 3 or 4 daies. Wee digged For the Catterpillar and Found it prettie deep. I put it into a boxe expecting it would have produced an Ichneumon, but it dried away and nothing came of it. Wee lately observed a sort of ichneumones or rather Vespae,[6] which prey upon severall sorts of Flyes. When they Fly with them they hold them by the heads and carrie them under their bellies. These make Holes a great depth in the ground, in which they lay their young and Feed them with the Flys they catch creeping backwards into the ground and drawing the Flys after them. I suspect they may at First lay their Eggs in the very bodie of a Fly. but one Fly being not enough to bring ye young one to its Full growth they feed it with more: their theca's are at last all covered over with the Wings legs and other fragments of Flys. You will oblige mee very much by sending mee one of Mr Listers Viviparous Flys,[7]

Your most Faithfull servant
Francis Willughby

ADDRESS

    For Mr Henry Oldenburgh,
    Secretary to the Royall Societie
    at his house in the Pellmell
        London

NOTES

1 Compare Letters 1646 and 1648 (Vol. VII).
2 Pupa.
3 See Letter 1589 (Vol. VII, p. 352), Qu. 10.
4 Chrysalis.
5 Caterpillar.
6 Wasps.
7 See Vol. VII, p. 350.

1778
Lister to Oldenburg
25 August 1671

From the original in Royal Society MS. L 5, no. 37
Partly printed in *Phil. Trans.*, no. 76 (22 October 1671) 2281-84

Yorke August 25 1671

Sir

I am indebted to you a great many particulars you have enquired of me. And to answer what remains of your former Letter.

I have observed ye 2 Insects, wch Mr Wray tells you smell of Musk, wch, indeed they doe in a high degree. The small Bees are very frequent in ye Wooles[1] in Lincolnshire & about ye latter end of April are to be found in pastures & meadows upon ye early-blowne flowers of a sort of Ranunculas, as you have been rightly informed, but it is something improper to say Bees feed on flowers & likewise ye same Bees are noe lesse frequent on ye flowers of *Den leonis*[2] etc. The sweet Beetle is a very large Insect & well known about Cambridge. All ye Tryalls I have made to preserve ym wth their smell have proved ineffectual: for both sorts of these Insects will of ym selves in a very few weekes become almost quite sent-lesse. To these I shall add an other sweet-smelling insect, wch is a Hexapode-Worme feeding on *Gallium luteum*.[3]

The Observation of *Vespae Ichneumones*, as it hath relation to spiders, I willingly reserve for other papers:[4] yet I may tell you in general, yt this kind of Insect is one of ye greatest puzzels in nature: there being few Excrescencies of plants & very many births of Insects wherein these slender Wasps after divers strange wayes are concerned.

Though I be at present from my bookes, yet, I well remember ye passage wch Mr Willoughby referrs you to in Mouffet:[5] & he is well able to judge whether ye observation be made upon ye same sort of Insect. I conceive it a fault not consistant wth an ingenious spirit to passe by in silence ye industrie of modernes, as well as of ancient writers, according to yt of C. *Celsus*. "Oportet neque recentiores viros in his fraudare, quae vel repererunt, vel recte secuti sunt; et tamen ea quae ab antiquiores aliquos posita sunt, authoribus suis reddere."[6] You can best informe me, whether *Swammerdam* be a trespasser or noe. Where I read in ye account given us by you of his booke N. 64.[7] That snails are both male & Female: That Catterpillars may teach us, by their feeding, ye correspondancie of ye Vertues of plants etc. I am desirous to know whether he quote Mr Wray for ye former, as having published ye Observation 10 yeares agoe at least:[8] & for ye latter, ye learned & noble Virtuoso F. Columna,[9] who did propose ye way of essaying ye vertues of plants by ye palates of Insects ye beginning of this age. By ye by let me aske of you, whether Swammerdams H[istory] of Ins[ects] be translated yet or noe.[10] for he seemes to have imployed his time to good purpos on yt subject.

    I passe to some particulars in your last letter. I am very glad to understand, yt there is a Peice to be printed of ye German Ph[ilosophers] concerning ye Tinctures or Essences to be extracted out of ye dung of Insects. as for ye passage of ye Letter wch you was pleased to transcribe, I doubt whether I well understand it or noe: for there it is said (as it seemes to me) as tho ye putrification of plants was ye author & parent of ye wormes whose dung was to be extracted: wch thing I thought F. Redi had put out of all question, yt meere putrefaction begetts nothing. I doe not doubt but yt some Insects may be happily found, wch may make some alterations upon ye plants they feed on for ye better, at least for a different use. The experiments I have made of this nature in order to ye obtaining colours more fixed have not succeeded. ex. gr. I fedd Catterpillars on ye leaves of *Glastum*,[11] purposely soed in my Garden; these eat lustly & excerned[12] much: but ye infusion of their dungs differed not at all, (yt I could discerne) from yt of ye bruised leaves: ye like I have experienced of roses: & I sent you formerly a note of certain Catterpillars found in Corne, excerning pure white flower.

    I did much admire ye Experiment of ye Speedy & sure healing of cut-eyes by ye juice of Celandine; & yet, pardon my diffidence, if I thinke we can scarce be too much cautioned against ourselves, we very often, especially in Medicinall matters, take *non causa pro causa*[13] & it is most certain, though ye Eye be beleeved a very tender part, it will suddainly heale of it selfe, as is frequently observed by Cock-masters[14] but since ye Experiment is reduced to Celadine alone by ye G[erman] P[hilosophers] without ye addition of any Vitriolick misterie, I am in great hopes it is no delusion. Celadine is a plant of its owne kind & not to be sampled[15] in Nature yt I know of: & although it has been delivered to us by ye Ancients, as a good Eye-herb: yet its yellow juice is soe exceeding keen & bitter, yt most Practioners have been distrustfull & forborne ye application of it, nay I could name some authours to you who have writ discourses purposly against yt very vertue of it, & particularly F. Columna If I well remember.

Thus far I have been indebted to you. I am willing to subjoyne a remarke of my owne: & it shall be, if you please concerning petrified shells, I meane such shells, as I have observed in our English stone Quarries. But, Sr, let me praemise thus much, yt I am confident, yt you at least will acquit me & not beleeve me one of a litigious nature. This, I say, in reference to what I have lately read in Steno's *Prodromus* yt, if my sentiments on this particular are somewhat different from his, it proceeds not from a spirit of contradiction, but from a different view of Nature. First than we will easily beleeve, yt in some countreys & particularly along ye shores of ye mediterranean sea, there may all manner of sea-shells be found *promiscuously* included in Rocks or Earth & at good distances too from ye sea. But for our English-inland Quarries, wch alsoe abound wth infinite number & great varieties of shells; I am apt to thinke, there is noe such matter, as petryfying of shells, in ye businesse, (or as Steno explains himselfe p. 84 et alibi) That ye substance of these shells, formerly belonging to Animals, hath been dissolved or wasted by ye penetrating force of juices, & yt a stony substance is come in ye place thereof, but yt those Cockle-like stones ever were as they are at present *Lapides sui generis*[16] & never any part of an Animal. That they are soe at present is in effect confessed by Steno in ye above cited page; & it is most certain, yt our English-quarrie shells, to continue yt abusive name, have noe parts of a different Texture from ye rock or quarrie they are taken, yt is, yt there is noe such thing as shell in these ressemblances of shells, but yt Iron stone Cockles are all Iron stone, Lime or Marble all limestone & marble, Sparr or Chrystalline shells all sparr etc. And yt they never were any part of an Animal, my reason is. That Quarries of different stone yeild us quite different sorts or species of shells, not only one from an other (as those Cockle-stones of ye Iron stone Quarries of Adderton in Yorkshire differ from those found in ye lead mines of ye neighbouring mountains, & both these from yt Cockle Quarrie of Wansford bridge in Northamptonshire & all three from those to be found in ye Quarries about Gunthrope & Beavour Castle etc) but I dare boldly say from any thing in nature besides yt either ye land, salt or fresh water does yeild us. 'Tis tru I have picked out of yt one Quarrie of Wansford very resemblances of *Murices, Telinae, Turbines, Cockles* etc.[17] & yet I am not convinced when I particularly examined some of our English shoares for shells, alsoe ye fresh waters & ye fields, yt I did ever meet wth (N.B.) any one of those *Species* of Shells any where else but in their respective Quarries, whence I conclude ym *lapides sui generis* & yt they were not cast in any *Animal Mold*, whose species or race is yet to be found in being at this day.

This argument perhapps, will not soe readily take place wth those persons, yt thinke it not worth ye while exactly & minutly to distinguish ye several *species* of ye things of Nature, but are content to acquiesce in figure, resemblances kind & such general notice but when they shall please to condescend to heedfull & accurate descriptions, they will, I doubt not, be of yt opinion, wch an attentive view of these things lead me into some yeares agoe.

Though I make noe doubt but ye repository of ye R.S. is amply furnished wth things of this nature, yet if you shall command ym, I will send you up 2 or 3 sorts of our English Cockle stones of different Quarries, nearly ressembling one ye other & all of ym very like a Common sort of sea shell: & yet if there shall not be enough specifically to distinguish ym & hinder ym from being sampled by any thing of ye spoiles of ye sea or fresh water or ye land snailes, my argument will fall & I shall be hapily convinced of an error. I am Sr

your most humble servant
Martin Lister

Sr

I shall be glad to heare yt Mr Willoughby has sent you up his observations about Vegetable Excrescences. I should desire, if it might not be too great trouble to you, to know what they are: for possibly I may have something to adde, at least I would have noe contradiction betwixt us.

ADDRESS
These
For his honoured friend
Mr Henry Oldenburgh
a his house in ye Palmal
London

POSTMARK AU 30

NOTES

Reply to Letters 1748 and 1757.
1 Wolds.
2 Dandelion (Fr. *dent de lion*).
3 Lady's bedstraw (*Galium verum* L.).
4 See Letter 1746 and its note 5, and Letter 1748.

5 See Letter 1746 and its note 4.
6 "And one should not be unfair to those more recent exponents of these matters, who have either discovered something or, at least, developed it in a proper manner, yet whatever has been established by older authorities should be attributed to them." This Celsus is probably the pagan apologist (second century A.D.) against whom Origen wrote, and in those work alone Celsus' arguments survive. Celsus frequently accuses Christians of not attributing to their true, older authors (including Plato) ideas or principles they had adopted as their own. But we did not hit on this exact passage.
7 *Historia insectorum generalis* (Utrecht, 1669) is reviewed in *Phil. Trans.*, no. 64 (10 October 1670), 2078–81.
8 The only work of Ray's published so far before was *Catalogus plantarum circa Cantabrigiam nascentium* (Cambridge, 1660), where, however, he does not seem to mention snails. Lister was perhaps forgetful, and remembered a conversation. Ray's priority was later accepted by Swammerdam.
9 Fabio Colonna (*c.* 1567–1650); see Letter 1656, note 9 (Vol. VII).
10 The Latin translation was only published (at Leiden) in 1685.
11 Woad, modern *Isatis*.
12 Excreted.
13 "what is not the cause for the cause."
14 Rearers of fighting cocks.
15 Paralleled; a use of the word becoming obsolete at this time.
16 "Stones of their own kind."
17 "Murices" is plural of *Murex*, a genus of shellfish; "Telinae," *Tellins*, another genus; "Turbines" are from *Turbo*, a genus of gasteropod.

1779

Oldenburg to Cassini

26 August 1671

From the original in Observatoire MS. B 4, no. 11 bis
Copy in Royal Society MS. O 2, no. 55

Celeberrimo Viro
Joh. Domenico Cassino
H. Oldenburg Salutem

Ingenti sane perfundebar laetitia, Vir Clarissime, cum novae tuae de Maculis Solaribus nuper visis Observationes impressae una cum amicissimis tuis literis mihi reddebantur. Quanquam Societatis Regiae Caetus, ob suetas hac anni tempestate ferias, impraesentiarum non celebrentur, copia tamen mihi non defuit, Scriptum tuum peraccuratum Nobilissimo Praesidi nostro, Domino Vice-Comiti Brouncker, nonnullisque aliis e Caetu illo praeclaris Astronomis exhibere, idem ipsi Societati, conventibus publicis restitutae, superis faventibus, exhibiturus. Spero, Nostrates operam suam tuae certatim sociaturos, qua tum haec Macularum, tum Saturni phaenomena, in rei Astronomicae decus et incrementum, sedulo observentur. Socii interim nostri pro tempore sparsi uberrimas una mecum gratias pro transmisso munere tuo Astronomico reponunt, quae, dante Deo, instauratis caetibus, ampliori Tibi forma persolventur.

Caeterum, ex pagellis insertis intelliges, Illustrem Boylium Ao 1660. postremas, quod scimus, in Sole maculas hic observasse.[1] Paenitet sane, me Observata illa sermone Latino non edidisse. Sed facilem earum Interpretem habebis Dominum Vernonem, utrique nostrum conjunctissimum, quem Parisiis jam reducem omnino crediderim.[2]

Inspicienti mihi Saturnium Hugenii Systema, occurrit p. 74, eum tunc existimasse, debere Saturni brachia julio aut Augusto 1671. gracilescere, prorsusque tandem disparere, et Planetam illum rotundum relinquere.[3] At colligere mihi ex literis tuis videor, Saturnum a primo hujus anni Ortu Heliaco jam visum fuisse rotundum ad diem usque undecimum Augusti [N.S.], die vero 14to brachia, quae indies illustriora fiant, suscepisse.

Perscripsit mihi non ita pridem Celeberrimus Hevelius,[4] se 1. junii st. n. 1671. Saturnum a Luna tectum ex voto observasse: Initium Occultationis accidisse Gedani hor. matut. 3.h 38.′ 27.″ circa montem Germanicianum: Lineam, ut vocat, itinerariam, quantum ex solo ingressu colligere ipsi licuit, per M. Ætnam transiisse; centrum fere Lunae per M. Horminium, M. Herculis, et superiorem partem Maris Caspii. Addit, spectaculum fuisse perjucundum, Sole Oriente Saturnum occultari, appulsumque, 20 pedum Tubo, distincte admodum dignoscere; genuinam tamen Saturni faciem, ejusque annulos eo tempore, ob diluculum, Solemque Horizonti adeo vicinum, haud satis clare apparuisse; unde etiam factum, quod Planetae illius exitum deprehendere nequaquam potuerit, praesertim cum Sol ad 12. propemodum gradus jam elevaretur.

Eidem phaenomeno Astronomi quidam nostrates quoque invigilaverant, sed frustra, caelo non annuente. Quid apud Vos eam in rem factum fuerit, si non sit incommodum, perscribi nobis rogamus. Vale, Vir Illustris, et me Tibi addictissimum crede. Dabam Londini die 26 Aug. 1671.

P.S.

His vixdum scriptis redduntur mihi literae Domini Fogelii Hamburgensis,[5] qui significat, Dominum Picardum, jam tum Hamburgi agentem, Maculas Solares prope Texellam conspexisse, idemque phaenomenon sibimet in ipsa urbe Hamburgensi comparuisse; adhaec modo laudatum Dominum Picardum asseverasse, se mense Octobri A.1661. ultimas in sole maculas observasse; quod tempus tempore Boyliano, supra commemorato, posterius est.

Misit mihi idem Fogelius, Picardo id petente, Satellitum Jovialum Eclipsis a Reverenda Tua praedictas; quas hisce iisdem Transactionibus bona tua venia inserere non dubitavi.[6]

Jam modo edoceor, quosdam ex Astronomis nostratibus hesterno die (Aug. 15.) et hoc ipso die, quo haec scribo, maculam unam in Sole, Orientalem ipsius limbum recenter ingressam, conspexisse.

TRANSLATION

H. Oldenburg greets the very celebrated Jean Dominique Cassini

I was truly filled with great delight, famous Sir, when your new printed observations about the sunspots seen recently were delivered to me, together with your most friendly letter. Although the Royal Society is not meeting at present because of the holidays usual about this time of year, I was not lacking in opportunities for showing your highly accurate paper to our most noble President, the Lord Viscount Brouncker, and several other distinguished astronomers of that assembly; and that same paper will, God willing, be presented to the Society itself when its ordinary meetings are resumed. I hope that our Fellows will indeed combine their efforts with yours, so that both these sunspots and the phenomena of Saturn may be carefully observed for the improvement and adornment of astronomy. Meanwhile, our Fellows, scattered for the time being, return you most copious thanks for this astronomical present you have sent which, God willing, will be conveyed in fuller words when the sessions are resumed.

Moreover, you will gather from the pages enclosed here that the illustrious Boyle observed in 1660 the last sunspots seen here, so far as we know.[1] I regret very much that I did not publish those observations in Latin. But you will have a ready interpreter of them in Mr. Vernon, who has the closest relations with both of us and who is now I fully believe returned to Paris.[2]

As I was persuing Huygens' *Systema Saturnium* I happened to notice that he then thought (p. 74) that Saturn's "arms" ought to become thinner in July or August 1671 and finally disappear altogether, leaving that planet in its rounded shape.[3] But I seem to gather from your letter that Saturn was seen to be round from his first heliacal rising of this year until 11 August [N.S.], and that he acquired "arms," becoming more brilliant day by day, on the fourteenth.

The very celebrated Hevelius wrote to me not long ago[4] that on 1 June 1671, N.S., he had observed as perfectly as one could wish an occultation of Saturn by the Moon; the beginning of the occultation occurred at Danzig at 3h 38′ 27″ A.M. near the Mons Germanicianus, the line of its path (as he calls it) passing through Mount Ætna, so far as he could judge from the ingress alone, and by the center of the Moon, Mount Horminius, Mount Hercules, and the upper part of the Caspian Sea. He adds that the spectacle was a most agreeable one, the sun rising as Saturn was occulted, and that he followed the appulse most distinctly with a twenty-foot tube. However, the true shape of Saturn and his rings at that time did not appear very clearly because of the dawning day and the sun's proximity to the horizon; for the same reason he was quite unable to perceive the planet's egress, especially as the Sun had then risen almost to twelve degrees.

Some of our astronomers waited up for the same phenomenon, but in vain for the skies were unfavorable. We beg you to give us an account of what was done about this among you, if convenient. Farewell, illustrious Sir, and believe me your most devoted. London, 26 August 1671.

P.S. When I had barely written this there was delivered a letter from Mr. Vogel at Hamburg,[5] who tells me that Mr. Picard (now passing through Hamburg) observed the sunspots while off Texel, and had shown him the same phenomenon in the city of Hamburg itself; and that the worthy Mr. Picard had further asserted that he had himself seen sunspots last in October 1661, which is a later time than that of Boyle's [record], noted above.

The same Vogel has sent me at Picard's request the eclipses of Jupiter's satellites as predicted by your reverend self; and I have not doubted of your kind forgiveness for inserting them in these name *Transactions*.[6]

And I may now inform you that certain of our astronomers did yesterday (25 August) and this very day that I am writing this to you observe a single spot on the Sun, recently entered upon its eastern limb.

NOTES

Reply to Letter 1769.
1 *Phil. Trans.*, no. 74 (14 August 1671), 2216–17, mentions Cassini's observations of 1, 2, and 3 August—from what source we do not know, since Oldenburg had not then received Letter 1769—and prints Boyle's account of sunspots observed from 27 April to 9 May 1660.
2 See Letter 1752 and its note 2.
3 See *Œuvres Complètes*, XV, 338, 339.
4 See Letter 1718.
5 Letter 1771.
6 Again, no. 74, p. 2238.

1780
Oldenburg to Hill
? 30 August 1671

Letter 1747 from Thomas Hill reached Oldenburg on 16 August 1671 according to the endorsement he made upon it, and he noted the date of his answer as 30 August. However, Hill's reply (dated 31 March 1672, N.S.) records the date of Oldenburg's letter as the twentieth.

This letter of Oldenburg's contained as an enclosure Letter 1780a, which was intended for the unknown Jesuit in Brazil, together with (possibly) a personal note to the same Jesuit.

Oldenburg was (presumably retrospectively) directed by the Royal Society to request such information when Letter 1747 was read to the Society on 14 December 1671.

1780a
Inquiries for Brazil

Enclosure with Letter 1780
From the draft in Royal Society Classified Papers, XIX, no. 73

Inquirenda per Brasiliam Commendata curae Domini Thomae Hill, qui ea se Bahiam ad Jesuitam N. N. transmissurum promisit in literis Ulyssipone datis julij 23. 1671 [N.S.] scripta ab H. Oldenburg, Aug. 19. 1671.

I. Circa *Aerem*;

Quaenam sit usitata salubritas vel Insalubritas Aeris? Quaenam sint caeli mutationes pro diversis Tempestatibus Anni diversisque partibus diei? Verumne sit, noctibus aestivis, frigora intensiora, hybernis vero mitiora saepe persentisci? Quibus mensibus Pluvialis tempestatis sit initium et finis? Quale caelum eo praecise tempore, quando Sol transit Zenith Brasiliensium, mense Octobri et Februario? Num in eadem Caeli Brasiliensis plaga, pari Solis accessu et recessu,[1] iisdemque anni mensibus, Aestas sit et siccitas ab Orientali parte circa Oceanum; ab Occidentali vero trans juga montium Brasileae, Hyems et pluviae? An noctes plaerumque adeo sint clarae, ut uno eodemque die Luna vetus et nova conspici, literaeque ad Lunam quadratam satis recte legi queant? An serenitas Brasiliensis ea sit, ut Astronomis ad caelestia intentis percommoda sit instituendis compluribus magni momenti Observationibus circa Eclipses, Nubeculas Magellanicas, Venerem post emersionem a Sole falcatam, Mercurium scintillantem et corniculatum accessus denique Lunae ad stellas tum Fixas tum Erraticas, aliaque phaenomena, rarentur Europaeis conspecta.

Quae Meteorum genera potissimum ibi gignantur? An crebris, ut scribitur, fulguribus Caelum sub vesperam coruscet, tempestate vel maxime serena, sed sicca? Num in *Maranham*,[2] prope Aequatorem, vehementius crebriusque intonet? Num frequentes appareant Irides, Halones, Dracones ignei volantes? Num verum sit, Grandines vix unquam ibi conspici, nec altissima montium cacumina nive tecta observari? Num pluviarum guttae sint pergrandes, gravique impetu decidant? Num Ros Brasiliensis Europaeo sit multo fertilior, penetrantior, tenuiorque, ferrum aliaque sub dio posita facillime corrodens et excedens; tantae interim sit efficaciae, ut et pecara et homines aestuantes, et spirituum jactura fractos mirifice roboret?

Qui Venti imprimis flare soleant? Num hiberno sive pluvioso semestri, ex nubilosa plaga Austrina intendantur et Vulturni velut naturam induant, indeque vehementius, quam Aquilo mensibus aestivis, dominentur, adeo ut ductus aquarum inde a mense Martio ad Octobrem obsequia illis praestent? An reliquo anni tempore ex Septentrione in Austrum maria cogantur? An major observetur ventorum inconstantia circa Aequatorem, quam alibi? An pluvia sub Aequinoctiali circulo decidat faeda, adeoque contagiosa ut si collapsa corpus attigerit enascantur pustulae, vestesque faede mavolentur?

Quibus Morbis praecipue Regio sit obnoxia? Verumne quod perhibent, singulis septenis annis, humidos admodum et morbosos menses hibernos dari, hisque sex alios salubriores succedere? An immunis sit a morbis Epidemicis, et nominatim a Peste? An frequentes ibi affectus Dysenterici nunquam in Epidemios transeant? An Plenilunio et Novilunio, quin et singulis quadrantibus, alterationes manifestas corpora recipiant? An verum sit, motum Lunae diurnum non minus quam menstruum, mutationes adeo evidentes suscitet, ut singulis sex horis, accedent mari morbi ingravescant recedente vero, cruciatus mitigentur? An, licet dolores exacerbentur in morbis, ad maris affluxum, vix tamen eo tempore quisquam interent; contra vero, ad refluxum ejus, aegroti plaerique exstinguantur; idemque in partu fieri ab Obstetricibus sit observatum? An prae aliis morbis in Brasilia grassentur Catharri, Haemarrhagiae, Dysenteriae, Opthalmiae, Spasmi, Obstructiones viscerum, Febres acutae, Hydrops, Tenesmus, Cholera, Lumbrici, Lues Venerea, Impetigines? Nulli vero Calculi, nullae Arthritides, nullus Scorbutus? An multi Brasilienses ultra centesimum aetatis annum viridi senecta fruantur?

Quae remediorum genera, eorumque parandorum ratio? Num omnes passim Brasilienses inoclae medicinam faciant, morborumque notitiam ex symptomatibus venentur, et communi quaenam animi notione indicationes ex morbis eruant, iisque satisfacere pro morbi indole satagant? An seniores quique Brasiliensium eximii sint Botanici, facilique negotio omnis generis medicamina ex undequaque conquisitis parent? An ea norent tanta sagacitate intus et extus adhibere, praecipue in morbis a veneno natis, ut quis illorum manibus tutius se credat, quam Medicis, qui Rationales dici amant? An verum sit quod saepe membra militum sanciata, et jamjam ab Europaeis chirurgis amputanda, Barbari recentibus gummis, succis et balsamis, a ferro et igne praerepta feliciter restituerint? An crebro in nosocomiis relicta ulcera et gangraenae ab iisdem solo Tabacci succo curentur? An complures ex venenatorum fungorum aliorumque toxicorum esu moribundos, solo potu infusi recentis *Jaborandi* derepente a mortis faucibus vindicent?[3] An religiosi sint admodum in praescribenda aegris diaeta? An, si purgandi sit necessitas, a medicamento fortiori abstineant, et vix ultra Tamarindes[4] et Mahoacannae recentis condituram,[5] similiave laxativa, vix progrediantur? Num careant Pharmacopoliis et remedia ex variis composita aversantur, simpliciora remedia a quibus corpora non adeo irritentur, amplexantes? Num moris ibi sit, nativi medicamenti Infusum raro Igni sed Aeri et rori nocturno verus Orientem exponere? Num in Phlebotomiae usu parce, an vero liberaliter sanguinem mittant? An hirudinibus utantur, vel scarificatione, an modo utroque? Quaenam sint praecipua ipsorum Emetica, Diaphoretica, Opiata? Num loco Opii, ad conciliandum somnum, et dolorum vehementiam retundendam utantur totius corporis, praecipue vero capitis, frigidae irroratione, et unctione viscidae cujusdam et frigidae materiae, e planta quadam, *Urucatu* dicta,[6] et ex Cardui littoralis ramis contusae? Verumne sit, incolas Luem suam, corpore debite praeparato, feliciter curare solo Decocto cujus basis *Caaroba* et *Sarsaperilla*?[7] Num optato successu balsamis illis fragantibus *Copaiba*[8] et *Cabureiba*,[9] vulnera sanent, haemorrhagiam sistant, iisque interne et externe exhibitis nervos corroborent? Num Gummi illud perquam familiare, *Icicariba* dictum, (quod *Elemni* aliis vocatur) capitis affectibus, prae caeteris, medeatur?[10] Num *Tipioca* pota, fluxus sanguinis hepaticos et dysentericos internos coerceat et incrasset; nec non haemorrhagias a vulnere concitatas, sive hausta, sive plagis, emplastri in morem applicata, mundificet sanetque?[11] An foliis recentis *Tabacci* contusis, desperata restituant mala; et generatim Tabacco tanquam polychresto utantur Brasiliani; dum decoctis ejus sive intus assumptis, sive extus per fomenta adhibitis, plurimos morbos frigidos curent; gangraenos quoque, ulcera cancrosa, vulnera antiqua et sordida, succo et cineribus opis feliciter sanent? Quinimo vulneribus ab Indorum sagittis, letali toxico imbutis, morsibus quoque virulentorum animalium, beneficio foliorum tabacci tritorum, eorumque succi praesens remedium, dummodo tempestive adhibeatur, afferant? Num Incolae pulverem ejus et succum loco balsami peregrinantes circumferant?

Rogamus, ut plantarum balsamorum, gummi, et succorum, hoc paragraphi memoratorum, specimina, si commode id fieri possit, nobis trans mittantur; quod omni officiorum genere quae proficisci a nobis possunt, compensare annitemur.

II. Circa *Aquam*

In genere de Aqua marina quaeritur, An illa, si lardum, haleces, aliave carnium et piscium genera valde salita in ea maceres, dulcescant, idque citius quam in fontana?

Quaenam sit profunditas Maris circa littora Brasiliae? Quis salsedinis ejusdem gradus? An ut plurimum tranquillum sit aequor Brasiliense, adeo ut Barbari gemino ligno suberoso, *Jangada* dicto,[12] insidentes, piscaturam aliquot leucis a littore remoti secure exerceant? An agitatum noctu valde ignescat, magnoque lumine refulgeat? An adeo sit pellucidum, ut pisces ultra 20. orgyarum profunditatem aureo colore micantes, ex altis pupibus commode conspiciantur meridiano tempore, soleque lucente? Et an tum simul intueri liceat, quam motus in profundo mari subinde diversus sit et contrarius ei, qui in superficei a tumultuariis ventis cietur; id quod jactas bolides aliasque artis nauticae conjecturas non parum eludat?

Quinam sint Currentes, ut vocant? Quae Aestuum marinorum ratio? Quodnam praecise tempus Accessus et Recessus maris? Quam plagam versus mare in Aestibus volvatur? Quaenam sit distantia perpendicularis inter summos Tumores et imas subsidentias, durantibus summis incrementis et extremis decrementis? Quinam sint gradus Affluxus et Refluxus aquarum in aequalibus temporis spatiis, quaeque motus earundem Velocitas in diversis altitudinibus? Quo die Aetatis Lunae, quibusque temporibus Anni, summi Aestus infimique Recessus contingant? An verum sit, quod ibi mensibus aestivis Accessus; hibernis vero, Recessus sint longiores et vehementiores?

Quoad *Flumina*, quaenam sit eorum longitudo, et latitudo, quis cursus, quae inundationes, quae salubritas? An verum sit, fluvium, qui Pharnambucensem praefecturam terminat, et D. *Francisco* sacer est, mensibus aestivis rapidissimum esse simul et altissimum, ruptisque obicibus valentius in campos et mare ruere; mensibus autem pluviis decrescere modiceque tantum in pelagus exonerari? An fluvius Argenteus, *Rio de la Plata* dictus, exundet singulis annis, et terram faecundet *Nili* in modum? An Brasiliae flumina majora, ut sunt *Amazonum* et *Maranhan*, necnon D. *Francisci, de la Plata* et *de Janeiro* aliquando ad 30. milliaria in Oceanum labantur tanto impetu ut in ipso mari dulces hauriantur latices, etsi e fonte aliquo salirent.

Quoad *Fontes, Aquas fluviales, Aquas Minerales, Thermas, Lacus*; quaenam eorum qualitates et vires? Et an verum sit, in Lacum illum mediterraneaum, qui omnes Brasiliae fluvios, et inter eos modo dictum S. Francisci, ab altissimis Peruviae montibus Ortum versus demissos recipit, aureas arenas, a rupibus auriferis, Peruviam versus jacentibus, detritas per complures torrentes copiose devehi?

An Aquae ex imbribus collectae facillime ibi putrescant, ravimque subinde inducant nisi excoquantur? An Lacus ibi juxta littus reperiantur, qui mari licet vicini et quasi contigua aquis tamen sunt dulcissimis; puteique circa ipsum littus et quo aestus maris pertingit, effossi, qui potabiles dulcesque aquas largiuntur? An in desertis rivuli quidam e lacubus oriundi, hieme sint dulces, aestate subsalsi, eo quod stagnantes assiduo solis aestu adurantur?

Quos Pisces alant Aquae Brasilienses, tum marinae tum fluviales tum stagnantes? quae eorum varietas, copia, magnitudo, bonitas? An verum sit, Rajarum Brasiliensium duas familias, quas *Ajereba* et *Jabebirete* appellant,[13] licet carnis sint probatissimae, utrasque tamen radiis circa caudam haerentibus instructas esse, quorum punctiorae admodum malignae, exquisitos dolores adferant, quas radix arboris *Mangue*,[14] et Oleum imprimis frunctuum *Urucuri* mirum in modum mitiget?[15] Item, verumne sit, Zoophytum illud marinum pellucidum, quod *Moucicu*[16] vocant, talem habere urendi qualitatem, ut si qui nudis pedibus littora obambulent, Bullamque hanc venenatam minus provide concalcent, ingenti ardore afficiantur, qui non solum callosas pedum plantas, sed et totius corporis cutem magno confestim crucciatu infestet, malo ad aliquot horas durante, quovis remedio refrigerante anodyno frustra adhibeto; qui tamen feliciter causticis calidisque, nominatim vero mordaci illo oleo castaneae de *Acaju*,[17] in spiritu vini dissoluto, curetur? Item, num piscis, *Guamajacu Atinga*[18] dicti, folliculus fellis adeo sit venenatus, ut ejus particula vel ciceris magnitudine assumpta tam horrenda symptomata inferat, ut oculi mox caligent, mens vacillet, lingua tardescat, membrorum tremor frigidusque sudor subsequatur, vires omnes resolvantur, moxque veneno illo extinguantur; nisi illo Cancrorum genere quos *Aratu* nuncupant,[19] uno scilicet eorum contuso, et ex vino propinato, vomitumque ciente, remedium praesens afferatur? Item, deturne alterius indolis, ejusdem tamen speciei, piscis, *Guamajacu-Ape* dictus,[20] cujus caro tantae sit malignitatis, ut si immediate a coctione comedatur, mentem perturbet, ebriisque et phreneticis similes efficiat; per integram vero noctem a coctione servata tuto edatur? Item, an caro piscis, *Piraque* vocati, non vesca per inscitiam comedatur, per aliquot dies infatuet; quin et piscis hic, mediante licet baculo longo, attactus, crepitum articulorum, in medio vero tactus, artuum tremorem efficiat?[21] Rogamus, ut pisces rariores exsiccati ad augendum Pinacem nostrum transmittuntur.

III. Circa *Terram*;

Quaenam sit regionum *Brasiliae* facies? Quaenam sit summa Montium inibi celsissimorum altitudo? Num montes jaceant sparsim, an jugatim? Num Juga montium diposita sint Boream et Austrum, an vero Eurum et Zephyrum versus? Quaenam dentur montes Ignivomi, quae Promontoria?

Quaenam sit Natura Soli, num Argillosa, Arenosa, Cretacia, Levis et ferax? quae grana, quos fructus, quae alia vegetabilia, nostris oris insueta, proferat; imprimis, quae ligna aedificiis vel tincturis apta? Qua arte et industria Incolae promoveant foveantque Soli fertilitatem, et medeantur sterilitati?

Num verum sit ex arbore *Copaiba*,[8] cortice ejus ad medullam usque inciso, liquorem balsamicum, tanta quantitate sub plenilunium destillare, ut trium horarum spatio ad 12. libras olei effundat? Cum quibusvis vulneribus sanandis frigidis crucciatibus colicis fungadis, stomacho languido corroborando, gonorrhaeae sistendae etc. valere praedicetur, copiam ejus nobis transmitti exoptamus. Idem de Balsamo Peruviano, ex arbore, quae *Cabareibae*[9] dicitur, collecto nec non de Gummi arboris *Icicaribae*,[10] deque Gummi arboris *Ietaibae*,[22] de lacryma sive resina, Fruticis *Caaopia*,[23] petimus.

An succus pomi *Acaju*, arbori *Acaiaiba*[17] innascentis, linteamina ferrugineo colore maculans, nulla elici arte queat, priusquam arbores denuo floreant? Numque in ejusdem castraneae cortice oleum lateat adeo mordicans, ut si quis id incautus ore attigerit, labia et linguam, ignis ad instar, urat?

Num grana fructus arboris *Urucu* (quae eadem habetur cum *Achiotl*,)[24] urinae mixta, tam pertinaci colore tingat pannos linteos, ut elici non possit? Hujusmodi grana aliqua, una cum aliquot plantae radicibus, nobis transmitti rogamus.

Num arbor *Janipaba*,[25] mense Decembri follis spoliari caepta, mox nova prioribus multo laetiora, idque singulis mensibus, acquirat?

Num lignum arboris *Tapiae* putredinis sit expers, ideoque navibus construendis dicatum sit?[26]

Num ex ligno arboris *Ambaibae* exiccato ignem sine pyrite et chalybe eliciant incolae, foraminique excavato immittant bacillum ex duro aliquo ligno fastigiatum, quod quasi terebrando circumagunt donec vel apposita arborum folia exiccata, vel gossypium accendantur.[27]

An pulvis ligni arboris *Ibabirabae*,[28] in carbonem redacti, oculis insufflatus, et succus spinarum contusarum arboris *Saamounae*,[29] mirifice conferant oculorum inflammationibus aliisque eorum morbis? Paululum utriusque transmitti petimus.

An radix arboris *Guaiaba*,[30] una cum cortiae ejus, in aqua communi cocta et pota, eximie medeatur dysenteriae, quando indicatio est adstringendi et roborandi? Et hujus specimen desideramus. Cumque Piso innuat, dignam omnino esse Arborem, quae Europae importata, Magnatum hortos exornet, scire avemus annon possit commode in Europam, cum spe succretionis, transvehi? An fructuum ejusdem arboris grana (ut affirmat *Piso*) ab avibus et pecoribus deglutita, et mox per alvum cum excrementis egesta, losic licet arenosis, laetissime proveniant?

An arbores, *Ibixuma* et *Quitus*,[31] sint saponariae, priorisque cortex et posterioris pulpa, vicem saponis egregie praestent?

An faeminae utantur in balneis cortice arboris *Avaramo-temo*,[32] ut laxis pudendi partibus tonum restituant, aetatemque quin et virginitatem (ut Piso scribit) hac ratione mentiantur?

Num arbor *Camara-miri*,[33] flore sit unico, qui quovis anni tempore se aperiat de die hora undecima, maneatque expansus ad secundam usque pomeridianam, omnesque simul istarum arborum flores tunc eadem hora claudantur usque in diem posterum? Id quod *Piso* verissimum esse, floremque hunc sibi per deserta peregrinanti defectum horologii ex parte supplevisse scribit.

Annon arbor *Cambuy*[34] sive *Myrtus Americana sylvestris* (quae tam insignes praestat usus medicos perhibetur ab omnibus, in reficiendo stomacho, in sanandis ulceribus, in sistendo fluxu alvi juxta ac uteri, etc.) possit commode in Europam, ut ibi plantetur, transportari?

An nullum habeant Brasilienses praesentius remedium curandis equorum vulneribus, quam est pinguis illa substantia quae emanat ex foliis arboris *Paiomiriobae* sive *Tareroqui*, aqua maceratis et putrefactis?[35] Specimen hujus remedii desideramus.

Num frutex *Aminiju* ferat fructum, qui maturus inque capsulas aliquot dissiliens, Gossypium largiatur, in cujus flocco immersi sint septem nigri fructus, pistaceorum magnitudine et figura, quibus contineatur nucleus sapore amygdalino?[36]

Num ex foliis arboris *Caraguatae* conficiatur pannus lineus ideo bonae notae, ut nostro vix cedat?[37]

An Brasiliani, si cui forte necem molientur, momentum exiccatae herbae, *Sylva de Praya* dictae,[38] in pulverem tritae, epulis indant, et sic vitam eripiant; nec ullum huic malo remedium hucusque repertum, ipsi hujus plantae radici praeferendum? Numque folia ejusdem plantae, venenata licet, in emplastri formam redacta, strumas resolvant et curent?

An *Cereibunae*,[39] quae species *Manguae* est, fructu amaro vescentes palumbi, carnem inde nanciscantur adeo amarem, ut vix esculenta sit?

Nam *Petum* sive *Tabacum* experientia cognitum sit in Brasilia, mederi malis sequentibus; nempe, recentia ejus folia eorumque succus et balsamum ulceribus cancrosis frenum imponere, et venenatis morsibus mederi; aquam aliumve liquorem convenientem, in quo maceratum fuit Tabacum, pediculos enecare, et multa capitis mala cutanea mundificare; cineres foliorum exiccatorum vermes enecare; masticata folia lassitudinem et famem sedare peregrinantibus in desertis; ventriculum et cor roborare; Tabaci syrupum asthmati et hydropi multum prodesse, vi sua incidendi et abstergendi validissima? Numque iis solis non prosit, qui vel bilioso vel delicatiori fuerint temperamento?[40]

Num *Mirabilis Peruana* media nocte ad lumen aperiatur et patentissima fiat, nec sole delectetur, quod ejus calorem qui paucum quippe tenuemque florum humorem dissipet ferre nequeat?[41]

Num semina *Quigombi* sive *Alceae muscatae* masticata vel manus attacta incalefacta fragrantissimum odorem moschi referant? Specimen eorum desideratur.[42]

An radix *Jaborandi*,[3] prima speciei apud *Pisonem*, eximie valeat contra venena frigida, ejusque recentis pugillus contusus atque e convenienti liquore haustus, cujuscunque fere veneni emi per sudores et urinas exturbet? Hujus quoque aliquam quantitatem expetimus.

An radix fruticis *Acutiguepo-obi* sola,[43] absque alio remedio, ulcera male morata sanet? Specimen ejus transmitti rogamus.

An verum sit, succum floris et foliorum plantae *Nambi*[44] tergo bufonis leviter instillatum, confestim eum enecare; et praeterea, hominum praecordia adversus venena, si ventriculo jejuno hauriati, munire? Paululum ejus nobis transmitti petimus.

An per experientiam revera constet, radices adeo decantatas plantarum *Ipecachanhae* et *Caa-apiae*[23] insigni pollere facultate purgatrice per superiora et inferiora, omnique veneno eximie adversari; nec praestantius facile remedium adversus plurimos morbos, ex longa obstructione ortos, in Brasilia reperiri?

An integra herba *Murucuia-miri*,[45] species Granadillae, leviter attrita, et ex aqua vel vino assumpta, tuto et jucunde secundinas expellunt, et robur visceribus mox restituat; numque folia ejus contusa, et fervente aquae, donec tepescat, indita, atque podici aliquoties applicata, praesentissum contra haemorrhoidas remedium praebeant? Specimen ejus petimus.

Num radix herbae *Caapebae*, a Lusitanis dicta *Erva de nossa Senhora*,[46] in taleolos secta, et per aliquot dies sub dio in liquido convenienti macerata, et pota usque adeo calculi expellat materiam, ut magnates Lusitani aliud nullum medicamentum huic praetulerint? Quantitatem ejus aliquam nobis transmitti rogamus.

Hactenus de Vegetabilibus.

Progrediamur ad *Animalia*, et inquiramus, Quibus Animalibus Brasilia abundet, sive feris, sive domesticis; quaeque particulatim *Insecta* ibi abundent? Verumne sit, Gallinas, Columbas aliasque aves palmipedes, in Brasiliam ex Europa illatas magis esse prolificas, nec non incubatum minori temporis spatio, quam in Europa absolvere?

Rogatur, ut avis illa in vertice cornigera, quae *Anhyma* vocatur,[47] cujus cornu antidotalem qualitalem obtinet, nobis exsiccata transmittatur, una cum aliis insignioribus istius regioni peculiaribus avibus. An avis *Urubu*,[48] ita faeteat, sive viva, sive mortua, ut haud impune feratur, et quandoque nauseam et vomitum cieat?

De *Quadrupedibus*, scire avemus, An soli *Porci* inter pecora Europaea Brasiliae invecta, in melius ibi mutentur, adeo ut non faecunditatis solum, sed et nutrimenti ratione eam praerogativum obtineant, ut aegris aeque ac sanis tutae sint delitiae, carnique ovillae praeferantur? An compertum sit, emplastrum paratum ex rasura pilosa tophorum sphaericorum, quae in boum imprimis ventriculis reperiuntur, contra haemorrhagias feliciter applicari? An verum sit, animalculum illud, *Maritacaca* dictum,[49] viverram referens, Ambramgriseam avide devorare, tantum tamen abesse, ut gratum inde odorem spargat, ut e contra vel leviter irritatum, erepitum ventris emittat cum faetore intolerabili, alliique aemulo; qui faetor adeo inficiat vestes, capillos, arma etc. ut ne quidem fortissimo lixivio, 20 dierum spatio, faetorem exuant. An Capreae Brasilienses lapidem Bezoardicum ventriculo gignant, eoque contra venena incolae cum successu utantur?

An Apri Brasilienses vulnerati soleant infinitos sui generis convocare tunc Venatores, vel Tigrides, perpetuos hostes, gregatim adoriri?

Verumne sit, Tigrides Brasilianas, imprimis quae rufescentibus sunt maculis instar carni vitulinae non solum a Brasilianis, sed et omnibus passim Europaeis aestimari?

An Lacerti Brasilienses adeo sint inediae patientes, ut ad 6. vel etiam 8. mensium spatium asservati, ne ulla quidam capta musca vel culice necdum alio cibo hausto, vitam tolerent? Numque eorum, fructibus et ovis crudis vescentium, caro elixa vel frixa inter delicias expetatur? Porro, an haec animalia mactata et excoriata, diu adhuc moveantur, cordaque eorum excepta admodum subsiliant? Adhaec, An quandoque in ventriculo Lacertorum inveniatur Lapis ovi fere gallinacei extrinsecus figura et magnitudine, intus vero Lapidis bedoardici colore et substantia, qui contusus a tunicis, quibus constat, facile separetur? Et si ita sit, an lapis hic aestimetur ab incolis?

An Testudines inediam ferre possint ad biennium usque, dummodo tantillum aquae sorbeant. Verumne sit, Locustas *Gaayara* dictas,[50] in plantas transformari, pedibus primum terrae affixis, unde radices exeant, quae terrae infigantur, ex quo paulatim parvo temporis spatio totae convertantur? An Erucae Brasilienses, Lagartas des *Verças* dictae, transmittentur in aviculas pulcherrimas, *Guainumbi* dictas?[51]

Quoad Incolas *Homines*, tum Viros tum Faeminas; quid eorum indoles, statura, forma, fortitudo, agilitas, lingua, arma, religio, vivendi ratio, supellex etc quibus rebus et exercitiis maxime incumbant?

An nunquam assent carnem veru affixam, sed foveam faciant in terra, ejusque fundo imponunt grandia alicujus arboris folia illisque imponant carnem assandam, quam itidem foliis tegunt terraque obruant, super ea focum struentes luculentum, eumque continuantes donec probe assatam esse carnem judiciaverint? Annon bibant inter edendum sed a parte demum potum adjiciunt?[52]

Verumne sit, incoles mature pubescere, senescere tarde, idque sine caritie aut calvitio? An matres Brasilienses rideant nostrates in vestiendis et educandis parvulis curam, eaque perspirationem impediri et catharros multos generari dicant?[53] An nulli, inter eos, strabones, lusciosi, claudi, gibbi, inveniantur; cum tamen infantes nunquam aut linteis involvantur, aut involuti fasciis ligentur, sed frigida frequenter laventur? An Brasilienses raro adversa valetudine afficiantur? An eorum callentiores longaevitatem et bonam valetudinem suam his causis tribuant, viz. quod fortibus nascantur, et eximiae Aeris Ventorumque serenitati et aequalitati exponantur; tum etiam, quod tantum non ignorent, quid curae sint, quid animi affectus et corporeae voluptates; quodque eodem semper victu et amictu, eoque simplici gaudeant? An nulla in ipsis plus habendi cupido percipiatur, atque ea invicem aequitate vivant, ut cui plus est, lubens impertiatur minus habentibus, pari dandi et poscendi invicem facilitate? An faeminae inter illos pudicae ab octennio ultra sexagesimum annum sint faecundae; imo septuagenareae orbos infantes lactare conspiciantur? Num facili negotio et nemine obstetricante pariant, rarissime abortientes? An plaeraeque puerperae statim in partu surgant, ad proximum flumen ad corpus abluendum properent, et impigre ad officia domestica redeant.[54]

Cum characterum et literarum ignari dicantur, quomodo antiquitatis memoriam, resque tam pace quam bello gestas conservent?

An Brasilienses Mediterranei sine lege, sine religione, ferino ritu in hunc usque diem, nulla stabile sede, morentur, et sub dio perpetuo victitent? An *Tapujae* jacula sine arcu validissimis lacertis torquere norint? Sintne adeo strenui Urinatores, ut, re ferente, patentibus oculis totius horae spatio urinentur?[55]

An *Ovetacates*, gens una Brasiliensium, adeo sint pernices, ut inter venandum, cervos assequi valeant? An omnes fluminis *Platae* accolae sint statura gigantea et sua velocitate capreas fugientes retinere possint?

An passim in ipso mortis articulo laetabundi quasi de Euthanasia glorientur? Num verum sit, illos prae amore in parentum, veneno non extinctorum, cadavera involare, eaque dilaniata intra se sepelire?[56]

An qui a Veneris aestu temperare sibi nesciunt, in Brasilia, illius caeli temperiem ferre nequeant?[57] Num ibidem tam advenae quam indigenae cavere sibi debeant a vini et carnium usu quotidiano? An incolarum potus maxime uscitatus et saluberrimus sit aqua eorum fontanum vel fluvialis limpidissima, quaeque largius et crebrius pota nullos in ventre vel hypochondriis flatus aut tormina excitet, neque ventriculum debilitet, sed contra egregie refocillet?

An infantes juvenesque frequentioribus morbis ibi infestentur, senes vero rarioribus?

Insuper inquirendum, quaenam *Fossilia* ibi reperiantur majori copia, quaenam fodinae lapideae, lapidumque qualitates, quique eorum, respectu plagarum mundi, positus etc? Qualis glebas tellus illa largiatur, ut sunt

Margae, Terrae fulloniae, Terrae fictiles, Boli, aliaeque terrae medicatae? Quaenam alia fossilia regio suppeditet, puta Carbones fossiles, Salinas, Alumen, Chalcanthum, Stibium, Sulphur etc? Quaenam metalla ferat; circa quae indagandum, quae Fodinarum Metallicarum constitutio, varietas, quis situs, quae profunditas, signa, aquae, qui halitus; quae methodus ex globis metallicis metalla eliciendi etc?

An in littore regionis *Maghe*, rupes quaedam Smaragdina, in turris modum se attollat, quae Sole tacta mire radiet?

Verumne sit, quod Ambra grisea ex Oceano copiose in Brasiliae littus eructetur, ibique non-nisi procelloso mari alluat; quodque, tempestate vix cessante, aves (imprimis, Struthiones)[58] et quadrpuedes nonnullae in ipso littore certatim eam devorent, priusquam ipsi maris accolae eo perveniant?

An omnis ante insolationem Ambra molle tantum gluten sit, ingratoque adeo adore nares feriat, ut ab inexpertis plane respuatur; animalia tamen illa dulcem ejus saporem, prius persentiscant, ejusque sapore mire delectentur?

Inquiratur porro, quaenam sit *Magnetis* Declinatio in diversis partibus Brasiliae, quaeque Declinationis variatio in loco eodem?

Circa *Venena* investigetur, Verumne sit, liquorem ex radica *Mandihoca* expressum,[59] sapore dulcem, ab animalibus avidissime haustum, statim ea extinguet, ex radice tamen non expressum caetera animantia nutriat, praeter homines quibus lethalis sit, nisi humorem ejus penitus expresserint, quo facto et panem et potum inde salubrem conficiant?

An ex eadem radice, maximo licet scatente veneno, optimum tamen non modo alimentum, sed et antidotum *Carima* dictum, paretur.[60]

An a solo hepate piscis Brasiliensis *Uruti*, punctura ejus venenata curetur, cum caetera remedia respuat?[61]

An celebris illa herba, *Juquiri*, Oves et Capras pinguefaciat, homines interimat?[62]

An Nux Vomica Feles, Mures et Aves enecet, hominibus, vero medicina sit?[63]

An folia, flores, et fructus herbarum *Tangaraca*[64] et *Juquiri*, venena Brasiliae facile prima, propriam suam unaquaeque radicem pro opposito habeat Antidoto?

An Bufoni Cururu aliisque Insectis Venenatis habitis, solius *Nhambi*, decantatae illius panaceae, succus suffusus, vel cinis Tabaci aspersus, praesentem mortem inferant.[65]

An verum sit, aliquis Venenatorum animalculorum puncturas nulli cessisse remedio, quam hepati ejusdem animalis, et ea potissimum parte applicato, qua vesiculae fellis est continuum?

An Brasilienses passim serpentum, viperarum, bufonum et piscium venenatorum ictus pinguedine, capitibus et jecinoribus eorundem applicatis curent?

An nonnullae, quae in *Europa* sunt venenata, in *Brasiliae* vesca reperiantur, et vice versa, et quaenam illa sint? Adhaec, num formicae illae grandiores, tum carnes aliquot serpentum, lacertorum, vermium et glirium sylvestrium, principibus Brasiliae incolis inter delicias habeantur? Nominatim, an Centipedes illi, *Carasitu* et *Caromouritu* dicti, virides et nigri, eviscerati tostique, inprimis autem Vermes illi *Jarumai* et *Caramatori*, pingues et albicantes, inque medullosis sylvestrium Palmarum truncis viventes, ipsis sint in pretio?[66]

An Brasilienses dicto citius, ubi de natura veneni constiterit, in sylvis efficacissimas herbas colligere norint, quas contusas, portionis[67] forma, aegris subministrant, animasque pene extinctas suscitent?

An viperae et Angues insito quodam timore a Cancris abhorreant, tum Porci quoque ab istis laesi, instincta naturali se esu Cancrorum curent?

Verumne sit, serpentum illum sonorum sive crepitaculo instructum Brasilianis *Boicininga*, nobis *Rattle-snake* dictum,[68] caudae extremitate in anum hominis immissa, mortem confestim inferre, veneno autem suo, quod ore vel dentibus infundit, multo lentius vitam tollere? Numque praesentissimum prae caeteris remedium, quod Barbaris contra hujus aut qualiscunque Serpentis morsus restat, sit ipsius nocentis caput contusum atque emplastri forma vulneri calens applicatum, virentibus Tabaci foliis partibus vicinis impositis?

An revera constet, Serpentem *Boicuaiba*,[69] cum comnibus fere serpentibus, maxime venenatis perpetuum bellum exercere, eosque insidiose opprimere, imo venenatissimum *Boicininga* aliquando devorare, ipsum tamen adeo veneni expertem deprehendi, ut incolae carnem ejus comedere non extimescant?

Verumne sit, ictis a serpentibus *Curucucu, Ibiracoa* et *Boipeba*, sanguinem bullientem mox e naribus, oculis auribusque, imo manuum et pedum unguibus, profluere?[70]

Num serpens ille immanis *Boiguaçu* dictus feris hominibusque adeo terribilis a Formicis tamen, patulum ejus os turmatim ingressis, necetur;[71] cum istiusmodi formicae a parva vipera, *Ibiiara*, in fugam vertantur?

An viperae, *Jararacae* dictae, muscum fortiter redoleant, adeo ut dolorem capitis inferant?[72] Specimen ejus exisiccatae petitur.

An vipera, *Ibiiáram* dicta, capitibus duobus sit instructa, et Utroque ore venenum fundat?[73]

Num crocodili, *Jacaré* dicti, vulnera adipe ipsius animantis coalescant; ipsiusque testes myrothecium redoleant; nec non omasus ejus siccatus et in pulverem redactus, calculo medeatur? Num caro et ova ejus ad esum expectantur?[74]

Verumne sit, Icheumonem, muris genus, Crocodili dormientis fauces intrare ventremque exedere?[75]

An caudae Lacertarum ex parte amputatae renascantur, sed integrae abscissae non item?

Verumne sit, illa Lacertarum genera, quae *Taraguira* et *Tejunhana* appellantur, celerrime accurrant, quando hominem vident dormientem, cui Serpens aut aliud venenatum animal laedendi causa appropinquat, illumque expergefaciant ne saucietur?[76]

An Araneae illae, *Nhamdú* dictae, ni caute apprehendantur, veneni liquorem primo attactu spargant, qui, si oculum feriat, totalem visus privationem minetur?[77]

An passim receptum sit, oleo mordacissimo, ex immaturis et crudis glandibus, qui pomis *Acaju* adnascuntur, extracto praecavere irreptionem minutissimorum illorum insectorum, quae Lusitanis *Bicho* dicuntur, ne scilicet plantas pedum et manuum cutem penetrant, inque iis se recondant; ubi vesicula orbiculata inclusi, postquam ad iustam magnitudinem excrevere, aciculae vel argenteae cuspidis beneficio a Brasilianis facile exciduntur, ea adhibita cautione, ut vermis folliculo inclusus eximatur integer, antequam sobolem progeneret; cum folliculo rupto nova oriantur symptomata, unde vel ipsa quandoque gangraena nascitur?[78]

An serpentes quidam integras formicarum myriadas deglutiant; et num formicae tostae et assumptae difficultatibus urinae, aeque ac millipedes, succurrant?

An compertum omnino sit, Brasilienses nosse tanta solertia praeparare venena, ut ocius vel tardius operentur, quinimo ut stato tempore interimant, postquam ad dies et menses aliquot sepulta quasi mansere, priusquam vires exercerent? Et an possint sagittas, vestres, cibos, et fructus crescentes, aquam et integros fluvios sic inficere, ut pedetentim, non statim, homines extinguant?

An scelestiores Brasiliensium, dicti Bufonis, ad solem suspensi, bilem et spumam colligant, eaque inter secretiora et lente necantia venena reservent?[79]

An passim id observetur, quod Piso semet observasse scribit, tempore scilicet imbrido, comitante suffocativo tepore veris, corruptionem accelerante, ex unaquaque gutta aquae crassae, in momento quasi generari Bufones, tot myriadas simul, ut solum universum sub iis lateat; neque illi Bufonibus ex coitu natis ullo modo differant?

Verumne sit, radices herbae Castae sive Mimosae[80] tutum praebere antidotum, folia vero ejus pernicioso veneno turgere, si saepe in usum adhibeantur. Ita

> ——— Qui mihi vulnera fecit,
> Solus Achilleo tollere more potest.

Soleantne venefici Brasilienses tantillum pulveris foliorum exiccatorum herbae Mimosae, clam inditum fistulae una cum Peto sociis propinare, qui nullam exinde longo temporis spatio noxam sentiunt; attamen, nullo licet accedente effectu manifesto, tandem emaciati mortem obeantur?

An *Manipuera*, i.e. succus radicis *Mandehocae*, adeo venenosus est, ut famulis hanc radicem praeparantibus, necesse sit esculentis et potulentis admiscere flores *Nhambi* et radices *Urucú*, ad muniendum cor et ventriculum, ne a noxiis vaporibus inficiantur? Et num Venefici ex succo hoc usque ad totalem ejus putredinem reservato, altiorem corruptionis gradum ex vermiculis inde nascentibus quaerant, iisque in pulverem redactis hominum vitae insidientur, ita ut, exigua licet quantitate, vitam certo citoque adimat, si exhibeatur simplex; si vero compositum, et viribus imminatis (quod potissimum pulvere herbae *Caapeba* et *Nhambus* fieri solere dicitur) longo post tempore interimat?[81]

Verumne sit, succum hunc, *Manipueram*, adeo venenosum esse, ut, si crudus assumatur, statim enecet; nutritivus vero fiat, si percoquatur?

An nuclei fructus arboris *Ahoay*,[82] in pulverem redacti, qualitate sint adeo venenosa, ut tantilla ejus quantitas ore hausta omne antidotum respuat? Specimen eorum petitur.

An herba *Nhambi* sit quasi Panacea adversus plaeraque venena? Insigniorem ejus quantitatem nobis transmitti rogamus, ut et herbarum *Caapiae, Caacicae, Jaborandi, Caapebae,* quae et valde Antidotales haberi dicuntur.

An Erinaceorum, qui, *Cuandú* vocantur,[83] spinae adeo venenosa sint qualitate, ut irritate tam profunde eas ejaculentur, ut sensim in carnem penetrent, et viscera inficiant, transfixosque lente perimant: contra vero, tela haec emortua prosint, ita quidem ut eorum pulvis, drachmae plus minus pondere assumptus, familiari isti Indiarum dysenterico malo medeatur, si aliquoties reiteretur cum liquore convenienti?

Appendix

An verum sit, Apes Brasilienses ceram nigram conficere? Et si sic, aliquantum ejus transmitti rogamus.

An planta, *Hetich* dicta,[84] unde farinam conficiunt Brasilienses (perinde atque ex *Maniocha*), semine careat, propagetur vero radicibus orbiculatim concisis, atque hoc modo per agrum satis?

An apud Brasilienses nulla animantia, sive terrestria, sive aquatica; nec ullae arbores, herbae, fructus reperiantur, quae a nostris non sint dissimiles, exceptis his tribus plantis, portulaca, ocymo, et filice?

Quibus animalibus utantur Brasiliani loco equorum, quibus omnino carere scribuntur?

An faeminae Brasilienses nullis menstruis laborent, sed fluxum illum arte quadam divertere norint, et quaenam illa sit.

TRANSLATION

Inquiries for Brazil, commended to the charge of Mr. Thomas Hill, who in his letter from Lisbon of 23 July 1671 [N.S.] promised that he would send them to the Jesuit N—— N—— at Bahia, written by H. Oldenburg on 19 August 1671.

I. Concerning the Air: What is the usual healthfulness (or otherwise) of the air? What changes take place in the sky according to the various seasons of the year and different times of day? Is it true that during summer nights a pretty sharp chill is often felt, and in winter quite a mild one? In which months does the rainy season begin and end? In what state are the heavens when the sun is exactly overhead in Brazil, in February and October? In the same region of the Brazilian sky, with an equal approach and recession of the sun,[1] and in the same months of the year, is it always summery and dry in the eastern part near the ocean, and wintry and wet in the western part on the other side of Brazil's mountain range? Are the nights for the most part so clear, that the old moon and the new may be seen on one and the same day, and that print can be read pretty well by the light of a quarter moon? Is the stillness of the air in Brazil such as to be very proper for astronomers wishing to make very important observations in the heavens to do with eclipses, the Magellanic Clouds, Venus when she is sickle-shaped after emerging from the sun, and Mercury when it is scintillating and horned, the appulses of the moon to both stars and planets, and other phenomena rarely seen by Europeans?

What types of meteors are most usually generated there? Is there brilliant lightning flashing in the evening sky, as has been written, even when the weather is very calm and dry? Does it thunder very loudly and frequently at Maranhão,[2] near the Equator? Do rainbows, haloes, and fiery flying dragons appear frequently? Is it true that hail is seen hardly anywhere, and that the tops even of the highest mountains remain free from snow? Are the raindrops very big, falling with great violence? Is the Brazilian dew much more fertile, penetrating, subtle than that of Europe, and does it corrode and wear away iron and other things exposed in the open very easily, yet being of such vigor that it marvelously strengthens both men and cattle when they are hesitant and downhearted?

What winds generally blow? Do they come in the winter or rainy season from the cloudy southern region and, assuming a southeast by south character, thence prevail more strongly in the summer months than the north wind, so that the drawing of the waters from thence in the period from March to October obeys their behest? And in the remainder of the year are the seas driven from north to south? Is there a greater uncertainty in the winds near the equator than elsewhere? Is the rainfall at the equator so foul and infectious that if it falls upon the body it causes pustules and damages clothing?

What chief diseases does the region suffer from? Is it true as they say that every seventh year the winter months are very damp and sickly, and that then six healthier years follow? Is it immune from epidemic diseases and plague in particular? Do the frequent outbreaks of dysentery there never become epidemic? Are there obvious alterations in the [human] body at full moon and new moon, indeed at the quarters too? Is it true that the moon's daily and monthly motions provoke such marked changes [in a patient] that every six hours, as the sea flows in, an illness grows more serious and as the sea ebbs again the suffering declines? Although the sufferer's torments increase with the flowing of the sea, do hardly any sick die at that time, while on the contrary many perish with the ebb tide? And is the same observed by midwives at time of birth? Are the diseases that rage in Brazil catarrhs, hemorrhages, dysenteries, ophthalmias, spasms, obstructions of the bowels, acute fevers, hydropsies, tenesmus, cholera, intestinal worms, syphilis, impetigo? Is there no stone, arthritis, nor scurvy? Do many Brazilians enjoy a green old age beyond one hundred years?

What are the remedies and how are they prepared? Do all the natives up and down Brazil practice medicine, do they seek after knowledge of diseases from their symptoms, and do they try to deal with them according to the character of the disease, after they have considered its symptoms according to some common intellectual principle? Are the older Brazilians excellent botanists, able with ease to prepare every kind of medicine from materials gathered in all places? Do they know how to apply them both internally and externally with such wisdom that anyone may with greater safety entrust himself to them, than to the physicians who like to be called rational, especially when the sickness is caused by a poison? Is it true that the natives often heal successfully (using fresh resins, juices, and balms and leaving aside knife and cautery) the wounded limbs of soldiers, even when the European surgeons say they ought to be amputated? Are the hospital cases of ulceration and gangrene often cured by them with the sole aid of tobacco juice? Are many persons dying as a result of eating poisonous fungi and other toxic substances suddenly snatched from the jaws of death merely by drinking freshly infused *jaborandi*?[3] And are they very strict in controlling the diet of the sick? If purgation is necessary do they abstain from strong drugs, rarely employing anything more than fresh preparations of tamarind[4] or *mechoacanna*,[5] or a similar laxative? Are they without druggists and averse to remedies made from many ingredients, preferring simpler remedies that irritate the body less? Is it the custom there rarely to expose infusions of indigenous remedies to fire, but rather to the air and nightly dew towards the east? Are they sparing of bloodletting, or do they let blood freely? Do they use leeches, or scarifiers, or what method? What are their most important emetics, diaphoretics, opiates? In order to induce sleep or numb the agony of suffering, instead of using opium, do they [apply to] the whole body, and the head especially, a cool lotion and a thick ointment of some cool material bruised out of a certain plant called *urucatu*[6] and the seashore thistle? Is it true that the inhabitants cure the pox successfully, after preparing the body properly first, by a mere decoction whose basis is sarsaparilla and *caaroba*?[7] Do those fragrant balms *copaiba*[8] and *cabureiba*[9] cure wounds as well as one could wish, stop hemorrhages and strengthen the nerves, when taken either internally or externally? Does that very common resin, called *icicariba* or (by others) *elemi* heal afflictions of the head particularly?[10] Does the drink tapioca restrain and thicken the internal bloody flux in dysentery or disease of the liver, and does it (either when drunk, or when applied to the injury like a plaster) cleanse and heal hemorrhages bursting out of wounds?[11] Do bruised fresh tobacco leaves cure desperate diseases, and do the Brazilians in general use tobacco as a panacea? Do they cure many chilling diseases either with decoctions of tobacco taken internally, or with foments of it applied externally, and also treat successfully gangrenes, cancerous ulcers, old foul wounds with its juice and ashes? And indeed carry with them a present remedy, provided it be timely employed, for the wounds caused by Indian arrows coated with a deadly poison and for the bites of poisonous creatures, in the shape of the ground leaves and juice of tobacco? Do the natives when traveling carry this powder and juice instead of a balm?

We ask that if it may conveniently be done, some samples of the balsamic plants, resins, and juices mentioned in this paragraph may be sent to us; we will strive to make recompense with every kind of service within our power.

II. Concerning water; in general it is asked of seawater, if you steep bacon, salt fish, and other kinds of salty meats and fish in it, do they become sweet more quickly than in fresh water?

What is the depth of the sea off the coast of Brazil? What degree of saltness has it? Is it so very calm and smooth that the natives, sitting on a pair of timbers of a corklike wood called *jangada*,[12] safely paddle out fishing to a few leagues distance from the shore? When it is disturbed at night, does it sparkle much and shine brightly? Is it so clear that from the high poop [of a ship] about midday, with the sun shining, fish can easily be seen twenty fathoms down, gleaming with a golden color? And then at the same time one can perceive how different the movement deep down in the sea is, and contrary to that upon the surface which is excited by the boisterous wind; which upsets the hurling of missiles and other schemes of naval artifice not a little?

What are the currents, as they are called? And what is the rule of the tides? At what times exactly does the sea ebb and flow? In what direction does the tide set? What is the vertical distance between the highest flow and the lowest ebb at spring tides? What is the amount of flow or ebb in equal time intervals, and what is the velocity of the movement of the water at various heights? At what age of the moon and season of the year do the highest tides and lowest ebbs occur? Is it true that in the summer months the rising tide is long-lasting and violent, while in winter the reverse is true?

What rivers are there, what is their length and breadth, what is their course, their healthfulness, their liability to flood? Is it true that the river called after St. Francis which bounds the province of Pernambuco is very swift and full in the summer months, so that breaking its dikes it rushes violently into the fields as well as the sea; while in the rainy months it subsides and makes only a moderate stream? Does the "silvery river," the River Plate, flood each year and fertilize the land as the Nile does? Do the greater rivers of Brazil, namely the Amazon, the São Francisco, the Plate, the Rio de Janeiro, and the Maranhão, sometimes run up to thirty miles into the ocean with such force that out at sea a sweet fluid may be drawn up as though straight from a spring?

As to springs, river water, mineral waters, hot springs, and lakes: what are their characteristics and virtues? And is it true that gold-rich sands are brought down in quantity, from the gold-bearing rocks lying over towards Peru as they are worn away by mountain streams, into that inland lake which receives all the Brazilian rivers and among them the São Francisco mentioned before, running down from the very high mountains of Peru, farther west?

Does water collected from roofs readily putrefy there, and bring on hoarseness unless it is boiled? Do lakes occur near the seashore there which contain fresh water although so near, almost contiguous, to the sea; and can wells be dug near the shore within the tidemark, which yield a potable fresh water? Are there in the deserts certain streams arising from lakes, which are fresh in the winter, but brackish in the summer because being stagnant they are dried up by the constant heat of the sun?

What fish flourish in the waters of Brazil, whether the sea, rivers, or still water? What is their variety, plenty, size, and goodness? Is it true that there are two families of the Brazilian ray, called *ajereba* and *jabebirete*,[13] which although most certainly fleshy are both provided with stings attached near the tail, the venomous points of which cause exquisite torments, which may be wonderfully eased by the root of the *mangue* tree[14] and especially by the oil of the fruit *urucuri*?[15] Also, is it true that that transparent marine zoophyte they call *moucicu*[16] has such a burning quality in it that if anyone walking barefoot on the beach happens to tread carelessly on this poisonous blob he is seized with a violent burning pain, not only in the hardened sole of the foot but tormenting the whole surface of the body for a period of several hours, during which the application of cooling anodynes is quite vain; and yet the pain is readily removed by hot, caustic medicaments, especially that vesicant oil from the cashew nut, dissolved in alcohol?[17] Also, is the membrane of the gall bladder of the fish called *guamajacu atinga*[18] so poisonous that if a particle no bigger than a chick-pea be swallowed it causes such dreadful symptoms that the eyes soon become clouded, the mind wanders, the speech becomes thick, and the limbs are affected by a trembling and cold sweat, so that all bodily vigor is first weakened, then extinguished by that poison, unless one of those crabs they call *aratu* is applied as an immediate remedy— bruised, and drunk with wine, provoking a vomit?[19] Further, is there another variety of fish of the same species, called *guamajacu-ape*,[20] whose flesh is so hurtful that if it is eaten straight after being cooked it disturbs the mind, causing as it were a fit of drunkenness or frenzy; but if it is laid aside all night after cooking it may be eaten safely? Also, does the flesh of the fish called *piraque* fuddle one for several days if eaten by mistake, and besides this, if this fish is touched, even with a long stick, does it cause a crackling of the joints and a trembling in the limbs?[21] We ask that dried fishes may be sent to us for the enlargement of our repository.

III. Concerning the earth: what is the appearance of the regions of Brazil? What is the height of its most lofty mountains? Do the mountains rise in isolation, or form a chain? Is the chain of mountains aligned north and south or east and west? What volcanoes are there, what headlands?

What is the nature of the soil, is it sandy, chalky, clay, poor, or fertile? What corn, fruits, and other plants does it yield, unknown in Europe? Particularly, what timber is there useful for building or as dyestuff? By what art and labor do the natives promote and maintain the fertility of the soil, and remedy any infertility?

Is it true that at the time of full moon such a quantity of liquid balsam may be tapped from the tree *copaiba*[8] (by cutting through the bark to the heartwood) that in three hours time up to twelve pounds of oil may flow out? As it is said to be excellent for healing any kind of wound, driving away cold, agonizing colics, strengthening weak stomachs, and stopping gonorrheas we much desire a supply of it. We also wish for some of the Peruvian balm collected from the tree called *cabureiba*[9] and of the resin of the *icicariba* tree,[10] of that of the *ietaiba*[22] tree, and the oozings or resin of the *caaopia* shrub.[23]

Does the juice of the cashew nut growing on the *acaiaiba*[17] tree stain linen with a rusty color that can be removed by no artifice before the trees flower again? And is there in the bark of the same "chestnut" tree an oil so stinging that if anyone should carelessly put some to his mouth it would at once burn his tongue and lips as if it were fire?

Do the seeds of the fruits of the *urucu* tree (which is thought to be the same as the *achiotl*)[24] when mixed with urine dye linen cloths with such a fast color that it cannot be removed? We ask for some of these seeds, together with a few roots of the plant, to be sent to us.

When the leaves of the *janipaba* tree begin to wither in December, does it soon acquire new ones, much more attractive than the former, and thus every month?[25]

Is the wood of the *tapia* tree nonputrefying, and so thought to be highly suitable for shipbuilding?[26]

Do the natives draw fire from the dry wood of the *ambaiba* tree without flint and steel, for making a hole in it they place in that a stick of some hard wood which they twirl round as though drilling, until some dried leaves or cotton placed nearby catch light?[27]

Does the wood of the *ibabiraba* tree,[28] when reduced to charcoal and powdered, if blown into the eyes, and also the juice of the pounded thorns of the *saamouna* tree,[29] marvelously benefit the eyes in cases of inflammation and other diseases? We ask for a little of both to be sent over.

Does the root of the *guaiaba* tree,[30] together with its bark, boiled in ordinary water and drunk, have a notable curative effect in dysenteries, when the signs warrant a drying and strengthening action? We also desire a sample of this.

And as Piso suggests that this tree is very worthy of being imported into Europe to adorn noblemen's gardens, we desire to know whether it can conveniently be transported into Europe, with some hope of its growing up? Do the seeds from the fruit of this tree (as Piso alleges), when they have passed through the alimentary canals of birds or cattle and fall even on sandy ground, spring up most cheerfully?

Are the *ibixuma* and *quiti* trees of a soaplike quality, the bark of the former and the pulp of the latter serving excellently instead of soap?[31]

Is the wood of the *avaramo-temo* tree used by women at the baths in order to restore the tone of their organs, feigning in this way (as Piso writes) youth and all but virginity itself?[32]

Does the *camara-miri* tree have so unique a flower that every year at a certain time it opens itself each day at eleven o'clock, and stays open till two o'clock in the afternoon, when all the flowers of those trees close themselves at the same moment until the following day?[33] This Piso writes is most true and that he himself when traveling in these wastes partly supplied the want of a clock by observing these flowers.

Can the *cambuy* tree,[34] or wild American myrtle (which is said by all to have such great medical usefulness in restoring the appetite, curing ulcers, stopping an intestinal or uterine flux, and so on) be conveniently transported to Europe, in order to be planted there?

Have the Brazilians no better remedy for curing wounds in horses than that fatty substance which exudes from the leaves of the *paiomiroba* or *tareroqui* tree,[35] when they are mashed in water and rotted? We desire a specimen of this remedy.

Does the *aminiju* bush bear a fruit which when it is ripe and a few are bursting from their shells releases a cotton, in whose strands are embedded seven black fruits, in shape and size like the pistachio, in which there is a kernel having an almond taste?[36]

Is "linen" cloth made from the leaves of the *caraguata* tree of such good repute, that it is hardly inferior to ours?[37]

Do the Brazilians, in striving to put a person to death, slip a very small amount of the dried and powdered herb called *sylva de praya*[38] into his food and so steal his life away; and, in the case of such a crime, has any remedy been found hitherto to be used in preference to the root of this very plant? And though this plant is poisonous, do its leaves when made up into a poultice wonderfully resolve tumors, and cure them?

Does the *cereibuna*,[39] which is a species of mangrove with a bitter fruit, make the flesh of pigeons eating its fruit so bitter, that it is scarcely edible?

Is *petum* or tobacco known by experience in Brazil to cure the following ailments; that is, to inhibit with its fresh leaves and their juice and balsam cancerous ulcers, and heal poisonous bites? Does tobacco mashed in water (or any fluid to hand) kill lice and cure many skin infections of the head? Do the ashes of its dried leaves kill worms, and its leaves when chewed relieve the fatigue and hunger of the traveler in the wilderness? Do they strengthen the heart and viscera? Does the syrup from tobacco benefit asthmatic and dropsical people greatly, by its great vigor in cutting and cleaning? And does it only not benefit persons of a bilious or delicate temperament?[40]

Does the "Peruvian marvel" open to the light in the middle of the night, and become very broad, not rejoicing in the sun because it cannot bear the sun's heat which dissipates the little and thin humor of the flowers?[41]

Do the seeds of *quigombi* or *alcea muscata* when chewed or warmed in the hand give off a most fragrant odor of musk? A specimen of them is desired.[42]

Does the root of the *jaborandi*,[3] the first of the species according to Piso, work wonders against chilling poisons, a handful of the fresh root bruised and drawn into a convenient liquid driving out any kind of poison that has been swallowed by sweating and by urine? Of this also we beg some quantity.

Does the root of the *acutiguepo-obi* bush,[43] without any other remedy, hea persistent ulcers? We ask for a sample of it to be sent.

Is it true that the juice of the flowers and leaves of the plant *nambi*,[44] lightly dropped on a frog's skin, kills it at once? And furthermore, that it protects the human viscera against poisons, if it is taken into an empty stomach? We beg for a little of it to be sent to us.

Does it appear true by trial that the so-much-talked-of roots of the plants ipecacuanha and *caa-apia*[23] have a singularly powerful faculty for purging both upwards and downwards and combating strongly every kind of poison, and that there is to be found in Brazil no more effective remedy against many ills arising from a long-standing obstruction?

Does the whole plant *murucuia-miri*,[45] a kind of granadilla, slightly beaten and taken in wine or water, expel the afterbirth in a safe and pleasant manner, and soon restore strength to the viscera; and are its leaves, bruised and steeped in boiling water till it is cool and then applied to the fundament from time to time, a good remedy against hemorrhoids? We wish for a specimen of it.

Does the root of the *caapeba* plant (called by the Portuguese Our Lord's Herb),[46] cut into strips, steeped for a few days in a suitable liquid in the open and drunk, so expel the matter forming stones that the chief of the Portuguese prefer no remedy to this? We ask that some quantity of it may be sent to us.

So far concerning plants.

Now let us move on to animals and we ask, what animals abound in Brazil, both wild and domestic, and particularly what kinds of insect? Is it true that hens, doves, and other broad-footed birds brought from Europe to Brazil become more prolific, and incubate [their eggs] in less time than in Europe?

It is requested that a dried specimen of the bird called *anhyma*,[47] bearing a horn on its head possessing the quality of an antidote, may be sent us, together with the other notable birds peculiar to that part of the world. Does the *urubu* bird[48] stink so offensively, dead or alive, that it can hardly be borne with impunity, and sometimes causes nausea and vomiting?

Concerning the quadrupeds, we long to know whether pigs alone among the European cattle brought to Brazil are changed for the better there, so as to be superior not only in their fecundity but in their value as food also, [their meat] being agreeable to the sick as well as the hale, and preferred to mutton? Is it discovered that poultices made from the hairy shavings of the spherical concretions found in the stomachs of oxen especially are successfully exployed against hemorrhages? Is it true that the little animal called *maritacaca*,[49] resembling a ferret, eats ambergris eagerly but is itself so far from scattering a pleasant odor that, on the contrary, when even slightly alarmed it emits a discharge from its belly making an intolerable stink, like that of garlic; which stink so infests clothes, hair, weapons, and so on that not even the strongest lye will remove it in under twenty days? Do Brazilian goats generate the bezoar stone in their stomachs? And do the inhabitants use it successfully against poisons?

Do Brazilian bees have the habit, when injured, of gathering together an infinite number of their own kind, and of then attacking their perpetual enemies, hunters or tigers, as a swarm?

Is it true that Brazilian tigers, especially those bearing reddish spots, are reckoned [to taste] like veal, not only by the [native] Brazilians but by all the Europeans everywhere?

Are the Brazilian lizards so tolerant of fasting that they may be kept for six or eight months, supporting life without capturing a fly or a gnat or taking any other food? And is the fried or boiled flesh of others which live on fruit and raw eggs sought after as a delicacy? Further, when these animals have been killed and skinned are they still capable of moving for a long time, and does the heart beat after being excised? And again, is there sometimes found in the stomach of a lizard a stone almost like a hen's egg in size and external form, but within rather resembling the bezoar stone in color and substance which, when struck, easily breaks into the layers of which it is composed? And if so, is this stone prized by the inhabitants?

Do turtles go without food for two years, so long as they can take in a little water? Is it true that the locusts called *gaayara*[50] are transformed into plants, their feet first being planted on the ground, then roots growing out into the soil, after which in a little while the whole is transmogrified? Do the Brazilian caterpillars called "cabbage lizards" turn into very pretty little birds, called *guainumbi*?[51]

As to the human inhabitants, both men and women, what are their characteristics, stature, shape, strength, agility, language, weapons, religion, manner of living, household gear? What occupations and practices do they chiefly pursue?

Do they never roast meat on a spit, but making a pit in the ground and placing at the bottom of it the large leaves of a certain tree, place the meat to be roasted upon them, covering it again with more leaves and earth; then making a bright fire over it, they continue the fire until they judge that the meat is thoroughly roasted? Do they not drink between mouthfuls, but take their drink at the end?[52]

Is it true that the natives grow to puberty early and age slowly, and then without loss of teeth or hair? Do Brazilian mothers laugh at our way of dressing and bringing up small children, which, they say, impedes the perspiration and causes much catarrh?[53] Are no squinting, purblind, lame, or hunchbacked persons found among them because infants are never swathed in linen or bound up in swaddling clothes, but are frequently washed with cold [water]? Are the Brazilians rarely afflicted with ill health? Do the more thoughtfull among them attribute their good health and longevity to these causes, namely, that they have strength from birth, and are exposed to the excellent calmness and constancy of the air and winds, as also, that they hardly know what care is, what is heaviness of heart or bodily delights; that they always enjoy the same dress and diet, and those of the simplest? Is no desire for possessions found among them, and do they not on the contrary live in a state of mutual equality, so that he who has more gives freely to him who has less, giving and taking being equally easy? Are not the modest women among them fertile from the eighth to past the sixtieth year, so that even septuagenarians are seen nursing orphan children? Do they not bear their children easily, without a midwife, rarely losing a child? Do not many women get up straight after childbirth, and go to wash in the nearest river, and then return actively to their household tasks?[54]

As they are said to be ignorant of both letters and numbers, how do they preserve the recollection of the past, and of acts of war or peace?

Do the inland Brazilians remain to this very day without law or religion like wild beasts, living always in the open without settled habitation? Do the *Tapujae* with their powerful shoulder muscles know how to fling javelins without aid from a bow? Are there such tough divers, that they can remain below for a whole hour with their eyes open?[55]

Are the *Ovetacates*, a Brazilian tribe, so fleet of foot that, when hunting, they keep up with deer? Are all the dwellers by the river Plate of gigantic stature and can they by their speed catch fleeing goats?

Do they everywhere make merry even in their death throes, as it were rejoicing in making a good end? Is it true that, moved by affection, they seize the bodies of parents not killed by poison and having dismembered them, bury them inside themselves?[56]

Are those in Brazil who cannot temper their libido unable to bear the climate of that region?[57] And should both the natives and the settlers there be cautious in the daily consumption of meat and wine? Do the natives mostly employ as their usual healthful drink the very clear water of their rivers and springs, which even when drunk frequently and copiously causes no wind nor pains in the belly or abdomen, and far from weakening the stomach on the contrary fortifies it remarkably?

Are children and young people frequently plagued with illness there, and elderly people only rarely?

Moreover inquiry should be made as to what minerals are found there in good supply, what stone quarries there are and the qualities of the stone from them, their relation to the points of the compass, situation, and so on. What types of special earth are to be found there, such as marl, fuller's earth, potter's clay, or boles and other earths of medical value? Does the region supply other minerals such as coal, brine, alum, copperas, antimony, sulphur, and so forth? What metals does it produce, concerning which the constitution, variety, situation, depth, signs, water, and damps of their metal mines should be looked into; what method is used for extracting the metal from its ore, etc?

In the *Maghe* region, by the seashore, is there a certain rock of emerald thrusting itself up like a tower, which shines with extraordinary brilliance when touched by the sun?

Is it true that ambergris is copiously thrown up by the sea on to the shores of Brazil, and washes about on the shore there when the sea is stormy; and that when the storm has barely subsided birds (ostriches particularly)[58] and several quadrupeds eagerly devour it upon the beach, before those who dwell near by can get to it?

Is all this ambergris before sun-drying soft, gummy stuff having so disagreeable an effect on the nose that the inexperienced throw it aside altogether; but do those animals first sniff its sweet savor, of which they are wonderfully fond?

Further, it is to be inquired what the magnetic declination in various parts of Brazil is, and what is the variation of the declination at the same place?

Let it be looked into concerning poisons, whether it is true that the fluid sqeezed from the manioc root,[59] having a sweet taste and eagerly drunk up by animals, kills them instantly; but when it is not squeezed from the root it is food for other living things but not for man, to whom it is fatal unless the juice is completely extracted; when this has been done, are wholesome food and drink made from it?

Is there prepared from the same root, though absolutely dripping poison, not only very good food but also the antidote called *carima*?[60]

Is a poisoned prick by the Brazilian *urutu* fish only cured by the liver of the same, all other remedies failing?[61]

Does that famous plant the *juquiri* fatten sheep and goats but slaughter men?[62] Is nux vomica death to cats, mice, and birds but a medicine for men?[63]

Do the leaves, flowers, and fruits of the plants *tangaraca*[64] and *juquiri*, easily the principals among Brazilian poisons, each have an antidotal root opposed to them?

Do the painted-on juice of that much-vaunted, all-curing herb, *nhambi*, by itself, or scattered tobacco ash, bring immediate death to the *cururu* toad and to other insects considered to be poisonous?[65]

Is it true that there is no remedy for the stings of poisonous little animals but the livers of the same creatures, particularly if that part which is next to the gallbladder is applied to the place?

Do the Brazilians everywhere cure the sting of poisonous snakes, vipers, toads, and fishes by applying the fat, heads, and livers of the same creatures?

Are some [kinds] which are poisonous in Europe found to be edible in Brazil, and vice versa, and which are they? Moreover, are those large ants, as well as the flesh of a number of snakes, lizards, worms, and forest dormice regarded as delicacies by the native chiefs in Brazil? Particularly, are those centipedes called *carasitu* and *caromouritu*, which are green and black, gutted and baked; and are those fat, white grubs called *jurumai* and *caramatori*, living in the pith of the trunks of palm trees in the forest, valued highly by them?[66]

When the nature of a poison has been settled, do the Brazilians know how to gather most powerful herbs as quick as lightning from the forest, which when bruised they administer in the form of a drink[67] to the sufferers and revive life when it is almost extinct?

Do vipers and snakes have an innate fear and loathing of crabs, and when pigs are bitten by them do they have a natural instinct to cure themselves by eating crabs?

Is it true that if a man is impaled on the end of the tail of that noise-making or rattle-bearing snake called by the Brazilians *boicininga* and by us the rattlesnake, it kills him at once, whereas the poison itself (injected into him from the mouth or teeth of the snake), works much more slowly?[68] And is the best remedy above all others that these savages have against the bite of this or any other serpent the bruised head of the harmful creature itself, applied hot to the wound in the form of a plaster, with the efficacious leaves of tobacco covering the surrounding parts?

Does it seem to be true that the *boicuaiba*[69] snake carries on a perpetual feud with almost all other serpents, particularly poisonous ones, catching them by stealth and even devouring the very poisonous *boicininga* sometimes, yet is itself found to be so free from poison that the natives do not fear to eat its flesh?

Is it true that when people are bitten by the snakes *curucucu*, *ibiracoa*, and *biopeba*, frothing blood soon flows from their nostrils, ears, and eyes and even from the nails of their feet and hands?[70]

Is that enormous serpent the *boiguacu*, so terrible to both wild animals and men, killed by troops of ants entering its jaws?[71] For ants of this kind are put to flight by the little viper called *ibiiara*.

Does the viper called *jararacae*[-miri] smell so strongly of musk that it brings on the headache?[72] A dried specimen of it is requested.

Does the viper called *ibiiaram* have two heads, and emit poison from both mouths?[73]

Does the fat of the crocodile called *jacare* knit together the wounds made by the same animal, and do its testes smell of myrtle? Do its tripes, dried and powdered, relieve the stone? Are its eggs and flesh used as food?[74]

Is it true that the *ichneumon*, a kind of mouse, enters the throat of the sleeping crocodile and goes out through the belly?[75]

Are the tails of lizards regenerated from the part cut off, but not if the whole is cut off?

Is it true that those sorts of lizards called *taraguira* and *tejunhana* quickly run up when they see a snake or other dangerous animal approaching a sleeping man with intent to harm him, and arouse him to prevent his being hurt?[76]

Do those spiders called *nhamdu*, if caught hold of carelessly, scatter a poisonous fluid at the first touch, which threatens the loss of vision should it reach the eyes?[77]

Is it everywhere agreed that that very biting oil extracted from the unripe, raw acorns produced by the *acaju* fruit protects one from infestation by those very small insects which the Portuguese call *bicho* ["worm"] lest they penetrate the soles of the feet or the skin of the hands and bury themselves there; whence, after they have enclosed themselves in round cysts, they are (when they have grown to the proper size) easily removed by the Brazilians with the aid of a small pin or needle of silver, with this precaution, that the whole worm enclosed inside the cyst must be extracted before it produces offspring, and that if the cyst is broken the symptoms recur, whence sometimes even a gangrene may result?[78]

Do some snakes swallow down ants by the thousand, and do ants (baked and eaten) relieve difficulties in urination, just as millipedes do?

Is it absolutely certain that the Brazilians are masters of such skills in preparing poisons that they [cause the poisons to] operate sooner or later, so that they actually cause death at a determined time after remaining dormant for some days or months until they unleash their strength? And can they so taint arrows, clothes, food, growing fruits, water, and even whole rivers that they will destroy men by degrees, not all at once?

Do the more villainous Brazilians hang the aforesaid toads in the sun, collect their bile and foamy spittle, and keep these for their more secret and slow-acting poisons?[79]

Is it there noticed everywhere, as Piso writes he observed, that in the rainy season which coincides with the stifling heat of spring and increasing corruption, toads are generated from each and every drop of viscid water as it were instantaneously, so many thousands together that they hide the ground beneath them; nor do these differ in any way from sexually generated toads?

Is it true that the roots of the herb casta, or mimosa,[80] furnish a safe antidote, although its leaves are full of a dangerous poison, if they are often brought into use? Thus
>Only that which has done me harm.
>Can, like the yarrow, be my balm.

Do Brazilian poisoners secretly cause their companions to smoke a very little of the dried leaf of the mimosa plant, concealed in a pipe together with tobacco, who feel no ill effect from it for a long time afterwards, yet without there being any obvious symptoms fade away and die of emaciation?

Is *manipuera*, that is the juice of the manioc root, so poisonous that it is necessary for the servants who prepare the root to take *nhambi* flowers and the *urucu* root in their food and drink to strengthen their heart and internal organs, lest they be affected by the noxious vapors? And do poisoners aim at a higher degree of corruption by keeping the juice until it putrefies and reducing the maggots generated in it to a powder, with which they gain power over a man's life? For if administered alone, it will destroy life quickly and surely, but if administered in a compound so that its strength is diluted (which the plants *caapeba* and *nhambi*, powdered, are said to do particularly) it will kill after a long lapse of time.[81]

Is it true that this juice, *manipuera*, is so poisonous that if swallowed raw it kills instantly; yet when well cooked it becomes nutritious?

Is the kernel of the fruit of the *ahoay* tree,[82] when reduced to powder, of so poisonous a virtue that the tiniest amount of it taken into the mouth defeats all antidotes? A specimen of it is requested.

Is the plant *nhambi* as it were a panacea against many poisons? We ask for a good quantity of it to be sent to us, as of the plants *caapia, caacica, jaborandi, caapeba* also, as they too are said to be powerful antidotes.

Are the prickles of the "hedgehogs" called *cuandu*[83] so poisonous that, when provoked into ejecting them with sufficient force to penetrate deep into the flesh, they infect the viscera, and those so struck die slowly? Yet on the contrary when these prickles are removed after death, and a drachm more or less of powder made from them is taken, they alleviate dysentery, that familiar ailment of the Indies, if [the dose is] several times repeated with a suitable liquid?

Appendix

Is it true that Brazilian bees make a black wax? If so, we ask for a little to be sent to us.

Is the plant called *hetich* whence the Brazilians make a flour (in addition to manioc) without a seed, and actually propagated by cutting the roots into little round pieces which are sown in the fields?[84]

Is there in Brazil not one creature, either terrestrial or aquatic, nor one tree, plant, or fruit to be found, which is not dissimilar to ours, excepting only these three plants: the purslane, clover, and fern?

As writers declare that the Brazilians utterly lack horses, what animals do they employ instead of them?

Do Brazilian women suffer no catamenia, but prevent it by some art, and what is that art?

NOTES

Reply to Letter 1747.

This inquiry into the natural history of Brazil and the pharmacological knowledge of its native inhabitants, which reflects a well-read European's impression of what was most strange and remarkable in tropical South America, his inclination to entertain the concept of the noble savage while at the same time attributing mysterious, even diabolical powers to him, is based largely on two volumes by the chief authorities on Brazil, particularly the first; we have designated the four chief works they contain by letters invoked in the notes below:

I. *De Indiae utriusque re naturali et medica libris XIV* (Amsterdam, 1648), containing *inter alia*:

A. Wilhelm Piso, *Historiae naturalis & medicae Indiae occidentalis libri V* (pp. 3–327);
B. Georg Marggraf, *Tractatus topographicus & meteorologus Brasiliae . . . quibus additi sunt commentarii . . .* (pp. 3–39).

II. *Historia naturalis Brasiliae* (Leiden and Amsterdam, 1648), containing:

C. W. Piso, *De medicina Brasiliensis libri IV* (pp. 1–122);
D. G. Marggraf, *Historiae rerum naturalium Brasiliae libri VIII* (pp. 1–292).

There is a good deal of duplication among these four works which we have not attempted to explore in detail. Fortunately the three major ones contain indexes enabling us to locate the passages in which Oldenburg's Indian names for species may be found, together with descriptions providing the sources for his questions; however, we have not tried to locate the source of every question.

Useful studies of these two seventeenth-century naturalists were made more than a century ago, as regards the zoology by Karl Martin Lichtenstein ("Die Werke von Margrave und Piso über die Naturgeschichte Brasiliens," *Abhandlungen der Königlichen Akademie der Wissenschaften zu Berlin*, 1814–15, 1816–17, 1820–21 (2), and 1826), and as regards the botany and pharmacology by C. F. P. von Martius in "Ueber die Pflanzen-Namen in der Tupi-Sprache" (*Bull. Kön. Bayer. Akad.*, 1858; separate, Munich, 1858, pp. 1–18) and in *Systema materiae medicae vegetabilis Brasiliensis* (Leipzig, 1843), not to say his *Flora Brasiliensis* (Munich, 1840–1906).

In attaching modern scientific names to the Indian terms used in this document we have leaned heavily on the above works, the *Index Kewensis*, and the recent book by Walter B. Mors and Carlos T. Rizzini, *Useful Plants of Brazil* (San Francisco, 1966).

1. That is, in the same latitude.
2. Maranhão is a state, of modern Brazil but Oldenburg may mean São Luiz do Maranhão, its chief city, formerly often called simply Maranhão.
3. *A*, pp. 215–16. The plant is a species of *Pilocarpus*, yielding an alkaloid, pilocarpine, still used in ophthalmology.
4. *A*, p. 157. Piso's name is *jubay*; the plant is *Tamarindus indica* L., an introduction to Brazil.
5. *A*, pp. 252–53; the plant, also called *jiticucu*, a convolvulus and one source of jalap, is almost certainly *Operculina macrocarpa* (L.) Urban. The whole passage follows *A*, pp. 24–25.
6. A type of orchid (the picture of a lily at *A*, pp. 235–36, is a mistake; compare *D*, p. 35).
7. Sarsaparilla, the root of a trailing vine (*Smilax* spp.) was presumably an introduction to Brazil. It is now regarded as inert medically. *Caaroba* (*A*, p. 143; *D*, pp. 11–12) is *Jacaranda copaia* (Aubl.) D. Don.
8. *A*, pp. 118–19. Copaiba is a balsam (still known by this name) deriving from plants of the genus *Copaifera*.
9. *A*, pp. 119 20. This plant, called "Peruvian balsam," is *Myroxylon balsamum* (L.) Harms (= *M. peruiferum* L.f.).
10. *A*, p. 122; this is another balsam, of the Burseraceae family, probably *Protium icicariba* (DC) March.
11. Tapioca (*tipioca* is the original Indian form) is, of course, the prepared starch or flour of the cassava root, *Manihot utilissima* Pohl, a native of South America.
12. Not identified. Possibly a kind of balsa wood is meant.
13. All this passage follows *A*, pp. 293–94; we have not identified the species: *Trygon?*
14. *A*, p. 204; Indian name *Guapariba*, Portuguese *mangue*, Spanish *mangle*: the mangrove; the dominant species is *Rhizophora mangle* L.
15. *A*, p. 127; this is a palm, either *Syragus coronata* (Mart.) Becc. or *Attalea excelsa* Mart.
16. *A*, p. 296; some kind of jellyfish, not identified.
17. "Castanea" literally means chestnut; see *A*, pp. 57–58. The tree (also called *Acaiaba*) is *Anacardium occidentale* L.
18. *A*, p. 299. This is some form of Diodon, or globefish.
19. *A*, p. 300; not identified.
20. *A*, p. 301; some form of Ostracion, or trunkfish.
21. Presumably one of the electric rays, family Torpedinidae.
22. *A*, p. 122; a species of *Hymenaea*, possibly *H. courbaril* L.
23. *A*, p. 122–25; a species of *Dorstenia* (probably *D. brasiliensis* Lam., a shrub used for dyeing).
24. *A*, p. 133; *D*, pp. 61–62. This versatile plant, *Bixa Orellana* L., yields a red pigment

annatto, which was used to flavor chocolate, and was supposed to act as a febrifuge. *Achiotl* is, of course, the Mexican name for it.

25 *A*, p. 138; *Genipa americana* L.
26 *A*, p. 141; *Crataeva tapia* L.
27 *A*, p. 147 (exactly); *Cecropia* spp., now called *imbáubas*, and used for paper making.
28 *A*, p. 149; a species of Myrtaceae, according to Martius.
29 *A*, p. 175; *Chorisia crispiflora* H. B. & K.
30 *A*, p. 153 (the whole of this passage); probably the tree is the common guava (Spanish *guyaba*: *Psidium guayava* Raddi), which is of no known medical value.
31 *A*, p. 162; *ibixuma* is *Guazuma ulmifolia* Lam. and *quiti* is *Sapindus saponaria* L. (soapwood).
32 *A*, p. 168; Piso wrote "meretrices"; the plant is *Pithecolobium avaremotemo* Mart., still known in nineteenth-century Europe as "Brazilian astringent bark."
33 *A*, p. 177 (exact copy): some kind of *Lantana*.
34 *A*, p. 178; another of the Myrtaceae, perhaps *Eugenia velloziana* Berg.
35 *A*, pp. 184–86; *Cassia occidentalis* L. or *C. sericea* Sw.
36 *A*, p. 186: *Gossypium* sp., perhaps *G. barbadensis* L.: cotton.
37 *A*, pp. 192–94; probably *Aloe vera* L., certainly from the illustration an aloe; an introduction to Brazil.
38 *A*, p. 205, Indian name *Inimboja*: *Caesalpina bonduc* L., a maritime shrub.
39 *A*, p. 204; *Avicennia nitida* Jacq., a tree having an astringent bark found in the mangrove swamps.
40 *A*, pp. 206–7.
41 *A*, pp. 208–9.
42 *A*, pp. 210–11; possibly *Hibiscus esculentis* L., and if so, an introduction from Africa.
43 *A*, p. 224; *Maranta* or some other genus of *Scitaminea*.
44 *A*, p. 229; *Piper bartlingianum* (Miq.) C. DC., a shrub.
45 *A*, p. 248; genus *Passiflora* L., the term *granadilla* is applied to both the passion flower and its fruit.
46 *A*, pp. 261–62; *Cissampelos pareira* L. (or possibly *C. glaberrima* St. Hil.).
47 *A*, p. 91 (figure) and p. 325; *Palamedea cornuta*.
48 *A*, p. 326; a vulture, *Cathartes* (*Vultur*) *aura*.
49 *A*, p. 324, exactly; this is clearly a skunk.
50 *A*, pp. 316–17; the creature is perhaps the praying mantis.
51 *A*, p. 318; *D*, pp. 196–99, describes nine species of hummingbird (without the fable quoted here).
52 *B*, p. 17.
53 *A*, p. 12.
54 *A*, p. 13.
55 *A*, p. 13; *D*, p. 20.
56 *A*, p. 14; the original passage makes the reference to cannibalism plainer. The savages, says Piso, with equal delight devour their enemies out of hate and their parents out of a disgusting affection. Oldenburg has confused two consecutive sentences and rather spoiled the sense.
57 *A*, p. 16.
58 The Indian name is *nhanduguacu*; *D*, p. 190. These birds are, of course, rhea.
59 The sap of the common cassava (manioc, note 11) contains hydrocyanic acid, which is removed by leaching and squeezing to make the starch of the root edible. The extracted juice is also concentrated and made harmless by prolonged heating as a basis for sauces.

60 For all the above, see *A*, pp. 114–17. *Carima* is simply a name for baked cassava flour.
61 *A*, p. 65; not identified.
62 *A*, p. 202; the plant is doubtful, but is possibly a *Mimosa*.
63 *D*, pp. 96–97; nux vomica comes from an East Indian tree (*Strychnos nux-vomica*); however, "Brazilian nux vomica" was derived from other species of *Strychnos* (e.g. *S. toxifera* Schomb.), whence the Brazilians also derived the arrow poison curare.
64 *A*, pp. 301–3. *Tangaraca* is *Boerhavia hirsuta* L.; it is not poisonous.
65 *A*, pp. 228, 298; for *nhambi*, see note 44.
66 This passage was not identified.
67 *Read*: "potionis."
68 *A*, p. 274.
69 *A*, p. 275; not identified.
70 *A*, pp. 276–77; it is suggested that *curucucu* is a species of *Trigonocephalus* or *Crotalus*.
71 *A*, pp. 276–78; a large boa, possibly the anaconda.
72 *A*, p. 280; not identified.
73 *A*, pp. 280–81; some kind of *Caecilia*.
74 *A*, p. 282.
75 Compare Letter 1785, note 1.
76 *A*, p. 284; not identified.
77 *A*, p. 285.
78 *A*, p. 289.
79 *A*, p. 298.
80 This is the same plant as the *juquiri* (note 62 above).
81 *A*, p. 305, for the whole passage.
82 *A*, p. 308; *Thevetia ahouai* A. DC., a strong poison.
83 *A*, pp. 324–25; the animal is, of course, a porcupine.
84 *A*, p. 254; "Ietica vulgo Batata"—this is simply the sweet potato (*Ipomoea batatas*); obviously Oldenburg was not familiar with any form of the potato.

1781

Oldenburg to Ray

31 August 1671

Ray's Letter 1738 of 3 July is endorsed as received on 7 July 1671 and answered on 31 August. As Ray's Letter 1786 makes plain, Oldenburg's letter was lost in the post, but contained a request for a description of the porpoise mentioned in Letter 1738.

1782
Oldenburg to Willughby
31 August 1671
From the memorandum in Royal Society MS. W 3, no. 44

Written again Aug. 31. 71.

NOTE

This endorsement to Letter 1746 indicates that Oldenburg sent his third reply to it on this day.

1783
Oldenburg to Vogel
1 September 1671

Vogel's Letter 1771 of 11 August is inscribed as having been received on 20 August and answered on 1 September, but although Oldenburg has written "v. copiam" there does not appear to be a surviving copy.

1784
Beale to Oldenburg
2 September 1671

From the original in B.M. MS. Add. 4294, ff. 44-45

Sept. 2. 71

Dear br.

You excuse yr slownes, whilst yu continue to heape very greate favours on me. My time hath beene somewhat diverted this fortnight wth interchanges of Epistolary Addresses wth our Revd Deane of Wells, Dr Bathurst,[1] nowe there, & some others there, Who are concernd for ye R.S.

If yu please to enquire aftr a letter, wch I send by this very post to *Honble Mr Boyle, directed to my L Vic Ranaleghs house in Pell Mell*,[2] perhaps it will be needefull, yt yr favour should rendr it legible. And then yu will therein find better hopes from Dr Bathurst, *at Oxford*, then yu and I did conceive. It would ease us somewt, if we could yet believe ye best. But He wilbe stinging, to make his word good.

It did not become me to write much to Mr Boyle, but yu, if yu please, may adde *this*, by way of discourse.

That, since I read his booke, I reade *Miscell[anea] Curiosa Germ. Leips.* &, though I have seene stranger, & greater Rarityes, & better composed; Yet I conceive they may do much good; chiefly by a fresh examination; & by exciteing a generall, & vigilant attendance to all extraordinary occurrences; by recording them; & by their ingenuous applications to ye designes of ye R.S. in some Considerables, where our Physicians are apt to be shy: The observations are pregnant; The Scholia (wch are many) learned & full of instructive references, & usefull citations. May they & ye Venetians[3] hold on, & yn I shall retract my former advise & not make haste to wish More forreigne Accompts of *Phil. Transactions*; Yrs affoording ye largest compasse & ye greatest variety; but spare not to give us a hint at least of all yt is very excellent, & usefull in othre.

If any other Phil Trans were to be published, It were to be wished in Spaine & towards their Westerne Colonyes, or rather in Portugal in relation to Brasile, or ye East Indyes.

Yu wilbe mindefull upon all occasions to addresse fayrely to Dr Sachs & yt curious Society. To wish them a prosperous furniture from all their surrounding neighbourhood, as far as good letters beare credite in ye North, in Sweden, Denmarke, Poland, Muscovy, Russia. You may wthout offence minde them of ye *Enquiryes yu published* in yr First & 2d Vol For *Hungary & Transylvania* &c.⁴ You may sollicite ye recovery, (or some fresh attempt for ye designe) of *Procopius Bonanus, De Admirandis Rebus Hungariae*, cited in their Obser. 131.⁵ You may recommend Mr Ray's Industry in his *Catalogus Plantarum Angliae* wch he continues to advance, & wt is done, & nowe under ye hands of *Dr Sharroc* & others. *Not to ingage them on ye same trouble*; But, if only upon ye viewe of such plants as are obvious in England some diligent persone would collect a *Catalogue of such plants as are peculiar to any place of yt large Empire*; or do much *differ in shape*, or vertue from these *in England*, though *by other circumstances* seeming of ye same kind; & *wth emendations, or supplements for their owne best Herbarists*; such a worke were worthy to roll on all over ye world; & to rayse fresh Colleges of *Vertuosi* for these & other usefull matters allover & round about our Globe. Or, if France & Italy would followe ye English Example, in these particulars, or, *as Dr Merret hath begun.*⁶ This would be *Groundworke*; & *tis allwayes ye surest way, though lesse splendid*, to lay *ye foundations deepe*, & *strong*. I suppose they have these bookes of Mr Ray & Dr Merret in Italy, France & Germany.

[I heare] yt Dr Sharroc hath another Tract of Vegetables in ye presse, & Dr Morison & Mr Ray promise more.⁷ And, Sr Hugh Platt written two small Tracts of Experiments [of] planting grafting inoculating & Mr Childrey is [*paper worn*] to advance his Britannia Baconica.⁸[. . .]

But yu may have far better instructions from Honorable Mr Boyle & others of ye RS, to engage ye *Curious*, wthout *offence* or *suspicion*, & yet to assist their designe, wch will taske all ye world, & hold out to ye end of ye world, in despight of ye Mewes of Maevius,⁹ or ye Gall pourd out upon yu by pale & envyous Mumpsimus.

Sr In ye *Catalogue of Prints* Stubs booke is thus entitled *A reply to Geo Thomson pretender to Physic & Chymistry*, &c.¹⁰ Never was there a fitter match for Impudence, foulenes of tongue, mouth & pen. Let them fight it out. Two blind Cocks in a pit. Neyther can ayme one stroke aright, but breath mischiefe all about them. The price is 6s, wch will surely cracke ye stationer. Were I concernd for my Lord Bacon, or my selfe personally, I should disdeigne to reflect one eye upon ye Sycophant, or to spend more than a sheete or two at most wth my face directly towards those staunch men, who have not been ashamed to set on ye Cur, by authorising, & Patroniseing his first disloyaltyes & sacriledge. To them I could render ye busines contemptible, or themselves odious to all nations. But there is hope they will repent, & learne to blush.

Nowe to yr last Tract.[11] Yu begin in a newe & excellent methode, to give us breefely ye substance of forreigne Essayes. In my opinion, Dr. Wallis hath answered, & yet declined ye answere, wth greate iudgement, & necessary prudence. But to do full right to Mr Boyle, should we not take notice, yt though *in generall* he ascribeth Fluidity to ye motion of visible particles, & Firmness to an apparent reste, yet he denyes not a new *perpetuall motion* in ye parts of Firme bodyes, wch may sometimes have very swift, or *brisk vibrations, as wn ye solid Diamond blazeth wth Light*. There may be more Cosmicall Affections than we have yet discovered. But some men have a Metaphysicall zeale against free enquiryes; They can explicate all Physicall Phaenomena wth their Metaphysicall Salve, as cheape as water, *Deus e machinis*. I would only learne of them, Wn they can grant, yt ye Author of all things could make a long-lasting Watch, & could settle & regulate ye poises of all things for ye best Cosmicall Advantages. If soe, ye remoter parts of ye world may have some poises a kin & some much differing from ye Magnetismes we have lately found, nay more we may find hereafter, & other more particular tendencies wch are nowe in grosse attributed to Gravity. But I run too [long]. Deare Sr

Yr ever oblieged servant
B

If my superscription to my L Raun[elagh]'s lodgings be a mistake by change of lodgings &c I pray yu let yr servant secure ye letter from ye post officers. I durst not enclose it in yrs, least ye price should tempt our Trusty boyes.

[P.S.] To provide fit greatings & usefull advises for Dr Sachs & ye curious society.

[*illegible*] I intend to greete worthy Mr Chamb[erlayne] I am glad yu take notice of Gale. I heare yt he angers Mumpsimus [by] degrading ye Stagyrite. He ascends higher then ye Jewish church even to ye Patriarchall Age. [*illegible*][12]

ADDRESS
For my much honoured friend
Henry Oldenburg Esqr
at his house in Pell Mell
Westminster   Post is paid 3d

NOTES

The letter to which this is a reply is lost.

1 Ralph Bathurst (1620–74) was ordained priest in 1644 but being a royalist practised medicine under the Commonwealth (he became M.D. in 1654). He is mentioned by Wallis as one of those who took part in scientific meetings at Oxford in the 1650s, and became F.R.S. in 1663. He had returned to his orders after the Restoration, being appointed Dean of Wells in 1670, while President of Trinity College, Oxford.
2 This letter dated 2 September is printed in Birch, *Boyle*, VI, 431–32; Beale sought to interest Bathurst in compiling a list of forgotten inventions.
3 Probably he means the editors of the *Giornale de' Letterati*.
4 See *Phil. Trans.*, no. 25 (6 May 1667), 467–69.
5 See *Miscellanea Curiosa*, I, 292, in a paper by Sachs, who, however, indicates that the work mentioned by Beale (whose author was a physician in the royal mines of Hungary), illustrated by over two hundred plates, probably was never printed off owing to its author's death.
6 That is, in Christopher Merret's *Pinax* (London, 1666).
7 For Morison's work, see Letter 1701, note 4; Robert Sharrock's *History of the Propagation and Improvement of Vegetables* appeared in a second, enlarged edition at Oxford in 1672; Ray wrote many works on natural history.
8 Sir Hugh Platt had died about 1611. Possibly Beale had heard of the forthcoming reprint of his *Garden of Eden, or an Accompt of the Culture of Flowers and Fruits now growing in England* (in two parts; London, 1675); see *Phil. Trans.*, no. 113 (26 April 1675), 302–4. There was in fact no second edition of Childrey's work; about two sentences are here lost, where the paper is worn.
9 Maevius was a mean-spirited and sarcastic Latin poet of the time of Virgil and Horace.
10 George Thomson (c. 1620–76), M.A. Edin. 1647, M.D. Leiden 1648, was a vigorous exponent of chemical medicine and critic of the "Galenic" remedies preferred by the College of Physicians. His writing excited much controversy. His dispute with Stubbe began when his attention was called to some passages in which Stubbe as a stalwart Galenist denounced all chemical physicians generally and Thomson in particular in *Campanella revived, or an inquiry into the History of the Royal Society* (London, 1670); Thomson replied in Μισοχυμίας Ἔλεγχος; *or a Check given to the insolent Garrulity of Henry Stubbe: in vindication of My Lord Bacon and the author* (London, 1671). Stubbe replied to this, and incidentally criticized Thomson's earlier Αιματιασις: *Or, the True way of preserving the Bloud* (London, 1670), dedicated to "the Disciples of Bacon," in two works, often bound together, *The Lord Bacons Relation of the Sweating Sickness Examined, in a reply to George Thomson Pretender to Physick and Chemistry* (London, 1671; the dedication is dated 12 January) and *An Epistolary Discourse concerning Phlebotomy. In opposition to—— G. Thomson, Pseudo-Chymist, a Pretended Disciple of the Lord Verulam* (London, 1671; the dedication is dated 14 February, but the date at the end is 3 April). There was more than one issue of each of these works, with very slightly differing title pages.
11 *Phil. Trans.*, no. 74 (14 August 1671); Beale alludes to Wallis's remarks on Leibniz's *Hypothesis physica nova* (that is, our Letter 1673; Vol. VII, pp. 559–64).
12 This postscript is scrawled in the marginal folds, and is nearly illegible.

1785
Oldenburg to Lister

4 September 1671

From the original in Bodleian Library MS. Lister 34, f. 33

London Sept. 4. 71.

Sir,

Yr very material Letter of Aug. 25. is well come to my hands; for wch as I return you most hearty thanks, so I shall take care, that the weighty contents thereof may be, as they deserve, laid up in the Books of the R. Society, as well as preserved by ye presse in the Phil. Transactions.

I shall at the present, for some return, transcribe for you the particulars, I lately received from Mr Willughby, concerning ye *Vespae Ichneumones*, after I have desired yr favor of informing me, why they are called *Ichneumones*.[1]

He writeth thus;

[*Oldenburg here quotes, practically word for word, all the material content of Letter 1777.*]

So far this worthy and inquisitive gentleman. To wch I have not now leasure to add any thing, safe yt I am Sir

Yr very humble and faithf. servt
Oldenburg

Mr. Willughby hath sent me up ye specimina of ye particulars, contain'd in his letter.

I intreat you, Sir, to doe me ye favor, to send me one more [of] yr viviparous flys, as soon as conveniently you can. It is for a curious friend;[2] and I cannot now get any of those, you formerly sent to ye R. Society; they being in their Repository, out of wch nothing can be had wthout the consent of the Body, wch now meets not, nor will meet till Michelmas.

What you observe upon Steno, is very considerable to me, and doubtles will appear so to others, when publisht in ye Transactions.

ADDRESS
> To his honor'd friend Martyn
> Lister Esquire, at his house
> wthout Michel-gate barr
>> at
>>> York

NOTES

Reply to Letter 1778.
1 The word means, in Greek, "tracker" and was applied to a mongooselike animal living in Egypt, popularly supposed to creep into the mouth of a sleeping crocodile to kill it by eating its viscera. The name ichneumon was transferred to a parasitic insect only about ten years before this time.
2 Willughby; see Letter 1777, and its note 7.

1786
Ray to Oldenburg
12 September 1671

From the original in Royal Society MS. R 1, no. 14
Printed in *Phil. Trans.*, no. 76 (22 October 1671), 2274–79

Sr,

About ye latter end of Aprill 1669 being at West-chester with my Lord Bishop of the Diocesse in the company of F. Willughby Esquire, I had the good fortune to meet with a young Porpesse of a convenient size for dissection, brought thither by some fisher-men, who caught him upon the sands where the tide had left him, in the Anatomy whereof I observed some things omitted by Rondeletius in his description of the Dolphin.[1]

The length of this fish was by measure 3 feet & 7 inches. A string of 2 feet & 2 inches girded him in the thickest place. The shape of his body was not much unlike that of a Tunnyfish, only his snout longer & sharper. His skin was thin smooth & without scales. In an old and well grown fish it's like the skin may be thick and tough, as Rondeletius represents it.

His fins are cartilagineous & flexible, not sharp or prickly as the Ancients report them. On his back he hath only one, wch was distant from the tip of his snout 1 foot & 9 inches, & the basis of it in length 5 inches & an half; so that measuring from the tip of his snout to the end of the tail it was situate somewhat below the middle of the fishes length. On the belly it had only one pair of fins, 9 inches & an half distant from the tip of the lower mandible; much about the place, where ye foremost pair of fins in other fishes usually grow. The tail is forked, of the figure of a crescent, the breadth thereof from angle to angle 11 inches. The situs or position of it contrary to that of all other fishes, except those of this kind. For whereas the plain of ye tail of other fishes when they swim stands erected perpendicularly to the plain of ye horizon, in this fish (and I suppose in all others of ye cetaceous kind) it lies parallell thereto. The reason whereof I conceive to be partly to supply the use of the hindmost pair of fins in other fishes, wch serve to ballance the body & keep it up in the water, answering in proportion to the hinder legs of a Quadruped. Hence we see, that those fishes wch have long bodies & but one pair of fins, as Eels & the like, cannot keep themselves up in the water, but lie always grovelling on the bottome. partly, to facilitate the fishes ascent to ye top of the water (to wch he can immediately raise himself by a light jerk of his tail thus placed) for the use of respiration, wch is necessary for him as for Quadrupeds. For doubtlesse if violently deteined under water he would in a short time be suffocated or drowned.

Immediately under the skin lay the fat, wch as I remember, our Seamen call the blubber. It was firm full of fibres, & in this small fish of an inch thicknesse, encompassing & enclosing the whole body belly and sides. The use whereof I conceive to be 1. to keep the cold water at a distance from ye blood, wch is I believe actually & to the touch hot in a degree not much inferiour to that of Quadrupeds, & therefore by immediate contact of ye water would be apt to be chill'd. 2. to keep in the hot steams of the blood from evaporating; by that means also preserving & maintaining its natural heat. As we see water & any other liquor in a close vessell will retain its heat much longer then in an open: and nothing is more proper to detain the finest & subtillest evaporations & spirits then oil or fat. 3. Perhaps also to lighten or counterpoise the body of the fish wch would otherwise be to heavy to move & swim in ye water. Under the blubber lay the musculous flesh like to that of Quadrupeds but of a darker colour. The body was divided into 3 Regions or *Ventres* like a Quadrupeds, viz. Head, Breast, & belly. The vessels & *viscera* in each *venter* for ye main the same as in Quadrupeds. 1. The Abdomen was compassed about with a strong *Peritonaeum*. The guts joyned to the mesentery & of a very great length, by measure 48 feet, without any difference or distinction of great & small; neither was there any blind gut or Appendix that I could find. The stomack was of a strange make, being divided into two large bags beside other smaller ones. I found nothing in it, but a good number of those little long fishes wch our fisher men dig out of the sands at low water & therefore call in some places Sandeeles;[2] by some they are called Launces, and by Gesner, *Ammodytae*.

The liver was of a moderate size, situate in the right side, & divided into two lobes, having no *cystis fellea* or receptacle of gall annexed. The *Pancreas* large, sticking close to the 3d bagge of ye stomack into wch also its *ductus* enters, and empties it self. The spleen small and roundish. The kidneys large, sticking close to the back, & lying contiguous one to the other, made up of many little kernels, like to, but much lesser then those of an oxe, of a flat figure, having no *pelvis* in ye middle, but the ureters going out at ye lower end. The urine-bladder oblong & little for the bulk of the Animal; having on each side a round ligament made of the umbilicall arteries degenerating. The *Penis* long, slender, having a small sharp *Glans*; it appears not outwardly, but lyes hid in its sheath within ye body, doubled up or rather reflected in the form of ye letter S, as is that of a Bull. The testicles lye within ye *Abdomen* on each side, as they doe in ye Hedgehog & some other Quadrupeds; of an oblong figure; for their internall substance, seminall vessels both *praeparantia* & *deferentia, Epididymides, Vas pyramidale, corpus varicosum,* & *glandulae prostatae* exactly like to those of Quadrupeds. The seminall vessels perforate the *urethra* with many little holes, whereof 4 are most conspicuous, somewhat above the neck of the bladder. The Diaphragm was musculous as in Quadrup. The heart large, included in a Pericardium, had its two Ventricles; its *valvulae sigmoides* & *semilunares, tricuspides* & *mitrales*; its coronary arteries & veins: in a word the whole structure & substance of ye heart & lungs agreed exactly with that of Quadrupeds. The Windpipe was very short, as it must needs be, the fish having no neck; the Larynx at top was of a singular figure running out with a long neck & a nob at ye end like an old fashioned ewer.

The pipe in the head through which these kind of fish draw their breath & spout out water, lies before the brain, & ends outwardly in one common hole, but inwardly it's divided by a bony *septum* as it were into two nosthrills: but below again it opens into the mouth in one hole. This lower orifice is furnished with a strong *sphincter*, whereby it may be shut

& opened at pleasure, & above this *sphincter*, the sides of ye pipe are lined with a glandulous flesh: wch if you presse you shall see start out of many little holes or *papillae* into ye cavity of ye pipe a certain glutinous liquour, wch serves as I suppose to keep ye parts thereabout slippery. Above the nosthrills is a strong valve or membrane like an *Epiglottis*, wch serves to stop the pipe, that no water may get in there against ye fishes will. Within the *fistula* are 6 blind holes having no outlet, 4 tending toward ye snout, 2 above the valve that stops the nosthrills & 2 beneath it: 2 tending toward the brain, having a long but narrow cavity, for the use of smelling, as I conjecture; though opening ye brain I could find neither olfactory nerves, nor *processus mammillares*.[3] The eyes are small considering the bigness of the fish, & situate at a good distance from the basis of the brain. The snout is long, & furnished with very large & strong muscles, to root or turn up ye sand at ye bottom of the Sea for to find fishes, as appears in that we found nothing in his stomack but Sandeeles, wch as was intimated before lie buried in the sand. The Brain & *Cerebellum* are for the substance & *anfractus*[4] of them the same with those of Quadrupeds, only differing in ye figure as being shorter: But what they want in length they make up in breadth. They have also the like teguments called *dura* and *pia mater*. the same ventricles. 6 or 7 pair of nerves besides the optick: the same ventricles, only in the *medulla oblongata* we observed not these protuberances called *nates* and *testes*. The skull *Cranium* is not so strong & thick as in Quadrupeds, but articulated after ye same manner to ye first *Vertebra* of the back-bone. This largenesse of ye brain & correspondence of it to that of man argue this creature to be of more then ordinary wit & capacity; & make to seem lesse fabulous & improbable those ancient stories related by Herodotus concerning Arion:[5] by Pliny the elder concerning a dolphin enamoured of a boy, whom he was wont to carry crosse a bay of the Sea from Baiae to Puteoli to School; &c.[6] by Pliny the younger of another enamoured of a boy at Hippo in Africa whom he was wont to carry upon his back in like manner.[7] The story is worth ye noting. But proceed; this fish had in each jaw 48 teeth standing in a row, like to little blunt pegs. The tongue was flat above, of an equall breadth to ye very tip, wch was toothed or pectinated about the edges, tyed firmly down to ye bottome of ye mouth all along ye middle, as Aristotle truly saith:[8] whence I cannot but wonder that Rondeletius should heerin contradict Aristotle; & affirm contrary to the truth, as I believe, quod Dolphinis lingua est mobilis, quae modo exeri, modo condi potest.[9] Unlesse perchance in this particular the Dolphin differs from ye Porpesse. For the

Porpesse is as I take it, the *Phocaena* of the Ancients, wch is a lesser sort of Dolphin, & not the *Dolphinus*; at least if the fish we are describing were a porpesse; for the teeth of this fish were lesser then, & of a different figure from those in ye jaw of a Dolphin we got beyond Seas. Yet is the difference not great between the Dolphin & *Phocaena*. As for that fish wch our Seamen now adayes call the Dolphin, and wch, as it is described by Mr Terry & Ligon, hath teeth on its tongue, small scales, is finn'd like a rock, of a pleasant smell & tast, what it is I know not, but I am sure it is *toto genere* different from the Dolphin of the Ancients.[10]

We observed not in this fish any nosthrills beside those in ye *fistula* nor any Ear-holes or *meatus auditorij*[11] at all, wherein also Aristotle agrees with us; wch yet Rondeletius found out near to ye eies. It being manifest (saith he) that a Dolphin doth hear; & seeing no creature can hear without a passage for that purpose to convey sounds to ye brain: Hac ratione impulsus, cum Delphini cranium diligentissime contemplatus essem, manifestissimum andiendi meatum, qui ad cerebrum usque patet inveni statim post oculum, tam exiguum ut fere oculorum aciem fugiat.[12] And we observed in the skull a bone answering to ye *Os petrosum*, wch most certainly was for the use of hearing. It had 6 short ribs that had no cartilages, & 7 that had Cartilages (on each side I mean). The Breast-bone was very small. As for the name Porpesse, I agree with Gesner that it was so called, quasi *Porcus piscis*, most nations calling this fish *Porcus marinus*, or Sea-swine. Indeed it resembles a swine in many particulars, as the fat, the strength of the snout, &c.

The book & Epistle of Pliny I have forgotten, & have not now the book by me; wherefore I desire, if you think fit to publish it, you would supply them. Mr Willughby returns you thanks for yr Lr.[13] He hopes to see Mr Lister next week. Your letter to me wch you mention in your last to Mr Willughby never came to my hands, else you had received the enclosed description sooner. I have no more at present but to assure you that I am Sr

Your very humble servant
John Ray

Middleton Sept. 12. 1671.

NOTES

1 Found in Guillaume Rondelet's *De piscibus marinis* (Lyons, 1554–55).
2 Fishes of the genus *Ammodytes*.

3 "corpus mammillares"?
4 "convolutions."
5 See the beginning of Book I of the *Histories*; Arion was a musician who rode on a dolphin.
6 *Natural History*, Book IX, c. 8.
7 *Epistles*, no. 33, 1. 9.
8 *History of Animals*, Book IV, c. 8.
9 "That the dolphin's tongue is movable and capable of being now protruded, now concealed."
10 Edward Terry, *A Voyage to East India* (London, 1655); Richard Ligon, *A true and exact history of Barbadoes* (London, 1650, 1657); "rock" is "rock fish," any one of a number of species; "toto genere," "in every way."
11 "auditory passage."
12 "Reasoning in this way, when I had examined the dolphin's cranium very diligently, I found a very obvious auditory passage immediately behind the eyes leading as far as the brain, so slender that it almost escapes the sharpness of sight."
13 Letter 1782.

1787
Lister to Oldenburg
13 September 1671

From the original in Royal Society MS. L 5, no. 38
Printed in *Phil. Trans.*, no. 76 (22 October 1671), 284-85

Yorke Sept. 13. 1671.

Sir

In my last paper about Vegetable Excrescencies,¹ I was wholly silent of ye opinion wch Mr Willughby is pleased to favour,² & because yt Worthy Gentleman hath soe farr made it probable, yt now it seemes only to depend upon ye good fortune of some lucky Observer, I am willing to reassume my former thoughts, yt all those odd Observations, we have made of the Births of *Ichneumones*, doe but begett in me a strong beleife, yt they have a way yet unheeded wherby they doe as boldly as subtly convey their Eggs within ye bodies of Insects & parts of Vegetables.

A 5 & last proposition of yt Paper was, yt ye substance of many Vegetable Excrescencies seemed not to be ye food of ye Worms to be found in ym: my meaning was yt ye substance of the Vegetable Excrescencies in wch those *Ichneumones* wormes were to be found, was rather augmented than diminished or worme eaten. And ye like conformity of their feeding within Insects is well observed by Mr Willughby, yt ye impraegnated Catterpillars seem not to be concerned, though their bodies are full of Insects of a quite different Kind, but goe on as farr as they may towards the atchievement of the perfection of their owne species. Thus I have seen a Poppie head swolne to a monstrous bulke & yet all ye Cells were not receptakles of *Ichneumones* but some had good & ripe seed in ym.

 I shall not refuse Mr Willughby (though you know upon what grounds I have twice done it to you) ye satisfaction of an Answer to my 10th Quaere by him resolved negatively. It is true ye swarmes of *Ichneumones* coming out of ye sides of Catterpillars doe immediatly make ymselves up into bunches, & each particular *Theca*, from ye Cabbage Catterpillar for example, is wrought about wth yellow silke, as those from ye black and yellow-*Jacobaea*-Caterpillar with white; but as for Webb to cover those bunches of *Thecas* I never observed it, but in ye Green Caterpillar soe common in our Lincolnshire heaths, wch are affixed to Bents or other plants. These in truth neever deceived but my expectation; for I verily thought I had found, when I first observed ym, a Caterpillar equivalent to ye Indian silk-worme: but having cutt ym in two & expected to have found a Caterpillars Chrysalis in ye midle, there presented ymselves a swarme of *Ichneumones*. These are as large many of ym as my thumb, yt is, at least 4 times bigger then ye *folliculus* or Egg-bagg of any English spider yt I ever saw yet. By good fortune I have not throwne away ye Boxes, wherin I made ye Observation concerning *Ichneumones* feeding upon ye eggs of certain Spiders; I have had ym in several boxes some 8 some 10 some 12 dayes in Vermiculo feeding upon ye very Cakes of Spiders eggs before they wrought ymselves *thecas* for further change; yt they seldome exceeded ye number of 5 to one cake of eggs etc. soe yt you may assure Mr Willughby this is noe conjecture but a real Observation accompanied wth more circumstances yn I am willing at present to relate. Sr I am

Your most humble servant
Martin Lister

 You may expect some sprigs from me, as soon as I am able to goe abroad; for I have been very dangerously ill & ye last Friday had an incision made under my Tongue, whence my surgeon tooke a stone out as bigg as a bean. I could be content to gratify your curiosity wth ye circumstances of this odd distemper, upon promise it may not be published by ye presse.

ADDRESS
    These
For his honourd freind
Mr Henry Oldenburgh
at his house in ye Palmal
    London

POSTMARK SE 18

NOTES

Reply to Letter 1785.
1 Letter 1751.
2 See Letter 1777.

1788
Oldenburg to Beale
14 September 1671

Beale's Letter 1784 is endorsed as answered ten days after its arrival on 4 September 1671.

1789
Winthrop to Oldenburg
September 1671?

From the copy in the Winthrop Papers, V, 100, and the draft, *ibid.*, 159

Salem in N: England Sept:

Sr

Yours of Apr: 11: 1671: I have received together wth all those bookes, wch were mentioned in yt letter and the transactions of the last yeare, as also the list of the Royall Society: I am greatly obliged, and its a most contenting kindnes to have such information of the Progresse of literature

& good intentions in those parts of ye World: I returne most humble thankes for those favours of much valew. The reception of those things by mr Fairwether[1] is certified in your letter and I had since oportunity to speake wth him & thanke him for his care, & careful delivery of them: I find no intimation of some other things sent some monthes before by Capt. Peirse his ship, for the repository of ye Royall Society, wth letters also to your selfe:[2] There were in a round boxe a Rattlesnake skin or 2; and a little of that kind of Snakeweed, wch is most ordinarily used here for the cure of such as are bit[ten by] yt serpent: there was also severall eares of a kind of Maies, or Indian Corne, wch comes from some northern parts of this country, where the ordinary sort of Indian corne wch is planted in these colonies, doth not ripen, but doth ripen well, and if planted heere very late in the summer wilbe fitt to gather, as soone, as the other wch was planted early in the spring; after Turnepseed hath beene ripe & gathered it hath beene planted in the same ground, and beene ripe wth the former of ye spring planting therefore I suppose it may doe well in England, if planted the beginning of Aprill or possibly the begining of May (If the frost should happen after it springeth up it will hurt it) but triall may be made in these monthes some weekes distance. I thinke I might send an eare of it if not more formerly, but had then little of it, having had but one eare sent me some yeares since, the produce of wch I have caused to be reserved unmixt: and intend to send more of them, except I understand yt those were delivered to your hands: wch I may hope might be since your letter was written: for in a letter received from my cousin Adam Winthrop[3] of a much later date than yours, I am informed that he had my letters by Capt: Peirse, & had delivered what was directed to him wth those letters, wch might not come to his hands till a good while after their arrivall, for I now understand, yt he resided then far from ye Citty, when yt ship came thither, wch I knew not when I directed my letters to him. That wch is intimated in your letter, that some gentlemen upon veiwing that shelfish called Horsfoot, questioned whether, that wch I called the sharpe taile of that Creature might not be the fore part of it, requireth me to satisfy that doubt, and why I apprehend it to be as I wrote in my former letters, for wch I [advance] these following reasons: First their progressive motion is alwaies the other part the round part foreward, when they goe, they draw that sharp spike after them, as I have my self seene often & thousands of others & is to be dayly[4] [...]

Here is a sort of wood wch groweth in low swampy places in many parts of this Country, wch they commonly call Poyson Wood.

I am sorry those Cranberries were spoyled by the tast of the Caske, I intreated a freind to put them up by whom [I] am since informed, [they] were put in a new caske first scaled⁵ & prepared and water put wth them as was directed by your selfe, & is usuall here so as to be put up not only for England but for Barbados & those hott countries, wch was inquired into by those yt put them up, so as I know not what occasioned that accident: I am greatly disadvantaged for such correspondencies being up in the inland so remote from the place of shipping.

I had prepared some few other things heere, but [these] might be deferred till [there is] some good oportunity of sending them hence to Boston, the port from whence the ships saile. there is a sort of wood wch growes in low swampy places in many parts of the country, wch hath a very malignant quality upon the very touch of it for it causeth very bad swelling on the face & other parts of the body touched by the hand, wch hath handled that wood, though the inside of the hand handling it I have knowne noe hurte by it, I had thoughts of putting up some pieces in some case or bonet box, intending to wrap them well in papers & write on the outside Nole me tangere,[6] but shall defer it till I may be informed whether it be desired such an [ill thing][7] should be sent wch for the venemous quality it hath as above mentioned is commonly called heere [the poysone wood][8] I wish I had oportunities to make returnes sutable to that acceptable correspondence, whereof you greatly oblige

your most affectionate servant
J. Winthrop

I crave the favour of Intelligence about Dr. Keffler & his family, where & howe he is, if alive, & what he doth. as also of Mr Dureus, & Dr Comenius[9]

I am not unmindfull of those commands about a naturall history of this Country, & am collecting what I can, but I humbly conceive it is too soone for such a Worke, wch would be very imperfect untill more experience & the Inland parts better discovered & knowne.

NOTES

Reply to Letter 1675 (Vol. VII).
Although this letter is without date, we have placed it here as the most probable year for its composition, assuming that it predates Letter 1834, concerning which Winthrop has (probably later) noted at the head of the present draft "That by John Hale was Nov: 28: 1671"; the second letter presumably repeated the contents of the

first. The recipient of this letter is deduced by internal evidence, confirmed by an annotation in a later hand on the copy. The copy is quite clearly written, but the draft is peculiarly illegible even for Winthrop. This letter cannot belong to 1672, or Winthrop would not have described events in 1670 without further comment (see note 2, below).

1 Previously mentioned as a ship's captain in Letters 1532 and 1538 (Vol. VII).
2 See Letter 1514 (Vol. VII), describing the curiosities sent by Captain Peirce, and safely received in October 1670. There is no trace of any acknowledgement by Oldenburg.
3 See Letter 1514, note 2. "Cousin" is no doubt used here in the loose sense.
4 Here the text of the copy ends, and the next page of the draft is quite illegible.
5 Probably, "scalded."
6 "Touch me not."
7 The actual expression is illegible.
8 The square brackets here are in the original.
9 J. S. Küffler has often been mentioned in the correspondence; see Letter 1688 and its note 5. John Dury, Oldenburg's father-in-law, was at this time in Germany, perhaps at Cassel where he was to die in 1680. For J. A. Comenius (1592–1671), see Vol. IV, p. 389, note.

1790
Kirkby to Oldenburg
16 September 1671

This is mentioned in Kirkby's Letter 1838 of 9 December; it no longer exists.

1791
Flamsteed to Oldenburg
Late September 1671

From the original in Royal Society MS. F 1, no. 74

Mr. Oldenburge

By ye same hand¹ which brought me the inclosed calculus of Bullialdus I returne it, together with a representation of the same appearance from ye Caroline numbers, which if I have calculated accurately, exhibits yt phaenomenon as well as ye Philolaick tables. You may if yu please (with my thankes for his paines,) returne mine to him, intimateing if yu may be so bold wth him that hee might doe well to use some stricter method for collecting his parallaxes then that hee has prescribed in his Astronomy & made use of in this paper, which has falsified them above halfe a minute in this calculation; & would (as I tried in a calculation of a lunar appearance to happen on Feb. 25 next) so wrest them yt ye parallax of longitude should be two minutes greater, of latitude allmost as much lesse then a strict or demonstrative method will permit, & I have just cause to feare yt in some appearances where ye moons latitude shall be great neare ye horizon ye error will be greater. I intended to have sent yu ye calculations of ye moones transit over ye said star observed by Hevelius 1660 Junij 7/17: which I have ready by mee formerly calculated from Streets tables & intended this evening to have performed from the Philolaick, but my friends jorney anticipateing my expectations two dayes defeates mee of time & yu of it for this present but if yu require it hereafter it shall be ready at yr service. I observed ye late Eclipse of ye moone[2] as well as I could haveing no helpe & by reason of my frequent absence from home of late my instruments being out of order. at 7h. 04′ ye moone in ye earthe shadow appeared very red on ye easterne side; on ye opposite more dusky: and I saw ye same light still encreaseing till 7h. 20′ when a small parte was freed from ye shadow.

7.28 a 3d of her periphery enlightened
8.00 a 4th of her periphery still darke
8.07 ye westerne Caspian spot uncovered
8.11 fully light: but some penumbra neare the I Major of Hevelius[3]
8.15 I could se no more penumbra

the night after I saw ye emersion of ye middle star in cauda arietis[4] but by reason of ye cloudes suddenly covering ye moone could not make any better note then that shee was lower then ye Westerne spot its whole lenght & alike distant from her limbe when her upper brimme was 37.36 high: I feare some mistakes in both these observations which I could not avoid by reason yt since I find ye Pole of my object glasse (through which I cast ye moones species to take her height) is not exactly in ye middle of it, so yt ye appearance might be cast higher or lower then ye center of ye glasse which, then, because I did not perceave I tooke no heed of but shall carefully endeavour to try & remedy for ye future. Pray let mee heare what of these have been observed at London if yu can spare so much time as to write back by my freind who will carefully convey whatever yu direct for

yr most obliged freind & servant
J Flamsteed

I am busy in my calculations for ye next yeare which I can scarce get time for betwixt my more necessary affaire & a frequent headach joynd with much untoward distempers.

J.F.

ADDRESS
  To Henry Oldenburge Esq
  at his house in ye middle of
  ye Pell mell in St James's
     Westminster these
          present.

NOTES

Oldenburg has endorsed the letter as received on 28 September 1671. It continues Letter 1776.
1 Mr. Sargeant.
2 Of 8 September 1671.
3 Insula Major in the Caspian Sea, probably corresponding to the ridge of the large crater Langrenus near the Mare Fecunditatis.
4 "the tail of Aries [the Ram]."

1792
Hevelius to Oldenburg
27 September 1671

From the original in Royal Society MS. H 2, no. 27

Illustri Viro
Domino Henrico Oldenburg
Regiae Societatis Secretario
J. Hevelius salutem

Quanto desiderio hactenus, ut ut frustra, Microscopium una cum libris, atque isto instrumento, pro dimetiendis distantijs minoribus,[1] nec non responsum ad meas 19 Junij scriptas exspectaverim,[2] vix Tibi perscribere possum; praeprimis cum Excell. dominus Mareschallus Regni expetitum illud Microscopium toties ad nauseam usque urgeat. Scripsisti quidem die 12 Junij Mercatori Kock res illas traditas esse.[3] Sed ut percepi rerum suarum admodum est negligens: sic ut putem nihil adhuc transmissum esse, sed omnia adhuc penes ipsum latere. Quamobrem hocce unum abs Te magnopere peto contendoque, ut cures quo primo quaque tempore res illas omnes habeam, simul significes qua Navi, et quo Nauclero transmitti debeant. Si dictus Mercator promptius desiderata promovisset, iam pridem etiam illud promissum Succinum, cum alijs quibusdam observationibus notatu dignis habuissetis. Non latere vos puto, dominus Picard ex destinato missum esse Uraniburgum ad Observationes quasdam peragendas, pro differentia Meridianorum Parisios inter et Uraniburgum, elicienda;[4] nec dubito Vobis Parisienses ut mihi transmisisse Immersiones illas satellitum Iovis, quas observare constituerunt.[5] Quicquid Vostri Astronomi hucusque obtinuerunt, rogo ut communicetis, ego rursus, ut feci, officio meo etiam hac in parte non deero. Occultationem Saturni die 1 Junij animadversam, iam 19 Junij Vobis transmissi.[6] Die 6 Maij nec stellam illam sub ventre virginis, nec Eclipsin nuperum (quod valde doleo) Lunarem,[7] nec Stellam in Lino piscium die 19 Sept. ob caelum continuo nubilum et pluviosum observare potui; sed immersionem primi Comitis in umbram Iovis feliciter mihi deprehendere obtigit: prout ex ipsis observationibus hisce transmissis videbitis.[8] Precor, ex animo, ut nos omnes coelum magis benignum, ad observationes proximis Mensibus peragandas, habeamus. Aer ille turbidus etiam obstitit, quo minus post 1 Junii ad 11

Sept. me semel quidem Saturnum Luna silente notare ac delineare potuerim: quale autem facie, quam rectissime et diligentissime, prout etiam anno praeterito (crede) delineavi, apparuerit, hisce transmitto.⁹ Oportet ut Vobis eodem tempore simile forma Saturnus visus fuerit. An vero mense Iunio,

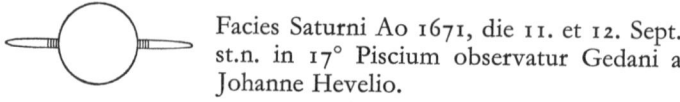

Facies Saturni Ao 1671, die 11. et 12. Sept. st.n. in 17° Piscium observatur Gedani a Johanne Hevelio.

Iulio, et Augusto eum plane rotundum conspexeritis, ut volunt Parisienses, vix mihi imaginari possum.¹⁰ Quippe omnino sum persuasus ut ut brachia Saturni ad latera arctissima apparuerunt, etiam Tubo 60 et 70 pedum; tamen haud credo omnino evanuisse, ut ne vestigium aliquod fuisse reliquum. Forte Parisienses brevioribus Telescopiis in ipso crepusculo Luna praesente, Saturnum contemplati sunt; quo tempore vix ac ne vix datur subtilissimum illud phaenomenum, ut mihi primo Iunii Tubo 20. ped. Saturnus cum occultaretur a Luna, obtigit, rite ac distincte cognoscere. Scripsi hac de re nuper ad dominum Cassinum, et dominum Picard, quid responsuri, avidissime exspecto. Nova illa stella sub capite Cygni die 16 Augusti plane visui se se rursus subduxit, ut modo nusquam appareat; altera vero in collo Ceti hactenus satis clare micuit, imo hucusque adhuc videtur. Machina mea Coelestis a tribus fere Mensibus sub praelo jam sudat, faxit DEUS O.M. ut fusissimum hocce opus, in Nominis Sui Gloriam, feliciter ad finem perducatur: sed cum plane solus sim, et nullum modo habeam ab auxilijs, et a Calculis: quippe Suecum istum, quod admodum doleo, mente plane captum, in Sueciam remittere coactus sum.¹¹ Hinc lente gradu res meae nunc procedunt. Caeterum non adeo pridem binas litteras a domino Iohanni Donellan ex Hungaria obtinui,¹² quas simul transmitto; citius aliquanto id fieri potuisset nisi responsum Tuum ad meas, resque illas hucusque exspectassem. Denique iterum iterumque officiose rogo, ut Microscopium resque reliquas quam diligentissime curetis; inprimis primo quoque tempore construi detis, si nondum factum est, tale instrumentum, ut scitis, pro minoribus distantijs, Tubo meo 50. ped. applicandum; sed meis sumptibus, lubentissimo animo omnia restituam: profecto ad quaevis gratissima officia atque studia me vicissim nunquam non habebitis promptissimum. Vale Vir honorande mei memor, et saluta decenter Totam Illustrissimam Regiam Societatem a Socio Illi devinctissimo. Dabam Gedani Anno 1671, die 7 Octob. st.n.

TRANSLATION

J. Hevelius greets the illustrious Mr. Henry Oldenburg, Secretary of the Royal Society

I can hardly express to you the urgency of eagerness with which I have awaited, though in vain, the microsope and the books, and also that instrument for measuring small distances,[1] together with a reply to my letter of 19 June [N.S.],[2] especially as His Excellency the Lord Marshal of the realm presses his request for his microscope until I feel distracted. You did indeed write that on 12 June the things were delivered to the merchant Kock.[3] But I have found out that he is very negligent in the conduct of his business, so that I think nothing has been sent on here yet, but is all thrust to one side in his place. Hence I must beg and beseech this of you once for all, that you will see to it that I get all those things at the earliest possible moment, and at the same time let me know by what ship and which mariner they are to be sent. If that before-mentioned merchant had done what was asked of him more promptly you would already have had that promised amber, with some other observations worthy of note. I think you must know that Mr. Picard has been sent on purpose to Uraniburg to make certain observations, in order to determine the difference in the meridians between Paris and Uraniburg;[4] and I don't doubt that the Parisians have sent to you as to myself those immersions of the satellites of Jupiter which they have resolved to observe.[5] Whatever your astronomers have accomplished so far you will, I beg, impart to me and I in return will, as I have done in the past, not be wanting in my duty in this respect. I have already transmitted to you the occultation of Saturn observed on 1 June, on the nineteenth [N.S.].[6] Because of wet weather and a continuously cloudy sky I could observe neither that star in the belly of the Virgin on 6 May]N.S.], nor (to my great regret) the recent eclipse of the moon,[7] nor the star in the line of the Fishes on 19 September. But I happened to follow the immersion of the first satellite in Jupiter's shadow very successfully, as you will see from the observations here enclosed.[8] I hope with all my heart that we may all have favorable skies for carrying out the observations of the next few months. That turbidity of the air also obstructed my being even once able to note and delineate Saturn in the moon's absence during the period from 1 June to 11 September; I here send you [a sketch of his] appearance [then], drawn most correctly and diligently just as (believe me) I drew it last year[9] Saturn should have revealed himself to you in a similar

The shape of Saturn in 17° Pisces observed at Danzig by Johannes Hevelius on 11 and 12 September 1671, N.S.

[For the figure, see page 272]

shape at the same time. I can hardly imagine that you will have seen him quite round in the months of June, July, and August, as the Parisians claim [to have done];[10] confident as I am that the "arms" [the ring] at the side of Saturn appeared very narrow even through a tube of 60 or 70 feet, yet I can hardly believe they have vanished quite away so that no trace of them is left. Perhaps the Parisians have observed Saturn with shorter tubes in the evening light when the moon was up, at which time it is hardly, if at all, possible to recognize that subtle phenomenon clearly and correctly, as happened to me on the first of June (with a tube of twenty feet) at the time of Saturn's occulation by the moon. I wrote about this business recently to Mr. Cassini and Mr. Picard, whose replies I eagerly await. On 16 August that new star under the head of the Swan had plainly withdrawn itself from sight again so that it was now nowhere to be seen; the other in the neck of the Whale has shone pretty clearly hitherto, indeed it seems even brighter than before. My *Machina coelestis* has been in press for almost three months; may God bring this very big book, dedicated to the glory of His Name, to a happy conclusion! But I am quite single-handed, without any aid from assistants or computers, for I was compelled to send that Swede home to Sweden, to my great regret, after he quite lost his senses.[11] Hence my concerns go forward at a very slow pace. Furthermore, I received two letters not so long ago from Mr. John Donellan in Hungary,[12] which I will send at the same time; this would have been done rather more promptly had I not been waiting for the answer to my letter, and the other things. Finally, I do most earnestly beseech you again and again to be really diligent in seeing after that microscope and the other things; and especially, if it is not yet done, have that other kind of instrument you know of for measuring small distances fabricated as soon as may be for use with my fifty-foot telescope; the expenses on my behalf will be most cheerfully repaid, and you will never find me other than most willing to perform any desired services or duties in return. Farewell, honored Sir, be mindful of me and present the whole of the most illustrious Royal Society with greetings from its most obliged Fellow. Danzig, 7 October 1671, N.S.

NOTES

This letter was read to the Royal Society on 2 November.
1 This micrometer was first mentioned as far back as Letter 1015 (Vol. V, p. 187).
2 Letter 1718.
3 See Letter 1723, where Oldenburg writes "Cock."
4 Compare Letters 1769 and 1771.
5 See Letter 1771 and its note 3.
6 See Letter 1718.
7 See Letter 1792a (1).
8 See Letter 1792a (2).
9 This passage was revised by Oldenburg and printed in *Phil. Trans.*, no. 78 (18 December 1671), 3032–33. The figure is taken from the *Philosophical Transactions*, the original having been lost.
10 See Letter 1769.
11 Presumably the young Swede named Skütt; see Letters 1536 (note 9) and 1557 in Vol. VII.
12 See Vol. VI, p. 484, and Vol. VII, p. 468, note 1, and p. 476.

1792a
Astronomical Observations

Enclosures with Letter 1792
From the original in Royal Society MS. H 2, no. 28
Printed in *Phil. Trans.*, no. 78 (18 December 1671), 3028–33

(1) Eclipsis Lunae Totalis Anno 1671, die ♀, 18 Sept. st.n. observata GEDANI a Joh. Hevelio

. . . .

(2) Occultatio Primi Jovialium ab umbra Jovis

. . . .

(3) Jovis & Lunae Transitus Anno 1671, die 30 Sept. st.n. mane observatus Gedani a Joh. Hevelio

. . . .

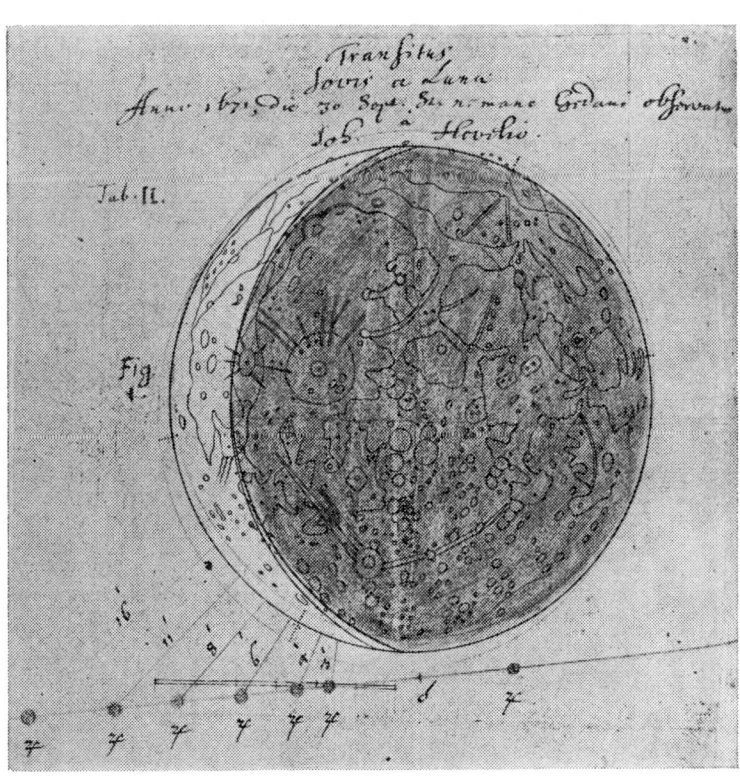

TRANSLATION

(1) A total eclipse of the moon observed at Danzig on Wednesday, 18 September, N.S., by Johannes Hevelius.

[A rainy evening prevented observation of the eclipse, but a glimpse of the moon about 8.30 P.M. indicated that emersion of the moon from the shadow had occurred more than half an hour before the time (9h. 6′ 27″) predicted by the *Rudolphine Tables*.]

(2) An occultation of the first [satellite] of Jupiter by the planet's shadow.

[Hevelius observed on the cloudy night of 25 September, N.S., as he knew Cassini was to do at Paris and Picard at Uraniburg. At first, about 4.30 A.M., he saw four satellites, three on the left, one on the right (his telescope giving a reversed image). At 5.12 A.M. he saw, at dawn, the innermost satellite on the left vanish in the shadow. He doubts whether the satellites are as useful for determining longitude as lunar appulses.]

(3) A transit of Jupiter and the moon observed at Danzig on 30 September 1671, N.S., in the morning, by Johannes Hevelius.

[Although the phenomenon was predicted as visible only from the Americas, Hevelius determined to observe, and witnessed a close passage at 7h. 26′ (after dawn), the moon coming within two minutes of the planet. Distances were measured with a 9-foot radius brass octant].

A passage of Jupiter by the Moon
observed by Johannes Hevelius at Danzig on 30 September 1671 N.S.
in the morning

[For the figure, see page 275]

NOTE

As the Latin text of these observations is printed in the *Philosophical Transactions* and also in *Machina coelestis, pars posterior* (Danzig, 1679), pp. 571–75, we have here given only their salient features in English summary.

PLATE 1. Franciscus de le Boe Sylvius
A contemporary crayon drawing, presumably
after the engraving by Cornelis van Dalem
B.M. Sloane MS. 5238, no. 64
See Letter 1698
By courtesy of the Trustees of the British Museum

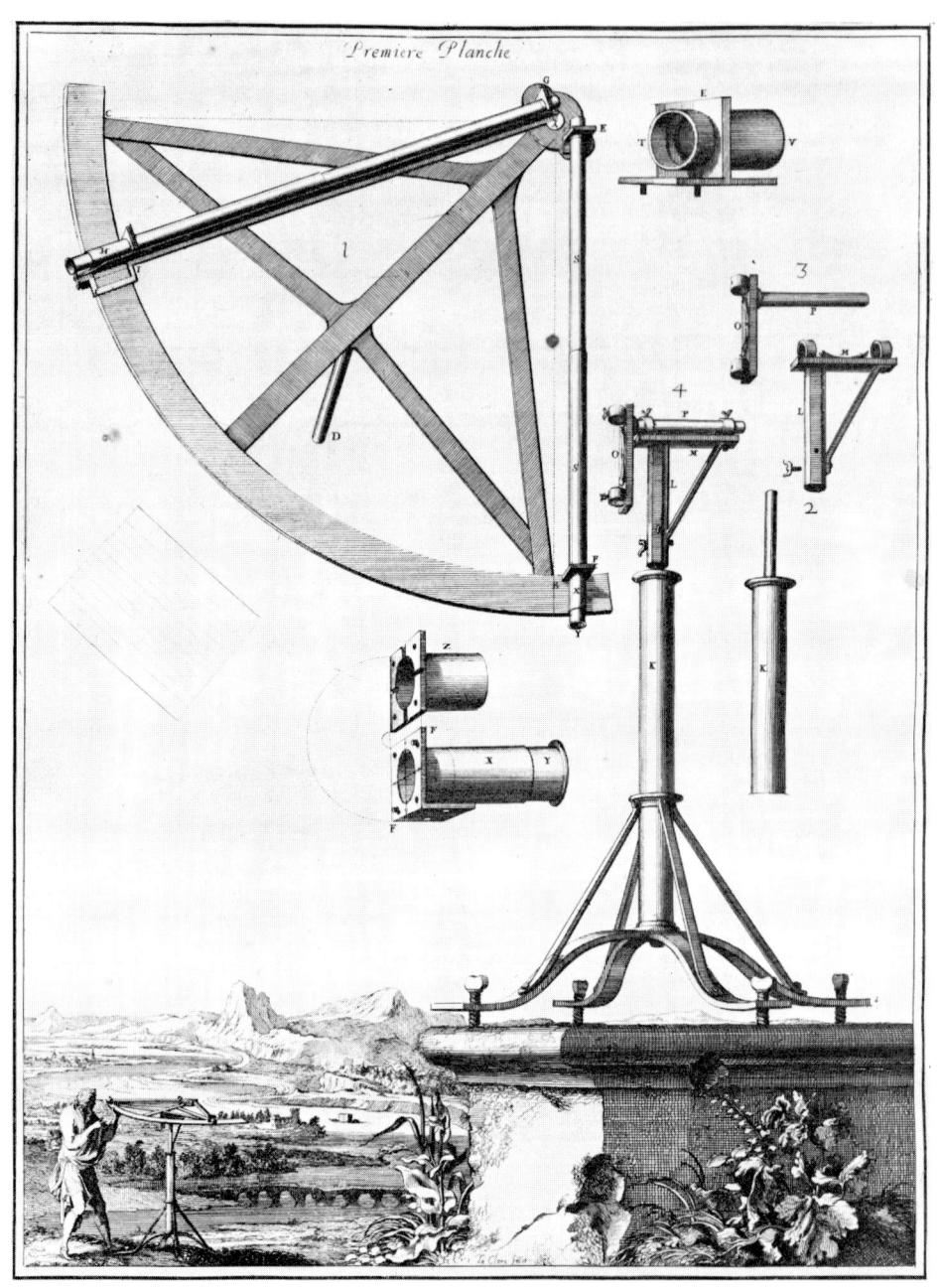

PLATE II. Picard's Quadrant
From *Mesure de la Terre* (Paris, 1671), Plate I
See Letter 1854
By courtesy of the Trustees of the British Museum

1793
Oldenburg to Leibniz
28 September 1671

From the original in Hannover MSS., ff 13-14
Printed in Gerhardt, pp. 67-69

Amplissimo et Consultissimo Viro
Domino Goth. Guil. Leibnitio J.U.D. et Consil. Moguntino
Henr. Oldenburg Sal.

Tardius aliquanto binis tuis novissimis, 18. Junii et 20. ejusdem ad me datis, respondeo, quod rusticari ad tempus, deinde complura negotia, nullam ferentia moram, expedire debuerim.

Gaudeo interim, quae antehac ad Schultzium Hamburgensem in usum tuum transmisi, rite Tibi dudum fuisse reddita. Ex eo tempore, Numero 74. Ephemeridum mearum Philosophicarum, Doctoris Wallisii de Hypothesi tua Physica judicium inserui,[1] quem libellum ab eodem bibliopola Hamburgensi ad Te curatum quoque fuisse plane confido.

Caeterum quod artem illam attinet, quam Amicum Tuum callere scribis, Chalybem scilicet ex ferro in quantitate cum magno emolumento parandi, scire te velim, Serenissimum Principem Rupertum Palatinum hic Londini artificium illud perquam facili negotio in praxin deduxisse, et quoties lubet deducere.[2] Quaevis enim Instrumenta ferrea, penitus jam confecta, integra etiam tormenta bellica grandia aeque ac parva, etc. novit Ille in Chalybem perfectum, multo minori quam secus fit sumptu facili negotio convertere, ad eamque quam libuerit temperiem, citra ullum instrumenti damnum, reducere.

Grandamici Experimentum a Te recitatum, fidei adeo sublectae habetur a Nostratibus, ut neminem hactenus reperim, qui dignum judicet, cui peragendo tempus impendatur.

Certum est, quod Monconisius de pulvere Küfleriano, ingentes naves duorum triumve minutorum spatio in fundum agente, commemorat; revera enim id praestitum fuit, imperante Cromwello, qui in eo erat, ut cum Inventore de certo precio contraheret; morte tamen rei executionem praeoccupante.

Compos fieri non possum libri a te desiderati, cui titulus, Gabriel Plat de thesauris subterraneis.[3] Interim edocuit me vir Philosophus et in

Chymicis versatissimus, qui eum totum evolvit expenditque, nullam ea in re, quam Tu indigitas, transmutationem intercedere, sed totum negotium in eo consistere, quod Aurum ex Antimonio parva quantitate, perinde atque ex Ferro, elici sive extrahi possit.

Experimentum Becheri impressum, de methodo scilicet ferrum ex limo lateritio et lini oleo parandi, in oras nostras pervenit, et jam modo sub examine versatur; cujus eventum suo tempore perscribam.

Vidisti sine dubio, quae Cassinus nuper de Maculis in Sole, Augusto novissimo observatis commentatus est;[4] quaeque de eodem argumento Ephemeridibus meis Philosophicis, No. 74. eodem mense evulgatis annotavimus. Non dubium, quin et Tu eas inspexeris; uti eaedem et Amstelodami, Hamburgi et Londini observatae fuerunt.

Clarissimus Wallisius tertium et ultimum volumen edidit operis sui de Motu et Mechanice, ubi, inter complura alia, tractat de quinque Potentiis Mechanicis, ad motum facilitandum comparatis, de Vecte scilicet, Axi in Peritrochio, Trochlea, Cochlea, et Cuneo; deque aliis, quae ad has reduci possunt. Inserit non-nulla de Hydrostaticis, de Gravitate et Elatere Aeris, deque Atmosphaerae contrapondio; unde ea derivat effecta, quae Naturae a vacuo abhorrentiae philosophorum vulgus attribuit; addita complurium Experimenti Torricelliani phaenomenum Explicatione; multarumque Quaestionum Mechanicarum Solutione etc.

Exemplaria ejus quamprimum sine dubio Hamburgum transvehentur; unde brevi poterunt Moguntiam curari.

Telescopia et Microscopia Anglica quod attinet, scire Te velim, Artificem hic esse unum alterumve, qui talia elaborent, quae hactenus Nostratium non modo, sed et Advenarum atque Extraneorum applausum meruerint. Arduum nonnihil est quid ea praestent, examussim designare. Dominus Hevelius non ita dudum Telescopium 50 pedum, triginta libris sterling; nec non Microscopium eximiae magnitudinis et praestantiae, decem libris sterling a nobis procuravit; mihique nuper scripsit, utroque sibi abunde satisfactum. Ni fallor, Telescopium 60 pedes longum probe elaboratum, statuitur amplificare objectum 1000000es: Et Microscopium, quale supra dixi, tantundem. Specula concava Ustoria quod spectat, Artificum nostrorum unus offert, velle se, precio 10. librarum Anglicarum, tale speculum conficere, cujus diameter sit 16. pollicum, quodque ad duorum pedum distantiam urat efficaciter. Nosti, in Gallia jam quid amplius fuisse praestitum. Forte et nostri homines majora praestarent, si consimili praemio stimularentur. Hisce vale, meque virtutis ac doctrinae tuae Cultoribus accense. Dabam Londini d. 28. Septembr. 1671.

TRANSLATION

Henry Oldenburg greets the very worthy and wise Mr. Gottfried Wilhelm Leibniz, LL.D., Councilor at Mainz

I am replying rather tardily to your two recent letters to me of 18 and 20 June because I was in the country for a time, and then had to deal with some business that would brook no delay.

Meanwhile I am glad that what was formerly sent for you to Schulz at Hamburg has at length reached you safely. Since then I have inserted Dr. Wallis's opinion of your *Hypothesis physica* [*nova*] into No. 74 of my *Philosophical Transactions*,[1] and I have every confidence that the same Hamburg bookseller will have taken care [to send] that little volume to you.

Moreover as to that art which, you say, your friend has mastered of preparing steel from iron in a very profitable way, I wish to let you know that His Highness Prince Rupert of the Palatinate has made that process practicable here in London, by a very simple method, repeatable as often as you like.[2] For he knows how to convert any device made of iron, quite finished, whether one as big as a whole cannon or some little thing, into perfect steel, using a simple method much less costly than any alternative; and he can give it any temper he chooses without any damage to the object.

Grandami's experiment that you relate is so little credited by our people that I have so far found no one who thought it worth while to spend any time upon it.

What Monconys records of Küffler's powder sending large ships to the bottom in the space of two or three minutes is true; for the thing was really done when Cromwell was ruling, who was about to do a deal with the inventor; but his death prevented its coming to anything.

I cannot lay hands on the book you want whose title is, *Gabriel Plattes on Subterraneal Treasures*.[3] Meanwhile, a natural philosopher much skilled in chemistry who has read and considered the whole book informs me that there is no transmutation involved in that business you wrote of, for it only deals with the fact that gold can be drawn or extracted in small amounts from antimony [stibnite], and in like manner from iron too.

Becher's printed experiment dealing with the way of making iron from brick clay and linseed oil had already reached us and is being put to the test at present; I will let you have the result in due course.

You have no doubt seen Cassini's recent remarks on the sunspots observed last August,[4] and our comments on the same topic in my *Philosophical Transactions*, no. 74, published in the same month. No doubt you examined them too, just as they were observed at Amsterdam, Hamburg, and London.

The famous Mr. Wallis has published the third and last volume of his work *Mechanica, sive de motu*, in which among many other matters he treats of the five mechanical powers applied to the easing of motion, of the lever, the windlass, the pulley, the screw, and the wedge that is to say, and of the others that can be reduced to these. He has inserted some things concerning hydrostatics, the weight and spring of the air, and of the atmospheric counterpoise, whence he derives those effects that the bulk of philosophers have attributed to Nature's abhorrence of a vacuum; there are besides the explanation of many phenomena of the Torricellian experiment, the solution of many problems in mechanics, etc.

Copies of it will no doubt soon be transported to Hamburg, whence they can easily be taken to Mainz.

As for English telescopes and microscopes, I wish to inform you that there are one or two craftsmen here who make such things, which have deserved the praise hitherto not only of our countrymen but of travelers and foreigners also. It is no trouble to state exactly what they offer. Not long ago Mr. Hevelius procured from us a fifty-foot telescope for thirty pounds sterling and a microscope of outstanding size and excellence for ten; he recently wrote to me that he was very satisfied with both. Unless I am mistaken a well-worked sixty-foot telescope is supposed to magnify an object a million times and a microscope, such as I have just spoken of, as much. As for a concave burning mirror, one of our craftsmen says he is willing to make such a mirror for ten English pounds whose diameter will be sixteen inches, to burn effectively at a distance of two feet. You know how much larger is one already completed in France. Perhaps our people would provide larger ones too, if they were encouraged by a similar reward. Farewell now, and count me among the admirers of your virtue and learning. London, 28 September 1671.

NOTES

Reply to Letters 1688, 1716, and 1721.
1 See Letter 1673 (Vol. VII).
2 The usual methods of making steel at this period involved the addition of small amounts of carbon to relatively pure (wrought) iron. However, steel can also be made by removing excess carbon from cast iron. This is what Prince Rupert attempted to do, in a process whose details are not known whereby cast iron was heated for long periods in his own glasshouse. The product was also called "malleable cast iron."
3 This is the book mentioned in Letter 1716, note 8.
4 See Letter 1769.

1794
Pardies to Oldenburg
10 October 1671

From the original in private possession
Printed in Rigaud, I, 170–72

Paris 20 Octobre 1671 [N.S.]

Monsieur

Je ne scaurois vous exprimer les sentimens de reconnoissance que je ressent moy mesme pour les faveurs singulieres qu'il vous a plu me faire en m'envoyant les deux livres du mouvement et en m'escrivant une lettre si obligeante. Vous pouvez vous assurer Monsieur que je ne souhaitterois rien plus que de pouvoir vous faire connoitre combien je vous honore et combien je me sens vostre obligé de l'honneur que vous m'avez fait particuliérement en voulant bien me permettre que je vous escrive de temps en temps et en m'invitant mesme à le faire.

J'ay lu le petit livre *de motu abstracto et concreto*[1] vous me dispenserez s'il vous plaist de vous en dire mon sentiment. Je ne ferois pas las mesme difficulté a l'egard du livre de M. Wallis ou de M. Wren si je les avois lus, car je suis deja fort prevenu de l'excellence de leurs esprit et de leur profonde erudition. J'ay autrefois estudié avec grand soin les ouvrages de M. Wallis de Arithm. Infin. de Sect. Conicis. de Cycloide, et ça esté avec une satisfaction extraordinaire et un tres-grand profit de ma part.[2] J'ay vu aussi quelques inventions de M. Wren que feu M. Fermat m'avoit fait connoitre:[3] Il n'y a rien de plus beau.

J'ay esté aussi charmé du tour hyperbolique qu'il taille avec une ligne droite inclinée d'une certaine maniere, au moins m'a-t-on dit que c'est M. Wren qui en est autheur.[4] Tout ce que j'ay vu de la plus part de vos autres messieurs me paroit extremement beau et me donne une grande inclination pour vostre nation et mesme pour apprendre vostre langue, qui sera dorenavant necessaire à tous les mathematiciens et physiciens. Comme nous n'avons en nostre bibliotheque presque aucun de vos livres, j'ose bien m'adresser à vous pour les faire venir. M. Justel sera mon garant et il pourra vous respondre que le prix de tous ces livres sera mis entre ses mains comme vous le marquerez. Je vous supplie donc de vouloir nous envoyer tous les livres qui sont imprimez en Angleterre depuis 6. ou 7.

ans qui concernent les mathematiques ou la physique soit en latin soit en anglois.

nous avons ici *Astronomia Britannica*,5 *Algebra Pell Lower de Corde Tabula Ulugh*,6 *Ougtreds Clavis, Barrow Euclid*.7 *Wallisi Arith. infin.* etc. *Commerc. Epist. de Cycloide.* et les ouvres de M. Hobbes. Ainsi il ne faudra pas nous envoyer ceux-là. Mais bien les autres s'il vous plaist, scavoir les ouvrages de M. Hooc. de M. Barrow, de M. Boyle, de Mercator, Gregory etc. de M. Morus,8 et sur tout vos excellentes Philosophical transact. ramassées depuis le commencement. et vous nous obligerez de nous les envoyer par aprés à mesure qu'elles se feront. Il n'est pas besoin que ces livres soient reliez on les fera relier icy à nostre mode. Je vous envoye un petit livre du P. Rapin, avec des theses *de Motu locali*.9 Je voudrois de tout mon coeur avoir quelqu'autre chose à vous envoyer, un de nos peres qui est à Negrepont m'a promis une relation exacte de l'Euripe. Il m'en avoit deja escrit quelque chose,10 mais il me dit qu'il a fait quelques observations plus exactes que les premieres. Je ne manqueray pas de vous l'envoyer incontinant. Je voudrois bien scavoir, si vos Messieurs ont fait des experiences pour le son dans le vuide tant avec les cordes qu'avec les fluttes. Dans les experiences de florence je trouve qu'ils ont experimenté que les cordes et les fluttes sonnent dans le vuide en mesme ton que dans l'air; ce qui me paroit bien remarquable. Vous m'obligerez infiniment de me communiquer quelque chose de ce que vous scavez là dessus. Je suis resolu de travailler à la continuation du traitté du mouvement et de vous le dedier. ce premier discours que j'ay fait n'est qu'un commencement d'un traitté complet que j'ay medité depuis long temps et ou je panse avoir trouvé quelque chose de nouveau. J'aurois bien de la satisfaction si je scavois que mon dessein peut agréer à vostre fleurissante academie et à vous de qui je suis avec respect Monsieur

Vostre tres-humble et
tres-obeissant serviteur
Pardies

Je ne scay si vos libraires voudroient se charger d'imprimer deux petits traitez en latin l'un in 12° De Antiquis mensuris, monetis et ponderibus quae olim fuerunt in usu apud Romanos, Graecos Hebraos et alias gentes clariores, cum eorum omnium reductione ad mensuras, monetas et pondera nostri temporis. l'autre in 8° Speculum geographicum in quo Nativa effigies Terrarum et Marium conspicitur. Je connois l'autheur qui est assurément un excellent home de nostre Compagnie et qui a de fort beaux ouvrages de physique et de mathematique tous prets à imprimer; mais il voudroit commencer par ceux-cy pour lesquels il a plus d'affection. Nos libraires d'ici ne veulent quasi plus imprimer que des livres françois mais sur tout ils ne peuvent se resoudre à se charger de ces livres de doctrine. Si quelqu'un de vos imprimeurs me vouloit promettre d'imprimer ces deux ouvrages je les luy envoirois esperant qu'il m'en envoiroit de sa grace au moins une cinquantaine en blanc de chacun. neanmoins ce ne seroit que de sa grace.

ADDRESS
    A Monsieur
Monsieur Oldemburg
    A Londres

TRANSLATION

Paris, 20 October 1671 [N.S.]

Sir,

I do not know how I shall express the gratitude I myself feel for the extraordinary favors which you have been pleased to do me, by sending me the two books on motion and by writing such an obliging letter to me. You may assure yourself, Sir, that I shall wish for nothing more than to be able to let you know how much I respect you and how much I feel myself indebted to you for the honor you have done me, particularly in so kindly permitting me to write to you from time to time, and even inviting me to do so.

I have read the little book *De motu abstracto et concreto*.[1] You will excuse me, please, from telling you my opinion of it. I should not make the same difficulty with respect to the book by Mr. Wallis or that by Mr. Wren if I had read them, for I am already strongly convinced of the excellence of their intelligence and of their profound learning. I formerly studied very carefully the treatises of Mr. Wallis [entitled] *Arithmetica infinitorum, De sectionibus conicis, De cycloide*, and that to my extraordinary content and very great profit.[2] I also saw some discoveries of Mr. Wren made known to me by the late Mr. Fermat;[3] there is nothing finer.

I was also delighted with the hyperbolic lathe which he forms with a straight line inclined in a certain way—at least I have been told that Mr. Wren is its author.[4] All that I have seen from the greater number of your other Fellows seems to me very fine and gives me a great partiality toward your countrymen, and even an inclination to learn your language, which henceforward will be essential for all mathematicians and physicists. Since we have hardly any of your books in our library, I venture to address myself to you to secure them. Mr. Justel will vouch for me and he will be able to tell you that the price of all these books will be put in his hands as you indicate it. I therefore beg you to be so good as to send me all the books printed in England in the past six or seven years dealing with mathematics or physics, either in Latin or English.

We have here *Astronomia Britannica*,[5] Pell's *Algebra*, Lower's *De corde*, Ulug Beg's *Tabulae*,[6] Oughtred's *Clavis mathematica*, Barrow's *Euclid's Elements*,[7] Wallis's *Arithmetica infinitorum*, etc., *Commercium epistolicum*, *De cycloide*, and the works of Mr. Hobbes. Thus it is not necessary to send these. But certainly the others, if you please, that is to say, the works of Mr. Hooke, Mr. Barrow, Mr. Boyle, Mercator, Gregory, etc., of Mr. More[8] and, above all, the whole of your *Philosophical Transactions* collected from the beginning. And you will oblige us in sending them afterwards as they are printed. There is no need to send bound volumes; they will be bound here after our fashion. I send you a little book by Père Rapin, with some theses "on local motion."[9] My heartfelt wish is to have something else to send you; one of our Fathers at Euboea has promised me an exact account of Euripus. He has already written something about it for me,[10] but he tells me that he has made some observations which are more precise than the first ones. I shall not fail to send it to you instantly. I should very much like to know whether your Fellows have made any experiments on [the transmission of] sound in the vacuum, using both strings and pipes. In the Florentine experiments I find that they learned by trial that strings and pipes sound with the same pitch in the vacuum as in the air, which seems to me very surprising. You will very much gratify me if you will let me hear what you know on this point. I have determined to work on the continuation of my treatise on motion, and to dedicate it to you. This first discourse of mine is only the beginning of a complete treatise which I have long planned and in which I think I have found out something new. I should be very pleased to think that my plan could be acceptable to your Society, and to you, to whom I am, with respect,

Your very humble and obedient servant
Pardies

I do not know whether your booksellers would be willing to undertake the printing of two little treatises in Latin: one in duodecimo, "De Antiquis mensuris, monetis et ponderibus quae olim fuerunt in usu apud Romanos, Graecos Hebraeos et alias gentes clariores, cum eorum omnium reductione ad mensuras, monetas et pondera nostri temporis." The other in octavo, "Speculum geographicum in quo Nativa effigies Terrarum et Marium conspicitur."[11] I know the author who is indeed an excellent member of our order, and who has some very fine works on physics and mathematics ready to print; but he would like to begin with these for which he has a greater affection. Our booksellers here want to print almost nothing but French books, and above all cannot resolve to undertake such academic books as these. If one of your printers would promise me to print these two works I would send them to him, hoping that he would send me as a favor at least fifty of each in sheets. But this would be only as a favor.

ADDRESS
>To Mr. Oldenburg
>>London

NOTES

>Reply to Letter 1767.
1 By Leibniz.
2 These were to be found in Wallis's *Opera mathematica* (Oxford, 1656–57), except *De cycloide*, published in 1659.
3 Known to Pierre de Fermat through his correspondence with Wallis, later published in the latter's *Commercium epistolicum* (Oxford, 1658).
4 See Vol. VI, p. 55, note 4 and *passim*.
5 By Vincent Wing, published at London in 1669.
6 See Vol. II, p. 165, note 2.
7 Probably Isaac Barrow, *Euclidis elementorum libri XV breviter demonstrati* (Cambridge, 1655).
8 Presumably Henry More.
9 Possibly René Rapin, S.J., *La comparaison de Platon et d'Aristote* (Paris, 1671), which contains some material on the ideas of Aristotle and Gassendi concerning motion.
10 The first account by P. Jacques Paul Babin, S.J., had already been printed in English translation by Oldenburg; see Letter 1722, note 3.
11 "On the ancient measures, coins, and weights formerly in use among the Romans, Greeks, Hebrews, and other better known peoples, with the reduction of all of them to the measures, coins, and weights of our own time." . . . "The geographical glass, in which may be seen the natural aspect of lands and seas."

1795
Oldenburg to Ray
11 October 1671

From the copy in Royal Society MS. O 2, no. 56

For Mr Wray
Answer to Mr Ray's Letter of Sept. 12. 1671.

London Oct. 11. 1671

Sr

I must differ no longer ye Acknowledgment of ye receipt of your favour, expressed by your letter of September 12. wch contains so accurat a description of ye Porpess yt it ought by no means, I think, to be left unpublished; in wch publication I shall be mindfull to supply ye quotations out of Pliny. And as soon as the R. Society shall open their publick assemblyes again, they also, I dare presume, will be glad of such a communication.[1] If Mr Willughby be returned from Mr Lister, I pray, Sr, let him read ye few lines at ye end of this letter.[2]

I have at present nothing to returne to you, but a relation of a Meerman, wch I lately received from my correspondent at Paris,[3] & shall here deliver in his owne words:

"On a veu à la Martinique dans les Indes Occidentales un Homme marin. Deux Francois et 4 Negres l'ont consideré fort long temps. Il estoit dans l'eau à huict pas d'eux. La moitié de son corps paroissoit estre hors de la mer; ce qui les estonna fort. Il avoit la figure d'homme, depuis la teste jusque à la ceinture; la taille petite et comme celle d'un Garçon de 15 ans; la teste proportionnée au corps; les yeux un peu gros, mais sans difformité; le nez large et camus; le visage plein; des cheveux gris meslez de blanc et de noir, plats, qui luy flottoient sur les epaules; et luy pendoit une barbe grise fort large sur l'estomac, qui estoit couvert d'un poil gris comme aux vieillards. Monsieur de Bois, General de la Martinique, a fait interroger les Negres separement, qui luy ont dit la mesme chose que les Francois. Avec tout cela, à moins que de l'avoir vû, on a dela peine à le croire. On m'en a envoye une relation dont j'ay fait cet extrait."

We are here as incredulous, as possibly they can be in France, about such stories. However, they may minister occasion to make further inquiry into ye truth of ym, & to consult all sorts of Navigators, examining what they have recorded concerning it, & their attestions, comparing together all the particulars.

I shall not conclude without acquainting you, yt Monsr *Bourdelot*, a famous French Physitian in his answer to Signr *Redi's* Italian letter, replying to Monrs *Charra's* book about vipers,[4] takes notice, that an *Afflatus Malignus et Halitus teter*[5] may very much envenome the bilious liquor, let fall by Vipers when they bite; & alledgeth in confirmation of it, a Relation of a Gardiner, who commonly found but halfe of his grafts to thrive, of wch, upon examination, the cause was thought to be yt yt Gardiner took allways 2. grafts to inoculate, of wch he first grafted yt, wch he held in his hand, and afterwards yt wch he held in his mouth, wch smelled very strong, as having very rotten teeth, wch might corrupt ye benignity of ye Vegetable juice, at ye end of ye 2d graft; so yt upon diligent research yt second stick never prospered. but allways withered away.

This also deserveth further observation, & for yt reason is commended to your care by Sr

Your Faithfull servant
Oldenburg

TRANSLATION

. . . .

"A merman has been seen in Martinique in the West Indies. Two Frenchmen and four Negroes studied him for a very long time. He was in the water eight paces away from them. Half his body seemed to be out of the sea, which surprised them very much. He had the shape of a man from the head to the waist; his stature small, like that of a fifteen-year-old boy; his head in proportion to his body; his eyes rather big, but without deformity; his nose large and snub; the face full; hair grey mixed with white and black, straight and floating on his shoulders; and his very large grey beard hung down to his stomach, which was covered with grey hair, as is common with old men. M. de Bois, Governor of Martinique, had the Negroes questioned separately, and they told him exactly the same things as the Frenchman. With all that, [the story] is accepted only with difficulty, except by those who saw the man. I was sent an account of which I made this extract."

. . . .

NOTES

Reply to Letter 1786.
1 Letter 1786 was read to the Society on 9 November 1671, in Ray's presence.
2 See Letter 1796.
3 There is now no trace of any such letter, or any indication of which correspondent was responsible for this tale; there are no surviving letters from Justel, Huet, or Vernon for this period. A full account of the sighting of the merman (attributed to 23 May 1671, N.S.) was to appear in Denis, *Mémoires*, no. 7, dated 11 April 1672, N.S.
4 The Abbé Bourdelot's *Recherches & Observations sur Les Viperes* (Paris, 1671) is reviewed in *Phil. Trans.*, no. 77 (20 November 1671), 3013–16. For Redi's letter, see Letter 1556, note 24, in Vol. VII.
5 "malignant breath and noisome exhalation."

1796
Oldenburg to Willughby
11 October 1671

From the memorandum in Royal Society MS. W 3, no. 45

Answ. Oct. 11. 71. in a postscript to a letter for Mr Ray of ye same date,[1]

NOTES

Reply to Letter 1777.
1 Letter 1795; the postscript was omitted from the copy preserved by Oldenburg.

1797
Oldenburg to Lister
12 October 1671

From the original in Bodleian Library MS. Lister 34, ff. 37-38

London Oct. 12. 1671.

Sir,

I understand, yt our noble friend Mr Willughby hath given you lately a visit, in wch I doubt not but you have had ample discourses touching those many particulars, yt have of late been the Subject of our letters, viz. ye Musk-insects, ye Vespae Ichneumones, ye anomalous production of many sorts of Caterpillars, petrified shells, ye English kermes, ye English black etc. I hope, Sir, you and he will oblige the R. Society (now to be open'd again very shortly) wth the result of ye conferences of such important Arguments; as I shall not omit communicating to ym yr two last letters of Aug. 25, and Sept. 13.[1] stored wth such variety of observables, as they will certainly be much pleased wth. At ye end of yr last letter, you make me exspect some things, wch, when they shall come to hand, shall be added to ye rest, when they come to be produced in publick. I have very little to return to you in recompence of yr rich communications. There was lately imparted to me a relation of a Meer-man, wch I shall here deliver in the very words of my Parisian Correspondent, thus:[2]

[*Oldenburg here quotes again the French passage in Letter 1795, p. 286, above; for the translation, see p. 287.*]

We are as incredulous here, as they can be in France, about such stories. However they may minister occasion to make further inquiry into ye truth of ym, and to consult all sorts of Navigators examining what they have recorded concerning it, and comparing their attestations.

Another thing I shall adde, wch perhaps will not displease you, viz.[3] That Monsr Bourdelot, a famous French Physitian, in his Answer to Sigr Redi's Italian Letter, replying to Monsr Chara's book about Vipers, taketh notice, yt an *Afflatus malignus* & *halitus teter* may much envenom the bilious liquor, let fall by biting vipers; and alledgeth, in confirmation of it, a relation of a Gardiner, who commonly found but half of his grafts to thrive; of wch upon examination, ye cause was thought to be, yt yt

Gardiner took always two grafts to inoculate, of wch he first grafted yt wch he held in his hand, and then yt wch he held in his mouth, wch smelled very strong, whereby ye benignity of ye vegetable Juyce was supposed to have been corrupted; it having been found, upon diligent research, yt yt second stick never prospered, but always wither'd away.

This also deserveth further Observation, and for that reason is likewise recommended to ye care by Sir

Yr faithful servt
Oldenburg

ADDRESS

   To his honor'd friend
   Martin Lister Esquire,
   At his house wthout Mickelgate-barr
   at York

NOTES

Reply to Letters 1778 and 1787.
1 Letter 1778 was produced before the Society on 2 November, its first meeting after the summer vacation; there is no mention of Letter 1787 in the Society's minutes.
2 For this quotation and its translation, see Letter 1795.
3 This is also contained in Letter 1795.

1798
Oldenburg to Huygens
14 October 1671

From *Œuvres Complètes*, VII, 111
Original in the Huygens Collection at Leiden

Monsieur,

Celle-cy n'est que pour vous faire bailler par la main de Monsieur Rancher,[1] de la part de Monsieur Wallis, son 3me et dernier volume de Motu, lequel vous est envoyé si grossierement relié, pour le faire mettre avec ce qui a precedé. Je suis. Monsieur

Vostre tres humble serviteur
Oldenburg

A Londres le 14 Octobre 1671

ADDRESS

A Monsieur
Monsieur Christian Hugens de Zulichem
à
Paris.

TRANSLATION

Sir,

This is only to have you receive, by the courtesy of Mr. Rancher,[1] and from Mr. Wallis, his third and final volume *De motu*, which is sent to you so crudely bound in order to go with what came before. I am, Sir,

Your very humble servant
Oldenburg

London, 14 October 1671

ADDRESS

To Mr. Christiaan Huygens
Paris

NOTE

1 He is mentioned in Letter 1866, to Huygens, as a close friend of Justel.

1799
Leibniz to Oldenburg
15 October 1671

From the copy in Royal Society Letter Book V, 15–21
Printed in Gerhardt, pp. 69–73

Vir Amplissime,

Literas Tuas, quibus mihi Dn. Wallisij, acerrimi ingenij et profundissimae doctrinae viri, judicium transcribis, dudum accepi. Responsum distuli, dum hoc quod vides Schediasma Opticum addere possem, quod Illustri Societati Regiae communicari peto.[1]

Memini in Transactionibus Philosophicis mentionem fieri Propositae ab *Auzuto* rationis opticae metiendi ex una statione;[2] sed qualas illa sit, mihi incompertum. Lentes sive *Vitra Pandocha*[3] nemo quod sciam, unquam consideravit; multo minus *Tubos Catadioptricos*, quales mihi in mentem venerunt. Illis confusio radiorum tollitur; his, unio augetur.

Amicus mihi est *Johannes Ottius*,[4] juvenis egregie doctus, vobis non ignotus, qui praeclaras habet meditationes Opticas, quanquam mihi Ellipsibus et Hyperbolis plus aequo tribuere videatur. Idem proponit rationem quandam a se inventam, solis circulis id efficiendi quod Cartesius Ellipsibus et Hyperbolis; imo plus etiam, ut scilicet omnes radij singulorum in totidem distincta puncta ordinate recolligantur; sed *hoc in certa tantum distantia figuraque tum objecti, tum fundi excipentis*. Caeterum meae Lentes Pandochae illud, fateor, praestare non possunt, ut vel unius puncti omnes radios in unum punctum recolligant, nedum ut singulorum; sed interim hoc praestant, ut quantum Lentes vulgares efficiunt in puncto objecti unico, in axe optico sito, tantum Pandochae praestent in punctis omnibus etiam ab axe optico remotis, *quantascunque sit apertura Lentis, aut Magnitudo, figura, distantia objecti*. Idem Ottius mihi niper misit dissertationem suam eruditam de morbis Visus;[5] quemadmodum et Henr. Screta, studiorum Ottio socius (qui eodem quo Ottius tempore de visu, ipse de Auditu Cogitationes Physico-mechanicas publicavit) suam de morbis Auditus.[6]

Quod celeberrimi Wallisij, acerrimi ingenij et profundissimae doctrinae Viri, judicium de Hypothesi mea qualicunque transcribis, accepi Tibique maximas gratias debeo. Siquid vicissim imperabis, nihil promtitudinis a me desiderari patiar. Si quae aliorum censurae ad vos pervenerunt (eorum inprimis quibus id negotij dedit Illustris Societas) beneficio tuo rescire spero. Clarissimus Wallisius mentem meam egregie cepit. Video, eum potissimum subsistere in hac propositione: *nulla est cohaesio quiescentis*. Fateor, Cartesium alia omnia sentire, cui videtur corporibus ad cohaesionis firmitatem nullo alio Glutine opus esse praeter quietem. Ego contra; hoc Gluten esse motum.

Sententia Illustrissimi Boylij de fluiditate et firmitate non difficulter, opinor, conciliabitur meae. Fateor ego, motu res fieri fluidas, quiete firmas; sed motu irregulari vario, crasso externo, perturbante proprium intestinum, quo cessante restituitur intestinus, id est *quies sensibilis*, seu potius *motus insensibilis conspirans*. Recte dubitat ipsemet Boylius, an detur absoluta quies in corporibus: Consistentiam ergo a quiete oriri, certum ei esse non potest. Imo, nequid dissimulem, quanto rem considero profundius, tanto persuadeor magis, nullam esse quietem absolutam in corporibus, et quod a nobis appellatur *corpus quiescens* id in rei veritate *esse spatium vacuum*, quicquid dissentiant Cartesiani. Hinc infero, ad essentiam corporis requiri aliud aliquid quam extensionem (id est magnitudinem et figuram,) alioqui a spatio non differet. Ostendam autem, illud nihil aliud esse posse quam motum. Possum ergo demonstrare has propositiones alicujus in Philosophia momenti; (1) *datur vacuum*; (2) *quod quiescit, est spatium vacuum*; (3) *quicquid movetur cohaeret in linea motus*; (4) *Tellus movetur*. Quae propositiones ex se invicem pendent, aut consequuntur. Ausim me primum asserere, qui demonstravit Motum Terrae. Si demonstrationes harum propositionum Illustri Societati Regiae non ingratas esse intellexero, transmittam aliquando.

A Cartesij regulis motus, fateor, me non posse non magnopere dissentire; quanquam de caetero maximi faciam illum virum, cui inter Heroes statuam dedicandam censeo. Ante omnia ei non concedo, corporis Essentiam consistere in Extensione (sed in motu;) nec proinde spatium et corpus esse idem, neque ergo vacuum esse impossibile: Nec proinde materia illa subtili, in indefinitum se actu comminuente, solius spatij implendi causa conficta, opus arbitror. Nec illud admitto, quod ait, motum tantum consistere in mutatione vicinitatis, ac non magis dicendum, moveri terram immoto caelo, quam caelum immota terra, mutari enim situm amborum inter se, ergo moveri utrumque. Unde sequeretur, spatium quoque vacuum moveri, quoties a corpore deseratur; ac proinde esse corpus; contra priora. Nego etiam, tantundem requiri actionis ad quietem, quantum ad motum: Omnis enim actio mutatio est, mutatio nulla quiescentis. Nec a Cartesio demonstratum est, eandem semper quantitatem motus in universo a Deo conservari; ratiocinatio enim ab immutabilitate Dei valde infirma est. Accedo jam ad leges naturae a Cartesio allatas. Prima vera est, *princip. part.*

2 n. 37. sed a Cartesio non demonstrata. Demonstravit eam primus Hobbius, quod semel moveatur, semper, quantum in se est, moveri.⁷ Secunda *n. 39.* vera est, sed a nemine demonstrata. Demonstrabitur autem a me; motui curvo inesse conatum in rectum; Cartesius iterum recurrit ad immutabilitatem, et regularitatem Dei. Tertia lex, *n. 40*, falsa est, et partim experimentis male intellectis, partim rationibus debilibus asserta; nec admitto, quae asserit (*part. 2. princip.*) *n. 43* quod quiescit, quod alteri conjunctum est, habere in se vim ad resistendum moventi, disjungenti; et *n. 44.*, motum non esse motui contrarium, sed quieti. Porro ex 7. regulis, quas habet *n. 46.* et sequentibus, ne unam quidem per omnia approbo; neque magnitudinem unius corporis continui ad rem pertinere censeo. Quieti vim resistendi abnuo. Nec quietem pro glutine agnosco. *Baroni Nulandio, tum ei qui contra Cartesii 7. regulas scripsit*,⁸ in eo non assentior, quod partim quietem considerant velut aliquid activum, partim putant in abstracta motus ratione corporis majoris, esse vim majorem eadem manente celeritate motus, cum tamen majorum vis major sensibilis longe aliud principium habeat, scilicet turbatam magis aetheris circulationem. Sed hic tam multiplex dissensus nihil apud me detrahit opinioni de tam insignibus viris. Scio enim, si tantum dissentiamus in principijs paucis, necesse esse ut dissentiamus in conclusionibus multis.

Quid de me vestris Transactionibus insertum est, nosse opto. Hypothesin meam magis magisque polio et emdendo: faxo aliquando, Deo volente, ut in paulo meliore habitu prostet. Gerickius noster scribit mihi, opus suum jam prope praelo exiturum,⁹ misitque mihi Indicem capitum: Ex quo disco, sequi eum systema Copernicanum, sed quodammodo emendatum,¹⁰ recensere varia experimenta comparandi vacuum, et unum ex ijs, comparandi vacuum quod putat summum. Ego, ut dicam quod res est, cum totum mundum globulis, bullis, gyris, orbibus constare credam, pro certo habeo, vacuum intercipi; sed vacuum aliquod sensibile procurari posse ullo experimento, non puto. Habeat ex[11] Experimentum, quo Nubes, ac ventus, coloresque Iridis possunt in vitro excitari; item Experimentum de Consumptione Aeris per Ignem: Experimentum ingens pondus elevandi: item, Experimentum novi et antea nunquam usitati sclopeti:[12] Thermometrum novum, Magdeburgicum dictum: *Globum* quem vocat *Sulphureum* (Schwefel-Kugell) qui miras illas operationes in distans exercet; plumam ad certam distantiam in aere libero sustinet, et secum gyrat.[13]

Non dubito quin ad Te pervenerint binae quaedam literae meae, eodem circiter tempore missae a me, quo datae sunt tuae.[14] Memini, me in ijs multa scribere, ad quae responsum desidero. Inprimis quis sit status rei opticae apud vos; quantam faciat Lunam optimum apud vos Telescopium, salva claritate; quae sit maxima magnitudo pediculi per optimum Microscopium; quae ut inquirerem imperaverat mihi Eminentissimum Elector Moguntinus rei opticae curiosissimus, qui de Instituto vestro praeclarissime sentit, ut est Princeps talium valde intelligens; item in quanta distantia legi possint literae maximae impressae, ut in libris Ecclesiasticis. Vellem etiam nosse, quis eventus fuerit destinationum Wrenni, et Dusonij, Celeberrimorum Virorum in poliendis sectionibus Conicis.[15] Ego quae de his politionibus sentiam in Schedula adjecta breviter expressi.

Sed nihil est nunc quidem quod magis a Te, Vir Amplissime, optem scire quam successum *Experimenti Magnetici Grandamici*. Exposui Tibi, ni fallor, literis praecedentibus, et repetam brevissime. Ait nimirum Grandamicus (libro, *demonstratio immobilitatis Terrae*), si Terella Magnetica ipso puncto suo polari collocetur in subere, ita ut alter polus Magnetis respiciat Nadir, seu Centrum Terrae, alter Zenith, suber autem in aqua libretur: certas Terrellae partes in Septentrionem, certas in meridiem *sine ulla declinatione* dispositum iri; ac proinde designari posse in Terrella Meridianum quendam, qui ubique monstret Meridianum loci *sine ulla*, ut dixi, *declinatione*: Quasi scilicet declinatio Magnetica in solo polo ejus hospitetur, quo nunc fixo reddito, ut unum perpetuo mundi punctum, nimirum centrum Terrae praecise respicere cogatur, caeteras etiam magnetis partes praecise respicere certas mundi plagas. Meminit etiam hujus Experimenti, sed, ut solet, sine nomine Inventoris, Cartesius in *Princip. Philos. part. 1. Artic. 145.* inter caetera magnetica phaenomena ibi recensita *n. 21*; dubitat tamen, an omnis omnino absit declinatio, et rationem reddere conatur *artic. 271*. Non dubito, quin Mercator, Powerus,[16] Henricus Philippi,[17] alijque apud vos insignes Magnetici hoc Experimentum sumpserint, quorum judicia si ad me pervenire feceris, magnum in me beneficium contuleris.

Unum superest, quod bona tua venia quaero: Scis, Illustrem Boylium multa Experimenta sumpsisse in Recipiente exhausto: sed in ijs quae edita sunt, non potui observare, tentatum ab eo unquam *discrimen inter Refractionem Aeris Communis et exhausti*. Si vel ipse, vel Celeberrimus Hookius, vel alius eruditorum vestrorum aliquid certi de eo argumento comperit, fac, quaeso, ut id ad me perveniat. Quod restat, vale faveque; si qua in re servire possum, audacter impone ac rescribe etc.

Cultori Tuo
Gottfredo Guilielmo Leibnitio

Francofurti
15/25 Octobris 1671.

TRANSLATION

Very worthy Sir,

I not long ago received the letter in which you copied out for me the opinion of Mr. Wallis, a man of keen intelligence and profound learning. I have delayed my reply until I could add this optical paper you see here, which I desire you to communicate to the illustrious Royal Society.[1]

I remember that in the *Philosophical Transactions* mention was made of a proposal by Auzout of an optical method for measuring distance from a single station;[2] but of what kind it was I do not know. No one, so far as I am aware, has ever considered using lenses or "universal" glasses,[3] still less reflecto-refracting telescopes such as came into my head. The confusion of the rays is removed by the one, and their union increased by the other.

Johannes Ott is a friend of mine,[4] a remarkably learned young man who is not unknown to you; he has some excellent ideas about optics though he seems to me to expect too much from ellipses and hyperbolas. He puts forward some method discovered by himself for doing by circles alone what Descartes [would do] by ellipses and hyperbolas, and indeed even more, so that all the rays from single [objects] may be gathered together again in due order in as many distinct points, but this only at a certain distance and when both the object and the screen receiving [the image] have a certain shape. I confess that my "universal" lenses cannot do as much, so as to be able to collect all the rays from even one single point into a point, much less from [multiple] individual points; yet this they will do, that is, whatever ordinary lenses will do for one unique point of the object situated on the optical axis the universal lenses will do for all points, even those remote from the optical axis, whatever the aperture of the lens, or the size, shape or distance of the object. The same Ott lately sent me his erudite dissertation on diseases of the sight,[5] while Heinrich Screta, Ott's fellow research worker, who published some physico-mechanical reflections on hearing at the same time as Ott printed his on sight, has likewise sent me his dissertation on diseases of the ear.[6]

I have received and owe you many thanks for your copy of the opinion of the very famous Wallis, a man of keen intelligence and profound learning, concerning my hypothesis such as it is. If you demand something of me in exchange I shall leave nothing to be desired in my readiness [to comply]. If the criticisms of any other persons reach you (especially from those to whom the Royal Society entrusted this matter) I hope to learn of them through you. The celebrated Wallis has followed my thoughts remarkably well. I see that he mainly sticks at this propostion: no cohesion comes from rest. I confess that Descartes perceived everything otherwise, since it seemed to him that no other cement than rest is needed for the solidity of cohesion in bodies. I take the contrary view: motion makes the cement.

The views of the very illustrious Boyle on fluidity and firmness are not, I believe, difficult to reconcile with my own. I agree that motion renders things fluid, while rest makes them solid; but this is a varied, irregular motion, coarse [and] external, upsetting the proper internal motion, and when it ceases the internal motion is restored, that is to say an observable state of rest or rather a contributory unobservable motion. Boyle himself is rightly doubtful whether there is an absolute state of rest in bodies, and therefore he cannot be certain that solidity is caused by a state of rest. Indeed, to hide nothing from you, the more deeply I have considered the matter the more convinced I am that there is no absolute rest in bodies and that what we might call a body at rest is in truth a vacuous space, however much the Cartesians disagree. Hence I infer that something other than extension (that is, size and shape) is required for the essence of corporeality, otherwise a body does not differ from space. I show, however, that this can be none other than motion. Therefore I can demonstrate these three propositions, of some importance in philosophy: (1) there is a vacuum; (2) whatever is at rest, is a vacuity; (3) whatever moves, coheres in the line of motion; (4) the Earth is in motion. These propositions depend one upon the other, or follow [from each other]. I may be so bold as to call myself the first to demonstrate the motion of the Earth. And if I am informed that the demonstrations of these propositions will not be unwelcome to the Royal Society, I will send them sometime.

I confess that I cannot but greatly dissent from Descartes's laws of motion, although otherwise I have a high opinion of that man, whom I judge worthy of being numbered among the heroes. Above all, I do not concur with him that the essence of body is to be found in extension (rather, in motion); nor, therefore, that space and body are the same nor again that a vacuum is impossible. Nor, accordingly, do I think there is any need for that subtle matter, continually grinding itself smaller by its action, imagined solely for the sake of filling up space. Nor can I admit what he says of motion's being only a change of surroundings, so that one cannot rather say, the Earth moves while the heavens stay fixed, than the heavens [move] while the Earth remains at rest; for if the position of both is moved with respect to each other, then both are moved. Whence it should follow that a vacuum can be moved too, whenever it is left empty of body; and so it is a body, contrary to [what was said] before. I also deny that as much action is required for rest, as for motion; for all action is a change, and a change is no kind of rest. Nor is it demonstrated by Descartes that God always maintains the same quantity of motion in the universe; for an argument based on the immutability of God is very weak. I at once accept the laws of nature alleged by Descartes. The first (*Principia*, Part II, § 37) is true but not demonstrated by Descartes. It was first demonstrated by Hobbes that whatever is once moved will always move, as much as it can.[7] The second (§ 39) is true, but demonstrated by no one. It will, however, be demonstrated by myself that in a curvilinear movement there is an endeavor towards the rectilinear. Descartes again has recourse to the immutability and regularity of God. The third law (§ 40) is false and founded partly on poorly comprehend experiments, partly on weak reasoning. Nor do I admit what he asserts (*Principia*, Part II, § 43) that a body joined to another has in itself a force of resistance against a movement that would separate them; and, § 44, that motion is not contrary to motion, but to rest. Further, of the seven rules contained in § 46 and the following sections I cannot wholly approve even of one, nor do I judge that the size of a single continuous body has anything to do with the matter. I deny the force of resistance in a body at rest. Nor do I acknowledge rest as a cement. I cannot agree with what the Freiherr von Nuland has written against the seven rules of Descartes[8] because they partly consider the state of rest as though it were something active, and partly reckon that in the abstract theory of motion there is a greater force maintaining the same velocity of motion in a larger body, whereas the greater force of larger bodies has a different, very obvious origin in the more disturbed circulation of the ether. But these complicated dissensions in no way lower my opinion of these excellent men. For I know that if we disagree over a few basic principles, we must differ over many conclusions.

I long to know what you have published about me in your *Transactions*. I improve and correct my hypothesis more and more; sometime, God willing, I will have it set out in better state. Our Guericke writes to me that his work is almost come from the press,[9] and he sends me a list of its chapters, from which I learn that he adopts the Copernican system, emended in some way,[10] and relates various experiments on making a vacuum; in one of them he makes what he thinks is the limiting vacuum. For my part, to state things as they are, as I believe the whole world to be made of globules, bubbles, vortices, and spheres I hold it for certain that vacuous spaces are included [in it]; but that an observable vacuum can be obtained by any experiment I do not think. He has an experiment showing that clouds, winds, and the colors of the rainbow can be produced in a glass vessel; also, an experiment on the using up of the air by fire, an experiment on raising a massy weight; an experiment concerning a new and hitherto unknown gun;[12] a new thermometer, named after Magdeburg; a "sulphur ball" (as he terms it) which effects those marvelous [electric] phenomena at a distance; it holds up a feather at a certain distance in the open air, so that the feather revolves with the sphere.[13]

No doubt two letters that I wrote about the same time that you wrote to me have reached you.[14] I remember that I wrote many things upon which I desired your answer. Firstly, what is the state of optical science with you; how big does the best of your telescopes make the moon without loss of clarity; what is the extreme size of a louse seen through your best microscope? These inquiries I was ordered to make by His Eminence the Elector of Mainz, who is most deeply interested in optical matters; he is very well aware of your design, as befits so markedly intelligent a Prince. Also, at what distance can the largest printed letters be read, like those of service books? We also wish to learn what was the result of the schemes of Wren and De Son, celebrated in the grinding of conic sections.[15] I have briefly expressed my views on this kind of [lens-]grinding in the annexed paper.

But there is nothing I would rather learn from you, Worthy Sir, than the success of Grandami's magnetic experiment. I explained it to you, if I am not mistaken, in previous letters and I will repeat it very briefly. Grandami says, then (in his book on the demonstration of the Earth's immobility), that if a magnetic terrella has its poles so mounted in cork that one pole is directed to the magnetic nadir, or to the center of the Earth, and the other to the zenith, and the cork is set to float on water, one section of the terrella will point to the north, and another to the south, without any declination, and so a certain meridian can be drawn on the terrella which will always show the meridian of that place, without any declination, as I have said; just as though the magnetic declination resided in its pole alone, which now being made fixed so that it perpetually points to one point in the Earth, that is, it is forced to point exactly to the center, the remaining parts of the magnet direct themselves precisely to determinate parts of the Earth. Descartes recalled this experiment (though, as usual, without its inventor's name) in *Principia philosophiae*, Part IV, § 145, as the twenty-first of the magnetic phenomena related there; but he doubts whether the declination is wholly removed and tries to give a reason for that in § 271. I don't doubt that Mercator, Power,[16] Henry Phillips[17] and others among you who are distinguished for knowledge of magnetism have undertaken this experiment, and you will confer a great benefit upon me if you will let me know their conclusions.

There is one more matter, for which I beg you to excuse me: You know that the illustrious Boyle has performed many experiments in an exhausted receiver; but I could not discover, among those that have been published, that he has experimented on any distinction between the [optical] refraction of ordinary air and [the contents of] an exhausted [receiver]. If he, or the famous Hooke, or any other learned man among you has found out anything certain on this head, please let me know of it. For the rest, farewell and cherish me; if I can serve you in any way, boldly call on me and write back, etc., to

Your admirer,
Gottfried Wilhelm Leibniz

Frankfurt, 15/25 October 1671

NOTES

Reply to Letter 1724.
1 This was *Notitia opticae promotae. Autore G. G. L. L.* (Frankfurt, 1671), a four-page pamphlet.
2 See *Phil. Trans.*, no. 7 (4 December 1665), 124, and Vol. II, pp. 467, 473.
3 The literal meaning is "all-gathering." Leibniz explains in his paper (which he also sent to Spinoza) that he used this term because his proposed new lenses would bear any aperture, that is, they would not need to be "stopped down."
4 See Letter 1688, note 10, and Letter 1867.
5 We were not able to trace this book on defects of vision by Johannes Ott.

6 Heinrich Screta published an M.D. thesis (Heidelberg, 1670), *Dissertatio physico-mathematica de causis ac natura auditionis*; but again we could find nothing on diseases.
7 The four words *quantum in se est* are quoted from Descartes's statement but originated in Lucretius; they were again used by Newton in formulating the First Law of Motion. For Hobbes, see *Elementorum philosophiae sectio prima: De corpore* (London, 1655), Ch. VIII, § 19.
8 The book is mentioned in Letter 1733, note 19.
9 Otto von Guericke, *Experimenta nova (ut vocantur) Magdeburgica de vacuo spatio* (Amsterdam, 1672).
10 This is in Book I; the "emendation" consists only of a brief note on discoveries with the telescope since 1609.
11 This preposition is an error in writing.
12 Guericke's pneumatic experiments are all in Book III; the air gun works by atmospheric pressure into an empty receiver, rather than by release of compressed air from the receiver.
13 This is in Book IV.
14 Letters 1716 and 1721 (lost).
15 Wren's paper was published in *Phil. Trans.*, no. 48 (21 June 1669), 961–62; see Vols. V and VI; for De Son, see Vol. II, p. 478, note 4.
16 The third part of Henry Power's *Experimental Philosophy* (London, 1664) is concerned with magnetic experiments, including a refutation of Grandami's views (but not a rejection of his meridian experiment based on trial).
17 See Vol. IV, p. 427, note 8.

1800

Lister to Oldenburg

16 October 1671

From the original in Royal Society MS. L 5, no 39
Partly printed *Phil. Trans.*, no. 77 (20 November 1671), 3002–3

Yorke Oct. 16. 1671

Sr,

I know not but my last to you might miscarry,[1] although indeed, it required noe answer. but to confesse to you, I have an uneasy & restlesse ambition to be of your illustrious body, & therefore begg pardon for putting you in mind of a begun favor, as once you wrote me word.

You may put this Quaery (yt this Letter be not without all matter of Philosophy) to your correspondants of Italy, viz.

Whether ye Tarantula be not a *Phalangium* (yt is, a 6-eyed-skipping-spider)² as Mathiolus³ & others seem to tell us; if soe whether some later authours impose not on us by giving us a Cutt or Figure of a Nett or *Reticulum orbiculatum*,⁴ wch our English *Phalangia* are never observed (yt I know off) to weave or make use of in hunting: & whether ye person bitt wth a Tarantula, be not ever, when on his Feet, disposed & actually dancing after ye nature of a *Phalangium*, wch never moves but by skipping, even as it happens wth such as are bitten wth a madd-dogg, who have been sometimes observed to barke like a Dogg etc: & if soe what we are to think & credit concerning such & such musical Tunes said to be most agreable & tending to ye cure of persons bitt wth a Tarantula.

Thus farr of this Letter I had writ to you ye other day, before yours of ye 11 of Octob. came to hand.⁵

'Tis true Mr Willoughby has twice honoured me wth visits of late; but yet made very short stayes much to my greife. indeed yt little time we were togather we spent (as you guessed) in conference about our common studies & veiwing Mr Brookes's rich & well stored Cabinet of Art & Nature.⁶

Amongst other things I had ye good fortune to present him wth a Musk-Ant, an Insect observed by me not many dayes before his first Visit. And though I cannot send you of ye Insects ymselves, as having parted wth all I had, yt I will ye Note.

Sept. 2d. I found on a sandy-ditch-bank ye first hollow beyond ye Ring-houses in ye high road to London about a mile & a halfe from Yorke, a sort of exceeding small Pismire (by wch note alone I think they may be sufficiently distinguished from all at least yt I have seen). Those without wings were of a light-yellow or flaxen, & broaken at ones nostrills, they emitted, like others, an Acid or sower smell. but those of ye same banke wth wings, were cole-black. these (I say) bruised & smelt to, emitted soe fragrant a sent like Musk, yt I must confesse they were too strong for me to endure: yet having kept ym sometime by me, ye more delicate sex were not displeased wth ye smell; And an Apothecary in this Cittie, famous for his dilligence in Chymical Operations, did compare ym (unseen & not yet made know to him) to an excellent balsome he is wont to praepare.

Mr Willoughby informed me, yt he had found ye Goat-chaffer or sweet-beetle out of season as to yt smell: & therupon asked me what I had observed as to ye time of their sweetest & strongest smelling. I answered yt I beleived it to be at ye time of ye Coit, for as much as at ye time yt I tooke ym highly perfumed, I had observed ye female to be full of Egg.

I shall trouble you noe further at present but thanke you for ye particulars of your letter. I am

>your most humble servant
>*Martin Lister*

I have by me 3s.[7] of ye English black to send you & it is ye 4th time I have repeated ye Experiment wth constant & like successe.

You may be pleased to put into ye next *Errata* N. 73. p. 2197. line 2. viz. "whereas ye true Kermes-husk seemes to be peirced but in one place." wch line is to be totally expunged.[8] That hole in some of ye shop Kermes being accidentall only, and ever on ye bottom [p]art cleaving to ye branch; & ye time of gathering ym for colo[ur is] without doubt before they are peirced & whilst ye animal is yet in Vermiculo and consequently ye Husk intire.

ADDRESS
>These
>For his honoured friend
>Mr. Henry Oldenburg
>at his house in ye Palmal
>>London

NOTES

1 Letter 1787; Oldenburg answered in Letter 1797, which Lister had not yet received.
2 The modern genus *Phalangium* is of the order Phalangidea, which includes spiders without poison glands or spinnerets; the "harvestman" is a typical species.
3 Pietro Andrea Mattioli (1501–77), naturalist.
4 "Spherical net."
5 Letter 1797; the second figure of the date is badly written.
6 John Brooke (*c*. 1635–91), whose father was Mayor of York when he went up to Cambridge in 1652, was one of the Original Fellows of the Royal Society, though expelled in 1685. He was M.P. for Boroughbridge in 1679 and 1680, having been created Baronet in 1676. He lived in or near York, and in later years corresponded with Lister.
7 If Lister used "s." as an abbreviation for "semis," this would signify half a dram.
8 Lister had used this phrase in Letter 1726 (p. 106). Oldenburg inserted his amendment at the end of *Phil. Trans.*, no. 76 (22 October 1671), 2294.

1801
Oldenburg to De Graaf
16 October 1671

De Graaf's Letter 1729 of 19 June is endorsed as received on 12 July and answered on 16 October. No copy of Oldenburg's reply survives. It is acknowledged by De Graaf in Letter 1931.

1802
Becher to Oldenburg
16 October 1671

From the original in Royal Society Boyle Letters I, no. 57

Nobilissime Domine,

Anni, ni fallor elapsi sunt viginti, quando honorem habui, Dominationem Vestrum Moguntiae cum ViceComite Ranalaug videndi,[1] & postea Parrhysiis, ac Londino aliquod commercium literarium variis epistolis habendi, quod postmodum temporum injuria interruptum praesertim mea ex parte, variis itineribus & occupationibus publicis, verum cum audiam Dominationem suam[2] etiamnum in vivos superesse, quod gaudeo, meque heic Amstelredami praesentem ac per mensem integrum forte morantem video, amicitia petere, loci vicinitate multas curiositate ductus, non potui non has ad Dominationem suam exarare, atque responsum expectare, num pareo hoc tempore praesentia literaria frui liceat, literae possent dirigi ad Omphalium Pharmacopolam Amsterodamensem op het huck van den kolck in den rosenbom, quibus me commendans & responsum expectans permaneo Dominationis Vestrae

Observantissimus amicus
Joh. Joachim Becher Dr.
Sacr. Caesar. Maj. Camerae &
Consiliarus & Commissarus

Amsterodami 26 8br 1671 [N.S.]

P.S. utrum physica mea subterranea cum duobus supplementis nota sit scire questio.

ADDRESS
   Phylosopho & Nobillissimo Domino
   Henrico ab Oldenburg, Soc Regiae
   Anglicana Secretario, Domino suo
         Londinum

TRANSLATION

Very noble Sir,

Unless I am mistaken, twenty years have passed since I had the honor of seeing your worship at Mainz together with Viscount Ranelagh,[1] and afterwards of exchanging some letters [with you when you were] in Paris and London, which correspondence was interrupted by the misfortunes of the times, especially on my side through various travels and public affairs. When I heard that your worship[2] was still in the land of the living, at which I rejoice, being myself here at Amsterdam to look up some friends and because of the curiosities in the neighborhood of this place likely, so far as I can see, to remain here for a whole month, I could not but write this to your worship and await a reply; if it is permitted me to enjoy a literary present at this moment a letter may be addressed to the Amsterdam pharmacist Omphalius, on the corner of the sluice in the Rosenboom. With which commending myself, and awaiting an answer I remain your worship's

                    Most obedient friend
                    Johann Joachim Becher, M.D.
                 Councilor and Commissary of His
                    Imperial Majesty's Chamber

Amsterdam, 26 October 1671 [N.S.]

P.S. I would like to know whether my *Physica subterranea* with two supplements is known [to you].

ADDRESS
   To the philosopher and most noble gentleman
   Henry von Oldenburg, Secretary of the
   English Royal Society, my Lord,
            London

NOTES

For the writer of this letter, see Vol. I, p. 210, note; Oldenburg corresponded with Becher in 1659 and 1660 (Letters 108, 177, 199, and 223). The style of the letter is very imperfect.
1 In the summer of 1658.
2 In the Latin there is a change from second to third person.

1803
Wait Winthrop to Oldenburg
17 October 1671

From the original in Royal Society MS. W 3, no. 28

Sr

My Father being remote from Boston when the ships sayled, ordered me to send those things which I have put on bord Mr Fairewether directed to yourself for the Royall Society;[1] which are, an Indian bow and quiver of arrowes, the sword of a fish, and a smale fish with a horne on the back, alsoe a mong the arrowes there is a sea thorn. the quiver is made of an Indian doggs skinn the arrowes are headed according to the Indian manner some with horsfoot tayles[2] some with stones and others with deere horn and sharks teeth: I have not els to trouble you with but remaine

Your very humble servant
Wait Winthrop

Boston Octob. 17th 1671

ADDRESS
    For
Mr Henry Oldenburg
att the Pelmeal nere
  London
      these

POSTMARK NO 28

NOTES

The envelope is endorsed "Leave this with Mr Daniell Colwell at the searchers office at the custome house to be conveyed as above," possibly by Wait Winthrop. Daniel Colwall (d. 1690), a London merchant, was the Royal Society's Treasurer.

Wait Winthrop (1641/2–1717) was John Winthrop's most successful son. He attended Harvard University (though he took no degree) and later accompanied his father to England in 1661. On their return, he assisted his father, and became a respected landowner and Justice of the Peace.

1 This letter and objects were presented to the Royal Society on 7 December 1671.
2 The tails of horseshoe crabs.

1804
Oldenburg to Lister
21 October 1671

From the original in Bodleian Library MS. Lister 34, f. 39

London Octob. 21. 71.

Sir,

Yr three last favours in writing, were of Aug. 25. Septemb. 13. and (Wch I received yesterday) of Octob. 16. If you have sent any between these, they have miscarried; and if so, I must solicite ym to be supplied by a fourth.[1]

If ye R. Society had not discontinued their publick Assembly's in this long Vacation, you had been one of them long agoe. And I can assure you before-hand, from the universall applause, wch all yr communications have met wth there, yt you will be as welcome amongst ym, as any. Nor shall I omit, at the first opening of their meetings again, to put ym in mind, both by their Journal and yr late Letters, yt you stand Candidat; and I am most confident, yt then you will be presently elected, in case there be but a *Quorum* requisite for yt purpose. Nothing hath retarded yr reception so long, but that before the Vacation, our meetings were so thin, yt no Election whatsoever could be made; wch just excuse I have satisfied divers other Candidats wth, yt have been Exspectants for many months.

I shall not faile, God permitting, to transmit yr quaere of Tarantula's to my Italian Correspondents by ye first conveniency. One of ye last letters,

I received from Venice, written by his Majies Resident three,² gives me this account, wch somewt surprised me; viz. That by means of a friend at Naples he endeavoured to procure ye best History he could of ye Bitings and Effects of the Tarantula; and yt they had written to him from the mouth of Dr Cornelio, a most Eminent man and very Curious in all Enquiries into Nature, yt the bittings of Tarantula's are fabulous, and yt there is no such disease as is reputed; but yt yt wch is, proceeds from ye heat and driness of ye Climat: Further, yt last year Dr Cornelio went on purpose into *Apulia* to satisfy his Judgement, a man yt seldom takes any thing upon trust; and yt he saw many Tarantula's, but found ye effects of their bitings to be nothing but ye fancies of ye credulous Vulgar. *So farr he.*

What shall we say then of ye several Tracts written of this kind, if all be fictitious?

I am exceedingly pleased to find ye stock of Musk-Insects encrease; as also yt yr Experiments of ye English black have a constant and like success. When you shall please to send us yt second specimen, you promise, I doubt not but you will specify somewt of ye kinds and particulars of those Experiments, you have made therewth; and especially, whether yt Black may be made in good quantities?

Yr answer to Mr Willughby's question about ye time of ye sweetest and strongest smelling of ye Goat-Chaffer, seems to me very like truth; it being observ'd in all sorts of Animals, yt about the time of Generation they acquire another sent from yt of other times: But, why this Insect should then get a musk-smell, will still remain a question.

I take particular notice, yt Mr Brookes, a member of ye R. Society,³ hath, by yr description, a rich and wellstored Cabinet of Art and Nature. Many such Collections, in all parts of ye world, made by judicious and diligent men, will at length make up such a Store-house, as our Society designeth for an Universal History of Nature, and consequently for a due Substratum to raise, in time, a True and Solid System of Natural Philosophy upon.

I shall be mindfull to take notice of what you have suggested to be expunged in N. 73; and always approve myself Sir

Yr faithful servt
Oldenburg

I pray, Sir, acquaint me by ye first, whether in yr letter of Sept. 13. ye word be *Beets*, to wch you say, yt, among other plants ye green Caterpillar affixeth his theca to. For I am not sure, whether I read yt word aright.

NOTES

Reply to Letters 1778, 1787, and 1800.
1 There is no indication that any of Lister's letters written in this period were lost.
2 Dodington; see his Letter 1695, of which the following lines are a paraphrase.
3 See Letter 1800, note 6.

1805
Malpighi to Oldenburg
22 October 1671

From the original in Royal Society Malpighi Letters, no. 11
Partly printed in *Opera Omnia*, I, Appendix, p. 13.

Eruditissimo et Praeclarissimo Viro
Domino Henrico Oldemburg Regiae Societatis Anglicanae Secretario
Marcellus Malpighius S.P.

Plantarum anatomen, cuius in indagine me iamdudum insudasse, alias te monui,[1] tandem in actuariolum informe congestam hic habes, Vir Clarissime.[2] Hanc (si tamen tantorum Virorum congressu non indignam agnosces) Regiae Societati meo nomine exhibeas, rogo, eiusque sincerum mihi aperire sensum ne renuas; si enim supervacaneos meos indicaveris labores, corpus aegritudinibus perpetuo fessum conquiescere sinam; at si non omnino inutiles agnosces reliquum vitae in his perficiendis insumam, prout ut tenuitas mentis, corporis, et fortunae permittent.[3] Aliam observationum seriem quamprimum transmittam.

Excellentissimus Dominus Montanarius accademicam edidit dissertationem circa sidera fixa, quae diversas magnitudines subeunt, cuius causas in vapores, et quasi maculas refundit.[4] Clarissimus Dominus Mengolus nunc sub praelo exercitationes elapso anno promissas habet.[5] Eruditissimi Domini Cassinij opuscula nunquam luce gavisa sunt.[6] Diu vivas, et mea studia fovere ne desinas.

Dabam Bononiae Calendis Novembris 1671 [N.S.]

Gelatorum Academiae opuscula varia transmittam quamprimum[7]

TRANSLATION

Marcello Malpighi sends many greetings to the very learned and famous Mr. Henry Oldenburg Secretary of the English Royal Society

Here, famous Sir, you may see the anatomy of plants, on the investigation of which I have been laboring for some time as I told you on a previous occasion,[1] put together at last in a clumsy little document.[2] I request you to present this to the Royal Society in my name (if you allow it to be not unworthy of an assembly of such great men), and to be so kind as to make the sincerity of my intention known to them: for if you shall hint that my labors are superfluous, I shall permit my body, worn out by constant sickness, to repose; but if you agree that they are not without value I will devote the rest of my life to perfecting these investigations, so far as the frailty of my intellect, frame, and fortune permit.[3] I will send over another series of observations as soon as possible.

The very excellent Mr. Montanari has published an academic dissertation on the fixed stars that pass through a range of magnitudes, whose causes he assigns to vapors and (as it were) sunspots.[4] The famous Mr. Mengoli now has the essays that were promised last year in press.[5] The little studies of the very learned Cassini have never enjoyed the light of day.[6] Long may you live, and continue to encourage my studies.

Bologna, 1 November 1671 [N.S.]

I shall as soon as possible send the diverse publications of the Accademia dei Gelati.[7]

NOTES

1 Oldenburg already knew of Malpighi's interest in the structure of plants in 1668 (Vol. V, pp. 279–80); Malpighi mentioned it again obscurely in April 1670 (Vol. VI, p. 629).
2 This was the work published by Oldenburg at London in 1675 to which he gave the title *Anatomes plantarum idea*, adding it to the first part of the *Anatome plantarum*.
3 The paper and the present letter were exhibited to the Royal Society on 7 December; besides thanking and encouraging Malpighi warmly, the meeting ordered Oldenburg to inform him of Nehemiah Grew's similar researches; see Letter 1842.
4 The book is *Prose de' Signori Accademici Gelati di Bologna* [ed. G. B. Capponi] (Bologna, 1671); see Vol. VII, p. 270, note 3. Montanari supposed that "sunspots" might become dense enough to diminish notably or obliterate a star's light.
5 Probably the book in question was *Speculazioni di Musica*, though its imprint is Bologna, 1670. Oldenburg received it only three years later; see *Phil. Trans.*, no. 100 (9 February 1673/4), 6194–7000.
6 These unpublished papers by Cassini had been frequently mentioned previously by Malpighi.

7 Malpighi subsequently sent the *Prose de' Signori Accademici Gelati di Bologna*; this copy is now in the British Museum. There were also published *Memorie, imprese e ritratti de' Signori Accademici Gelati di Bologna* (ed. G. B. Capponi] (Bologna, 1672), with biographies and bibliographies of its members.

1806
Thevenot to Oldenburg
28 October 1671

From the original in Royal Society MS. T, no. 44

Monsieur

J'ay quelque chose à vous envoier et à Monsieur Boyle,[1] i'attendois toujours qu'il fut en estat pour avoir cette occasion de vous ecrire et de satisfaire à mon devoir; mais limprimeur va trop lentement, et ie vous suis trop obligè et à Monsieur Boyle pour differer plus long temps mon remerciment des beaux livres qu'il m'a fait la grace de m'envoier; outre que ses livres nous donnent touiours de nouvelles veues ie vouderois fort aussi que les gens de lettres profitassent de son exemple, et qu'au lieu de perdre leur temps en raisonnemens faux et inutils, ils l'employassent à faire comme lui, des experiences, et à mettre la main à l'oeuvre, qui est le seul moyen de tirer quelque usage de l'etude et de l'aplication des Philosophes. Je vous diray Monsieur, pour répondre a ce que vous me mandez de sa part, que je me suis trouvè engagè à la traduction de l'Abulfeda,[2] qui est une entreprise ou la difficultè de la langue est la moindre, le peu d'historiens et de geographes que nous avons eus jusques à cette heure des Orientaux, m'a donnè plus de peine que tout le reste. Je le fais imprimer maintenant, et je fais estat d'en envoier les feuilles a Mr. Bernard à mesure qu'elles s'imprimeront car il m'a offert de les conferer avec quelques manuscrits que vous en avéz en vos quartiers: ma copie à deia estè conferée sur trois, ou quattre M.SS. qui m'ont passè par les mains et je n'en scay point d'autres en Europe outre ceux que jay veu que ceux que vous avez en Angleterre et celui de Vienne. Cette geographie à un peu retardè la suite du receuil de voyages, j'en suis maintenant ala quatrieme partie ou je fais estat d'inser quelques pensées que me sont venues sur l'art de la navigation, l'une de faire une nouvelle observation de la mesure dela Terre sur une plaine que ie pretends avoir trouvée, ou l'on pourra mesurer l'etendue de plusieurs degréz Nord et Sud, en y appliquant une mesure actuelle. J'attens tous les jours d'apprendre ce que mon amy qui est sur les lieux aura pû faire, et il y auroit deja 2. ou 4. ans que la chose seroit executée si i'avois pû souffrir la fatigue d'une observation qui se doibt faire sur les glaces qui se rencontrent fort souvent depuis le fonds de Sinus Botnicus, iusques bien avant dans la Mer Baltique.

L'autre pensée estoit de transmettre ala posterità la connoissance des mesures dont nous nous servons maintenant, de l'oster dela peine ou nous ont laissè tous ceux qui nous ont precedè, et d'etablir dés cette heure une mesure commune, par laquelle toutes les Nations se puissent entendre sur le fait des mesures ceque ie pretends faire par les cellules des Abeilles particulieres, s'il est vray qu'elles soient partout egales comme je trouve quele sont celles des mouches de hollande, de l'isle de france, et de florence; Mais vous verréz la chose mieux expliquée dans les feuilles que l'on imprime maintenant de la suite du receuil,[3] que ie vous enveray au premier jour, ceque i'en touche ici n'estant que pour satisfaire ala question que vous me faites de la part de Monsieur Boyle. I'espere au premier intervalle de loisir que ie pourray prendre, de faire un voyage en vos quartiers pour vous aller entretenir l'un et l'autre, et voir les autres amis que i'ay en Angleterre.[4] Je m'imagine que mon bon amy Monsieur Vossius y est encore[5] et ainsi je prens la libertè de mettre dans vostre pacquet le billet cy ioint que ie lui recis.

Croyez moy tousiours Monsieur, je vous prie, et soyez bien persuadè que c'est de tout mon coeur que ie suis Monsieur

Vostre tres humble et
tres obeissant serviteur
Thevenot

A Paris ce 7. Novembre 1671 [N.S.]

Si vous me faites la grace de m'ecrire je vous prie daddresser vos lettres a M. Andrè Cramoisy libraire demeurant dans la rue des vieilles boucheries au sacrifice d'Abraham pour me les faire tenir.

TRANSLATION

Sir,

I have something to send to you and to Mr. Boyle;[1] I have kept waiting until it was in a fit state to take the opportunity of writing to you and doing my duty, but the printer goes on too slowly, and I am under too heavy an obligation to you and to Mr. Boyle to defer any longer my thanks for the excellent books which he has kindly sent me. Besides the fact that his books always give us new insights, I very much wish that men of letters would profit by his example and that instead of wasting their time in false and useless reasoning they would employ it in making experiments, like him, and in putting their hands to the job, which is the only way of extracting any use from the study and application of philosophers. I should tell you, Sir, in reply to what you let me know from him, that I find myself engaged in the translation of Abulfeda,[2] which is an undertaking in which the difficulty of the language is the least [impediment]; the scarcity of Oriental historians and geographers up to the present has given me more trouble than anything else. I am now having it printed, and am making ready to send the sheets to Mr. Bernard as they are printed off, for he has volunteered to collate them with several manuscripts you have in your parts; my copy has already been collated with three or four manuscripts which have passed through my hands and I know of none in Europe beside those I have seen except those you have in England and the one in Vienna. This geography has rather held up the continuation of my collection of travels; I am now at the fourth part where I am ready to insert some ideas at which I have arrived on the art of navigation, one of making a new observation of the measurement of the Earth on a plain which I claim to have invented, by which one will be able to measure the extent of various degrees North and South by applying an actual measuring instrument. I await every day news of what my friend who is on the spot had been able to do; the affair would have been dealt with two or four years ago if I had been able to endure the fatigue of [undertaking] an observation which ought to be made on the icebergs which are often to be met with from the depths of the Gulf of Bothnia well into the Baltic Sea.

The other idea was to transmit to posterity knowledge of the measures we use nowadays, to relieve them of the difficulty in which we have been left by all our predecessors, and to establish from now on a common measure, so that all nations can agree on the reality of measures; this I claim to do on the basis of the cells of certain bees, if it is true that they are the same everywhere, as I find that those are of the flies of Holland, the Isle de France, and Florence. But you will see the thing explained more clearly in the leaves now being printed at the end of the collection [of *Voyages*][3] which I shall send you as soon as possible; what I touch on here is only to answer the question which you put to me on Mr. Boyle's behalf. I hope in the first leisurely interval available to me to make a journey into your parts, to converse with you both and to see the other friends I have in England.⁴ I suppose that my good friend Mr. Vossius is still there,⁵ and so I take the liberty of putting the enclosed letter which I have written to him into your packet.

Believe me always, Sir, I beg you, and be convinced that it is with my whole heart that I am, Sir,

Your very humble and obedient servant
Thevenot

Paris, 7 November 1671 [N.S.]

If you do me the favor of writting to me, I ask you to address your letters to Mr. André Cramoisy, bookseller, living in the Rue des Vieilles Boucheries, at [the sign of] Abraham's sacrifice, to be delivered to me.

NOTES

The only previously recorded letter from Melchisédec Thevenot (see Vol. I, p. 399, note 4) was in 1661 or 1662, but there may well have been other correspondence, now lost. Oldenburg's preceding letter to Thevenot is likewise lost.
1 Probably his *Relation de divers Voyages Curieux, IVe Partie* (Paris, 1672). See (for the earlier discourses) *Phil. Trans.*, no. 89 (16 December 1672), 5128–30.
2 This was included in the work just noted; see Vol. III, Letter 665 and note 14, p. 488.
3 There are no such leaves in the copy we examined.
4 We have not traced such a visit.
5 See Letter 1743, note 21.

1807
Huygens to Oldenburg
28 October 1671

From the original in private possession
Printed in Rigaud, I, 173–75

A Paris ce 7 Nov. 1671. [N.S.]

Monsieur

Je vous remercie treshumblement de ce que non obstant ma paresse a escrire presque inexcusable, vous ne laissez pas d'avoir la bontè de me faire part des productions de vos Illustres. Il y a à la veritè quelquechose qui m'a fait retarder d'une semaine a l'autre de vous faire cellecy, qui est l'imprimè dont vous la voiez accompagnée.¹ Car ce qu'il y a la dedans des Observations de Saturne, je l'avois donnè il y a deux mois, devant que m'en aller a la campagne, mais Mr. Cassini s'estant proposè de publier en mesme temps la suite de ses observations des taches du soleil, la gravieure des figures et autres circonstances y ont apportè cette longueur, que tout cela ne paroit que maintenant, et a mon grand regret, parce qu'ayant predit le retour de la forme ronde de Saturne vers la fin de l'année, peu s'en faut que la prediction ne soit accomplie devant qu'on en ait estè averti. Je dis pour les pais estrangers, car nos Messieurs scavent bien qu'aussi tost que Mr. Cassini m'eut appris que les bras de Saturne estoient revenues, je dis que assurement ils disparoitraient devant la fin de l'année. Je les observay encore hier au soir mais si foibles et obscurs qu'on avoit de la peine a les discerner. de sorte que dans peu de jours ils ne paroistront plus de tout. Cecy confirme tout a fait mon hypothese de l'Anneau qui presentement disparoit a nos yeux a mesure que les rayons du soleil en esclairent obliquement la surface plate tournee vers nostre vue. Et les apparences de cette année donneront moyen de predire le retour de la figure ronde avec bien plus de justesse qu'auparavant.

Je vous suis bien obligè de la construction de Mr. Sluse sur le probleme d'Alhazen.² Elle vient, comme il a bien remarquè de la mesme analyse que la mienne, et n'en est pas beaucoup differente. Il me semble tousjours que la mienne est la plus naturelle a cause de la disposition des asymptotes de l'Hyperbole, et il n'y a pas plus de facon aussi qu'à celle qu'il a donnée. Mais il faut que j'en communique avec luy mesme, qui est le plus scavant et le plus sincere de tous les Geometres que je connoisse, quand ce ne seroit que pour le prier de me faire part d'une analyse encore plus facile qu'il dit avoir trouvée de ce mesme probleme.

Je suis marry qu'on a tant de peine a avoir icy les livres qui s'impriment par de la. J'ai prie le bon Monsieur Vernham de m'en procurer quelques uns et nommement cette seconde partie du Traite de Mr. Boile³ mais jusqu'icy je n'ai encore pu l'obtenir. Pour la derniere partie de l'ouvrage de Mr. Wallis, j'espere qu'il aura la bontè de se souvenir de moy, quand il sera achevè d'imprimer, et il peut s'assurer que je suis un des plus grands admirateurs de ses profondes speculations.⁴

J'attens le volume entier de vos Transactions que j'ay priè mon Pere de m'apporter d'Angleterre. Je suis marry que nostre Monsieur Gallois ne continue pas ses nouvelles⁵ avec la mesme dilligence que Vous. Il y a 2 mois qu'il est a la campagne et que nous ne l'avons pas vu.

Mon Pere m'a envoiè une feuille de vos Transactions c'est pag. 631.

ou vous dites des choses merveilleuses de certains verres non spheriques.[6] J'ay bien de la peine à croire qu'ils puissent faire un bon effect en qualitè d'oculaire, et beaucoup moins en celle d'objectifs. Je vous prie de me dire quelle suite a eu cette nouvelle fabrique, dont je ne laisse pas d'admirer l'industrie, de ce qu'au moins ces verres sont assez regulierement taillez pour faire quelque chose de plus que les spheriques lors qu'on s'en sert a lire a travers. car c'est de quoy mon pere rend tesmoignage et en attend un de cette facon.

Je me recommande a vos bonnes graces et suis tresveritablement, Monsieur

Vostre treshumble et tresobeissant serviteur
Hugens de Zulichem

Nos observateurs pour l'Amerique partent dans peu de jours.[7] Et je leur donne une pendule ajustée d'une maniere nouvelle pour observer les Longitudes. Elle resistera mieux a l'agitation du Vaisseau que les precedentes.

TRANSLATION, partly by Oldenburg in *Phil. Trans.*, no. 78 (18 December 1671), 3026

Paris Novemb. 7. 1671. (st.n.)

Sir,

[I thank you very humbly for never failing kindly to share with me the results of your distinguished Fellows, in spite of my almost inexcusable laziness about writing.] There is something indeed, that hath kept me, week by week, from writing to you; which is the Printed paper, accompanying this Letter.[1] For the Observations of *Saturn*, therein contained, I had deliver'd two Months ago [before going into the country]; but Signor *Cassini*, purposing to publish at the same time the sequel of his Observations of the *Solar Spots*, the Engraving [of the figures], and other circumstances have caused such a retardment, that all this appears not till now, and that to my great regret, because having predicted the Return of the *Round* Figure of Saturn towards the End of this year, there wants but little but that the Prediction is accomplish't before others have been advertised thereof. I say this as to Forraign Countries; for our Philosophers here know very well, that as soon as Signor *Cassini* had told me, that the *Arms* of *Saturn* were returned, I said, that assuredly they would dis-appear before the End of this Year. I still observed them yesterday in the evening, but they were so faint and obscure, that it was hard to discern them; so that within a few days they will appear no more at all. This confirms altogether my *Hypothesis* of the *Ring*, which now disappears in proportion that the rays of the Sun do obliquely illuminate the *flat* surface of it, obverted to our sight. And the Appearances of this year give occasion to predict the Return of the *Round* figure with much more exactness, than before.

[I am very much obliged to you for Mr. Sluse's construction of Alhazen's problem.[2] It derives, as he rightly remarked, from the same analysis as mine, and is not very different. It still seems to me that mine is the more natural because of the disposition of the asymptotes of the hyperbola, and also it involves no more fuss than his does. But I must communicate directly with him since he is the most knowledgeable and candid of all the geometers I know, if only to beg him to share with me the still simpler method of analysis which he says he has found for the same problem.

I am annoyed that it is so troublesome to get here the books printed with you. I have asked kind Mr. Vernon to get me some, and notably the second part of Mr. Boyle's treatise,[3] but so far I haven't been able to obtain it. As for the last part of Mr. Wallis's book, I hope that he will be so kind as to remember me when it is printed off, and he may rest assured that I am one of the greatest admirers of his profound speculations.[4]

I await the complete volume of your *Transactions*, which I have asked my father to bring back from England. I am annoyed that our Mr. Gallois does not continue his journal[5] with the same faithfulness that you do yours. He has now been in the country for two months during which time we have not seen him.

My father sent me a sheet of your *Transactions*, page 631, where you say wonderful things about certain nonspherical lenses.[6] I find it very difficult to believe that they could give a good result as eyepieces, and even less as objectives. I beg you to tell me the results of this new method of making them; I cannot fail to admire the industry involved in it, at least in so far as these lenses are worked sufficiently accurately to perform rather better than spherical ones when they are used for reading. For this is what my father assures me of, expecting to have one of this kind.

I commend myself to your good graces and am very truly, Sir,

Your very humble and obedient servant,
Huygens of Zulichem

Our observers leave in a few days for [central] America.[7] I am giving them a pendulum clock adjusted in a new way for observing longitudes. It will bear the motions of the ship better than the preceding ones.]

NOTES

Reply to Letters 1545, 1571, and 1663 (Vol. VII), and Letter 1752. The text in *Œuvres Complètes*, VII, 115–19, was copied from Rigaud. The passages within square brackets have been translated by the editors.

1 This was the rare pamphlet *Suite des Observations des taches du Soleil faites à l'Academie Royale. Avec quelques autres Observations concernant Saturn* (Paris, 1671); compare Letter 1769. It was presented to the Royal Society on 2 November. The first portion was composed by Cassini, the second by Huygens (writing in the third person), whose contribution, dated 19 September 1671, is printed in *Œuvres Complètes*, VII, 118–19. Oldenburg printed a slightly condensed English version of the whole pamphlet in *Phil. Trans.*, no. 78 (18 December 1671), 3020–24.
2 This was sent in Letter 1752.
3 That is, *The Usefulnesse of Experimental Naturall Philosophy . . . The Second Tome* (Oxford, 1671).
4 Huygens had not yet received Letter 1798.
5 The *Journal des Sçavans*.
6 See *Phil. Trans.*, no. 33 (16 March 1667/8), dealing with the lenses of Francis Smethwick, and Vol. IV, p. 223.
7 Although the expedition to Cayenne was determined on before the end of 1670 (compare also Vol. VI, pp. 143–44, 212), the preparations consumed much time; Jean Richer and his assistant, Meurisse, left Paris for La Rochelle in mid-November 1671 and their vessel (a West Indian merchantman) sailed on 8 February 1672.

1808

Lister to Oldenburg

28 October 1671

From the original in Royal Society MS. L 5, no. 40

Yorke. Oct. 28. 1671.

Sir

I send you a 2d Paper about Vegetable Excrescencies, ye shortnesse of ye former[1] & some things therin perhapps lyable to exception obliging me therto.

1. Concerning ye 5 & last proposition of ye first paper it might be more intelligibly expressed thus viz, That ye substance or fibrous part of many Vegetable Excr. seemes not to be ye food of ye wormes to be found in ym: my meaning is, yt ye wormes in those Vegetable Excrescencies wch produce *Ichneumones* (to wch kind of Insect we would limit this proposition & therefore expunge all other Instances) these wormes, I say, doe not seem to devour ye substance or fibrous part of ym, as other Wormes eat ye kernells of nutts etc. but yt (whatever their manner of

feeding is & we doubt not but yt they are nourished in & upon some part of ym) ye Veget. Excresc. still mightily encrease in bulke, & sise as ye wormes feed.

It is observable (to endeavour a solution) yt some of ye Ichneumones delight to feed of a liquid matter as ye eggs of Spiders, & juices (if not eggs) within ye bodies of Catterpillars & Maggotts; whence we conjecture yt those of ye same *Genus* to be found in Vegetable Excrescencies may in like manner suck in ye juices of ye equivalent parts of Vegetables. And this ye dry & spongie Texture of some of those kinds of Excrescencies seemes to evince: for if you cut in pieces a Wild-poppie head for example (or ye great & soft balls of ye Oake) you will find in those partitions, wherin these wormes are lodged nothing but a pithy substance like yt of yong Elder, & if there chance to be any Cells yet unseased[2] (wch I have sometimes observed) the seeds therin will be found yet entire & ripe. Whence very probably they feed upon or suck-in by little & little ye yet liquid pulp of ye tender seeds & leave ye substance or fibrous part, to be expanded into an Excrescence.

As for matter of Fact to cleer ye truth of yt opinion, yt ye divers races of Ichneumones are generated by their respective animal parents & particularly yt those wch ye divers Excrescencies of Vegetables produce, are not plantigenous.[3] I am in great hopes, yt instance of Poppie-heads, swolen into Excrescencies, will favour us yt next season. my expectation is cheifly grounded upon ye condition & nature of yt plant; wch is such yt nothing can peirce ye skin of it & wounde it, but it must necessarily leave a marke of its entry, ye milkie juice springing upon ye lightest puncture & dryes or concreets suddainly into a red scarr. And this I thinke I may affirme, yt of ye many heads grown into Excrescencies wch I gathered this summer, all had more or lesse of those markes upon ym. but our aime is here only to make way for ye Observation against ye next season. To wch purpos alsoe we propose ye following Quaeries

1. Whether ye shagged-balls[4] of ye Wild-rose are not Excrescencies grown from ye budd & very fruit of ye plant: like as ye wild poppie heads are apparently not designed for wormes but seed

2. Whether ye large & soft balls of ye Oake are not in like manner ye budd & Acorn wth all ye parts of a sprouting branch thus monstrously perverted from ye first designe of nature.

3. Upon what parts or juices ye Ichneumones Wormes supposed to be thrust into Catterpillars & other Maggotts can be thought to feed: & whether there be not actually eggs in Catterpillars & Maggotts; (as there

are to be observed in their respective chrysalis's) sufficient to serve ym for food.

Concerning ye name ἰχνευμων,⁵ although I could willingly referr you to Mr Wray, who is another Hesychius,⁶ yet for your present satisfaction, I shall transcribe what yt excellent Critique G. Vossius saies (c. 16 de inimicitia)⁷ "Ichneumonis (id est mus pharaonis sive aegyptiacus) Crocodili ct Aspidis ova indagat, unde Illis Ichneumonis nomen quasi dicas Indagatorem (ἀπὸ τοῦ ἰχνευτου). Reperta utriusque ova conterit: ut est apud Oppianum in tertio de Venatione: Nitander tamen ait eum Aspidis Ova humi mandare."

Now a like Observation of certain Insects of ye Waspe kind, made noe doubt by some of ye Ancients, occasioned ye application of yt name to waspes, as well as to yt Ægyptian Mouse. Yet cannot I remember to have met wth in any of ye Ancients of more than one Text concerning those Wasps. viz. Aristotle *de Hist. Animal* lib. 5. c.xx. wch Pliny (Vide lib. 11. c. 21) hath rendered in a manner varbatim thus "Vespae, quae Ichneumones vocantur (sunt autem minores quam aliae) unum genus ex araneis perimunt Phalangium appellatum, et in nidos suos ferunt: deinde illinunt, et ex ijs incubando suum genus procreant."⁸

How farr this relation is tru & agreable to moderne observations we shall have perhapps occasion to discourse of else where: our designe here is only to tell you, yt we have enough to make us believe, yt these very Insects, we have been treating of, are for kind ye *Ichneumones* of ye Ancients. I am Sr

your most humble servant
Martin Lister

You must read *Bents* (yt is ye stalkes of grasse) or rushes and ye like—

I know from Mr Wray yt Dr Cornelio of Naples is an excellent person & very curious in Natural philosophy: witnesse his Experiment about Manna communicated by him in a letter to Mr Wray when he was at Rome & by this last published in his late Catal. of Engl. Pl. *vide ad Fraxinum*.⁹ Yet I cannot but thinke there is more in ye biting of ye Tarantula (if a phalangium) than he did discover: & wt he would have discovered if he had been assisted by some such Quaerie as I put & due consideration of ye Tables I drew.

ADDRESS
>These
>For his honoured friend
>>Mr. Henry Oldenburg
>at his house in ye Palmal
>>London

NOTES

Reply to Letter 1804.
1 Letter 1751.
2 Unoccupied.
3 Generated from the plant.
4 Robins' pincushions.
5 "ichneumon."
6 Hesychius (fifth century A.D.) was a Greek lexicographer of Alexandria, who has left the explanation of many uncommon words.
7 "The ichneumon (that is, the Egyptian mouse or mouse of the Pharaohs) searches for the eggs of asps and crocodiles, whence the name of ichneumon is applied to them as you might say "seeker" or "tracker." When found, the eggs of both [creatures] are destroyed [by it], as may be found in the third book of Oppian on hunting, whereas Nicander says that they eat the eggs of asps [lying] on the ground." The *Cynegetica* of Oppian of Apamea (third century A.D.) is a Greek poem about hunting; Nicander (second century B.C.) wrote a poem about venomous animals. We could not trace the chapter cited by Lister among the voluminous collected works of G. J. Vossius; however, in Vossius's *Etymologicon linguae latinae*, s.v. "ichneumon," there is a very similar derivation of the name (*Opera*, Amsterdam, 1695, I, 301).
8 Pliny's text is almost a translation of Aristotle's: "The wasps called ichneumons, which are smaller than others, destroy a kind of spider called phalangia, carrying them off to their nests, where they smear them over [with mud] and by hatching out from them procreate their own species."
9 "see under *Ash*." The reference is to Ray's *Catalogus plantarum Angliae* (London, 1670), p. 118. Ray had met Cornelio at Naples in 1664.

1809
Sachs to Oldenburg
29 October 1671

From the original in Royal Society MS. S 1, no. 35

Magnifice Nobilissime Amplissime OLDENBURGE, Fautorum Ocelle

Hactenus per plurales menses Litterarium nostrum commercium cessare visum est, tum quod Magnificae Dominationis Tuae Litteras Hamburgum cum fasciculo oblatas Vratislaviae expectarem, tum quod Secundo Ephemeridum Germanicarum Anno fidem solvere illiusque exemplar Londinum transmittere constitueram. Sed ubique novercantem inveni fortunam. Litterae M. Domin. Tuae cum Transactionum Philosophicum volumine 24. April. Londini conscriptae,[1] demum his nundinis Autumnalibus Lipsiam, et 20. Octob. tandem Vratislaviam tardissimo devenerunt gressu: Ephemeridum Germanicarum secundus Annus prelum Typographi quidem exceperat, sed ob inopinam mortem Sculptoris Francofurtensis, cujus operam in effingendis Tabulis aeneis adhibueramus sors impedivit, ob defectum Tabularum, quo minus Exemplaria distrahi potuerint et alio divehi, quod impedimentum molestissime fero, hac vice tamen evitari non potuit. Vereor enim ne sinistre aliqui ominentur quasi prima opera fervens fuerit, altera penitus tepescat. Spero intra mensem, certo futurum ut Tabulae aeneae, quae ad 40. numerum excreverunt, in nostras deveniant manus, dabimus operam ut quantocyus Exemplaria postmodum hinc inde transmittantur; unde per Scholzium Hamburgensem procurabo ut Magnif. Domin. T. promissum debitum solvam et Exemplar Londinum promovere possim. Interim ut promulsidis loco διαγραφίας quandam exhibeam, praemisi secundo Huic Anno brevem Historiam ortus et progressus Collegij Curiosorum, una cum Legibus, Hominibus Colligantis et Judicijs Virorum Excellentissimorum circa novum hocce institutum. Subsequuntur 260. observationes miscellaneae a 50. Medicis communicatae Tabulis ultra 40. aeneis illustratae. Accesserunt Analecta quaedam ad Observationes secundi Anni non minus quam Appendix ad Secundum Annum Omissorum Curiosorum. Addidi versionem Latinam Illust. Redi tractatus de Novis Experimentis circa Viperas, ut et experimenta ejusdem de Lacrimis vitreis.[2] Concludimus Catalogo Librorum Physico-Medicorum ab Anno 1665. usque ad presentem Annum, tum quorum mentio in Transactionibus Anglicis facta fuit, tum quorum notitia aliunde ad nos devenit. Speramus imposterum ex fideli communicatione reliquis Observationibus accessura varia Germanorum Experimenta, ut et hac in multorum desiderio satisfiat; qualia Chymica aliquot Anno secundo exhibuimus, plura in Tertio Anno notatur. Prioribus meis Litteris mense Martio scriptis,[3] ni fallor, a Magnif. Dominatione T. petieram, ut praemissa ad Exc. Dn. D. Willisium salute, tentaret an expiscari liceret bona cum ipsius venia secretiorem ipsius calcinationem ferri oculorum cancri ut absque corrosivo liquore eorum compages soluta vim medicam in quemvis liquorem facile deponant summo aegrorum cum commodo; cujus medicamenti mentionem facit in tractatu de Febribus secretum tamen non revelat. Hic si Mag. T. Domin. patrocinio Oedipus[4] fieri possem maximopere me sibi obstringeret, ex alijs secretioribus remedijs redimerem, e quorum numero Spiritus cephalicus volatilis, qui hactenus in affectibus capitis multum commodi praestitit. Nec verendum ut processus ille Willisianus communicatus publicam statim visurus sit lucem; siquidem si ita visum fuerit ut paucis innotescat, etiam sub fide silentij tanquam in fano Hippocratis apud me custodiendus esset. P. Athanasius Kircherus e Roma datis Litteris promisit se procuraturum ut Itali commercium Litterarium circa res naturales sint nobiscum instituturi, unde non dubito magnum emolumentum Academiae nostrae accessurum, si promissa reipsa vera praestiterit, Vir Germani candoris ut nativitate Germanus. Fasciculus Ill. Lambecio[5] destinatus Viennam migrabit propediem, quando Exemplaria Secundi Anni rursus S. Caes. Maj. Domino nostro Clementissimo destinata Aulam Caesaream intrabunt; interim Ipsi nuntiavi fasciculum Vratislaviae appulisse. Imposterum a Magnif: Dom. T. Transactionum Philos. Continuationem expecto non minus si quid aliud notatu dignum occurrerit, pro exornandis Laboribus nostris Germanicis, ut simul communicetur dabimus operam ut Beneficia a Magnif. T. Dominat. non minus quam toti Illustrissimo Collegio Regio nobis praestita omni officiorum cultu prosequi et devenerari possimus. Vale Vir Amplissime, et fave ulterius

                           Magnif. Dominat. T. addictissimo
                              Philippo Jacobo Sachs a
                              Lewenheimb D. et Physic.
                              Reipublicae Vratislavensi.

Vratislav. Siles. 1671
   29 Octobris

ADDRESS

    Viro
Magnific. Praenobili, Amplissimo
Dn. HENRICO OLDENBURGIO
Ill. Societat. Regiae Anglicae Secretario
Spectatissimo, Padrono Magno
               LONDINUM

TRANSLATION

Most noble, eminent, worthy Oldenburg, dearest of patrons

For several months until this moment it has seemed good to suspend our correspondence, both because I was awaiting your worthy lordship's letter and package being conveyed to Breslau through Hamburg, and because I had resolved to carry out my promise to the second year of the German *Miscellany*, and to send a copy of it to London. But everywhere I met ill fortune. Your worthy lordship's letter written at London on 24 April,[1] together with the volume of the *Philosophical Transactions*, arrived at the last Leipzig autumn fair and reached Breslau at last by very slow steps on 20 October. The second year of the German *Miscellany* would even now have come from the printing press had not fate been against it, through the unexpected death of the Frankfurt engraver whose labor we had employed in making the copperplates, because of the loss of the plates, so that copies could not be distributed and sent to other places; I bear this delay as a great burden, but this time it was unavoidable. For I am fearful that some may maliciously deduce that although there was enthusiasm for the first collection, it has flagged with the second. I hope to be certain of having the copperplates (which have grown to the number of forty) to hand within a month, and we will make an effort to get copies sent away from here as soon as possible thereafter; whence I will arrange things with Schulz of Hamburg so as to redeem my promise to your worthy lordship and send a copy to London. Meanwhile, to serve as an appetizer I present you with a kind of sketch: I have introduced this second year with a brief account of the rise and progress of the Investigators' Academy together with the Laws, the men who are combined together, and the opinions of the learned about this new enterprise. There follow 260 miscellaneous observations communicated by fifty medical men, illustrated by more than forty copperplates. Certain fragmentary notes are added to the observations of the second year as well as an appendix to the second year containing omitted curiosities. I have added a Latin version of the illustrious Redi's treatise concerning new experiments upon vipers, and also his experiments on Prince Rupert's drops.[2] We have concluded with a catalogue of the books on physic and medicine from 1665 to the present, both those mentioned in the English *Transactions* and those of which word reached us from elsewhere. We hope in the future [to have] with the remaining observations from reliable sources an addition of various experiments by Germans, so as to satisfy the desire of many in this respect. More of the kind of chemical [matters] of which we have given a few [examples] in the second year are to be noted in the third. Unless I am mistaken, in my letter of March[3] I asked your worthy lordship that, after greeting the excellent Dr. Willis, you would try to ferret out from him (with his goodwill) his secret of calcining iron [and] crab's eyes so that without any corrosive liquor their structure is opened and they yield their medical virtue readily to any fluid, with great benefit to the sick; of this medicine he makes mention in his book on fevers, yet he has not revealed the secret. Hence if with your worthy lordship's advocacy I can play the part of Oedipus[4] you will put me under the greatest obligation, which I shall redeem with other secret remedies, among which is a volatile head-spirit which has up to now showed much benefit in diseases of the head. Nor is it to be feared that if that process of Willis's be communicated it will at once be broadcast publicly, for if it is thought fit for the process to be known to few I will be as silent as though I were its custodian in the shrine of Hippocrates.

In a letter from Rome Fr. Athanasius Kircher has promised that he will arrange for the Italians to undertake a correspondence about scientific questions with us, whence I don't doubt a great flow of advantages to our Academy, if the promise is kept in fact by one who is as German in trustworthiness as in his birth. The package intended for the illustrious Lambecius[5] will shortly move onwards to Vienna when the copy of the Second Year (destined once more for his Imperial Majesty, our most clement Lord) shall enter the Imperial Court; meanwhile I have informed him that the package has reached Breslau. I await the further continuation of the *Philosophical Transactions* by your worthy lordship; nevertheless if anything else noteworthy should occur that might adorn our German endeavors, let it be imparted to us at once. We shall strive to acknowledge with every kind of courteous service and to respect the kindnesses received from your worthy lordship and the whole of the most illustrious Royal Society. Farewell excellent Sir, and contiue to cherish

Your worthy lordship's most devoted
Philipp Jacob Sachs von Lewenheimb
Dr. and Physician to the State of Breslau

Breslau in Silesia
29 October 1671

ADDRESS
To the very worthy, noble, and excellent
Mr Henry Oldenburg,
Most distinguished Secretary of the illustrious Royal Society,
My great patron,
London.

NOTES

1 We noted this lost reply in Vol. VII (Letter 1671) from Oldenburg's endorsement; it seems as though he may have held it back and then altered the date.
2 Francesco Redi, *Osservazioni intorno alle Vipere* (Florence, 1664), and *Esperienze intorno a diverse cose naturali* (Florence, 1671). The latter book contains an account of experiments in which glass drops were used to investigate digestion (see *Phil. Trans.*, no. 92 (25 March 1673), 6001–6).
3 Letter 1657 (Vol. VII) was written in March; however, this request was in fact made in Letter 1727 (see also its note 5).
4 Oedipus *guessed* correctly the riddle of the Sphinx; Sachs asked to be *told* the solution.
5 There is no record of this in the surviving correspondence; perhaps it was mentioned in Letter 1671 (Vol. VII).

1810
Esaie le Bourgeois to Oldenburg
31 October 1671

From the original in Royal Society MS. B 2, no. 12

De Chatham Ce dernier Jour d 8 bre 1671

Monsieur

Je vous suis extremmement obligé de vôtre bienveillance, Je vous en demande la Continuation avec toute lardeur dont Je suis Capable.
La diversité qu'il y a entre la maniere de vivre dIcy et Celle de france n'est pas une des moindres Choses qui Contribuent a m'ennuyer. Je ne puis mempescher de regretter Cette Charmante Liberté avec laquelle on se voir Les uns Les autres en france, Lorsque Je voy qu'icy les Visittes é les Conversations sont rares é tres Contraintes. si L'on voie des femmes elles seront ou muettes ou enfoncez dans le dernier serieux. Je vous asseure que J'en Conez dont Je ne suis pas encor Certain si ce sont autre chose que machines mangeantes é beuvantes, pour ne leur avoir veu faire que ces actions La: point d'enjoument, point de politesse, point de galanterie. Pour les hommes point de familiarité avec eux que le verre d'une main é la pipe de l'autre, boire comme des trous et fumer Comme des Dragons, Encor Je Croy qu'ils tiennent que de souffler de la fumee de Tabac au nez des gens est un trait de Civilite Je pense que si Javez eu les yeux Chassieux J'en serez desia guery a force de recevoir de ces sorte d'encens.

Tout Cela me contraint a passer La plusgrande partie du temps a Lire des Livres Anglez que Je Commence a entendre: Jay voulu d'abord me servir de Grammaire, Jay pris la francese de Mauger qui est a mon goust une asses mauvaise Grammaire,[1] mal digeree é pleine de Cent facons de parler qui me sont nullement du bel usage, avec des Entretiens fades et mal Conduits.

Il m'est tombé entre les mains un Certain Livre de Chiromance de Physiognomie fait par souunders, Imprimé cette annee et qui se vend devant la bourse,[2] Je seres bien aise de scavoir ce quon dit de ce livre La: Jay apris un peu de ces sortes de sciences estimant qu'il ya quelques raisons pour ne les pas reietter, mais Comme Je ne l'ay pas encor Leu Je ne puis vous en rien dire.

Les Livres dont vous me parlez sont asseurement Curieux é ne traittent pas de petits Sujets, J'ay principalement envie de voir celuy de mr Willis de anima brutorum:[3] Jay eu autrefois des pensees sur ce suiet autres que celles que Jay presentement, et Jay de lImpatience de scavoir celles de monsieur Willis; faittez moy Je vous prie la grace que J'en sache le prix et le lieu ou Il se vend affin que Je le fasse achetter.

Je suis bien aise qu'on ecrive encor sur le scorbut,[4] plusieurs en ont desia traitté, mais Il sera avantageux de le Conestre bien, estant a mon avis d'assez grande Consequence. Ces sortes de Corruptions de sang sont fort frequentes quoy quelles viennent rarement Jusquau degré du scorbut.

Je souhaitterez que le traitte des vents[5] sortist de la plume dun homme qui sceut egalement bien la philosophie de Descartes é la marine, sans cela Je ne voy pas qu'on puisse bien rendre raison de certaines constances dans LInconstance des Vents.

Je ne pensez pas que La Societé Royale eut tardé si Longtemps a recommancer ses assemblées. Je souhaiterez qu'on y voulut parler des sorciers, s'Il y en a, et Comment Ils peuvent faire. Nous avons veu cette annee grand nombre de personnes soupconnées de L'estre en basse Normandie, et le parlement de Rouen etet presque d'humeur a en faire mourir une bonne partie, mais Celuy de Paris L'en a empesché. Cela a exercé les Curieux en des recherches s'il y en peut avoir, mais Je trouve que les plus avisez non Croyent point, pour moy Je suis du mesme sentiment, é principalement depuis que Je les ay veus a Rouen et Les ay Interroger assez pour me faire Juger que ce sont pauvres fous qui abusent les autres apres avoir esté abusez eux mesmes: Les hommes les plus raisonnables d'entreux nient fermement qu'ils ayent aucune Communication avec Le diable, et les plus Jeunes au contraire le soutiennent, et font des histoires qui partent a mon avis de Leur Cerveau blessé; C'est une chose asseuree qu'ils ont une marque tirante sur le noir Insensible, et qui se dissipe avec le temps lorsqu'ils sont desabusez, Je croy qu'on peut expliquer Cela aussy bien que leurs visions de sabat sans parler de communication avec le diable. Je serez ravy de scavoir vos sentiments la dessus.

J'ay remarqué que ce qui cause cette Lumiere que produit la violence des rames dans la mer, n'est point ce qu'en a Creu Monsieur Descartes: Je trouve que c'est une glaire fort nette et fort Claire, qui samasse dans L'eau par petits globes, et ne fait lumiere que lorsque les rames ou les efforts des vagues la Jettent dessus L'eau; Cette glaire est tout a fait semblable a celle qui se trouve dans le ventre du Lampyris horsmis la Couleur qui est Jaune dans ce Vermisseau, et la raison pourquoy Ils jettent de la lumiere est la mesme; La glaire que se trouve dans l'eau éclaire encor quelque temps apres qu'on L'en a retiree aussy bien que celle du Lampyris apres qu'on la arrachee.

Je vous direz encor autre chose si Je n'avez desia trop passé la longueur d'une lettre. Je finiray en vous asseurant de mes treshumbles respects, et en vous priant de vous souvenir de moy sil se presente quelque occasion: Je ne me soucie pas si c'est pour sortir dehors ou pour demeurer, ayez cette bonté la pour moy que de vouloir bien vous en enquerir; voicy le temps que toutes les personnes de qualité sont a Londre. obligez de Cela Je vous conjure Monsieur une personne qui fera gloire d'estre toute sa vie vôtre treshumble serviteur

Esaie le bourgeois

Monsieur Gregory est a Londre Je croy que vous Ly aurez veû;[6] nous esperions pendant ces Jours passés voir icy Le MyLord Brounker mais Il n'est point encor venu.

J'ay entendu quelques uns dire que Le Duc de Mommouth Ira en france Commander Les troupes Anglezes si cela est et que je puisse aller avec luy J'en Seray bien aise.[7]

ADDRESS
    For Mr Oldemburg
  att his house In Paill-maill
        In
           London

POSTMARK NO 1

TRANSLATION

Chatham, the last day of October 1671

Sir,

I am extremely obliged to you for your benevolence; I ask for its being continued with all the ardor of which I am capable.

The difference in the mode of living here and in France is not the least of the things which contribute to my boredom. I cannot prevent myself regretting that delightful freedom with which people visit one another in France, while here I observe that visits and conversations are uncommon and constrained. If one visits ladies they are either dumb, or plunged into the utmost solemnity. I assure you that I am not yet certain whether some of those with whom I am acquainted are anything other than eating and drinking machines, not having seen them do any actions other than these: no sprightliness, no good breeding, no badinage. As for the men, there is no close acquaintance with them except glass in one hand and pipe in the other, drinking like fish and smoking like dragons. Indeed I think that they hold it an act of civility to blow smoke in people's faces; I think that if I had suffered from bleary eyes I should already be cured by the reception of this sort of incense.

All this forces me to spend the greater part of my time reading English books which I begin to understand. At first I wanted to make use of a grammar; I took Mauger's French grammar[1] which is, to my taste, a pretty bad grammar, badly digested and full of a hundred phrases not at all in good usage, with mawkish and badly designed conversations.

I have come across a certain book on chiromancy [and] physiognomy, written by Sanders, printed this year and sold in front of the Exchange.[2] I should be very glad to learn what is said of this book with you. I have learned a little about these sorts of science, reckoning that there is reason not to reject them, but as I have not yet read it I cannot tell you anything about it.

The books you describe to me are truly worthy of interest and treat no small subjects. I am chiefly curious to see that by Mr. Willis, *De anima brutorum*;[3] I formerly held opinions on this subject different from those I now hold, and I am impatient to know those of Mr. Willis. Please, I beg you, do me the favor of letting me know the price and the place where it is sold so that I can have it bought.

I am very glad that someone is writing on scurvy;[4] many have already discussed it, but it would be a great advantage if it were thoroughly known, it being in my opinion of pretty great consequence. This kind of corruption of the blood is very common, although it rarely gets to the point of scurvy.

I shall be glad if the treatise on winds[5] issues from the pen of a man who understands equally well the philosophy of Descartes and maritime matters; otherwise I do not see how certain constancies in the inconstant winds can be made clear.

I did not think that the Royal Society would have been so late in resuming its meetings. I wish that it would chose to discuss witches, whether there are any and how they can do [what they do]. This year we have seen many people suspected of being witches in Lower Normandy and the Parlement of Rouen was of a good mind to condemn to death a good number of them, but that of Paris prevented it. This has forced inquiring persons to investigate whether there can be any [witches], but I find that better advised people believe not. For myself, I am of the same opinion and more especially since I saw them in Rouen and questioned them enough to let me judge that these are poor, mad people who mislead others after having been themselves misled. The more reasonable among them deny strongly that they have any communication with the devil, while the younger ones on the contrary maintain it and tell stories which, in my opinion, come from their damaged brains. It is certain that they have a blackish, insensitive spot which vanishes in time when they are undeceived; I think that this can be explained, as also their fantasies of the [witches'] Sabbath, without talk of communication with the devil. I should be delighted to learn your opinion on this.

I have noticed that the cause of that light produced by oars striking the sea is not at all what Mr. Descartes thought. I find it to be a very clear and shiny slime which collects in the water in little globules and only shines when oars or the force of the waves throw it on top of the water. This slime is exactly like that found in the stomach of glowworms except for the color which is yellow in the worms, and the cause of their glow is the same. The slime found in water shines for some time after it is pulled out just as that in the glowworm does after being extracted.

I should tell you something else if I had not already exceeded the length proper to a letter. I shall end by assuring you of my very humble respects and by begging you to remember me if any occasion arises. I do not care whether it involves going abroad or staying here, be so kind as to take it upon yourself to make inquiries on my behalf—it is now the season when all persons of rank are in London. Oblige in this I entreat you, Sir, a person who will count it an honor to be, all his life, your very humble servant,

Esaie le Bourgeois

Mr. Gregory is in London; I think you will have seen him there.[6] We have been hoping during these past days to see My Lord Brouncker here, but he has not yet come.

I have heard some say that the Duke of Monmouth will go to France to command the English troops; if this is so and if I could go with him I should be very pleased.[7]

NOTES

All that we know of this young man, presumably a Huguenot, besides what he reveals in his correspondence, is contained in a letter written to Oldenburg by Mr.

de Brieux on 26 May 1673. It appears that he was a citizen of Caen and had been trained in medicine and surgery.

1 Claude Mauger's French grammar appeared in many editions, both French and English, with various titles, from the 1650s onwards. It was particularly aimed at travelers.
2 Richard Saunders, *Physiognomie, and Cheiromancie, Metoscopie* . . . (London, 1653; 2nd ed. London, 1670–71).
3 See Letter 1649, note 5.
4 Presumably Oldenburg had spoken of Walter Charleton, *De scorbuto liber* (London, 1671).
5 Very likely R. Bohun, *A Discourse concerning the Origins and Properties of Wind, &c* (Oxford, 1671), reviewed in *Phil. Trans.*, no. 90 (20 January 1672/3), 5147–50.
6 James Gregory the mathematician was in St. Andrews—at least Collins wrote to him there on 16 October. But there were other learned contemporaries of the same surname.
7 Hostilities in the Third Dutch War opened in March 1671/2; Monmouth became commander of the British regiments serving Louis XIV.

1811
Vogel to Oldenburg
1 November 1671

From the original in Royal Society MS. F 1, no. 34

Viro Nobilissimo & Doctissimo
HENRICO OLDENBURGIO
S.P.D.
Martinus Fogelius

Et tuae binae recte mihi redditae fuerunt.[1] Interea Macula Solaris iterum nobis apparuit, nunc tamen non amplius visibilis.[2] Mitto Clarissimi Henrici Siferi Observationes Telescopio mediocris longitudinis hic factas.[3] postremis quidem Caelum feliciter favit, ut fere a primo die, quo iterum apparere cepit, ad 5 usque Septembris, quod ad Limbum quam proxime accessit, continuo quasi filo tum motus tum Figura ejus repraesentari potuerit. Priores vero Observationes non nisi valde mutilae esse possunt, quod serius quam nos reliquos Caelum inspiciendum esse resciverit.

Illustrissimus Hevelius noster haec adscititia, ut vocat, Caeli Corpora nihil prorsus modo curat, Fixarum & Planetarum Calculo tantum intentus.

30 Septembris Calen. Greg. Jovis & Lunae Transitum accurate observavit, Phaenomenon sane ut rarum admodum, sic quod observantur, dignissimum;[4] eoque vel maxime Hevelii solertia laudanda est, quod diurno tempore, hora scilicet matutina 7. 26' eum inobservatum dimittere noluerit, quamvis Ephemeridum scriptores Americanis tantum conspicuam fore praedixerint Jovis Occultationem. non fuit autem Occultatio, sed arctissimus tantum transitus Lunae Falcatae decrescentis ad 2 propemodum digitos. Si librarium tam cito invenire licuisset, misissem tibi Historiae integrum exemplum una cum Observationibus quibusdam aliis, videlicet Eclipseos Lunaris proximae, & Jovis Satellitis Immersionis in ipsius Umbra factae mensis ejusdem Septembris & Saturni brachiorum tenuissimorum, 11 & 12 Septembris observatorum. Sed mittendae erant hae Clarissimo Picardo, adhuc Uraniburgi haerenti, quem ab Hevelio jam diu literas exspectare noveram.[5]

Aeque nos hic ac Hevelius Gedani, calculum Rudolfinum in Eclipsi quam dixi aberrasse deprehendimus. Emersisse enim jam Lunam ex umbra Terrae ante nonam etiam hic vidimus. cum tamen secundum illum calculum Gedani emersisse debuerit h. 9. 6.' 27." Tempus autem utrobique nubilum accuratiorem observationem utrobique invidit.

de Hispanorum Toxico responsa ex Hispania quam avidissime exspecto, multum lucis inde doctrinae de Veneno Sanguinis accessurum spero.

Si Galilaei Vita prout impressa est, integre & distincta describi a diligente scriba posset, te imprimis curante, ut absque erratis describatur, libens precium pro opera solverem, cum spes omnis impressi Exemplaris accipiendi decollaverit. Annon superesse amplius credis, quae Editori ex Italia submissa sunt a Viviano, de vita Galilaei? haec mihi alias sufficere possent. Fore, Integrum opus ut huc transmittatur, pignore deposito, sperare forsan non audeo. intra mensem alias me redditurum sponderem.

Quod Nobilissimi Boilei dissertationem a Germano illo Studioso accipere debuerim, ex literis quas reddidit, cum Ephemeridibus injectis, minime intelligere potui. Aut alius igitur fuerit ab hoc, aut pro dissertatione Ephemerides Maji mensis miseris. Utut sit, pro affectu tuo erga me gratus iterum ero.

Quod si eam una cum Borelli Historia Incendii Ætnaei (Si quidem examplari uno abundabis) proxime itura navi ad me mittendam curares, aliis libellis lubens commutarem. non deerit occasio hoc tempore, reditum ad nos meditante Presbytero Ecclesiae Anglicae, quod hic est.

An Pocokii folium de Caave & Sche apud vos prostat?[6] an idem in Garziam ab Orto Notas edidit?[7]

Morhofium negligentiorem paulo fuisse non miror. nam admodum festinata est ista Versio,[8] & Animus a Sponsae suae amore alio facile versus videtur. pro 8 a Typotheta 8° videris substituta, cujus Errata in parvum volumen quam plurima irrepserunt. Non tamen praeter rem foret, Versionis reliqua Vitia cum Sculzio communicari, ut in Exemplaribus reliquas emendentur.

Video te Ephemerides, mense Augusti meae etiam Epistolae fecisse mentionem, (pro quo honore gratias, quas debeo, ago) sed male ibi ad Calendarium Gregorianum Hamburgenses observationes factas legitur, *7, 8, 9 Aug. n. st.*; quas Juliani diebus debentur.[9]

Audivi Geoponicos Scriptores in Anglia recudi.[10] Clarissimus Gudius aliquot loca ad Manuscripta optima correxit, qui rogatus libens comminicabit.[11] Quod tibi significandum duxi, ut cum Editore loquaris, si ita videbis.

Quid Hovi vestri scriptis Botanicis fit?[12]

An nondum innotuit, quid sit Nux Vomica,[13] qualis sit arbor Thuris, Myrrhae, Bdellii, &c?[14] Credo per Consules Angliae qui in Oriente degunt, haec facile indagari posse, modo Societas Regia jubeat.

de Actorum Philosophicarum Versione Schulzius ipse prolixe scribet.[15] Vale, Vir Nobilissime, & me amare perge. Scrib. Hamb. Cal. Nov. 1671.

TRANSLATION

Martin Vogel sends many greetings to the very noble and learned Henry Oldenburg

Your two [letters] were also delivered to me safely.[1] Furthermore, the sunspot has revealed itself to us again but now it is no longer visible.[2] I send you the observations made here by the famous Heinrich Sivers with a telescope of modest length.[3] These last days the skies have been kindly, so that almost since the first day when it began to appear again to 5 September when it approached close to the limb it has been possible to delineate without break both its movement and its shape almost to a hair's breadth. The earlier observations can only be very imperfect because he had learned later than the rest of us that the sky was to be examined.

Our very illustrius Hevelius, intent only on calculations relating to the planets and fixed stars, now pays no further attention to this fortuitous event among the heavenly bodies, as he calls it. On 30 September, N.S., he observed accurately a transit of the moon by Jupiter;[4] as this phenomenon is exceedingly rare it is well worth observing. On that account Hevelius' skill is most praiseworthy, for he was reluctant to leave it unobserved, [though occurring] in the daytime, in fact at 7.26 A.M., and even though the writers of ephemerides predicted the occultation of Jupiter as visible only in the Americas. However, it was not an occultation but a very close passage within about two digits of the waning sickle moon. If I could have found a copyist in time I would have sent you a full transcript of the story together with some other observations, namely, an eclipse of the last moon, the immersion of Jupiter's satellites in his shadow that occurred in this same month of September, and the observation of Saturn's "arms," very thin, on 11 and 12 September. But these things had to be sent to the famous Picard, who still remains at Uraniburg, and who, I hear, has long awaited a letter from Hevelius.[5]

We here and Hevelius at Danzig have alike discovered that the *Rudolphine Tables* were in error as to the eclipse I spoke of. Here also we saw that the moon had already emerged from the Earth's shadow before nine o'clock, whereas according to that calculation [of the *Tables*] it should have emerged at 9h. 6′. 27″. However, cloudy weather in both places spoiled accurate observation at either.

I await replies from Spain about the Spaniard's arrow poison most eagerly, hoping to receive much light thence on the theory of blood poisoning.

If the life of Galileo can be clearly and completely copied by a careful scribe just as it is printed, especially if you inspect the work, so that it may be transcribed without errors, I would gladly pay for the work as I have lost all hope of receiving a printed copy. Do you suppose that there remains anything else of what Viviani supplied to the editor from Italy, concerning the life of Galileo? This might otherwise satisfy me. Perhaps I hardly dare hope that the whole of the material might be sent to me, after I had offered some surety. I would promise to return it in a month, if so.

I could not at all gather from the letter delivered by that German student (with the *Transactions* enclosed) that I was to receive the very noble Boyle's dissertation from him. Either he took it elsewhere or you sent the *Transactions* of May in mistake for the essay. However that may be, receive my renewed thanks for your kindness towards me.

If you will take the trouble to send that to me together with a copy of Borelli's *Incendium Aetnaei* (if you can spare a single copy) by the next boat that sails, I will gladly send other books in exchange. There is no lack of means at present as the chaplain of the English Church here is thinking of returning to us.

Is Pocock's sheet on coffee and tea available with you?[6] And has the same person published notes on Garcia da Orta?[7] I am not surprised [to hear] that Morhof has been pretty careless, for his translation was done in a great hurry,[8] and his mind has been easily set on another interest by his love for his bride. You will have seen that the printer whose many errors have crept into the small volume put 8º for 8. Still it would not be amiss to impart the remaining errors to Schulz so that they may be corrected in the rest of the copies.

I see that in the August *Transactions* you also mentioned my letter (for which honor I return you due thanks), but the Hamburg observations are wrongly given there as made by the Gregorian calendar ("7, 8, 9 August N.S."), which should be Julian.⁹

I have heard that the agronomic writers are being reprinted in England.¹⁰ The famous Gudius corrected a few readings from the best manuscripts which, on request, I would gladly communicate.¹¹ I am induced to let you know this so that you may have a word with the editor, if you think fit.

What does your countryman How do as regards botanical writings?¹²

Does he yet know what *nux vomica* is,¹³ and what kinds of tree are frankincense, myrrh, and bdellium?¹⁴ I believe that these matters could easily be looked into through the English consuls living in the East, if only the Royal Society would so ordain.

Schulz himself is writing at length about the translation of the *Philosophical Transactions*.¹⁵ Farewell, noble Sir, and continue to love me. Hamburg, 1 November 1671.

NOTES

1 We can only record a memorandum (Letter 1783).
2 See Letter 1771. This and the following sentence were printed in *Phil. Trans.*, no. 78 (18 December 1671), 3033.
3 The enclosure is a separate sheet, reproduced here as Letter 1811a.
4 See Letter 1792.
5 The meaning seems to be that Vogel received an open letter from Hevelius intended for Picard.
6 Presumably Vogel has in mind Edward Pocock, *The Nature of the drink Kauhi or Coffee* (Oxford, 1659)—largely a translation from Arabic. Pocock did not write on tea. See further Letter 1828.
7 Garcia da Orta's best known work was *Colóquios dos simples e drogas* (Goa, 1563); Pocock had no connection with it.
8 Of the *Cosmicall Qualities* (Hamburg, 1671); see Vol. VII.
9 See Letter 1771 and *Phil. Trans.*, no. 74 (14 August 1671), 2238. There is a correction in no. 77 (20 November 1671), 3018.
10 The Greek tradition of writing on agriculture was summarized and concluded by the Byzantine author of the *Geoponica* (tenth century), in turn based upon a sixth-century compilation of Cassianus Bassus. For a further reference to this abortive edition, see Oldenburg's letter to Gude of 28 April 1673.
11 Marquard Gude (1635–89) was a celebrated German polymath.
12 William How (b. 1620) had died in 1656; his *Phytologia Britannica* (London, 1650) was the first work devoted purely to British plants.
13 See Letter 1780a, note 63.
14 Bdellium was the name given by Dioscorides and Pliny to an aromatic gum; it is still so applied.
15 We have not found such a letter.

1811a

Sivers' Observations

Enclosures with Letter 1811
From the original in Royal Society MS. F 1, no. 34

Macula in Sole observata Hamburgi diebus Augusti Ao 1671
— 8   hor. 1 pomerid. sed non distincte
— 9   hor. 6 matut:
sed die 10   hor. 7 matut: non amplius aderat

H.S.

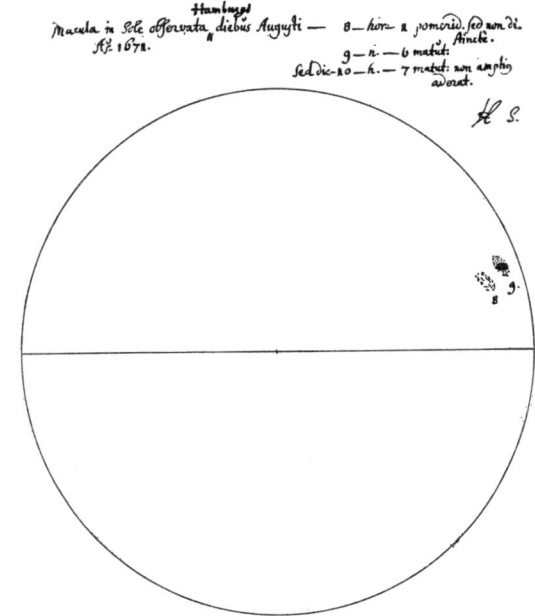

Macula in Sole observata Hamburgi Anno 1671 diebus mensis

Augusti
{
26 — hora 8 matut.
27 — h. 1 pomerid.
28 — h. 1 p.
29 — h. 11 antemer.
30 — h. 11 a.
31 — h. 1 pom.
}
&
Septembris
{
1 — hora 1 pomer.
2 — h. 2 p.
3 — h. 11 antem.
4 — h. 12 merid.
5 — h. 11 antem
& h. 4 pomeri.
}

diana non amplius visa est mihi,

H.S.

[*For the figure, see page 336*]

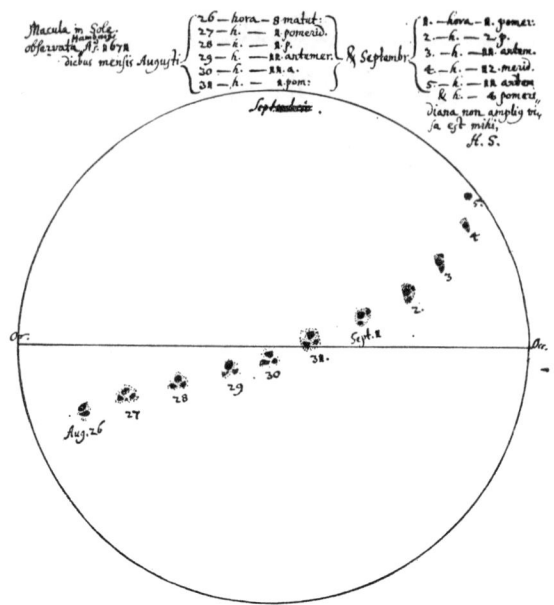

TRANSLATION

A sunspot observed at Hamburg in August 1671
on 8 August at 1 A.M., indistinctly
 ,, 9 ,,   ,, 6 A.M.,; but
 ,, 10 ,,   ,, 7 P.M., it was no longer present.

H.S.

[*For the figure, see page 335*]

A sunspot observed at Hamburg in 1671 on

August		and September	
26 at 8 A.M.		1 at 1 P.M.	
27 ,, 1 P.M.		2 ,, 2 P.M.	
28 ,, 1 P.M.		3 ,, 11 A.M.	
29 ,, 11 A.M.		4 ,, 12 noon	
30 ,, 11 A.M.		5 ,, 11 A.M. and	
31 ,, 1 P.M.		,, 4 P.M.	

The moon [*read* sun] was not seen any more by me

H.S.

[*For the figure, see top of this page*]

NOTE

The second figure only was reproduced in *Phil. Trans.*, no. 78 (18 December 1671), 3033, when Oldenburg printed the above record prefaced by a couple of sentences extracted from Vogel's covering letter.

1812
Oldenburg to Borelli
2 November 1671

From the copies in Royal Society MS. O 2, no. 57
and Letter Book V, 32–33

Celeberrimo Viro
Dn. Joh. Alphonso Borello Mathem. Italo, e Primarijs
H. Oldenburg S.P.D.

Non licuit ante diem hodiernum R. Societati munus illud, quo locupletare Ipsam voluisti, offerre, cum ei commodum non fuerit, caetus suos publicos mensibus aestivis intermissos, citius instaurare. Fronte perquam serena operam tuam utramque, tum de motibus a Gravitate pendentibus, tum de Ætnaei montis Incendio, doctissime tractantem, accepit, jussitque protinus, ut citra omnem moram debitas pro singulari tuo in ipsam studio gratias Tibi redderem, significaremque nihil sibi potius fore, quam doctrinam et Virtutem tuam uberrimis suae in Te benevolentiae testimonijs cohonestare.

Ad Umbilicum nuper perduxit Wallisius noster suum de Motu et Mechanice Tractatum, tribus voluminibus constantem; quorum ultimum, necdum a Te visum, Dn. Collinsius noster ad Te transmittendum suscepit. Cui Illustris Boylii accedit libellus, nuper Latino sermone editus, de Formarum et Qualitatum Origine, nec non ejusdem Tractatuli aliquot de Mira Aeris (etiam citra calorem) rarefactione deque Novis circa Durationem Virtutis Elasticae Aeris expansi Observatis, nec non de Condensatione Aeris, solo frigore facta &c. compositi.

Habet et alia parata, quae caeteris hac occasione junget, de quibus ipse fusius, ni fallor, ad Te scribet.[1] Adjeci Ego Symbolam meam, utut tenuissimam, nempe Clarissimi Leibnitij, Consilarij juxta ac Philosophi Moguntini, Hypothesin Physicam Novam, ad multa circumspicientem, atque utrique Societati Regiae, Britannicae et Gallicae, inscriptam. Tuum de ea judicium avide praestolamur, certique omnino sumus, Authorem mente gratissima id ipsum amplexurum, curaturumque, ut intelligas te beneficium ejusmodi haud male collocasse. Vale, Vir Clarissime, et a Tibi devinctissimo, plurimum salve. Dabam Londini die 2°. Novembris Anno 1671.

TRANSLATION

H. Oldenburg sends many greetings to Mr. Giovanni Aphonso Borelli, one of the leading mathematicians of Italy

Only today could I present to the Royal Society the gift with which you wished to enrich it, because it was not convenient to the Society to resume earlier its ordinary meetings, broken off during the summer months. It received very gratefully both your works, learnedly treating of the motions arising from gravity and of the burning of Etna, and at once instructed me that I should return you thanks for your singular goodwill towards the Society without any delay, and assure you that no object was dearer to it than to honor your learning and virtue by copious testimonies of its warm feelings towards you.

Our Mr. Wallis recently brought to an end his treatise on motion and mechanics in three volumes, of which our Mr. Collins has undertaken to send you the last, which you have not yet seen. To this the illustrious Boyle adds his volume on the *Origin of Forms and Qualities*, recently translated into Latin, as also some little treatises of his dealing with a remarkable expansion of the air (even beyond heat) and new experiments on the duration of the elastic virtue of the air, and also on the condensation of the air by cold alone, etc.

He has others ready which he will at the same time annex to these, about which he will, unless I am mistaken, write to you himself.[1] I have added my contribution, slight as it is, namely the *Hypothesis physica nova* of the famous Leibniz, Councilor and Philosopher of Mainz, which traverses many topics and is dedicated to both the Royal Societies of England and of France. We eagerly await your judgment of it, being assured that the author will receive it gratefully and will take care to have you know that such a kindness is not ill bestowed. Farewell, famous Sir, with many good wishes from your most obliged [friend]. London, 2 November 1671.

NOTES

Reply to Letter 1666 (Vol. VII).
1 There is no record that Boyle ever corresponded directly with Borelli.

1813
Oldenburg to Wallis
4 November 1671

Mentioned in Wallis's reply, Letter 1815 of 6 November, as received that morning.

1814
Oldenburg to Lister
4 November 1671
From the original in Bodleian Library MS. Lister 34, f. 41

London Novemb. 4. 71.

Sir,

On the first day of ye R. Society's opening their meetings again (wch was Novemb. 2.) you were wth great applause, nemine contradicente, elected into yt body, according to your merit; and you'l find, when ever your occasions shall permit you to come to London, as cordiall a wellcome amongst ym, as you can wish. Our Anniversary Election-day, for changing the Council, and chusing new Officers, is approaching, as falling upon ye 30th of this month: I should be very glad, you had no impediment to keep you from giving us a visit, if it can not be sooner, about yt time.[1] Whenever you come, you will please to remember ye English black, and ye Experiment, you so generously offred in one of yr letters to shew before this Society; who heard, wth much satisfaction, severall of yr late letters, to me, read before ym on Thursday last,[2] and made it a part of their philosophical entertainment, to debate the question of ye original of petrify'd shells, upon the occasion of yr letter wch discourseth upon yt subject.

Concerning yr 5th and last proposition about ye Vegetable Excrescencies, I am very sorry, it came not soon enough to be thus, as you have last of all altered it, inserted in the Transactions of October, just then printed off: How-ever, it is there printed, as you had worded it in yr letter of Sept. 13th,[3] differingly from yt of July 17:[4] wch I think is warily enough penned; and if it should not be thought so, I can easily in my next book take notice of yr last alteration; when I shall have occasion and take the liberty of publishing yr three Queries, inserted in yr last letter, together wth ye contents of yrs of Oct. 16 about Tarantula's:[5] All such inquiries and hits very much awakening the minds of sagacious and observing men. I intended to have conversed somewt longer wth you, but yt I am called away by a business yt will not bear to be delayed by Sir

Yr faithfull servant.[6]

ADDRESS

To his honored friend
Martyn Lister Esquire
At his house wthout Mickel-
gate barr
      at
           York

POSTMARK NO 4

NOTES

Reply to Letter 1808.
1 In fact, Lister never signed as a Fellow in the Charter Book.
2 Only Letter 1778 is noted in Birch, *History*, II, 487.
3 Letter 1787.
4 Letter 1751.
5 Letter 1800.
6 Oldenburg did not sign the letter.

1815
Wallis to Oldenburg

6 November 1671

From the original in Royal Society MS. W. 1, no. 131
and the copy in Letter Book V, 33–35

November 6. 1671. Oxford.

Sir,

I have yours of Nov. 4 this morning. I have written to ye Bishop of Oxford[1] to send to you for one of ye 2 Copies in your hand, paying 16s. 6d. and to Dr. Lamphigh[2] to send to you for ye other paying 16s. (They have each them in their letters an order to you to deliver ye books.) & I send you herewith an order on my son to pay you 11s. which with ye two former summes makes up ye 2. lb. 3s. 6d. for which I was Debitor to you on ye foot of your last account: And I am further obliged to you for your pains in ye busyness.

D. Leibnitium quod attinet: num quies an motus sit principium cohaesionis, non libet ultra disputare; neque de conciliatione sententiarum DD. Boylij et Leibnitij ea de re, aut utriusvis cum Cartesiana. Quippe in quaestionibus Physicis non ea certitudo demonstrationis esse solet quae in pure Mathematicis: Adeoque in illis dissentiendi locus. Motum esse cohaesionis principium, jam ante Leibnitium (uti nosti) per aliquot annos, contendebat G. Nelius noster. De quo quid senserim jam olim dictum est in literis quae inter me et illum te mediante intercesserunt. Malim adhuc hac de re ἀπέχειν, quam in utramvis partem determinare. Hactenus tamen assentio, vix aut ne vix quietem ullam absolutem in corporibus reperiri, saltem ijs quibuscum nos versamur. Spatium item Vacuum quin dari possit, nihil in contrarium video; quicquid sentiant vel Peripatetici vel Cartesiani. Huic autem, non minus quam Corpori, si Extensio concedatur; concedenda videtur et Magnitudo, (quippe Extensionem esse ubi nulla est Magnitudo, non satis assequor quo possit concipi;) sed et, si Vacuum illud Terminatum sit, etiam Figuram habet, non minus quam terminatum Corpus quod propterea erit et Figuratum; sin Vacuum intelligatur non Terminatum sed in infinitum extensum, Figuram quidem non habebit; sed nec Corpus, si concipiatur sic extendi, habebit Figuram. Non video igitur quomodo Figura et Magnitudo, magis quam Extensio, Corpus (seu Spatium plenum) a Spatio Vacuo distinguat. Dixerim ego potius, eo distingui, quod alterum Materialem sit, alterum non sit. Sin quaeretur, quid illud sit quod Materiam dicimus; dico illud magis a communi apprehensione quam sibi concipit animus ex vocis illius in communi sermone usurpatione animo innotescere quam ulla definitione explicari; idemque de Spatio, Loco, Tempore, alijsque notionibus simplicibus non paucis dicendum existimo. Alicubi enim sistendum erit in vocum significationibus, et rerum incomplexarum notionibus, non minus quam in notionibus complexis seu propositionibus: utrobique scilicet dicendum, esse κοινὰς εννοίας.[3] Nam, ut nullas concedentibus praemissas (tamquam per se notus, aut a notis ante probatas) nulla potest probari conclusio seu propositio; ita nulla verba quasi primitus nota concedentibus, nihil potest verbis explicari; nullasque rerum notiones simplices quasi primitus notas concedentibus, nulla res poterit definiri. Quidni itaque dicamus conceptus Simplices Temporis; Spatij; Materiae, Motus &c. non minus esse menti Apprehendenti congenios; quam conceptus complexos, Totum esse majus sua parte, Æqualia aequalibus addita conficere aequalia, &c, menti Judicanti? Motus autem quomodo corpus a Vacuo distingueret non video. Utut enim concesserim nullum forte corpus de facto esse quod non vel ipsum Totum, vel Partes saltem ipsius, moveantur: non tamen id concesserim ita ad Materiae Corporisve naturam spectare, ut, siquando quiesceret, desinerit esse corpus materiave. Habes itaque (quod petis) quid de his sentiam (ea libertate animi quam ab alijs expeto eisque vicissim concedo) raptim expositum.

Tuus
Joh. Wallis.

ADDRESS
   For Mr. Henry Oldenburg
      in the Palmal near St. James's,
                London

TRANSLATION

. . . . . , ...

As for Mr. Leibniz, I won't argue any more whether rest or motion is the cohesive principle, nor about the reconciliation of the opinions on this point of Messrs. Boyle and Leibniz or of either of these with that of Descartes. Indeed, in problems of physics the certainty of demonstration normal in mathematics is unattainable and so there is, in them, room for difference of opinion. That motion is the cohesive principle was (as you know) argued by our William Neile several years before Leibniz. What I then thought of that is recorded in the letters that passed between him and me by your intercession. I should prefer to remain aloof rather than conclude either way. This however I can accept, that there is hardly ever if at all an absolute rest to be found in bodies, at least in those with which we are familiar. Nor do I see anything contrary to the view that there may be a void space, whatever the Peripatetics and Cartesians think. To this, no less than to bodies, magnitude must be granted, it seems, if extension be granted, for I do not understand how one can conceive of there being extension where there is no magnitude. But also, if that void space be bounded it must have shape, no less than a bounded body which also has shape; unless the void space is taken to be unbounded and extending to infinity, when it will have no shape, as a body would not either if conceived to be thus extended. Therefore I do not see how shape and magnitude rather than extension serve to distinguish a body (or a plenum) from a void space. I would rather have said that they are distinguished because the one is material and the other is not. If the question is put, what is that we call matter, I say *that* is better known to the mind from the ordinary understanding which the mind itself develops from the use of that word [matter] in common speech, than can be explained by any definition; and I think the same of space, place, time and other simple ideas not to be expressed in a few words. For one may stick fast anywhere in the meaning of words and the ideas of elementary things, no less than in complex notions or propositions; of both categories it is to be said that they are ideas common to all.[3] For, as no conclusion or proposition can be proved, for those who concede no premises (as known *a priori*, or proved from what is already known) so for those who concede no word as understood from the beginning, nothing can be explained in words; and for those who concede no simple notions of things as understood from the beginning, nothing at all can be defined. Why then may we not say that the simple concepts, time, space, matter, motion, etc., are no less acceptable to the mind that apprehends them than the complex concepts: The whole is greater than its part; Equal quantities added to equal quantities make equals, etc., to the mind that reasons? However, I do not see how motion would distinguish a body from a vacuum. For, should I concede that perhaps there is, in fact, no body that does not move as a whole, or in its parts at least, still I have not made this concession in such a way as to involve the nature of matter or body so that, should it come to rest, it would cease to be body or matter. So you have what you asked for, my opinion on these points, hastily expressed with that freedom of thinking that I seek from others and in return allow them.

Yours,
John Wallis

NOTES

1 Nathaniel Crew (1633–1721), a high churchman. The copies were presumably volumes of Wallis's *Mechanica*.
2 Probably John Lamphire (1614–88), M.D., principal of Hart Hall.
3 The phrase is said to be used by Origen in *Contra Celsus* meaning moral conceptions common to all men.

1816
Tenison to Oldenburg
7 November 1671
From the original in Royal Society MS. T, no. 38

Holy-well Novemb. 7. 1671

Sr.

I know you will excuse my delay in writing, so soon as I have told you the reason of it. Almost ever since ye time of yr last to me,[1] I have bin deteind in Norfolk, &, in such circumstances as made no other Philosophie proper for me, beside that of Plato, in ye most literall sense, the Meditation of death. Being now return'd into ye Countie of Huntingdon, I bethink my self of yr desire & my own promise, concerning the Agriculture there practic'd. But having inquir'd a while into this matter, I find so little worth ye writing down, &, so much obstinacy in our countriemen in persisting in ye methods of their Fore-fathers, that, merely to avoid ye suspition of laziness & of a will to decline your commands, I send what follows.

Answer to Querie ye first.

The Land-countrie-part (as they call it) of this Shire is a strong clay for the greater part of it. Concerning this, Dr. Fuller has written, though imperfectly, somwt: "Although (sd he) Stiffclay (commonly called Steukly) be but ye name of one or two villages in ye midst, yet their nature is extensive all over ye Countrye".[2] But he is mistaken both in ye name of those villages (wch in ancient Records are called Stevocle) & in ye extensiveness of ye soyl. for This shire takes in no inconsiderable Part of ye great Levell of ye Fenns.

A. to Q. 2.

For ye preparation of Land-countrie-ground when first broken up, we use not any besides ye common one of ploughing & harrowing. but in ye Fenns their manner is this. they plough up ye Turf & then, gathering it in heaps, they sett it on fire: the Ashes being spread about, they plough again & sow Coleseed for a year or two, then barley, wheat, Oats. If ye burned Turf yeilds a yellow sort of Ashes, they like it well, & expect ye lasting of ye ground in heart for 6 or 7 yeares wthout manure. If ye Ashes be white, they expect good Cropps but half that Term of years.

For ye manure of ye Terra firma, ye husbandmen use it very promiscuously, though they know that Foldage[3] & hors dung is best for ye Clay, & Cow muck for ye Sand. An Acre, not Folded, takes wth us 20 & sometimes 30 loads of muck. Foldage is esteemed best for wheat, but its virtue reacheth only to one Cropp.

A. to Q. 3.

For wheat & barley they usually plough four times; & they express them in these Terms. Fallow, Stirr. Sett up.[4] Sow. They Fallow usually in Aprill. Stirr in June. Sett up in August for wheat, for barley in November. They sow, wheat in October; Barley a fortnight before & after our Ladyday; for Peas they plough but once & sow them at Candlemass. Our Ploughs are foot ploughs wth little Shears;[5] we use no wheels to them, not using to make little Ridges as is ye manner in Norfolk & other Places. Coleseed is sown in ye beginning of August.

A. to Q. 4.

All sorts of soyls are, for ye greater part, layd fallow one year in three.

A. to Q. 5.

We have some mountainous grounds so call'd, but few of them have so much beggerie on them as to be properlie Heaths. Some part of them have formerly bin broken up & sown (wth Rye & oats especially) & improv'd no otherwise then grounds by common both ploughing & manure. Most are now layd, there being little Encouragement to use them in tillage, because the Fenns are so very much plough'd, & cloy us wth plenty & cheapness.[6]

A. to Q. 6.

I know not of any marl in use with us, though we have many sandy grounds wch it might bind & fatten.

A. to Q. 7.

In ye Terra firma we sow most sorts of grain, but most ordinarily, Red Kentish, & Gray, wheat; barley, gray-peas, & Hors-beans. In ye Fenns are sown, Coleseed, Rape-seed, Barley, oats, & wheat 'though in lesser Quantities then ye other grains. The Coleseed we tast in our Pigeons & honey combs. In very drie seasons they steep their seed, some in Mud-pitt water, others in brine of bay salt, others in urine. In cold seasons, they lime it.

A. to Q. 8.

The Redwheat thrives best in a gentle sand. ye Gray in a Clay. Barley thrives well in any soyl, best in a mixt clay; Peas prosper in ye strongest Clay.

A. to Q. 10.

Upon an Acre we sow, a comb or 5 bushells of barley; 2 bushells & an half of wheat; a Comb of Peas. They sow in any Quarter of ye Moon.

A. to Q. 11.

We rowl after a good showr when ye corn is about an hand high; & we have none but the ordinary Instruments.

A. to Q. 9. misplac'd by me.

We avoid, as all other people, forrein seeds intermix'd & stingy kernels. We take seed from sand to sow on clay & vice versa. The Fenn corn, wch yields little flour, is yet used much with us for seed: & their barley we sow on a sandy land to best purpose, & their wheat on a clay. the more curious sort of Husbandmen Whipp out their seed-wheat, as they are wont to phrase it. that is, they take handfulls of the prime of ye sheaf, & lash it against an hurdle a few times 'till only ye Plumper kernells come away. & Lands sown wth this do from time to time afford them good seed. for ye seed of ye fenns it is not good, in ye Terra firma, ye first cropp, for any thing but seed; but in 2 or 3 years it proves full & yielding of flour. We sow, as others; after wheat barley, after that, pease.

A. to Q. 12.

An excellent year brings, from an acre, ten comb of wheat, tenn of barley, or oats, 6 of Peas. A good year, six of wheat, seven of barley, 5 of Peas. If it comes to 4 or three comb we pittie the husbandman very much.

A. to Q. 13.

They suppose much wett to be ye cause, generally, of Smutt; & sometimes over much manure of earthy Muck. They lime their seed against this inconvenience, & against ye Vermin. Against meldew (wch coming from the air they cannot wholly prevent) Nature has provided a tolerable remedie, our Fields being much exposed to ye motion of ye air. where we sow Bearded wheat under ye hedges, what it wanteth of air, it hath in ye virtue of its beard, wch is thought to keep of ye dew from insinuating into ye Kernell. I suppose that somwt may be prevented by such hott manure as Pigeonsdung, whose nitre renders ye kernell less apt for putrefaction by that oyly dew wch soaks into ye more porous & soft kind, & hinders it from that life & nourishment it might suck in from ye air.

A. to Q. 14.

We have no uncommon Remedies in use amongst us.

A. to Q. 15.

When ground is lusty & early sown, ye Corn, fedd or cutt before its spindling,[7] is strengthend in its stalk, & less apt to be layd by storms, & ye Ear is betterd; for otherwise all runns out into Stalk & chaff.

A. to Q. 16.

In some Places they reap a week before ye Corn be come to its full ripeness, & lett it lay exposed to ye weather. but in most, they cutt their wheat & carry it ye same day, fearing ye worser sort of Gleaners. When it lays a week, ye Kernell becomes slippery, bright, & firm or (as they call it) Glassie. This Glassiness promoteth its sale, it being a sign of ye soundness of ye grain, & that it is more capable of improvement then that wch is moister & more sluggish, wch they think is extended too much already.

A. to Q. 17.

Some tinn ye posts on wch their hovels[8] of wheat are supported. Wthin doors some have strawed sand betwixt each Layer of wheat, & have found it effectuall against mice & ratts. Against heating, they, as others, use a basket in ye middle, drawing it up as ye Mow riseth.

A. to Q. 18.

We use ye common waies of Thrashing, Casting, ridling, Skreening.

A. to Q. 19.

I find none but ye Ordinary waies of stopping wormes wth glassie mortar, frequent Turning, Skreening, &c.

A. to Q. 1. about Meadows.

They sow oats or fetches. some Hayseed wth very good event; others Think wintergrain ye best before ye ground be layd down, that ye grass may have ye better time for rooting.

to Q. 2.

We use nothing but Stubbing[9] or Drayning. In other Countries I have known wett rushy ground exceedingly improved by drains cutt throughly & soap ashes layd on.

to Q. 3.

They have usd cheifly Dutch-mills,[10] & such great Cutts as are most convenient for speedy conveighance to ye sea.

to Q. 4.

We here are strangers to saint foin, Lucern, Non such & ye like. ye common Cinque foil, as it grows wthout art, is our best, & so reputed.

A. to Q. 5.

We have here less art then in other Places. We bestow not so much as the making of it up in little grass cocks, whereby it abateth of yt curious greeness wch otherwise would have.

A. to Q. 6.

The short grass is best for sheep such as penny grass, & Burnet if not roasted too much in ye sunn. The grass of ye most & longest joynts is best for cows & horses.

After all these tedious (because very ordinary) particulars, I will releive your patience by a little story not unpleasant. I do, then, assure you, that In repeating some of your Queries to a good wealthy & knowing Yeoman; when I come at ye 12th about ye Quantity of corn produced by an Acre, he desir'd me to proceed no further, & he told me, in good earnest, that he would make no answer if I propounded any more Queries. For I see plainly (said ye over-politic old man) that there is more reason of state in this Royall societie then at first I was aware of. Verily it appears by these Queries that They have a design to spie out ye Riches of ye Land.

Thus Sr. you have wt occurrs to me at present in answer to your Queries. but I am sensible that this long Paper contains so very little to your Purpose, that I would desire it might be condemn'd, after your first perusall, ad spurcos usus.[11] Time I hope will enable me to serve you better. in ye mean while I have as great an inclination as any person, to be

yr Faithfull Friend & servt
T. Tenison

ADDRESS
These
For his honoured Friend Henry
Oldenburg Esqr at his house
in ye Palmal
in
Westminster

POSTMARK NO 8

NOTES

1 Tenison last wrote Letter 1672 (6 April 1671; Vol. VII); no record of Oldenburg's answer survives. This, or an earlier letter, contained a copy of the *Enquiries concerning Agriculture* printed in *Phil. Trans.*, no. 5 (3 July 1665), 92–94, to be found in Vol. II, pp. 224–26.
2 The two villages of Great and Little Stukeley are northwest of Huntingdon; see Thomas Fuller, *The History of the Worthies of England* (London, 1662), "Huntingdonshire, The Farewell."
3 The folding of sheep on land.
4 Hand-setting of the seed, as distinct from broadcast sowing.
5 Shares.

6 The drainage and hence the agriculture of the Fens had been much improved by the completion of the Bedford Level in 1653.
7 Before the ear-bearing stalk has shot up.
8 Sheds or open barns for storing grain; stacks or ricks.
9 Removing stumps and roots.
10 Probably a windmill with a scoop wheel for raising water. Drainage mills in the Fens are described by Walter Blith in *The English Improver Improved* (London, 1652).
11 "to foul uses."

1817
Oldenburg to Hevelius
9 November 1671

From the copy in BN MS. Lat. 10348, ff. 47–50

Per-Illustri Viro
Domino Johanni Hevelio Gedanensium Consuli dignissimo
Henricus Oldenburg S.P.

Impense doleo, Vir Clarissime, exspectationem tuam, hominum quorundum nostratium incuria tam diu fuisse protelatam. Meamet certe negligentiam incusare nequaquam possum, cum creberrime, et ad taedium usque, rerum in usum Tuum a me dudum comparatarum transmissionem inculcaverim, aegerrimeque tulerim, et diligentiam et curam meam, in utriusque nostrum fraudem tam diu clusam fuisse. Iam vero dubitare amplius nolim, quin cistula nostra, tum microscopium, tum librorum a Te desideratorum fasciculum continens, nautaeque Vestrati Martino Zachun, cujus navis Elephantis insignia gerit, commissa, duosque ante menses hinc Dantiscum profecta, dudum illaesa ad manus tuas pervenerit.¹ Rite accepi quicquid literarum, tum 19 Junij tum 7 Octobris ad me dedisti, omniaque tua communicata et observata Illustrissimae Societati nostrae caetibus suis publicis post aestivas ferias restitutae, exhibui.² Magna certe animorum lubentia, uti solent, quicquid a Te proficiscitur, illarum epistolarum argumenta auscultarunt debitasque Tibi gratias, pro perenni tuo in ipsam studio jugique Uraniae nostrae cultu, reponerem, jusserunt. Non parum nos afficit, Philosophis Parisiensibus, una cum aliis tantopere cordi esse Astronomiae incrementum, ut eam in rem destinato consilio accuratissimum Picardum, ante aliquot menses Uraniburgam amandaverint, unde sine dubio perscripta Tibi jam fuere quocunque *tum* Parisiis a praeclaris Viris Cassino et Hugenio de maculis Solaribus, deque Saturni apparentiis, nec non de nupera Eclipsi Lunae, *tum* ab ipsomet Picardo observata fuerunt.[3] Dominus Hugenius novissimis suis literis nobis significavit, reapse se deprehendisse formae Saturni rotundae reditum, hujus scilicet anni finem versus, prout ipse praenuntiaverat.[4] Adjicit idem, quamprimum Dominus Cassinus observaverat Saturni brachia rediisse (quod 14 Augusti contigit) se pronuntiasse, ipsa omnino ante exitum hujus anni esse disparituras adeoque se die 6. Novembris observantem comperisse, fuisse ea adeo exilia et obscura ut intra paucorum exinde dierum spatium omnem oculorum aciem fugere debeant. Existimat itaque phases hasce suam de Saturni ansis hypothesin mirum in modum confirmare, cum illae oculis nostris sese subducant, prout radii Solis planam ipsius superficiem, visui nostro obversam, oblique illuminant;[5] adhaec anni hujus apparentias copiam praebere uberrimam figurae sphaericae restitutionem multo, quam ante accuratius praenuntiandi.

Quae hic apud nos de phasibus illis observata fuere, non abludunt ab iis, quae nuper Parisiis ea de re lingua Gallica in lucem sunt emissa, Tibique omni procul dubio, jam communicata.[6]

Doctissimus Hookius noster, praeter ea, quae de nupera Eclipsi Lunae observarunt alii, insertis schedis contenta,[7] impertiit quae sequuntur:[8]

"Sept. 8. 1671 (ait ille) hor. 7 $27\frac{1}{2}'$ primitus Lunam Eclipsin passam observavi, quando illuminari jam coeperat, totali ejus obscuratione jam tum praeterita. Umbra transibat medium maculae Montis Porphyrii,[9] maculae hujus dimidio extra umbram apparente, alteroque dimidio ab eadem obscurato. Hor 7 49' umbra transibat medium montis Sinaij[10] mediumque omnium Orientalissimi ex 3 lacubus,[11] qui mare Adriaticum nuncupantur, ac praecise montium Appeninorum[12] jugae stringebat. Hor. 7 54' transibat medium I. Besbici in Propontide,[13] Hor. 8 $0\frac{1}{2}'$ transibat ponti Euxini fretum ad Archerusiae et Aristis promontoria.[14] Hor. 8. $6\frac{1}{2}'$ Paludem Maeotidem[15] tangebat, quae Palus tum distabat a margine Lunae proxime adjacentis una parte tertia diametri suae brevioris. Hor. 8 17' umbra deferebat corpus lunae (ad intimam lineam marginalem Tabulae majoris Lunae, ab Hevelio adornatae, ad divisionem scilicet 290am, praecise scilicet extra I. Majorem Maris Caspii).[16] Fusca penumbra non penitus relinquebat Lunam ante hor. 8 29', quo tempore illam Lunae partem, quam umbra novissime deseruerat aeque lucidam claramque, ac alteram deprehendi. Minuta circiter 4 vel 5, ex quo umbra evanuerat, effluxerunt, quando languidam percepi colorum speciem super ea Lunaris corporis parte, quae maxime penumbra afficiebatur, non nihil illi referebant colores diluti circa Lunam Halonis elanguescebat ipse magis ac magis, et post pauca quaedam minuta non amplius conspiciebatur. Non videbatur productus ab illis in aere nostro nubibus halitibusve, Coelo tunc circa Lunam perquam serenante, coloribus istis nonnisi in fusca phasi ejus parte apparentibus. Forte factum id fuit a lucis Solaris per Atmosphaeram Terrae circumdatam refractione."

Video, Te aegre ferre, promissum jam dudum ab Hookio nostro instrumentum, dimentiendis minoribus distantiis aptum tamdiu retardari. Causatur Inventor, si tantum non obrui negotiorum turba: promisso tamen se satisfacturum, quamprimum licuerit, spondet. Ego urgere non desinam. Gratias agimus pro literis Hungaricis tua cura ad nos transmissis. Vale. Dabam Londini 9 Novembris Anno 1671.

TRANSLATION

Henry Oldenburg greets the very illustrious Mr. Johannes Hevelius, most worthy Senator of Danzig

I very greatly regret that the negligence of some of our people should for so long a time have defrauded your expectations. I really cannot take any of the blame on myself, for I have very frequently wearied myself in urging on the conveyance of the things long ago prepared for your use by myself, and I take it very hard that my care and diligence have been stultified for so long, to the disappointment of both of us. I cannot but think that our box containing both the microscope and the package of books you wanted, consigned to your seaman Martin Zachun (master of a boat called the *Elephant* which sailed for Danzig two months ago), must have reached you safely long since.[1] I have received correctly the letters you wrote to me on 19 June and 7 October [N.S.], and I presented all your communications and observations to our distinguished Society after the resumption of its ordinary meetings following the summer holidays.[2] Whatever comes from yourself is, as always, very much to their taste; they listened to your letters and ordered me to return appropriate thanks for your continual zeal on their behalf and devotion to the pursuit of astronomy. We are not a little struck by the fact that the Parisian philosophers and others have the advancement of astronomy so much at heart that they decided some months ago to send the very exact Picard to Uraniburg, whence he has no doubt written you an account not only of what the celebrated Cassini and Huygens have observed by way of sunspots and the appearance of Saturn as well as the recent lunar eclipse, but also what was seen by Picard himself.[3] In his very recent letter to us Mr. Huygens told us that he had actually detected the return of the round shape of Saturn towards the end of this year that is, just as he had himself predicted.⁴ He adds, that as soon as Mr. Cassini had observed the reappearance of the "arms" [ring] (which was on 14 August) he [Huygens] at once declared that they would have quite vanished before the end of this year, and so, observing them on 6 November, he found them so thin and dark that within a few days from that date they must disappear from the sharpest sight. Accordingly he is of the opinion that these phases wonderfully vindicate his hypothesis of Saturn's anses, which withdraw themselves further from our eyes as the rays of the sun illuminate their plane surface, turned towards our eyes, [more and more] obliquely.⁵ Moreover, he believes that the appearances of this year afford a useful means of predicting the restoration of the round shape much more accurately than before.

What we observed here of these phenomena did not depart far from what was recently published in Paris concerning this question, in French, and that no doubt has been communicated to you.⁶

Our very learned Mr. Hooke, besides what others have observed of the late eclipse of the moon which is contained in the enclosed sheets,⁷ has imparted to me what follows:⁸

"Septemb. 8. 1671. H. 7. 27'¼ I first observed the Moon Eclipsed when it began to be enlightened, the total darkness being already past. The shadow passed through the middle of the Spot called by Hevelius Mons Porphyrius,⁹ half of the said spot appearing without the shadow and the other half being darkened thereby.

"H. 7. 49'. The shadow passed through the middle of Mons Sinai,¹⁰ through the middle of the Easternmost of the three Lakes¹¹ called Mare Adriaticum, and just touched the ridge of the Appennine Mountains.¹²

"H. 7. 54', It passed the middle of the Insula Besbicus in the Propontis.¹³

"H. 8. 0'½. It passed through the streights of the Pontus Euxinus at the Promontories Acherusia and Aristes.¹⁴

"H. 8. 6'½. It touched the Palus Maeotis,¹⁵ which Palus Maeotis was then distant from the limb of the Moon next adjacent one third part of its shorter diameter or breadth.

"H. 8. 17'. The shadow went off the body of the Moon upon the innermost limb-line of Hevelius his large chart of the Moon at the 290 division¹⁶ just without the Insula Major of the Caspian Sea. The duskish Penumbra left not the limb of the Moon quite without some kind of darkness, till 8. 29'; at which time I found that side of the Moon, which the shadow last left, was full as light and clear as the other.

"About four or five minutes after, the shadow was gone off, I perceived a faint representation of Colours upon that part of the body of the Moon, which was most affected with the Penumbra somewhat resembling the colours of a faint Halo about the Moon; this grew fainter and fainter, and after a few minutes was no more visible. It did not seem to be caused by any clouds or exhalations in the Air, the sky near the Moon being very clear, and the said colours not appearing any where, but upon the dusky part of its Phasis. Possibly it might be caused by the Refraction of the light from the Sun through the Atmosphere about the Earth."

I see that you take it ill, because that instrument for measuring small distances, promised long ago by our Hooke, has been so long delayed. The inventor of it makes excuse, that he is overwhelmed by a mass of business, but he promises that he will fulfill his pledge as soon as possible. I do not fail to urge it on him. I thank you for the letter from Hungary sent us by your kindness. London, 9 November 1671.

NOTES

Reply to Letters 1718 and 1792.
1 In Letter 1723 it was stated that they were entrusted to a merchant named Cock; this new information suggests that the instruments only left London in September, rather than June.
2 On 2 November, with so many other communications.
3 See, for example, Letters 1769 and 1771.
4 See Letter 1807.
5 The "anses" (handles) are, of course, the ring of Saturn.
6 See Letter 1807, note 1.
7 *Phil. Trans.*, no. 76 (22 October 1671).
8 Hooke's communication is printed in *Phil. Trans.*, no. 77 (November 1671), 2296, whence we take the English version, with slight modifications.
9 Hevelius named it Mons Porphyrites: the crater Aristarchus.
10 The crater Tycho.
11 The region of the crater Mösting, near the center of the disk.
12 This high ridge is still so called.
13 Hevelius' Propontis is the Mare Vaporum, south of the center, which has no obvious feature to identify with the imaginary "Isle of Besbicus."
14 So both MS. and print, but Hevelius' map has "Arietis"; in other words, the shadow passed (roughly) through the crater Plinius, in the "streight" between the Maria Tranquillitatis and Serenitatis.
15 The Mare Crisium.
16 "29" incorrectly in the print. The "Insula Major" is the crater Langrenus.

1818

Oldenburg to Wallis

11 November 1671

The endorsement on Wallis's Letter 1815 indicates that it was received on 8 November and answered on the eleventh; the answer is also mentioned in Wallis's reply, Letter 1828. Oldenburg made enquiries of Wallis on behalf of Thevenot (see Letter 1806) and Vogel (see Letter 1811).

1819

Lister to Oldenburg

11 November 1671

From the original in Royal Society MS. L 5, no. 41

Yorke Novemb 11th 1671

Sir

I am very sensible of ye great honour, ye R.S. hath done me in making me one of their body. You will please to adde this to many other favours, to make my acknowledgments in a compliment of your excellent fashion. I shall take care to returne ye *Dues*; but cannot promise a personal visit this Winter.

I had designed to send you ye Specimen of ye black Resin by ye Carrier; but Dr *Trout-becke* would needs have it from me about 10 dayes agoe.[1] I sealed it up & he promised to deliver it safe into your hands, to whom I told him I had engaged to send it. If ye Prince,[2] for whom he much desired it, vouchsafes to make any Tryal wth it to imitate ye Black-China-Varnish (to wch Mandelslo[3] saies none in Europe could ever yet arrive) I should be glad to have an account of ye successe; for 'tis ye only instance known to me of a Vegetable resin Naturally black.

I endeavoured to have preserved some of it liquid, by exactly stopping it in an essence bottle; but it had fermented & broken ye Glasse, yet had not changed its colour.

It cost me much pains to procure you these 30 graines: yet ye plant admitts of easy culture & it may be made wth little cost in great quantities were it cultivated for ye purpose. but it is too soon yet to thinke of yt, unlesse we can find out a real use. I am

> Sir your most humble servant
> *Martin Lister*

ADDRESS
    Thes
For this honoured friend
    Mr. Henry Oldenburg
     at his house in ye
      Palmal
       London

POSTMARK NO 17

NOTES

Reply to Letter 1814.
1 See Vol. VII, p. 383, note 7.
2 Prince Rupert, who was much interested in technical processes. When this letter was produced on 16 November the sample was divided between the Prince and Boyle for examination.
3 Presumably Lister had read the account of J. A. Mandelslo's travels in the English edition (London, 1662 and 1669) of Adam Olearius, *Voyages and Travels of . . . Ambassadors.*

1820

Oldenburg to Le Bourgeois

11 November 1671

Oldenburg endorsed Le Bourgeois's Letter 1810 as received on 2 November and answered on 11 November 1671.

1821
Oldenburg to Vogel
14 November 1671
From the copy in Royal Society MS. O 2, no. 59

Celeberrimo Viro
Domino Martino Fogelio Phil. et Med. Hamburgensi
H. Oldenburg S.P.

Exhibui R. Societati, quas de Solaribus Maculis observatione, Clarissimus Siferus vester descripsit, tuusque in eam affectus huc transmisit. Gratulatur illa Civitati Hamburgensi, quod tales nacta est viros, qui provehendae Astronomiae, atque excolendae toti Philosophiae tum gnaviter incumbunt. Agedum incessanter ut caepisti pergite, nec unquam permittite, vos et vestrum similes, ut unanimi hoc Europaeorum ad Scientias augendas flagranti fervore, Germania nostra post principia latere et otiari dictitetur: Incumbite in id, quantum fieri potest, ut Manuscripta jungiana a squalore et situ vindicentur, et in eruditorum examen cedant. In eo, si placet, estote, ut Sylvae Herciniae, inter alia plura, intimi recessus, quoad fossilia, vegetabilia, et animalia a viris solertibus vestigentur, et vestigata in justam Historiam compingantur. Ignosces, Vir Eximie, libertati meae, quae rationis humanae et solidae Philosophiae cultum, dignitatem et amplitudinem medullitus spirat.

Accepimus Lutetiae Parisiorum eas de maculis solaribus, de Saturno, et de nupera Eclipsi Lunae, observationes, quas Cassinus, Bullialdus, et Hugenius inibi instituerant. Dominus Hevelius non modo suas de Jovis et Lunae transitu, sed et de aliquibus stellarum Medicaearum in Umbram jovis Immersionibus observationes transmisit, juncta hac significatione, Machinam suam, ut vocat, Caelestem, jam trium mensium spatio sub praelo sudasse.[1] Inquisivi, possimne Galilaei vitam Anglice impressam in Tui usum ad Tempus comparare. Spero me voti compotem fore, rogoque ut persuasissimum tibi habeas, si ullum mei juris exemplar penes me esset, me summa cum lubentia, citra ullius pignoris (quod tu offers) depositionem, illud transmissurum; at quia non est, poteris, quod spondes, in rem vertere, et quid hac in re praestiteris, mihi quantocius significare. Dabo operam, ut intelligas, me Tui et rerum tuarum esse studiosissimum. Non putem, inveniri ea posse, quae forte Editori vitae istius ex Italia submissa fuere, nec operae pretium judico, librum tam amplum describendum curare.

Nullum profecto Historiae Incendij Ætnaei Borellianae Exemplar, quo quidem Ego potiri queam, superest: si Lutetiam Parisiorum eo nomine scribas, absque dubio aliquot exemplaria procurare poteris.

Scripsi Oxonium de Pocockij folio, quod de Caave tractat, sciscitatus insuper, num eidem quicquam, praeter vulgaria, de arbore Thuris, et Myrrhae, sit cognitum. Bdellium quod attinet, cum sit inter ἅπαξ λεγομενα, vix certi aliquid de eo explorabimus, alijs pro margarita, alijs pro gummi, alijs pro gemma &c. id habentibus. Quid de ijs edoctus fuero, proxime transcribam. Vale et me Tui cultoribus accense. Dabam Londini Novemb. 14. 1671.

TRANSLATION

H. Oldenburg greets the celebrated Mr. Martin Vogel, philosopher and physician at Hamburg

I presented to the Royal Society the account your famous Sivers had composed of his observation of the sunspots, which your regard to the Society led you to send. The city of Hamburg is to be congratulated on giving birth to men who strive so eagerly to advance astronomy and cultivate the whole of philosophy. Go on, then, continue without fail as you have begun; never should you and others like you let it be said that our Germany lags behind the leaders in this hot enthusiasm of all Europe for the advancement of science, or that she is lazy. So far as may be, see to it that the manuscripts of Jungius are rescued from mustiness and dirt, and laid before the learned for examination. See to it, please, that the deepest recesses of the Harz mountains (among many other places) are investigated by skilled persons with an eye for their minerals, plants, and animals, and let their findings be brought together into a proper narrative. Forgive my freedom of speech, worthy Sir, which expresses my heartfelt sense of the reverence, dignity, and excellence of human reason and solid philosophy.

We have received from Paris those observations of sunspots, Saturn, and the recent lunar eclipse which Cassini, Boulliaud, and Huygens have carried out there. Mr. Hevelius sent not only his observations of the transit of Jupiter and the moon, but those of some immersions of Jupiter's satellites in the planet's shadow, together with the information that his *Machina coelestis*, as he calls it, has already been in the press for three months.[1] I have enquired whether I can furnish a copy of the printed life of Galileo for your use over a period. I hope that I shall obtain my wish, and I beg you to be absolutely confident that if I had a copy of my own in my hands I would send it to you with the greatest pleasure and without any laying down of a pledge such as you offer. But as the case is otherwise, you will be able to make an exchange your surety, and what you shall prefer in this way, let me know as soon as possible. I will make every effort to convince you that I am most zealous for you and your concerns. I do not think that what was (perhaps) sent from Italy to the editor of that biography can now be found, nor do I judge it worthwhile to arrange to have so large a book transcribed.

There is absolutely no copy of Borelli's *Incendium Aetnaei* of which I am master; if you write to Paris on that account you will surely procure a few copies.

I have written to Oxford about the sheet concerning coffee written by Pocock, and the enquiry was also made, whether the same person had some knowledge beyond the usual of the frankincense tree, and myrrh. As for bdellium, as it is mentioned once only, we shall hardly find out anything certain about it, some taking it for a pearl, others for a gum or a gem, etc. What I shall learn on these points I shall transcribe in my next. Farewell, and count me among your admirers. London, 14 November 1671.

NOTES

Reply to Letter 1811.
1 See Letter 1792.

1822
Oldenburg to Dodington
14 November 1671

Mentioned in Dodington's Letter 1902.

1823
Helmfeld to Oldenburg
15 November 1671

From the original in Royal Society MS. H 3, no. 4

Dabam Madriti die 15. Novembri anno 1671 [N.S.]

Nobilissime Domine, Amice plurimum colende

Vix me explicare possum quanto cum gaudio epistolam Tuam et acceperim et perlegerim, sane aut meas Tibi plane non redditas aut Tuas responsorias perditas esse credidi.[1] Sed cum ita rerum mearum incertus jam in ipsis Hispaniae limitibus migrarem bonis advenit avibus felix tuae in me amando constantiae nuncius, et comitatus quidem benevola ad Dominum Godolphin epistola. Mirabar initio apicibus literarum nomen inscriptum Viri scilicet illius quem Gallia paulo ante bis mortuum praedicaverat, nunc mihi non est cur mirer ulterius, cum illum optima gaudentem valetudine Madriti invenerim. Rumori ni fallor ansam dedit morbus ille quo non ita pridem ad vitae usque periculum laboravit. Deo sint gratiae quod pristinae nunc restitutus sanitati videatur. Vir sane, ut sine palpo loquar, summa laude dignus est, et qui Tui gratia eo me effecit honore ut vel inde facile colligere possim quantum virtutes Tuas admiretur et colat.

Recordor hic quorundam quae in itineris hujus cursu vidisse memini, meo quidem quantulecunque judicio notatu dignorum, et adderem ea nisi scirem omnia Tibi jam satis explorata et cognita esse. Sed quidquid hujus sit, ne negligens fuisse videar dicam me duos in Gallia invenisse fontes fluxu et refluxu maris gaudentes, quorum quidem alter in Comitatu d'Anjou prope urbem Saumeur 45, alter in Episcopatu Perigordensi 40 milliaribus a mari distant.[2] Innumeras insuper in limitibus Hispaniae in urbe quadam Gallici juris Dax dicta Vidi scaturigines quibus longe ferventissima aqua per magnum terrae spatium prosiliebat et ea quidem copia ut rivi speciem obtineat.[3] Relatum mihi est quosdam curiosorum frustum plumbi cum fune quodam immisisse iste foraminibus sed nullum invenire potuisse fundum. Canis itidem immisus eodem momento ex fervore isto omnes perdidit capillos, nullum tamen in re medicae usum obtinet ob nimium uti dicunt calorem. Pistores hac acqua utuntur ad coquendum panem qui certe optimi est saporis. Lotricibus ad lavenda lintea vicem lixiviae praestat. Lubentissime experimenta quaedam physica hic tentassem sed prout in itinere non omnia licent quae libent, oportuit ut et ego foro et scenae hic servirem. Vale, Vir Nobilissime, et pauca haec aequi bonique consule

Tui obsequiosissimus
Gustavus Helmfeld

ADDRESS
> A Monsieur
> Monsieur Grubendol
>   a
>   Londres

TRANSLATION

Madrid, 25 November 1671 [N.S.]

Most noble Sir, very dear Friend,

I can hardly tell you how joyfully I received and read your letter, for I quite believed that either mine to you was never delivered or your answer went astray.[1] But as I was departing to the very borders of Spain, uncertain of my plans, there comes borne by kind doves your lucky message of constancy in affection to me, accompanied too by a nice letter to Mr. Godolphin. I marveled at first to see inscribed at the head of the letter the name of a man whom France had twice pronounced dead, shortly before; now I have no reason for marveling further since I find him at Madrid in the best of health. The basis of the rumor was, if I mistake not, that illness which a little while ago endangered his life. God be praised, he seems now to be restored to his former health. He is indeed a man worthy of the highest praise (I speak without flattery), who honors me for your sake so that I can easily judge from that how much he admires and respects your merits.

I am mindful here of certain things that I remember seeing in the course of this journey, worthy of note in my poor opinion, and I would add them here did I not know that all have been made known to you and examined already. But however that may be, that I may not seem to have been neglectful I may say that I discovered two springs in France rejoicing in the ebb and flow of the sea, of which one in the Province of Anjou near the city of Saumur was 45 miles from the sea, and the other in the bishopric of Perigord was 40 miles away.[2] Moreover, on the borders of Spain in a certain town under French jurisdiction called Dax I saw innumerable springs from which sprang jets of scalding hot water over a large space of ground, and that in such plenty that it forms a kind of stream.[3] I was told that some inquisitive persons had dropped a plumb line in at the mouths, but could find no bottom. A dog thrown into this place was instantly deprived of all its hair by the boiling heat; no medical use is made of it because of the excessive heat, they say.

Bakers employ this water for baking bread, which certainly has an excellent taste. It serves washerwomen in place of lye in washing linen. I would gladly have attempted some scientific experiments here, but the traveler cannot do as he pleases in everything, and I also was to observe the market and stage here. Farewell, most noble Sir; think well and kindly of these few words from

Your most obsequious,
Gustav Helmfeld

ADDRESS
   To Mr. Grubendol,
      London.

NOTES

1 There is no record of this letter, or of the recommendation to "Mr. Godolphin," who was not Sidney Godolphin but Sir William Godolphin (1634?–1696), who had been in Madrid since 1669 as envoy extraordinary and ambassador. His severe illness induced at least a temporary conversion to Roman Catholicism.
2 Saumur is in fact about 75 English miles from the port of Nantes; Périgueux (seat of the bishopric) is rather nearer Bordeaux.
3 Dax (Les Landes) is still a notable thermal station and resort. The water is at 64° C.

1824

Flamsteed to Oldenburg

15 November 1671

From the original in Royal Society MS. F 1, no. 75

Derby: No: 15: 1671

Mr Oldenburge
Sr

With this yu have my praemonitions of the next yeares appearances,[1] so contracted yt they may take up but a little roome in ye transactions; to which, since yu have inserted them 2 yeares I hold them now a due. ye Synopsis in ye conclusion I hold as necessary as the praedictions, therefore desire it may beare them company in ye presse: since without it little of theire worth or qualities can be understood: I have inserted, yu will find, a diurnall transit of ye moone at Cor Leonis:[2] which since yu required some calculation of such appearances for Mr Hooke I have commended to him I understand yt his way of observeing has nothing extraordinary in it but ye observers disposeing himselfe & his telescope in a darke roome, or so as all light, but what passes from ye object, may be excluded from ye eye: but this I have concealed lest I should discover what perhaps hee makes a secret of & which I had not his permission to disclose. tho indeed I am not bound to conceale what I reaceaved not from him but at ye 3d hand, & of which I can bring an experiment of mine owne to confirme it. I have added no schemes but if you or Mr Hooke desire them I shall delineate & send them yu I intended once to have composed all these calculations in an Ephemeris, but my other affaires & studies takeing up the best parte of my time, I had not leasure to performe what I intended. Yet I hope to get so much time as to performe it in parte the next yeare if providence permit mee health as hitherto: but to make so specious & prolix calculations as I have done, againe, I intend not; scarce each other appearance being by reason of the clouds observable & I not reaceaveing except from yrselfe & Mr Townely any observation of ye easiest. I designe therefore for the future to waite for such appearances as by revolveing[3] my ephemerides I hope will be visible. & to observe those, & afterwards commit my tables to triall by my observations yt so I may find the better where any thing is to [be] introduced or corrected and how in my numbers.

I have in prosecution of this designe praepared instruments fit for my purpose. 2 tubes one of 7, ye other of 14 foote with which & a micrometer I have measured the distances of the Pleiades for correcteing their places. Mr Townely is measureing the same in Lancashire whose observations as soone as I reaceave I will send yu ye calculations of ye [moons] remaineing transits over ye Pleiades: I have sometimes measured her diameters which I find larger them [*sic*] Streets numbers and made some such observations as require no great praecisenesse of time: I have likewise observed ye Satellits, 2 of those Morneings yt Mr Cassini praedicted his appearances to, of which ere long I shall give you an account: In the meane [time] pray what yu find amisse in my language correct freely & as freely informe mee of what I erre or write amisse in: I have last night & ye 10 & 12 of this moneth observed Saturne in 15 minutes lesse longitude then Heckers Ephemerides;[4] of all which I shall within a weeke informe yu further. I want at present some red glasses to save my eyes else I would view ye Sun sometimes, to see if I could descry any spots which as yet I have never seene: if Mr Collins can promise mee two one about $\frac{1}{2}$ an inch ye other $\frac{2}{3}$ or a little lesse broad Mr Sargeant who will come up within 3 weekes will pay him for them againe.⁵ for I would gladly have them speedily that I may observe ye Suns perigaeon diameters. if they be deare I would have but one ready polisht: till ye next opportunity I rest

Your obliged friend & servant
John Flamsteed

ADDRESS

    For my worthy good freind
    Henry Oldenburg Esq
    at his house in ye middle
    of ye Pell mell neare
    St James's Westminster
        these present
            London

NOTES

1 "Lunae ad fixas appulsus visibiles, nec non arctiores juxta eas Transitus, observabiles A. 1672" ("The visible appulses of the Moon to the fixed stars, and its close passages near them, observable in 1672") was printed in *Phil. Trans.*, no. 77 (20 November 1671), 2297–3001. The original is Royal Society MS. F 1, no. 78a (ii).
2 Predicted for 18 June; Hooke's interest in making this daylight observation of the moon and Regulus is noted in the printed paper (pp. 2298–99).
3 Turning over or reviewing.
4 Johannes Hecker, *Ephemerides motuum coelestium ab anno 1666 ad annum 1680*... (Danzig, 1662).
5 On the points just mentioned, compare Flamsteed to Collins, 8 November 1671 (Rigaud, II, 122–25).

1825

Oldenburg to Lister

18 November 1671

From the original in Bodleian MS. Lister 34, f. 43

London Nov. 18. 71.

Sir,

I have not only received yr letter of Nov. 11. wherein you gave me notice of yr present of the black Resin, to be received from Dr Trautback [*sic*], but also the present itself, after I had sent more then once for it. On Thursday last it was by me exhibited to ye R. Society, together wth yr letter; who not only wth much kindness embraced yr sense of being received into their body, but also yr very curious and probably usefull present, wch they order'd to be in part deliver'd to the Prince,[1] in part to Mr Boyle for Tryall; desiring wthall to know from you, whether you have ever stain'd any cloth, linnen or woollen, wth it, and if so, what ye successe thereof was? We were glad to understand, yt it may be made wth small cost in great quantities if cultivated for the purpose. If you think well of it, I would give notice to ye publick of this discovery in general; being persuaded, it will awaken some publick-minded and wealthy persons to inquire after you, and to concurr wth you in the propagation of ye Plant, and in rendring it of publick utility. But herein I shall not make a step further, than you allow me; and yt not only in this particular, but in all other things, wch yr generosity shall impart unto the Society by ye hands of Sir

Yr faithfull servant
Oldenburg

Mr Willoughby and Mr Ray are at present both in London, and speake wth much kindness and respect of you.

What ever I shall learn of the successe of the tryals, made wth yr black resin, I shall soon give you notice of, as I ought.

ADDRESS

To his honor'd friend
   Mr Martin Lyster, at
   his house wthout Mickel-gate
   barr at York
        York

NOTES

Reply to Letter 1819.
1 Sir Robert Moray, present at the meeting on 16 November, was charged with delivering this specimen to Prince Rupert.

1826

Flamsteed to Oldenburg

21 November 1671

From the original in Royal Society MS. F 1, no. 76

                                  Derby No. 21. 1671

Mr Oldenburge

The Errant of this is, to convey the observations of the circumjovialls I promised & some others: last Saturday[1] haveing from Mr Townelys diurnall and annuall motions made tables for my owne use & framed Radix'es from some observations I met with in Borellus[2] I found yt ye occultations of ye satellits are praedicted by Cassini after New Stile;[3] which before I esteemed old, & yt observation I made ye 7th day in ye morneing was on ye 17th, when at 5h. 39' mane, alto Jupiter 35°. 15', I observed their positions thus:[4]

                      ✶   ✶   ↑◯✶   ✶
                      d   c   m a   b

m.a. by estimation was ½ diameter *l.c.* 2 diameters or more. *d.c.* rather greater than *l.c.* with my long tube & micrometer Jupiter himselfe was in diameter 100 or 105 = 36" or 37".[5] I measured: *bd* 1706 = 10' 09":*lb* 1246 = 7' 25": but Jupiter being elevated 41° 06 or rather a ¼ of an hour before the star *a* had disappeared but when I know not precisely for after my first observation I returned to warme mee it being a frosty cold morneing & comeing again to ye tube after a little search for ye satellit *a*, & not findeing [it] I tooke Jupiter's height 41–06 whence I deduce the hour 6.14: so I am confident it had disappeared before 6: but when I know not: I have some other observations of ye satellits, but not findeing them much worth ye view I cease to trouble yu with them:

No: 6: hora 4–46 p.m. the moone being in ipso fere perigaeo⁶ & but 2 days at most past ye opposition of ye Sun: I measured with my short tube, its length 86 $\frac{1}{3}$:⁷ ye distance of the moones north limbe from ye brightest of ye Pleiades 45 16: ye height of ye orientall star of them being 7° 45′: and afterwards ye same height being 10.30 tubes length 85 $\frac{7}{10}$, ye like distance 5436: I observed ye moone both yt evening & ye next morneing severall times; & with both my tubes, & never found, yt her horizontall semidiameter could be lesse then 16′ 47″, nor more then 16–53, I resolve on 16–49 or 50″, which I had ye most frequently; whence I conclude alta orientali in cuspido 7° 45′ hora 4h–46′: lucida a limbo lunae 51′ 16″: a centro 1°–08′–05″ alta eadem Pleiadum 10° 30 hora 5–07 eadem a limbo 1.°–02–04 a centro 1–18–54.⁸

No: 10 in the evening I observed ye distance of Saturne from 2 fixed stars, the Superior *b* in Tychoes Catalogue Anno 1600 is in 11° 38′ with 1–00 lat: Aust. ye inferiour *a* in Pisces 11° 33′ with South lat. 2° 49′: on ye 12th day at 8h vesperi:

	PISCES	13°	12°
			ECLIPTIC
		∗b	
		∗♄	
		∗a	1671 No. 12. 8h

with my short tube & micrometer I measured ♄*b* 70′ 12″, and ♄*a* 43′–43″ whence I find him 12′ 43″ in consequence of ye superiour [star] with with 1°–09′–03″ more South lat. & allowing a praecise degree for ye motion of the fixed from 1600 till now:⁹ I determine him in

       Pisces 12–50–43 with 2–09–03 lat
Heckers Ephemerides¹⁰ give him Pisces 13–08 or 17′–17″ ⎫ lat 2–10 error 0′–57″
Wings   "   " " Pisces 13–05 or 14 –17 ⎭ lat 2–11 error 1 –57

The deviations in longitude are so large as I should not have beleived my observation tho Confirmd two severall nights had I not been fortified wth ye like observations in his Mercurius sub sole[11] whither rather then enlarg needlessly I refer you.

October ye 12th last past at my first viewing Saturne with my lesse tube I thought I saw something on each side him amidst ye colours of my glasse & ye spurious raies of his body: moveing my long tube to him I could see his anses somewhat more distinctly but very exile,[12] & to one that thought not of them scarce discernable

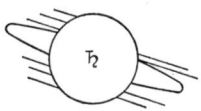

they were something further extended from his body then in this figure, & of a dusky color, not at all light like ye rest of his body but rather as ye obscure part of ye Moone first appeares after her change: save that I saw a little part on ye extremity of one of ye anses, about ye bignesse of a great pins head, more radiant. I have not of late veiwed him againe but I shall ere long when I [have] finished my observations of [ye] Pleiades which as ye weather permits I reiterate.[13] Last Sunday I receaved Cassini's tables,[14] lent mee by Mr Townely which I am now transcribing: pray thereof present my services to Mr Collins & desire him if hee have not yet procured me them to trouble himselfe no farther. but if hee please to procure mee a colored glasse or two against Mr Sargeant comes up which hee tells mee will be within this fortnight I will get him for them & pay him what they cost no more but yt I am

your servant to command,
John Flamsteed

ADDRESS
To Henry Oldenburge Esqr
at his house in ye midde of
Pell-Mell in St James's
Westminster these
present:

pd 3d.

NOTES

1 November 18.
2 No doubt G. A. Borelli, *Theorica medicearum planetarum a causis physicis deducta* (Florence, 1666)—the first allusion so far to this important book.

3 Obviously Flamsteed employed the hastily printed table at the end of *Phil. Trans.*, no 74 (14 August 1671), p. 2238, where the style of the dates is not stated.
4 "Alto" signifies altitude; *a* is the first satellite, whose immersion Cassini had predicted for 6:49 A.M. (see Letter 1771). But the *Phil. Trans.* table has a misprint and in any case Flamsteed missed the precise moment. And there was a difference in latitude.
5 Flamsteed means 100 or 105 divisions of his micrometer screwhead, each of which measures about 0.357 seconds of arc.
6 "almost in her perigee."
7 Inches, of course.
8 "At 4:46 A.M. the height of the eastern star in the point [of the Pleiades] being 7° 45', the bright star was distant from the moon's limb 51' 16", and from its center 1° 8' 5"; but at 5:07 A.M. when the height of the same star in the Pleiades was 10° 30', the bright star was distant from the limb 1° 2' 4" and from the center 1° 18' 54"."
9 That is, for the precession of the equinoxes; Flamsteed neglects the change in latitude. In the figure, we have added coordinate lines for clarity's sake.
10 See Letter 1824, note 4. Flamsteed goes on to give first the predicted longitude, then the deviation from his observation; next the predicted latitude and the deviation.
11 See Letter 1776, note 5.
12 Slender; this sentence was printed in *Phil. Trans.*, no. 78 (18 December 1671), 3034.
13 For these observations, see his letter of 8 November 1671 to Collins, printed in Rigaud, II, 122-25.
14 Cassini's *Ephemerides mediceorum syderum* (Bologna, 1668).

1827

Oldenburg to Sluse

21 November 1671

From the copy in Royal Society MS. O 2, no. 60

Per-Illustri et Reverendo admodum Viro
D. Renato Francisco Slusio Canonico Leodiensi &c.
H. Oldenburg Salutem

Postremis tuis literis locupletissimis, Vir Illustris, d. 18. Julij [N.S.] ad me datis, responsum citius maturassem, ni fuissem veritus occupationes tuas graviores meis affanijs nimium frequenter interpellare. Pergrata fuere, quae de libris nuper editis significasti; ea praesertim, quae de Gomezij Pereirae libro[1] transmittere dignatus es. Plurimum quoque tibi debemus; quod et Stibij, a Te insigniter adeo sublimati, Specimine, et curioso illo circa Nitrum Experimento augere nos voluisti. Vix quicquam nunc suppetit, quo redhostire liberalitatem tuam possim; Accipe interim, si placet, Illustrissimi Boylij modum non injucundum gravitatis Aeris Mutationes dignoscendi, qui hic est;

Ceram vulgarem et Minium ita commiscebat, ut globulus inde confectus aquae praecise innataret; ipsum phialae, libram aquae continenti, immittebat, eoque sic relicto deprehendebat, unius horae spatio eum duodecies mergi et emergere, singulis fere binis minutis positu istius mutato; Num vero hoc semper ita eventurum, de eo nil affirmat.

Ex literis Clarissimi Hugenij, nuper Parisijs ad me scriptis, intellexi, pergratam ipsi fuisse tuam de Alhazeni Problemate constructionem.[2] Ait, Te recte observasse, illam ex eadem cum Sua Analysi manare, nec a sua multum differre; adjicit interim, se arbitrari, suam magis esse naturalem, idque ob Hyperbolae Asymptoton dispositionem, nec tamen plus operae requirere, quam a Te suppeditatam. Putem, ipsemet jam ad Te hac de re scripsisse (id quippe se facturum spondebat,) Teque rogasse ut Analysin illam adhuc faciliorem, quam de eodem Problemate Te invenisse significavas, ipsi communices. Eandem generositatem, et Nos a Te petimus, Tibique gratitudinem nostram pro re nata testificandam stipulamur.

Idem Hugenius, si ad Te scripsit, haud dubie sua de Saturno observata nupera Tibi impertiit quamque ea systemati suo egregie respondeant, significavit. Autumat interim, Anni hujus phases magno usui fore, ut exinde tempus rotundae figurae reditus multo majori, quam prius ἀκριβεία praedicatur.

Latere Te non putem, quae Cassinus, Picardus, Siferus et Hookius noster de maculis Solaribus nuper observarunt. A Doctore Medico Hamburgensi, Martino Fogelio intellexi, Siferum, doctum Urbe illa Mathematicum, dictarum macularum ad limbum Solis Orientalem reditum Aug. 26. (st. v.) et observationes suas ad usque 5. Septembris quando iterum ad limbum Occidentalem disparebant, continuasse.[3] Non dubito, quin et Tu, Vir Illustrissime, huic contemplationi caelesti pro excelso Tuo Genio indulseris, nobisque observationum tuarum summam sis communicaturus, quemadmodum et Nos nostras, Actibus meis Philosophicis insertas, prima quaque occasione commoda transmittemus.[4]

Celeberrimus Hevelius nequaquam otiatur, sed in expedienda Caelesti sua Machina impense desudat, eandemque jam per tres quatuorve menses sub praelo laborare affirmat. Clarissimus Wallisius noster, edito jam volumine tertio suum de Motu et Mechanice opus absolvit, cujus exemplar Tibi transmittendum D. Collinsius noster (qui Te perquam officiose salutat) suscepit.

Dn. Willisius inprimendum jam curat Tractatum geminum, *De Brutorum Anima* unum, *De Morbis Capitis* alterum. Dominus Charletonus *de Scorbuto* nuper edidit libellum, in quo de Morbi illius triplici differentia tractat, ipsius scilicet ex rancido sanguine, sale fixo, et sale acido genealogiam edisserens. Insuper exspectamus indies D. Bohuni Historiam *Ventorum*, Anglice perscriptam; mox tamen, ni fallor, in Sermonem Latinum vertendam.[5]

Quae omnia sua tempore, si ita Tibi libuerit, per nostrum in Hollandia amicum ad Te curabimus. Vale, Vir Eximie, nos porro ama, et quando vacat, has Tibi traditus esse significa. Dabam Londini d. 21 Novembris 1671.

TRANSLATION

H. Oldenburg greets the very illustrious and reverend René François de Sluse, Canon of Liège, etc.

I should have prepared my reply to your recent very rich letter of 18 July [N.S.] more promptly, illustrious Sir, had I not been fearful of interrupting too frequently your more serious affairs with my trifles. The information you imparted about recently published books was most welcome, especially what you were so good as to communicate about Gomez Pereyra's book.[1] We are also much indebted to you for deciding to enrich us with that specimen of antimony so remarkably sublimed by yourself and that curious experiment concerning niter. I have hardly anything in stock with which to recompense your generosity; but meanwhile accept, please, the very illustrious Mr. Boyle's not inelegant way of detecting the atmosphere's changes in weight, which follows:

He mixes red lead and common wax so that the little ball thus formed will just float in water; he puts it in a vessel containing a pound of water, and letting it be, has known it sink and rise a dozen times in the period of an hour changing its position every minutes; but he does not assert that it will always behave thus.

I have gathered from a letter of Mr. Huygens, recently addressed to me from Paris, that your construction of Alhazen's Problem was most welcome to him.[2] He says, you have correctly noted that it derives from the same analysis as his own, and does not greatly differ from it; but he adds that he is of the opinion that his own construction is the more natural because of the arrangement of the hyperbola's asymptote, without requiring any more effort than that furnished by yourself. I think he will have written to you himself about this matter already (as he undertook to do), and have asked you to impart to him that more simple analysis which, you report, you have discovered for that problem. We beg you to be equally generous to ourselves, and covenant an appropriate manifestation of gratitude to you.

If the same Huygens has written to you, no doubt he has imparted his recent observations of Saturn and told you how notably they correspond with his system. Meanwhile he thinks that the appearances of this year will be of great value since from them the time of the return of the round shape will be predictable with much higher accuracy than before.

I think I must not conceal from you what Cassini, Picard, Sivers, and our own Hooke have observed of the recent sunspots. I have heard from the Hamburg physician Martin Vogel that Heinrich Sivers, a learned mathematician of that city, observed the return of those spots to the eastern limb of the sun on 26 August (O.S.) and continued his observations until 5 September when they again disappeared at the western limb.[3] No doubt you too, illustrious Sir, with your lofty genius, devoted yourself to viewing this celestial phenomenon and will communicate a summary of your observations to us, just as we will send you ours, inserted in my *Philosophical Transactions*, at the first convenient opportunity.[4]

The celebrated Hevelius is by no means idle, for he labors hard at expediting his *Machina coelestis*, and he says that that book has been in the press for three or four months. Our famous Mr. Wallis has finished his work *Mechanica, sive de motu* with its third volume, now published, of which our Mr. Collins (who greets you most dutifully) has undertaken to send you a copy.

Mr. Willis is at this moment seeing through the press his double treatise, *De brutorum anima* and *De morbis capitis*. Mr. Charleton lately published a small book *De scorbuto*, in which he discusses the diversity of that triple disease, speaking of its derivation from rancid blood, fixed salt, and acid salt. Further, we daily expect the *History of Winds* of Mr. Bohun, written in English but soon, unless I am mistaken, to be translated into Latin.[5]

All these things, if it will please you, I shall take care to send you in due course by our friend in Holland. Farewell, worthy Sir, continue to love us, and when you have leisure let us know that these have been delivered to you. London, 21 November 1671.

NOTES

Reply to Letter 1745. The date is given as 22 November in Sluse's reply, Letter 1843.
1 See Letter 1745a.
2 Letter 1807.
3 See Letter 1811a.
4 The sunspot outbreak was treated in *Phil. Trans.*, nos. 74 (August), 75 (September) 77 (November), and 78 (December).
5 We could not find a Latin version.

1828
Wallis to Oldenburg
23 November 1671
From the original in Royal Society MS. W 1, no. 132

Oxford. Nov. 23. 1671

Sir,

To yours of Nov. 11. I had sooner answered but that I was willing to have answered more fully than yet I can. By *Pocockij folium de Caave et She*, (that is, of Coffee and The)[1] I suppose they mean a paper of half a sheet, printed here in Arabick and Latin, out of an Arab Physician concerning their *Kawha* or (as wee call it) *Coffee*, (but nothing of *The* or *Tea*,) I have endeavoured to get one of these papers, both from the Dr. and from the Printer, but I cannot yet light upon one: when I do, I will send it to you. I have attempted to meet with Dr. Morrison,[2] once or twice, but have missed of him; and so can give you as yet no account of those Trees.

Concerning Abulfeda:[3] where Mr. Grave's[4] copy is, I cannot tell, nor how much paines hee took about it. But Dr. Pocock hath two excellent copies of it. And Mr. Clark[5] had (before his death) taken a great deal of paines in comparing them, and other Geographers with them; in order to an Edition of it. But his death, as in other regards,(he being a person of very good worth & industry,) so particularly in reference to this happened unluckyly, before it was ordered and digested, so that I doubt that labour will be lost. Dr. Pocock's copies (I think, both of them,) are not pointed for ye pronunciation; but so accurate are they that (in a distinct Column) the names of these points are in words at length set down. But as to Mr. Grave's copy, I doubt there may be some mistake (for if any such were, Mr. Clark surely would have indeavoured to have gott a sight of it, but I do not remember yt hee ever spake of other than Dr. Pococks 2 Copies:) But if any such bee I suppose it is in his Brothers hands Mr. Edward Graves, a Minister (I think) in Leicestershire (or Lincolnshire)[6] But I mean to inquire further of it. Dr. Pocock desires yt when you have occasion or opportunity of sending anything to Mr. Vernon at Paris, that you would send to him one of those Books you have of his, to Mr. Vernon to present from ye Author to Monsieur Thevenot.7 No more at present but that I am

> Your very humble servant
> *John Wallis*

ADDRESS

For Mr. Henry Oldenburg
   in the Palmal near St. James's
      London

NOTES

Reply to Letter 1818.
1 See Letter 1811, note 6.
2 Presumably Robert Morison (1620–83), Professor of Botany at Oxford, often mentioned as an author.
3 See Letter 1806, note 2.
4 This was John Greaves (1602–52), the mathematician and orientalist.
5 Samuel Clarke (1625–69), another oriental scholar.
6 As Wallis points out in Letter 1833, this was Thomas Greaves (1612–76), also an orientalist, who held livings in Northamptonshire.
7 See Letter 1836.

1829
Urban Hjärne to Oldenburg
23 November 1671

From the original in Royal Society MS. H 3, no. 9

Paris le 2 Decemb. st. n. 1671

Monsieur

Je crains bien que mon long silence ne me rende suspect aupres de Vous, et qu'il ne vous donne lieu de croire que j'aye oublié les grandes amities que vous m'avez temoignées en plusieurs facons pendant que i'estois a Londres, et c'est pour eviter le malheur, que i'ay pris la hardiesse de vous importuner par ces lignes et afin aussy en meme temps de vous remercier treshumblement de la grande faveur que vous m'avez faite, ayant este le principal autheur de l'honneur que i'ay eu d'entrer dans l'illustre Societé Royale: Et comme ie n'ay jamais merité de vostre bonté une telle faveur, ie vous asseure que i'en ay de si grands ressentissements de reconnaissance dans le coeur, lesquels i'espere avec le temps si le bon Die me conserve la vie de Vous faire voir; que ie n'auray point de repos que ie n'aye trouve les moyens de Vous les faire connoistre par mes services. Et par la de vous donner lieu de n'avoir point de regret de m'avoir ainsy obligé. Je Vous supplie donc de considerer que ie sois encores voyageur dans les pays estrangeres, ou ie ne puis faire aucune chose qui meritte de vous estre adressée. I'espere que quand Dieu m'aura fait la grace d'estre de retour chez nous ie me ressouviendray de mon devoir et ie Vous proteste que ie seray soigneux de m'acquitter de ce que i'ay promis. Ce n'est pas que ie n'aye ramassé et recuilly ca et lá quelque chose trescurieux et méme en assez grand nombre. Mais comme la pluspart de ces choses sont medicinales, et que le reste n'est pas d'assez grande consequence pour Vous estre presenté, ou s'il y en a quelques une, que Vous en avez peut estre deja la connoissance, C'est le sujet pour lequel ie ne vous en ay pas encores voulu faire part

I'espere toutefois en tirer un iour plusieurs connoissances, et plusieurs pensees pour inventer quelque chose de nouveau. Il se trouve icy tous les jours des personnes qui apportent ou proposent quelques inventions nouvelles, dont quelques unes reussissent. Il y a quelque temps qu'un Hollandois proposa au Roy de fournir de leau autant qu'on en pourroit avoir affaire dans un lieu, ce qu'il promettoit de faire par le seul travail d'un petit garcon, ce qui seroit fort avantagieux a versailles, ou il ny a de l'eau que par artifice dans les fontaines les jets d'eau et les grottes, et méme dans la pluspart de canaux. Ie n'ay pas encores veu la machine de cet homme, mais on asseure qu'il peut venir au bout de sa proposition. Il y en aussi un autre qui a deja fait quelques experiences pour resusciter une persone ou une beste noyée, et meme apres trois jours. Il y a deux ou trois mois qu'il en fit une, qui reussit en partie. Il prit un chien qui apres esté noyé trois iours auparavant, Il le fit remuer, mais il ne luy rendit pas la vie tout a fait. Je crois que cela vint de ce qu'on n'avait pas noyé ce chien dans une fleuve ou dans une riviere, mais dans un tonneau ou il n'a pas eu autant d'air comme il en avoit besoign pour l'entretien de la vie, et ce fut sans doute ce quil fut cause qu'il mourut. Quoyque il y en ait plusieurs qui nient qu'il se puisse trouver aucun air dans l'eau, ie sçay bien toutefois, qu'il n'y a aucun bon naturaliste qui le nie, et qui ne soustienne que les poissons ne peuvent pas vivre sans air. Ce que l'on peut bien voir chez nous dans les grandes hyvers, ou les petits estangs se gelent par tout en sorte qu'il ny peut entrer aucun air et ainsi les poissons demeurent étouffer, de sorte que dans le printemps quand l'eau est degelée on les trouve morts et corrumpus dans l'eau, et quand il arrive que l'on troue la glace dans ces lieux, les poissons viennent en trouppes mettre le tete hors du trou pour respirer et prendre l'air, et alors on les prends en grande quantité. Outre cela il y a plusieurs exemples, que ie n'ay pas besoign de vous rapporter, et qui vous sont assez connues. L'unique Histoire que Monsr Adam Olearius raporte dans son livre intitulé Die Hosteinische Kunstcammer[1] dans le discours du chien marin et des polypes (qu'il a tiré, si ie ne me trompe, de la chronique de Sicile) et dans laquelle il parle de ce Petrus qui nageoit ca et la par tout dans la mer, et presque toujours et qui sçavoit raconter plusieurs choses de ce qu'il avoit veu dans la mer, et qui est enfin peris dans ce grand goufre charybdis proche la Scylle, ou il se hazardat et allat deux fois a la sollicitation du Roy de Sicile, qui pour l'exciter a y aller y iettat par deux fois de grands bocals d'or, et dont le dernier rempli de pieces d'or fut ietté au milieu de ce goufre, ce que ce Roy faisoit afin de mieux sçavoir les circumstances de ces lieux, et la cause de cet effroyable bruit qu'on y entend, et qui s'y fait, ce qui seroit une preuve convaincante de la verite de mon opinion, si on estoit bien asseure de la verité de cette histoire. Mais pour revenir a nostre discours, et a cet homme qui est icy et qui entreprend de ressusciter ainsy les noyez, et qui fait un grand mistere de son secret, du quel pour moy ie ne fais pas tant de cas, veu qu'en finlande et autres pays circonvoisins il se trouve bien souvent, que des personnes apres avoir estè noyees et mortes durant deux ou trois iours, reviennent en vie. Le principal de la chose pour les gairer consiste a les tirer hors de l'eau, de laquelle i'ay assez amplement entretenu Monsr. le Conseiller Leyonberg Resident de Suede,[2] lors que i'estois a Hamtoncourt il y a deux ans. Et quoyque l'on puisse dire que ceux qui sont pendus ou estrangler meurent vistement, ie puis dire que c'est autre chose, puisqu'il ne manque pas d'air tout a fait a un homme noyé comme a ceuxcy. Cependant il demeure dans l'eau sans grand sentiment, et presque comme un enfant de huict mois dans le ventre de sa mere, et quasiment évanouy ou comme dans un assoupissement ou presque comme dans un extase, et qui plus est, quelquefois ils entendent tout ce que font les personnes qui sont proche d'eux, et qui les cherchent etc. de méme comme on peut voir en ceux qui tombent dans un evanouissement ou defaillance, qui quand ils sont eveillez sçavent dire tout ce que ceux qui estoient proche d'eux ont dit. Je sçay aussy que ceux qui ont esté delivrez de l'eau ont bien souvent recite la meme chose, et encores ressenti dans l'eau plusieurs autres incommoditez, comme entre autres dans l'hyver, s'il arrive qu'il soient tombez dans l'eau, et glissez sous la glace, ils se pleignent fort du bruit qu'on a fait dessus la glace, et quasi comme des douleurs que l'on ressent lorsque l'on entend quelque chose qui fait grincer les dents et quasi faillir le coeur, et autres choses semblables qu'ils sçavent raconter, et qui seroit inutile de vous écrire. Mais quoyque les poulmons a cause de la quantité d'eau que le patient avale, et dont ils sont tout remplis, ne poussent pas faire leur fonction: neantmoins leau ne pouvant pas entrer dans le coeur, dans les arteres ny dans les veines, cela n'empesche pas la circulation du sang, qui d'autre part estant empeschée ne se fait que petit a petit et insensiblement, de méme comme dans l'apoplexie ou suffocation hysterique, ou le patient est tout a fait étouffé. Si le passage de la nourriture est coupé et que le chile ne puisse passer, il faut considerer que le feu de la vie est aussy feuble, et par consequent, la consumption du sang des esprits et de la nourriture fort petite, et quasi de meme, comme celle des ours dans Lepponie et Finlande, qui dorment des mois tout entiers sans manger. J'avoue pourtant que c'est tout autre chose quand on tombe dans la mer, ou dans l'eau impure et trouble, ou les pores sont remplis d'autres matieres et que par consequent ne peuvent pas prendre tant d'air, comme quand on tombe dans l'au fraische ou de riviere. Il arrive aussy bien souvent que ceuxcy qui tombent meurent d'abord, quoyqu'on les tire de l'eau vistement. Mais cela arrive par ce qu'en tombant ils se rompent le cou, et pour lors ils deviennent bleux alentour de cou; ainsi que ie l'ay veu, et remarque moy méme quelque fois. J'ay dit cy dessus que la principale chose pour les guerir estoit de les tirer de l'eau, ce que nos Finlandois scavent fort bien observer: car si tost qu'ils sont trouvés l'homme noyé, ils le tirent doucement de l'eau et ne le mettent point a l'air, afin que l'air cru et grossier ne puisse pas entrer impetueusement, et se méler avec l'eau qui reste dans les poulmons, et afinque quand la circulation du sang vint a faire les fonctions avec force, elle ne rompe et ne creve les veins poulmoniques, ou par le crudite de l'eau n'esteindre la chaleur et feu vital dans le coeur, ce qui se fait que l'on remarque presque dans tous ceux qui sont noyéz, et ne sont pas retires á propos, que le sang leur sort par la bouche, ce qui est aussy arrivé au chien d'ont i'ay parlé cy dessus, et duquel cet homme s'est voulu servir pour faire son experience. et quand cela arrive, il ny a aucun remede ny aucune esperance de les pouvoir sauver. Ces pourquoy quand ceux de Finland ont touve le noyé, ils le tirent doucement iusques sur la surface de l'eau et le couvrent aussytost d'une grosse couverture et le portent dans une etouve, ou ils le mettent sur un tonneau[3] et le roulent çà et la fort doucement d'abord fort lentement et augmentant l'agitation dans le suitte par degrez et ainsy font sortir l'eau par la bouche le nez et les autres endroits, et quand l'eau est sortie et que les pores sont ouvertes ils le frottent avec avec [*sic*] des linges chauds et autres fomentations, et ainsy le noyé recommence a prendre la vie petit a petit, et apres avoir langui quelques jours ou quelques semaines (les uns plus, les autres moins, selon la force du patient) ils revivent fort souvent. Ils observent aussy fort dans ces pays de ne laisser pas approcher des corps que l'on traitte ainsy toutes sortes de personnes et particulierement les homicides ou ceux qui sont suspect d'aucune meutre ou acune autre grand crime; Mais ce n'est pas une chose que ie veille examiner icy, c'est pourquoy ie la laisse lá. L'on remarque que ceux qui l'ont rechappé de ces accidents perdent beaucoup de leur esprits, qu'ils sont ensuite quasi tousiours resueurs et estourdis, que leur memoire diminue beaucoup, ce qui arrive sans doutte, par ce que la teste qui est plus pesante que les autres parties du corps demeurant tousjours en bas, le sang s'y jette en abondance, et pousse les esprits animaux de costé et d'autre, et par la il destruit les detours et les petites canaux qui servent a ces esprits pour faire leur fonction, comme la memoire et la fantaisie. Et deplus la fraischeur de l'eau ainsy que ie le croy y contribue beaucoup lorsqu'elle entre dans le nez et dans les oreilles. Mais pour revenir a celuy dont iay parle desia plusieurs fois cydessus qui veut faire voir ces experiences, ie ne scay pas encores les moyens dont il se sert pour faire reussir son secret. Je scay seulement qu'il se sert de lavements pour mieux faire evacuer l'eau par les boyaux, ce qui n'est pas en usage dans les pays dont i'ay parle. Car ces sortes de remedes y sont presque in connus parmy les petites gens. Je sçay aussi qu'il met de la cendre sur le corps, ce qu'il fait sans doute a limitation des mouches qui se revivifient y estant mise, ce qui s'entend quand elles ont esté noyées. Je croy que cela peut un peu ouvrir les pores, et que la cendre par son acrete peut irriter les esprits et porter a un movement, ce que ie croy toutefois se pouvoir mieux faire par un frotement avec les linges chaudes. Je ne puis non obstant la longueur de ma lettre obmettre de vous faire le recit d'une chose qui est bien forte pour prouver mon sentiment. Monsr. Oxehuwud[4] Gentilhomme Suedois fort iudicieux et tout a fait digne de foy m'a reconté depuis peu, qu'il y a quelques annees qu'estant dans la paroisse de Bottnare ou il demeuroit, et qui est situé a trois lieues de la ville de jönkoping, un garçon agé d'environ 15 ou 16 ans, tomba en peschant dans l'eau, dou il ne fut tiré, que le troisieme iour d'apres, et fut gueri de la meme façon que ie l'ay dite cy dessus, et il m'assura que ce garçon disoit avoir reposé dans l'eau avec beaucoup de tranquilité, et sans aucune peine, quil entendoit distinctement tout ce que l'on disoit au dessus de luy, et racontoit meme tout ce que son pere avoit dit en le cherchant, neantmoins il ne vescut que six mois apres cet accident et estoit tout change d'humeur. Car avant quil tombast dans l'eau, il estoit fort gay, et apres il devint fort triste, et n'aimoit que la solitude. Un autre Suedois m'a aussy recité, qu'estant a Ubsala il tomba dans la riviere, ou il fut environ une heure et que pendant cette temps la il entendoit tout ce que l'on disoit au bord de la riviere. Je pourrois vous rapporter quantite d'autres histoires semblables pour prouver mon sentiment, mais ie ne le veux pas faire crainte de vous ennuyer; et parce qu'elles ne sont pas si recentes que cellecy. Et vous sçavez aussy ce que Monsr. Stiernhielm Conseiller suedois écrivit de Stockholm il y a un an[5] de ce jardiner qui estoit tombe dans l'eau proche de cette ville là. Je croyrois mal employer le temps de vous faire d'autres narrations semblables.

Cest pourquoy vous aura la bonté de me pardonner toutes les importunitez que ie vous fais, et de recevoir cette lettre en bon part, la quelle n'a esté qu' pour ebaucher cette matiere, laquelle i'espere perfectioner avec le temps, ainsi que plusieurs autres quand Dieu m'aura fait la grace d'estre de retour chez nous, et dy exercer ma charge, la quelle me donnera le moyen de pouvoir mieux m'instruire de toutes choses. Vous sçavez que iusques a present je n'ay fait que voyager, et qu'ainsi ie n'ay pui m'appliquer qu'a fort peu d'exercises, et particulierement dans celuy de la chimie, la quelle requierre beaucoup de temps. J'espere bientost retourner au pays, et de passer par chez vous en m'en allant, et d'y estre instruit de beaucoup de choses de vostre tendre bienveillance, laquelle je vous supplie de me conserver, et d'estre asseuré que ie seray toute ma vie de tout mon coeur et de toute mon ame et avec tout le respect que ie vous dois Monsieur,

Vostre treshumble et
tres obeissant serviteur
Urbain Hiärne

TRANSLATION, chiefly by Oldenburg, from Royal Society MS. H 3, no. 10, printed in Birch, *History*, III, 5–7

Paris Decemb. 3. 1671. N.S.

[Sir

I fear lest my long silence may have roused your suspicions about me and given you occasion to believe that I may have forgotten the great friendship you demonstrated for me in various ways while I was in London, and it is to avoid this misfortune that I have been so bold as to importune you with these lines and also, at the same time, to thank you very humbly for the great favor you have done me, having been chiefly responsible for the honor I have received of being] a member of ye Illust. R.S.. [And as I have never deserved your kindness in receiving such a favor I assure you that I have very great feelings of gratitude in my heart which I hope in time, if God preserves my life, to reveal to you, and I shall never rest until I have found means of letting you know this by my services. And so never to give you occasion to regret having thus obliged me. I beg you then to bear in mind that I am still a traveler in foreign lands where I can accomplish nothing worthy of being addressed to you. I hope that when God has benevolently permitted me to return to my own country I shall remember again what my duty is, and I swear to you that I shall take care to acquit myself of what I promised. It is true that] I have met wth many curious things [here and there, but most of them were medicinal and] I doe not think [the rest] of importance enough to present you wth them. [If there were any, you perhaps already know of them and this is the reason why I did not wish to impart them to you as yet.

I still hope one day to extract much knowledge from these and to have some ideas for discovering something new. There are here people who every day bring forth or propose some new inventions, some of them successful. Some time ago a Dutchman made an offer to the King to supply as much water as could be made use of in a place, which he promised to do by the work of one single little boy, a thing that would be very advantageous at Versailles, where there is no water except that supplied artificially for the cisterns, fountains, and grottoes, and even most of the canals. I have not yet seen this man's mechanism, but am assured that he can carry out his proposal. There is another] yt hath already made some Experiments... of reviving [people or] animals drown'd, and yt even after they have been so [three days]. He made one 2. or 3. months agoe, wch succeeded in part. He took a Dog, wch having been drown'd 3 days before, he made him to stir, though he brought him not quite to life again. It was thought, yt ye reason why he reviv'd not altogether, was, because ye dog had not been drown'd in a river [or stream], but in a barrel, in wch there was not air enough to entertain life [and this was without doubt the cause of his death. Although there are some who deny that any air can be found in water, I very well know that no good natural philosopher denies it, or does not hold that fish cannot live without air. All of which can be seen with us in hard winters, when the little ponds are frozen solid and no air can enter, and thus the fish stifle, so that in the spring when the water unfreezes they are found dead and putrifying in the water; and if it happens that a hole is broken in the ice in these places, the fish troop there to stick their heads out of the hole to breath and take the air, and then they are caught in large numbers. Besides this, there are several examples which I need not recite to you, since they are sufficiently well known to you. There is the singular story which Mr. Adam Olearius tells in his book entitled *Die Holsteinische Kunstcammer*[1] in the discussion of the dogfish and of the octopus (taken by him, if I am not mistaken, from the chronicle of Sicily) and in it he speaks of a certain Peter who swam here, there, and everywhere in the sea, almost continuously, and could tell many stories of what he had seen in the sea, and who finally perished in that great whirlpool Charybdis near Scylla, where he ventured to go twice at the request of the King of Sicily who to incite him to go there twice threw in there great jars of gold, the last of which filled with gold pieces was thrown into the middle of this whirlpool. This the King did to learn more about the details of these localities and the cause of the dreadful noise heard there and how it was made, which would be a convincing proof of my opinion if one could be assured of the truth of this story.

But to return to our account and to] this person [who is here and who undertakes to resuscitate the drowned; he] maketh as yet a secret of his art; but I know [there is no reason for this, since] yt in Finland and ye neighb[oring] contries it often coms to passe, yt persons, after they have been drown'd two or 3 days, come to life again. The main of ye art consists in the manner of drawing ym out of ye water, about wch I once discours'd largely wth Monsr Lyonberg, ye Resident of Sueden [when I was at Hampton Court two years ago.[2] And] though those yt are hanged and strangled, dye soon, yet yt is another thing, because there wants not all air to a drown'd animal, as there doth to one yt is strangled. [Nevertheless he remains in the water without much feeling, almost like an eight-months' fetus in the womb of its mother, and as it were in a faint or coma or almost as if in a trance; and what is more, sometimes they understand what is done by people near them, who search for them, as may also be seen in those who fall into a faint or swoon, who on being awakened can repeat what those near them said. I also know that those who have been safely delivered from the water often say the same thing, and have even felt the effects of many other discomforts while in the water; among others, if in the winter, they have fallen into the water and slid under the ice, they complain bitterly about the noise made on top of the ice, almost like the suffering felt on hearing something which sets the teeth on edge and makes the heart almost stop. And there are other things they tell, which would be useless to write about to you.] And although ye Lungs, by reason of ye abundance of water, got in, cannot perform their function, yet since ye water cannot enter into ye heart, nor ye arteries and veins, ye circulation of ye bloud is not quite stopp'd, but only hindred, so yt it can not be made but very slowly and insensibly, after ye manner as in apoplexies or hysterical suffocations [where the patient is entirely suffocated]. If ye passage of ye nourishment is obstructed, and yt the chile cannot passe, it is to be consider'd, yt ye vital heat also is very weak in this case, and consequently yt ye consumption of ye bloud, spirits, and nutriment is but smal, and in a manner yesame, as it is in ye bears of Lapland and Finland, wch sleep whole months wthout eating any thing.

Mean time, I asknowledg, yt tis quite another thing, when persons fall into ye sea, or into foul and troubled waters, ye pores whereof are fill'd wth other parts and consequently cannot contain so much air, as fresh and clear water doth. [It also happens pretty often that those who fall in die straight away, although they are pulled out quickly. But this occurs because they break their necks in falling, whence they turn blue around the neck, as I have seen and noted for myself sometimes.

I said above that the main thing to cure them was to pull them out of the water, as our Finlanders understand very well, for] as soon as they have found ye person drown'd, they draw him up very gently, towards ye surface of ye water, yet wthout bringing him hastily into ye Air, to ye end, yt ye raw and grosse Air, may not get into him impetuously, and mingle wth the water yt is yet in ye lungs, and least, when ye circulation of ye bloud coms to be made again, ye bloud doe not burst ye pulmonick veins, and so by ye crudity of ye Water the vital warmth of ye heart be not extinguisht. Whence it is observ'd in almost all drown'd persons, yt are not drawn up wth yt care, yt ye bloud issues out of their mouth: wch also happen'd to ye dog above mention'd [wch that man chose to use for his experiment] And when this case happens, there is not any hope left of recovery. Wherefore the Finlanders having found ye drown'd body, they draw him gently towards ye surface of ye water, and presently cover him wth a thick cover, and carry him into a hot stove, where they put him upon a ton,[3] and role ym gently to and fro, beginning first of all wth a very gentle motion, and afterwards by degrees increasing ye agitation; whereby the water coms out of ye mouth, nose, and other orifices: And the water being come away, and ye pores open'd, they rubb ye patient wth hot linnen cloaths and use other fomentations, and then he begins to live again litle by litle, and after some days or weeks (some sooner, some later, according to the force and constitution of ye patient) they often are reviv'd [They are also very careful in this country not to permit close to the body they are treating thus every sort of person, and particularly not homicides nor those suspected of any sort of murder or other major crime. But this is not anything which I want to examine here, so I leave it at that point.] It is observ'd, yt those wch thus escape, have lost much of their vivacity, and yt they are afterwards almost always very dull and estourdys, yt their memory is much impaired, wch doubtless happens, because ye bloud hath been plentifully cast into the head [which is heavier than the other parts of the body and so remains always lower, and pushes the animal spirits in various directions and hence destroys the passages and little canals which permit these spirits to carry out their functions, like the memory and the imagination.] To wch also may much contribute the coldness of ye water entering into ye nose and eares.

But to return to ye Parisian Artist [of whom I have already spoken several times above, who wants to show these experiments], I doe not yet know ye means he useth [to make his secret succeed]. I know only thus much, yt he maketh use of Clysters, the better to evacuate the water out of the bowels, wch is not practis'd in the contrys, I spoke of. [For this kind of remedy is almost unknown to humble folk.] This I know also yt he puts ashes over ye body; wch doubtless he doth in imitation of what happens to flys, wch are revived, being put in warm ashes, after they have been drown'd. Perhaps ye ashes may open ye pores, and by their sharpness may somewhat irritate ye spirits and bring ym into motion again: ye wch yet I think may be better done by rubbing wth hot linnen cloaths.

Before I conclude my letter [in spite of its length], and this account, I cannot but impart to you one thing more relating to this matter. Monsr. Oxhuwen,[4] a Suedish Gentleman very judicious and of great veracity, hath lately assur'd me, yt some years agoe in ye parish of Botnare in Sueden, ye place of his residence, situate 3. leagues from Jonkoping, a youth of 15. or 16 years of age, fell into ye water when he was fishing; whence he was not drawn up but ye 3d day after, and was recover'd after ye manner above described; And he added, yt ye Lad said, he had lain in ye water wthout any trouble, hearing what was said concerning him above water, and relating what his father had said in seeking him. But he lived but 6. months after this accident, and was quite changed in his temper, being very melancholy, [and loving solitude] whereas before he had been very cheerfull. An other Suede assur'd me likewise, yt being at Upsal he fell also into ye river, whence he was drawn up an hour after, having heard, during yt time, all what had been said on the river side.

I could tell you many more histories of this nature [to prove my views] but I would not be tedious [and they are not so recent as these]. You know, what Monsieur Stiernhelm, a Suedish Concellor living at Stockholm, one of ye R. Society, wrote to you a year agoe,[5] of a Gardner, yt was fallen into ye water near yt town, and how he was reviv'd a good while after. [I should think I was employing my time badly if I gave you other similar accounts.

This is why you will be so good as to forgive all my importunities and to receive this letter kindly, which was only intended to sketch out this material which I hope to improve with time along with several other matters when God is so good as to permit me to return to our country and there practise my profession, which will give me the means and ability to instruct myself better in all things. You know that hitherto I have done nothing but travel and consequently have been able to apply myself to very slight studies and especially in chemistry, which demands much time. I hope soon to return home and to pass through your country in going there, and so to learn many things by your tender care. This I beg you to preserve towards me, and to rest assured that all my life, with all my heart and soul, with all possible respect, I shall be, Sir,

Your very humble, obedient servant
Urbain Hiärne]

NOTES

Urban Hjärne (1641–1724) was the outstanding Swedish scientist of the late seventeenth and early eighteenth centuries. He studied medicine at Upsala, and had inaugurated a theater at Stockholm before starting his travels in 1667. In England he was elected F.R.S. (on the motion of Leijonberg; see note 2) on 18 November 1669; the following year he proceeded M.D. at Anger. He helped develop Sweden's mineral resources and founded a chemical laboratory at Stockholm in 1683. Through his office as royal physician he also played a considerable role in politics.

The portion of the translation within square brackets is ours.

1 Correctly, Adam Olearius, *Die Gottorfische Kunst-Kammer* (Schleswig, 1666), tabula XXVI, pp. 50–52; the King was the Emperor Frederick II, and the pearl diver was named Nicholas, not Peter.
2 Johan Leijonberg (*né* Barckman, 1625–91) came to England as a diplomat in 1653, and accompanied Whitelocke on his embassy to Sweden, 1653–54. He was resident from 1661, envoy from 1672, and died in London. He was elected F.R.S. on 21 November 1667.
3 "barrel."
4 Oxehufvud is the modern Swedish form of this name.
5 See Vol. VII, p. 17.

1830
Vernon to Oldenburg
23 November 1671

From the original in Royal Society MS. V, no. 18

Paris December 3d 1671 [N.S.]

Sr

I am forced to make wide gaps in my Correspondence (my businesse will have it soe however I doe not faile ever & anon as I have leisure to make visits to the learned & heare what passeth among them.) I doe not doubt, butt the discourse of a new planet makes a great noyse among you.[1] I waited upon Sigre Cassini to know the circumstances of it & found him not at home. however wthin a day or two hee did mee the Honour to give mee a visit & then hee told mee that as hee was intent upon observing the Position of the ansulae of Saturne concerning wch hee hath Printed a paper wch I believe you have seene,[2] as hee one day came to observe & was looking about Saturne, hee perceived a starre smaller then Saturne's Satelles to move in his glasse & was much surprised at it. However the Noveltie was gratefull to him. hee resolved to make closer applications to it, & see what it might bee. Saturne, at the time hee made this observation, was in aquarius; neere that Starre, wch beeing one of those wch make the water wch runs out of Aquarius his urne in Bayerus is marked wth the greeke letter χ³ & thus they bore one to another as that *A* should bee Saturne *B* Saturnes Satelles [Titan] *C* This new starre, wch moves, lesse then Saturnes

```
            *
       *  * B
       C  A
```

Satelles, placed in a Right line wth Saturne, & wch held that same course, butt moved something swifter then Saturne. Saturne was then retrograde & moved from east to West. This first night observation then putt a firme impression in him that it was either a Satelles of Saturne, or a new planet. Hee continued to observe it two nights more, & then hee was out of all doubt. For though his senses clearly discovered the motion to him, yet he was fearfull to trust them in a matter of such noveltie & importance, till repeated examinations had confirmed him in the certainty of them. Having then this assurance & the pleasure of this new discoverie, hee resolved to make it publique the next assembly of the Royal Academie, & did soe; told them, what hee had seene & heere every one was joyfull at the newes of soe great a curiositie, & desired to bee eyewitnesses of it themselves. Wch hee promised, they should bee at night if it were faire weather as it had beene all along heretofore. Butt, see the force of ill luck, from that time to this, there hath beene nothing, butt Clouds, & mists, & drisling weather, & not one cleare Starry night, wch is to them a great subject of impatience, butt to him of despaire: for, you must know, that in some two dayes Saturne was to finish his Retrograde, & returne to his direct motion. If it bee soe that this bee a planet & not a satelles of Saturne it is feard, that by this misfortune hee shall quite come to loose it, especially if the motion of it bee, as he supposeth. For, first that moved directly before Saturne: Saturne, when his retrograde motion is finisht, turnes one way, & that, as hee conjectures another for example

```
      *    * *       *    * *
      C    B A       C    A B
         obs. 2nd        obs. 1st
```

A. Saturne

B. his satelles: At the first observation on the right hand; at the 2d, come about towards the left. Now when the retrograde motion is spent hee supposeth they may move thus. That is saturne downewards towards *B*. &

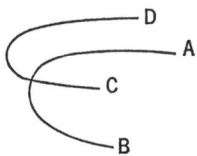

that upwards, towards *D*. For his part, for the little time hee observed it, hee conjectured it a planet & noe Satelles; because its motion did not at all agree wth that of the Satelles; neither did it move about Saturne, butt from it in a direct line, & something swifter. Soe that hee observd some 8 minutes difference in the distance.

This is what concernes this new Starre; of wch I shall give you a clearer account, as I heare farther. For new pieces wee have [not] any that I know wch concerne your inclinations. In Italy Sigre Montanari is said to have putt out his observations about the stelle fisse,[4] & Redi to have finisht his historia degli Animali chi nascono dalle Piante.[5] Pere Pardies, who is professor here in the Colledge of Clermont, & whose small treatise about locall motion hath beene translated into english,[6] hath a mind to putt out a second part, wch hee tells mee will bee farre more Physicall & curious, & wherin hee will demonstrate severall propositions concerning sound, & light, & the descent of heavy bodies; in a manner wch none yet hath thought upon. Hee seemes to bee very fond upon this treatise; the materialls of wch hee saith hee hath already collected, & only wants some little order & digestion, wch hee is now giving it. Besides hee hath another curiosity wch may bee said in a matter [*sic*] to bee quite finisht. Hee intends to project the spheare of fixt starres in 6 mappes: they are already done excepting only some of the Constellations in Southerne latitude, whose right ascensions hee must calculate, butt that hee saith will quickly bee done.[7] The maine Obstacle is, that Pailly[8] who hee intends shall grave them because hee is very able is sick. & till hee recovers, hee cannot proceed butt his distemper is butt a feavour wch hee hopes may quickly come to a crisis. There is a gentleman here, one Monsr Garibal,[9] desires to know whether that Treatise of Kinkhuysen wch the Transactions say is translated into latine bee extant for hee would faine have it[10] this same gentleman tells mee, hee hath one volume of our Transactions translated into latine it is that of anno 1669. Hee saith they have not translated the former yeares. Monsr Justel hath received a letter from you[11] wherein you tell him: you have sent him a Pacquet wch is addrest to Calais to Monsieur Pothou, God knowes whether it will not miscarry if it bee soe addresst. Monsieur Justel writes his letters cruelly in hast wch sometimes causeth mistakes when you send any other Pacquet addresse it

            a Monsieur
            Monsieur Ponthon Marchand
            a Calais

Yesterday my Ld Gray[12] went from hence I gave him a pacquet for you wch Monsieur Justel prayed mee to send you. Pray my humblest Respects to the Bishop of Sarisbury if hee bee in towne to Mr Surveyour[13] to Dr Wallis & Mr Hooke. Butt I must not forgett one who is neare to you & whom I instantly Honour Mr Boyle whose hands I kisse and Rest

most affectionately yours
Francis Vernon

NOTES

1 It is unlikely that the English could have heard as yet of Cassini's discovery of the satellite Japet, made in mid-October (see Letter 1848). Huygens only imparted the discovery (of whose reality he was still dubious) to his brother Constantijn on 4 December, N.S.
2 See Letter 1807, note 1.
3 Approximately, RA 23h 15', decl. 8° 30' S. (1950); it is thus slightly south of the ecliptic.
4 See Letter 1805, note 4.
5 Redi did not in fact publish any "History of Animals generated in Plants." His study of parasites in animals appeared in 1684.
6 See Letter 1744, note; and, for the new work, Letter 1859.
7 I. G. Pardies's *Globi coelestis in tabulas planas redacti descriptio...Opus posthumum* (Paris, 1674) was published in Latin and French by P. de Fontenay, S.J. The plates were engraved by Guillaume Vallet; the portrait of the Duke of Brunswick (to whom Pardies dedicated the atlas) was painted by Michelin and engraved by Nanteuil.
8 Possibly Pierre Paillet or Palliot (1608–98), but he seems to have moved already from Paris to Dijon.
9 Probably this was the Mr. de Garibal of whom Pierre Petit wrote to Huygens in 1668 (*Œuvres Compèltes*, VI, 235), saying he was brother-in-law to N. G. de Lareynie, a *maître des requêtes*.
10 See *Phil. Trans.*, no. 49 (19 July 1669), 998; also Letter 1522, note 4 (Vol. VII), and the Introduction to Vol. V, xxv. The translation was never published.
11 This is now missing.
12 It is impossible to be positive, but it seems likely that the title might be applied to Thomas Grey (1654–1720), son of the Earl of Stamford; he became a politician and (in 1708) F.R.S.
13 Christopher Wren.

1831
Oldenburg to Flamsteed
25 November 1671

From the memorandum in Royal Society MS. F 1, no. 76

Rec. Nov. 24. 71.
Answ. both these letters Nov. 25. 71.

NOTE

Reply to Letters 1824 and 1826.

1832
Oldenburg to Wallis
26 November 1671

Wallis's Letter 1828 was, according to Oldenburg's endorsement, received on 24 November and answered on the twenty-sixth.

1833
Wallis to Oldenburg
27 November 1671

From the original in Royal Society MS. W 1, no. 133

Oxford November 27. 1671.

Sir,

Since I sent away my last,[1] I have received from Dr. Pocock the inclosed Paper in Arabick & (not Latine, but) English, wch therefore (because you desire it for a forraigner) I have in two blank pages, put into Latine.[2]

He tells mee that Mr. John Grave's Abulfeda, (much inferiour to those copies of his,) Mr. Clark had the use of, as allso of that at Cambridge which had been Erpenius's written (he thinks) by Erpenius own hand.³ That of Mr. John Grave, he supposeth is still in ye hands of his brother Dr. Thomas (not Edward) Grave, to whom, if you have occasion to send, it may be done by his brother Sr. Edward Grave, a Physician,⁴ about Henrietta Street in Covent-Garden. As to what I wrot on occasion of your Letter concerning Leibnitius, you may use your discretion.⁵ That (wch you conjecture, and not unlikely, may be his meaning,) yt Matter, wch when in Motion, is Body, should become, when at rest, but Voyd Space; seems hard: and though he should so distinguish ye words, I doubt the Thing will be ye same: & if, contrary to ye old opinion in appearance, he affirm a Vacuity, & mean nothing by it but Quiescent Matter, he will not be thought to overthrow their sentiments, who never denyed Quiescent Matter: but did allways allow this, even when they most denied Vacuity. So yt if you send him what I wrote last, you may adde this to it:⁶ sin forte velit, (quod insinuas,) Corpus, a Vacuo, eo tantum distingui, quod eadem Materia, quae, dum in Motu, Corpus erat, fiat, Quiete, Vacuum: Hoc durum dictu videtur: nec Vacuum negantibus adversatur. Quippe, qui hoc negant vel maxime, minime tamen negaverint Materiam Quiescentem: Sed, Spatium ea refertum, non Vacuum, sed Plenum vocant: Ut, de solo Nomine, non Re, sit controversum. I desired, in my last, that you would send, for Dr. Pocock, one of his Bookes to Mr. Vernon for Monsr Thevenot. You may intimate allso to Mr. Vernon, yt since they are so greedy of those books (as appears) at Paris; if hee think fit, some number of them (a dousen or twenty) may be sent him to put off to some Book-seller there at a price, but move it as from your self, or mee, not as from Dr. Pocock, who is loth to take ye confidence of giving him that trouble, unlesse he should intimate his willingnesse to undertake it. If ye Bishop of Oxford have not yet sent for his book, I suppose it is but his forgetfullness.⁷ For it was his own desire when he was here, to have that delivered him at London rather then at Oxford: &, if you think fit, you may send it to his lodgings in White-hall, & receive ye mony there. I had written thus far, when I received from Dr. Pocock the inclosed to Mr. Vernon, wch he desires you to transmit. You may to him allso present ye service of Sir

Yr humble servant
John Wallis

ADDRESS
For Mr. Henry Oldenburg
   at his house in the
   Palmal near
   St. James's
   London

NOTES

1 Letter 1828.
2 No doubt the sheet mentioned in Letter 1811, note 6.
3 See Letter 1828; Thomas Erpenius (or van Erpe, 1584–1624) was a Dutch orientalist, author of an Arabic grammar and Professor of Oriental Languages at Leiden from 1613.
4 Edward Greaves (1608–80), M.D. 1641, F.C.P. 1657, was physician to Charles II. He is somewhat dubiously said to have been created baronet in 1645.
5 See Letter 1815.
6 "If (as you hint) he perhaps means that a body is only distinguished from a vacuum by the fact that the same matter while in motion constitutes a body and when at rest a vacuum; this seems a hard saying, nor is it opposed to those who deny the vacuum. For indeed those who deny that most do not deny that matter may be at rest, but call that related space not a vacuum but a plenum; so that the dispute is about words only, not things."
7 See Letter 1815, note 1.

1834
Winthrop to Oldenburg
28 November 1671

This is mentioned in Oldenburg's reply of 18 March 1671/2. According to a note on the draft of Letter 1789 it was sent by John Hale.

1835

Flamsteed to Oldenburg

2 December 1671

From the original in Royal Society MS. F 1, no. 77
Partly printed in *Phil. Trans.*, no. 78 (18 December 1671), 3034

Derby Dec 2: 1671

Mr Oldenburge
Sr

I have yr last and cannot but returne yu all reall thanks for your constant favours, & Acknowledgements for ye good opinion yu are pleased to have of my slender tho tedious labors. Understanding yt yu would provide mee ye glasses I want I have desired my freind Mr Sargeant to deliver yu this which may informe yu yt Mr Collins to whom I had allso intimated my want of them[1] writes me word yt hee would procure them for mee I suppose yu understand so much & I hope betwixt yu both I shall have those I want good ones but not more then I need. I have last thursday night[2] (the onely cleare one of late yt hath blest us) observed Saturne with my 14 foot tube an aperture of $1\frac{1}{2}$ inch,[3] & an eye glasse yt drew two inches, hee appeared perfectly round free from ye perewigge of raies & colours, but no Anses to be seene. My worthy & generous freind Mr Townley in his last to mee writes Pray continue yr observations of Saturn, I onely looked at him one night and could hardlie distinguish his line of ye ansulae, but plainly saw a darke line through him neare his upper part. this apparently, yt is inverted, &c. His letter beares date Nov: 20: 71: ye observation I sent yu[4] was made October 12 & within a weeke or two after I had frequently the same appearance tho with a wider aperture then I use at present. I have not seene Hugenius his peece, so am no farther acquainted with his Systeme then by what I find of it in Fabris easie Opticks.[5] Not findeing yt Mr Townlys Micrometer is so devised as to be convenient for some observations I intend I have devised a new one in which I can have thread sights or other as I please & parallell threads disposed perpendicular to ye ostensors like a kind of rete which is very convenient;[6] & I hope by it to escape some inconveniences & faults which in ye use of our micrometer at present wee frequently undergoe & commit; but I may not at present impart it till I have found a smith yt can make mee neat screws, & tried ye successe of my devise, which if I cannot doe in a convenient time I will send a scheme of it to yu & Mr Hooke for yr opinions of my contrivance, as I shall allso to Mr Townly, to whom I am much engaged, ere long: I thanke yu for what yu informed mee concerneing Hevelius his Machina, I would gladly heare whether Tychoes workes, which I heard were to be printed at Amsterdam last yeare, goe on with like successe.⁷ Yu will oblige me by informeing what yu hear of them I have no more at present but to wish that my future endeavours may better deserve the thanke you returne mee from ye illustrious Society then those contracted ones did, & to assure yu that it shall be my endeavour they may & that I may some way [cor]respond [to] ye good opinion yu [are] pleasd to have & the courtesies yu have showed to Sr

Your obliged servant
John Flamsteed

I shall ere long send yu my calculations of ye moons residuall transits over ye Pleiades which I am readie to dispatch as soone as I have another cleare night *J:F:*

ADDRESS

To Mr Henry Oldenburge
Esq, at his house in the
Middle of ye Pell mell
in St James's Westminster
these
    present

NOTES

Reply to Letter 1831.
1 See Flamsteed to Collins, 1 August 1671 (Rigaud, II, 120–21).
2 November 30.
3 Hence the magnification would be about 80 diameters.
4 In Letter 1826.
5 Huygens' *Systema Saturnium* (The Hague, 1659) was criticiced by Honoré Fabri in *Brevis annotatio in systema Saturnium Christiani Eugenii* (Rome, 1660); Fabri's *Synopsis optica* (Lyons, 1667) contains a further long discussion, pp. 49–59 (Prop. xxiv).
6 For Towneley's micrometer, see Vol. III, pp. 436–39, and the figure in *Phil. Trans.*, no. 29 (11 November 1667). The use of threads (hairs) for sighting was already envisaged by Towneley in place of metal pointers ("ostensors"). "Rete": net.
7 No such edition is recorded; the last was of 1648.

1836
Oldenburg to Vernon
4 December 1671
From the memorandum in Royal Society MS. V, no. 18

Answ. Decemb. 4. 71. yt his letter shall be produc'd before ye Society; yt I lay hold on his promise of further information: yt Cassini by reason of his skil and acc[uracy] deserves to be a member of all ye best ph[ilosophicall] Academies. yt Sr. Malpighi sent a MS. de Anatome plantarum exc[ellently] written:¹ yt I will send him *Grew* of yesame subject,² and Pococks Philosophus Autodidactus for Thevenot;³ yt I shall be glad to see Pardies of sound and light; and his projections of fixt stars; yt I send him N. 77. of Transactions⁴ to shew Flamsteds pred[iction] to Cassini; of Witsen's Archit. Navalis;⁵ of Charleton de Scorbuto;⁶ of Willis's books in ye presse; of Sr S. Moreland's tromp;⁷ yt hee would tell me, what animals dissected, and wt ye measure of ye Earth is; yt I will inquire, whether Kinkhuysen be actually done in Latin; and yt A. 1669 of ye Transact. is very falsely done.

NOTES

Reply to Letter 1830. There is no record of the reading of Vernon's letter.
1 See Letter 1805, read on 7 December.
2 See Letter 1720, note 3.
3 Edward Pocock, *Abu Bakr ibn Al Tufail, Al Ishbili. Philosophus autodidactus sive epistola Abi Jaafar Ebn Tophail... in linguam latinam versus ab E. Pocockio* (London, 1671).
4 Dated 20 November 1671.
5 Nicolaas Witsen, *Aeloude en hedendaegsche Scheeps-bouw en Bestier* (Amsterdam, 1671); there is a long account of this book in the issue of *Phil. Trans.* just noted, pp. 3006–12. See also Letter 1839.
6 See Letter 1810, note 4.
7 About this time Sir Samuel Morland published *Tuba Stentoro-phonica. An Instrument of excellent Use as well at Sea as Land* (London, 1671); see *Phil. Trans.*, no. 79 (22 January 1671/2), 3056–58, and Letter 1648 (Vol. VII).

1837

Oldenburg to Wallis

5 December 1671

Wallis's Letter 1833 was received on the twenty-eighth and answered on 5 December.

1838

Kirkby to Oldenburg

9 December 1671

From the original in Royal Society MS. K, no. 8
Partially printed in *Phil. Trans.*, no. 83 (20 May 1672), 4069–70

Dantzigk 19 December 71 SN

Sr,

If mine 26 7ber past came [safe] you would know that your welcome Letter of ye 29th May was not then come to mine, (nor did it till about 3 weekes agoe;) Though by the Philo. Trans. I could perceive you had Received mine,[1] and by Mention there made could judge of your indulging Kindeness for which my thankes are due, yett would crave your waveing the name of your humble servant, who encouraged by: is emboldened once more to trouble, you, with a relation as true as to mee strange; for to bee more certaine I made a Jorney purposely to the place: and This I must Beg of you to Comunicate to Mr Boijle to whom I have formerly Mentioned Something of it—

Neare a Small Village called Tuckum $2\frac{1}{8}$ German miles distant from this cittij Westward; There is an inland Sea (made by the Conjunction of 3 Rivoletts, Some Springs from the adjoineing scarce to bee accounted Hills & the Descending Raine & Snow water) of about halfe a german mile Long & $\frac{1}{8}$ broade, it stretcheth NWN. & SSW. about the middle of the Bow on the East Side it dischargeth it selfe with a pretty streame as it also doth in another place more Southerly; the Soyle of The grounde all Rounde about Seemes to bee sand mixt with claij, its shore Generally

Sandij as its bottom alsoe; its Depth at Deepest 4 most part 1 & ⅓ fathom 'tis stored with Delicate & wholesome fish as pearch Roche² Eels &c & famed for a Small fish (much esteemed here and not much unlike a pearch onely it is not soe party coulored & hath a Larger head proportionable to its body) called cole pearch; The water sweete & wholesome: yett in the 3 monthes of June July & August is yearelij Dureing the Dry weather rendred greene in the middle with an hairij efflorescence (occasioned as I suppose by the fermenting water at that Season becomeing more Stagnant the Supplyes to it beeing less:) which greene substance beeing by a Violent winde forced to the shore, and with the water drunke by any Cattell greate or small dog or poultrij causeth certaine & sudden Death: though at the time that a knoweing & ingenious person (who acquainted mee first with it) did see three dogs poijsoned with it, the horses that were ridden into the water beyond where this greene substance floted: Drunke without any Danger; yea Dureing that Season the water in The Streames that flow from it, are wholesome; I dare not undertake to give you my opinion what this greene Substance may bee, but if you Desire it: the next season, God spareing life, shall endeavour to procure some of it, and make it undergo a chijmicall analysin; One thing more I must ad; (which confirmes the Conjectures that Amber procedes from a Bijtuminous fluid Substance endurated by the operation of aqu-aereall particles upon it) That the cheife Fisher tolde mee in fishing 2 or 3 yeares agoe the Nett brought up with it a considerable Large piece of white amber, which as a Raretij hee presented to one of The chief Fathers of the Olive's Abbij to which the Sea belongs; and which cannot bee suspected to be a product of the Ocean, it lying so high, and remote at least 3 German miles distant from the Ocean; and since also the neighbouring Woods, [contain] none such as are highly Resinous Trees, cannot be reasonably said to furnish such Amber; that Conjecture may receive some Confirmation from this Account [*paper torn*] Rivolets it is compounded of [*torn*]³ here Dwells in this Cittij a meere [*torn*] requisite will needs pretend to make [*torn*] nes than any yett made, but he wants good glass and encouragement; have [*torn*] lately to any certaintij in this arte his knowledge beeing the product of his own [*torn* con]tinued endeavours; I am resolved to try what he can doe; if you would bee pleased to procure for mee halfe a dozen plates of best English glass fitt to make Glasses & Microscopes; upon Conveyance whereof to Mr. Samuell Lee⁴ hee will pay the Costs and take care to send them mee—

Monsr Hevelius presenteth you with his best respects hath received your Late Letters⁵ & will suddenly write answere; hee Desires you to gather up for him Monsr Cassini printed Letters Concerneing his arte as also all things that are now pertaineing to it hee will gladly pay for them; but hath noe Convenience to procure them here and The French Vertuosi seeme not willing to Comunicate to him as hee judges haveing writt himselfe to Monsr Cassini for them but Receives noe answere This from him; and now I judge it time to Beg your pardon for beeing soe Tedious and Remaine

Sr, your humble servant
Chri Kirkbij

I pray if you chance to meete with Colonel Kirkbij⁶ tell him I am well; but may dye before gett one Line from him. Adieu. The inclosed to Ox[ford] pray send forward per post.⁷

ADDRESS
>   Monsieur
> Monsieur Grubendol
>   a
>   Londres
> per post Franco Anvers

NOTES

The top of the sheet is torn, evidently in opening, and a number of words in the penultimate paragraph are thus irretrievably lost. The bottom of the sheet is also partly torn away, evidently later, as it is partly contained in the early eighteenth century copy in Royal Society Letter Book Supplement V, 281–84; this however omits some sentences and paraphrases others. We have included all Kirkby's own text as far as it survives.

1 Letter 1664 in Vol. VII; in *Phil. Trans.*, no. 71 (22 May 1671), 2158–59, are two observations sent by Kirkby. The earlier letter of 26 September is lost.
2 Perch, roach. The lake, now called Jeziorny Tuchomskie, is about 22 km. NW of Danzig (about 3 German miles).
3 The printed version reads here, "that conjecture, which imports that Amber is a bituminous fluid substance, hardned by the operations of the aqu-aerial particles upon it, may receive some confirmation from this account"; but Kirkby's original was heavily edited by Oldenburg.
4 The merchant mentioned in Letter 1709.
5 Presumably Letter 1817 is meant; Hevelius did not write until February 1671/2.
6 See Letter 1664, note 9 (Vol. VII).
7 Oldenburg's endorsement indicates that this was a letter for "Mr George Hickes fellow of Lincoln Coll. in Oxford," and that he forwarded it on 2 January 1671/2.

1839
Nicolaas Witsen to Oldenburg
10 December 1671
From the original in Royal Society MS. W 3, no. 51

Viro doctissimo et delectissimo
D. Henrico Oldenburg
S.P.D.
Nicolaus Witsen

Vir Clarissime

Ut Steni promissim,[1] mitto vobis volumen istud cujus mentionem in meis litteris feci de insula sejlon nuperrime hic editum,[2] cui addidi alphabetum Moscoviticum una cum figura magnae urbis Novogardicae, olim a me in Russia ad vivum depicta, nunquam ut credo a vobis visa. Rogo ut boni consulas meam audaciam et librum in observantiae testimonium, grati animi et amicitiae tesseram accipias. caeterum si qua in re vobis inservire possim rogo ut mandes. vale dabam Amstelodami anno MDCLXXI die XX decembris

P.S. brevi vobis mittam varias figuras anatomicas johan. Swammerdam de bombycibus apum genitalibis etc.

TRANSLATION

Nicolaas Witsen sends many greetings to the very learned and distinguished Mr. Henry Oldenburg

Famous Sir,

As I promised Steno,[1] I send you that volume recently printed here about the island Ceylon which I mentioned in my letter,[2] to which I have added the Russian alphabet together with a sketch of the great city of Novgorod made by me years ago just as it was, and never seen by you, I believe. I beg you to take my boldness in good part and to accept the book as a testimony of my regard and a token of my gratitude and friendship. Moreover if I can serve you in any way, command me, I beg you. Farewell. Amsterdam, 20 December 1671.

P.S. I shall soon send you the various anatomical sketches made by Jan Swammerdam, of the silkworm, the reproductive system of the bee, etc.

NOTES

Nicolaas Witsen (1641–1717) visited England with his father, who was sent on a diplomatic mission from Holland to Cromwell. He made another visit in 1668. Meanwhile he had studied at Leiden, reading law with Oldenburg's nephew Coccejus. In 1664–65 he traveled to Russia, Switzerland, France, and Italy. In 1671 at Amsterdam he published *Aeloude en hedendaegsche Scheeps-bouw en Bestier*, a beautiful book with a long notice in *Phil. Trans.*, no. 77 (20 November 1671), 3006–12. He was later burgomaster of Amsterdam and involved in the English revolution of 1668–89.

1 The reference to Steno (if that is the word) is inexplicable.
2 Philippus Baldaeus, *Naauwkeurige beschryvinge van Malabar en Choromandel, der zelver aangrenzende ryken, en het machtige cyland Ceylon* (Amsterdam, 1672). There is an account of this book in *Phil. Trans.*, no. 80 (19 February 1671/2), 3088–94.
3 The further entomological researches of Jan Swammerdam (Vol. VII, Letter 1537, note 9), after his book of 1669, were with the exception of his monograph on the mayfly (*Ephemeri vita*, Amsterdam, 1675) published only long after by Herman Boerhaave in the *Bybel der Natuure* (Leiden, 1737–38.) Moreover, Swammerdam did not first appear before the Royal Society as an entomologist but as a student of human anatomy, as will be seen below.

1840
Oldenburg to Vernon
11 December 1671

From the memorandum in Royal Society MS. V, no. 18

Dec. 11. writ to him again; and sent Pococks letter, and ye Society's being pleas'd wth his communications of ph[ilosophical] occurr[ences].

NOTE

Second reply to Letter 1830.

1841
Oldenburg to Flamsteed
12 December 1671

From the memorandum in Royal Society MS. F 1, no. 77

Rec. Dec. 9. 71.
Ans. Dec. 12. and sent N. 77. and Vernons acct of ye new planet.[1]

NOTES

Reply to Letter 1835. Probably Oldenburg also sent Flamsteed the red glasses he had requested, and offered him the loan of Huygens' *Systema Saturnium*.
1 See Letter 1830.

1842
Oldenburg to Malpighi
14 December 1671

From the copy in Bologna MS. 2085, VII, ff. 6–7
Partly printed in *Opera omnia*, I, Appendix, p. 14

Celeberrimo Viro
Domino Marcello Malpighio Philo. et Med. Bonon.
Henr. Oldenburg S.

Scriptum illud tuum de Anatome Plantarum, Vir Clarissime, quod Amplissimo Regis nostri apud Venetos[1] Mandatario huc transmittendum commendaveras, rite mihi traditum, tuoque nomine Societati Regiae caetum publicum celebranti exhibitum fuit.[2] Cum Illa partem eius sibi praelegendam iussisset, indeque argumenti intellexisset dignitatem et momentum, protinus secum reputavit, altioris indaginis rem esse, quam quae publica eiusmodi et festina praelectione pro merito expendi posset. Consultum proinde iudicavit, more suo uti et Exercitationem hanc tuam Sociorum suorum nonnullis, talium imprimis rerum studiosis, et gnaris, privatim per otium evolvendam atque excutiendam committere. Quo reliqua facta, mox in mandatis mihi dedere, ut, dum eruditi illi Viri Commentationem hanc tuam enucleatum irent ego sine mora tibi significarem, permagna se animorum lubentia munus hoc tuum Philosophicum esse amplexatos, daturosque operam, ut magis, magisque prolixam suam in te benevolentiam, paremque de egregijs tuis studijs existimationem persentiscas. Etenim abunde iam palam fecisti (quod prona mente agnoscimus) dignum te esse, qui prima inter rite philosophantes subsellia occupes, quique reconditioribus Naturae penetralibus rimandis aetatem absumas. Ea sane quae hactenus e scientiae tuae penu deprompsisti, talem jure suo inter doctos plausum meruere, ut animus inde sumere omnino possis meditationes, et studia tua, et hanc imprimis de Plantis Diatribam, citra haesitationem illam, quae prae se fert epistola tua provehendi.

Quamprimum Socij illi nostri, quibus id pensi datum Anatomen tuam sub examen revocandi,[3] suam de ea sententiam exposuerint, officio meo nequaquam deero, eam Tibi sine fuco, ut postulas, perscribendi. Hoc interim celare te nolim Vir Praestantissime, quemdam e Societate nostra Virum Medicum idem argumentum tractandum suscepisse, quinimo ea ipsa hora (quod forte miraberis) qua tuum a me scriptum proferebatur, libellum suum sermone Anglico iam editum laudatae societati exhibuisse:[4] in quo *Plantarum Anatomen* tum ab ipso arcessit semine, tum singulis earum partibus earumque vegetandi ratione consideratis, cum semine claudit.

Animus certe est, prima quaque occasione hunc tibi Tractatulum nave, Liburnam velificatura transmittere; cuius interpretem Anglicum te in Urbe vestra haud difficulter nacturum confido. Mihi certe persuasissimum, binas has Exercitationes, utut discrepanti methodo elaboratas, eum apud Philosophos sagaciores locum esse inventuras, ut uberem ex inde Vegetationis argumento Lucem esse illatam sint existimaturi, uberioremque adhuc illatum iri, si et Tu, et concivis hic noster certatim porro hanc materiam, eadem, qua caepistis cura, excolere pergatis, aliisque viris solertibus hoc ipso ansam praebeatis, sua quoque meditamenta et symbola in rem eandem conferendi. Indefesso igitur studio Telam hanc eximiam pertexe, et Nostrates Philosophos Tibi studiosissimos crede. Vale. Dabam Londini d. 14. Decemb. 1671.

TRANSLATION

Henry Oldenburg greets the very celebrated Mr. Marcello Malpighi, Philosopher and Physician of Bologna

That essay of yours on the anatomy of plants that you entrusted to our King's very worthy representative at Venice[1] for conveyance hither, famous Sir, was safely delivered to me and presented on your behalf to the Royal Society at its ordinary meeting.[2] When the Society had given order that a part of it be read aloud and thence perceived the dignity and importance of its argument, it immediately reflected that the merits of the essay demanded a more searching examination than could be given it at an open meeting of that kind after a hasty perusal. Hence the Society judged it prudent to follow its custom and refer your essay to some of its Fellows for private study and examination at leisure, especially to those who are attentive to and skilled in such matters. When the rest of the business had been done I was at once instructed that while these learned persons were penetrating to the bottom of this exacting study of yours, I should let you know without delay that the Society had accepted your philosophical present with great intellectual satisfaction and that it would make every effort that you should be more and more sensible of the Society's warm goodwill towards you and its like estimation of your outstanding researches. You have made it abundantly clear to all that (as we freely acknowledge) you are worthy of occupying the first place in the ranks of those who philosophize correctly, and that you spend your life in disclosing the most intimate of Nature's secrets. What you have hitherto taken out from your store of knowledge surely deserves such applause from the world of learning that you can quite make up your mind to extend your meditations and studies, especially this dissertation on plants, overcoming the hesitation that your letter reveals.

As soon as those of our Fellows to whom your *Anatomy* was given for consideration shall have declared their opinion of it,[3] I shall not fail in my duty to transcribe it for you without dissimulation, as you request. Meanwhile I could not conceal from you, excellent Sir, that a certain physician in our Society has taken the discussion of the same problem upon himself, and indeed in that very same hour at which your paper was laid before the Society by myself (you will perhaps be amazed at this) a little treatise in English already published by this man was presented to it.[4] In this he traces the anatomy of plants from the very seed, and having considered their individual parts and their manner of growth he concludes with the seed.

I certainly intend to send this little treatise to you by the first convenient opportunity of a vessel sailing for Livorno, for I am confident that in your city you will easily meet with someone to interpret the English. I am absolutely sure that these two essays, though developed along different lines, will have the same place in the minds of the wiser philosophers so that they may be thought of as throwing a bright illumination on the subject of plants, and a still brighter one will be shed if you and our fellow-citizen here will continue to work on this topic with the same diligence as at the beginning; and you will also by so doing furnish an occasion for other skilful persons to bring out their ideas and contributions upon the same theme too. Accordingly, you should weave this exceptional fabric with tireless zeal, believing that our philosophers are most zealous on your behalf. Farewell. London, 14 December 1671.

NOTES

Reply to Letter 1805.
1 Dodington
2 On 7 December 1671.
3 Part of Malpighi's work was actually read to the Society on 21 December 1671, when it was given to Goddard for consideration, to be passed on to Hooke.
4 Grew; for the book, see Letter 1720, note 3.

1843
Sluse to Oldenburg
17 December 1671

From the original in Royal Society MS. S 1, no. 74
Partly printed in *Phil. Trans.*, no. 97 (6 October 1673), 6123–26
Printed in Boncompagni, pp. 668–73

Nobilissimo et Clarissimo Viro
D. Henrico Oldenburg Societatis Regiae Secretario
Renatus Franciscus Slusius Salutem

Antequam ad literas tuas XXII mensis elapsi datas respondeam, officii mei ratio postulat hoc anni novi principio, ut faustum illum ac felicem cum longa similium serie, Tibi, Vir Nobilissime, ac Illustrissimae Societati et ὄντως βασιλικῇ, apprecer, quo ea quae felicibus adeo auspiciis coepta sunt, porro prosequi, ac tandem, magno reipublicae literariae emolumento ad exitum perducere Vobis liceat.

Literas vero tuas quod attinet, gratias primum habeo maximas, pro ijs quae solita humanitate voluisti. Caeterum a Clarissimo Hugenio nihil adhuc accepi, alijs, ut existimo, studijs occupato. quoniam autem Tu, Vir

Clarissime, videri vis meas esse aliquid putare nugas, accipe quae circa Alhazeni Problema, curis secundis, meditatus sum.

Datus sit circulus, cujus centrum A: puncta data sint D et d. Supponatur factum quod quaeritur, sitque radius incidens DE, reflexus Ed; et ex

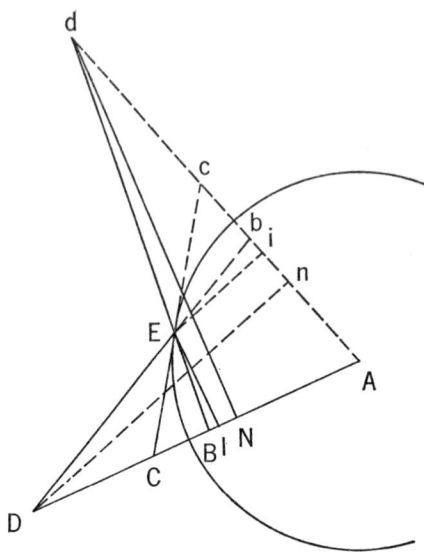

puncto reflexionis E cadat in junctam DA normalis EI, et in eandem ex d normalis dN, occurrantque eidem tangens EC et radius dE productus in B.

Sit nunc $DA = z$. $AI = a$. $NA = n$. $EI = e$. $dN = b$. $BA = y$. $AE = q$. $CA = x$. Igitur cum anguli DEC, CEB, sint aequales, et angulus CEA rectus, ex hypothesi, erunt tres DA, CA, BA, harmonice proportionales (hoc enim facile ostenditur). erit itaque ut DA ad BA ita DC ad CB. Sive in terminis analyticis, $z:y = z-x:x-y$, et $2zy-xy = zx$ sive $\frac{2zy}{z+y} = x$.

Cum autem rectangulum CAI, sive xa sit aequale quadrato AE sive qq, erit $x = \frac{qq}{a}$, et per consequens $\frac{2zy}{z+y} = \frac{qq}{a}$ sive $\frac{zqq}{2za-qq} = y$. Porro est ut dN ad EI, ita NB ad IB, sive $b:e = y-n:y-a$.

Itaque $ye-ne = yb-ba$. et $y = \frac{ba-ne}{b-e}$. Igitur

$\frac{zqq}{2za-qq} = \frac{ba-ne}{b-e}$ sive $2zbaa-2znae-qqba+qqne = bzqq-zqqe$. Quae aequatio est ad hyperbolam circa asymptotos, cujus constructio cum circulo dato,

Problemati satisfacit. Cum vero, ob circulum, sit $qq = aa+ee$, si loco $2bzaa$ ponatur ejus valor $2bzqq - 2bzee$, habebitur alia pariter ad hyperbolam circa asymptotos, $bzqq - 2bzee - 2znae - qqba + qqne = -zqqe$; et hac methodo, atque illa, quam in libello nostro de Analysi[1] exposuimus, prodibunt infinitae aequationes ad hyperbolas et ellipses, quae cum circulo dato problema absolvent. nisi quod effectiones plaerunque intricatiores evadant, quam ut operae precium sit illas aggredi. Construi tamen poterunt eo modo, quo usi sumus in Ellipsi, ejusdem libelli nostri p. 62.

Retulimus, ut vides, calculi nostri summam, ad lineam DA, sed satis animadvertis, non majori difficultate referri potuisse ad dA (quae pariter data est) ductis scilicet lineis, quas in Schemate punctis adumbravimus. Verum novo calculi labore non est opus. Si enim rectae dA ejusque partibus, eosdem ac prius terminos analyticas adhibeas; hoc est, si ipsam dA facias aequalem z, $Dn = b$, $nA = n$, $Ai = a$, $Ei = e$ &c prodibit eadem aequatio quae prius; et infinitas alias hyperbolas et ellipses obtinebis, quae cum circulo dato Problemati satisfacient.

φορτικὸς essem, si singulos casus prosequi vellem, cum illorum aequationes sola signorum $+$ et $-$ variationes discernantur. Unum tamen excipio, nimirum cum angulus dAD est rectus; ejus enim aequatio habetur, expunctis a priori aequatione partibus, in quibus n (quae in nihilum abit) invenitur: nempe haec $2zbaa - qqba = bzqq - zqqe$, vel (pro $2zbaa$ posito ejus valore) $zbqq - qqba = 2zbee - zqqe$. Sed animadvertendum est, quod, licet referendo analysin ad rectam DA, statim sese offerant in aequatione duae Hyperbolae; et aliae totidem a prioribus diversae, cum refertur ad rectam dA; easdem tamen omnino parabolas haberi, ad utramvis rectarum dA vel DA referatur analysis: cujus rei ratio levi consideratione tibi occurret.[2]

Patere nunc, Vir Clarissime, ut superiorem analysin omnibus, quae circa speculorum sphaericorum reflexionem proponi solent Proplematibus applicem, novo facto schemate.

Sit igitur, ut prius, circulus cujus centrum A punctum D datum et ab eo radius incidens DE, cujus reflexus sit EQ; juncta DA, ducatur ad illam tangens EC, et normalis EI; et producatur ad eandem, recta QEB. Denominentur partes ut prius, $DA = z$. $CA = x$. $AE = q$. $BA = y$. $AI = a$. $IE = e$. Igitur propter tres DA, CA, BA, harmonice proportionales, et tres CA, AE, AI, Geometrice, semper habebitur aequatio $y = \dfrac{zqq}{2za - qq}$, in quodcumque circuli punctum cadat radius DE. Itaque si quaeratur punctum E, in quod si radius DE incidat, reflectatur παραλλήλως

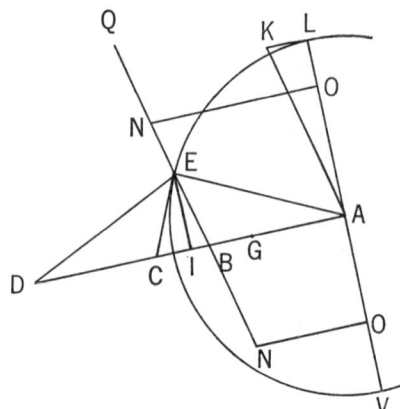

diametro LAV normali ad DA; reflexus QE productus transibit per I, ut patet, et I ac B coincident. Igitur $a = y = \dfrac{zqq}{2za-qq}$, sive $aa - \dfrac{\frac{1}{2}qqa}{z} = \frac{1}{2}qq$, et problema per plana solvetur.

Si quaeratur punctum, a quo radius reflectatur parallelus alteri cuilibet lineae, ut AK (ducta ex centro A;) ducatur ad illam ex puncto L, tangens $KL = d$. evidens est, triangula ALK, EIB, fore similia, cum omnia latera unius parallela sint lateribus alterius &c. Itaque AL ad LK ut EI ad IB, sive $q:d = e:a-y$. et $\dfrac{qa-de}{q} = y = \dfrac{zqq}{2za-qq}$. et $zq^3 = 2qzaa - 2zdae - q^3a - qqde$. Sive pro aa posito $qq-ee$. $zq^3 = 2zq^3 - 2zqee - 2zdae - q^3a + qqde$. Utraque autem aequatio est ad hyperbolam circa Asymptotos, quae cum circulo dato Problema absolvit.

Proponatur nunc efficere, ut radius reflexus transeat per datum punctum N (ut in Problemate Alhazeni) vel ut productus versus punctum reflexionis E, occurat dato puncto N. Ex N cadat in AL normalis $NO = n$, sitque $AO = b$. Patet esse ut AO, ad differentiam ipsarum ON, AB, ita EI ad IB. hoc est, $b : n-y = e : a-y$, vel $b : y-n = e : a-y$. Igitur $\dfrac{ba-ne}{b-e} = y = \dfrac{zqq}{2za-qq}$. Unde $2zbaa - 2znae - qqba + qqne = bzqq - zqqe$, nimirum illa ipsa aequatio Problematis Alhazeniani quam supra invenimus. Vel 2do casu $\dfrac{ba+ne}{b+e} = y = \dfrac{zqq}{2za-qq}$ sive $2zbaa + 2znae - qqba - qqne = zbqq + zqqe$: de quibus aequationibus plura non addo, cum vel nimia sint fortasse quae supra diximus.

Atque haec sunt Problemata, quae circa punctum reflexionis proponi solent; in quibus tamen finitam puncti D dati distantiam supposuimus. Sed facilior erit Analysis, si supponamus infinitam. Secta enim CA bifariam in G, constat ex proprietate trium DA, CA, BA, harmonice proportionalium, tres DG, CG, BG, fore geometrice proportionales, supposita quacumque puncti D distantia. Itaque si supponatur infinita, BG abibit in nihilum, et punctum B cum puncto G coincidet. Igitur AB erit perpetuo aequalis BC; erit itaque $CA = 2y$, et rectangulum CAI aequale quadrato AE dabit in terminis analyticis $2ay = qq$, sive $y = \frac{qq}{2a}$; cumque distantia puncti D supponatur infinita, erit ED parallela AC. Itaque si quaeratur radius reflexus parallelus AL, quoniam eo casu a et y coincidunt erit $a = y = \frac{qq}{2a}$ sive $aa = \frac{1}{2}qq$.

Si quaeratur ut parallelus sit AK, erit rursus $q : d = e : a - y$. et $\frac{qa - de}{q} = y = \frac{qq}{2a}$. Sive $2qaa - 2dae = q^3$. Si petatur ut transeat per N, erit ut supra $\frac{ba + ne}{b + e} = y = \frac{qq}{2a}$ et $2baa \pm 2nae = bqq \pm qqe$. Quae aequationes sunt quoque ad hyperbolas circa asymptotos, nisi N punctum esse supponatur in AL: nam cum tunc n aveat in nihilum, sublatis ab aequatione partibus in quibus n continetur, residuae dant aequationem ad parabolam, ut supra quoque monuimus.

Non exspectas, Vir Clarissime, ut cum specula concava hactenus in exemplum adduxerim, nunc agam de convexis.[3] Scis enim eandem esse prorsus analysin, et aequationes sola signorum $+$ et $-$ variatione distingui. Scis parabolam vel ellipsin, quae uni satisfacit, satisfacere alteri; et si hyperbola in convexo Problema adsolvat, ejus oppositam paria facere in concavo. His itaque omissis, addo tantum eadem analysi haberi in speculis concavis focos et spatia, quae radii occupant in axe, data qualibet puncti lucentis distantia: sed mira facilitate cum radii supponuntur paralleli; quod tamen nonnullo circuitu a quibusdam demonstrari vidi. Nam in speculo concavo EE, cujus centrum A, si radius extremus reflecti intelligatur ad axem AR in B, ducta tangente EC, erit CB aequalis BA. Bisecetur semiaxis AR in Q; erit itaque Q focus et QB spatium quaesitum. Est autem QB dimidia CR (ob aequales AQ, QR, AB, BC) hoc est dimidia excessus secantis arcus ER supra sinum totum. Igitur si arcus ER sit exempli gratia grad. 9, erit AC 101246, et BQ $\frac{623}{100{,}000}$ ipsius AR. Sed

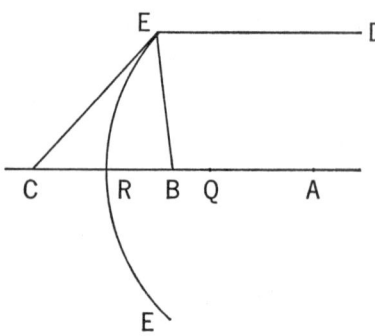

nimium te moror in tricis hisce Geometricis, quibus me defunctum existimabam, nisi quod occurrant saepe vel aliud agenti. Itaque si Deus vitam et otium dederit, hoc vere fortasse in publicam emittam mea de Problematum determinatione, περί μοναχοῦ⁴ λογοῦ de tangentibus curvarum μελετήματα. praesertim cum Clarissimus Riccius me moneat, a se, studijs alijs occupato, nihil expectandum esse; et nuper ἀπροσδοκήτως inciderim in methodum facillimam ea demonstrandi, quae longiore circuitu olim inveneram; utraque tamen via in brevissimam ac facillimam regulam desinente. Sed quid futurum sit θεῶν ἐν γούνασι κεῖται: ego enim Pyrrhoniano more hactenus οὐδεν ὁρίζω.

Experimentum Illustrissimi Boylij, cum cera ad aquae gravitatem arena vel plumbo adducta, saepe feci; non in aqua simplici tantum, sed etiam varijs salibus imbuta; ac deprehendi κοινῶς, globulum ascendere calore, mergi frigore: caeterum non adeo definitis ac spatio tam brevi repetitis vicibus. Accidere nihilominus potest, ut initio ludos similes exhibeat, bullularum causa, quae ferme invisibiles, ipsi adhaerent, eumque attollunt, et quibus expirantibus rursus mergitur. id enim mihi saepe compertum est.

Plures anni sunt ex quo ad solares maculas non respexi, Scheinerij diligentiae confisus cui nihil addi posse, cum Cartesio existimabam.⁵ Intelligo tamen ex tuis aliquid novi observatum fuisse: adeo verum est quod ait Seneca, verum naturam sacra sua non simul tradere. quid autem sit istud, fac me quaeso certiorem; hac tamen lege, si absque tuo incommodo fieri possit. Plurimam quoque ut a me salutem dicas rogo, Clarissimo Collinsio, a cujus humanitate, quando ita jubet, expectabo J. Wallisij τοῦ πάνυ tertiam partem de motu.

Curabo ut Bibliopolae nostri libros alios, quorum meministi, ex Hollandia petant; ibi enim eos inventum iri confido. magno sane eos videndi desiderio teneor; illum praesertim qui in Scorbuti caussas inquirit. Varia enim ac mira sunt hujus morbis, olim pene ignoti, nunc autem frequentissimi συμπτώματα,[6] quorum rationes a Viro Doctissimo post eximium Willisium scribente, libenter intelligam. qualia sunt, pulsus intermittens, adeo frequenter ut meminerim aegro (qui tamen lecto non detinebatur) id trium vel quatuor horarum spatio, plusquam quadringentis vicibus accidisse. Dolor sub sterno, non ille quidem valde acutus, sed pertinax, et qui mirum in modum aegros fatigat; quem (ut hoc obiter addam) externae applicationi aquae ex lumbricis terrestribus cum vini spiritu et absque eo distillatae ac frequenti usui interno spiritus salammoniaci tandem cessisse memini. Sed haec sunt alterius fori.

Spiritus hujus salammoniaci mentio in memoriam mihi revocat φαινόμενα duo non iniucunda, quae fortasse observasti. quod scilicet, quamvis coloris sit expers, si vino albo infundatur, illud extemplo grato rubore tingat: et quod cum spiritu salis culinarij mixtus, non mediocriter effervescat, (licet uterque volatilis sit) ac tandem exhalatione coaguletur in salem valde volatilem et οξύπικρον. Vale Vir Nobilissime meque, ut soles, ex asse tuum amare perge. Dabam Leodii VI Kal. Januarij Anno MDCLXXII [N.S.]

TRANSLATION

René François de Sluse greets the very noble and famous Mr. Henry Oldenburg, Secretary of the Royal Society

Before I answer your letter of the twenty-second of last month, the course of my duty requires me at the opening of this new year to wish for you, most noble Sir, and the illustrious and truly Royal Society, that it may be fortunate and happy, with a long series of similar years, so that you may be enabled to continue further those things that have been so auspiciously begun, and to bring them to a conclusion of great profit to the republic of learning.

As to your letter, in the first place I am most grateful for what your customary kindness led you to attempt. Further, I have as yet received nothing from the famous Huygens who is, as I suppose, intent on other studies. However, since you, Sir, seem to wish to think of my trifles as something, here are my second thoughts on the problem of Alhazen:

Let there be a circle given whose center is A; the given points are D and d [see the figure, page 402]. Let it be supposed that what is sought is accomplished, the incident ray being DE and the reflected ray Ed. Let the normal EI fall on DA joined from the point of reflexion E, and the normal dN upon DA from d; let the tangent EC and the ray dE produced to B also meet DA.

Now let $DA = z$; $AI = a$; $NA = n$; $EI = e$; $DN = b$; $BA = y$; $AE = q$; $CA = x$. Therefore, as the angles DEC, CEB are equal and the angle CEA is right, by hypothesis, the three lines DA, CA, BA are in harmonic proportion, as is easily proved. Thus $DA:BA = DC:CB$. Or in analytical terms $z:y = z-x:x-y$,

$$2zy - xy = zx, \text{ or } \frac{2zy}{z+y} = x.$$

However, as the rectangle CAI, or ax, is equal to AE^2 or q^2, $x = \frac{q^2}{a}$ and by consequence

$$\frac{2zy}{z+y} = \frac{q^2}{a} \text{ or } \frac{zq^2}{2za-q^2} = y.$$

Further, $dN:EI = NB:IB$, or $b:e = y-n:y-a$.

Thus $ye - ne = yb - ba$. And $y = \frac{ba-ne}{b-e}$. Therefore

$$\frac{zq^2}{2za-q^2} = \frac{ba-ne}{b-e}$$

or $2zba^2 - 2znae - q^2ba + q^2ne = bzq^2 - zq^2e$. This equation is that of the hyperbola upon the asymptotes, the construction of which with the given circle solves the problem. Since indeed, because of the circle, $q^2 = a^2 + e^2$, if instead of $2bza^2$ we put its value $2bzq^2 - 2bze^2$, we shall have another similar equation to the hyperbola upon the asymptotes, $bzq^2 - 2bze^2 - 2znae - q^2ba + q^2ne = -zq^2e$. By this method and that which we have expounded in our little book on analysis[1] an infinite number of equations to hyperbolas and ellipses are produced, which together with the given circle solve the problem; but some of them come out with complex powers so that it is not worth while to attack them. However, they can be constructed by the method used for constructing the ellipse on p. 62 of our little book.

As you see, we have referred the basis of our calculation to the line DA but you will notice clearly enough that we could with equal ease have chosen dA (which is also a given line) by drawing the lines which we have shown dotted in the figure. There is in fact no need for a fresh calculation. For if you apply the same analytical terms as before to dA and its divisions, that is, if you make dA itself equal to z, $Dn = b$, $nA = n$, $iA = a$, $Ei = e$, &c then the same equation will yield itself as before; and you will obtain an infinite number of other hyperbolas and ellipses which, with the given circle, solve the problem.

I should be tedious if I went on to develop individual cases, when their equations differ only by the variations in the signs plus and minus. But I make one exception, that is when the angle dAD is a right angle; for its equation is obtained by removing the terms from the first equation in which n (vanishing to nothing) is found; namely this,

$$2zba^2 - q^2ba = bzq^2 - zq^2e, \text{ or}$$

(substituting for $2bza^2$ its value), $zbq^2 - q^2ba = 2zbe^2 - zq^2e$. But it is to be observed that, although when referring the analysis to the straight line DA two hyperbolas immediately present themselves in the equation, and others quite different from these when the analysis is referred to dA, yet absolutely the same parabolas may be obtained by referring the analysis either to dA or to DA; the reason for this will appear to you upon a moment's reflection.[2]

Be patient now, famous Sir, while I apply the above analysis to all those problems that are usually propounded about reflection from spherical mirrors, first drawing a new figure.

Therefore, let there be as before a circle, center A, the given point D, and the incident ray from it DE, which is reflected to Q [see the figure, page 404]. Join DA, and draw to it the tangent EC and the normal EI, and QE produced to B. Let its parts be denominated as before, $DA = z$, $CA = x$, $AE = q$, $BA = y$, $AI = a$, $IE = e$. Therefore because the three lines DA, CA, and BA are in harmonic proportion, and the three lines CA, AE, and AI are in geometric proportion, on whatever point of the circle the ray DE falls, the equation obtains $y = \dfrac{zq^2}{2za - q^2}$. Thus, if the point E is sought such that when the ray DE strikes it, the ray may be reflected parallel to the diameter LAV normal to DA; the reflected ray QE produced will pass through I, as is obvious, and I and B coincide.

Therefore $a = y = \dfrac{zq^2}{2za - q^2}$, or $a^2 - \dfrac{\frac{1}{2}q^2 a}{z} = \frac{1}{2}q^2$, and the problem is solved by plane loci.

If the point from which the ray is reflected parallel to any other given line is sought, as to the line AK drawn from the center A, let the tangent $KL = d$ be drawn to it from the point L. It is obvious that the triangles ALK, EIB will be similar, as all the sides of one are parallel to sides of the other, &c. Thus $AL : LK = EI : IB$, or $q : d = e : a - y$, and $\dfrac{qa - de}{q} = y = \dfrac{zq^2}{2za - q^2}$. And $zq^3 = 2qza^2 - 2zdae - q^3 a - q^2 de$. Or, putting $(q^2 - e^2)$ for a^2, $zq^3 = 2zq^3 - 2zqe^2 - 2zdae - q^3 a + q^2 de$. Either equation is that of an hyperbola upon asymptotes, which with the given circle solves the problem.

It may now be proposed: construct the reflected ray so that it passes through the given point N (as in the Problem of Alhazen) or so that when produced on the other side of the point of reflection E it meets the given point N.

From N let the normal $NO = n$ fall upon AL, and let $AO = b$. It is clear that $AO : ON - AB = EI : IB$. That is, $b : n - y = e : a - y$, or, $b : y - n = e : a - y$. Therefore,

$$\dfrac{ba - ne}{b - e} = y = \dfrac{zq^2}{2za - q^2}. \text{ Whence,}$$

$2zba^2 - 2znae - q^2 ba + q^2 ne = bzq^2 - zq^2 e$, which is the very same equation as in the problem of Alhazen, which we discovered above. Or in the second case,

$\dfrac{ba + ne}{b + e} = y = \dfrac{zq^2}{2za - q^2}$, or $2zba^2 + 2znae - q^2 ba - q^2 ne = zbq^2 + zq^2 e$; I say nothing more about these equations, because I have perhaps already said too much above.

And these are the problems that are usually posed about the point of reflection, in which, however, we have supposed the point D to be at a finite distance. But the analysis would be easier if we suppose it to be infinite. For let CA be bisected at G; it follows from the property of harmonic proportionality between DA, CA, and BA that the three lines DG, CG, and BG will be in geometric proportion whatever distance be assumed for the point D. Thus if it is supposed to be infinite, BG vanishes to zero and the point B coincides with the point G. So AB is always equal to BC, $CA = 2y$, and the rectangle CAI equal to the square AE gives in analytical terms, $2ay = q^2$, or $y = \frac{q^2}{2a}$, and as the distance of the point D is supposed to be infinite, ED will be parallel to AC. Thus if the reflected ray parallel to AL is sought, since in that case a and y coincide, $a = y = \frac{q^2}{2a}$, or $a^2 = \frac{1}{2}q^2$. If it is to be parallel to AK, again

$$q : d = e : a - y \text{ and } \frac{qa - de}{q} = y = \frac{q^2}{2a}. \text{ Or } 2qa^2 - 2dae = q^3.$$

If it is demanded that it pass through N, as before

$$\frac{ba + ne}{b + e} = y = \frac{q^2}{2a}, \text{ and } 2ba^2 \pm 2nae = bq^2 \pm q^2 e.$$

These equations are also those of hyperbolas upon asymptotes, unless the point N is supposed to be in AL; for, as n then vanishes to zero, on removing the terms containing n the remainder form the equation to a parabola, as we gave notice above.

You will not expect me, famous Sir, to go on now to deal with convex mirrors after having hitherto used the concave mirror as my example.[3] For you will know that the analysis is exactly the same, and that the equations are distinguished only by changes in the signs plus and minus. You know that a parabola or ellipse that solves the one problem also solves the other; and if an hyperbola solves the problem for a convex mirror, its opposite branch will do the like for a concave one. So, omitting all that, I shall only add that from the same analysis the foci of concave mirrors may be obtained and the spaces that the rays fill along the axis, given the distance of any luminous point. And this falls out with wonderful facility when the rays are supposed to be parallel, which is yet something I have seen demonstrated by no one, however circuitously. For [see the figure, page 406] in the concave mirror EE whose center is A, if the extreme ray is understood to be reflected to the axis AR at B, and the tangent EC be drawn, CB will be equal to BA. Let the radius AR be bisected at Q; Q will be the focus and QB the space to be found. However, QB is half CR (because AQ, QR, AB, and BC are equal), that is, half the excess of the secant of the arc ER over the whole sine. Therefore if the arc ER is, for example, $9°$, $AC = 101246$, and $BQ =$

$\frac{623}{100{,}000}$ of AR. But I delay you too long in these geometrical conundrums, from which I thought I had freed myself, except that they are often met with even when one is about other things. So if God give me life and leisure, I may this spring publish my studies on the solution of problems, on the singular ratio,[4] [and] on tangents to curves, especially as the famous Ricci advises me that nothing more is to be expected from himself because he is engaged on other studies. And recently, unexpectedly, I met with a very easy way of demonstrating those things that I formerly discovered in a roundabout way; either method however ends in a very short and easy rule. But the future lies on the lap of the gods; for as yet in the Pyrrhonian fashion I myself make no claims.

I have often performed the experiment of the very illustrious Boyle, adding sand or lead to wax to bring it to the [specific] gravity of water, not only using plain water, but even water imbued with various salts; and in common with him I gathered that the little ball ascended with heat and descended with cold, but not with such definite alternations repeated at such short intervals. Nevertheless it can happen that it may play tricks like that at first because of the bubbles, quite invisible, adhering to it; these bear it up, and when they burst it sinks again. I have often found this.

I have not observed sunspots for many years, thinking like Descartes that nothing could be added to the diligence of Scheiner.[5] However, I gather from your letter that something new has been observed, so true is Seneca's saying: Indeed, Nature does not betray all her rites at once. Please tell me what that is, I mean, if you can without inconvenience to yourself. I beg you also to give many greetings from me to the famous Collins, from whose kindness in his own good time I shall expect the third part of the *Mechanica* of Wallis, our torchbearer.

I will see to it that our bookseller seeks in Holland for the other books you mention, where I am sure he will discover them. I have a great desire to see them, especially the one examining the causes of scurvy. For the symptoms of this disease, once almost unknown but now very common,[6] are varied and strange, and I shall willingly learn the reasons accounting for them from this learned author who writes in succession to the distinguished Willis. They are such as: an intermittent pulse, so rapid that I remember one sick person (who nevertheless did not keep his bed) in whom [the intermissions] happened [at the rate of] 400 times in the space of three or four hours. A pain under the chest bone, not terribly sharp but continuous so that it wearies the patient; which (as I may add in passing) I remember ceasing in time through the external application of a water distilled from earthworms with or without spirit of wine, and the frequent internal use of spirit of sal ammoniac. But these things are irrelevant here.

This mention of spirit of sal ammoniac recalls to me two not inelegant phenomena which perhaps you have observed. That is to say although it is colorless, if white wine is poured on it, it immediately takes on a pleasant pink; and when it is mixed with spirit of common salt it effervesces considerably, although both are volatile [salts], and in the end through this exhalation congeals into a very acrid and volatile salt. Farewell, most noble Sir, and continue as usual to love me, being wholly yours. Liège, 27 December 1671 [N.S.]

NOTES

Reply to Letter 1827. Copies were sent by Collins to James Gregory and by Oldenburg to Huygens (on 12 February 1671/2).
1 The second edition of his *Mesolabum* was published at Liège in 1668; the reference is to *De analysi*, an addendum to it.
2 The hyperbolas are not symmetrical with respect to b and z; the parabolas on the other hand are symmetrical.
3 Sluse has inadvertently transposed the two types; he has treated the convex mirror.
4 Compare the use of the word *monachos* in Letter 1548 (Vol. VII, p. 255). Pappus (*Mathematical Collections*, Bk. I, Prop. 61) was the first mathematician to use the word in the sense of "singular [least] ratio," a use puzzling mathematicians after Commandino published the text in 1588 until the meaning was established by Pierre de Fermat. In general a curve (say, a conic) meets an indefinite straight line at two points; in the case of the tangent these reduce to a single point, the monachos; similarly the two roots of an equation may reduce to one. The monachos, then, determines a minimal or maximal condition. (For the above we are indebted to D. T. Whiteside.)
5 Christoph Scheiner, S.J. (1575–1650) claimed original discovery of sunspots, about which he wrote a huge, diffuse book, *Rosa Ursina* (Bracciano, 1630).
6 Scurvy had, of course, become a common maritime disease in a severe form because of the length of ocean voyages to the Indies; mild scurvy was endemic everywhere. For Willis's book, see Vol. IV, p. 11, note 4.

1844
Oldenburg to Pardies
18 December 1671
From the draft in Royal Society MS. O 2, no. 62
and the copy in Letter Book V, 74–75

A Londres le 18. Dec. 1671.

Monsieur,

La vostre du 20. Octob. ne me fut rendue que le 13. du courant, par ie ne scay quel retardement, qui a empesché la personne, que M. Vernon en avoit chargé, pour me le donner icy. Elle vint accompagné de vostre Geometrie et du beau livre du P. Rapin et des Theses de Motu locali. Comme ie vous suis bien obligé de ces presents, ainsi ie ne scaurois vous celer la Joye, que nous avons d'entendre les nouvelles de vostre beau dessin de travailler à la continuation du Traité du Mouvement, que [...]¹ dont vostre premier discours a esté trouvé digne icy d'estre traduit en Anglois. Je vous puis assurer, que la Societé Royale ayant sceu le respect, que vous luy avez tesmoigné par vostre lettre, et faisant grand estat de tous ceux, qui s'employent à l'avancement des sciences solides et utiles, ne manquera iamais d'agreer les belles productions d'une personne de vostre Esprit et doctrine, principalement sur un sujet, come celuy que vous avez entrepris et qui est de si grande importance à toute la philosophie, asscavoir le Mouvement, ses Regles et ses Principes.² Vostre sagacité propre vous precautionera assez de ne vous ietter pas dans les labyrinthes de la Metaphysique dont les subtilitez sont plus propres d'embarasser et d'obscurcir, que de developper et esclaircir les choses. Et, si i'ose declarer ma petite pensée du discours du P. Rapin, ie suis persuadé, que ce docte personage, apres avoir derechef bien consideré la Nature, et comme ses operations et phaenomenes dependent quant aux causes secondes, du Mouvement et de la figure il ne fiera pas tant á l'Antiquité et à la Metaphysique, qu'il semble faire dans son livre, parce qu'anciennement et dans les Ecoles on n'a presque rien fait iusques icy, que d'entretenir le Scepticisme, et d'estaller des pures reveries et speculations du cerveau abstraites de ce qui se fait reellement dans la nature.³

Tout homme bien advisé ne fera point de difficulté, come je croy, d'advouer, que les effets, qui se voyent dans l'univers mesme, et les particularitez qui s'y rencontrent, estant attentivement observéz et par apres judicieusement comparez ensemble, sont le meilleur moyen de trouver de veritables principes et de bastir une bonne philosophie lá dessus. Je ne doubte pas, Monsr, que vous n'avez pris ce chemin pour cultiver et parfaire ce que vous avez commencé; à quoy s'il y a quelque chose icy qui vous puisse servir, et qui depende de moy, vous n'avez que me commander. Quant aux livres de philosophie, imprimez en ce pais icy, ie suis prest de vous fournir tous ceux que vous m'avez marquer dans vostre lettre, avec tout ce qui sera publié dorenavant de cete nature lá. Il vous plaira seulement de me faire scavoir, si vous demandez indifferemment ceux qui ont esté escrit icy en Anglois et en Latin, ou seulement ceux de la derniere sorte. De plus, si vous voulez, que ie vous envoye les Transactions par la poste, ou que i'attende quelque amy, qui passe d'icy á Paris.

Quant aux experiences pour le son dans le vuide, ie vous diray que ie trouve que parmy ceux de la Societé Royale Monsr Boyle a peut estre le plus examiné cete matiere, et telle est sa generosité et encor l'estime qu'il fait de vostre personne et merite, il ne fera point de scrupule de vous communiquer quelques unes de ces Experiences sur ce sujet. J'ay sa permission de vous dire à present, qu'ayant mis une horologue de poche dans un recipient appliqué à sa machine pneumatique, et bien espuise l'air, il a trouvé que quoy que le mouvement de la dite horologue y continuoit visiblement, le son pourtant n'en fut nullement entendu: lequel neantmoins fut bien ouy lorsque ledit recipient estoit plein d Air.[4] De plus, que par le moyen de la mesme machine il a fait donner le mouvement à une chorde qui estoit l'unison d'une autre, en frappant seulement une de ces deux la: ce qu'il scait faire par un artifice qu'il mettera sans doubte au public avec d'autres particularitez de cete nature là si Dieu luy donne et continue la santé.[5]

Pour les Experiences de ces Messieurs de Florence, ie vous laisse penser, s'ils ont esté capables, par les moiens et instruments dont ils se sont servis, d'empescher l'entrée de l'air principalement dans celuy là, qu'ils firent avec leur organette, p. 97. 98.[6] Il me semble, qu'il y avoit trop d'endroits pour l'acces d'une substance si subtile et penetrante que l'Air.

Pour les livres, que vostre Amy voudroit donner à imprimer icy, ie ne scay, qu'en dire, nos libraires semblant estre aussi difficiles à imprimer des livres Latins, principalement ceux, qui surpassent le commun, que les vostres. Je ne manqueray pourtant pas de soliciter cette affaire, et si j'y reussis, ie vous en diray des nouvelles, estant Monsieur

      Vostre treshumble et tresobeissant serviteur
       Old.

ADDRESS
 Au Pere Pardies
 de la Compagnie de Jesus
 au College de Clermont
   à Paris

TRANSLATION

Sir

Yours of the twentieth of October was not delivered to me until the thirteenth of this month; some delay unknown to me prevented the person whom Mr. Vernon charged with it from giving it to me here. It came accompanied by your

Geometry and by the fine book of Père Rapin and the theses *On Local Motion*. I am very much obliged to you for these presents and so cannot conceal from you the joy we felt on hearing the news of your fine plan of working on a continuation of the treatise on motion, [. . .]¹ your first discourse on which subject was deemed worthy of being translated into English. I can assure you that the Royal Society, knowing the respect to which you have borne witness in your letter, and making much of those who employ themselves in advancing solid and useful science, will never fail to accept the fine work of a person of your intelligence and learning, especially on a subject like that you have taken on, which is of such great importance to all philosophy, that is to say Motion, its rules and principles.² Your own shrewdness will be enough to caution you against plunging yourself into the labyrinths of metaphysics, whose subtleties are better at hampering and obscuring than at developing and clarifying things. And if I may state my own humble opinion of Père Rapin's discussion, it is that this learned person, after having once again carefully reflected on Nature and how her operations and phenomena depend as to secondary causes on motion and shape, will not rely so much on antiquity and metaphysics as he seems to do in his book, because by the ancients and by the Schoolmen almost nothing has been done until now except to maintain skepticism and air pure fantasies and abstract speculations of the mind of what actually happens in Nature.³ No well-advised man, I think, will make any difficulty over acknowledging that to observe attentively and then compare judiciously the effects observable in the universe itself and the peculiarities found there is the best means of finding out truer principles and building a sound philosophy thereupon. I do not doubt, Sir, that you have taken this road to the cultivation and completion of what you have begun; if there is anything here which can help you and which is in my power you have only to ask me. As for the books on philosophy printed in this country, I am ready to supply you with all those you have marked for me in your letter, together with all those which shall be published hereafter of this kind. Only please let me know if you are requesting those written in either English or Latin, or only those of the latter kind. Further, whether you would like me to send the *Philosophical Transactions* by post, or to wait for some friend who is going from here to Paris.

As for experiments of sound in the vacuum, I must tell you that I find that among the Fellows of the Royal Society Mr. Boyle has perhaps examined this subject most of all; and such is his generosity and the esteem in which he holds you and your deserts that he makes no scruple of communicating some of his experiments on the subject to you. I have his permission to tell you now that when he put a pocket watch into the receiver of his pneumatic engine and carefully exhausted the air, he found that although the motion of the said watch visibly continued, yet no sound was heard—and nevertheless the sound was easily heard when the said receiver was full of air.⁴ Further, that by means of the same engine he has caused a string which was in unison with another to vibrate, only by striking one of these two, which he knows how to do by a trick which he will doubtless publish with other particulars of this nature if God gives him continued health.⁵

As for the experiments of the Florentine gentlemen, I leave you to reflect whether it was possible for them, with the means and instruments which they used, to keep the air from entering, especially that which they made with their little organ pp. 97 and 98.⁶ It seems to me that there were too many points of access for so subtle and penetrating a substance as air.

As for the books which your friend would like to have printed here, I do not know what to say: our booksellers seem to make as much difficulty over printing Latin books as yours, especially those out of the ordinary. Nevertheless I shall not fail to make enquiries in this matter and if I succeed therein I shall send you news of it, being, Sir,

Your very humble and obedient servant
Oldenburg

ADDRESS

To Père Pardies, S.J
at the College de Clermont
Paris

NOTES

Reply to Letter 1794.
1 "Que" is possibly crossed out; for some reason a little slip of paper is pasted on the page here.
2 When Oldenburg read Letter 1794 to the Society on 14 December 1671 the Fellows instructed him to encourage Pardies to continue his work on motion.
3 This sentence has been crossed out in the draft.
4 This is in fact described in Experiment 27 of Boyle's *New Experiments Physico-Mechanicall, Touching the Spring of the Air, and its Effects* (Oxford, 1660); see Birch, *Boyle*, I, 62–63.
5 Boyle had proposed this experiment in Experiment 41 of *A Continuation of New Experiments Physico-Mechanical,...* (Oxford, 1669); see Birch, *Boyle*, III, 262. Boyle described both these experiments to the Society after the reading of Pardies' Letter 1794.
6 The members of the Accademia del Cimento made a one-pipe organ worked by a bellows which they put in cylindrical brass box with a handle to work the bellows protruding from the box; when the box was partially evacuated by means of a suction pump they still heard sounds.

1845
Oldenburg to Sachs
22 December 1671

From the draft in Royal Society MS O 2, no. 63

Celeberrimo Viro
Domino Phil. Jacobo Sachs a Lewenheimb. Med. D. etc.
Henricus Oldenburg Salutem

Novissimas tuas, 29. Octobris ad me datas, nonnisi 27. Novembris accepi. Citius iis respondissem, ni negotium illud, quod tuo me nomine apud Clarissimum Willisium nostrum expedire jusseras, scriptionem meam aliquamdiu sufflaminasset. Non enim datur quolibet tempore viros medicos, in praxi, ut est ille, occupatissimos, domi offendere, atque iis amicorum desiderata exponere. Cum tandem eum compellarem, atque quod injunxeras ab ipso peterem, respondit, rem eandem multoties a se quaesitam, nec hactenus ulli, ob justas rationes concessam fuisse; proindeque se sperare, nec Te id aegre laturum vel etiam tuam erga ipsum benevolentiam remissurum.

Ni fallor, eo res ista redit, ut ejusmodi Calcinationis Martialis beneficio, Aquae parentur factitiae, Spadanis virtute similes paresve; quanam adminiculo aegris aeque consulatur, ac si ipsas aquas Minerales haurerent.

Caeterum magno nos perfundis gaudio, dum scribis, Ephemeridum Germanicarum Annum secundum tantum non expeditum esse, Historiaque ortus et progressus Collegii Curiosorum etc. locupletatum Acta mea Philosophica quod attinet, lubentissime singulorum Exemplar Tibi transmitterem, ni Bibliopola noster Martinus, cujus impensis ea hic imprimuntur, singulis mensibus illa Hamburgum ad Georgium[1] Schultzium transmitteret; unde ea, si res tanti videatur, poterunt commodissime ad Te curari.

Inventa nuper hic fuit ab Equite Anglo, qui Samuel Moreland vocatur, Tuba quaedam, Stentoro-phonica dicta, cujus beneficio Vox humana ad unius, duorum, trium etc. milliarium Anglicorum (pro majori vel minori longitudine et opificii praestantia) distantiam ita potest diffundi, ut ab omnibus, intra Activitatis illius sphaeram constitutis, distincte possit exaudiri: Res tota jam Anglice impressa, et brevi, ni fallor, in sermonem Latinum vertenda.[2] Hoc inter Mechanices ornamenta referendum. Subjungam illi Observationem physicam, satis, ni fallor, raram, quae nuper mihi fuit a Clarissimo Domino Denisio, Medico Parisiensi, communicata.³ Ait ille, se novisse hominem, Parisiis commorantem, qui, postquam integri biennii spatio, diros circa umbilicum dolores, pulsumque violentum et pondus perquam grave in eadem regione pertulisset, medicis nequaquam remedia sua administrantibus, tandem per sedes, veri animalis ossa exeruerit, quae non nisi per intervalla prorumpant. Ait, ipsum jam 30. vertebras integras, rite formatas et perforatas ejecisse; adesse duas homoplatas,⁴ os cranii, costas, ossa femoris, pedum plaeraeque esse fracta et cariosa. Difficillium judicat explicata, ex quanam corporis parte proveniant; atque in qua regione generari animal illud poterit, num intra aut extra viscera? quamdiu vixerit, cum ossa adeo dura deprehendantur: cum aeger semper tota vita quantum scilicet meminerit, hanc dolorem et hoc pondus se sensisse affirmet.

Totam, ni fallor, historiam laudatus Dominus Denisius gravi hoc casu finito, scribet et in publicum emittet. Interea, quid Tua, Vir Clarissime, et Tui geminorum de eo sit sententia, scirem lubenter. Vale et me Tibi Adictissimum crede. Dabam Londini die 22. Dec. 1671.

TRANSLATION

Henry Oldenburg greets the very famous Mr. Philip Jacob Sachs von Lewenheimb, M.D., etc.

I only received on 27 November your very latest letter to me written on 29 October. I would have replied to it more quickly if that business which you instructed me to go into with the celebrated Willis on your behalf had not delayed my writing somewhat. For it is not the done thing to accost medical men fully engaged with such a practice as his is, at home, at any hour one chooses, in order to explain the wishes of one's friends. However, when I had addressed myself to him and made him the request according to your instructions, he replied, that the same request had been made to him many times and that, for good reasons, he had never granted it to any one. And so he hoped you would not take it ill, or abate your goodwill towards him.

If I am not mistaken, that business amounts to this: that by such sort of calcination of iron artificial mineral waters are made, of a virtue similar to Spa water and the like, so that by their administration sick people are as much gratified as if they had drunk the [natural] mineral waters themselves.

Furthermore, we are greatly pleased by your writing that the second year of the German *Miscellanies* is very nearly perfected and is enriched with a history of the rise and progress of the Investigators' Academy etc. As for my *Philosophical*

Transactions, I would gladly send you a copy of each issue did not Martin, our bookseller at whose expense they are printed here, send them every month to Georg[1] Schulz at Hamburg, whence they can easily be procured for you if they seem worth the trouble.

There has recently been invented here by an English knight, Sir Samuel Morland, a certain tube called "stentorophonic," by which the human voice can be carried to a distance of one, two, or three English miles (according to its length, and the skill of the maker) so that it can be heard distinctly by all within its range; [an account of] the whole thing has already been printed in English and will soon, I think, be translated into Latin.[2] This may be numbered among advances in mechanics. To this I add an observation in medicine which is, if I am not mistaken, pretty uncommon, sent me by the famous Paris physician, Mr. Denis.[3] He says that he has known a man, living at Paris, who after the space of two whole years during which he suffered acute pains in the region of the navel, a throbbing pulse, and a sense of a great burden in that same region, at length, without taking any medicines, voided by stool genuine animal bones, which came out only at intervals. He says that this man has already voided thirty whole, perfectly formed and perforated vertebrae; there are also two scapulas,[4] a skull bone, ribs, femors, and many broken and carious feet[bones]. He believes it is difficult to explain from what part of the body they come, and in what region that animal could be generated (either within or without the viscera) while he lived, as the bones were found to be so hard, [and] as the sick man affirmed that he had felt this pain and sense of heaviness always throughout his life, or at least as long as he could remember.

The praiseworthy Mr. Denis will, if I mistake not, write and publish the full story when this serious case is completed. Meanwhile I would like to know the opinion of yourself and your colleagues concerning this. Farewell, and believe me most devoted to you. London, 22 December 1671.

NOTES

Reply to Letter 1809.
1 Correctly, Gottfried.
2 There does not appear to have been any Latin translation.
3 We have not found any other account of this, either published or unpublished.
4 Strictly, "omoplatas"; the "h" is redundant.

1846
Fermat to Oldenburg
22 December 1671

From the original in private possession
Printed in Rigaud, K, 182–84

Clarissimo viro D. Oldenbourg
S. Fermat S.P.D.

Quam in festa fuerit hoc anno populatio murium agris qui in conceranensi[1] diaecesi montibus subiacent, vix enarrari potest, tanta huiusmodi animalculorum solito minorum, subrufo colore copia subito e vicinis rupibus se effudit, ut torrentis instar segetes sternens ipsa gra[n]dine damnosior spicas radicitus corroserit; non te latet quid Aristotelis lib. 6°. hist. Animal. cap. 37°. et plinius lib. decimo cap. 65°. scripserint de Soricibus agrestibus et detrimento ab iis non solum messibus sed etiam quibusdam populis illato, parum autem fide dignum plerisque videbitur, quod de foecunditate murium ambo tradunt, praesertim ubi asserunt, apud Persas praegnantes et in utero parentis repertas fuisse, aut ut Julii Scaligeri verbis utar, matres fieri antequam nascantur, utinam inquit ille; tales apud nos vitulae forent;[2] hujus vero de qua agitur rei, cuius ipse quidem testis non fui, sed ab aliis omni Exceptione maioribus didici, causam inquirere, si vacat, te sagacissimum naturae indagatorem nec pigebit forsitan nec dedecebit. Abietibus id tribuunt regionis incolae; similem vero luem aiunt frumentis nocuisse viginti retro ab hinc annis; sed cum ibi adeo annosae sint hae arbores, idque tam raro eveniat, credibile est quaedam praeter consuetudinem tempestatis accessisse quoties hic prodiit effectus; cum igitur innumeri illi Terrigenae, ut ita loquar, vastatores nuper orti sunt, plura, Et ni fallor, insueta concurrere oportuit. Immodicum puta solis fervorem et diuturnam siccitatem vaporesque multo sale permixto & solo murium generationi aliunde apto, abiegni forte ligni putredine, praeter modum attractos qui deinde resoluti. Eodemque loco recepti fuerint.[3] Sic aestate nonnunquam improviso imbre velut Ebulliente pulvere stupendam ranunculorum multitudinem Erumpere videmus, quae phaenomena si eodem tempore contigissent, veteris illius et fabulosae batrachomyomachiae nova et vera imago potuisset Exhiberi.[4] Si vero cum haec leges tibi in mentem veniat tritum illud, Parturient montes, addere merito poteris, nascetur terribilis mus, non ridiculus ut vulgo dicitur. Vale et me ama.

Tolosae, Kal. Jan. 1672 [N.S.]

ADDRESS
    A Monsieur
        Monsieur Oldenbourg
    A Londres

TRANSLATION

Samuel de Fermat presents many greetings to the famous Mr. Oldenburg

I can scarcely relate to you how troublesome the population of mice in the fields lying below the hills in the district of Couserans[1] has been this year; so great a multitude of these little animals (usually pretty small and reddish in color) poured out of the neighboring crags that like a torrent flattening the crops worse than any hailstorm it gnawed the ears to the very roots. You cannot but recall what Aristotle (*History of Animals*, Bk. 6, ch. 37) and Pliny ([*Natural History*] Bk. 10, ch. 65) say about the field shrews and the damage they did not only to harvests but even to certain peoples. Yet many things narrated by both about the fecundity of mice will appear unworthy of belief, especially where they affirm that according to the Persians they were found to be pregnant even when within their parent's womb; or, if I may employ J. C. Scaliger's phrase, they were mothers before they were born; "would," says he, "that we had such calves."[2] It will perhaps be neither tedious nor unfitting for such a wise investigator of nature as yourself to inquire into the cause of this affair, if it is unknown, of which I was not myself a witness but of which I have learned from others, without exception men of weight. The inhabitants of the region put it down to the fir trees and they say that a like plague damaged the corn twenty years ago; but as these trees are there so venerable and this happens so rarely, it is credible that some unusual tempest occurred each time this effect was produced; accordingly, as so innumerable a horde of earth-born vandals (if I may so call them) has lately arisen, it must have been the case that many unusual circumstances concurred, if I am not mistaken. For example, excessive heat in the soil with long-continued drought and vapors with much mixed salt and a soil from elsewhere fitted for the generation of mice, perhaps rotten fir wood, drawn together in an unusual way which were then separated and received into the same place.[3] Thus sometimes in summer with unexpected rain as it were boiling the dust we see a fantastic multitude of frogs appear; if these [two] phenomena had happened at the same time they would have presented a new and genuine version of that ancient and fabulous "battle between the frogs and the mice."⁴ And if indeed you recall in reading this that tag: "The mountains are in labor . . . " you may properly continue " . . . and give birth to a terrible mouse," not *ridiculous* as the saying has it.⁵ Farewell and love me.

Toulouse, 1 January 1672 [N.S.]

ADDRESS
> To Mr Oldenburg
> London.

NOTES

As Rigaud remarked, the writing (though very neat) displays "several instances of inattention."

1 Properly Conserans, seat of a medieval bishopric, perhaps corresponding to the modern district of Couserans (Ariège), in the central Pyrenees, where the town of St. Girons has an ancient episcopal palace.
2 Julius Caesar Scaliger (1484–1558), classical scholar, author of a commentary on Aristotle.
3 It is very difficult to puzzle out this sentence, but it is at least clear that Fermat attributes the plague of mice to spontaneous generation. The ancients thought that female mice were fertilized by salt.
4 An allusion to a very old Greek mock-heroic poem.
5 The story is from Aesop, this well-known sentence from Horace *Ars poetica*, l. 139.

1847
Oldenburg to Dodington
22 December 1671

This is mentioned in Dodington's reply, Letter 1876; it probably enclosed Letter 1842.

1848
Cassini to Oldenburg
22 December 1671

From the original in Royal Society MS. C 1, no. 54

Clarissimo Viro D. Henrico Oldemburg
Regiae Societatis Anglicae a Secretis
J. D. Cassinus S.P.D.

Tuorum in me officiorum cumulo, Vir Clarissime, iamdiu respondere debuissem. Sed spes, dignum aliquid Te nobilissimoque caetu vestro rependendi, quam Caelum dederat, abstulitque; longam hanc nexuit moram. Videram a die 23 Octobris ad 6 Novembris errantem stellulam precedere Saturnum, tunc retrogradum ad occidentem, in distantia minutorum circiter octo quae hoc temporis spatio nonnihil aucta est, primo quidem in recta linea cum Saturni bracchijs, deinde vero cum deflexione aliqua ab haec eadem linea ad Austrum, cuius motus proprij certior factus sum, non modo comparatione ad Saturnum, verum etiam ad stellas fixas Telescopias, paulo Borealiores stella quintae magnitudinis, quae a Tychone ponitur in altero flexu australi aquae Aquarij,[1] quarum decem intra distantiam minutorum quinquaginta numeravi. Harum vero penultima ordine distantiae a praedicta stella Tychonica distititur a via novi huius planetae ad Austrum minus uno minuto: quam cum nondum assequuutus fuisset die 4 Novembris die 6 eam praeterierat reliqueratque ad ortum. Dum ex observationibus definiendum expecto, sitne planeta hic Saturni satellitio accensendus, an potius numero planetarum Principium, qui Saturno altior, illi fuse fuerit ante copulatus, qua ratione eiusdem cum alijs planetis copulationes statis temporibus possint contingere, an denique perpetuae sit vel brevis apparitionis Cometarum instar, ac potissimum quod de eo futurum sit instante statione, et directione Saturni, unde ista melius definiri posse sperabam; diuturnae caeli intemperies ipsum ulterius prosequendi omnem abstulit opportunitatem; et licet, redeunte per dies multos serenitate, et Saturnum et memoratas fixas Telescopicas, quas nova planeta praeterierat, diligenter circumspexerim, illum tamen ulterius deprehendere aut distinguere non potui, quamvis plerumque plures offenderim stellulas, expendendas, nisi Caeli obstitisset intemperies, necessariam observationum continuitatem iterum interumpens. Itaque cum ab ultima certarum ipsius observationum iam duo menses praeterierint, ac interim Saturnus cursum suum in ortem reflexerit, nisi is e Saturni comitatu fuerit, ipse procul a loco habitarum observationum in incertum remotus vix poterit inter fixarum Telescopicarum agmen deinceps distingui et recognosci. Descriptionem viae ipsius per fixas quousque eam observare mihi datum est tradidi nuper Domino de Vernon qui eam ad vos transmittet.[2]

De transmittis ad me Philosophicis tuis transactionibus honorificentissimaque mentione ibi habita mearum observationum macularum solis, successuque praedictionum tibi maximas gratias ago.[3] Vidi in ijsdem observationes Domini Hook in secunda apparitione,[4] meis nondum editis plane consentientes, et Observationem eiusdem lunaris eclipsis mensis semptembris cuius finis Londini hora 8.17′ comparatus fini observato a me Parisijs H. 8. 28. 20″ arguit differentiam meridianorum min. 11. 20″.[5] Eiusdem eclipsis finem observarunt Patavij Rinaldinus[6] h. 9. 36′ florentiae Vivianus H. 9. 8′. 20″ Taurini Turinus[7] h. 8. 47. Avenione Gallet,[8] H. 8. 45′. 36″. Quae ex Hevelij observationibus provenit apparens coniunctio lunae cum Jove die 30 Septembris mane[9] h. 7. 26′ eadem mihi hic in regio observatorio visa est h. 6. 3.′ 30″ differentia consurgente ex parallaxim et meridianorum differentijs, et mihi quidam Jupiter existens in linea recta per lunae cornua distitit a cornu eius austrino min. 7 quae Hevelio minus minutis 3. Saturnus qui hoc anno ab ortu Heliaco ad diem 11 Augusti visus fuerat rotundus et a die 14 eiusdem mensis deinceps cum brachijs, in tali figura permansit ad diem 8 Decembris, a die autem 13 Decembris deinceps visus est plane rotundus. Priorem rotunditatem tribuo nimiae obliquitati radiorum visualium supra planum annuli Saturni, cum is motu apparenti directe pervenisset ferme ad 20 gradum ♓. quae causa cessavit, cum motu retrogrado ad gr. 18 eiusdem signi fuit restitutus, cum adhuc a Sole videretur in gr. 16. posterioris rotunditatis causam magis tribuo nimiae obliquitati radiorum solis supra idem planum annuli cum a sole videretur saturnus excedere 19 gr. ♓ licet a terra conspiceretur in gr. 14 eiusdem Signi. Hi termini, quos pro Telescopiorum magnitudine et praestantia variari necesse est, Telescopio pedum 17 operis Campani Romani artificis definiti sunt. Vale, Vir Clarissime, et me Tibi Illustrissimoque caetui vestro addictissimum ama. Parisijs die 1 Jan. 1672 [N.S.].

TRANSLATION

G. D. Cassini sends many greetings to the famous Mr. Henry Oldenburg, Secretary of the English Royal Society

I should long ago have acknowledged your series of services to me, famous Sir, but I refrained in the hope of repaying you and your most noble assembly with some worthy gift from the sky; so ensued this long delay. From 23 October to 6 November I had seen a little "wandering star" preceding Saturn, then in retrograde motion to the west, at a distance of about eight minutes, which increased considerably over this stretch of time; it was at first in a straight line with Saturn's "arms" [ring] and afterwards had a slight deflection from that towards the south. Of its own movement I was the more convinced not only by comparison with Saturn but also by relating it to the fixed telescopic stars a little to the north of the fifth-magnitude star which is placed by Tycho in the alternate southern bend of Aquarius's water,[1] of which I have counted ten within the space of fifty minutes of arc. The last of these (counting in order from the above star of Tycho) is displaced less than a minute south of the path of this new planet; it had not yet reached this star on 4 November but on the sixth it had passed it and left it to the east. While I am waiting to determine from the observations whether this planet is to be reckoned as a satellite of Saturn or rather as one of the primary planets which, being more remote than Saturn, was for a long time previously [optically] joined to him in the same way that such [optical] unions can occur at stated times among the other planets, or lastly whether it is perpetual or a short-lived apparition like a comet, and particularly what will happen to it at the time of Saturn's station and direct motion, when I could hope that it would be better defined—for a long while the unkindness of the heavens denied me all opportunity of following up my observations further. And although with the return of many fine days I diligently examined both Saturn and the above-mentioned fixed telescopic stars which the new planet had passed by, I could neither discern nor distinguish it, yet I would have gone over those many little stars that had to be evaluated again and again had not the unkindness of the heavens frustrated me by breaking the necessary continuity of observation once more. And so, as two months had already slipped by since the last of the reliable observations of it, and meanwhile Saturn had curved his course back towards the east, unless it were a companion of Saturn's it must have moved away far from the place of observation to some unknown quarter where it could hardly be again discovered and recognized among the whirling multitude of stars. I have recently given Mr. Vernon a description of its path among the fixed stars in so far as I was permitted to observe it, and he will send it to you.[2]

I return you many thanks for your *Philosophical Transactions* you sent me and the very honorific mention there made of my observations of sunspots and the success of my predictions.³ In the *Transactions* I also saw the observations made by Mr. Hooke of the second appearance,⁴ fully consonant with my own unpublished ones, and also his observation of the lunar eclipse during September, concluded at London at 8h. 17'. Since the end was observed by myself at Paris at 8h. 28'. 20" it appears that the difference of the meridians is 11.' 20".⁵ Renaldini⁶ observed the end of the same eclipse at Padua at 9h. 36', Viviani at Florence at 9h. 8'. 20". Turini at Turin at 8h. 47', and Gallet at Avignon⁸ at 8h. 45'. 36". The apparent conjunction of the moon and Jupiter on the morning of 30 September at 7h. 26', figuring in the observations made by Hevelius,⁹ was seen by me at the Royal Observatory here at 6h. 3' 30", the difference arising from the parallax and difference in latitude; to me, indeed, Jupiter seemed to be in a straight line through the horns of the moon at a distance of seven minutes from its southern horn, which Hevelius made less than three minutes. Saturn was seen as rounded from its heliacal rising until 11 August, and after the fourteenth of that month with "arms," remaining in that form until 8 December; however, since 13 December he has again been seen as quite round. I attribute the first period of roundness to the excessive obliquity of the visual rays [striking] the plane of Saturn's ring when, in his direct apparent motion, he had quite reached the twentieth degree of Pisces; this cause disappeared when in his retrograde motion he had gone back to the eighteenth degree of the same sign. Since he was up to now seen from the sun in the sixteenth degree, I rather attribute the cause of the later period of roundness to the excessive obliquity of the solar rays upon the same plane of the ring, since Saturn was seen from the sun to be beyond the nineteenth degree of Pisces, although from the Earth he was observed in the fourteenth degree of the same sign. These limits (which must be variable according to the size and quality of the telescope) were defined by a telescope of 17 feet made by the optician Campani of Rome. Farewell, famous Sir, and love me as one who is most devoted to yourself and your most illustrious assembly. Paris, 1 January 1672 [N.S.].

NOTES

1 See Letter 1830, note 3.
2 See Letter 1854a; presumably Cassini did not know of Vernon's Letter 1830.
3 *Phil. Trans.*, no. 74 (14 August 1671), 2216–17, and possibly no. 75 (18 September 1671), 2250–53.
4 *Phil. Trans.*, no. 77 (20 November 1671), 2295 and 2296.
5 This makes the difference in latitude between the two cities 2° 50', whereas the true value is roughly 2° 16'—but the method was very approximate.
6 Carlo Renaldini; see Vol. IV, p. 483, note 7.
7 Possibly Giulio Turini of Nice, who had a flourishing medical practice at Turin.
8 Jean Charles Gallet (1637–1713), a religious of the church of St. Symphorien at Avignon, wrote a number of works on astronomy, some of them absurd.
9 See Letter 1792a (3).

1849

Flamsteed to Oldenburg

23 December 1671

From the original in Royal Society MS. F 1, no. 78

Derby Decem: 23 1671

Worthy Sr

I have reaceaved the glasses & booke from Mr Sargeant which I esteeme cheape of ye rates & hold my selfe obliged to yu for providing them onely the receipt was needlesse since I can not but hold it an indignity offered yu by any yt will not credit yu without such certificates: I thanke yu for ye corrextions of my exorbitant latin & wish yu would bestowe the same castigations on the included where yu find them requisite. I have to my praedictions added ye observed distances of ye Pleiades which may be annexed or left out as yu please since I have so ordered it that the rest will be absolute without them.[1] I have not seene a star light evening till this instant of a long time so have made few observations but what yu are acquainted with, next weeke I must visit some freinds afterwards I shall be attendant on ye heavens for those observations I have foreseene, & will not, God willing, permit a sun shine day to passe without seekeing for his spots of which I never yet could see any: I thanke yu for your information of ye new planet neare Saturne but I wonder yt I never heard of more companions then his ansulae when yu mention his satelles as a thinge indifferently knowne & common I should be glad therefore to heare from yu whether hee has such a satelles as Jupiters,[2] & to see Hugenius his systema which if yu please to lend me for a perusall I will get my schole fellow Mr Sargeant [to] waite on yu for when hee comes up to London next after Christmas for my selfe have no hopes of seeing it in hast: Pray if yu see Mr Collins informe him yt I have his last letter & that tho my occasions permitte mee not at present I will ere long write both to him & Mr Nuns[3] a transcript of whose letter, to a freind of his hee was pleased to send me; concerning ye writeing of an Ephemeris. but wanteing time at present I must conclude subscribeing my self as alwaies

Yr obliged servant
John Flamsteed

I shall send yu a draught of my micrometer ere long: and with my first opportunity write to Mr Townly: pray if Hevelius send yu any account of ye lunar Eclipse[4] let us have it publick for ye English observations agree all very well togeather & I doubt not but his will shew us ye difference of our Meridians better then most have yet.

ADDRESS

To Henry Oldenburg Esq
at his house in ye middle
of ye Pellmell in St
James's Westminster
   these present

NOTES

Reply to Letter 1841.
1 See Letter 1824 and its note 1; the additions were printed in *Phil. Trans.*, no. 79 (22 January 1671/2), 3061–63: "De Lunae ad Pleiades reliquas Applicationibus, Anno 1672 observandis, promissa appendicula Johannis Flamsteed" ("J. F.'s little appendix concerning the moon's appulses to the rest of the Pleiades to be observed in 1672"). The original is Royal Society MS. F 1, no. 78a(i).
2 Flamsteed means, of course, that he was till then unaware of Huygens' discovery of Titan, announced in 1659, never having seen *Systema Saturnium*.
3 The same person is mentioned in a letter of Flamsteed to Collins of 17 April 1672 (Rigaud, II, 137). A Thomas Nunnes of Northampton was a surveyor and mathematical practitioner.
4 See Letter 1792a (1).

1850

Oldenburg to Lister

23 December 1671

From the original in Bodleian Library MS. Lister 34, ff. 47–48

Sir,

I herewth send you Mr Colwal, Treasurer of ye R. Society, his receipt of the 3 lb 5. shillings, wch you so generously paid in, by my hands; wch was looked upon as a very handsom action, I assure you.[1]

We have lately received from Signr Malpighi, the Author of ye *Historia de Bombyce*, a very curious and considerable piece *de Anatome Plantarum*,[2] wch, for the most part, agrees wth the thoughts and considerations of Dr *Nehemiah Grew*, a Fellow of ye R. Society, in his book lately publisht, under the title of, *The Anatomy of Vegetables, wth a General Account of Vegetation, founded thereon*; printed for Spencer Hickman, at ye Rose in Pauls Church-yard. Of wch latter I give some short description in the Transactions, now in ye presse.[3] I am of opinion, that these two Authors will be found to have exceedingly cleared the whole matter of vegetation, they having descended and penetrated into all the particulars and the most minute observables in plants. Malpighi hath only sent us an abstract of his meditations; wch he intends to enlarge, and illustrate wth figures, representing to ye Eye, whatever he discourseth of.

Besides this, there is come abroad Sr Samuel Moreland's Loud-Speaking Trumpet, wch he also calls *Tuba Stentorophonica*,[4] an instrument likely to prove very usefull both at Sea and Land, in conveying Humane Voyce so, that it may be heard distinctly, one, two, three, or more miles off, according to the length of ye Instrument and the strength of ye voyce, speaking in it. The thing being in print, and to be had at *Moses Pit's* in Litle Britain; I forbear to say more of it here, being persuaded, you will send for one of ye books, thereby to satisfy yrself as well about the Construction, as the Uses of this Organ.

Of ye black rezin I cannot yet give you any account, those Noble persons, to whom it was recommended, having made no report of it hitherto:[5] wch when it comes in, shall be signified to you by Sir

Yr faithf. servt
Oldenburg

London
Dec. 23. 71.

ADDRESS
  To his honored friend
  Mr Martyn Lister at his
  house wthout Mickel-gate-bar
      at
        York

NOTES

1 Presumably five quarters' subscription at the rate of one shilling per week, to 25 March 1673.
2 See Letter 1805.
3 See *Phil. Trans.*, no. 78 (18 December 1671), 3037–43.
4 See Letter 1836, note 7.
5 See Letter 1819, note 2.

1851
Oldenburg to Tenison
23 December 1671

Tenison's Letter 1816 is endorsed by Oldenburg as answered on this date.

1852
Oldenburg to Vogel
26 December 1671

From the memorandum in Royal Society MS. O 2, no. 59

Scripsi rursus d. 26. Dec. 71. et misi folium Pocockii de Caave, et catalogum de libris nunc sub proelo sudantibus. Boyle, Willis, Bohun, nec non nova de Morelandii Tuba Stentor-phonica. Non retinui copiam hujus novissimae epistolae.

TRANSLATION

I wrote again on 26 December 1671 and sent the sheet of Pocock on coffee, and a list of books now being printed: Boyle, Willis, Bohun, as well as Morland's *Tuba Stentoro-phonica*. I did not keep a copy of this latest letter.

NOTE

Second reply to Letter 1811.

1853
Vernon to Oldenburg
27 December 1671

This letter is known only from the mention of it in the next letter from Vernon, Letter 1854.

1854
Vernon to Oldenburg
30 December 1671
From the original in Royal Society MS. V, nos. 19, 20, and 22

Paris Jan. 9th 1672 [N.S.]

Sr

I told you in my last of the 6th Current That I would give you what account I could concerning the measure of the earth.[1] I am sorry Monsieur Picart is not here, for if hee were He would not scruple to lett mee see what hee had done at Leisure: now there is a secret made of what hee compos'd & soe I am faine to snatch what otherwise I might have gatherd.

Hee like a learned man, as hee is, gives a plaine title to his booke & wthout any more bussle calls it

Mesure dela Terre.

His name is not at it: all that is besides in the Frontispiece is

a Paris
Del imprimerie Royale

The booke is bound up wth some Anatomicall Observations wch the Royal Academie have made & is the same wth that wch is before extant & Printed by Leonard[2] & you have it I am sure being the account they give of the particularities they have observed in 6 animals among wch are a dromedarie & a gazelle beeing bound together & in a large Print they make a folio wch is very broad, but the thicknesse is butt moderate not neere soe thicke as a large commonprayer booke.

Hee divides his treatise into 13 articles in the first hee begins wth a preamble wherein hee shewes that this probleme concerning the just dimensions of the circumference of the earth, is noe new thing butt hath beene the enquiry of severall ages in wch Princes have beene curious & learned men have been encouradged to the search & clearing of this difficulty, to this purpose hee brings a passage out of Abulfeida where hee saith that Almamon[3] a Prince of the Arabes desiring to know what the true measure of a degree might bee commanded the experiment to bee made in the plaines of Sanjar where a Station beeing chosen 2 trouppes of horsemen sett out from thence & went in a Streight line till one had raysed a degree of latitude & the other had depresst it & at the end of both their marches they who raysed it counted $56\frac{2}{3}$ miles, they who depresst it 56 iust. they supposed there might bee some errour in their reckoning of their marches, & therefore both parties at last shot up into this conclusion that $56\frac{2}{3}$ of a mile might bee justly allowed to a degree. Hee makes an observation that the antient computation of miles to a degree run alwaies upon the decrease as for Instance Aristotle counted to a degree 1111. stadia Eratosthenes 700. Posidonius 666 Ptolomee 500, at last Fernelius[4] brought it to 56746 Toises de Paris, Snellius to 55021 T[5]

Article 2d. This Snellius his way of measuring hee iudgeth to have been the most artificiall wch was by a scale of Triangles butt in one thing he iudgeth it deficient because hee tooke his obser[vations] only by Pinnules wch doe not point it out soe distinctly.

Article 3d. hee begins to speake of his owne Method & the exactnesse of it, that when the Resolution was taken of measuring a degree hee chose his meridian (out of wch hee intended to take his measure, betweene Sourdon in Picardie & Malvoysine wch lies upon the confines of the Gastinois & Hurepois.[6]

To attaine the exact measure of this arc of the Meridian lying betweene Sourdon & Malvoysin, hee saith hee measured actually a way wch lay very streight, betweene Villijuif & Juvisy, hee begun to measure from the middle of a mill at Villejuif & continued till hee came to the pavillon at Juvisy. The distance betweene these 2 termes hee found in going forward 5662 Toyses 5 feet, in coming back hee found it 5663, 1 Pied wch because it was measured wth great exactnesse, hee stated the distance between these two places in round reckoning 5663 Toyses. Note, 1 Toyse = 6 feet Parisian.

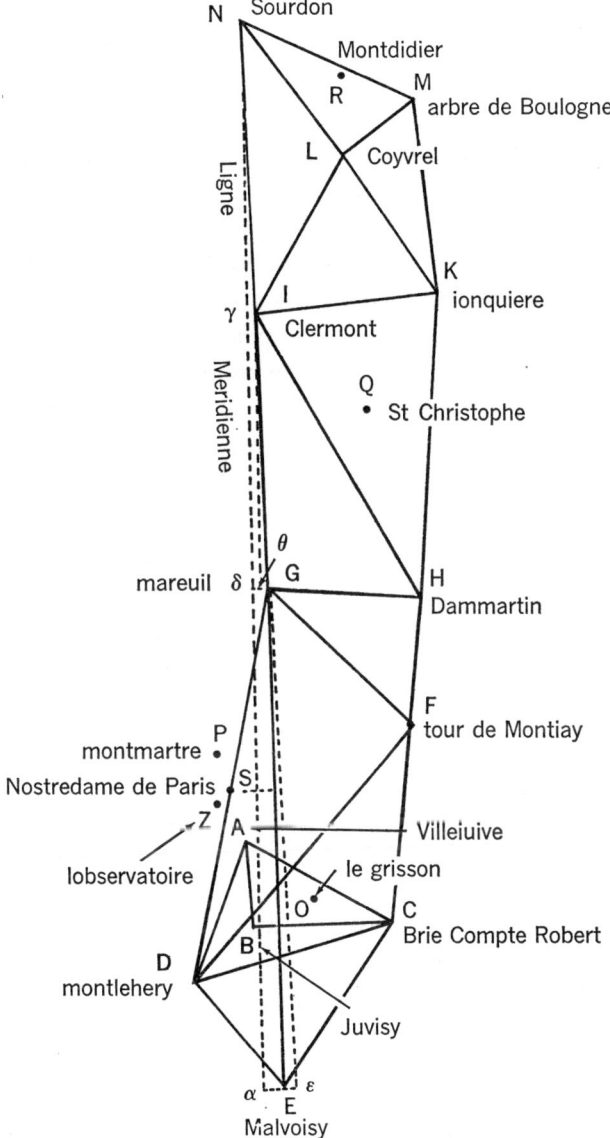

The instrument hee measured wth was Pikes ioyned together at their ends by a scrue wch measure was 4 Toyses long. this hee applied along a cord stretched horizontally at the end of every such Pike had a fiche, hee had in all 10 Fiches or stakes soe every grand fiche made 80 Toyses.[7]

This distance of 5663 T. was the base of the first triangle, upon wch the measure of all the depending scale was formed.

Hence hee proceeds to talke of measures & saith that the Length of a Pendulum each of whose Vibrations is a second of time computed according to the meane motion of the Sun, is 36 pouces 8½ lignes, mesure du Chastelet de Paris,[8] hee alledgeth that this measure may serve in all Countries probably, because the same Length of a pendulum served for a second both at the Hague & at Paris and hee conjectured, the same might serve in other latitudes also.

Hence hee saith, that if one had a mind to constitute an universal measure wch might bee common to all countries, one might make it thus.

Call this Pendulum for seconds of 36 Pouces 8½ Lignes the Radius Astronomicus. the ⅓ of this radius the pes Universalis.[9]

The double of the Radius might bee called the Universall Toyse, wch will be in proportion to the Parisian Toyse as 881 to 864.

The quadruple may bee called the Universal Perch, wch is equall to the Length of a pendulum for two seconds, in short the universal mile might containe a 1000 of these perches.

The Instrument wth wch the Angles were taken in the measuring of these Triangles was a quadrant of 38 Inches radius. wth prospective glasses fastned to point out the Objects this Instrument never misst a minute in taking an angle sometimes it came wthin 5″.

Article 6th. Relates the manner of taking the distance betweene malvoysine & Sourdon. wth the Triangle & Stations observed in it. This distance is 68347 Toyses 3 Pieds.[10]

7 Article containes the continuation of the same measure from Sourdon to Amiens to the End that Fernelius his account might bee liquidated whether it were true or noe.

8 Article After having measured the particular distances betweene Malvoysine, Mareuil, Sourdon & Amiens, hee comes to examine the Position of each of these lines of distance in respect of the Meridian The measure of this meridian hee finds to bee 68430 Toyses 3 Pieds.[11]

9 Article Compares the meridian distance already measured & reduced to the Parisian Toyse wth minutes & secondes in the heavens wch were taken by help of a Limb beeing a 20th part of a circle whose radius was 10 feet.

10th Article relates that the Knee of Cassiopeia was the Starre hee pitcht on, to measure the minutes & seconds of a degree in the heaven from, & the Reasons why hee chose that Starre.

11 Article gives the Resolution of the Quaestion, that is to say how may Toyses Paris measure answer to a degree of the circumference of the earth, as for Instance

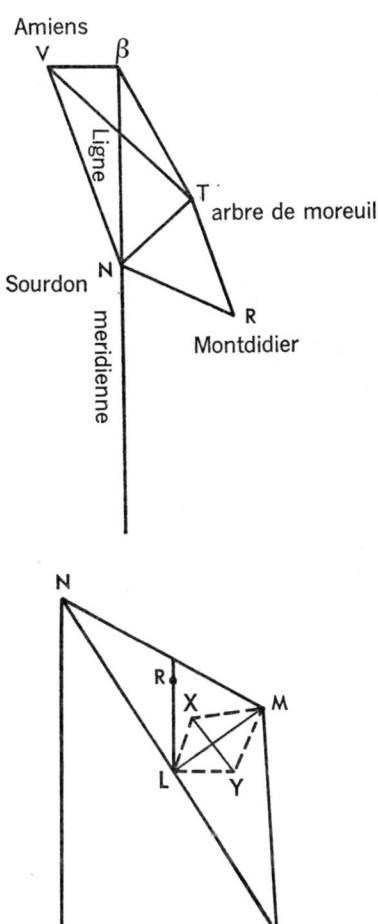

The difference of Latitude betweene Malvoysine & Sourdon is
found by observation made in the heavens to bee . . 1° 11′ 57″
between Malvoysine & Amiens 1 22 55

The meridian distance betweene Malvoysine & Sourdon calculated from measures taken upon earth was 68430 Toys. 3 Pieds

Hence he concludes that . . . . 57064 Toys 3 foot = to a degree
numero rotundo.[12]   57060   = gradus

If you would reduce this to Universal measure you must remember, that the universal Toyse is to the Parisian as 881. to 864. hence 1 degree = 55959 Toyses universelles

The Reduction of this to forrein measures is thus.
Suppose the Paris foot to consist of 1440 Parts

The Rhinelande (or Leyden foot) containes of these	1390
The London foot	1350
The Bolognian	1686
La brasse de Florence	2580

Hence each degree in a grand circle of the earth according to the measure of different countries is

Toyses du Chastelet de Paris	57060
Pas de Bologna	58481
Verges du Rhin de 12 pieds chacune	29556
Lieues Parisiennes de 2000 Toyses	$28\frac{1}{4}$
Lieues moyennes de France d'environ 2282 T	25
Lieues de marine de 2853 T	20
Milles d'Angleterre de 5000 pieds chacun	$73\frac{7}{200}$
Milles de Florence de 3000 brasses	$63\frac{7}{10}$

Hence the circumference of the Earth

Toyses de Paris	20541600
Lieues de 25 au degré	9000
Lieues de marine	7200

The Diameter of the Earth is

Toyses de Paris	6538594
Lieues de 25 au degré	$2464\frac{56}{71}13$
Lieues de marine	$2291\frac{59}{71}$

Hee putts a table where hee shows the correspondent value in measure to the parts of a degree for example

Minute		Toyses	seconde		Toyses
1	=	951	1	=	16
2		1902	2		32
	&c			&c	
60 or a degree	=	57060	60 or a minute		951

A table followes of the difference of the elevations of the Pole.
Betweene malvoysine & the observatoir at Paris difference of latitude . . . . 19′ 22″

betweene malvoysine & Nostredame de Paris		20′	22″
& mareuil		33	32
& Clermont		52	
& Sourdon		71	52
& Nostredame d'Amiens		82	58
betweene nostredame de Paris & of Amiens		62	36

Table of Elevations of the Pole

The Elevation of the Pole in the garden of the Royall Academie at Paris is	48°	53′	
at Nostredame at Paris	48	52	10″
at St. Jaques de la Boucherie	48	52	20
At Malvoysine	48	31	48
at the observatoir of Paris	48	51	10
at Mareuil	49	5	20
Clermont	49	23	48
Sourdon	49	43	40
Nostredame d'Amiens	49	54	46

Differences of Longitudes

Sourdon more easterly then Amiens by		5′	54″
Clermont then Sourdon		1	9
Mareuil then Clermont			34
Mareuil then malvoysine			20
Mareuil then Paris		4	37

Article 12 is framed upon an objection wch might bee made, whether the measure is the same taken here at paris, or if it were taken upon a levell by the sea side. here hee computes upon the fall of the seine & iudgeth the place where hee measured to bee raysed above the sea not more yn 80 Toyses. & concludes the difference betweene measuring here, & by the sea, not above 8 feet per degree. here hee makes a table of levells, describes an Instrument to take levells wth. Speakes about Refractions & how to Correct them.

Article 13 hee examines the opinions wch were different from his as of Fernelius, Snellius, & Riccioli, & gives some hints as to what may have given the occasion to their mistakes & the difference of their measures from his.

Certainly this methode of Monsieur Picarts is the exactest of any yet made use of, for the stating of a degree. next post, It may bee I may shew you how hee did it. now the wheather is very cold, & I straine my self much to doe what I have done butt because I promised you I would not faile you. my Service & Respects to all my Friends of your Society I am,

> Your most affectionate Servant
> *Francis Vernon*

Pray shew this to Mr Collins. what I have written is only to serve for an information for you & your Friends, butt not to have printed in the transactions.[14] adieu.

NOTES

1 Vernon had several times referred previously to Picard's geodetic survey and the publication of the book in which it was described; see especially Letter 1370 (Vol. VI, pp. 432–36).
2 See Vol. VII, p. 499, note 3.
3 The great Abbasid caliph of Baghdad, Abdullah al-Mamun (786–833). The trial was made near Palmyra.
4 See Jean Fernel, *Cosmotheoria* (Paris, 1527).
5 Willebrord Snel (1591–1626) measured (1615–17) the length of a degree between Alkmaar and Bergen-op-Zoom by triangulation; the work was described by him in *Eratosthenes Batavus* (Leiden, 1617).
6 For the places, see the map (p. 433) and the notes in Vol. VI, p. 436; see also, Letter 1870 below.
7 What Vernon means is that *two* measuring rods were placed end-to-end ten times till 80 toises had been marked out.
8 "36 inches and $8\frac{1}{2}$ lines [one line equals one-twelfth of a French inch], measure of the Chatelet in Paris."
9 "universal foot."
10 This figure is given in Art. VIII as the distance between the parallels of Malvoisy and Sourdon; Art. VI gives only the (greater) sum of the three distances actually measured.
11 This figure is found in Art. XI as the final distance on the ground between the two parallels.
12 "in round numbers."
13 $2864\frac{56}{71}$ in the original book, which is correct.
14 In fact Oldenburg read this letter to the Royal Society on 11 January 1671/2.

1854a
Cassini's Discovery of Japet

Enclosure with Letter 1854
From the original in Royal Society MS. C 1, no. 56

Dn. Cassini Ulterior deductio eorum, quae in proxime praegressa epistola continentur, de planeta nova[1]

Prope stellam, quae in Tychonis Catalogo est in altero flexu aquae Aquarii magnitudinis quintae, et hodie reponitur in gradibus 12.33 Piscium cum latitudine Australi gr. 2. 49′ in Uranometrica vero Bayeri notatur χ in primo flexu Australi,[2] sunt decem stellulae bono Telescopio visibiles, intra distantiam minutorum quinquaginta, ab hac stella Tychonica Boream versus, a nemine hactenus descriptae, nescio an visae. Illustris namque Hevelius, qui stellas sibi Telescopio visas, in hoc Coeli tractu cum praedicta stella Tychonica anno 1642 & 1643, quam diligentissime descripsit; et in Prolegomenis Selenographiae aere incisas dedit, ne unam quidem istarum bi annotavit.[3] Ad Orientalissimas harum stellularum Saturnus retrogradus

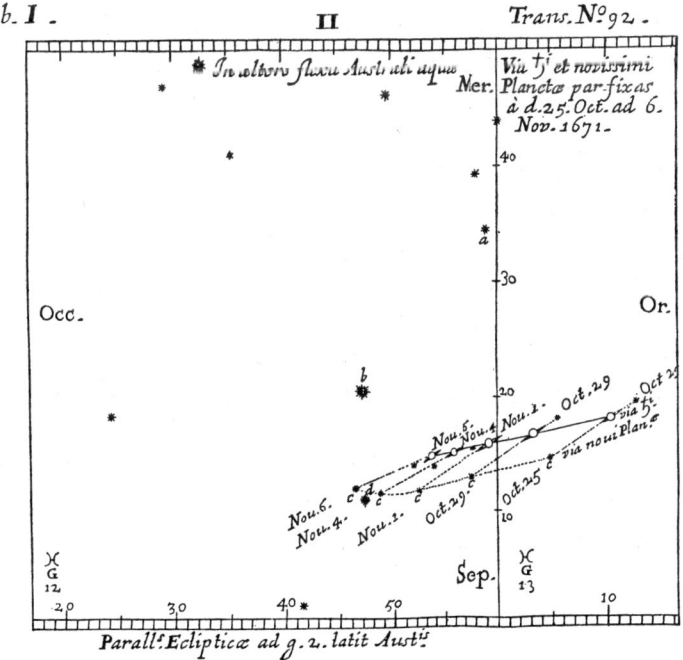

observatus est accedere intra aperturam Telescopii pedum 17, quae tanta est ut totum Solem comprehendat, die 24 mensis Octobris anni hujus 1671 hora 8. 45′ notataeque sunt duae Saturno viciniores *a* & *b*, a quibus Saturnus magis distabat quam ipsae inter se, quarta circiter parte distantiae ipsarum, propior tamen erat aliquanto ipsi *a* quam *b*. Videri non potuit Saturni satelles vel quia in ejus umbra versabatur, ut ex praecedentium dierum observationibus videbatur conjici posse, vel quia representari non posset Telescopio vento tunc agitato. Sequenti die 25 Octobris 7. 37′ Saturnus visus cum brachiis & comite Orientali, qui Septentrionalior erat a linea brachiorum in mediocri ab ipso distantia.[4] Ipse autem cum stellis notatis *a b* faciebat triangulum fere Isosceles, in cujus vertice versabatur, paulo vicinior dictis stellis quam die praecedenti. Praeter consuetum Satellitem vidi stellulam *c* Saturno Occidentalem, in recta linea brachiorum distantem ab ipso plus duplo distantiae satellitis ad oppositam partem, sic erat autem aliquanto minor ipso satellite[5] • ⌒ •

Die 29 Octobris hora 7 30 Saturnus propior erat stellae *b* quam *a* faciebatque triangulum Isosceles cum stellis *b d*, cuius basis *b d* distantia fixarum inter se erat dimidia distantiae Saturni ab iisdem. Erat inter Saturnum & stellam *d* paulo borealiora linea ducta per ipsos stellula *c*, & paulo vicinior Saturno quam stellae *d*. Satelles autem consuetus erat Orientalis, aliquanto Australior a linea brachiorum.

Die prima Novembris h. 7. 53. Saturnus visus cum brachiis valde tenuibus & fuscis, comite Occidentali, vix una diametro Saturni ab ipso distans qui a linea brachiorum deviabat nonnihil ad Austrum: Stella *c* quae die 29 Octobris magis distabat a stella *d* quam *d* a *b* nunc ab eadem distabat sola medietate distantiae *b.d.*

Die quarta Novembris vespere hora 7. Vidi Saturnum cum brachiis tenuibus, et comite consueto Occidentali prope maximam digressionem. Saturnus cum stellis *b d* faciebat triangulum fere Isosceles, & parum differentem ab Equilatero. Stella autem *c* valde vicina erat ipsi *d*, vix ab ipsa distans sexta parte distantiae stellarum *b d*.

Die 6 hora 7. 40′ Saturnum vidi cum brachiis valde tenuibus, comite Occidentali, & stellam *c* quae jam praeterierat stellam *d*, eamque reliquerat ad Ortum. Exinde dies permulti nubilosi omnem observationum continuandarum opportunitatem ademerunt, nec redeunte serenitate potuit ulterius mobilis haec stellula recognosci.

TRANSLATION

Mr. Cassini's later discussion of the matters contained in the next preceding letter, concerning the new planet[1]

Near the fifth-magnitude star which in Tycho's catalogue is in the alternate bend of Aquarius's water, denoted by the letter χ in the first southerly bend [of the water] in Bayer's *Uranometria*,[2] today resting at 12° 33' of Pisces with south latitude 2° 49', are ten starlets visible through a good telescope lying within the distance of fifty minutes north of this star of Tycho's and, if seen by anyone, certainly not yet described. For the illustrious Hevelius, who described very carefully in 1642 and 1643 the stars in this region of the sky containing Tycho's star visible to him through a telescope, and published an engraving of them in the prolegomena to his *Selenographia*, recorded no single one of them there.[3] Saturn was observed to reach the easternmost of these little stars in his retrograde motion at 8h. 45' on 24 October of this year 1671, using a telescope of seventeen feet of such an aperture that it will include the whole of the Sun, and two [stars] *a* and *b* were observed closer to Saturn, the distance from him being greater than the distance between them by one-fourth part, roughly, Saturn being however a little nearer to *a* than to *b*. It was impossible to see Saturn's satellite [Titan], either because it had moved round into the shadow (as it seemed might be guessed from the observations of the preceding days) or because the telescope then vibrating in the wind could not reveal it. On the following day, 25 October, Saturn was seen at 7h. 37' with his "arms" and his companion to the east, which was

> The path of Saturn and the newest planet
> through the fixed stars
> from 25 October to 6 November.
>
> [*For the figure, see page 439*]

north of the line joining the two "arms" at a little distance from him.[4] With the stars marked *a*, *b*, Saturn formed an almost isosceles triangle about the vertex of which it was moving, being a little nearer to those stars than on the previous day. Besides the usual satellite I saw the little star *c* to the west on the line joining the "arms" and distant from Saturn, more than double the distance of the satellite on the opposite side. Thus it was a little smaller than the satellite.[5] [*See the small drawing on page 440.*]

On 29 October at 7h. 30' Saturn was nearer to the star *b* than to *a* and formed an isosceles triangle with the stars *b* and *d*, whose base *bd* (the distance between the two fixed stars) was half the distance of Saturn from them. The star *c* was between Saturn and the star *d*, a little north of the line drawn between them, being a little nearer to Saturn than to the star *d*. The usual satellite however was to the east, a little south of the line joining the "arms."

On 1 November at 7h. 53'. Saturn was seen with his "arms" very thin and dark, his satellite being to the west deviating quite a lot south of the line between them and distant barely one diameter of Saturn from him. The star *c* which on 19 October was further from *d* than *b* from *d*, was now only half as far from *d* as the distance *bd*.

On the evening of 4 November at 7 o'clock I saw Saturn with very slender "arms" and the usual satellite to the west at maximum deviation. Saturn made an almost isosceles triangle with the stars *bd*, indeed nearly equilateral. However the star *c* was very much nearer to *d*, scarcely being further from it than a sixth part of the distance between the stars *b* and *d*.

On 6 November at 7h. 40' I saw Saturn with extremely thin "arms," his satellite to the west, and the star *c* which had already passed the star *d* had left it behind to the west. From that time onwards very cloudy weather has spoiled every opportunity for continuing the observations and when fine weather returned I could not detect that little star any longer.

NOTES

When this paper was produced at the meeting of 11 January 1671/2 (Birch, *History*, III, 3) Oldenburg recorded it as a "letter" of 9 January 1671/2, N.S., which is also the date of Letter 1854. It is not endorsed as a letter. It seems clear that it is the document mentioned by Cassini in Letter 1848, and was transmitted by Vernon. The handwriting is not English, nor Cassini's autograph. The heading was added by Oldenburg. The dates are New Style in the Latin, the figure, and our translation.

1 This refers to Letter 1848.
2 See Letter 1830, note 3.
3 See *Selenographia* (Danzig, 1647), fig. D, facing p. 34.
4 The figure is missing from the manuscript and the Letter Book; indeed, it was handed to Hooke for study when the paper was read on 11 January 1671/2. However, a printed figure (reproduced here) which exactly fits the text was reproduced in *Phil. Trans.*, no. 92 (25 March 1673); in this issue Oldenburg at last printed an account in English—not a translation of the present document—of Cassini's discovery of Japet and its subsequent confirmation. The diagram runs from Pisces 12° 17' to 13° 16' and (vertically) from 2° S. Lat. to about 2° 50' S. Lat. North is towards the *bottom* of the diagram, which is an inverted mirror image.
5 The little diagram is very roughly sketched on the paper.

1855
Oldenburg to Wallis
30 December 1671

This letter is answered in two from Wallis, Letters 1865 and 1872; it dealt with some botanical questions raised by Vogel in Letter 1811, described Oldenburg's barometical readings and Newton's new telescope, and mentioned the new publications by Morland and Ralph Bohun. This is the first allusion in the correspondence to Newton's reflecting telescope, which was examined by the Royal Society in late December 1671 and was probably the occasion of Isaac Newton's being proposed a Fellow on 21 December. Before 1 January 1671/2 it had been examined at Whitehall by the King, Brouncker, Moray, and others. The exact date and manner of the telescope's arrival in London are not known; on 14 December John Collins was able to write a slightly garbled hearsay account of the instrument to Vernon in Paris, but he had clearly not seen it with his own eyes (Rigaud, I, 176). The statement in Newton, *Correspondence*, I, 72, note 1, that Newton presented a reflecting telescope to the Royal Society "late in the year 1669" is a mistake.

1856
Oldenburg to Huygens
1 January 1671/2

From *Œuvres Complètes*, VII, 124–26
Original in the Huygens Collection at Leiden

A Londres le 1. Janvier 1672

Monsieur,

Je me trouve obligé de ne differer pas plus longtemps ma responce à la vostre du 7 novembre, vous ayant d'abord souhaité, avec cete nouvelle annee, une nouvelle confirmation de vostre santé et un accroissement de toute autre felicité. Les observations de Monsieur Cassini touchant la suite des Taches solaires, accompagnees de celles qui regardent Saturne (pour la communication desquelles nous vous sommes bien obligéz) s'impriment presentement en Anglois dans les Transactions qui appartiennent au mois de Decembre, mais qui ne sont pas encore achevées, à cause de l'interruption que ces iours de festes donnent aux ouvriers.¹ Je vous les pourray envoier la semaine qui vient, avec quelques lettres latines de Monsieur Hevelius touchant ses propres observations du mesme Planete; la derniere Eclipse de la lune; une occultation de la 1ere des Jovialistes par l'ombre de Jupiter; un transit de [Jupiter] et [Lune]; comme aussi les observations faitez à Hamburg touchant les taches du soleil retournees etc.

Au mesme temps ie fais estat de vous expliquer l'invention d'une nouvelle sorte de Telescope par Monsieur Isaac Newton, Professeur de Mathematiques à Cambridge.² Tout ce que ie vous en diray à present, c'est, que par le premier Essay, qui en a esté vû et examiné icy, il apparoit, qu'un telescope d'environ 6 pouces, a representé l'object 9 fois plus grand qu'un Telescope ordinaire de 25 pouces, en comparant la mesure de l'une et l'autre image.³ Cela se fait, par deux reflexions, dont l'une, refleschit l'object d'un concave metallin à un miroir metallin plan, l'autre, de ce miroir à un petit verre oculaire plano-convexe, qui envoye l'object à l'oeil, et l'y represente sans aucune couleur et fort distinctement en toutes ses parties. Vous en aurez la figure, et une entiere description, par le prochain ordinaire, s'il plait à Dieu.

Touchant la suite des verres non-spheriques, auxquelles Monsieur Smethwick travaille, ie vous diray, que l'autheur pousse tousiours son dessein, et croit d'y pouvoir reussir, ayant depuis peu fait un petit Tube d'environ 6. pouces, qui fait voir l'object aussi bien et aussi nettement qu'une lunette ordinaire, assez bien travaillée, de 18. pouces, à ce que quelques personnes intelligentes l'estiment. Il y va lentement, par ce qu'il ne se sert de personne que d'un valet pour travailler dans sa chambre, voulant perfectionner la chose en particulier, devant que de la faire publique et commune.

J'ay receu cejourdhuy une lettre de Monsieur Sluse,⁴ qui respond à la mienne, ou ie luy avois mandé ce que vous m'escrivistes dans vostre derniere touchant la construction dudit Sieur Sluse sur le probleme d'Alhazen; vous vous proposant alors d'en communiquer avec luy mesme. Sur quoy il m'a envoyé un discours fort docte, contenant ses posterieures meditations sur le dit probleme, qui estant trop longues pour estres copiées dans le peu de temps, qui me reste acetheure, il faut que i'en remette aussi le detail iusques à une autre fois. Cependant ledit Hugens⁵ adjoute ces paroles: A Clarissimo Hugenio nihil adhuc accepi, aliis, ut existimo, studiis occupato. La lettre fut datée VI. Cal. Januar. 1672.

Au reste, i'ay la 3me partie du livre de Monsieur Wallis pour vous l'envoyer de sa part: ce que i'executeray par le premier amy, qui passera d'icy à Paris.

Vos amis icy seront tres-aises d'entendre des bonnes nouvelles touchant vostre pendule, que vous ditez estre ajustée d'une maniere nouvelle pour observer les longitudes et estre envoyée dans un voyage en Amerique.

J'ay depuis peu envoyé a Monsieur Vernon la figure et la description imprimée de la Trompe de Monsieur Moreland, l'ayant prié de vous la faire voir, et d'entendre vos pensées la dessus particulierement sur le probleme, qu'il y a inseré, touchant la veritable figure, et les dimensions d'un instrument, qui aggrandit le mieux et le plus la voix humaine. Je ne doubte pas, que vous ne l'ayez desia vû et consideré, et que vous n'ayez la bonté de nous en dire vostre sentiment; ce qui obligera particulierement Monsieur

Vostre treshumble et tresobeissant serviteur
Oldenburg

ADDRESS

> A Monsieur
> Monsieur Christian Hugens de Zulechem
> à la Bibliotheque du Roy
> á
> Paris

TRANSLATION

London, 1 January 1671/2

Sir,

I feel obliged to defer no longer my answer to yours of 7 November [N.S.], having first wished you with this new year a new confirmation of your health and an increase of all other happiness. Mr. Cassini's observations on the continuation of the sunspots accompanied by those concerning Saturn (for communicating which we are much obliged to you) are at this moment being printed in English in the *Philosophical Transactions* for December, which are not yet printed off on account of the interruption to the workmen created by these holidays.[1] I shall be able to send them to you in the coming week, with some Latin letters of Mr. Hevelius concerning his own observations of the same planet, the latest eclipse of the moon, an occultation of the first of Jupiter's satellites by the shadow of Jupiter, a transit of Saturn and the Moon, and also the observations made at Hamburg on the return of the sunspots, and so on.

At the same time I have it in mind to explain to you the invention of a new kind of telescope by Mr. Isaac Newton, Professor of Mathematics at Cambridge.[2]

All that I can tell you now is that at the first attempt to see and examine it here, it seems that a telescope of about six inches represented an object nine times larger than an ordinary telescope of 25 inches, comparing the size of the two images.³ This is accomplished by two reflections, one of which reflects the object from a metal concave to another plain metal mirror, the other from this mirror to a small plano-convex glass eyepiece which sends the object to the eye and represents it without any color and very distinctly in all its parts. You shall have a drawing and a complete description by the next post, God willing.

Concerning the continuation of the nonspherical lenses on which Mr. Smethwick is working, I shall say that the inventor is pressing on with his plan and believes he can succeed, having recently made a little tube of about six inches which permits the seeing of an object as well and as distinctly as an ordinary, well-worked telescope of eighteen inches, as several intelligent people believe. He gets on slowly, because he makes use of no help except from a servant working in his room, wanting to perfect the thing in private before making it public and common knowledge.

Today I received a letter from Mr. Sluse⁴ in reply to mine in which I told him what you wrote me in your last about the said Mr. Sluse's construction of Alhazen's problem, and your intention of communicating with him directly. He has written me a very learned discourse on this subject which being too long to be copied in the small amount of time now remaining to me, I must also defer sending you the details until another time. However the said Huygens⁵ adds these words: "I have so far received nothing from the famous Huygens, who is, as I suppose, intent on other studies." The letter was dated 27 December 1671 [N.S.].

For the rest, I have the third part of Mr. Wallis's book to send you on his behalf, which I shall do by the first friend who goes from here to Paris.

Your friends here will be very glad to hear good news of your clock which you say has been adjusted in a new manner for the observation of longitude and is to be sent on a voyage to America.

I recently sent Mr. Vernon the figure and printed description of Mr. Morland's trumpet, having asked him to show it to you and to learn your ideas upon it, and especially on the problem he has introduced into it concerning the correct shape and dimensions of the instrument which best and most magnifies the human voice. I don't doubt that you have already seen and considered it, and that you will kindly tell us your opinion of it. This would especially oblige, Sir,

Your very humble, obedient servant,
Oldenburg

ADDRESS
  Mr. Christiaan Huygens
    At the King's Library
      Paris

NOTES

Reply to Letter 1807.
1 *Phil. Trans.*, no. 78, is dated 18 December.
2 See Letter 1855.
3 As is clear from the diagram accompanying Letter 1866a, the increase is about three diameters.
4 Letter 1843.
5 *Sic*; read: "Sluse."

1857
Oldenburg to Newton
2 January 1671/2

Printed in Newton, *Correspondence*, I, 73, from
the copy in Royal Society MS. O 2, no. 64

Oldenburg reports to Newton the interest his reflecting telescope has aroused at Court and in the Royal Society, and informs him of the proposal that he, Oldenburg, should send a formal statement of the invention to Huygens "thereby to prevent the arrogation" of foreigners. He enclosed a draft diagram and description of the new instrument, prepared in London, for his approval. (This, corrected by Newton, was later transmitted to Huygens with Letter 1866.) Oldenburg also reported some difficulties that had been raised about the optical properties of Newton's telescope.

1858
Johann Ludwig Hannemann to Oldenburg, King Charles, and the Royal Society
3 January 1671/2

From the original in Royal Society MS. H 3, no. 11

Rex potentissime, invictissime, principes
serenissimi, Comites celsissimi,
Vosque caeteri Generosissimi societatis
Regiae assessores

Ætherea fama serenissimae vestrae societatis Regiae, Rex potentissime invictissime, principes serenissimij; Comites celsissimi; Barones perillustres, Generosissimi, et Vos Doctores excellentissimi, Amplissimi, Vostrum, inquam fama sydera dudum tetegit, ac omnium mortalium traxit oculos animosque: Montem parnassum Musarum, Heliconem pieridum in vestram societatem Regiam, duplici nomine Regiam demigrasse fatemur: Regem Vestrum serenissimum principem, Collegii vestri supremum praesidem etiam Apollinem vivum, et quid hercle eo divinius repraesentare infallibilis spei est, sed quo vehor an in laudem tanti collegii? ibi profecto nec mens, nec lingua, nec manus suum officium facerent amplius, intraque vota nostra et merita vestra starent. quare illud redivivis ciceronibus nepotum dissertissimis demandatum volumus, ut caetera, qua vellemus, in limine tam splendidissimae societatis illa perorant pectora devotissima. Et si liceat heic pauca balbutire (annuente Rege praeside serenissimo, caeterisque celsissimis, illustrissimis membris) Sanguis succus ille noster vitalis per totum corpus nostrum sparsus et fluxu Euripi indefesso circularis juxta Clarissimum Harveum Anglorum Aristotelem, adhuc dum, ubinam generetur inter doctos controvertitur, hactenus et antequam ductus Lactei Thoracici a Pequeto Gallo et Bartholino Dano detecti, Epati sanguificandi facultas adjudicata postea autem cordi hoc munus sanguificandi ringente Veritate obtrusum, quam sententiam minime amplecti possumus: Glissonius vester, ni fallor, sanguificandi facultatem ipsi sanguini acceptam refert merito,[1] quam opinionem et nos ut omnium verissimam hactenus propugnatus adversus incomparabilem virum Fridericum Hoffmanum Medicum Hallensem excellentissimum deque republica medica optime meritum, ut olim publice constabit,[2] neque hanc sententiam adhuc mutaturus sum, nisi Vestra Societas Regia contrarium jubeat, cujus sententiae unice acquiescemus, hic ergo vestrum judicium, cui nos subjicimus, anxie moramur, plura adderemus Sed haud licet, respondere paucis placeat, supplices rogando rogamus.

>Florete Musarum principes
>Vestrae Societatis addictissimus
>et humillimus cultor
>*Johannes Ludovicus Hannemann*
>urbis Buxtehudae physicus

Dabam Buxtehuda in Ducatu
Bremensi Die 3 januarii anno 1672

ADDRESS
> Illustrissimae Societati
> Regiae Curiosorum
> In Britannia.
> hujusque Secretario dignissimo,
> Viro Generoso Henrico Grubendol
>> pateant
>>> Londinj

TRANSLATION

Most mighty and victorious king, most serene highnesses, most highborn counts, and you other noble Fellows of the Royal Society

O most mighty, victorious king, most serene highnesses, most highborn counts, very illustrious barons, knights, and you, most excellent doctors, worthy Sirs, the fame of your most serene Royal Society has almost reached the heavens; I say, your fame has touched the stars, and it attracts the eyes and minds of all mortals. We confess that the Muses' Mount Parnassus and their Helicon have migrated to your Society, which is twice over named Royal. Your king, a serene highness, is, as its chief president, a living Apollo, and, by Hercules, what hope have we of representing him more divinely? But whither am I led in praise of such a college? In truth, to a point where neither mind nor tongue nor hand performs its function any longer, falling between our hopes and your accomplishments. Wherefore we wish for help from some reincarnated, most eloquent descendant of Cicero, so that devoted minds may declaim the remainder of our meaning on the threshold of so very splendid a society. And if it is permitted to stammer out these few words (by leave of the serene kingly president and the rest of the high-born and illustrious Fellows): Where that life-giving blood-juice of ours—diffused throughout our body and circulating like a tireless Euripean tide, according to the famous Harvey, the English Aristotle—is generated, has been hitherto debated between learned men; before the lacteal ducts of the thorax were discovered by the Frenchman Pecquet and the Dane Bartholin the faculty of bloodmaking was assigned to the liver, but afterwards this gift of bloodmaking was forced upon the heart in the teeth of truth, an opinion we could never embrace. Your Glisson, unless I am mistaken, rightly referred that received faculty of bloodmaking to the blood itself,[1] and this opinion we also have defended hitherto as most true of all against the incomparable Friedrich Hoffmann—most excellent physician of Halle, greatly deserving of the world of medicine—as has been shown in public before now,[2] nor shall I modify this opinion unless your Royal Society ordains the contrary; to whose judgments alone we must bow. Hence we here anxiously await your decision, to which we have subjected ourselves. We could add more but it would not be fitting. As begging supplicants we beseech you to send us a few words in reply. May you flourish, chief among the Muses!

> Your Society's most devoted and humble supporter,
> *Johann Ludwig Hannemann*
> Physician of the town of Buxtehude

Buxtehude in the Duchy of Bremen, 3 January 1672

ADDRESS

Let this be laid before the most illustrious Royal Society
of Investigators in Britain,
and its very worthy Secretary,
the wellborn Henry Grubendol,
    at London

NOTES

When this letter was read on 8 February 1671/2, Oldenburg was instructed to reply that the Society was grateful for the writer's respect, but "it is not their custom to be hasty in delivering their judgment in any philosophical matters; but that all things of that nature are committed by them to observations and experiments frequently and carefully made "(Birch, *History*, III, 10).

Johann Ludwig Hannemann (*c.* 1640–1724) was born at Amsterdam and studied theology before turning to medicine. He practised medicine in Germany from 1668 onwards, becoming Professor of Medicine at Kiel University in 1675 and M.D. of Copenhagen. He was a member of the Academia Curiosorum. He wrote much on medicine, hermetic chemistry, the philosophers' stone, and other esoteric topics.

1 See Francis Glisson, *Anatomia hepatis*... (London, 1654), Ch. XXXV (in the Amster-

dam, 1659 reprint, pp. 358–62). Glisson maintains that the blood is not made by liver, heart, veins, or arteries but by the vital spirit in the blood itself, which originated from the vital seed and preceded all the organs of the body.

2 Presumably this refers to medical disputations, not yet printed. Hannemann was to publish *Fasciculus 60. quaestionum miscellanearum. Una exhibens mantissam anti-Hoffmannianam de vero sanguificandi organo* (Bremen, 1672). This Friedrich Hoffmann is probably the man who was physician at Magdeburg before accepting a post at Halle; he was born in 1626 and died in 1675. Hannemann more than once referred to Hoffmann's "Mantissa Cardianastrophes," published at Leiden only in 1740 under the title *Cardianastrophe admiranda*.

1859
Pardies to Oldenburg
3 January 1671/2

From the original in Royal Society MS. P 1, no. 74

A Paris 13. de l'an 1672 [N.S.]

Monsieur

On ne peut pas en user d'une maniere plus obligeante que vous faites n'y d'une façon plus genereuse que fait le tres-illustre et tres-excellent Monsieur Boile Certainement Monsieur, j'avois auparavant une veneration bien profonde pour la doctrine et pour les grans merites de vos personnes: mais maintenant je suis si touché de la bonté obligeante dont vous en usez envers moy quil n'y a rien que je ne voulousse faire pour vous témoigner ma reconnoissance. Je vous supplie de me faire encore cette grace de vouloir assurer Monsieur Boile de mes tres humbles respects et de luy dire qu'outre le rang que je puis tenir dans le nombre de ses admirateurs il me fera un singulier plaisir s'il veut me conter pour un de ses plus fideles serviteurs.

Vous me ferez plaisir de m'escrire toujours par la poste quand il vous plairra de me faire cet honneur. pour mon adresse vous pourrez mettre comme il vous plairra pourvu qu'avec mon nom ou bien avec ma qualité de Professeur de Mathematique vous mettiez au College de Clermon á Paris

Pour les livres que vous me faites la grace de vouloir prendre soin de m'envoyer, je vous prie que ce soient tous ceux qui ont esté imprimez en Angleterre depuis 7 ou 8. ans touchant les mathematiques ou la philosophie soit en latin soit en Anglois. Le libraire qui nous fera emplette peut vous donner le memoire de ces livres et de leur prix que vous prendrez la peine de m'envoyer par la poste. et incontinant, mesme devant que les livres soient partis, je vous feray tenir l'argeant par M. Justel ou par telle autre voye qu'il vous plairra, suivant tout ce qui sera marqué dans le memoire, parce que je me persuade que vos libraires ne vous marqueront rien que le juste prix qu'il desireront avoir de leur livres. Pour les Transactions qui ont esté faites je vous prie qu'elles soient toutes mises avec les autres livres. Mais pour celles qui se feront dorenavant il suffira de me les envoyer par la voye de M. Justel ou de quelque amy à mesure qu'elles se feront ou la commodité se presentera.

Vous et Monsieur Boyle m'avez sensiblement obligé en me communiquant l'observation du son dans le vuide. Il est trop visible que la maniere de Florence n'est pas exacte pour empescher l'entrée de l'air. Mais il y a grande apparence que du moins l'air dans leur machine est extremement rarefié. Cependant ils disent que les fluttes de leur organello sonnent toujour en mesme ton. c'est ce que je voudrois bien qu'on experimentast. Le P. Kircher raporte une experience d'une clochette de verre qui sonna fort distinctement dans le vuide fait par le moyen de l'eau. quoy qu'il en soit de cette experience je m'en rapporte infiniment plus à M. Boyle parce que je scay qu'il y va avec une certitude qui luy est toute particuliere.

Comme je vous voy d'une humeur si obligeante je vous demanderay encore une grace. Je scay que M. Hook a fait de belles experiences sur les refractions de diverses liqueurs.[1] n'y auroit-il pas moyen d'avoir une petite table de ces refractions? un mot seulement pour l'esprit de vin pour l'huile de therebentine &c. Item si en rectifiant l'esprit de vin ou en le meslant il peut faire telle refraction qu'il voudra ou enfin s'il ne scait pas la maniere de temperer tellement une liqueur qu'elle fasse la refraction qu'on desire. Cela me seroit tres utile pour une petite invention que je m'en vay faire imprimer.[2] C'est une Horloge au dedans d'une chambre où une Iris marque toute sorte d'heures et tous les autres cercles coelestes. Cette Iris doit toujours estre dans un plan perpendiculaire aux rayons du soleil. J'ay divers moyens de le former, mais le plus aisé de tous seroit une phiole ronde de verre remplie d'une liqueur transparente qui fit la refraction d'un certain degré que je desirerois. J'ay trouvé sur cela quelque chose que j'espere qui ne desagrêra pas aux intelligeans.

Pour mon dessein du traitté du mouvement Je profiteray du sage avis que vous me donnez de ne m'embarrasser pas aux questions metaphysiques et déstablir ma doctrine sur de bonnes experiences. Ça toujours esté mon dessein et quoique dans ce premier discours j'ay fait profession de vouloir tout prouver par les seuls principes dela metaphysique et de prevenir toutes les experiences; je n'ay pas laissé d'avoir egard à ce qui se passe en effect dans la nature, et je croy mesme avoir fait sur ce sujet toutes les experiences necessaires et avec autant d'exactitude qu'on pourroit souhaitter. Mais quand les experiences certaines nous ont appris une fois ce qui est dans la nature; il ya plaisir de rechercher la cause de ces effects, et comme si on ignorait ce que l'experience nous a appris, prouver *à priori* ce qui doit s'en ensuivre. C'est ainsi qu'Archimede à demonstré les loix de l'equilibre dissimulant de scavoir ce qu'il ne pouvoit ignorer des experiences communes à tout le monde.

Mais puis que vous avez bien eu la bonté d'approuver en general mon dessein, je veux vous en faire ici un petit détail pour scavoir de vous plus en particulier vostre sentiment et recevoir vos avis. Je veut L'intituler *La Mechanique ou la Science du mouvement local appliquée à quelques questions importantes de la Nature et a quelques inventions curieuses de l'art*.[3]

aprés le premier discours, jen mets un second *de la Statique* où j'explique le plus clairement qu'il m'est possible les lois de l'equilibre et de toutes les forces mouvantes que ie reduits toutes à la ballance. cela est commun. Des corps suspendus; de la figure des cordes suspendues par les deux bouts: je croy avoir ladessus quelquechose de particulier et je demonstre dans quel cas cette figure seroit Parabolique comme Gallilée l'a souhaitté. et en quel cas elle seroit hyperbolique ou Elliptique.[4]

Le 3e discours est du mouvement des corps pesans. de leur acceleration dans la cheute et de leur retardement dans leur montée. Je demonstre à priori la proportion de leur vitesse ce que Galilée n'a fait qu'en supposant une definition que Baliani, le P. Le Casre le P. Fabri et plusieurs autres luy contestent.[5] Vous scavez les longues contestations qui ont esté la dessus entre Gassendi et le P. le Casre.[6] M. Fermat termina leur different par une demonstration qui est parmi les lettres à de Gassendi où il prouve fort geometriquement que le mouvement dans l'hypothese du P. le Casre est impossible et qu'il ne faudroit pas moins d'une eternité à une pierre pour tomber de la hauteur d'un pied.[7] Le P. Lalouvere est survenu la dessus et a demonstré que le mouvement se peut fort bien faire dans l'hypothese du P. le Casre pourvu que le Corps ne passe pas par tous les degrés de tardiveté.[8] et en effet il pretend que la pesanteur du corps estant determinée dans un certain degré de force, cette pesanteur aussi pousse en bas le corps avec un certain degré de Vitesse dez le commencement de la cheute: et cela a paru si raisonnable que M. Fermat mesme n'y trouva rien à redire. Mais je demonstre geometriquement que cette pesanteur determinée qui pousse ainsi dez le commencement avec un certain degré de force et d'une certaine vitesse, est impossible: du moins si l'on suppose que la pesanteur agit perpetuellement et sans interruption.

En tous ces discours je mesle plusieurs questions de physique de Geometrie et de Mechanique. comme ici de la force des percussions d'un coup de marteau qui passe aussi par tous les degrez de foiblesse. du mouvement des astres á scavoir s'ils peuvent se mouvoir par une *forme interieure* comme quelques uns veulent; et si en ce cas leur mouvement ne seroit point acceleré comme celuy des corps pesans &c. Je demonstre qu'un grain de sable tombant sur un plat de ballance feroit soulever l'autre plat où seroit le poid le plus enorme du monde et je donne la hauteur jusques où le poid s'eleveroit.

Le 4e discours est des Liqueurs. Je demonstre à priori que leur vitesse au bas des tuyaux est en raison sous doublée de la hauteur des tuyaux. mesme dés le commencement de leur chutte, pourvu que le tuyau soit plus grand que le trou par où sort l'eau en bas. Car si le tuyeau est tout uniforme aussi grand en bas qu'en haut la vitesse augmentera à mesure que l'eau sortira. J'explique aussi leur equilibre dans les tuyeaux inegaux: je les compare les unes avec les autres pour rendre raison des experiences du vuide. Je traitte de leur saillies. je donne quelques inventions curieuses des fontaines artificielles: et enfin je donne quelque avis et quelques regles pour la conduitte des eaux, des machines pour les élever &c.

Le 5e des Librations soit des pendules, soit des cordes, soit des ressorts et de toute autre sorte de corps. Je demonstre à priori que les vibrations des cordes tendues sont uniformes, c'est à dire que les petites durent autant que les grandes dans une mesme corde: que les vibrations de deux cordes egales en grosseur et egallement tendues sont en mesme raison que leur longueurs. qu'une mesme corde tendue par divers poids fait les vibrations en raison sous doublée des poids: en un mot je demonstre tout ce que l'experience nous fait voir dans les consonances des cordes ayant egard à leur grosseur, longueur tension et pesanteur. pour les pendules outre ce qu'on scait communément je demonstre aussi ce qu'on m'a dit que M. Hugens à trouvé scavoir que le mouvement d'un poids seroit toujours egal dans les divers arcs d'une cycloide.[9] la demonstration en est tres belle et si vous voulez je vous l'envoiray. Item qu'un poids *a* suspendu par un filet *ab* se mouvroit par une cycloide *ace* egale à celle qui seroit en *bde* en sorte que le filet s'appliquast toujours a ladite cycloide *bde*. Pour la pratique

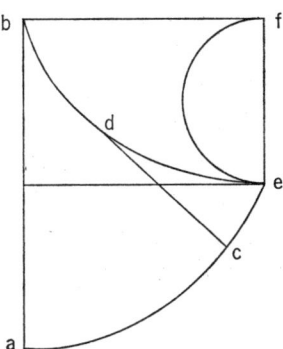

cela ne seroit pas plus juste que si le poids se mouvoit tout seul dans son cercle. le filet *ba* en double du diametre *fe*.

Le 6e discours et du mouvement d'Ondulation, par lequel j'explique toute la nature et toutes les proprietez du son et de la Lumiere. Je fais entendre pour quoy dans les consonances les octaves font un son de mesme espece ce qui n'arrive pas dans les autres consonnances. ce qui me revient le plus en cecy est la proprieté des refractions de la lumiere que je demonstre geometriquement par là. Il ya deja plusieurs années que j'ay enseigné publiquement tout cecy et mesme je l'ay imprimé dans des theses. Depuis peu j'ay lu l'excellent ouvrage de M. Hooc de Micrographia. j'y ay lu avec plaisir ce qu'il y dit des ondulations pour expliquer la lumiere et j'ay bien eu de la complaisance de voir que j'avois concouru avec un si docte homme en plusieurs choses. mais dans la suitte j'y ay trouvé des choses qui m'ont un peu surpris. Il veut que la refraction des rayons se fasse par les ondulations vers la perpendiculaire entrant dans un corps ou les ondulations vont plus vite ou plus aisément.[10] Il veut aussi que les rayons ne soient pas toujours perpendiculaires aux ondulations, et il explique les couleurs par les diverses inclinations. or je croyois avoir demontré le contraire. A scavoir 1º que les rayons sont toujours perpendiculaires. 2º.que la refraction se fait vers la perpendiculaire lors que les ondulations s'y font plus lentement. quoy qu'il en soit je feray juge M. Hooc luy mesme de nostre petit different, et je suis prest á luy deferer en toute chose.

Je ne vous parle pas de plusieurs incidens qui se trouvent meslés par cy par la ny des questions geometriques qui peuvent s'y resoudre. comme de la figure que fait une liqueur qui file en tombant en bas. ou de la methode generalle de mesurer le temps sur les vitesses dans le mouvement acceleré, ou vicissim. par le moyen des vitesses et des temps comparez ensemble je fais cette proposition generale. Datam figuram (cujuscumque generis planam, solidam) cubare/quadrare ex data tangente certae cujusdam curvae quae ad datam figuram certam habeat analogiam. cette proportion s'applique à une infinité de figures extraordinaires.

Voila Monsieur un destail de mon dessein. Je vous demande pardon si je vous importune par une si longue lettre, le desir que j'aurois de profiter de vos lumieres et de vos avis m'a fait prendre cette liberté. J'imprime actuellement un discours de la connoissance des Bestes.[11] que je vous envoiray incontinant qu'il sera fait.

ADDRESS
   A Monsieur
   Monsieur Grubendol
      Londres

TRANSLATION

Paris, the thirteenth of 1672 [N.S.]

Sir,

One could not be treated in a more obliging manner than you have done, nor in a more generous fashion than the very famous and excellent Mr. Boyle has done. Certainly, Sir, I formerly held the learning and high personal merits of both of you in the most profound respect; but now I am so touched by the obliging kindness you both show me that there is nothing I should not willingly do to testify my gratitude. I beg you to do me yet another favor by kindly assuring Mr. Boyle of my very humble respects and informing him that besides the status I can hold among the number of his admirers, it would give me singular pleasure if he would count me among his most faithful servants.

You will give me pleasure by always writing to me by the post when you are pleased so to honor me. As for my address, you can put it however you please provided that with my name or else my rank as Professor of Mathematics you put "at the Collège de Clermont at Paris."

As for the books you are doing me the favor of kindly taking care to send me, I beg you to let these be all those printed in England during the past seven or eight years relating to mathematics or philosophy in either Latin or English. The bookseller who will make the purchase for us can give you the list of these books and their price and I will trouble you to send them to me by the post. And immediately, even before the books have started on their way, I will see that you have the money through Mr. Justel or by any other route that suits you, according to all those which are marked in the list, because I am convinced that your booksellers will not mark other than the just price which they wish to receive for their books. As for the *Philosophical Transactions* please put all those already published in with the other books. But those to be published in the future may be simply sent to me via Mr. Justel or by some friend, according as opportunity serves.

You and Mr. Boyle have decidedly obliged me by communicating to me the observation of sound in the vacuum. It is all too obvious that the Florentine method is not exact enough to prevent the entry of air. But it seems very likely that at least the air in their contrivance is extremely rarefied. However, they say that the pipes of their little organ always sound in the same pitch. This is something I would very much like to have tested. Father Kircher reports an experiment with a little glass bell which rang very distinctly in a vacuum created by means of water. However it may be with that experiment I take very much more to that of Mr. Boyle, because I know that he works with a precision which is unique to him.

Since I find you in so obliging a frame of mind, I shall ask you for another favor. I know that Mr Hooke has made some fine experiments on the refractions of different fluids.[1] Would there not be a way of having a little table of these refractions? Only a word on spirit of wine, on turpentine, and so on. Also, if by rectifying spirit of wine or by mixing it he can produce any refraction he wishes, or, finally, whether he knows the way so to treat a fluid that it will produce any desired refraction. This would be very useful to me in connection with a little invention I am going to have printed.[2] It is a sundial in a room on which a spectrum marks every sort of hour and all the other celestial circles. This spectrum must always be in a plane perpendicular to the rays of the sun. I have various methods of forming it, but the easiest of all would be by a round flask of water filled with a transparent fluid which made a refraction of the precise degree I require. I have in this connection found out something which, I trust, will not be unacceptable to intelligent men.

As for my plan for the treatise on motion, I shall profit by the wise advice you give me not to hamper myself with metaphysical questions, and to build my theory upon good experiments. This has always been my plan, and although in this first discourse I have put on a show of wishing to prove everything by the principles of metaphysics alone and to anticipate all experiments, I have not failed to pay attention to what actually goes on in nature, and I think that I have even made all the necessary experiments on this subject and that with all the accuracy one could wish for. But when sure experiments have once taught us what exists in nature there is pleasure in searching out the cause of these effects and, as if ignorant of what experience has taught us, to prove *a priori* what must follow. This is how Archimedes demonstrated the laws of equilibrium, pretending not to know what he could not have been ignorant of, from experiments known to everybody.

But since you have been so very kind as to give general approval of my plan, I should like to describe it for you here in a little detail, to learn from you your exact opinion and to receive your advice. I propose to call it *Mechanics, or the science of local motion applied to several important questions of nature and to some interesting practical inventions*.[3]

After the first discourse I shall put a second "On Statics" in which I shall explain as clearly as I can the laws of equilibrium and all the moving forces which I reduce to the balance. That is usual. On hanging bodies; on the shape of bodies suspended by both ends; I believe I have found something special on that subject, and I shall demonstrate in which case this shape would be parabolic, as Galileo hoped, and in which case it would be hyperbolic or elliptical.[4]

The third discourse is on the motion of heavy bodies, their acceleration during fall, and their slowing down in ascent. I shall demonstrate *a priori* the ratio of their speeds, which Galileo only did by assuming a definition which Baliani, Father Cazré, Father Fabri, and several others dispute.[5] You know the long disputes which took place between Gassendi and Father Cazré.[6] Mr. Fermat ended their difference by a demonstration which is among the letters to Gassendi, in which he proves very geometrically that in Father Cazré's hypothesis motion is impossible and it would take not less than an eternity for a stone to fall from the height of one foot.[7] Father La Loubère came in on this and demonstrated that motion could perfectly well occur in the hypothesis of Father Cazré provided that the body did not pass through all degrees of slowness.[8] In fact he claims that as the weight of a body is determined at a certain degree of force, this weight also pushes the body downwards with a certain degree of speed from the beginning of its fall; and this seemed so reasonable that Mr. Fermat himself found no fault with it. But I demonstrate geometrically that this determinate weight which thus pushes from the beginning with a certain degree of force and at a certain speed is impossible, at least if one assumes that the weight acts perpetually and uninterruptedly.

I shall mingle with all these discourses various questions of physics, geometry, and mechanics. As here of the force of the percussion of hammer blows, also passing through all the degrees of weakness. Of the motion of the stars, to learn whether they can move themselves by an "internal form" as some propose, and whether in this case their motion would not be at all accelerated like that of heavy bodies, etc. I shall demonstrate that a grain of sand falling on the pan of a balance makes the other pan rise even if it has on it the most enormous weight in the world and I shall give the height to which the weight would rise.

The fourth discourse is on fluids. I shall demonstrate a priori that their speed at the bottom of a tube is as the square root of the height of the tube; even from the beginning of their fall, provided that the tube is larger than the hole through which the water issues at the bottom. For if the tube is quite uniform, as large at the base as at the top, the speed will increase in proportion as the water issues forth. I shall also explain their equilibrium in nonuniform tubes; I shall compare one with the other to explain the experiments on the vacuum. I shall treat their jets. I shall give several interesting inventions of artificial fountains and, finally, I shall give some advice and some rules for conducting water, on machines for raising it, and so on.

The fifth of oscillations: of pendulums, strings, springs, and every other sort of body. I shall demonstrate *a priori* that the vibrations of stretched strings are uniform, that is to say that the small ones last as long as the large ones in the same string; that the vibrations of two equal strings (equal in thickness and equally stretched) are as their lengths; that the same string stretched by different weights performs its vibrations as the square root of the weights; in a word, I shall demonstrate everything that experience teaches us about the consonance of strings, having regard to their thickness, length, tension, and weight. As for pendulums, besides what is commonly known I shall also demonstrate what I have heard that Mr. Huygens has found out, that is to say that the motion of a weight will always be equal in the different arcs of a cycloid.[9] The demonstration of this is very fine, and if you like I shall send it to you. Also that a weight *a* suspended by a thread *ab* would move in a cycloid *ace* equal to that which would be in *bde* if the thread were always applied to the said cycloid *bde* [*see the figure, page 455*]. In practice this would not be any more accurate than if the weight moved by itself in its circle. The thread *ba* is twice the diameter *fe*.

The sixth discourse will be on the motion of waves, by which I shall explain the entire nature and all the properties of sound and light. I elucidate the reason why in consonances the octaves give sounds of the same kind, which does not happen in the other consonances. What pleases me most in all this is the property of the refractions of light which I shall from this demonstrate geometrically. I have already taught all this publicly for several years, and even had it printed in the form of theses. Recently I read the excellent work of Mr. Hooke, *Micrographia*. I read with pleasure what he there says about waves to explain light, and I was very well satisfied to see that my opinion coincided with those of so learned a man in several matters. But in what followed I found things which a little surprised me. He wants rays to be refracted when perpendicular waves enter a body where the waves move faster or more easily.[10] He also wants the rays to be not always perpendicular to the waves, and he explains colors by means of the different inclinations. Now I think I have demonstrated the contrary. That is to say, first, that the rays are always perpendicular and second, that refraction always occurs towards the perpendicular when the waves travel more slowly. However this may be, I shall make Mr. Hooke himself judge of our little disagreement, and I am ready to defer to him in all things.

I do not speak of several problems scattered here and there nor of the geometrical questions that can be resolved therein. For example, the shape taken by a fluid which shoots out in falling down, or the general method of measuring time against speed in an accelerated motion or vice versa. By comparing together the speeds and the times I derive this general proposition: "To cube/square a given figure (plane or solid and of any kind) from a given tangent to a certain determinate curve having a determinate analogy to the given figure." This proportion is applicable to an infinite number of extraordinary figures.

Here, Sir, is a detailed account of my plan. I make my excuses for importuning you with such a long letter; my desire to take advantage of your knowledge and your advice has made me take this liberty. I am at this moment printing a treatise on the consciousness of animals,[11] which I shall send you instantly when it is ready.

ADDRESS
    To Mr. Grubendol
        London

NOTES

Reply to Letter 1844.
1 See Vol. II, pp. 208, 224, 248, etc.
2 This design for an unusual sundial—an artificial rainbow formed by admitting light through a hole and a refracting medium into a darkened room was to trace the hours by its motion—was described by Pardies in *Horologium thaumanticum duplex*. As this little work is stated by Pardies's biographers to have been printed at Paris in 1662, his manner of expression here is hard to understand. Certainly he alludes to it as already published in the preface to *Deux machines propres à faire les quadrans* (Paris, 1673), which he calls an extract from the earlier work.
3 Pardies did not live to see the publication of this complete work, as Oldenburg remarked in his notice of *La Statique ou La Science des Forces Mouvantes* (Paris, 1673) in *Phil. Trans.*, no. 94 (19 May 1673), 6042–46, in the preface to which Pardies describes the whole in terms very like those employed in this letter.
4 Pardies's first *Discours* corresponded to the previously published *Discours du mouvement local*, while the second is the already-mentioned *La Statique*. The remaining discourses were never published.

In his *Discorsi matematiche* (Leiden, 1638) Galileo was the first to consider the shape of a rope suspended by its ends; he guessed its curve to be a parabola. Pardies (wrongly) seems to suppose it may be any conic section. In fact the problem remained unsolved at this time.
5 See Giovanni Battista Baliani, *De motu* (Genoa, 1638); Pierre de Cazré, *Physica demonstratio, ... adversus nuper excogitatam a Galilaeo... de eadem motu pseudo-scientiam* (Paris, 1645); Honoré Fabri, *Tractatus physicus de motu locali* (Lyons, 1646).
6 Pierre Gassendi's answer to Cazré was *De proportione qua gravia decidentia accelerantur epistolae tres...Quibus ad totidem epistolas... P. Cazraei... respondetur* (Paris, 1646). See his *Opera* (Lyons, 1658), III, 564 ff.
7 This letter of Pierre de Fermat (of 1646) was first published in Gassendi's *Opera*, VI, 541–43. See Paul Tannery and Charles Henry, *Œuvres de Fermat* (Paris, 1894), II, 267–76. Fermat himself remarked: "ces deux personnages ont fait de gros volumes... J'ai tranché tout ce différend en trois ou quatre pages."
8 See Antoine de la Loubère, *Propositiones geometricae sex, quibus ostenditur ex cazraeiana hypothesi circa proportionem qua gravia decidentia accelerantur, non recte inferri a Gassendo*

motum fore in instanti... [Toulouse, 1658]. The point of all this discussion was (in modern terminology): is the instantaneous velocity of an accelerating body correctly represented by $\frac{ds}{dt} = at$, or by $\frac{ds}{dt} = as$? Galileo embraced the former alternative (leading to $s = \frac{1}{2}at^2$), rejecting the latter as yielding infinite velocities. His critics argued that this was not the case, but only at the cost of assuming (as La Loubère showed) that an accelerating body does not move from zero velocity smoothly to any given velocity, but "jumps" directly from zero to some (small) finite value. This is in conformity with the result derivable from the second alternative, $s = Ae^{at}$. See I. Bernard Cohen in *Isis*, 47 (1956), 231–35.

9 Huygens had discovered the isochronism of cycloidal motion in 1659; his proof of this (and of the fact that the evolute of a cycloid is an identical cycloid) was published in *Horologium oscillatorium* (Paris, 1673). Pardies's proof appeared as an appendix to the book under discussion, the "Privilege" of which is dated 19 October 1672.

10 See *Micrographia* (London, 1665), p. 57 and Scheme VI, fig. 1.

11 *Discours de la connoissance des bestes* (Paris, 1672), which opposes the theory of Descartes that animals are insensitive machines; see *Phil. Trans.*, no. 82 (22 April 1672), 4054.

1860

Dodington to Oldenburg

5 January 1671/2

Mentioned in Dodington's Letter 1902, as being in reply to Oldenburg's Letter 1822.

1861

Newton to Oldenburg

6 January 1671/2

Printed in Newton, *Correspondence*, I, 79–80, from the original in private possession

In this reply to Letter 1857 Newton expresses surprise at the Royal Society's estimation of the importance of his telescope. He corrects and amends Oldenburg's draft description to be sent to Huygens, and answers the difficulties raised about the optical properties of the telescope. He also explains how to keep the eyepiece clean. Finally, he expresses his appreciation of his proposed election as Fellow of the Society.

1862

Oldenburg to Wallis

9 January 1671/2

The writing of this letter in the weekly series is somewhat doubtful; according to Wallis (Letter 1872) it was mentioned in Letter 1869 (of which only a memorandum survives), but never reached him.

1863

Lister to Oldenburg

10 January 1671/2

From the original in Royal Society MS. L 5, no. 42
Printed in *Phil. Trans.*, no. 76 (22 January 1671/2), 3052-55

Sir

I am very much pleased, when you give me to understand, yt somthing is published of ye Anatomy of Vegetables, & yt more is designed by yt excellent person Signior Malpighi; And since ye receipt of your last, I have perused ye very ingenious Book of Dr Grew; &, as far as I have observed these matters, all things therin are faithfully delivered, & wth great sagacity. In turning over my Notes, made some yeares agoe, I find, amongst other things of this Nature, some few Observations concerning the Veines of Plants or such Ductus's as seem to contain & carry in ym ye noblest juices of Plants. Of these, there is little or noe mention made in this curious Tractate, unlesse under ye Notion of Pores. And because I am of ye opinion, yt they will prove Vessells analogous to our human Veines, & not meer pores, they shall, if you please, be ye subject of your entertainment in this Letter, & ye rather that, if they prove Veines (as I little doubt ym) they are not to be passed over in silence, but are early to be accounted for in ye Anatomy of Vegetables.

To avoid ambiguity, those parts of a plant wch Pliny (lib. 16. cap. 38) calls by ye Names of *Venae*, & *pulpae*,[1] are nothing else, in my opinion, but what our late Authour Dr Grew calls Fibres & Insertments, or ye *lignous* body interwoven with yt wch he takes to be the *cortical*, yt is, ye several distinctions of ye *Grain*. Now, yt ye Vessells, we are about to discourse of, are not any of ye pores of ye lignous body (to use ye Doctors Termes) is plain in a traverse cutt of *Angelica Sylvestris magna vulgatior J.B.*[2] (for example;) the Veines there very clearly shew ymselves to an attentive view to be distinct ye fibres observable in the *parenchyma* of ye same cortical body together wth ymselves; ye milkie juice still rising besides and not in any Fibre. Alsoe in ye like cutt of a Bur-dock in June, ye like juice springs both on this & on yt side of ye radij of ye woody Circle, yt is, in ye Cortical body & pith only. Again, where there is noe pith, there is none of this juice to be observed, & consequently none of these Veines as in ye roots of plants & trunks of Trees; but ever in ye barke of either. I need not here enumerate ye many Plants wherin these particulars are most plainly observable, as in *Sphondylium*,[3] *Cicutaria*,[4] many of ye Thistle kind, etc.

Further, neither are they probably of ye number of ye Pores described by our authour in ye Cortical body, or Pith; not surely of those pores extended by ye *breadth*, because ye course of ye juice in these Vessells is by ye *length* of ye plant; as I have sometimes very plainly traced in ye pith of a dryed Fennel-stalke, following ym by dissection quite through ye length of ye pith. It remaines, yt, if pores, they are of those pores of the Cortical body, yt are supposed to be extended by ye length thereof: wch yet seemes (to me at least) not enough, but we thinke ym Vessells, invested wth their owne proper membranes, analogous to ye Veines of our humane body; for these reasons,

1. Because they are to be found in ye Pith, and sometime in ye Cortical body of a plant not included within ye Common Tunickle of any Fibres, as is above noted; (yt Fibres, or ye Seminal root are cloathd, is most plain in some plants, as in *Fern*, & *Geranium batrachoides*;[5] ye fibres of ye *former* are coated at least in some parts of ye plant wth a black skin, in ye *latter* likewise wth a red one:) And in these cases, had they not, I say, their owne proper membranes, we see noe cause, why ye very porous & spongy body of ye pith & cortex, should not be in all places filled alike wth yt juice, & not rise (as most plainly it doth) in a few determinate & set places only, yt is, according to ye position and order of these Vessells. 2. Again ye Experiment I made, & wch you were pleased to publish, concerning ye effect of a ligature on *Cataputia minor Lobel*.[6] viz. the suddain springing of ye milkie juice out of infinite pores besides ye incision; (the cause of

wch Phaenomenon I take to be, ye dissected Veines impetuously discharging ymselves of part of their juice within ye porous *parenchyma* of the barke;) whence it is probable, yt, if there was no coated Vessel to hold this milkie juice, we might well expect its springing upon ye bare ligature; as when we squeeze a wet Sponge, ye external Cuticle of ye plant, as this Experiment shews, being actually perforated.

In ye next place, It is very probable, yt these Vessells are in all Plants whatsoever. For, as it is truth-like of all the other *substantial* parts of plants, yt they are actually in, & common to all plants, though specifyed by divers accidents in figure & texture; so of these *Veines*, which, though they be discernable mostly in those plants, where they hold *discoloured juices*, yet we may very probably thinke, yt they are not wanting, where ye eye finds not yt assistance in ye challenging of ym. As in these very plants, where they are *least* visible, there is yet a time when they are, if not in all, yet in some, parts of these plants plain enough to ye naked Eye: The tender shoots of the Greater & Lesser *Maple*,[7] in May, are full of a milkie juice, viz. ye known liquor of these Veines. Again to this purpose, if you apply a clean Knife-blade to a traverse cutt of ye like Shoots of *Elder*, ye Gummy liquor of these Veines will be drawn forth into visible strings, as is ye nature of bird-lime of ye barke of *Holly*, or ye milke of *Cataputia minor Lobel*. Further, ye leaf-stalks of our garden-Rhubarb doe sometimes shoot, (by what accident, we enquire not here,) a transparent & very pure chrystalline Gumm, though ye Veines, yt held this gummy juice, are by noe ordinary meanes visible in ym; & yet by comparing ye Nature & properties of this Gumm wth yt of ye Gumme of other Vegetables, we cannot doubt but this *Gum-Rhubarb* is ye juice of these Veines, as well as we are assured, ye Gumm of other vegetables to be of theirs, by ye same comparative Anatomy. Lastly, we thinke yt even *Mushromes* (ye seemingly inferiour & imperfect order of Vegetables) are not exempt & destitute of these Veines, some of ym yielding a milkie juice hot & fiery, not unlike some of ye *Spurge*-kind or *Euphorbium*.

It might be expected, yt I should add somethings at least concerning ye Original & Productions of these Veines, if not an exact Description of ym; ye course of ye juices in ym; & their more immediate & primary Uses in ye matter of Vegetation: But I must acquaint you, yt (besides ye season is not now proper to improve & verify, if I had leisure, ye observations formerly noted, & yt they were things thrown into my *Adversaria*[8] without other order, then yt nothing should slip from me in ye quest of medicaments yt might be of light) although I find indeed, many scattered particulars (besides ym already delivered) concerning ye Position, Order, Number, Capacity, Distributions, Differences, Figure, etc. of these Veines, you will be pleased to take in good part, if I thinke fitting to reserve ym untill ye opportunity of an other Summers review: It seeming to me noe small matter, to have fairly hinted ye existence of ym to such curious persons, as shall have ye leisure, & find ymselves in better circumstances, yn I can pretend to, as to those great advantages of Glasses, Designing, etc.

To conclude wth ye *primary* Use of these Veines; wch is, in my opinion, to carry ye *succus nutritius*[9] of plants, because where they are not, there is noe Vegetation; as is seen, if an Engrafted branch or Arme be bared & stripped off ye clay basse etc. in June, all ye course of Vegetation will appear to have been made only by ye barke & not by ye wood, yt is, in ye place only where these Veines are. A *secondary* use is ye rich furniture of our Shopps; for, from these Veins only it is, yt all our Vegetable druggs are extracted; & infinite more might be had by a diligent enquiry, & some easy meanes, wch I have not unsuccessfully put in practice; witnesse ye Black Resin, I not long since sent you a specimen of. I am Sir

Your most humble servant
Martin Lister

Yorke January 10th 1671.

ADDRESS

    These
For my much honored friend
    Henry Oldenburgh Esquire
at his house in ye Palmal
        London

POSTMARK IA 12

NOTES

Reply to Letter 1850.
1 "veins" and "pith."
2 The large, commoner, wild angelica of Jean Bauhin, perhaps *Angelica archangelica*.
3 Cow parsnip, *Heracleum sphondylium*.
4 Hemlock, *Conium maculatum*.
5 Crowfoot cranesbill.
6 Spurge (genus *Euphorbia*); compare Vol. VII, Letter 1634, note 4 (printed in *Phil. Trans.*, no. 70, 17 April 1671, 2121-23).
7 That is, sycamore.
8 Notebooks.
9 "nutritive juice."

1864
Oldenburg to Kirkby
12 January 1671/2

Oldenburg received Kirkby's Letter 1838 on 31 December 1671 and answered it twelve days later, according to his endorsement on the envelope.

1865
Wallis to Oldenburg
14 January 1671/2
From the original in Royal Society MS. W 1, no. 135

Oxford January 14. 1671.

Sir,

I have forborn to answere yours of December 30, in hope to have had some farther account from Dr. Morrice[1] to send you. I had first from him (concerning ye Nux Vomica, Arbor Bdellij, & Mirrhae,) only this general account, that in Piso, Johannes Margravius,[2] and Clusius in his second part de Exoticis,[3] you might have an account of them. I have since (with him) consulted Piso, but in him we found nothing. The other two hee promised mee to search and give mee an account, but hath not yet done it, though I have divers times called upon him for it. I think he will very shortly be at London, and I doubt whether I shall have any further account of him before he go; but there you may possibly have it of him, for I told him it was from you that I received the Quaere.

My Barometer, wch with yours was Dec. 24 at $30\frac{1}{8}$, was fallen ye next day to $29\frac{1}{2}$; & December 30, 31 below 28; but December 29 & January 1, about $29\frac{1}{4}$, and rose till at Jan. 5, 6, to $29\frac{3}{4}$ & Jan 7, a little higher; then fell, and is this morning at 29 or a little lesse (these two last night having been rainy;) I expect it will now rise all this week.

Mr. Newton's improvement of ye Telescope, by contracting it, (wch is very advantageous,) I have seen an account of, in a letter from Mr

Collins to Mr Bernard;[4] onely (I perceive) there is a difficulty to find ye object, and it is more dark by ye reflexion; these may perhaps by further improvement be rectified.

Sr. Samuel Morelands book I have not seen, but mention was made of the thing in ye same letter of Mr. Collins. The problem he mentions, must be solved by experience, (rather than demonstration,) there being a complication of so many physical accidents, yt ye neglect of some one unheeded may soon defeat a demonstration, deduced from some others of them. When you write to Mr. Vernon, you may desire him to let mee know whether what I have inserted from Mr. Hugens (in my last chapter of my book de Motu) be to his content;[5] I indeavoured it might be so. My service, with a happy New Year, to yourself and Lady, from Sr.

Your affectionate friend and servant,\
John Wallis

I did not hear, til I heard it from you, yt Mr. Bohun's Book was stopped in ye presse; It was, I am told, onely for two or three words (I know not what,) but is now abroad, though I have it not.[6] I presume it is at London before this time, else I would send you one.

ADDRESS

These For Mr. Henry Oldenburg, in
the Palmal, near St. James's
London

POSTMARK IA 15

NOTES

Reply to Letter 1855.
1 Presumably Robert Morison.
2 See Letter 1780a, note.
3 Probably Wallis meant Charles de L'Ecluse, *Exoticorum libri decem: quibus animalium, plantarum, aromatum, aliorumque peregrinorum fructuum historiae describuntur* (Antwerp, 1605).
4 That Collins was in correspondence with Edward Bernard in December 1671 is apparent from Rigaud, but this letter is not recorded; no doubt Collins' account was similar to that he wrote Vernon (above, Letter 1855, note).
5 In Chapter XIV—the penultimate chapter of *De motu*— Wallis discusses the anomalous suspension of mercury and the experiments upon it made by Huygens and others. Wallis attributes the first observation of the phenomenon to Boyle. (*Opera mathematica*, Oxford, 1695, I, 1050.)
6 For an explanation of this postscript, see Letter 1872.

1866
Oldenburg to Huygens
15 January 1671/2

From *Œuvres Complètes*, VII, 128–29
Original in the Huygens Collection at Leiden

a londres le 15 janvier 1672.

Monsieur,

Voicy l'effect de la promesse, que ie vous fis par ma derniere du 1 janvier.[1] vous verrez par la description et la figure ce que c'est, plus particulierement que ce que ie vous en dis grossierement dans la dite lettre. Vous aurez la bonté de nous en dire vostre opinion. Il y aura quelque difficulté de trouver une substance refleschissante, qui se puisse conserver nette. De mesme, il ne sera pas si facile, de trouver les objects par cete sorte de Telescopes. On croit pourtant, que l'on pourra trouver quelque expedient pour l'un et l'autre.

Je croy, Monsieur, que vous aurez vû la Description imprimée de la trompe de Monsieur Moreland. j'avois prié Monsieur Vernon de vous la faire voir, et de vous demander vos pensees sur le Probleme, que l'Autheur y a inseré, touchant la veritable figure, et les dimensions d'un Instrument, qui aggrandit le plus et le mieux la voix de l'homme.

J'ay envoyé au mesme les Transactions du mois de Decembre,[2] qu'il ne manquera pas de vous monstrer s'il vous plait de prendre la paine de les lire. Je ne manquerois pas de vous en envoyer un Exemplaire toutes les fois, qu'on en imprime, si ie croiois, qu'elles fussent dignes de vous, et que le pacquet n'en fut trop enflée.

Monsieur le Chevalier Moray vous fait ses humbles baisemains, et tous vous autres amis icy seront tres aises d'entendre la continuation de vostre santé, si importante au progres des sciences solides. Je vous baise les mains et suis Monsieur

Vostre tres humble et tres obeissant serviteur
H. Oldenburg

Si Monsieur Justel desire de voir, et mesme de faire copier la figure et la description de ce telescope de Monsieur Newton, ie vous prie de luy en faire part. J'espere que vous avez receu ma lettre du 1 janvier 1672;

et ie seray bien aise d'entendre, que celle-cy vous ait esté bien rendue.

P.S. Je m'estonne Monsieur, que vous n'avez pas encor receu la 3me partie du livre de Monsieur Wallis de Motu et Mechanice; dont ie vous envoiay, de la part de l'Autheur, un Exemplaire le 13me Octobre 1671, par la voye de Monsieur Rancher, grand amy de Monsieur Justel; comme ie fis au mesme temps, un autre à Monsieur Carcavy.[3] Je vous prie, d'en vouloir parler à Monsieur Justel, et luy monstrer ce que i'en dis icy. Je suis tres-assuré que i'ay fait ce que dessus, l'ayant marqué dans mes tablettes.

ADDRESS
A Monsieur
 Monsieur Christian Hugens de Zulichem
  à la Bibliotheque du Roy
   à
    Paris.

TRANSLATION

London, 15 January 1671/2

Sir,

Here is the fulfilment of the promise I made to you in my last [letter] of 1 January.[1] You will see by the description and the drawing what it is, in more detail than from what I told you more crudely in that said letter. You will be so kind as to give us your opinion of it. There will be some difficulty of finding a reflecting material which can be kept brilliant. Besides, it will not be so easy to locate objects with this kind of telescope. But it is thought that it will be possible to find remedies for both these [difficulties].

I imagine, Sir, that you must have seen the printed description of Mr. Morland's [speaking] trumpet. I have begged Mr. Vernon to show it to you, and to ask you for your thoughts on the problem introduced by the author, on the true shape and the dimensions for an instrument which will magnify the human voice most and best.

I have sent the *Transactions* for December to the same person,[2] which he will not fail to show you if you are pleased to take the trouble to read them. I should not fail to send you a copy every time that one is printed, if I thought that they were worthy of you and if the package were not thereby made too bulky.

Sir Robert Moray makes you his humble compliments and all your other friends here are very glad to hear of the continuation of your good health, so important for the progress of the true sciences. I kiss your hands and am, Sir

    Your very humble and obedient servant
    H. Oldenburg

If Mr. Justel wishes to see or even have a copy made of the drawing and the description of Mr. Newton's telescope, I beg you to share it with him. I hope that you received my letter of 1 January 1671/2, and I should be very glad to hear that this one has reached you safely.

P.S. I am astonished, Sir, that you have not yet received the third part of Mr. Wallis's book, *De motu et mechanice*; I sent you a copy with the author's compliments on 13 October 1671, through Mr. Rancher, a great friend of Mr. Justel, as I did another at the same time to Mr. Carcavy.[3] I beg you to be so good as to speak to Mr. Justel and to convey to him what I say here. I am very well assured that I did what I have said above, having written it down in my records.

ADDRESS
  Mr. Christiaan Huygens of Zulichem
    at the King's Library
      Paris

NOTES

1 Letter 1856; the enclosure here is Letter 1866a.
2 See *Phil. Trans.*, no. 78 (18 December 1671), containing a communication from Huygens. Any letter to Vernon accompanying this copy is lost.
3 See Letter 1798 (dated 14 October, however, which Huygens did receive); again, there is no record of a letter to either Justel or Carcavy.

1866a

Newton's Telescope

Enlcosure with Letter 1866
From *Œuvres Complètes*, VII, 129–31
Original in the Huygens Collection at Leiden

Explicatio figurae

AB speculum concavum metallicum, fundo tubi adhaerens cujus radius 13 digitorum Anglic. fere.

CD speculum metallicum planum ovale, bacillo ferreo affixum, et circulo aeneo, intra tubi cavitatem mobili, insertum. F lens vitrea, cujus latus superius planum inferius convexum, radius autem circiter $\frac{1}{12}$ digiti.

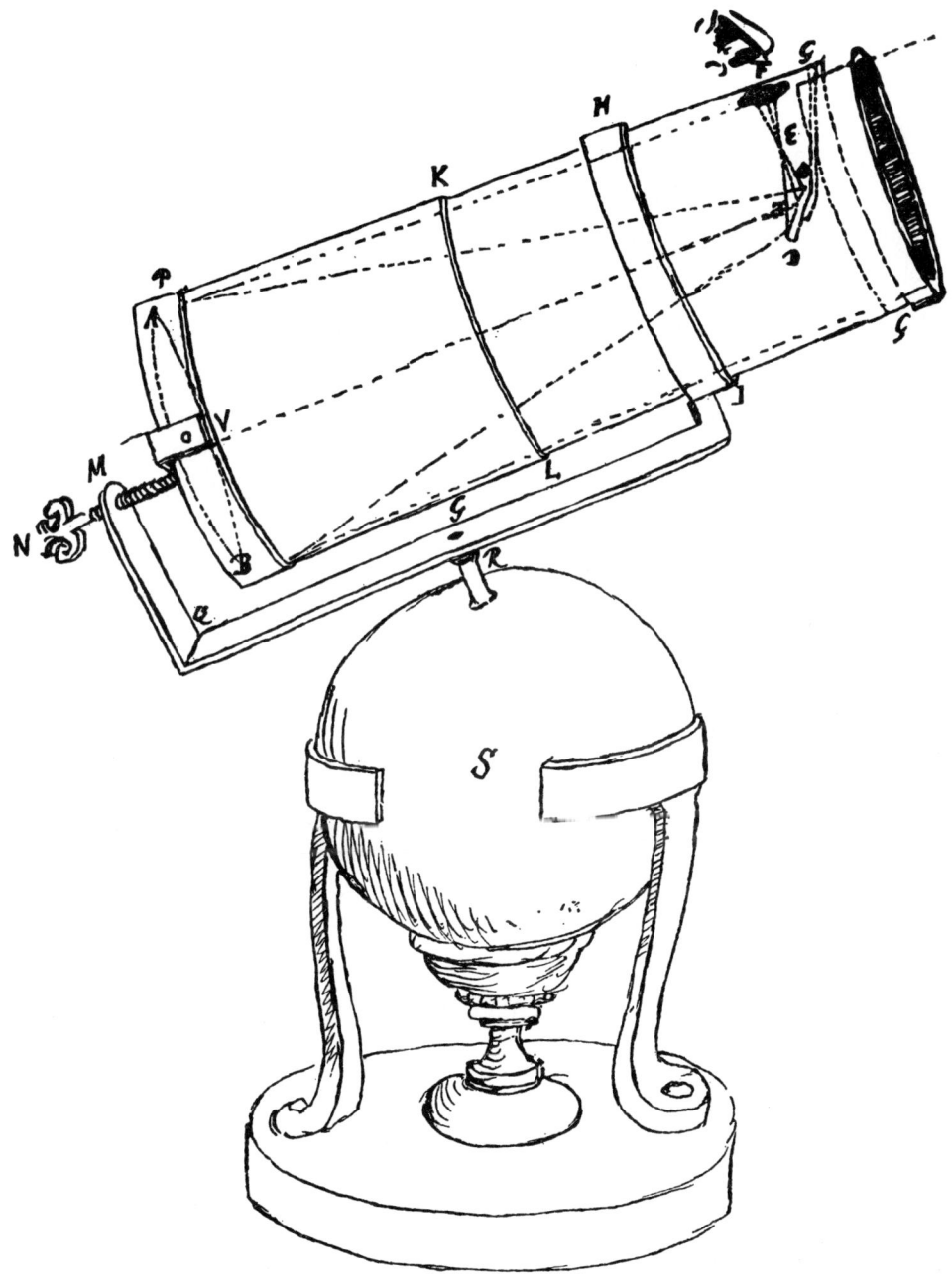

Metallum quippe colligit solis radios ad distantiam 6⅓ digitorum, et lens ocularis ad ⅙ dig. fere distantiam ab ejus vertice. Novi etiam dimensiones eorum ex vasis in quibus elaborata fuere; speciatimque diametrum haemispherici concavi, in quo elaborata fuit lens vitrea, dimensus illum $\frac{1}{6}$ digiti esse reperio.

G.G.G.G. pars tubi anterior, circulo aeneo *HI* firmiter constricta ita ut non facile moveri possit.

PQKL. Pars tubi posterior, circulo aeneo *PG* immobiliter affixa.

O uncus ferreus, circulo aeneo *PG* affixus, ultra tubi axem extensus, cui clavus cochleatus *N* immissus, tubi partem posteriorem antrorsum pellit, vel retrahit, ad speculorum debitam distantiam investigandam, parte priore fixa remanente.

NMGI[1] ferrum curvatum, quod tubum sustinet: glubo ligneo *S*, clavi *R* adminiculo affixum.

Centrum speculi *CD* locatur in axe tubi, ita ut in ipsum perpendicularis, a centro lentis demissa cum axe angulum rectum constituat, et objecti species a speculo concavo in idem repercussa, versus lentis focum *E* reflectatur.

Conferendo distantias foci istius a verticibus lentis et speculi concavi, h.e. *EF* $\frac{1}{6}$ digiti. et *ETV* $6\frac{1}{3}$ dig; prodit ratio 1 ad 38; qua indicatur, objecta 38 circiter vicibus ampliari.

Corona ferrea, ventilogio, ornamenti ergo, imposita, 300 circiter pedibus distans, cum uno oculo huic tubo admoto, spectabatur, altero in charta subjecta, 11 circiter digitis ab ipso distante, magnitudine et figura, *A* insignita apparebat[2] tubus autem vulgaris 25 digitos longus, lente objectiva convexa, oculari vero utrinque concava (cujus radius est 2 digitorum) oculo admotus, figuram coronae dictae magnitudine *B*. eadem observata chartae ab ocula distantia, alteri oculo exhibebat.

TRANSLATION

Explanation of the figure

AB is a concave metal speculum attached to the base of the tube whose radius is about thirteen English inches [*see the figure, page 471*].

CD is a plane oval metal speculum fastened to an iron stalk and mounted within a brass circle, movable within the hollow of the tube. *F* is a glass lens whose upper surface is plane and whose lower surface is convex, with a radius of one-twelfth of an inch, roughly. The metal [mirror] focuses the sun's rays at a distance of $6\frac{1}{3}$ inches and the eye lens at a distance of almost one-sixth of an inch from its vertex. I also knew their dimensions from the forms on which they were polished, particularly the diameter of the concave hemisphere in which the glass lens was polished, for having measured it I found it to be one-sixth of an inch.

G.G.G.G. is the front part of the tube, firmly clasped by the brass circle HI so that it cannot easily be moved.

$PQKL$ is the rear part of the tube, fixed immovably to the brass circle PG.

O is a bent piece of iron secured to the brass circle PG and extending beyond the axis of the tube, into which the screwed key N is inserted so as to move the rear portion of the tube backwards and forwards while the front part remains fixed, in order to find the proper distance between the mirrors.

$NMGI$[1] is a curved piece of iron supporting the tube: it is fastened to the wooden ball S by means of the pin R.

The center of the speculum CD is so placed in the axis of the tube that a perpendicular line let fall from the center of the lens makes there a right angle with the axis, and the image of an object reflected to the same point by the concave mirror is again reflected towards E, the focus of the lens.

Comparing the distances of this focus from the vertex of the lens and [that of] the concave speculum, that is, $EF = \frac{1}{6}$ inch and $ETV = 6\frac{1}{3}$ inches, the ratio works out at 1 to 38, which indicates that the object should be magnified about 38 times.

When an iron crown placed as an ornament on a weathervane at the distance of about three hundred feet was looked at by placing one eye to this tube, while the other eye was directed to a sheet of paper about eleven inches distant from it, the crown seemed of the size and shape shown at A.[2] When the eye was applied to a common telescope twenty-five inches long with a convex objective and a biconcave eye lens (whose radius is two inches) the form of the crown appeared of the size [shown at] B, when the other eye was directed to the same paper as before at the same distance.

NOTES

As already mentioned, this description was originally drawn up by Oldenburg, who revised it in accord with further information he received from Newton. The copy in the Royal Society (printed in Newton, *Correspondence*, I, 74–76) is an earlier "state" than the present paper, which was copied from it for transmission to Huygens.

The figure shows Huygens' copy, in his diary, of the illustration sent him by Oldenburg. The original is lost, because it was sent by Huygens to the Abbé Gallois for the *Journal des Sçavans*.

1 Read: "MQI."
2 The large and small images of the crown were omitted by Huygens in making his sketch. The one is about three times the size of the other.

1867
Oldenburg to Johannes Ott
15 January 1671/2

From the copy in Royal Society MS. O 2, no. 67

Doctissimo Viro
Domino Johanni Ott Philosopho Helvetio
Henr. Oldenburg Soc. R. Secr.
Salutem

Vidi non ita dudum Eruditas tuas Physico-Mechanicas de Visionis Natura Cogitationes, easque publice in Ephemeridibus meis Anglicis Numero 71. laudavi.[1] Testatum quippe inibi facis, mentem Te gerere authoritatibus emancipatam, atque rationis et experimentorum praesidio veritatem investigare. Genuinum hoc ipso societatis Regiae alumnum Te praestas, indeque amplissimam sine dubio studiorum tuorum mercedem reportabis. Elucere id jam ex ijs incipit, quae de Machina, elaborandis figuris Conicis apta, nec non de longissimis tubis, citra ipsarum fraudem, contrahendis, ad invenisse Te perhibes. Felicissimum porro ijs in rebus successum Tibi comprecamur, hortamurque impense ut inventa illa tua in rem vertere, eaque ratione scientiarum fines proferre ne renuas. Rem nobis pergratam praestabis, si exponere non graveris, quid reapse inventorum istorum beneficio peregeris; et si qua in re vicissim queam bene de Te mereri nequaquam detractabo. Prima hac vice, qua commercium literarium Tibi pando, brevis ero, postea, Deo dante, si ita libuerit, fusius liberiusque tecum collocaturus. Hisce vale, et me, Virtutis ac Doctrinae Tuae Cultorem, ama. Dabam Londini die 15. Januarij 1672.

TRANSLATION

Henry Oldenburg, Secretary of the Royal Society, greets the very learned Mr. Johannes Ott, the Swiss philosopher

Not long ago I came across your learned physico-mechanical reflections on the nature of vision, and praised them publicly in my English *Transactions*, no 71.[1] For truly you there prove that your mind works independently of authority and that you investigate truth under the auspices of reason and experiment.

In this you stand out as a true pupil of the Royal Society, and hence no doubt you will obtain a most ample profit from your studies. That already begins to stand out among them which you report you have discovered concerning a machine proper for polishing conic sections and shortening very long telescope tubes without spoiling them. We wish you a further happy success with these things and earnestly exhort you to reduce your discoveries to practice and not to deny the further extension of the frontiers of science in that way. You will act in a manner most welcome to us, if you will be good enough to explain what you have actually accomplished through those inventions; and if I can in return deserve well of you I shall not fail to do so. On this first occasion of opening a correspondence with you I will be brief, and afterwards, God willing, I shall if you wish write more freely and at greater length. Farewell now, and love me as an admirer of your learning and virtue. London, 15 January 1672.

NOTES

Although none of these biographical facts can be positively linked together, it seems likely that the writer on optics from Schaffhausen who so impressed Leibniz (see Letter 1688) was a member of the noble Ott family of Zürich, to be identified with the physician Johannes Ott (1639–1717), who was possibly the son of Franz Ott (1614–91) at one time an ambassador in Italy. He became *bailli imperial* in 1681. Besides his thesis (Letter 1688, note 10) he published several works on medicine.

1 See *Phil. Trans.*, no. 71 (22 May 1671), 2163–65.

1868

Oldenburg to Cassini

15 January 1671/2

From the original in BN, n.a.f. 6197, ff. 28–30

Ilustrissimo Viro
Domino Johanni Dominico Cassini Astronomo Celeberrimo
Henr. Oldenburg
Felicitatem

Intellexit ex novissimis tuis, 9 Januarii ad me datis, Regia Societas propensam tuam in Se voluntatem, indeque profectam insignium tuarum de Novo Planeta deque Saturno Observationum enarrationem. Voluit omnino, ut protinus Tibi significarem, Te rem gratissimam Ipsi praestitisse, cohortaturque, sponte quantumvis currentem, ut sueta tibi cura et solertia, quotiescunque caelum annuerit, istas de Errante stella Observationes consecteris, donec certi quid de ea definire concedatur.

Perplacet insuper, quod egregium adeo de novissima Eclipsi Lunae Observationum cumulum congessisti nobisque communicasti; quodque doctam tuam de iterata hoc anno Saturni rotunditate sententiam exposuisti. Vix quicquam Te dignum, quod remittam suppetit. Dicam tamen, in manus meas nuper incidisse epistolam, Hierapoli (vulgo Aleppo) scriptam, quae indicat, d. 8/18 Sept. 1671 circa hor. $7\frac{1}{4}$ vespertinam, Eclipsin Lunae incepisse, eamque h. 8.9' penitus obscuratam fuisse, inque eo statu continuasse adusque h. 9.50'; tunc vero lucem suam recuperasse; atque h. 10.45' sibi ipsi omnino restitutam fuisse.[1]

Insuper, celare Te nolem, me Clarissimo Hugenio per hunc ipsum tabellionem misisse descriptionem Inventi cujusdam Telescopici, cujus beneficio Inventor putat contrahi insigniter Tubospecilla posse, nec tamen quicquam eorum praestantiae et effectibus derogari.[2] Magni sane momenti Inventio, dummodo exspectationi par fuerit successus. Quaedam de eo Experimenta hic peregimus. Vestrum erit, rem totam, satis minute descriptam, expendere, vestrumque de eo judicium nobis imperteri.

Denique, ad Dominum Vernonium misi Ephemerides Anglicas, mense Decembri editas, petiique, ut eas Tibi communicaret, quo magnam earum partem imples.[3] Non ingratam forte fuerit inibi reperire, quae Cl. Siferus Hamburgensis de macularum solarium redita observavit.[4]

Vale, Vir Celeberrime, et me, Virtutis ac Eruditionis tuae Cultorem studiosissimum crede. Dabam Londini d. 15. Januar. 1672.

ADDRESS
> Illustrissimo Viro
> Domino Johanni Dominico Cassini
> Astronomo Celeberrimo etc.
>   Parisiis.

TRANSLATION

Henry Oldenburg wishes happiness to that very famous astronomer, the most illustrious Mr. Giovanni Domenico Cassini

From your most recent news addressed to me on 9 January [N.S.] the Royal Society learned of your ready goodwill towards it and then of the continued account of your remarkable observations concerning Saturn and the new planet.

It was insistent that I should at once inform you that you had furnished it with something most acceptable, and urge you (however eager you may be on your own account) to follow up those observations of that wandering star with your usual care and skill whenever the skies shall be favorable, until it may be possible to determine something certain about it.

The Society was very pleased, moreover, because you had assembled such a notable mass of observations relating to the last eclipse of the moon and imparted it to us; and because you had expounded your learned opinion of the round appearance of Saturn, renewed this year. I have hardly anything worthy of you at hand by way of return. I may report, however, that a letter recently came to my hands written from Aleppo, indicating that the lunar eclipse of 8/18 September 1671 began there about 7.15 P.M., that it became total at 8.9 P.M. and so remained until 9.50; then the moon began to recover its brilliance which was fully restored by 10.45 P.M.[1]

Further, I will not conceal from you that I have by this very post sent to the celebrated Huygens the description of a certain person's discovery relating to telescopes by which he thinks it will be possible to shorten them very much without at all diminishing their excellence and effects.[2] The discovery is obviously of great significance if the result comes up to expectations. We have made some trials of it here. It will be for you to consider my pretty minute description of the whole thing and let us have your judgment of it.

Lastly, I have sent my English *Transactions* published in December to Mr. Vernon, and asked him to communicate them to you, as you have supplied the greater part of their content.[3] Perhaps it will be not unwelcome to you to find there what the famous Sivers of Hamburg observed of the return of the sunspots.[4]

Farewell, famous Sir, and believe me a most zealous devotee of your learning and virtue. London, 15 January 1672.

ADDRESS

To the very illustrious Mr. Giovanni Domenico Cassini,
Most celebrated astronomer etc.,
Paris.

NOTES

Reply to Letters 1848 and 1854a, read to the Royal Society on 11 January.
1 We do not know the source of these observations, which seem to be otherwise unrecorded.
2 See Letter 1866a.
3 See Letter 1866, note 2.
4 Letter 1811a.

1869
Oldenburg to Wallis
16 January 1671/2

From the memorandum in Royal Society MS. W 1, no. 135

[Received] Jan. 15 71/2
Answered Jan. 16. 71.
Sent him a copy of Pardies letter about ye Book he is going to print.[1]

NOTES

Reply to Letter 1865.
1 Letter 1859.

1870
Vernon to Oldenburg
17 January 1671/2

From the original in Royal Society MS. V, nos. 19 and 21

Paris Jan 27. 1672 [N.S.]

Sir

I told you in my letter of the 8th Current[1] that I intended to send you the method by wch Monsieur Picart wrought when hee stated the measure of a degree to 57060 Toyses parisian measure. I intended to have beene quicker in what I promised you butt the cold growing troublesome & businesse intervening were the occasions that I could not comply wth my promise till now.

In this sheet then wch accompagnies this letter I have sent you the Diagrams taken out of Monsieur Picards booke wth as much exactnesse as I could. here are three of them, & I have marked them wth fig 1 fig 2 fig 3 & in these Diagrams you see all the connexion of triangles by wch he measured the distance from Malvoysine to Sourdon, & from Sourdon to

Amiens, & from this measure hee concluded what the Just length of a degree might bee reduced to the Paris Toyse.²

This is what Monsieur Picart Proposed to himself from this chaine of Triangles concerning wch I need adde nothing more butt onely proceed to the duplication of what the letters stand for

A. then is the middle point of the mill at Villejuive

B. is the neerest corner of the Pavillion of Juvisy

C. is top of the Steeple of Brie Compte Robert

D. is the middle of the Tower of Montlehery

E. is the top of the Pavillon of Malvoysine

F. is a pole placed for this purpose on the ruines of [the] tower of Montiay wth a lock of hay putt upon it, that It may bee seene at a greater distance.

G. is the middle of the Hummock of Mareuil where it was requisite to have a fire made to distinguish it at a distance

H. is the middle of the great ovall Pavillion of the castle of Dammartin

I. is the tower of St Sampson in Clermont

K. is the mill of Jonquieres neere Compiegne

L. is the tower of Coyvrel.

M. is a little tree on the Hill of Boulogne neere Montdidier.

N. is the tower of Sourdon.

O. is a little forked tree upon the point of the Grisson neere Villeneufe St. George

P. is the tower of Montmartre

Q. is the tower of St. Christoph neere Senlis

These are the names of the Points betweene malvoysine & Sourdon, at wch hee tooke his Stations, & from whence hee observed his angles.

The Base wch hee actually measured as I writt you before³ was AB, the high way lying betweene Villeiuive & Juvisy wch hee found to bee equall to 5663 Toyses de Paris. from this base hee deduced the measure of all the other 13 triangles as for Example.

in the Triangle ABC to find the side AC

Angle $CAB = 54°\ 4'\ 35''$
$ABC\quad 95\ \ 6\ \ 55$ } by observation
$ACB\quad 30\ \ 48\ \ 30$

Side $\quad AB\quad 5663$ Toyses of actuall measure

Hence $\quad AC\quad 11012$ [toises] 5 feet

$\qquad BC\quad 8954$ [toises]

In The second triangle ADC to find DC & AD

Angle   DAC = 77° 25′ 50″
        ADC   55   0   10
        ACD   47   34
the side AC 11012 Toyses 5 feet
Hence   DC 13121   3
        AD   9922   2

The third triangle DEC to find DE. CE.
Angle   DEC   74° 9′ 30″
        DCE   40   34
        CDE   65   16   30
The side DC 13121 Toyses 3 Pieds
Hence   DE   8870   3
        CE 12389   3

The fourth triangle DCF to find DF
angle   DCF 113° 47′ 40″
        DFC   33   40
        FDC   32   32   20
side   DC 13121 T. 3 P.
Hence   DF 21658.

The fifth triangle DFG to find DG. FG
angle   DFG   92° 5′ 20″
        DGF   57   34
        DGH   30   20   40
side   DF 21658 T
hence   DG 25643
        FG 12963 3 P.

The sixth triangle GDE to find GE
angle   GDE 128° 9′ 30″
side   DG 25643 T
        DE   8870 3 P
hence   GE 31897

Soe then the line of distance betweene malvoysine & Sourdon beeing divided into the 3 parts EG, GI, IN the part EG is already found.

The seventh triangle FGH to find GH
angle   FGH   39° 51′ 0″
        FHG   91° 46   30
        HFG   48   22   30
side   FG 12963 T. 3 P.
hence   GH   9695

the 8th Triangle GHI to find GI, IH

    angle GHI 55° 58′ 0″
               GIH 27 14
               IGH 96 48
side GH 9695 T.
hence GI 17557
          HI 21037

Thus the 2d part of the three GI is found.
the ninth triangle HIK to find IK

    angle HIK 65° 46′ 0″
               HKI 80 59 40
               KHI 33 14 20
side HI 21043 T
hence IK 11678

the tenth triangle IKL to find KL, IL

    angle LIK 58° 31′ 50″
               IKL 58 31
side IK 11683 T
          KL 11188 2 p.
          IL 11186 4

the eleventh triangle KLM to find LM

    angle LKM 28° 52′ 30″
               KML 63 31
side KL 11188 T 2 P
hence LM 6036 2

the twelfth triangle LMN to find LN

    angle LMN 60° 38′ 0″
               MNL 29 28 20
side LM 6036 T 2 p
hence LN 10691

Thus you see that the ligne of distance EN beeing divided into three unequall parts EG. GI. IN. The measure of all three are found by this scale of triangles. butt I am cutt short in time. this will serve to content your present Curiosity & give you a glympse how Monsieur Picart proceeded in the discovery of this measure. In my next[4] I shall continue this measure from Sourdon to Amiens. & give you an account of such other particularities as may bee you will bee delighted in contemplating now. I rest

                                    Your most Obedient Servant
                                             Francis Vernon

NOTES

1 See Letter 1854 (actually of the ninth, N.S.), *ad fin.*
2 See the figures of the triangulation already reproduced on pp. 433 and 435. What follows is a summary of Picard's *Mesure de la Terre*.
3 See Vol. VI, p. 435.
4 Letter 1877.

1871

Newton to Oldenburg

18 January 1671/2

Printed in Newton, *Correspondence*, I, 82–3, from the original in private possession

In this reply to a letter of unknown date from Oldenburg, in which he indicated that some of the Fellows were considering what metal might be used in making a larger reflecting telescope, Newton explains the necessity of getting a metal without pores visible in the microscope and discusses the possible composition of speculum metal, favoring the use of arsenic. He also inquires whether the Society is continuing its weekly meetings, since he intends (if it is) to send up an account of the "Philosophicall discovery" which, he says, led to his first making a reflecting telescope. He also inquires into the duties of a Fellow of the Society.

1872

Wallis to Oldenburg

18 January 1671/2

From the original in Royal Society MS. W 1, no. 137

Oxford. January 18, 1671/72

Sir,

To yours of Dec. 30, I answered in mine of Jan. 14.[1] But if you sent any of Jan. 9 (as yours of Jan. 16 intimates) it is not come to my hands. Your Barometer's hight at Dec. 24, Mr. Newton's Telescope, Sr. Sam.

Morlands Tuba, and Mr. Bohun's book, (to all wch particulars my last answered) were mentioned in yours of Dec. 30. If since you have written any thing before yt of Jan. 16, which I have just now received, I have it not. The words excepted at, in Mr. Bohun's book, were somewhat in favour of ye Royall Society, & of new Philosophy, wch were a little mollified, & then passed as they are now printed.[2] What Dr. Morison sayd of ye Authors mentioned, I suppose was at adventure; for when hee and I together did consult Piso, wee found nothing; ye other Authors were not at hand: & more (I think) hee had not to say at ye present.[3] My Baroscope at Jan. 14th, was under 29 inches ($28\frac{7}{8}$) ye next day at $29\frac{3}{8}$, and so ever since at $29\frac{3}{8}$ or $29\frac{1}{4}$; sunshine by day, but some rain in ye nights (for ye most part). My 3d part de motu, I do not find yt either Mr Hugens or Mr Vernon takes any notice; in your next to them you were best inquire whether they be received.[4] A particular account of Mr Pardies paper, you cannot expect by this Post; (there being not time enough to write it:) But I intend it by ye next.[5] In ye general; I do not expect much more than hath bee done allready; unlesse more application, of ye general principles to particular cases, (wch are infinite;) and such as (in ye methods I propose) are but meerly business of calculation. What you have published of late, I am ignorant, having seen none since yt of September. I am

Yours &c.
John Wallis

ADDRESS

For Mr. Henry Oldenburg
   in the Palmall near
   St. James's
   LONDON

NOTES

Reply to Letter 1869.
1 Letters 1855 and 1865 respectively.
2 See Letter 1865 *ad fin*. This presumably refers to the preface to Bohun's *A Discourse concerning the Origine and Properties of Wind*, in which he refers to what "we call the New Philosophy; not that it was Invented, but only Reviv'd, and Vindicated by the Moderns, from the Injuries and oppression of Time." As Bohun was a Fellow of New College, Oxford, he was presumably sensitive to the dislike felt for the Royal Society in some Oxford circles.
3 See Letter 1865.
4 See Letter 1866, postscript.
5 See Letter 1873.

1873
Wallis to Oldenburg
18 January 1671/2
From the original in Royal Society MS. W 1, no. 136

Oxoniae Jan. 18. 1671/2

Clarissimo Viro D. Henrico Oldenburg
Johannes Wallis Salutem

Clarissime Vir,

Perlegi quam misisti Synopsin operis, quod (ut ais) D. Pardisius jam molitur, in sex Tractatus distributum. Et quidem laudo conatus Clarissimi Viri rem Philosophicam et Mathematicam promovendi; atque illam quidem hujus ope. Quippe ex quo Galilaeus Mathesin accommodaverit rebus Physicis, mirum est quos progressus fecessit scientia naturalis. Et quidem tantum abest ut haec displiceant, ut eandem mihi proposuerim semitam calcandam in scriptis a me plurimis (quod ipse probe noveris) tum editis tum non editis.

Primum quod spectat; Mechanicen, seu de Motu doctrinam, rebus tum Natura tum arte factis accommodando, post Galilaeum Torricellium et alios, quid ipse (in Mechanica mea seu de Motu doctrina) praestiterim; annis continue tribus jam proximis, publici juris feci: etiam plura additurus multa, nisi quod nolim operis molem, adeoque et pretium, nimis augere. Utut autem ego principia ibidem posuerim, generaliter tradita, quae si particularibus casibus accommodentur (quorum et ego non paucos attigi) in immensum possint extendi: Non desunt tamen in quibus se exerceat Vir Clarissimus, vel eadem specialius exponendo, vel etiam suggerendo nova.

Idemque de secundo repetendum est: ubi speciatim Staticam (prioris partem) se expositurum ait. Quippe et hanc ibidem ego exposui; rem a primis principijs deducens; multaque ab alijs vel postulata vel gratis posita legitime demonstrans. Non tamen illos alios (magni nominis viros, et de re literaria optime meritos,) aspergens labe quod idem non fuerint ipsi. Eaque quae huc spectant, reduxi, si non ad Libram omnia, ad ea saltem unde ipsa Libra dependet principia. Funem autem utroque fine suspensum, non tracto, aut figuram quam sic suspensus faciat; quam rem jam ante tractavit

Galilaeus, et post illum (si memini) Stevinus in Sparto-staticis;[1] et siquid porro opus sit, poterit (credo) illud solo calculo (rite adhibito) satis expediri. Quod quin faciat Vir Clarissimus ego non repugno.

Et (quem ille tertio loco se tractaturum ait) de Motu Gravium Accelerato et Retardato, quid ego statuo ibidem videas; et, quo nitar fundamento; atque unde ego ea (ut loquitur) a priore demonstro. Quae autem Gassendum inter et Casraeum intercessit controversiam nominatim non attingo, et quidem consulto; soleo enim, quam possim commode, parcere nominibus, contentus sensa mea simpliciter exponere (adjunctis causis cur ita censeam;) cum Rectum sit et sui Index ex Obliqui: neque tam interest quid hac in re fecerint Gassendus, Casraeus, Ballianus, Fabrius, Fermatius, Lalovera, alijve; quam, quid sit verum.[2] Quod Gassendi partes potiores putem, satis inde colligas; Quid autem hac in re fecerint illi alij, neque scio, neque jam vacat inquirere. Quae autem ego trado, Demonstrative procedunt (Mathesin quod spectat) sed ex data hypothese Physica: Adeoque Hypothetice proponuntur. Quam cautionem ideo adhibeo, quoniam fieri potest ut Gravitas (de cujus natura et proprijs causis vixdum satis constat) aliud quid esse possit quam suspicemur adhuc: quod si olim aliquando constiterit, consideratio Mathematica accommodanda erit ei (cum innotuerit) Physicae Hypothesi. Vim item Percussionis ibidem tractavimus, cum capitibus adjunctis, (atque illud speciatim, quod innuit, Percutiens utut minimum, posse vel Maximum quadantenus movere; quatenus vero, calculo determinandum est, pro re nata:) Quam nova lege tracto, nova methodo. Non displicebit tamen ut Vir Clarissimus nostris, siquid deest, addat: vel siquid erratum est, meliora doceat. Quod autem ait, Percussionum vires debilitatis gradus omnes transire: potest forte, sano sensu, admitti. Verum si hoc vult, ut, sicuti Grave sponte cadens intermedios omnes a quiete gradus transit (quod nostris demonstratis congruit) sic et Percussa vel Projecta quaelibet: Ego plane non assentior.

Liquorum Descensum, quanta sit celeritate, sive a Latere sive per Fundum Tubi effluentium, (quem loco quarto aggressuros est,) ego speciatim non attigi: ut locus sit Clarissimo Viro multa hic speciatim supplendi, quae apud nos vel non occurrunt, vel in ijs tantum comprehensa quae de Hydrostaticis, de Gravium Descensu, et Motuum Declivitatibus, de Celeritatibus Arctis, Minutis, et Vi prementi proportionalibus habemus; unde ea quae huc spectant calculo accommodanda sunt.

Sed neque (cui locum quintum assignet) Reciprocationes sive Pendulorum sive Chordarum tensarum, et quae huc spectant, speciatim tracto: nisi quatenus ea deduci possunt a principijs generaliter traditis, de Gravium

Descendentium motu Accelerato, et Ascendentium Retardato, de Centro Percussionis, de Elatere indeque orta Resilitione, et quae sunt hujusmodi. Quamquam enim de his, eisque quae ad caput praecedens spectant, privatis literis ad D. Vicecomitem Brounker, D. Boyle, atque ad Te scriptis aliquando egimus, non tamen ea publici juris facta sunt. Neque est ut ea praejudicio sint Clarissimo Viro de his acturo. Speculationem autem illam quam primus monuit Hugenius, atque exinde jam ante multos annos demonstravit Honoratissimus D. Vicecomes Brounker, de Penduli motu apposita Cycloide moderato, et Cycloidem aliorsum describente;[3] utut aliquando in animo fuerit, de Cycloide tractanti considerasse, eamque quatenus ex Cycloidis natura deducendam esset, determinasse, (quod non foret difficile, propter lineae Cycloidalis, partiumque ipsius, longitudines notas, et tangentium positiones, adeoque ejusdem in singulis punctis declivitatem;) omisi tamen, quoniam de Cycloide jam fueram sat copiosus, nedum nimias; eamque rem jam ante consideraverat Hugenius primo, et post eum D. Brounkerus, quantum saltem opus videbatur; eratque jam iterum (sic saltem nobis nunciatum est) Hugenius ipse rem eam fusius mox tractaturus, neque erat (cum aliunde suppeteret tractanti materia satis abunde) cur illum hac in re anticiparem.[4]

Quam denique sexto adeoque ultimo loco habet, Undulationum doctrinam, indeque Sonorum et Luminis explicationem; ego hactenus intactam reliqui: sed quam edito Opere Micrographico (ut alios taceam) tractavit Hookius noster, cui (in plerisque saltem) concivit (ut videtur) Vir Clarissimus. Sicubi dissentiunt; nolim ego me statim arbitrum interponere, in re quam non ita penitus consideravi ut mihi per omnia satisfaciam ipse. De Figuris quadrandis et cubandis, multisque ad hanc rem spectantibus, egi jam olim in Arithmetica Infinitorum, in tractatu de Cycloide, de Curvarum εὐθύνσει et πλατυσμων; et fusius nuper in tractatu de Motu, ubi de Calculo Centri Gravitatis egimus; (et, praeter nos, alij multi:) Et quidem, ut alias, sic speciatim Tangentium ope; sed et subtensarum; ut in scriptis meis passim videre est. Quod autem ad calcem habet, de *Figuris, cujuscunque generis, planis quadrandis, et solidis cubandis, unius Tangentis ope*;[5] vel ego non satis intelligo quid velit, vel metuo re magna cum mitigatione intelligendum sit. Verum ego Clarissimi Viri laboribus praejudicare nolo. Sive volet eadem quae nos tractavimus, denuo tractare sua methodo; sive quae nos generaliter tradidimus volet ille ad particulares casus accommodare; vel fusius agere quae nos succincte; vel ea tradere quae nos omisimus: est quo se exerceat campus satis amplus. Interim haec sunt quae a te rogatus dicenda habui. Vale.

ADDRESS
   For Mr Henry Oldenburg
   in the Palmal near St James's
      London

POSTMARK [IA] 22

TRANSLATION

Oxford, 18 January 1671/2

John Wallis greets the famous Mr. Henry Oldenburg

Famous Sir,

I have read the synopsis you sent me of the work which, as you say, Mr. Pardies is now concerned with, divided into six treatises. And I do indeed praise the enterprise of this worthy man in promoting philosophy and mathematics, and doing so by this means. Certainly it is wonderful what advances natural science has made since Galileo applied mathematics to physics. And so far is this work from displeasing me that I have proposed following the same path myself in many of my own writings (as you know very well yourself), both published and unpublished.

As for the first [treatise], I have continually during the three last years published (in my theoretical mechanics, or *De motu*) what I had accomplished in succession to Galileo, Torricelli, and others in applying mechanics or the theory of motion to the works of Nature and of art; and much more could have been added, but that I was reluctant to increase the bulk and price of the work too much. For I there laid down general principles which, if applied to particular cases (of which I touched on not a few) could be extended enormously. Yet there are not lacking some upon which the famous author may practise, either by explaining them in more detail or by proposing novelties.

The same is to be said of the second [treatise], where (he says) he will in the first part explain statics in particular. For I have dealt with this too, deducing it from first principles and demonstrating properly many things that were either taken as postulates by others, or taken for granted. Yet I do not mean to cast blame upon those others (men of great repute, deserving much of the world of learning) because they did not do likewise. And, as to what is relevant here, I have reduced everything if not to the balance at least to those principles that depend on the balance. However, I do not discuss the rope suspended by its ends or the figure made by thus hanging it, a matter formerly treated by Galileo and after him (if I remember [rightly]) Stevin in his spartostatics.[1] If anything further is worthwhile he will be able, I believe, to supply it by calculation alone, properly applied. And I have no reluctance to the worthy man's doing this.

And concerning the accelerated and retarded motion of heavy bodies, which he says he will treat in the third place, you may in the same work see what I have laid down concerning it and upon what basis I rely and whence I demonstrate those things (as they say) a priori. I do not particularly touch on the dispute between Gassendi and Cazré, and on purpose, for it is my custom when I conveniently can to omit names, being content to explain my meaning simply (adding the reasons for my opinion); as it may be the nominative case and its index and indirect cases; nor does it matter so much what Gassendi, Cazré, Baliani, Fabry, Fermat, La Loubère and others did in this business, as what the truth is.[2] You may sufficiently gather from there that I think Gassendi had the stronger case; as for what the others did in that affair, that I do not know nor have I had leisure to find out. However, what I am concerned with proceeds demonstratively (as regards the mathematics) but upon a given physical hypothesis, and so is stated hypothetically. I give this warning because it might be that gravity (of whose nature and causes hardly anything is known as yet) is quite different from what we have hitherto supposed; so that if that shall at some future time appear to be the case, the mathematical discussion may be adjusted to that physical hypothesis (when it shall be discovered). I have also treated, in the same place, the force of percussion with some annexed headings (especially that which suggests that an impacting body, however small, can move another, however big, up to a certain point—how far may be determined by a calculation for that purpose). This I have brought under a new law, using a new method. But it will not be disagreeable if the worthy writer adds to our treatment, if anything is lacking, or gives better instruction where we have erred. When he says that the forces of impacting bodies may pass through all degrees of feebleness, this can surely be admitted in any reasonable sense. But if he means that, just as a freely falling body passes through all the intermediate degrees [of velocity] from rest (as is consonant with our demonstrations), so a body when struck or projected [moves through] each one, this I flatly contradict.

I have not specially touched upon the descent of fluids, and their velocities when flowing out from the side of a pipe, or from its base, the subject of his fourth section, so that there is room here for the famous author to supply many particulars which are not found in my work, or are embraced only under what we have included concerning hydrostatics, the descent of heavy bodies, the declivities of motions, [and] brief [or] small velocities, and [those] proportional to the force acting. Whence what is relevant here may be fitted to calculation.

Nor, turning to his fifth topic, have I dealt in particular with the vibrations of pendulums or taut strings, and related matters, except in so far as these may be deduced from the general principles concerning the accelerated motion of descending heavy bodies, and the slowing down of ascending ones, the center of percussion, elasticity and the force of springs, and other things of this kind. For although I have written about these things and others with which the preceding chapters are concerned in private letters to my Lord Brouncker, Mr. Boyle, and yourself sometimes, still these have not been made public. Nor should this be prejudicial to the worthy man in considering such topics in the future. However, with regard to that notion to which Huygens first drew attention, and which thereafter (but many years ago) was demonstrated by the Right Honorable Lord Brouncker, concerning the motion of a pendulum controlled by a cycloid applied to it and [itself] describing a cycloid in another place,[3] I formerly had it in mind to consider it when dealing with the cycloid and to have settled it in so far as it could be deduced from the nature of the cycloid (which would not be difficult because the lengths of the line of the cycloid and of its parts are known, and the positions of its tangents, and accordingly their slopes at particular points). But I left it out, having written enough about the cycloid, indeed too much; Huygens formerly considered the same question first of all, and then Lord Brouncker (at least so far as was worthwhile); and it was the case—or so it was reported to us—that Huygens himself was to treat the same subject soon at greater length a second time, and there was no need for me to anticipate him in this as there was plenty of other matter for discussion.[4]

And lastly for what he has in the sixth and final section, the theory of waves and from that the explanation of light and sound, I have so far left it quite alone; however, our countryman Hooke (to speak of no other) has dealt with this in his published book, *Micrographia*, with whom it seems the celebrated author agrees, on many points at any rate. But if they disagree on any issue I have no desire to rush at once as an umpire into a matter upon which I have not yet thoroughly reflected, so as to be satisfied myself about everything. I have formerly written upon the squaring and cubing of figures and many related matters in my *Arithmetica infinitorum*, in the treatise on the cycloid, on the rectification and flattening of curves, and recently at greater length in the treatise on motion where I have written of the calculation of centers of gravity; and besides myself there are many others. And, as by other means, so in particular by the method of tangents, and subtenses also; as may be seen here and there in my writings. As for what he adds at the very end, "concerning figures of any kind, squaring planes and cubing solids by means of a single tangent,"[5] either I do not sufficiently understand what he means or I fear the thing is to be taken with a large pinch of salt. But in truth I have no wish to prejudge the worthy author's efforts. If he wishes to discuss what I have discussed, let him do so by his own method; if he wishes to relate to particular cases what I have dealt with in general terms, or to be copious where I have been terse, or to deal with my omissions, there is room enough for him to practise in. Meanwhile this is what I had to say upon your request. Farewell.

NOTES

Further reply to Letter 1869; it is concerned with Letter 1859.
1 "Statics of cords"; see Letter 1859, note 4. *Spartum* was the Latin name for Spanish broom, from which plant cords and ropes were twisted. Simon Stevin printed his work *Van het Tauwicht* ("Of the cord weight") in Part IV of *Wisconstighe Ghedachtenissen* (Leiden, 1608); Wallis would have seen it in the Latin version of this book by Willebrord Snel, *Hypomnemata mathematica* (also Leiden, 1608). Stevin dealt with the suspension of weights by cords; he did not consider the form of the catenary, as Wallis here suggests.
2 See pp. 460-61, notes 5 through 8.
3 Huygens had discovered at the end of 1659 that the evolute of a cycloid is the same cycloid, but published no demonstration; Brouncker communicated a cumbersome proof to the Royal Society on 22 January 1661/2 (Birch, *History*, pp. 70–74), which also remained unprinted at that time.
4 Long before Huygens had let it be known that the theorems would appear in a second edition of his *Horologium* (first printed at The Hague in 1658); however, *Horologium oscillatorium* was to be published only in 1673.
5 These are not Pardies's own words: compare above, p. 455–560.

1874
Oldenburg to Dodington
18 January 1671/2

Mentioned in Dodington's reply, Letter 1901, as enclosing Letter 1875 to Malpighi.

1875
Oldenburg to Malpighi
18 January 1671/2

From the original in Bologna MS. 2085, I, f. 66
Printed in *Opera omnia*, I, Appendix, p. 15

Illustrissimo Viro
Domino Marcello Malpighio Philos. et Med. Bononiensi
Henr. Oldenburg
Felicitatem

Significavi Tibi, Vir Clarissime, per literas d. 14. Decembris novissimi ad Te datas,[1] Societatem Regiam Scriptum tuum de Anatome Plantarum nonnullis e Caetu suo sociis, perpendendum commisisse. Insimul promisi, me Virorum illorum, quibus id pensi impositum, sententiam, quamprimum ea dictae Societati fuerit exposita, candide perscripturum. Hujus itaque epistolae argumentum non erit aliud, quam datam tibi fidem liberare. Scire igitur Te velim, Philosophos illos nostros, rerum a Te in Exercitatione illa tua traditarum callentissimos, ad unum omnes statuere, Te subacto judicio eximiaeque cura rem propositam exegisse, eamque omnino mereri, quae in lucem publicam maturrime emittatur.[2] Dabis igitur, operam, Vir Doctissime, ut nostram, et aliorum, quibus haec res longe lateque jam innotuit, exspectationem, quamprimum fieri poterit,[3] impleas, eoque ipso manifestum facias, hanc Naturae partem uno hoc seculo amplius multo solidiusque, quam caeteris omnibus praegressis, quantum quidem nobis constat, excultam fuisse.

Promissi memor sum, quo ad libelli, de Plantarum etiam Anatome a Medico Anglo perdocte concinnati, transmissionem me nuper obstrinxi. In eo sum, ut de nave exquiram, in oras vestras profectura; qua occasione et plura forte perscribam, quae ad rei philosophicae incrementum facientia apud nos geruntur. Vale, Vir Optime, et me Tuum ex asse crede. Dabam Londini d. 18. januar. 1672.

Scire pervelim, Te binas meas literas recte accepisse.[4]

TRANSLATION

Henry Oldenburg wishes happiness to the most illustrious Mr. Marcello Malpighi, Physician and Philosopher of Bologna

That the Royal Society had entrusted your paper on the anatomy of plants, celebrated Sir, to certain of its own Fellows for their consideration I informed you in my letter of 14 December last to yourself.[1] And at the same time I promised that I would honestly report to you the opinion of those upon whom this consideration was imposed as soon as it should be laid before the Society. Thus the business of this letter is solely to fulfill that promise. Accordingly, I wish you to know that those philosophers of ours who are most skilled in the matters dealt with in that essay of yours are all of the opinion that you have handled the topic you chose with the most acute judgment and extreme care, and that the essay is worthy of being published as soon as may be.[2] Accordingly, learned Sir, you will make it your business to realize the expectation of ourselves and others, to whom the matter is now known far and wide, as soon as possible;[3] and thus also you will make it plain that in this one century this aspect of Nature has been much more, and more deeply, studied than in all preceding centuries, so far as we can tell.

I am mindful of a recent promise that I would send you a book, likewise on the anatomy of plants, put together with much learning by an English physician. I am in the process of enquiring for a ship sailing to your part of the world; perhaps I will then take the opportunity of writing at greater length of what has been going on here towards the advancement of philosophy. Farewell, and believe me wholeheartedly yours. London, 18 January 1672.

I am very anxious to know whether you have received my two letters safely.[4]

NOTES

There is a slightly variant draft of this letter in Royal Society MS. O 2, no. 69 and (as usual) in the Royal Society Malpighi Manuscripts.
1 Letter 1842.
2 The report of Goddard and Hooke was not formally noted in the minutes.
3 It will be recalled that Oldenburg had already suggested that Malpighi should perfect his paper for publication; notably, it lacked figures.
4 Letters 1654 (Vol. VII) and 1842.

1876
Dodington to Oldenburg
19 January 1671/2

From the original in Royal Society MS. D 1, no. 24

Much Hond Sr

As I promised you in my last,[1] I now send you the product of my eandeavours to serve the desires of the most Honble R.S. & yr worthy selfe.[2] I may well terme them most Honble. since I can assure you, They are so esteemed by all men on this side the Alpes, who have any insight in the Learning of nature or who studie the Knowledg of themselves, their Fellow Creatures, or their Creator.

I will goe on entertayning this Correspondence with Dr Cornelio, until I have gotten from him, & conveyed to you, wt he promiseth in his to me.

Yr of the 22. ultimo, I omitted to answere until now, to the end I might give you this proofe of my observance. ye sending me ye Scheames of Sr Sam. Morelands Tuba-stentoraphonica will be very wellcome.

I think I shall this day deliver to one Mr Aston[3] ye Book wch dr Malpighi sent me for you, I have caused it to be bound. It is 15 discourses by 15 several Gent. of Bologna, on divers subjects much after ye nature of Caelius Rhodaginus, Rossinus, A Gellius &c.[4] Those Academists had it seemes written much before in verse, and this they wrote in Prose. meerly to let ye world see they had not quite layd aside the use of Prose. Possibly had they putt this also into verse, it had not binn amisse. I conceive you'l find small satisfaction in it;

The Venetians as I foretold, have layd by all their Giornale & write no more.[5]

I am dear Sr

    The most Honble Royall Societies & yr
    Most humble servant
      John dodington

Mr Oldenberg

ADDRESS
These for Mr. Hen: Oldenberg
Secretary to ye R. Society
   In
   London

NOTES

This letter was received on 5 February. The date of its writing is given in Dodington's next. Letter 1902.
1 Presumably Letter 1860, now lost.
2 The enclosed letter from Tommaso Cornelio (Letter 1876a).
3 It is possible that this was Francis Aston (*c.* 1645–*c.* 1715), Fellow of Trinity College, Cambridge, since 1667, to whom Isaac Newton wrote in 1669 a well-known letter about traveling in Europe. He was elected F.R.S. in 1678 and was one of the Society's Secretaries from 1681 to 1685.
4 This is the book mentioned in Letter 1805, notes 4 and 7; it (or rather Montanari's contribution to it) is reviewed in *Phil. Trans.*, no. 89 (16 December 1672), 5125–28. For Aulus Gellius, see Vol. VII, p. 499, note 20; Ludovicus Coelius Rhodagini (1450?–1525) was an Italian scholar; Rossini we could not positively identify.
5 Dodington was mistaken.

1876a
Cornelio to Dodington
9 January 1671/2

Enclosure with Letter 1876
From the original in Royal Society MS. C 1 no. 106

Illustrissimo Signore Mio Signore Colendissimo

Io mi confesso multo obbligato alla benignita di V. Illustrissima che se e degnata di leggere il mio libretto de Progimnasmi e darli quelle maggiori lodi che io haverei potuto sperare[1] e quantunque io ben m'avveggia che quelle provengano piu tosto dell' humanita di V. Illustrissima che del merito del libro Non dimeno io non posso non compiacermene quando che non sappia riconoscere maggiore frutto della pubblicatione de' libri che l'approvatione fatta da huomini di gran talento. E'cio mi servirebbe di sprone a scrivere altre mie speculationi et osservationi curiose se una

Lunghissima infirmita che assai acerbamente mi molesta non me' svietasse. Mà se havero fortuna di recuperar la salute potro sperare di potere ciò eseguire, e sodisfare in buona parte agli quesiti che V. Illustrissima si degna d'impormi in materia della Natura et effetti delle Tarantole della Puglia: Le quali veramente altro non sono che una specie di falangij, molto grandi e dipinti in varie maniere e con diversita di Colori. Queste habitano entro alcune cavernole profonde della Terra le quali hanno un forame circolare della grandezza d'una noce. A'tempo di Estate facendosi un poco di sibilo nell'orificio delle dette Cavernole corrono velocemente le tarantole all'aria, et in questa maniera si prendono. Et io spero nel mese d'Aprile o' di Maggio de poterne mandare alcun numero di vive perche ho sperimentato che quelle si mantengano alcune settimane senza cibo veruno, e' se ne potranno ancora mandar delle morte esiccate entro lo spirito del vino o' altro simile liquore che le preserva dalla putredine. Per quello poi che appartiene agli effetti di coloro che si giudicano morsicati dalla Tarantole Io stimo altramente da quello che il volgo si persuade perche da molte osservazioni e congetture mi do à credere che senza precedere il morzo della Tarantola avenga tal sorte de' mali ad alcuni di Coloro che habitano in quei Paesi aredissimi e' che spessi fiate sono tormentati da lunghissima sete. Nè mai se è saputo che alcuna persona sia stata morsicata dalla Tarantola e' che poi appresso si temessero gli effetti del male: Mà sempre mai aviene che le persona, sentendosi in tempo d'estate travagliati da quegli strani accidenti che patissono gli attarantati, suppongano dopo' l'effetto del male esser stati feriti da quell' animale Lascio di raccontare più à lungo le mie osservazioni sperando di poter ciò fare su'l principio di Primavera allhora che il mio male non mi suole cosi acerbamente travagliare ritrovandomi adesso fortemente tormentato et inhabile allo scrivere Intanto prego V. Illustrissima a darmi alcuna contezza dello stato di salute in che si trova il Signor Roberto Boile e di ciò che di nuovo ha prodotto la famosa societa Reale d'Inghilterra: Perche se bene io per lo passato sono stato favorito d'essere avisato dal Signore Oldemburgo Segretario di quella Società, tuttavia hora per lo spatio quasi di due anni hò dismesso per caggione della mia infirmità, il commercio delle lettere e' per fine offrendomi sempre prontissimo a' commandi di V. Illustrissima con profonda riverenza me l'inchino Di Napoli a' 19 di Gennaro 1672.
D.V. Illustrissima

Divotissimo et obligatissimo Servitore
Tomaso Cornelio

TRANSLATION

Most illustrious Sir, my most esteemed Lord,

I acknowledge myself most obliged to your kindness, most illustrious Sir, in that you have condescended to read my little *Progymnasmata* [*Physica*] and give to it a greater praise than ever I could have hoped for;[1] and although I do indeed perceive that this rather springs from your kind heart, illustrious Sir, than from the merit of the book itself, still I cannot but congratulate myself since I recognize no greater reward from the publication of books than the approbation won from men of great abilities. And so it would be an incentive to me to write out my other speculations and curious observations if a very protracted illness that troubles me pretty severely did not forbid me. But if I have the luck to recover my health I shall be able to hope then to attend to and in large part satisfy the queries your excellency is good enough to transmit to me concerning the nature and effects of the tarantulas of Apulia. In truth these are no more than a species of phalangia which are very big and variegated in color. They live in a very deep burrow in the soil having a circular entrance as big as a walnut. In the summertime if you make a whistling sound at the entrance to the burrow the tarantulas come running into the open, and so they are readily captured. I hope that in the months of April or May I may send you a number of them alive, for I have learned by trials that they will live some weeks without food, and if they do not live I will send you some dead ones dried, put in spirit of wine or the like fluid to preserve them from putrefaction. As for the phenomena associated with persons who suppose themselves to have been bitten by a tarantula, I take a different view from the common one because a multitude of observations and reflections cause me to believe that, quite without being bitten by a tarantula, such afflictions fall on some of the inhabitants of those very dry regions who, panting for breath, are tormented with long-continued thirsts. Whenever it is known that some person has felt the bite of a tarantula he at once from then on fears the effects of the disease; but it always happens that the same person, feeling himself troubled in the summertime with those strange phenomena that occur to those bitten by a tarantula, then supposes the effects of the disease to have been induced by that creature. I forbear to recount my observations at greater length, hoping to be able to do so at the commencement of Spring when my sickness does not usually torment me so much, finding myself at present very much afflicted and unfit for writing. Meanwhile I beg your excellency to give me some account of the state of health of Mr. Robert Boyle, and also of what the famous Royal Society of England has produced recently. Because although I was in the past favored by the notice of Mr. Oldenburg, the Secretary of that Society,[2] nevertheless for the space of almost two years now I have given up correspondence by reason of my poor health; and to conclude offering myself always most obedient to the commands of your excellency, with profound respect I bid farewell as your excellency's most devoted and obliged servant,

Tomaso Cornelio

Naples, 19 January 1672 [N.S.]

NOTES

Tommaso Cornelio (1614–84?), professor at Naples since 1654, was one of the most enlightened persons in the south of Italy, and a great friend of Malpighi's. See also Vol. III, p. 441, note.
1 For Dodington's approach to Cornelio, see Vol. VII, p. 551.
2 Oldenburg first wrote to Cornelio in June 1667 (Vol. III, Letter 648).

1877
Vernon to Oldenburg
20 January 1671/2
From the original in Royal Society MS. V, nos. 19 and 22

Paris Jan. 30th 1672 [N.S.]

Sr

In my last of the 27th Current[1] I gave you an account how by a concatenation of triangles, Monsieur Picart came to find the length of the line EN which is the distance betweene Malvoysine & Sourdon. For if you reassume what was already discovered by the help of those triangles you will find that

EG was in length 31897 Toyses
GI 17557
IN 18905

These added together make the length of EN wch is the line of distance betweene malvoysine & Sourdon . . . . 68359.[2]

Let us proceed now to continue this measure from Sourdon to Amiens; & for the attaining of this you must make use of that Diagram wch is marked on the folio fig. 2.[3] In that Diagramme

R stands for the Steeple of St Peters in Montdidier,
T is a tree upon the Hill of Moreuil
V is the Lanterne of nostredame of Amiens

To find the distance *NV*. You must looke back upon *NLM* the last triangle of Fig. 1. & see how it [is] disposed in Fig 3 where

  in the triangle *LMR*

angle	*LMR*	58°	21'	50"
	MRL	68	52	30
side	*LM*	6037 Toyses		
hence	*LR*	5510	3 P	

  In the triangle *NRL*

angle	*NRL*	115°	1'	30"
	RNL	27	50	30
side	*LR*	5510 T	3 P	
hence	*NR*	7122	2	

goe on to fig 2d. in the triangle *NRT*

angle	*NTR*	72°	25'	40"
	TNR	67	21	40
side	*NR*	7122 T	2 P	
hence	*NG*	4822	4	

finally in the triangle *NTV*

angle	*NTV*	83°	58'	40"
	TNV	70	34	30
side	*NT*	4822 T	4 P	
hence	*NV*	11161	4 quod erat quaesitum.[4]	

to the distance betweene malvoysine & Sourdon	68359	Toys
adde the distance between Sourdon & Amiens	11161 4	Pieds
the whole will bee the distance betweene malvoysine & Amiens	79520 4	

    I must not omitt to hint to you that Monsieur Picart searches out the measure of those same lines by other stations & by other triangles to confirme himself in the truth of his operations: butt because at last they come to agree very neere wth these measures to avoide the trouble I passe them over. For I designe here to write noe more then what may just serve to give you a light to comprehend what hee hath done.

    Wee have then as I thinke now sufficiently stated the particular distances of these places lying betweene Malvoysine & Amiens; the next thing is from hence to deduce the Length of a meridian, intercepted betweene the parallels of Malvoysine & Amiens. This is done in the 8th Article & it was thus.

    In the moneth 7ber of the yeare 69 hee went to the Hill of Mareuil, & from the Hummock of it wch is marked wth the point *G.* from whence on can discerne on one side Clermont on the other side Malvoysine hee tooke the meridian. & wth a quadrant tooke the angles of declination from this meridian. the manner hee relates at length. The summe of all is hee found by these observations the angle EGE wch is the declination of EG from the meridian westward o gr 26′

the angle $GI\theta$ wch is the declination of GI from the meridian eastward 1° 9′

angle $IN\gamma$ ——— of IN from the meridian eastward   2° 9′ 10″
angle $VN\beta$ ——— of NV from the meridian westward 18   55

Soe that in all these four triangles $EG\varepsilon$. $GI\theta$. $IN\gamma$. βVN. You have two angles knowne (for the angles at ε . at θ . at γ . at β are right) & a side EG. GI. IN. NV.
hence he concludes.

the length of the meridian $G\varepsilon$ 31894 Toyses
                         $I\theta$ 17560   3 Pieds
                         $N\gamma$ 18893   3
                         $N\beta$ 10559   3

hence the length of the whole
meridian $\alpha\beta$ betweene the parallels
of Malvoysine & Amiens is   78907   3

here hee frames an objection & saith that these lines wch make up the meridian, are not in a strict sense a curve, butt in Reality the sides of a polygone circumscribed about the circumference of the earth. Yet hee affirmes the difference betweene these lines & a true curve to bee butt 3 feet per degree wch is scarce worth taking notice of. this hee proves afterwards in that article, where hee makes the table in wch hee calculates what difference there is betweene the reall levell & the apparent. another Note hee makes in this same article wch is that though hee tooke those meridians for greater exactnesse wth a quadrant, Yet hee did not omitt to use a compasse whose declination to the Westward hee saith in yeare 1670 towards the end of summer hee found   1° 30′
anno 66 hee observed little variation at all.

64 it varied eastward   40′
hee makes a pretty note & saith the difference of variation in a
yeares time amounts neere to — — — — — — — — — — — — — —   20′

The length of the meridian betweene malvoysine and amiens being thus stated his next businesse is to enquire what answers to it in the heavens.

And by the help of an Instrument whose Limb was an arch of $\frac{1}{20}$ of a circle & its radius 10 feet wch hee gives the figure of & his manner of

rectifying any errors, wch might deceive him in ye using of it, hee determines the difference of latitude betweene malvoysin & Sourdon 1° 11′ 57″
betweene malvoysine & Amiens 1 22 55
wch comparing wth what hath beene said before it is evident that 1° 11′ 57″ in heaven answer to a meridian of   68430 T   3 P on earth.
   Hence hee concludes a degree   57064.   3
     that is numero rotundo[5]   57060 hee allowes to a degree.
     This Fernelius computed to   56746. Toyses[6]
     Snellius . . . .   55021.[7]
     Riccioli . . . .   62900.[8]

of the three it is apparent Fernelius comes the nighest, wch in the last article where he discourses of other differences ex professo[8a] Monsieur Picart attributes to meere chance for hee used not halfe the exactnesse in his observation, that Snellius did. Snellius his differing hee attributes to too small a base hee tooke to measure & too small angles hee was to take afterwards & his instruments not soe good as here. Riccioli's deduction depends upon refraction wch hee shewes how it might very well have deceived him.

   I thinke I have given you some satisfaction as to this proposition of Monsieur Picarts about the measure of the earth, at least as to the most materiall parts of it. as to all the particular niceties wch it would bee to tedious to describe I hope the booke it self wch some time or other surely will come abroad may putt an end to your Curiosity. I commend you [illegible] what I have written [illegible] [the Fellows of the Royal Society] may have a designe of deducing the measure of a degree from their owne observations. [illegible][9] I would not for any good imaginable that this should putt a stop to their industry or deprive them of the pleasure of comparing their exactnesse with Monsieur Picarts, or the world, of the advantage of having soe important a probleme resolved to them by different artists, in different countries by different mediums, that soe when the whole comes to bee reflected upon one may conclude from the accuratenesse of the observers who have come the neerest to truth in their observations.

   I must Not forgett to tell you that Monsieur Pecquet of the Royal Academie is dangerously sick of a feavour.[10] it seemes he had a high opinion of spirit of wine & used it much as a restorative pray god send it dont act contrary to his intentions, & shorten his days as a destructive.

   The new discovery wch the Royall Academie hath made in the body of a woman wch you say is a secret is a ductus, from the Lower trunc of the Vena cava to the venae mamillares. & to the breast. Mr Huygens is now God bee thanked quite recovrd & goes abroad & is intent about having his treatise de Cycloide & about pendulum clocks made fitt for the presse.[11]

Signre Cassini told mee hee would write to the Royall Society & propose it to them, whether they would please to doe him the honour as to make him a member of it.[12] hee is now intent upon his observations about Jupiter. the Royall academie upon their Physicall dayes are imployed upon Plants & the Chymicall examinations & analysis of them. in their mathematicall exercises their greater speculations are in Dioptriques & considering the lawes of Motion. Monsieur Borelli one of the Academie[13] hath made glasses for a tube of 35 parisian feet wch is now fitting for them: wch glasses Sigre Cassini, who in these matters is Criticall, saith are very good. Monsieur Borell is extreamely taken wth Mr Newtons happy invention of shortening the Telescope. hee desires to [bee] satisfyed in one particular of it. wch is whether The objective glasse of a telescope wch performes the same effect wth one of 6 foot is ground as for a tube of 6 feet or only as for one of 6. or 7. inches to wch size wee heare prospective glasses of 6. feet are reduced pray satisfied him & mee as to that.

I must desire of you for a gentleman wch hath beene a long time importunate wth mee for it to have a draught of Sir William Petties ship wth two bottomes.[14] The model I know is in Mr Hookes Keeping at Gresham College. pray lett it bee drawne wth a Crayon or how you please wth the profile & crosse section of it & what ever It costs I will desire Mr Collins to reimburse you Pray my humblest respects to the Bishop of Sarisbury if hee bee in towne & my Reall acknowledgements to Mr Boyle for doing mee the honour to Remember mee wth soe much Kindnesse. my service to Mr Hooke. I am.

Your most affectionate Servt
Francis Vernon

NOTES

1 Letter 1870.
2 Oldenburg has noted here that this distance is 77 English miles.
3 The upper figure on p. 435.
4 "which is what was sought for."
5 "in round numbers."
6 See Letter 1854, note 4.
7 See Letter 1854, note 5.

8 See Giovanni Battista Riccioli, *Geographia et hydrographia reformata* (Bologna, 1661). Picard dealt with the weakness of his method, arising from atmospheric refraction, in § 13 of *La Mesure de la Terre*.

8a "intentionally, of set purpose."

9 Oldenburg struck out this sentence so that it can only be partially read. The words in brackets are required to make sense of the passage. Oldenburg altered the next sentence to read: "... stop to the industry of our friends in England or deprive..."

10 Pecquet recovered.

11 *Horologium oscillatorium* (Paris, 1673).

12 Cassini was proposed as a candidate by Oldenburg on 24 April and 1 May 1672, and elected on 22 May.

13 Jacques Borelly; see Vol. V, p. 509, note 7, and vol. VII, p. 60. Borelly won considerable repute for his work on practical optics. (This was not Pierre Borel of Castres, never a member of the Académie, who had died in October 1671.)

14 It appears from Letter 1900 that the "gentleman" was Nicolas Toinard. The development of Sir William Petty's double-bottom (catamaran) yachts can be traced in Vols. I and II (see the Indexes s.v. "Petty"). One model—probably that constructed by Petty for the information of the shipwrights—was examined by a committee in January 1662/3 (Birch, *History*, I, 184); it was two and a half feet long. Another, nearly five feet long, was preserved in the Royal Society's repository (Grew, *Musaeum*, 363–64). Henry Hunt, who apparently entered Hooke's or the Royal Society's service as a lad from the country in 1673, made a drawing (presumably from a model) now in the Pepysian Library, Magdalene College, Cambridge.

1878

Oldenburg to Newton

20 January 1671/2

Printed in Newton, *Correspondence*, I, 83, note 1, from the original in private posession

Rec. Jan. 19, 1671/2. Answ. Jan. 20. Desired to have his consent of printing his invention. Let him know ye duties of a fellow: and ye uninteruptednes of ye meetings of ye Soc. except long vacation.

NOTE

Reply to Letter 1871, on which this memorandum is written.

1879
Malpighi to Oldenburg
22 January 1671/2

From the original in Royal Society Malpighi Letters, no. 12
Printed in *Opera Omnia*, II, *De formatione pulli in ovo*, p. 13

Praeclarissimo et Eruditissimo Viro
Domino Henrico Oldenburg Regiae Societatis Anglicanae Secretario
Marcellus Malpighius S.P.

Observationum rude inchoamentum, quod elapsis annis placuit in incubatis ovis tentare, his iniunctum recipies, Vir Clarissime.[1] Scio, amplissimam hanc & perdifficilem esse provinciam, & iam fere ex toto occupatam; quae mihi tamen in re tam obscura visae sunt occurrisse, brevibus exarata percurrere ne graveris, &, si non omnino indigna reperies, Regiae Societati exhibere quaeso, cujus censurae singula subjecta intendo.[2]

Transmissam elapsis mensibus de Plantarum anatome epistolam sub censura Clarissimorum Virorum laborare libenter audio, ipsorumque sensum avide exopto. Eximias interim Tibi grates ago ob propensam officiorum tuorum erga me affluentiam. Librum, quem in Italiam [te] transmissurum indicas, libentissime excipiam: Absit tamen, ut quemadmodum innuis, cum Viro Doctissimo certatim, hanc eandem materiam excolere intentem, cum optime agnoscam, supervacaneos undique conatus meos succedere, ubi vel minimus aliorum labor effulsit. Litterarum exercitamenta apud nos silent, nec quidquam novi in lucem promitur. Tuis interim me solare epistolis, et tui addictissimum fovere ne desinas. Dabam Bononiae, Calendis Februarii, 1672 [N.S.]

TRANSLATION

Marcello Malpighi sends many greetings to the very famous and learned Mr. Henry Oldenburg, Secretary of the English Royal Society

You will find here enclosed, famous Sir, the roughly assembled observations of incubated eggs that I had decided in previous years to attempt.[1] I know that this is a vast and very difficult task which has been almost completely worked out already, but you will be so kind as to look through what I have happened to notice in this very obscure field, briefly expressed, and if you think it is not wholly unworthy I beg you to lay it before the Royal Society, to whose criticism I mean to submit each part.[2]

I am glad to hear that the letter on the anatomy of plants sent some months ago is to be subjected to the criticism of distinguished men, and I eagerly long for their opinion. Meanwhile I return you my best thanks for your ready wealth of services on my behalf. I shall give a welcome to the book which, you say, will be sent; however, I hope there will be no question of bitter rivalry between myself and that learned person, as you hint, in studying the same subject, since I very freely acknowledge that my endeavors may on every particular be rendered superfluous, whereon light is shed by even the slightest labors of others. Literary men with us keep mum, and no new work for the press is promised. Meanwhile, do not cease to comfort me with your letters and to cherish your most devoted [friend].
Bologna, 1 February 1672 [N.S.]

NOTES

Reply to Letter 1842.
1 This was the essay, illustrated with splendid drawings, entitled *Dissertatio epistolica de formatione pulli in ovo*. As Adelmann points out, Malpighi had made few observations on eggs before the summer of 1671, when most of the work for this essay was done; however, Malpighi only wrote that the *intention* to study embryology was formed in earlier years.
2 This letter and the *Dissertatio* were received before 22 February, on which day Oldenburg read the former and a part of the latter. The Royal Society was so well pleased with Malpighi's observations that "It was ordered that this discourse, and the figures ... should forthwith be committed to the printers of the Society to be printed; and that particular care should be taken by the secretary, of having the schemes exactly ingraven by the best ingraver to be had in London"; and that particular thanks should be returned to the author. The work was published in London in 1673.

1880

Oldenburg to Lister

24 January 1671/2

From the original in Bodleian Library MS. Lister 34, f. 12

Jan 24th 71.

Sir,

Yr Discourse about the Veines in Plants found so good acceptance wth our Society, (where it was read on Thursday last,¹)that I received order, not only to returne you their hearty thanks for it, but also to be carefull in having it enter'd into their Register-book.² Besides wch, I take the liberty of making it publick in the Transactions of this very month, to let the world know, that in England there are persons as well as elsewhere, that have made deep researches into the fabrick of Vegetables, and that have, as well as ye Italians, considered them as a kind of standing and movelesse Animals.

Sir, I have a great mind you should see and examine ye written Discourse of Sigr Malpighi upon this subject, now in our hands.³ And if you could direct me, how to send it to you wth safety, I would actually transmit it for yr perusall, not doubting but you would be carefull of returning it to me after you had read and considered it. Those of the Society yt have perused it, doe highly praise it: and I am persuaded, that, in some particulars at least, it may enlarge yr thoughts and observations, and confirme them in others. You will meet in this Dissertation not only wth Veins, but Arteries, Trachea's, Lungs, Peristaltick motion, Uterus, and what not?

The President of the Society, in the name of that Body, exhorteth you herewth, that you would not omit, when ye approaching Summer's opportunity serveth, to review and repeat yr observations of this argument, the better to clear up those particulars mention'd by you, concerning ye Position, Order, Number, capacity, Distributions, Differences, Figure etc. of those veines. Wch being well perform'd, caeteris paribus,⁴ the Doctrine and Philosophy of ye vastest part of ye Sublunary World, wch relateth to Vegetables, is like to be satisfactorily stated.

I am very sorry, I cannot give you any good account of ye black resin, yt you sent up. Mr Boyle saith that of so smal a quantity, as he had (wch was half of it) he could not make any tryal, worth speaking of. And from P. Rupert I can as yet obtain no answer at all. We hope, you will draw, when there is opportunity, a greater quantity of yt black, and furnish us wth more, or make tryals yrself, for further certainty and satisfaction. The Society hath a great kindness for you, and I am very particularly Sir

Yr very humble and faithf. servt
H.O.

ADDRESS
For his honored friend
Martyn Lister Esquire
at his house wthout Mickel-
gate-barr at
Yorke

POSTMARK IA 24

NOTES

Reply to Letter 1863.
1 January 18, 1671/2.
2 This letter was (as usual) copied into the Letter Book (Vol. V, p. 123) but not into the Register Book.
3 See Letter 1805, note 2.
4 "other things being equal."

1881

Oldenburg to Fermat

25 January 1671/2

From the copy in Royal Society MS. O 2, no. 70

Clarissimo Viro
Domino S. Fermato
H. Oldenburg Salutem

Accepi, Vir Praestantissime, tuam de nupera Agrorum conseranensium per mures edita populatione cum notis annexis. Quid referam pro illa gratia, nil suppetit aliud, nisi Samuelis Morelandi Equitis Inventum de

Sono articulato ad duo vel tria milliaria Anglica distincte et clare devehendo: Nisi velis ut adjiciam, Matheseos in Academia Cantabrigiensi Professorem, Isaacum Newtonum, pro nuper nobis communicasse novam, ut retur, Telescopij rationem Catadioptricam, qua scilicet Tubo-specilla longiora, citra effecti fraudem, insigniter contrahere novit. Praestat illud gemini speculi metallici, unius concavi, alterius plani, necnon lentis vitreae, plano-convexae, beneficio. Prius speculum reflectens, et fundo Tubi adhaerens (in illo specimine, quod confecit Author ipse, et nobis examinandum transmisit,) radium habet 13. digitorum Anglicorum fere. Alterum Speculum, reflexos radios prioris recipiens, et ad lentem vitream denuo reverberans, est ovale, et circulo aeneo, intra Tubi cavitatem mobili, insertum. Lens vitrea radium habet $\frac{1}{12}$ digiti: Metallum quippe colligit Solis radios ad distantiam $6\frac{1}{3}$ digitorum, et lens ocularis ad $\frac{1}{6}$ dig. fere distantiam ab ejus vertice. Exploratae sunt nobis hae dimensiones ex vasis, in quibus elaborata fuere, speciatimque diametrum concavi haemisphaerici, in quo elaborata fuit lens vitrae, dimensi, eam $\frac{1}{6}$ digiti esse deprehendimus.

Centrum speculi plani locatur in Axe Tubi, ita ut in ipsum perpendicularis, a centro lentis demissa, cum axe angulum rectum constituat, et objecti species a speculo concavo in idem repercussa, versus lentis focum reflectatur: conferendo distantias foci istius a verticibus Lentis, et speculi concavi; prodit ratio 1 ad 38; qua indicatur, objecto 38. vicibus circiter in isto Tubo ampliari.

Misi similem descriptionem Domino Hugenio Parisijs nunc degenti, cujus de ea judicium praestolamur;[1] cui si et vestrum sociare placuerit, rem omnino gratam praestabitis. Vale, et Tibi addictissimum Oldenburgium amare perge. Londini die 25. Januarij. 1672.

TRANSLATION

Henry Oldenburg greets the very famous Mr. S. Fermat

I have received your [letter], excellent Sir, about the recent overflowing of mice upon the fields of Conserans, with the adjoined notes. In returning thanks I have nothing at hand except Sir Samuel Morland's invention for carrying articulate sound distinctly and clearly over a distance of two or three English miles, unless you would like me to add that very lately the Professor of Mathematics at the University of Cambridge, Isaac Newton, communicated to us a supposedly new type of reflecto-refracting telescope in which he has discovered how to shorten long telescopes without spoiling their effectiveness. This is promised by means of a pair of metallic mirrors, one concave and the other plane, and a plano-convex glass lens. The first reflecting speculum, placed at the end of the tube, has a radius of nearly thirteen English inches in the example which the inventor himself constructed and sent to us for examination. The other speculum, receiving the rays reflected from the first and in turn redirecting them to the glass lens, is an oval one inserted into a brass circle which is movable within the hollow of the tube. The glass lens has a radius of one-twelfth of an inch. In fact the metal speculum focuses the sun's rays at a distance of $6\frac{1}{3}$ inches while the eye lens focuses them at nearly one-sixth of an inch distance from its vertex. These measurements are given to us from the forms in which they were ground, and in particular we found that the diameter of the concave hemisphere in which the glass lens was polished was one-sixth of an inch.

The center of the plane mirror is so located on the axis of the tube that a perpendicular dropped upon it from the center of the lens makes a right angle with the axis, and the image of an object reflected upon it by the concave mirror is redirected towards the focus of the lens. Comparing the focal lengths of the lens and the concave mirror yields a ratio of 1 to 38, which indicates that an object is magnified about 38 times by that tube.

I have sent a similar description to Mr. Huygens, now living in Paris, whose judgment of it we have sought;[1] you will do something very welcome to us if you will join yours to his. Farewell, and continue to love your most devoted Oldenburg. London, 25 January 1672.

NOTES

Reply to Letter 1846.
1 See Letter 1866.

1882

Oldenburg to Newton

27 January 1671/2

Printed in Newton, *Correspondence*, I, 83, note 1, from the original in private possession

Writ again jan. 27. 71. repeated what I said before, and desired ye proportions of arseneck and metal.

NOTE

Second reply to Letter 1871, on which this memorandum is written.

1883
Newton to Oldenburg
29 January 1671/2

Printed in Newton, *Correspondence*, I, 84, from the original in private possession

In reply to Letter 1882, Newton states that in a speculum metal arsenic should be added to between one-sixth and one-eighth part by weight of the copper, and describes his method of alloying the metals; he permits the printing of the description of his telescope in the *Transactions*, and sends his admission fee as a Fellow of the Royal Society. Finally, he promises a full account of his work in optics.

1884
Oldenburg to Pardies
29 January 1671/2

From the memorandum in Royal Society MS. P 1, no. 74

Resp. le 29 janv. 1672. diverses choses considerees de ces matieres, come la demonstration dela Cycloide faite par Hugens, et icy dans les registres de la Societé.[1] La figure des cordes suspendues des 2. bouts, parabolique par Wren.[2] Les librations des pendules ne sont pas isochrones dans l'air Mais bien dans le vuide.

Hook luy cedera, s'il donne des raisons plus fortes touchant la refraction des rayons. Sa proposition Latine traitée par Barrow dans ses lecons Geometriques, Mr Boyle luy envoye l'experience de l'huile de Terebinthe distillée sur le sel marin se mesle avec l'esprit du vin.

Hooke scait temperer une liqueur dans des certaines limites.[3]

Envoié la responce latine de Wallis.[4]

et promis de luy envoyer Willis de Anima brutorum. Vous escrire des livres par la prochaine.

L'air n'estoit pas bien rarifié dans l'Experience Florentine. Et on ne scait pas, si ce n'estoit par une continuation du mouvement du corps.

A distillé l'esprit de Terebinthine sur le sel marin bien sec par un feu bien lent dans une cucurbite, alors l'huile de Tereb. se mesle avec l'esprit de vin, peut estre par une separation d'une substance gummeuse qui fait nager l'huile sur l'esprit du vin.

Dans cete grande quantité d'eau, il y a beaucoup d'air.[5]

He desires,[6] not only to draw touch lines, but also to square all manner of figures so toucht, and hath performed it so well, yt by a very able mathematician of Scotland Gregory he is exceedingly applauded. See Barr[ow] in his Geometrical Lectures; wch certainly you have at Paris.

The general:

This doctrine of Tangents being compleated, we may truly affirm (wch wants exemplification) yt giving one propertie of a figure, all ye rest may be derived by a certain & regular method. Wch some call cribrum syntheticum.[7]

And young Pascal wrote a treatise of conicks,[8] mention'd in Des Cartes his Epistles, concerning wch Mersenne gives this Caracter, qua ab una propositione universalissima, 400 corollariis armata, totum Appollonium complexus est[9]

TRANSLATION

Replied on 29 January 1671/2. Various things considered about these matters, like the demonstration of the cycloid by Huygens, here in the Register Book of the Society.[1] The figure of cords suspended from the two ends: parabolic, by Wren.[2] The oscillations of pendulums are not isochronous in the air, but are indeed, in the vacuum.

Hooke will concede to him, if he gives stronger arguments about the refraction of rays. His Latin proposition treated by Barrow in his geometrical lectures. Mr. Boyle sends him the experiment of oil of turpentine distilled over sea salt mixing with spirit of wine.

Hooke knows how to order a liquid within certain limits.[3]

Sent the Latin reply of Wallis.[4]

And promised to send him Willis, *De anima brutorum*. To write you about books in the next.

The air was not very well exhausted in the Florentine experiment. And it is not known whether this might not occur by the continuation of the motion of the body.

[Boyle] distilled spirit of turpentine over very dry sea salt with a very low fire in a cucurbit; then the oil of turpentine is miscible with spirit of wine, perhaps by the separation of a gummy substance which makes the oil swim on the spirit of wine.

In this great mass of water there is a great deal of air.⁵

. . . .

... in which, from one most universal proposition, enriched with 400 corrollaries, the whole of Apollonius is included.⁹

NOTES

Reply to Letter 1859. The notes are not continuous.
1 Oldenburg must have confused himself; perhaps he was recollecting the anagrams, still undecoded, sent by Huygens in 1669 (Vol. VI, Letter 1277a) or the unpublished paper "De motu corporum ex motuo impulsu hypothesis" (Vol. V, p. 284, note 1) of which the Royal Society had preserved a copy. There is no sign that Huygens ever sent a manuscript copy of his crucial demonstration that motion along an inverted cycloid is tautochronous before the publication of *Horologium oscillatorium* in 1673, and there are many hints in the correspondence that he did not.
2 See Letter 1859, note 4. Wren does not appear to have left his opinion on record, but the record of the meeting of 12 January 1670/1 (Birch, *History*, II, 464) makes it likely that Oldenburg was well acquainted with Wren's progress in statics.
3 Possibly the meaning is that Hooke knows how to adjust the refractive index of fluids—for this was something Pardies had asked about.
4 Letter 1873.
5 This seems to be an afterthought related to the Florentine experiment.
6 These two words are hard to decipher. "He" is presumably Barrow.
7 "a synthetic sieve."
8 See Vol. IV, p. 323, note 5.
9 See Marin Mersenne, *Cogitata physico-mathematica* (Paris, 1644): *Hydraulica phaenomena*, Preface, p. 11, no. 12. It was Mersenne who introduced Pascal's work on conics to Descartes late in 1639. The quoted passage is slightly distorted (perhaps by Collins): the first word should be *qui* (Mersenne having praised the Pascals, father and son, says of Blaise: "who in a unique proposition... has embraced...").

1885
Vogel to Oldenburg
31 January 1671/2
From the original in Royal Society MS. F 1, no. 35

Viro Nobilissimo & Doctissimo
HENRICO OLDENBURGIO
S.P.D.
Martinus Fogelius

Quas superioris anni [mensibus] Novembri & Decembri ad me dedisti literas, recte mihi fuerunt redditae. Respondissem maturius prioribus, nisi aegrorum visitationibus, impeditus fuissem.

Quod nos ad Philosophiam excolendam adhortaris, agnoscimus tuum ad nos affectum, quo nos tali negotio non ineptos judicas. Et praestaremus sane aliquid, nisi Maecenatibus destitueremur, quibus vos abundare videmini.

Ego, quantum in me est, omnem moveo lapidem, ut Veritatem proveham longius, sed solus fere hic sum, omnis socii expers.

Siferus vel centies a me monitus fuit, ut Phoranomicam Jungii editioni fere paratam absolveret. Sed, nescio an fato, ad alia semper abripitur. Edidit nunc Joannis Adolfi Tassii Opticae sive potius Photonomicae Compendium, quo accuratius nullum hactenus prodiit.[1] Edidit etiam ejusdem de Proportionibus Doctrinam, sive Protomathesin. Mittam prima navi Photonomicae Compendium nam alterum libellum pridem, ni fallor, acceperis. Fuit hic (Tassius) Professor in Gymnasio nostro & Jungium Praeceptorem suum in Mathesi, quamvis jam aetate provectior, habuit, praecipue vero in Analysi. Totius fere Matheseos Scientiarum Compendia haec olim conscripsit, Empirico tamen processu, non Apodictico (quod hunc Tirones nostri non capere valeant) ad exemplum Geometriae Empiricae Jungii. Haec Compendia hereditate transiere ad Legatum Nostrum, qui vobiscum est, Amplissimum Vincentium Garmerum,[2] qui domi suae servat. Habeo ipse fere omnia, ex ultima Auctoris recognitione, inter mea κειμήλια, & ex meis exemplaribus bina haec edita sunt Compendia a Sifero. Quod si tibi detur occasio cum Syndico Garmero loquendi, da operam, ut ipsum ad editionem reliquorum impellas, & ab oblivione vindices tam praeclara Systemata.

Opus etiam erit, ut Siferum nostrum excites ad Phoranomicae Schemata delineanda, & fasciculos reliquos perlegendos. Quod prima quavis occasione te velim facere.

Bacenis seu Semana Silva, (quam cum plerisque Hercyniam vocas, ex prava pronuntiatione literae C male colligentibus, esse nostram Harz) remotior a nobis est, quam ut intimos ejus recessus perlustrare possimus.[3] Jam olim in colligendis Silvae hujus plantis diligentissimum se praestitit Joannes Thalius, Medicus Northusanus,[4] editio 1. Metallicorum Corporum Historiam ex Loeneisio praecipue licet petere et aliis.[5] Animalium Historiam desideramus. Excitandi tibi sunt Meibomius, Vir curiosus & doctus, Helmestadiensis Professor;[6] Bernhardides, Medicus Guelferbytius, olim Zellerfeldae ad Semanam silvam Medicinam exercens; Stochusius, Goslariensis Medicus, non unus e multis; Ramlovius Osterodensis Medicus, & Grylingius Stolbergensis Medicus.[7] Si Regio quopiam stipendio mihi prospiceretur, ipse repeterem loca olim a me in Silva hac lustrata, & conseriberem Historiam, in qua nihil forsan desiderari posset a curiosis talium. Nunc aegris visitandis occupor, ut familiam commode alam. Possem nihilominus historiae Silvae naturalem edere, qualem Childrey[8] Angliae dedit, si excerpta mea & Observata cum Thalii Catalogo, Loeneisii Excerptis &c. jungerem. Utinammodo socium laboris haberem!

De Galilaei exemplari mihi ad tempus concedendo cogites amplius, rogo, ut eo maturius Historia haec prodeat. Quantum argenti loco pignoris deponendum sit hic & apud quem; ex possessore inquiras. mitti poterit cum Schulzii libris.

Pro Pocockii folio gratias ago maximas. non opus fuisset Latine vertere, quia Lexico adhibito Anglicos libros intelligo. et Arabicae linguae olim operam dedi. Miror, vestros Medicos, & Phytoscopos non laborare, ut ex Oriente tandem habeamus accuratas Figuras & Descriptiones Arborum Thuris, Myrrhae, Myrobalanorum, Opopanacis, Sagapeni &c.[9]

Nescimus adhuc, an Vomica nux sit Fructus, an Fungus, an aliud quid. de Bdellio cum quaesivi, intellexi resinam Arboris, quae in Officinis reperitur. Schulzius libentissime Ephemeridum Versionem quam paras, imprimi curasset, quia jam sumtus aliquos fecerat ejus causa. Interpres ultimus aeque ineptus omnino est, ac primus.

de Tuba Morelandi pridem cognovi ex literis Justelli.

Clarissimus Morhofius Epistolam edidit de Scypho Vitreo per Humanae vocis Sonum fracto.[10]

Lachmundus edet Dissertationem de Ave Diomedae,[11] Amstelodami imprimenda. hanc excipiet Tractatus ejusdem de Lapide Judaico.

Habeo apud me Relationem de Groenlandia quam vocant, Germanice a Chirurgo descriptam, in qua omnes Plantae, Animalia, Nix varia ad vivum &c. curiose depinguntur. Respondit etiam ad pleraque capita, quae Societas Vestra proponit eo profecturis consideranda. Nihil ab ipso scribi volui praeterea, quae quam compertissima haberet.

Nihilne de Toxico Hispanorum accepisti?

Nihil respondes ad haec 2 quaesita, an Pocockius Notas scripserit ad Garziam ab Orto et quid Howi vestri Botanicis scriptis fiat.

Vale Vir Nobilissime & me amare perge. Scribam prid. Cal. Febr. 1672

ADDRESS
A Monsr
Monsr Grubendal
a
Londres

TRANSLATION

Martin Vogel sends many greetings to the very noble and learned Henry Oldenburg

The letters you wrote to me in November and December last year have been safely delivered to me. I should have replied more promptly to the former had not my attendance on the sick prevented me.

I discern your goodwill towards me in your urging me to the cultivation of philosophy, since you judge me not incapable of such an activity. And surely I should have come forward with something, if we were not lacking in wealthy patrons here, who seem to abound with you.

So far as in me lies, I move heaven and earth in order to advance the truth, but I am virtually singlehanded here, devoid of all companions.

Sivers has been advised by myself a hundred times to finish off the edition of Jungius' *Phoranomica* that is almost ready. But some turn of fate always carries him off to other things. He has now published the *Optica*, or rather compendium of photonomics, of Johann Adolf Tasse, than which nothing more exact has appeared.[1] He has also published the same author's *Doctrina de proportionibus*, or *Protomathesin*. I shall send the compendium of photonomics by the first ship, for the other book you will have received long ago, if I mistake not. He (Tasse) was a professor in our Gymnasium here, and Jungius was his teacher of mathematics, analysis particularly, though far advanced in years. He some time ago wrote a compendium of almost all the mathematical sciences, taught in an empirical manner, however, not formally (for this our beginners were not up to dealing with), following the example of Jungius' empirical geometry. This compendium was inherited by our envoy to you, the very worthy Vincent Garmers,[2] who keeps it at home. I have myself almost the whole of it among my own treasures, as it received the author's final touches, and from my copies these two compendia have been edited by Sivers. If you have any opportunity of conversing with Syndic Garmers, try to persuade him to agree to the publication of the remainder, and so preserve such an excellent system from oblivion.

It will also be worthwhile to exhort our Sivers to draw the diagrams for *Phoranomica* and read over the remaining fascicules. Which I would wish you to do at the first opportunity.

The Bacenic or Semanic forest (which you call "Hercynian," along with many others who from a depraved pronunciation of the letter C suppose it to be our Harz) is too far from us, for us to examine its deepest fastnesses.[3] Long ago Johann Thal, a physician of Nordhausen,[4] proved very diligent in collecting plants from this forest in a single edition. The history of metallic bodies, is chiefly to be sought in Lonicer and others.[5] We lack an account of the animals. You should excite Meibom, an inquisitive and learned man, professor at Helmstadt;[6] Bernhardides, physician at Wolfenbüttel but formerly practising medicine at Zellerfeld in the Thuringian forest; Stochus, physician at Goslar, not one out of many; Ramlovius, physician at Osterode, and Gryling, physician at Stolberg.[7] If I could look forward to some royal stipend, I would seek out again places I formerly examined in that forest and write a History from which perhaps nothing would be found lacking by lovers of such things. Now I am busy attending the sick, in order to nourish my family properly. Nevertheless I can publish a natural history of the forest, such as Childrey[8] gave of England, if I combine my extracts and observations with Thal's catalogue, the excerpts from Lonicer, and so forth. Would that I had the help of colleagues!

Please think further about granting me a copy of the Galileo for a time, so that this history may come out the more promptly. You may ask the owner how much money is to be deposited as a pledge, and with whom. It can be sent with Schulz's books.

I thank you heartily for Pocock's sheet. There was no need to translate it into Latin, because I can understand English books with the aid of a dictionary. And I once gave some study to the Arabic tongue. I wonder that your physicians and botanists do not strive to get us at last from the East accurate sketches and descriptions of the trees frankincense, myrrh, myrobalan, opopanax, sagapenum, etc.[9]

We have hitherto been ignorant whether nux vomica is a fruit, a fungus, or what. When I inquired about bdellium I meant the resin of the tree, which is to be found in shops. Schulz would very gladly take charge of the printing of the translation of the *Transactions* that you are preparing, because he has already been put to some expense on that account. The last translator was quite as incompetent as the first.

I first learned of Morland's trumpet from Justel's letter.

The famous Morhof has published a letter about breaking a glass goblet by the sound of the human voice.[10]

Lachmund is publishing a dissertation, to be printed at Amsterdam, on the bird Diomeda.[11] A treatise by the same author on Jew's-stone[12] is to follow this.

I have by me a relation of Greenland, as they call it, described in German by a surgeon, in which all the plants, animals, varieties of snow, etc. are curiously depicted in a lifelike way. He also answers many of the headings which your Society proposes for the consideration of travelers. I did not wish him to write anything beyond what he had ascertained very exactly.

You have heard nothing of the Spanish arrow-poison?

You make no reply to these two questions, viz. whether Pocock has written notes on Garcia d'Orta, and what has become of the botanical writings of your countryman How.

Farewell, noble Sir, and continue to love me. 31 January 1672.

ADDRESS
  To Mr. Grubendol,
  London

NOTES

  Reply to Letters 1821 and 1852.
1 For this mathematician, see Vol. VI, p. 621, note 4. The B.M. Library Catalogue lists by Tasse: *Arithmeticae empiricae compendium ex recensione H. Siveri* (Hamburg, 1673); *Photicae (quae vulgo optica dicitur) compendium* (Hamburg, 1678); *Opuscula mathematica ex recensione H. Siveri... de novo revisa et emendata* (Hamburg, 1699).
2 Vincent Garmers was a member of a notable family in Hamburg, others of whom were Syndics besides himself. He went on diplomatic missions to Denmark, Sweden, England, and the Emperor Leopold.
3 The geographical terms are Latin, of course; Vogel seems to apply both to the forests of Thuringia (as distinct from the Harz *Mountains*).
4 *Sylva Hercynia, sive catalogus plantarum sponte nascentium...* was published at Frankfurt-am-Main in 1588.
5 Presumably the work of Adam Lonicer, *Naturalis historiae opus novum* (Frankfurt-a-M., 1551) is meant; it was also issued in many German editions as *Kreuterbuch...*
6 Heinrich Meibom, the Younger (1638–1700), born at Lübeck, was Professor of Medicine at Helmstadt from 1664 onwards. Some works of this very voluble author have been mentioned previously.
7 We have not further identified any of these.
8 The reading is doubtful, but appropriate: Joshua Childrey's *Britannia Baconica* (London, 1660) has been several times mentioned before.
9 All these are names of resins, some of them used in medicine, rather than of the species of trees from which they are derived.

10 See Letter 1542 and note 2 (Vol. VII, pp. 229–34).
11 Friedrich Lachmund, *De ave Diomedes dissertatio* (Amsterdam, 1674). *Diomedea* are albatross or mallemuck.
12 This term is applied both to the fossil spine of a large sea urchin from Syria and to a form of iron pyrites or marcasite.

1886
Huygens to Oldenburg
3 February 1671/2

From the original in Royal Society MS. H 1, no. 71
Printed in *Œuvres Complètes*, VII, 140–43

A Paris ce 13 febr. 1672. [N.S.]

Monsieur

J'ai receu vos lettres du 1er et 15er Jan. dont la dernière porte l'accomplissement de la promesse de l'autre, qui est la description du merveilleux telescope de Mr. Newton.[1] dont j'ay beaucoup meilleure opinion maintenant que lors que par le raport imparfait qu'on m'en avoit fait je m'imaginois qu'il s'estoit proposè d'accourcir les lunettes ordinaires par la reflexion de ses miroirs. Je vois maintenant que son dessein a esté bien meilleur et qu'il a considerè l'avantage qu'a le miroir concave par dessus les verres convexes à assembler les rayons paralleles, qui certainement selon le calcul qui j'en ay fait, est fort grande.[2] De la vient qu'il peut donner une ouverture beaucoup plus grande au miroir qu'a un verre objectif de mesme distance de foier, et que par consequent il peut faire grossir d'avantage les objects par sa nouvelle lunette que ne feroit une lunette ordinaire de pareille longueur. Je vois de plus cet avantage dans son invention qu'il evite un inconvenient qui est inseparable des verres objectifs convexes, à scavoir l'obliquitè de leur deux surfaces, qui gaste la refraction des rayons qui passent vers les bords du verre et fait plus de mal que l'on ne pense.[3] Le verre aussi d'ailleurs, tant par les reflexions contre ses deux surfaces que par son obscuritè intercepte une bonne quantitè des rayons, qui ne se perdent pas de mesme par la simple reflexion du miroir. Mais il s'agit de trouver une matiere pour ce miroir qui soit capable d'un poli aussi beau et uni que celuy du verre, et la maniere de donner ce poli sans gaster la figure spherique. Jusqu'icy je n'ay point vu de miroirs qui l'eussent a beaucoup pres si beau que le verre, et si Mr. Newton n'a desia trouvée quelque invention pour le rendre meilleur qu'a l'ordinaire, j'ay peur que sa lunette ne distingue pas si bien les objects que ne font celles qui sont composees de verres. Mais il vaut bien la peine qu'on cherche de remedier a cet inconvenient, et je ne desespere pas qu'on n'en puisse venir a bout, sur tout quand je considere les nouvelles pratiques qu'ont trouvè quelques curieux d'icy pour la perfection du poli des verres. Le petit miroir plat intercepte une partie des meilleurs rayons, mais a cela il n'y a point de remede, et la grandeur de l'ouverture du miroir doit recompenser cette perte. Je m'estonne que dans la description on n'a pas marquè que les objects paroissent renversez, car cela doit estre ainsi suivant la disposition de l'oeil et de la lunette qu'on y a representées. Mais pour regarder aux astres il n'importe pas beaucoup. Je crois que Mr. Newton n'aura pas laissè de considerer l'avantage qu'auroit un miroir parabolique par dessus le spherique en cette construction, mais qu'il desespere comme moy de pouvoir tailler des surfaces autres que spheriques dans l'exactitude et perfection requise, quoyqu'autrement il soit plus aisè de faire la parabolique que les Elliptiques ou hyperboliques, a cause de certaine proprietè du conoide parabolique qui est que toutes les sections paralleles a l'axe font la mesme parabole.

Voila Monsieur tout ce qui me vient dans la pensée à vous dire sur cette nouvelle invention; dont je serois bien aise d'avoir vu l'effect, et en attendant je voudrois scavoir de vous si la lunette, dont la description marque la longueur et la multiplication, faisoit voir les objects bien distincts, et clairs, dont ce dernier depend de l'ouverture du miroir qui n'y est point exprimée. Pour ce qui est de la difficultè de trouver les objects il est facile d'y remedier en attachant une lunette ordinaire a cellecy qui luy soit parallele. Si Mr. Smetwick continue encore son travail sur les verres non spheriques je seray bien aise d'en apprendre le succes, mais a ce que je puis juger par l'experience que j'ay en ce mestier il n'y a rien a esperer que seulement des superficies spheriques; et qui les peut rendre parfaites et bien polies, j'estime qu'il n'a pas trouvè un petit secret.

Je ne scay qui peut vois avoir mandè que je n'avois pas encore receu le dernier volume du traitë de Mr. Wallis. Il est vray qu'en vous escrivant ma derniere je ne l'avois pas encore, mais Mr. Justel me l'apporta peu de jours apres, desorte que je fus estonnè de veoir que dans vostre penultieme lettre vous me promettez ce livre encore une fois. Mais en tout cecy ma negligence est la plus coupable, parce que je ne devrois pas avoir estè si longtemps sans vous escrire, car la maladie que j'ay eue du depuis ne suffit pas pour m'excuser. Il est vray qu'elle est cause de ce que je n'ay pas renouvellè le commerce avec Mr. Sluse, apprehendant de me remettre trop avant dans l'estude de geometrie dont il ne me vient que trop d'occasions tous les jours. Toute fois si vous avez la bontè de me faire part de ce qu'il vous a envoyè dernierement touchant le Probleme d'Alhazen, vous me ferez grand plaisir.

Mr. Vernon m'a monstrè la description de la trompette de Mr. Moreland, dont je voudrois bien voir l'effect, ayant de la peine a me l'imaginer si grand qu'il est assurè dans cet escrit. On m'a dit qu'on en fera venir une pour cette Academie. Le probleme touchant la meilleur figure pour cette Trompette seroit difficile a resoudre et il faudroit auparavant avoir bien des connaissances en ce qui regarde la nature du son que nous n'avons pas encore.

Mon Horologe de nouvelle fabrique n'a pu estre preste, a cause de mon indisposition, pour partir avec ceux qu'on a envoyè en Amerique pour les Observations celestes, et quand mesme elle auroit estè preste, le vaisseau estoit si petit et si peu accommodè pour cette experience que je n'aurois pas estè bien aise de l'y avoir embarquée.[4] Je crois que j'iray quelque jour moy mesme a quelque petit voiage, pour voir le succes de cette invention, car je vois qu'il depend beaucoup de la diligence de ceux a qui on en commit le soin desquels je ne suis pas fort satisfait jusqu'a present.

Jay estè bien aise de trouver dans vos dernieres Transactions[5] les diverses observations de Saturne qu'on vous a envoiees, qui confirment les nostres, et font qu'on ne pourra jamais les revoquer en doute. Cela m'a de nouveau fait faire reflexion sur l'utilitè du dessein de ces Nouvelles, qui est certainement tresgrande, et tous ceux qui aiment les belles sciences vous sont fort obligez de la continuation reguliere de ces escrits, et de la peine que vous prenez a en avancer la matiere par les correspondances que vous entretenez de tous costez. Je vous ay assurè plus d'une fois que vous m'obligerez en m'en envoyant des exemplaires et je vous le repete encore car j'aime mieux les avoir en propre que de me contenter de la lecture par emprunt.

Je suis de tout mon coeur Monsieur
Vostre tres humble serviteur
Hugens de Zulichem

Je remercie treshumblement Mr. le Chevalier Morray de l'honneur de son souvenir et luy baise les mains, comme aussi a tous vos Illustres Messieurs qui sont de ma connoissance.

ADDRESS
  A Monsieur
  Monsieur Grubendol
    A
      Londres

TRANSLATION, partly from *Phil. Trans.*, no. 81 (25 March 1672), 4008–9

[Paris, 13 February 1672 [N.S.]

[Sir,

I have received your letters of the first and the fifteenth of January, the latter of which brings the accomplishment of the promise in the other, that is, the description of the marvelous telescope of Mr. Newton.[1] Of this I now have a much better opinion than I did when, from the imperfect account made to me, I imaged that he proposed to shorten ordinary telescopes by the reflection of his mirrors. I now see that his plan was much better and] that he hath well considered the advantage, which a *Concave speculum* hath above *Convex glasses* in collecting the parallel rays, which certainly according to the calculation, I have made thereof, is very great.[2] Hence it is, that he can give a far greater aperture to that *speculum*, than to an Object-glass of the same distance of the *focus*, and consequently he can much more magnifie objects this way, than by an ordinary Telescope [of the same length]. Besides, by it he avoids an inconvenience, which is inseparable from convex Object-Glasses, which is the Obliquity of both their surfaces, which vitiateth the refraction of the rays that pass towards the sides of the glass, and does more hurt than men are aware of.[3] Again, by the meer reflection of the metallin *speculum* there are not so many rays lost, as in Glasses, which reflect a considerable quantity by each of their surfaces, and besides intercept many of them by the obscurity of their matter.

Mean time, the main business will be, to find a matter for this *speculum* that will bear so good and even a polish as Glasses, and a way of giving this polish without vitiating the spherical figure. Hitherto I have found no *Specula*, that had near so good a polish as Glass; and if M. Newton hath not already found a way to make it better, than ordinarily, I apprehend, his Telescopes will not so well distinguish objects, as those with Glasses. But 'tis worth while to search for a remedy to this inconvenience, and I despair not of finding one [especially when I reflect upon the new techniques found out here by some inquirers to perfect the polishing of lenses. The small flat mirror intercepts a portion of the best rays, but there is no remedy for that, and the size of the aperture of the mirror compensates for that loss. I am surprised that in the description it has not been noted that objects appear reversed, for it must be so considering the arrangements of the eye and of the telescope represented. But for observing stars this is of no great importance.] I believe, that M. Newton hath not been without considering the advantage, which a *Parabolical speculum* would have above a *Spherical* one in this construction; but that he despairs, as well as I do, of working other surfaces than spherical ones with due exactness [and perfection]; though else it be more easie to make a *Parabolical* than *Elliptical* or *Hyperbolical* ones, by reason of a certain propriety of the *Parabolick Conoid*, which is, that all the Sections parallel to the Axis make the same Parabola.

[Here, Sir, is all that came into my mind to say to you about this new invention; I should be very glad to have seen it in operation, and while waiting I should like to know from you if the telescope, whose length and magnification are given in the description, shows objects very distinct and clear, the latter depending upon the aperture of the mirror which is not stated. As for the difficulty of locating objects, this can easily be remedied by fastening an ordinary telescope to this so that it is parallel to it. If Mr. Smethwick still goes on with his work on nonspherical lenses I should be very glad to learn with what success, but as far as I can judge by my own experience in this art, nothing can be hoped for except from spherical surfaces, and I should consider it no small discovery if any one can make them perfect and very smooth.

I do not know who can have told you that I had not yet received the last volume of Mr. Wallis's treatise. It is true that when I wrote my last to you I had not yet received it, but Mr. Justel brought it to me a few days afterwards, so that I was astonished to see that in your last letter but one you promise me this book once again. But in all this my neglicence is the more culpable because I ought not to have been so long in writing to you, since the illness I have had since then is not sufficient excuse. It is true that it is the reason why I have not renewed the correspondence with Mr. Sluse, being apprehensive of getting myself too deeply involved in the study of geometry, for which I find only too many opportunities every day. Nevertheless, if you will be so good as to share with me what he has last sent you about Alhazen's Problem you will give me great pleasure.

Mr. Vernon has shown me the description of Mr. Morland's trumpet, which I should much like to see in operation, finding it difficult to suppose its effect to be as great as I am assured in that account. I have been told that one will be made for this Academy. The problem of the best shape for this trumpet is one difficult to resolve, and first it would be necessary to have a thorough knowledge of the nature of sound such as we do not yet possess.

My clock of a new design could not, because of my illness, be ready in time to leave with those being sent to America to make celestical observations, and even if it had been ready, the ship was so small and so little suited for this trial that I should not have been content to have had it aboard.[4] I think I shall one day go on a little voyage myself to see the success of this invention, for I see that it very much depends upon the diligence of those to whose care it is committed, and I am not so far very well satisfied with them.

I was very glad to find in your last *Transactions*[5] the various observations of Saturn sent to you, which confirm ours, and make it impossible ever to reject those as being in doubt. This made me reflect again upon the usefulness of the plan of these news sheets, which is certainly very great, and all who love true science are very much obliged to you for the regular continuation of these writings, and for the trouble you take in promoting the business by the correspondence you conduct on all sides. I have assured you more than once that you would oblige me if you sent me copies, and I repeat it once again, for I prefer to have them as my own than to be content with borrowing them to read.

I am, Sir, with all my heart

Your very humble servant,
Huygens of Zulichem

I thank Sir Robert Moray very humbly for the honor of his recollection and I salute him, as I do also all your illustrious Fellows with whom I am acquainted.

ADDRESS
To Mr. Grubendol,
London]

NOTES

Reply to Letters 1856 and 1866.
1 Letter 1866a.
2 See Huygens' notes on Letter 1866a, printed in *Œuvres Complètes*, VII, 131-32; he there calculated that if a plano-convex lens and a concave mirror have the same focal length and aperture, spherical aberrations are as 28 to 3.
3 Huygens at this time thought that this obliquity was the cause of the coloration of images.
4 Compare Letter 1807, note 7.
5 *Phil. Trans.*, no. 78 (18 December 1671).

1887
Bernard to Oldenburg
4 February 1671/2

From the original in Royal Society MS. B 2, no. 7

Honed Sr,

This gives you my hearty Acknowledgments for yr favours, & my advise yt Mr Hooke & Mr Newton make all hast to print their Methods in Dioptriques least our Neighbours clayme great shares in ye honr of their Inventions: The little booke of ye Tuba Stenterophonica is already printed in France with ye Cutts.[1] I find diverse persons here inclinable to Experimentall Philosophy: & ye news of ye Academy Royall at Paris will provoke more. I am assurd from thence of a Booke wch yt Society hath lately printed in ye Louvre conteyning ye Anatomyes of ye Rarer Animalls, and an exact dimension of ye Globe wee tread upon;[2] but yt it is intended onely as a Present to Princes & Benefactors: when one comes to your hands I would desire a small Account of ye latter Treatise. Shortly huyghens's Dioptriques is expected,[3] & ye Analytiques of father Pardes.[4] & a Treatise of Dr Pecquet's de Oculo.[5] They advise alsoe yt ye Ingenious at ye Observatory are makeing Metallines much larger yn ye famed one of France.[6] Dodart & Marchant are putting forth an Herball with excellent Cutts. Picart's observations at Uraniburge[7] confirme what our men have guessed at, namely ye Libration of ye Earth. The elegance of Mr Nicole in his writeings is greatly commended.[8] Thus I have wearied you, & yet further entreate yr Order for ye sending ye Enclosd to Sr John Wroth, at whose losse I must lament, & pray God hee may recommend himself to his Aged Unckle yt his Fortune may descend to him.[9]

Sr I am yr very affectionate Servtt
E. Bernard.

Febr. 4. 1671.

ADDRESS
  These
  For his Worthy Freind
  Henry Oldenburgh Esq
  att ye Pellmell near
      St James's
          London

POSTMARK FE 5

NOTES

Presumably this letter was written from Oxford; Bernard had close links with Paris. We have not found Oldenburg's letters to Bernard.
1 It was printed, in French, in Denis, *Mémoires*, no. 2 (15 February 1672, N.S.), 16–35.
2 Compare Vol. VII, p. 496.
3 Only published posthumously in 1703.
4 Compare Letter 1859.
5 This seems to be a ghost; for his dispute with Mariotte concerning the eye, see Vol. IV, p. 349, note 1.
6 Metallic burning mirrors.
7 See Letters 1769 and 1771.
8 Probably the Jansenist writer P. Pierre Nicole (1625–95); compare Vol. VII, p. 142, note 7.
9 For the illness of the elder Sir John Wroth, see Letter 1735 (and note 6); he was succeeded by his son of the same name. The aged uncle was Sir Thomas Wroth (1584–1672), who outlived his brother less than a year.

1888

Flamsteed to Oldenburg

5 February 1671/2

From the original in Royal Society MS. F 1, no. 79

Derby: Feb: 5 16$\frac{71}{72}$

Sr

Since I lost ye opportunitys of observeing those circumjoviall appearances yu communicated to us from Monsr Cassini I hold my selfe obliged to give yu an account of 2 which I observed very lately yt so it may appeare to yu that, it was not any neglect in my selfe but ye foulnesse of ye weather yt hinder'd mee from giving yu ye account yu might expect of those praedictions & that ye french astronomers (if yu thinke these observations worthy to be communicated to them) may esteeme of us as not unmindfull of ye heavens. Thursday last being Feb. 1st instant was very cleare so yt veiwing ye sun severall times I found his body cleared from spots. his diameter in my long tube of $164\frac{1}{2}$ inches, I measured severall times with ye micrometer $5435 = 32' 37''$. So his semidiameter $16' 18''$: Persuaded yt this clearnesse would continue, I sought for ye motions of ye Satellits from Cassini's Tables & found yt with us they ought to stand apparently as in this figure: viz. ye first 3. ye second 8. ye third

2. and ye 4th, $12\frac{1}{2}$ semidiameters of Jupiter from his center and that ye first would be ye same night observed in his shade ye third hid under his face. for these appearances I resolved to attend. at 8 aclock the Satellits appeared nearly as ye figure represents them onely ye dexter 3d satellit somewhat more removed from Jupiters limbe then is represented. I waited til 10.h 36' when Jupiter's height being 32° 30' the 1st satellit disappear'd at ye point neare *a*, but $\frac{1}{6}$ of Jupiters diameter from his limbe, & a little above a line drawne through ye center of Jupiter & ye utmost satellit. at 10h–$38\frac{1}{2}'$ haveing diligently sought it it was certeincly not to be seene Jupiter's height 32°. 50': in the meantime ye dexter satellit aproached neare Jupiters limbe from which at 10h. 52' alto Jupiter 34°. 20', it was onely distant $\frac{1}{8}$ of Jupiters diameter from [his] limbe somewhat under ye broad Zone as at *b*. perpendicular to yt point of [his] limbe which is cut by a line draw through ye remotest satellit & his center. So yt now I guessed it partly in ye plane of its orbe with ye utmost limbe of Jupiter. these apparently. for I have drawne ye satellits & describd ye appearances inverted as my tube presents it and Cassini delineates them. I foresaw some following appearances which ye variation of ye weather & ye skys constant thicknesse since have not permitted mee to observe. something may hence be deduced which I omit till what I conceive, may be either confirmd or redargued[1] by future observations.

I have severall informations from Cambridge yt Mr Newtons short telescope which performes so extraordinary is delivered into Dr Barrow's hands to be by him presented to ye R. Society.[2] I suppose yu have had it some while since. I hope you will please to informe us of the contrivance

I have had some rude descriptions of it but such as I cannot collect much from but that it augments ye image projected on a peece of mettall by reflecteing it on another polisht peece of brasse whereon it is veiwd by ye eye. what is wanteing in ye information concerneing ye dimensions of ye figures of ye metall plates & their position yu will much oblige mee if yu please to let mee understand yu may send ye letters to mee by ye post directed to my selfe but if too large by the carrier who still lodges as I understand at ye Bell in Smithfeilde.³ when ye heavens aford mee more phaenomena yu may expect to heare further from mee. till then I take my leave & subscribe

       Yr much obliged freind & servant
         John Flamsteed

 ye altitudes taken by a quadrant of 20 inches Rad[ius]. I durst not stay in ye keene frost till ye 3d was joynd to ye limbe it was so very cold. ye observation made in my longer tube.

ADDRESS
 To Henry Oldenburge Esqr
 at his house in the middle of the
 Pell mell neare St James's
 Westminster these
    present

NOTES

1 refuted.
2 Using almost identical words in a letter to Collins of 31 January, Flamsteed also adds that a kinsman of his had come from Cambridge (Rigaud, II, 126).
3 In the same letter to Collins Flamsteed fears that Oldenburg had ceased writing to him because Flamsteed had asked Collins not to write directly to himself but to a certain Mr. Lichfield, so that his father (Flamsteed senior) would not see all his correspondence coming to the house.

1889
Wallis to Oldenburg
5 February 1671/2
From Birch, *History*, III, 9

. . . .

Feb. 8. Five letters to Mr. Oldenburg were read:
1. Of Dr. Wallis, dated February 5, 1671/2, intimating, that from several late observations of his he conjectured, that the moon's perigee and apogee might much influence the rising and falling of the mercury of the barometer. This was recommended to those members of the Society, who had baroscopes, for further observation.

. . . .

NOTE

No manuscript of this letter has been found; it was not entered in the Letter Book, nor was it printed. It is worth observing that Wallis was not concerned with some occult influence of the moon, but with atmospheric tides (which, however, were imperceptible with the instruments then available).

1890
Oldenburg to Bernard
6 February 1671/2
From the memorandum in Royal Society MS. B 2, no. 7

Rec. Feb. 5. 71. Answ. Feb. 6. Desired acct. of ye letter of ye Rabbi (converted to Christianity) written to another Rabbi, shewing ye grounds of his leaving judaisme.

NOTE

Reply to Letter 1887. We know nothing of the religious pamphlet.

1891

Newton to Oldenburg

6 February 1671/2

Printed in Newton, *Correspondence*, I, 92–102, from *Phil. Trans.*, no. 80 (19 February 1671/2), 3075–87, and the copy in CUL MS. Add. 3970. 3, ff. 460–66

This is the celebrated letter or rather paper, many times reprinted, in which Newton fulfilled his earlier promise to describe the optical researches that had led him to the invention of his reflecting telescope.

Here he begins with an account of his prismatic experiments, culminating in the *experimentum crucis*, from which he learned that "Light it self is a *Heterogeneous mixture of differently refrangible rays*." This discovery [of chromatic aberration] convinced him that, however figured, lenses could not be made to give perfect images. Newton further laid down a "doctrine" or theory of light and colors which, he claimed, "is not an Hypothesis but most rigid consequence... evinced by ye mediation of experiments concluding directly & wthout any suspicion of doubt." Here he insisted that color was not a quality of light, that in each pure ray its color and refrangibility were both inseparable and inviolate, and that the union of all the colors was necessary to form white light.

1892

Oldenburg to Newton

8 February 1671/2

Printed in Newton, *Correspondence*, I, 107–8, from the copy in Royal Society Letter Book V, 157

In reply to Letter 1891, Oldenburg reports the reading of it to the Royal Society on the day of writing, and the Society's view that it should be printed, in order to establish priority. Oldenburg asks permission to print it in the *Philosophical Transactions* for February.

1893
Oldenburg to Cornelio
9 February 1671/2

From the copy in Royal Society MS. O 2, no. 71

Clarissimo Philosopho
Domino Thomae Cornelio
H. Oldenburg felicitatem

Intellexi ex spectatissimi nostri Dodingtonij literis,[1] Vir Celeberrime, in animo Tibi esse, Tarantulae naturam et effecta proxima aestate, quantum feret valetudo, ex vero nobis enarrare. Omnimodum Tibi sanitatem medullitus comprecamur, exploratum habentes Te eam magno cum fructu investigationi Naturae et Naturalis Historiae augmento esse impensurum.

Societas Regia Britannica Institutum suum Philosophicum quantumpote consectatur, et nonnulli ejusdem consortes, in Mathesi, Physica, et Medicina praecellentes, doctos quosdam Tractatus in lucem nuper emiserunt. Sunt inter eos Boylius (qui pristinae restitutus est santitati,) Wallisius, Willisius, et Grewius. Primus horum, edidit Tractatulos quatuor, ubi 1. Mira Aeris (etiam citra Calorem) Rarefactio detegitur: 2. Observata nova circa durationem Virtutis Elasticae Aeris expansi enarrantur: 3. Experimenta nova de Condensatione Aeris, solo frigore facta; ejusdemque sine machinis Compressione, traduntur. 4. Ejusdem quantitatis Aeris rarefacti, et compressi mire discrepans Extensio comprobatur.

Alter, Wallisius, totam jam expedivit et publici juris fecit Mechanicam, sive de Motu doctrinam; ubi parte prima, Generalia de Motu; de Gravium descensu et Motuum declivitate, et de libra traduntur; secunda, de centro Gravitatis, ejusque calculo, multa perdocte et demonstrative disseruntur; Tertia et ultima, integra doctrina de Vecte, de Axe in Peritrochio cum Potentijs cognatis, de Trochlea, et Cochlea; de motibus compositis, acceleratis, retardatis, et projectorum; de Percussione; de Cuneo, de Elatere, et Resilitione; de Hydrostaticis, et Aeris Æquipondio, varijsque Questionibus Mechanicis, continetur.

Willisius pronuper edidit libellum geminum, de Anima Brutorum alterum, alterum de Morbis Capitis. Grewius denique insignem vulgavit Tractatum de Anatome Plantarum; unde constare videtur, Plantas in multis referre animantia, nec immerito *Animalium Immobilium* nomine insigniri. Quaquidem in re consentientem habet celeberrimum Malpighium qui in eandem sententiam multa nuper observata eximia nobiscum communicavit.

Nobilis Boylius insuper praelo jam commisit dissertationem suam de Gemmis, earumque origine et viribus, quae duorum triumve mensium spatio lucem, sic spero, videbit.

Ad haec, Bohunus quidam, Vir doctus, diatribam edidit de Origine et Proprietatibus Ventorum, insignioribus annexis de Oracanis, ut vocant, alijsque ventibus procellosis, narrationibus, hominum fide dignorum authoritate nixis.

Denique Morelandus Eques, Tubam suam Stentoro-Phonicam publicavit, cujus adminiculo, ad unum, duo, vel tria milliaria Anglica, pro ratione magnitudinis instrumenti, vox humana perquam distincte propagari et diffundi potest.

Nec silere oportet nuperum Isaaci Newtoni, Mathematum in Academia Cantabrigiensi Professoris, Inventum Telescopicum, quo Tubo-specilla sic contrahuntur, ut Opticum hujusmodi instrumentum, sex pollices longum, Telescopij vulgaris, probe licet elaborati, et sex pedes longi, vicem praestare valeat. Qua de re plura brevi, Deo dante, in Adversarijs Philosophicis dicemus. Vale, Vir Doctissime, et me Tibi addictissimum crede. Dabam Londini die 9. Febr. 1672.

TRANSLATION

H. Oldenburg wishes happiness to the very famous philosopher, Mr. Tommaso Cornelio

I have learned from a letter written by our very excellent countryman Dodington[1] that it is your intention, celebrated Sir, to provide us with a relation next summer, health permitting, of the nature and effects of the tarantula, based on truth. We wish you with all our hearts every kind of good health, believing that your having explored that with great profit will be regarded as contributing to the investigation of Nature and the increase of natural history.

The British Royal Society pursues its philosophical purpose as well as it can, and several of its Fellows outstanding in mathematics, physics, and medicine have recently published various learned treatises. Among them are Boyle (whose health is restored to its former state), Wallis, Willis, and Grew. The first of these has published four little treatises in which 1. A marvellous expansion of the air (beyond that of heat) is detected; 2. New observations concerning the duration of the elastic virtue of expanded air are related; 3. New experiments on the condensation of air by cold alone and without any mechanical compression, are discussed; 4. The marvellously different extension of the same quantity of air when rarefied and expanded is demonstrated.

Another, Wallis, has now completed and published *Mechanica*, or the theory of motion, of which the first part deals with generalities about motion, the fall of heavy bodies and oblique motions, and the balance; the second speaks of the center of gravity and its calculation very learnedly and demonstratively; the third and last contains the complete theory of the lever, the windlass and related powers, the pulley and the screw, the compounding, accelerating, and retarding of motions and projectiles, percussion, the wedge, elasticity and springiness, hydrostatics and the weight of the air, and miscellanea.

Willis has very recently published a double volume, one work being on the soul of animals, the other on diseases of the head. Lastly, Grew has made public a notable treatise on the anatomy of plants, whence it seems to be established that plants in many respects resemble animals and are not unjustly called "motionless animals." Malpighi is of the same mind on this point, having communicated to us many remarkable recent observations supporting that same opinion.

Moreover, the noble Boyle has now committed his essay on gems and their origin and virtues to the press, whence it will I hope see the light in two or three months' time.

Further, a certain learned man named Bohun has published a work on the origin and properties of winds, with some extraordinary stories of hurricanes (as they are called) and other storm winds based on the authority of trustworthy men.

Lastly, Sir Samuel Morland has published his *Tuba Stentoro-phonica*, by means of which instrument the human voice can be very distinctly propagated and diffused over a distance of one, two, or three English miles, according to its size.

Nor must I fail to mention the recent telescopic invention of Isaac Newton, Professor of Mathematics at the University of Cambridge, by which telescopes are so much shortened that an optical instrument of this kind, six inches long, can excel an ordinary telescope of six feet, though a well-made one. We shall with God's blessing say more of this shortly in our *Philosophical Journal*. Farewell, learned Sir, and believe me most devoted to yourself. London, 9 February 1672.

NOTE

1 Letters 1876 and 1876a.

1894
Oldenburg to Dodington
9 February 1671/2
From the memorandum in Royal Society MS. D 1, no. 24

Rec. Feb. 5. 71/2
Answ. Feb. 9. 71.
retaind a Copy of my letter to Cornelio,¹ but none of yt to Dodington.

NOTES

Reply to Letter 1876.
1 Letter 1893.

1895
Flamsteed to Oldenburg
10 February 1671/2
From the original in Royal Society MS. F 1, no. 80

Derby Feb: 10: 16$\frac{71}{72}$

Sr

Mr Sargeants occasions drawing him to towne at this time I thought it not fit to let fly an occasion of conveiing a letter to you tho haveing wrote but a weeke agone¹ & ye weather haveing hindred my intended observations since, I have nothing now to informe yu worth yr knowledge: onely whereas yu proferred mee in one of yrs not long since a perusall of Hugenius his Systema Saturnium,² if now yu please to oblige mee with a perusall of it yu may deliver it to my freind who will procure it safe to mee & perhaps back againe to yu at his next returne to London. I shall be very carefull of it, & not ungratefull this is all at present from

Your servant to command
John Flamsteed

P.S. I desired Mr Collins in ye last I wrote to him to let yu know yt January 1st last part I saw Saturne then without any anses:[3] since I have not seene him nor shall till hee againe emerge from ye light of ye sun. *J.F.*

ADDRESS
   To Henry Oldenburge Esq
   at his house in the Middle of ye
   Pell mell in St James's
   Westminster these
        present

NOTE

1 Letter 1888.
2 Flamsteed's interest in borrowing this book was mentioned in Letter 1849.
3 See Flamsteed to Collins, 31 January 1671/2 (Rigaud, II, 127).

1896
Newton to Oldenburg
10 February 1671/2

Printed in Newton, *Correspondence*, I, 108–9, from the original in private possession

In answer to Letter 1892, Newton gives permission to Oldenburg for the printing of Letter 1891, and offers to send more experiments in support of his theory.

1897
Oldenburg to Lister
10 February 1671/2
From the original in Bodleian Library MS. Lister 34, f. 15

London Febr. 10. 1671.

Sir,

I shall not repeat here, what I have already said to Mr Brook in excuse of not sending at present a copy of Malpighi's Discourse De Anatome Plantarum; knowing, yt he will shew you my letter to him concerning that matter.[1] All I have now to impart unto you, is, a farther account of Sigr Cornelio at Naples, about ye nature and ye efforts of ye Tarantula; wch I will doe in his owne language, whereof I think you to be master:

His words are;[2]

"Le Tarantole veramente non sono altro che una specie de Falangii molto grandi, et pinti in varie maniere, e con diversita di colori. Queste habitano entro alcune cavernole profonde della terra, lequali hanno un forame circolare della grandezza d'una noce. A tempo di estate, facendosi un poco di sibilo nell' orificio delle dette cavernole, corrono velocemente le tarantole all' aria, et in questa maniera si prendono. Et io spero nel mese d'Aprile o' di Maggio di poterne mandare alcun numero di vive, perche ho sperimentato, che quelle si mantengono alcune settimane senza cibo veruno et se ne potranno ancora mandar delle morte esiciate entro lo spirito del vino o' altro simile liquore, che le preserva dalla putredine.

"Per quello poi che appartiene agli effetti di coloro, che si giudicuno morsicati dalle Tarantole, Io stimo altramente da quello che il volgo si persuade, perche da molte osservationi e congeturre mi do à credere, che senza precedere il morso della Tarantola, avenga tal sorte de'mali ad alcuni di coloro che habitano in quei paesi aridissimi, e che spesse fiate sono tormentati da lunghissima sete. Nè mai si é saputo che alcuna persona sia stato morsicata dalla Tarantola, et che poi appresso si temessero gli effetti del male: má sempre mai aviene che le persone sentendosi in tempo d'estate travagliati da quegli strani accidenti che patiscono gli attarantati, soppongono, dopo l'effetto del male, esser stati feriti da quell'aminale.

Spero di poter fare piu à lungo le mie osservationi su'l principio di prima vera, ritrovandomi adesso fortemente tormentato et inhabile allo scrivere etc."

If here be no mistake, 'tis a discovery of a monstrous fiction, yt hath been impos'd upon us by a general tradition and particularly by Epiph. Ferdinandus,[3] Kircherus, Sengwerdius[4] etc. I shall be very glad to hear yr further thoughts upon this matter, after this further account from Sir

yr faithf. servt
Oldenburg

NOTES

1 Compare Letter 1880: evidently second thoughts prevailed. For Mr. Brooke, see Letter 1800, note 6. We have no trace of the letter.
2 See Letter 1876a, where a translation will be found.
3 Epifanio Ferdinandi (1569–1638) was a native of Southern Italy who received the degrees of Ph.D. and M.D. from the University of Naples. He became a successful and fashionable physician, and published a number of works on medical subjects.
4 Wolferdus Senguerdius, professor and librarian at Leiden, was the author of, among other works, *Disputatio philosophica inauguralis de tarantula* (Leiden, 1667).

1898
Kirkby to Oldenburg
10 February 1671/2

Mentioned in Kirkby's Letter 1954 of 13 April 1672 as containing queries about a new way of making steel.

1899
Oldenburg to Huygens
12 February 1671/2

From *Œuvres Complètes*, VII, 145–6
Original in the Huygens Collection at Leiden

A Londres le 12/22 Fevrier 1672

Monsieur,

La vostre agreable du 13e courant me fut rendue hier ayant bien de la joye de vous y trouver en bonne sante. Estant presque las d'escrire, apres avoir transcrit moy mesme la lettre de Monsieur Sluse touchant le Probleme d'Alhazen,[1] à fin que vous l'eussiez correctement copiée, ie me trouve obligé de remettre a une autre fois la responce aux particularitez contenues dans la vostre. Cependant vous accepterez l'imprimé cy-joint;[2] et puisque i'ay pris la peine de transcrire la lettre de Monsieur Sluse, vous ne vous rebuterez point de me mander vos pensees la dessus.

Nos Messieurs pensent avoir trouvé une matiere pour le miroir de Monsieur Newton, capable d'un poli assez beau et uni, et la maniere de donner ce poli sans gaster la figure spherique.[3] Et pour les autres inconveniens: ils sont tels, que l'advancement de cete sorte de Telescopes ne s'en accrochera point, i'espere. Et il y a un autre de nostre societé qui pretend d'avoir trouvé une voye de perfectioner les Telescopes etc. au dela (de beaucoup) de l'invention de Monsieur Newton.[4] Dont, peut estre, vous aurez des nouvelles plus particulieres cy-apres. Ces choses detournent Monsieur Smethwick de sa facon de travailler des verres non-spheriques, comme il les appelle; croyant qu'il sera beaucoup surpassé par ces nouveaux pretendans. Le temps esclaircira tout. Je suis Monsieur

Vostre treshumble serviteur
Oldenburg

ADDRESS
    A Monsieur
Monsieur Chrestian Huygens de Zulechem,
  à la Bibliotheque du Roy à
      Paris

TRANSLATION

London 12/22 February 1671/2

Sir,

Your agreeable letter of the thirteenth of this month was delivered to me yesterday, giving me much joy to find you in good health. Being almost worn out from writing, after having myself transcribed Mr. Sluse's letter about Alhazen's Problem,[1] so that you might have it copied correctly, I find myself obliged to put off to another time any reply to the details of your letter. However, accept the enclosed printed matter,[2] and since I have taken the trouble to transcribe Mr. Sluse's letter do not be discouraged from letting me know your thoughts thereon.

Our Fellows think they have found a substance [suitable] for Mr. Newton's mirror, capable of a sufficiently good, smooth polish, and a method for giving it this polish without spoiling the spherical figure.[3] As for the other difficulties, they are such that, as I hope, the improvement of this kind of telescope will not be held up by them. And there is another of our Society who claims to have found a way of improving telescopes, etc., much superior to Mr. Newton's invention.[4] Of this, perhaps, you will have fuller news later. These things have turned Mr. Smethwick from his method of working nonspherical lenses, as he calls them, believing that he will be much surpassed by these new claimants. Time will clarify all. I am, Sir,

Your very humble servant
Oldenburg

ADDRESS

To Mr. Christiaan Huygens of Zulichem,
In the King's Library,
Paris

NOTES

Reply to Letter 1886.

1 Letter 1843; the transcript was sent with the present letter (and is printed in *Œuvres Complètes*, VII, 147–51).
2 *Phil. Trans.*, no. 79 (22 January 1671/2).
3 At some point in late December or early January the Royal Society ordered a four-foot Newtonian reflector to be made, probably by Christopher Cock. It was examined by the Society on 25 January, when the mirror was insufficiently polished and the eyepiece found to be too weak. On 1 February it was thought to be improved, and Hooke was instructed to see to its perfection. There are further references to this instrument in Hooke's *Diary*, but it never succeeded. The Society ordered another four- or five-foot reflector from Cock on 14 March.
4 On 18 January (the second meeting of the Society after Christmas, when Newton's new telescope was "examined and applauded") Hooke announced "a highly considerable improvement" of all lenses and devices using them, whose nature he concealed in an anagram. It never came to anything.

1900
Oldenburg to Nicolas Toinard
15 February 1671/2
From the draft in Royal Society MS. O 2, no. 73

A Monsr Toinard à Orleans

Londres le 15 Febr. 1671/2

Monsieur

Ayant sceu par l'avantage de l'amitié, que ie cultive des longues annees avec le Chevalier Southwel, le genie extraordinaire de vostre personne, et la capacité que vous avez à advancer toutes sortes de belles et utiles conoissances, J'ay promptement consideré la station, ou ie me trouve au regard dela Societé Royale la quelle m'obligeant à lier partout ou ie puis commodement, des alliances philosophiques pour unir ensemble par ce moyen les forces intellectuelles des beaux Esprits de l'univers ie me sens puissament porté à vous offrir le mesme commerce literaire, que i'ay le bien d'entretenir avec quantité d'autres par tout le monde.

Une des principales choses, où vise nostre Societé, est de faire composer une ample et sincere Histoire naturelle, comme la fondament d'un systeme solide de philosophie: c'est pourquoy nous taschons d'engager par tout des Esprits faits come le vostre, à fin d'observer avec soin et de consigner avec fidelite et exactitude tout ce qui se rencontre de remarquable dans les pais particuliers, à fin d'en faire par apres un amas et magazin complet pour fournir à ladite Histoire Universelle de la Nature.

C'est pourquoy ie serois bien aise d'apprendre de vous, Monsieur, s'il se trouve desia quelque bon Autheur Francois qui aye escrit et mis au public une telle Histoire de vostre excellent Royaume, touchant les mineraux, Vegetaux, animaux, comme aussi le temperament de l'Air, des Eaux de toutes sortes, des Meteores, des Maladies etc. Si non, ie souhaiterois fort, que vous, et vos semblables, chacun dans la province ou il reside, prendroit la peine dorenavant d'y travailler avec candeur et assiduité, pour en produire un ouvrage, qui fut digne d'un bon livre et d'un bon Francois.

Il y a un Medecin icy, appellé Monsr Merret, habile homme et curieux, que a commencé à travailler pour cete Isle, comme on peut voir dans son livre qui porte le tiltre, Pinax Rerum Britannicarum, Fossilium, Vegetabilium et Animalium; lequel en toute apparence sera augmenté avec le temps.¹

On travaille à present icy aux moyens de perfectioner les Telescopes, et les Trompes Stentoro-phoniques. Il est veritable par l'Experience, que la Lunette de la facon de M. Newton de 6½ pouces, fait pour le moins le mesme effect que les ordinaires de 5. pieds. Et il n'est pas moins vray, que la Trompe de Monsr Moreland de 6. pieds de long, se fait entendre distinctement à la distance d'une mille Angloise, que fait 5200 pieds d'Angleterre mais cela avec un vent favorable; et à la distance de demy mile, avec un vent de costé, dans un temps mediocrement calme. On en fait de ces Instruments entortillez, qui estant effectivement plus longues que les autres, respandent la voix clairement à la distance de 2½ miles Angloises.

Touchant la construction du navire double du Chevalier Petty, Monsr Southwell et moy tascherons de vous y servir en vous procurant ou un racourci au bois ou carton; ou pour le moins, les desseins en plan, en perspective, et de profil avec les proportions.² Et en toutes autres choses, où vous me jugerez capable, ie tascheray de vous faire voir, que i'estime la vertu par tout ou ie la trouve, comme il appartient à Monsieur

> Vostre tres humble et tres-obeissant serviteur
> *Oldenburg*

TRANSLATION

> To Mr. Toinard, in Orléans
>
> London, 15 February 1671/2

Sir,

Having learned by means of the friendship which I have maintained for many years with Sir Robert Southwell of your exceptional personal genius and of your ability in promoting all kinds of good and useful learning, I immediately bethought myself of the position which I hold in the Royal Society which constrains me to cement philosophical alliances, wherever I conveniently can, in order to unite by this means the intellectual powers of all the noble minds of the universe, so that I feel strongly moved to offer you the same literary correspondence which I enjoy with very many others throughout the world.

One of the chief things to which our Society aspires is the composition of a large and truthful natural history, as the foundation of a solid and philosophical system. This is why we try everywhere to involve minds constructed like yours in observing carefully and faithfully and exactly passing on whatever they find remarkable in their particular countries so that from these may afterwards be made a collection and complete store to supply the said universal history of nature.

This is why I should be very glad to learn from you, Sir, whether there exists some good French author who has written and published such a history of your excellent kingdom, touching on the minerals, vegetables, animals, as well as the character of the air, of all kinds of waters, of atmospheric phenomena, of diseases, etc. If not, I very much hope that you, and others like you, each in the province where he lives, will henceforth take the trouble to work to this end ingenuously and assiduously, to produce a work worthy of a good book and a good Frenchman.

There is a physician here named Mr. Merret, a clever and ingenious man, who has begun such work for this island, as may be seen from his book, which bears the title *Pinax rerum Britannicarum, Fossilium, Vegetabilium et Animalium*; it is probable that it will be enlarged in time.[1]

Here at present work is going on to perfect telescopes, and Stentorophonic trumpets. It has been found true by experiment that a telescope of $6\frac{1}{2}$ inches as designed by Mr. Newton has at least the same effect as an ordinary one of five feet. And it is equally true that Sir Samuel Morland's trumpet six feet long can make sounds distinctly audible at a distance of one English mile, which is 5200 English feet—but that is with a favorable wind—and at a distance of half a mile with a cross wind in moderately calm weather. Coiled instruments of this kind have been made, which being effectively longer than the others transmit the human voice clearly to a distance of $2\frac{1}{2}$ English miles.

As for the construction of Sir William Petty's double-bottom ship, Sir Robert and I will endeavor to serve you by obtaining for you either a model in wood or cardboard, or at least plans in plan, perspective, and profile, with the proportions.[2] And in anything else in which you judge me to be able to do so I shall try to show you that I value merit everywhere that I find it, as is proper in, Sir,

Your very humble, obedient servant
Oldenburg

NOTES

Nicolas Toinard (or Thoynard, 1629–1706) was born at Orleans, his family being a notable one in that city. He came to Paris for study in 1652. Some parts of his *Evangeliorum harmonia* (published posthumously at Paris in 1707) were printed for private circulation as early as 1669. He was an associate of the brothers Dupuy in Paris, and later a correspondent with Justel. John Locke met him in April 1678 and conducted a long correspondence with him, from which it appears that Toinard's traditional scholarly pursuits were compatible with virtuoso interests, especially in artillery. We do not know about his friendship with Southwell.

1 Christopher Merret's *Pinax* was published at London in 1666 and again in 1667, but not subsequently.
2 Presumably this was written in response to something Oldenburg learned from Southwell; compare Letter 1877, note 14.

1901
Oldenburg to Flamsteed
16 February 1671/2

From the memorandum in Royal Society MS. F 1, no. 79

Rec. Febr. 8. 71/2
Answ. Febr. 16. 71
And sent him Syst. Saturni Hugenii, and an acct of Newtons glass.

NOTE

Reply to Letters 1888 and 1895.

1902
Dodington to Oldenburg
16 February 1671/2

From the original in Royal Society MS. D 1, no. 25

Venice Febr. 26.72. [N.S.]

Hond Sr.

Yr letter of 9ber 14. I answered Janr. 15. That of xber 22, I answered on the 29 of the last month,[1] & in that I gave you an accompt how I had sent yr leter to Sigr Malpighi, as I doubt not but he hath acknowledged to you, in regard I sent you a packet from him, this 12. Instant.[2] Since when I have received yrs of the 18 January & too morrow I will send ye Inclosed to Bononia,[3] I will incourage him also to send me wt other Bookes or Papers he thinks fit, since a month hence I have a friend goeing for England, by whom I can conveigh them to you. I expect a more accurate minute discourse from Sigre Cornelio at Naples touching ye Bitings & effects of the Tarantulaes, though in mine of 29 Janr I sent you somwt under his hand.[4] Heere is reprinted a very curious Book of 3 ducates price in folio. The Natural Histoire of Ferrante Imperato,[5] wch I doubt not but you have seen, I esteeme it a most curious, true & exact peece, for wt it contaynes, The Author having taken little on trust, If you desire one or more, I will observe yr Comands, In ye Interim, This is its summarie

The first five Bookes treat of ye Earth, Its differencies, vertues, Gummes, Fatts, Minerals &c.

The 6 & 7 Bookes treat of The water, Its differencies and original, Its Colour, effects, qualities, Productions &c.

The 8 & 9th Bookes discourse of the Ayer, & of such Bodies as have a Beeing in that Region. of its use, qualities, differencies &c.

The 10 & 11 Bookes treat of Fire, Heat, Cold &c. of Light in ye Elementarie Continent, of the Various products and effects of Heat & Cold, natural & Artificial &c.

The 12 Book is a particular discourse of ye original of Fire & ye divers operations of Heat & Cold in Mechanics.

The 13 Book treateth of the Generation of Metalls: more particularly of Allom, Copperas, Nitre, of divers Salts, &c.

The 14 Book is full of observations of several veines or Fattnesses in ye Bowells of ye Earth, such as Cole Pitch, Bitume, Naphtha, Pinasphalto, Amber or succinum Salts &c.

The 15 is employed about The more sollid Mettals such as steele, Iron, Antimonie, Quicksilver, Lead, Brass, Brimstone &c.

The 16 is about veynes of Mettals & of substances consolidated & procreated in them.

The 4 followeing Bookes treat of ye Separation of Mettals & transubstantiating of them, as well as of ye refining of them, ful of curious experiments.

The 21 Book treats of Philosophical Medicine or Phisic, & therein more particularly of ye Philosophers stone, Chimical Phisic, & the like.

The following 5 Bookes treate of stones, theire divers Conditions, Qualities, Colours, originals, vertues uses and vallues. And, obiter,[6] of Gemms, very fully.

Then 27 Book is taken up in ye consideration of vegetives produced in ye Sea, as Coral, Sponge, Scylls,[7] onyons, Sea netts, Mushromes &c &c &c & some sensitive vegetals produced by ye sea.

The 28 wch is ye last Book, is applyed to ye consideration of several Plants and Creatures terrestrial, not much observed by other Authors, To this last Book, an Apothecary heare one Gio. Maria Forro, hath made some additions, full of Curiosity & Truth, & with observable Modesty.

This is wt I find necessarie for ye present to say of it and I think, I have doon a great deale, when I have comprised so much in so little roome; I am a sincere Honourer & Admirer of ye R.S. and to yr selfe Sr

a most assured humble servant
J. dodington

ADDRESS

For Mr Oldenburg, Secretary to
the Royal Society, my most
Honoured friend
    In London

NOTES

1 Only the last of these letters is extant (Letter 1876); however, Dodington's recollection of its content was at fault.
2 This was Letter 1879, accompanying *De formatione pulli*.
3 Letter 1875.
4 Letter 1876a.
5 Compare Letter 1695, note 6. The book was not reviewed in the *Philosophical Transactions*.
6 "in passing."
7 Probably the squill, *Urginea maritima*, a marsh and beach plant also known as sea onion.

1903
Oldenburg to Newton
17 or 19 February 1671/2

Printed in Newton, *Correspondence*, I, 109, note 1, from the original in private possession

Rec. Feb. 13. 71/2. Answ. Febr. 17 and sent him Mr Hooks observations upon his discourse.

NOTE

This is an endorsement on Letter 1896, to which it is a reply. Although Newton's answer (Letter 1904) describes Oldenburg's letter as being dated 19 February, this is probably a misreading by Newton. For Hooke's "observations," see Newton, *Correspondence*, I, 110–14, or Birch, *History*, III, 10–15.

1904
Newton to Oldenburg
20 February 1671/2

Printed in Newton, *Correspondence*, I, 116, from the original in private possession

Newton acknowledges curtly both Huygens' (Letter 1886) remarks on his telescope and Hooke's observations (Letter 1903) upon his theory of light. He doubted that there was force in their criticisms.

1905
Hill to Oldenburg
20 February 1671/2

From the original in Royal Society MS. H 3, no. 6

Worthy Sr

I have received yours of the 20th August Last wth the Several Inquiryes for the Brazeel[1] wch I transmitted by a Safe Hand to my friend of the Bahia who I am confident will provoke the Father of the Society to engage upon giving you satisfaction. I should not have omitted So considerable a Circumstance as the Jesuites name had I knowne it. but I did not then, nether do I yet. Att the Returne of the first shipps, wch probably may bee in six months I hope to send a Letter from himselfe. and when once your Correspondence is begun, I question not but hee will give you some frequent accounts of his diligence to serve you if hee bee so inquisitive a Person, as hee is represented to mee. I am Sr

Your very humble servant
Tho. Hill

Lisbon primo March. 1672. [N.S.]
Mr Oldenburgh.

ADDRESS
> For Henry Oldenburgh Esq
> Secretary to ye Royal Society
> London

NOTES

> Reply to Letter 1780.
1 Letter 1780a.

1906
Collins to Oldenburg
c. 20 February 1671/2
From the original in Royal Society Classified Papers XXIV, no. 20

Memorandum

In Writing to Slusius to acquaint him that a good while since I sent him Dr Wallis his 3d and last part of Mechanicks, and Bartholini Dioristice treating of the limits of Aequations[1] having then lately received a few Coppies from Denmarke the which Bookes were delivered to Simon Are Master of the young Trompe directed to be left with Mr Elziveer to be transmitted to Slusius at Leige, not long after which I received the two Bookes he sent me,[2] to witt Lalovera de Cycloide and his owne Mesolabe, hat here we have in ye Presse Horrox Astronomicall remaines digested by Dr Wallis[3] Dr Barrows Comment on ye 4 first Bookes of Apollonius fitted for the Presse[4] to which Mr Barnard will adde the latter 3 out of Arabick namely out of the Coppies of Beni Musa with the notes of Eutocius and Abdelmelech,[5] and ere long we expect to put Mr Newtons Introduction to Algebra, his generall Method of Analyticall Quadratures, and 20 Dioptrick Lectures into the Presse.[6]

To give him an account of Mr Newtons Telescope

And to mention that John Ott Scaphusa Helvetico in a little Treatise of Vision printed at Hedelberg in 1670[7] mentions that by the benefitt of his late Studies

Longissimi quique tubi in Compendium redigi possunt nequidquam laxa illorum perfectione[8]

And that he hath invented a simple Instrument that mooves pleasantly cujus beneficio cuiuscunque generis Hyperbola Ellipses ac Parabolae describi quaeant, ut et Circuli Segmentum quodcunque,[9] of which we should thankfully embrace a good Account.

That in the Transactions giving an Account of Dr Barrowes Bookes there is added an Additionall Theoreme about ye Cycloid[10] which either send, or so much of that Transaction, to which if the Dr had remembred he would have added these Theoremes.

If any two Curves as AB, CD be alternly placed about the same Axis AC, the greatest common Ordinate is that whose touch lines EG and FH

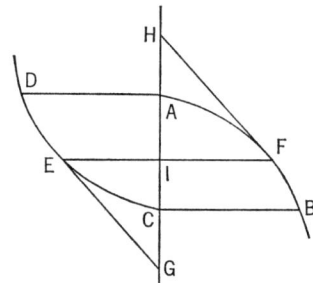

are parallell And the greatest Rectangle EIF is that, where the Segments of the Axis produced (as CG, AH) cutt off by the touch lines are equall.

We are very glad of his Intentions to publish his treatise de Maximis et Minimis et tangentibus Curvarum, earnestly desiring some of them as formerly to be paid for by Mr Daems of Amsterdam.

Mengolus his 4 Vols of Musick in folio we have no account of, nor of Gottignies Dioptricks printed at Rome where the Author is said to have made wonderfull Tellescopes, John Baptist Baliani's Opuscula Posthuma[11] is supposed to treat of Pendulum Clocks of which Argument the Excellent Hugenius is putting a treatise to the presse at Paris, at Lyons the learned Cursus Mathematicus of Claudius Millet de Chales is said to be in the presse, but of the Comments on Archimedes by those learned adversaries Borellius[12] and Honorato Fabry we heare nothing.

To give an Account of Sr Samuell Morelands speaking Trumpet.

That Dr Pell hath a table of Squares and a Canon of the sides of all rationall right angled Triangles whose Hypotenuse is less than 10000 in the Presse[13] which Bookes being in English if they will be acceptable to him shall be sent.

NOTES

This memorandum is undated, but precedes Letter 1916, for which it is the model. Nothing suggests that it was written long before the end of February. Collins wrote a similar letter to James Gregory on 23 February (Turnbull, *Gregory*, pp. 218–20).

1 Erasmus Bartholin, *Dioristice seu aequationum determinationes duabus methodus propositae* (Copenhagen, 1663).
2 Since the Wallis volume was sent about the end of November (compare Letter 1827) the two books from Sluse, sent long before (Letter 1687), must have reached London about the end of the year 1671.
3 For Wallis's work on Horrox's papers, see Vol. II, pp. 163–64, 165, note 5, etc: the *Opera posthuma* were published at London in the autumn of 1672, having been with the printer since at least May 1671. The book was presented to the Royal Society on 30 October 1672 and reviewed in *Phil. Trans.*, no. 87 (14 October 1672), 5078–79.
4 What Barrow actually published, three years later, was *Archimedis opera; Apollonii Pergae conicorum libri IV; Theodosii sphaerica, methodo novo illustrata et succinte demonstrata* (London, 1675). The *Apollonius* was completed by Barrow before August 1671 (Rigaud, I, 195).
5 Compare Vol. V, p. 235, and p. 237, note 8. This never appeared. The Beni Musa ("sons of Moses") were three brothers who lived in Baghdad c. 870, devoting themselves to translation from Greek and mathematical studies. Hunain ibn Ishaq and Thabit ibn Qurra were among the translators they employed. Eutocios (c. 500) wrote commentaries on both Apollonios and Archimedes, usually printed with editions of their writings: he was a Syrian Greek. 'Abd al-Malik al-Shīrāzī was a Persian mathematician, living in the latter part of the twelfth century, who wrote a summary of the *Conics*.
6 On the Kinckhuysen translation as improved by Newton, see Vol. V, p. xxv, and Vol. VII, p. 159; the publication of this work was confidently expected through the early part of 1672 (see D. T. Whiteside, *The Mathematical Papers of Isaac Newton*, Cambridge, 1967——, II, 277 ff.). The next work is probably the revised version of *De analysi* (see Vol. VI, p. 230, note 7), which Collins also hoped to publish in London; Newton never completed it, and it first appeared (in an English version by John Colson) as *The Method of Fluxions and Infinite Series* (London, 1736). The course of optical lectures at Cambridge was begun by Newton in January 1669/70; Collins's "20 lectures" simply represents a nominal series of ten annual lectures, given over two years. The *Lectiones opticae* were published at London only in 1729 (having been preceded by an English version in the previous year).
7 See Letter 1867.
8 "Any very long telescope may be reduced to a small one without any loss of its perfection."
9 "by means of which any kind of hyperbola, ellipse, and parabola can be described, and also any segment of a circle." Collins copied much more from this book for Gregory (Turnbull, *Gregory*, pp. 200–203).
10 See *Phil. Trans.*, no. 75 (18 September 1671), 2262; the addition is to the Appendix, no. 33, to Lecture XI in *Lectiones geometricae*.
11 See Vol. VII, p. 380, note 34.
12 See Vol. VI, p. 423, note 13. Much of this book news has appeared many times before and, as previously remarked, much of it is false.
13 *Tabula numerorum quadratorum decies millium, una cum ipsorum lateribus* (London, 1672) —see *Phil. Trans.*, no. 82 (22 April 1672), 4050–51.

1907
Oldenburg to E. Bartholin
22 February 1671/2

From the original in the Kgl. Bibliotek, Copenhagen, Boll. Brevs. U⁴, no. 731

Clarissimo Viro
Domino Erasmo Bartholino, Mathematico Hafniensi,
Henr. Oldenburg
Felicitatem

Bellam adeo, ac se nunc offert, occasionem evadere mihi nolebam, Vir Celeberrime, quin de Valetudine tua et praesentium studiorum tuorum ratione percontarer. Fit hoc per Amplissimum Regiae nostrae Legationis Secretarium, Dominum Thomam Henshaw, virum e Societate Regia, tum Philosophicae quam civilis rei callentissimum.[1] Exponere is Tibi pro re nata poterit praesentem Caetus nostri Philosophici statum et labores; nec non indicare Libros, a nonnullis ejusdem sociis, aliisque, nuper hic editos; quos inter eminent, Mechanices Wallisianae Pars tertia et ultima; Willisii de Brutorum Anima, Morbisque Capitis, Dissertatio gemina; Morisoni Plantarum Classis prima,[2] Bohuni Historia Ventorum; Henricus Morus de rerum Incorporearum Existentia[3] etc. Quibus brevi succedet Illustris Boylii nostri de Gemmarum Origine et Viribus Diatriba, tam Latine quam Anglice imprimenda;[4] aliaque indefessi hujus Philosophi opera, omnibus solide Philosophantibus summopere, ni admodum fallor expetenda.

Accepimus, Clarissimum Picardum, Regiae Parisiensis Academiae sodalem, in Dania, Astronomiae promovendae ergo, ad tempus fuisse commoratum. Expediverat ille, priusquam e Gallia excederet, novam suam de Terrae Mensura operationem; Cujus cum Exemplar Hafniam, ut audio, secum detulerit, Tibi sine dubio visum; pergratum equidem nobis feceris, si rei ab Ipso peractae summam, tuamque de toto ille opere sententiam, Nobis, ad quos nullum hactenus Exemplar pervenit, explicare volueris.[5] Adhaec, cum et insigniores quaedam Observationes Caelestes habitae ab ipso fuerint Uraniburgi, earum quoque copiam nobis a Te, pro humanitate tua, fieri impense rogamus.

Scire quoque percupimus, quibus studii Tu ipse, Vir Clarissime, jam occuperis; et quousque correctiores Typi Braheana opera provexerint.

Si nedum quicquam Tibi innotuit de Newtoniana Telescopiorum contrahendorum ratione, nuper Societati Regiae exhibita, harum Lator dignissimus eam Tibi exponere non detrectabit. Nec est, quod pluribus Te morer, cum viva Ejusdem voce alios Virorum hujus loci Illustrium conatus possis edoceri. Vale igitur, Vir Praestantissime, et Philosophiam gnaviter augere et ornare perge. Dab. Londini d. 22 Februarii 1672.

Si respondere visum fuerit per Tabellionem ordinarium, literae tuae, quaeso, sic inscribantur;

A monsr

Monsr Grubendol

à Londres

Nil praeterea; multo enim tutius hac ratione ad me pervenient, quam in nomine meo proprio inscribantur.

TRANSLATION

Henry Oldenburg wishes happiness to the very famous Mr. Erasmus Bartholin, Mathematician of Copenhagen

I was reluctant to lose so fine an opportunity as now presents itself of inquiring after your health and the present trend of your studies. I do this by means of the very worthy Mr. Thomas Henshaw, secretary to our King's ambassador, a Fellow of the Royal Society and a man as experienced in philosophy as in politics.[1] He can explain to you deliberately the present condition and efforts of our philosophical society, as well as make known to you the books recently published here by several Fellows of the Society and others, among which stand out the third and last part of Wallis's *Mechanica*, Willis's *De brutorum anima*, and *De morbis capitis*, a double work; Morison's *First Class of Plants*,[2] Bohun's *History of Winds*, Henry More, *De rerum incorporearum existentia*[3] and so forth. These will soon be succeeded by the illustrious Boyle's *Essay about the Origine and Virtues of Gems*, to be printed in both English and Latin,[4] and other works of this tireless philosopher, all much desired by all right-thinking philosophers, unless I am much mistaken.

We have heard that the celebrated Picard, a member of the Royal Academy at Paris, has remained in Denmark until the present time for the advancement of astronomy. Before leaving France he had sent us his new attempt upon the measurement of the Earth, of which [book] he has, I hear, carried a copy to Copenhagen, and so no doubt you have seen it. You would do something most agreeable to us if you would be willing to give us a summary account of everything he has done, and your opinion of the whole work, as no copy has so far reached us.[5] Moreover, as he has made some pretty important astronomical observations at Uraniborg, we also earnestly beg from you, out of your kindness, that you supply us an account of them.

We should also be very glad to know what studies you yourself, famous Sir, are now engaged upon, and how far that more accurate edition of the works of Tycho Brahe has proceeded.

If you have not yet heard of the Newtonian way of shortening telescopes, lately exhibited to the Royal Society, the very worthy bearer of this letter will not mind explaining it to you. Nor should we detain you with many things, since you can be informed by word of mouth from the same person of the other endeavors of distinguished people here. So farewell, excellent Sir, and continue strenuously to adorn and perfect philosophy. London, 22 February 1672.

If you think fit to reply by the ordinary post your letter should, please, be addressed thus:

   A Monsr,
   Monsr Grubendol
   à Londres;

nothing more, and your letter will come to me far more safely addressed in this way, than with my own name.

NOTES

1 Thomas Henshaw (1618–1700) has been often mentioned in the correspondence. He was to remain in Copenhagen as envoy extraordinary, and to write many letters to Oldenburg. The Ambassador was Charles Stuart, Duke of Richmond (1639–72).
2 *Plantarum umbelliferarum distributio nova*; see Letter 1701, note 4.
3 Presumably *Enchiridion metaphysicum, sive de rebus incorporeis dissertatio* (London, 1671).
4 The English edition was printed at London in 1672, the Latin in 1673.
5 This request of Oldenburg's seems very extraordinary, in view of the very complete summary of the *Mesure de la Terre* already sent by Vernon in Letters 1854, 1870, and 1877, which Oldenburg had received and reported to the Royal Society on 1 February.

1908
Oldenburg to Malpighi
22 February 1671/2

From the original in Bologna MS. 2085, I, ff. 83–84
Printed in *Opera omnia*, II, *De formatione pulli in ovo*, pp. 14–15

Celeberrimo Viro
Dn. Marcello Malpighio Philos. et Med. Bononiensi
H. Oldenburg S.P.

Praeclaram gratamque adeo testaris ingenii juxta ac industriae tuae ubertatem, Vir Clarissime, ut vix verba suppetant, quibus studiosum Animorum nostrorum in Te affectum prout par erat explicemus. Vix egregiam tuam de Plantarum Anatome Diatribam expenderamus, quin, ecce! novam et perquam elaboratam de Ovo et primis Pulli staminibus Dissertationem, ei succenturiatam, acciperemus. Et hanc citra moram Societati Regiae exhibui; quae non ambabus ulnis modo, sed intimis medullis, eam excepit. Patebat illud e confertis sociorum plausibus luculentissime;[1] quos ut quantocius Tibi significarem, confestim jubebar. Adeo ingeniose, adeo docte, adeo nitide (nec minus modeste tamen) scriptum hoc, ut soles omnia tua, adornasti, ut praelum, quo toti innotescat Orbi literato, protinus efflagitare videatur.

Nil ibi quicquam meritis detrahis aliorum, quin imo Majorum inventa et labores debitis laudare praeconiis accumulas. Tu interim ea prosequeris, quae indagine ulteriori vestiganda isti reliquere. Hoc ipso genuinum Te Societatis Regiae Alumnum, cordatumque Naturae Mystam praestas, dum scilicet Physiologiae locupletissimae et longe lateque patentis pomaeria extendere modis omnibus allaboras.

Nolimus profecto, Vir Doctissime, ut aliorum in iis ipsis, quae Te occupant, argumentis operae sociatae conatus et studia tua sufflaminent. Absit ut vel subeat mentem tuam, supervacaneos esse tuos (quod novissimae tuae videntur innuere) labores in Plantarum Anatome perficienda, eo scilicet nomine quod Socius quidam nostras eandam materiam excolere satagat.[2] Ille sua methodo et Observationibus suis; Tu alia tua, tuisque Observatis propriis, rem eandem elucidatum itis, dumque in praecipuis consona eruitis, hujus partis Naturae Theoriam eo firmiori consistere talo jubetis. Hinc est, quod unanimi suffragio nostra Te poscit Societas, ut, si quae Tibi suppetunt, quibus jam communicata fusius penitiusque a Te exponantur, ne ulla ratione dissimules aut luci publicae neges. Scripto illo tuo innueras, Iconismis compluribus, in rem ipsam ducentibus, tua illa de Plantis observata Te delineasse.³ Si ita visum Tibi esset, etiam Icones illas nobis concredere, operam sane daremus, ut omnia illa tua typis quam fieri posset nitidissimis, et summa quantumpote cura imprimerentur.

Saepius equidem id usu venit, dum Viri Illustres Sagacesque rectae philosophandi methodo et rationi insistunt, in easdem ipsos veritates incidere. Proclivi esset plura hujus rei Exempla, quae doctissimi quidam e Societati nostra Philosophi, aliique praebuerunt, recensere, ni id Epistolae limites exederet, nique persuasum mihi esset, Te similia omnino explorata habere.

Agedum igitur, Vir Praestantissime, semitam, quam caepisti, gnaviter et generose calcare pergas, Spartamque quam nactus es, pro virili exornare. Praeter egregia illa de Plantis, in penu tuo etiamnum reliqua, patet ex novissimis tuis Te plura adhuc in promptu habere lectissima de Animalibus Oviparis Observata, quae inibi sub-indicas. Non consulimus tantum (quae tua vox est) sed plane cohortamur ut quae etiam de istis pro solertia tua indagasti, exponere ne graveris. Indictam quoque velimus vocem illam tantum non desperabundam, quam edis, de Quadrupedum aliorumque Faetuum Viviparorum naturae perquirendae difficultate.⁴ Non diffitemur quidem, operam ejusmodi potiora exigere otia, sumptusque graviores; at reputabis Tecum, si placet, Viros, observandi artem callentes (quorum numero Te jure accensemus) insigniter posse tum labores tum sumptus compendifacere: Saltem non renues, aliquot circa id argumentum Observationum speciminibus luculentam aliis facem ad faeliciter caepta perficienda, in immortale nominis tui decus, praeferre.

En Tibi, Vir eximie, nostra de studiis et institutis tuis sensa. Dilemma tuum, quo Diatribam tuam posteriorem claudis, solutum, ni fallor, habes. Optionem dederas, vel novos ut indicemus labores, vel perpetuo Te feriari jubeamus. Prius horum, ut vidisti, nobis sumpsimus; posterius Tibi plane (id quod candidum ingenium tuum aegre ferre non potest) denegamus. Vale, Vir Optime, et a Societate Regia, Tui studiosissima, plurimum salve. Dabam Londini, d. 22 Februarii, A. 1672.
Responsi tui gratiam avide exspecto.

TRANSLATION

Henry Oldenburg wishes happiness to the celebrated Mr. Marcello Malpighi, Philosopher and Physician of Bologna

You display such extraordinary and welcome richness in your intellect and industry, famous Sir, that I can scarcely find words with which to express the eager goodwill of our spirits towards you as I should. We had hardly finished our consideration of your essay on the anatomy of plants when, lo and behold! we received as a supplement to it your new and fully finished dissertation on the egg and first stages of the chick. And this too I presented without delay to the Royal Society which not only embraced it with both arms but took it to its very heart. That was most agreeably obvious from the combined applause of the Fellows, who immediately ordered me to convey the same to you.[1] You have perfected this paper (as you do all your works) so learnedly, so ingeniously, with so much devotion, that it seems fit at once for the press, in order that it may be known to all the learned world.

So great is your fairness of outlook that nothing there detracts from the merits of others; rather indeed you pile up due praises for the labors and discoveries of your predecessors. Meanwhile, you press on with further investigation along their tracks. In this way you do emphatically prove yourself a pupil of the Royal Society and a true member of nature's priesthood, while you labor by all methods to extend far and wide the bounds of a well-stored natural science. Hence it is, most learned Sir, that we are absolutely against the idea that the parallel efforts of others, in those researches that engage you, should impede your own endeavors and studies. Let it never cross your mind that, because one of our Fellows strives to follow the same line of research, your own labors towards the perfection of the anatomy of plants are superfluous (as your most recent letter seems to suggest).[2] He is employing his own methods and observations and you others of your own in order to elucidate and explain the same subject, and while your chief findings are in agreement you place the theory of this aspect of nature on all the firmer footing. For this reason the Society speaking with one single voice begs you that if you have other things by you, which would enable you to explain more fully and completely what has already been communicated to us, you will not on any account conceal them or keep them from the public. In that paper of yours you hinted at drawings you have made[3] of your observations concerning plants in a large number of plates that will illustrate that same subject. If it should seem fit to you to entrust those plates to us we will without fail see to it that all of them shall be printed as elegantly as possible and with the maximum care.

Moreover, it happens quite often that when wise men pursue the way and method of philosophizing rightly, they come upon the very same truths. It would be easy to list many examples furnished by the learned philosophers of our Society, and by others, if to do so did not exceed the bounds of a letter, and if I were not sure you have had many similar experiences.

Come then, excellent Sir, and continue to tread the path upon which you have begun with diligence and warmth of heart, and with all your might adorn the post you have obtained. Besides those remarkable points concerning plants that you still have in your cabinet, it is obious from your latest essay on the incubated egg that you have by you many other choice observations on oviparous animals, as you there intimate. We do not merely advise you (to use your own term) but openly exhort you to be so good as to expound your own investigations of these topics, performed with your usual skill. Moreover, we would wish unsaid that word of yours, that all but despairing comment you throw out about the difficulty of investigating profoundly the nature of quadruped and other viviparous foetuses.[4] We do not deny that work of this kind demands rather considerable leisure and heavy expenses, but please remember that men skilled in observational science (among whom we rightly count yourself) can effect remarkable economies in both effort and money; hence you will at least not refuse to bring forward a bright torch (in the form of a few specimens of observations upon that topic) so that others may perfect what has been happily begun, to the undying glory of your name.

Here you have, excellent Sir, our opinion of your studies and intentions. You have here too, I fancy, a solution to the dilemma with which you conclude your essay on the egg. You offered us the choice of imposing fresh tasks upon you, or sentencing you to an endless holiday.[5] From what has just been said you will see that we have chosen the former of these [alternatives], while we quite deny you the latter (which cannot disagree with your candid temperament). Farewell, best of men, with many greetings from the Royal Society, which is most devoted to you. London, 22 February 1672.

I eagerly await the favor of your reply.

NOTES

Reply to Letter 1879. The draft is Royal Society MS. O 2, no. 77.
1 Letter 1879 and a part of *De formatione pulli* were read to the Society on 22 February; the Society thought the essay should be printed forthwith. Oldenburg had drafted this letter of thanks beforehand and brought it to the meeting.
2 The allusion is to the parallel work of Nehemiah Grew on plant anatomy. A week later (29 February) Croone spoke on his study of eggs whereby he had "found some such thing as the rudiments of a chick in the egg before incubation." Wilkins insisted that the honor of the discovery belonged to Malpighi, who had first announced, described and illustrated it. (A paper by Croone, now known to be founded on a mistake, was read on 28 March; see Birch, *History*, III, 30–40.)
3 The printed text has "delineare Te decrevisse" ("that you have decided to draw").
4 At the end of *De formatione pulli* Malpighi had made this remark, following the precedent of Harvey in *De generatione animalium*.
5 Compare Letter 1805, and the last sentence of *De formatione pulli*.

1909
Oldenburg to Dodington
23 February 1671/2

Mentioned in Letter 1912 as conveying Letter 1908 for delivery to Malpighi, with thanks to Dodington for his services, especially for acting as a postal agent on his behalf.

1910
Lister to Oldenburg
24 February 1671/2

From the original in Royal Society MS. L 5, no. 43
Partly printed in Birch, *History*, III, 17–18

Yorke Feb. 24 71

Sir

You will oblige me, if you save ye Longing, you gave me, by ye perusal of ye MS. of Signore Malpighj de Anatome Plantarum. As for ye further Account concerning ye *Tarantula* of Signore Cornelio at Naples I received it in Italian, as you was pleased to communicate it to me; & since you desire my thoughts upon this matter, I will briefly make reflections upon some of ye particulars & explain thereby ye Querie yt gave ye occasion.

It is here affirmed yt ye *Tarantula* is a *Phalangium*, wch yet does not plainly appear;[1] possibly it may, when ye Author shall please to give us his more particular Observations or transmitt any of ye Animals themselves. To be great, diversly painted & wth diversity of colours, to live in holes of ye earth etc. are Notes common to most sorts of Spiders even wth us. It is very necessary yt great heed be taken of ye Characteristical Notes we gave ym & by wch we know *Phalangia* from all ye other Tribes of Spiders: for in this consists (at least in my judgment) ye discovery of ye nature & effects of ye Tarantula.

We had undoubtedly been in ye darke still, but for yt one chance Note of Pliny (lib. 11 c. 24) viz. *assultim ingredi*,[2] & had never known what ye Antients had meant by their *Phalangia*. And yet having observed yt skipping motion in two or thre sorts of our English Spiders, we found, yt all those wch had yt peculiar motion, agreed too in ye *senary*[3] Number of Eyes, not to mention other distinguishing markes, those two being enough to reduce ym to order. Now that it being ye sole propertie of this Tribe of Spiders to move in Going as tho they *danced* & therefore to be (for kind) those wch ye Antients called *Phalangia* & whose biting they soe much dreaded, I thought it very material to enquire, whether ye Tarantula was not one of ym, yt is, whther ye Tarantula goe by Skippes, & have 6 eyes only, etc.

To tell you ye truth I had some reason to question this, (not but yt ye *phaenomena* or ye effects of yt miscellaneous bite (if really tru) did undoubtedly depend (in my thoughts) upon ye Nature of ye Animal) but yt I had seen a spider brought from Rome by ye name of a *Tarantula* & yet whose figure (as I remember) shewed it plainly to be of another Tribe & no *Phalangium*. Again because some late Authours yt I had seen of this matter had given us ye Cutt or figure of a *Reticulum orbiculatum* or Wheel-net wth a Tarantula in it: wch in truth is as an improper a thing (if a Phalangium) as

Delphinum sylvis appingere[4]

This Tribe [Phalangia] having yt in common wth some other Tribes of spiders, yt they scorne Netts & hunt openly & take their prey by ambush & agility of body. for an elegant description of their hunting I refer you to Mr Evelin in Mr Hookes Micrographie;[5] where alsoe I observe to you by ye by yt, yt grey *Phalangium* there mentioned is exceeding common all over England (where I have been) as well as at Rome.

We may well expect from ye ingenuity & diligence of Signore Cornelio ye full cleering of this matter, we being already beholden to him for yt other Raritie of his Native soil *Manna*, wch he has put beyond exception, to be a spontaneous exudation of ye Ash-Tree. Soe ye Expt registred, as he himselfe penned it in a Letter to Mr. Wray. Catalog. Plant. Angliae ad Fraxinum.[6]

However in ye meane time I may deserve your pardon, if I praepossess you wth my opinion. I agree wth him, yt ye matter will probably (when thoroughly examined) not prove, not only as ye Vulgar is persuaded, but not [as] Authours write neither: And yet, (he must excuse me) if I thinke it will prove more than a meer fiction & yt those strange accidents wch ye

Attarantati are said to suffer ae not to be attributed to ye great drought of ye country & thirst only, but possibly to ye bite of a certain Animal too. I am Sr

Your most humble servant
Martin Lister

ADDRESS
    These
    For my honoured friend
    Henry Oldenburg Esq
    at his house in ye
    Palmal
        London

POSTMARK FE 26

NOTES

Reply to Letters 1880 and 1897.
1 True spiders, distinguished by the possession of spinnerets and poison glands, are now placed in the natural order Areneae of the class Arachnida. Phalangids are members of the same class, but a different subclass and order (*Opiliones*). They lack spinnerets and poison glands. Harvestmen (daddy longlegs) are typical of the group. The tarantulas are true, large spiders, *Lycosa tarantula*, only slightly poisonous to man.
2 "they move by jumping". Pliny characterises phalangia as having a poisonous bite, thin, variegated body, and jumping motion.
3 Six.
4 "To depict a dolphin in woods" (Horace, *Ars Poetica*, 30); the poet gives this as an example of false or extravagant imagery.
5 See Robert Hooke, *Micrographia* (London, 1665), pp. 200–2. The subject there is called a grey hunting spider, which Lister here calls a phalangium.
6 See Letter 1808 and its note 9.

1911
Cornelio to Oldenburg
24 February 1671/2

From the original in Royal Society MS. C 1, no. 108

Clarissimo et Doctissimo Viro
Henrico Oldenburg Societatis Regiae
a Secretis
Thomas Cornelius Salutem

Quod amantissimis literis tuis antehac non responderim, Henrice humanissime, causa fuit magnus et diuturnus morbus, quo vehementius ingravescente corporis animique vires miserabiliter amisi: nam et insigni macie confectus jampridem extabui, et desidia atque longuore pene exanimatus obtorpui. Cave autem existimes me rationis ac humanitatis usque adeo inopem esse, ut plane non agnoscam, quanto nobis honori atque emolumento futurum sit commercium literarum, quod aliquando vobiscum inierim. At enim prae me fero atque profiteor me suspexisse jamdudum novitia Britannorum instituta conatusque in promovendis artibus, quae hominum generi fructum possint afferre. Gratulor itaque vestrae Societati, gratulor omnibus rerum naturae studiosis, gratulor huic seculo. Nam quid amplissimo philosophantium Caetui optatius contingere poterat quam potentissimi ac sapientissimi Regis Optimatumque conspiratio atque consensus in illustrandis disciplinis, civiumque animis ad bonarum artium studia, non opibus solum atque favore verum exemplo etiam alliciendis: etenim, ut Plato ait, quae apud principes viros studia vigent, ea reliqui cives alacriter amplectuntur et colunt. Ii vero qui ad exquirendam naturae rationem animum contulere habent unde admirabiles reconditarum rerum notiones consequantur: id est observationum disquisitionumque Thesauros, quos vestra passim expromit industria. Habet autem hoc seculum insigne quiddam, quo vetustatem plane vicisse videtur. Scilicet ille hodie mos philosophandi increbruit, ut naturae mysteria non legendo duntaxat hauriantur e veterum scriptis, et seu auctoritate seu levi conjectura pendantur, sed autopsia potius, siquidem liceat atque experimentorum pondere examinentur; et quandoque etiam mathematica apodixi, aut chemica probentur analysi: quod sane institutum, ceu ad veritatem in physicis vestigandam maxime appositum, vos egregii Regiae Societatis philosophi inviolate servatis. Porro autem quando hanc philosophandi rationem susceptam video, in spem magnam adducor tantam rerum naturae scientiam brevi nos adepturos, quantam nemini mortalium usque adhuc datum est assequi. Quid? quod possumus verissime dicere omnia aetatem hanc nostram Physiologiae incrementa sibi debere, nec profecto quicquam nobis traditum a Veteribus esse, quod ad rerum naturalium scientiam plane conferat. Ita me hercule nobis licet in nostris studiis, quae vindices assertoresque vos habent viros omnino praestantes, quodammodo gloriari; ne priscorum sapientiam semper admiremus. Equidem quod ad me attinet, incredibile est quanta tenear expectatione eorum, quae quotidie vestra isthaec luculenta officina depromit. Propterea summam cepi voluptatem ex literis tuis Henrice Clarissime, quibus tum ad jungendam vobiscum amicitiam, tum praeterea ad studia doctrinae pariter consocianda benigne humaniterque me allicis. Quocirca maximas tibi ac universae Societati gratias ago et habeo: utinam vero referre aliquando etiam possim. Sed quando vestris quidem laudibus, magnisque erga me meritis aliter suffragari non queo; studium saltem in vos meum voluntatemque usquequaque praestabo. Caeterum ut primum per valetudinem mihi licuerit animum ad intermissa jam diu literarum studia referre, enitar certe ut aliquid mentem observationum commentationumque Vobis impertiam: Nam etsi ego mihi tantum non tribuo ut cogitata mea vobis probanda fore confidam, tamen persuasum habeo non injucundas vobis futuras peculiares quasdam nostratium rerum notitias, quas aliunde nequeatis eruere. Ejusmodi arbitror ea esse, quae in puteolano agro, in Cumano et Bajano litore in Anaria insula atque in Vesuvio monte accurata inquisitione dudum notavimus. Vale Vir Clarissime et a nobis crebriores epistolas, si tibi eas haudquaquam ingratas fore significaveris, deinceps expecta. Neapoli III Non. Martii Anno MDCLXXII [N.S.].

ADDRESS
  Clarissimo et Doctissimo Viro
  D. Henrico Oldenburg Regiae
    Societatis Secretario
      Londinum

TRANSLATION

Tommaso Cornelio greets the very famous and learned Mr. Henry Oldenburg, Secretary of the Royal Society

The reason for my not replying before now to your most friendly letter, my good friend Henry, was a severe and prolonged illness, which as it grew more vehement robbed my mind and body of vigor most wretchedly, for long before it was over I had wasted away to an extraordinary degree of emaciation and being quite exhausted by languor and prostration I was almost paralyzed. But do not think me so lacking in reason and good feeling that I do not acknowledge how greatly we shall profit from and be honored by the correspondence I began with you some time ago. For I profess and declare that I have long admired the new endeavors and designs of the British people for advancing those arts which can prove fruitful to the human race. And so I rejoice for your Society, for all students of nature, and for this age. For what could be more desirable for that very worthy assembly of philosphers than the agreement and participation of your most powerful and wise monarch and nobility in clarifying the learned subjects and also in attracting the minds of citizens to the study of the useful arts, not by financial support only but by example. As Plato says, those studies that flourish among the leaders of society will be eagerly taken up and cultivated by other citizens. Indeed, those who apply their minds to the investigation of nature have that whence splendid ideas of hidden secrets result, that is to say stores of observations and essays which your industry displays at every turn. This age possesses one attribute to a notable degree in which antiquity seems obviously to have been defective. That is to say, the manner of philosophizing has become prevalent whereby the mysteries of nature are not derived merely by reading from the writings of the ancients and considered in the light of authority or trifling conjecture, but rather by personal examination whenever it is practicable to submit them to the test of experiments, and sometimes too they are probed by mathematical demonstration or by chemical analysis. And this method is that wholly relied on by your distinguished philosophers of the Royal Society, as that most appropriate for the investigation of the truth in physics. Further, when I see that way of philosophizing adopted a great hope is aroused in me that we shall soon be masters of so great a knowledge of nature as it has never before been given to mortal men to enjoy. Why so? Because we can truly say that this age of ours owes every improvement in natural philosophy to itself, and that in fact nothing was transmitted to us from antiquity that fully applies to the study of nature. Thus we may indeed, by Hercules! boast in some measure about ourselves with regard to our studies, which have in you as defenders and exponents men of really outstanding merit; lest we should always be marveling at the wisdom of the ancients. For myself at any rate, it is incredible how much I look forward to those things that are every day turned out from that same splendid workshop of yours. Moreover, excellent Henry, I gained the highest delight from your letter in which you most kindly and generously invite me to join in friendship with you, and likewise to combine our researches. For this I return the warmest thanks to you and to the whole Society; would that I could indeed, some time, return [something]. But when I cannot otherwise endorse your praises, even, or your great opinion of my merits, I shall at least constantly excel in my zeal and goodwill towards you. Furthermore, when my health shall permit me to resume my purpose of conducting our long interrupted correspondence I shall strive to impart to you some notions concerning observations and reflections. For though I have not such a high opinion of myself as to believe that my notions will be tested by yourselves, yet I am sure that some particular points will not seem inelegant to you, as giving knowledge of things in our region which you cannot evoke elsewhere. Among them, I believe, are our observations of long ago based on very exact inquiry in the neighborhood of Pozzuoli, on the shore at Cumae and Baiae, on the isle of Ischia, and on Mount Vesuvius. Farewell, famous Sir, and henceforth expect more frequent letters from us, if you shall have assured us that these will not be unwelcome to you. Naples, 5 March 1672 [N.S.].

NOTE

Reply to Letters 648 (Vol. III) and 1893.

1911a

Cornelio to Dodington

24 February 1671/2

Covering letter for Letter 1911
From the original in Royal Society MS. C 1, no. 107

Illustrissimo Signore mio Signore Padrone Colendissimo

Tardi rispondo alle lettere di VS Illustrissima perche lindebolezza nella quale mi hà lasciate il male non mi hà permesso di poter sino a questo giorno applicar la mente alle scrivere. Gia s'avvicina il tempo nel quale si potranno mandar le tarantole. E tratante io non voglio lasciar di riferir a VS Illustrissima quelche mi hà raccontato pochi giorni sono una Signora judiziosa e libera d'alcuni prejudizi volgari cioé che ritrovandosi ella in terra d'Otranto (ove sono in gran copia questi animaletti) vide un suo servitore che accortosi d'essere stato morsicato dalla tarantola, mostrana nel collo una picciola puntura o ferita intorno della quale in brevissimo tempo sorsera alcuni granellini pieni d'humor seroso, et indi a poche hore commincio quel pover huomo ad esser travagliato da sintoni fierissimi, cioè de sincopi, inquietudini grandissime vacillamenti di testa e vomito: ma senza haver giamai volonta di ballare o gusto di stromenti musicali so ne morí miserabilmente nello spazio di due giorni. Questa stessa Signora mi hà raffermato che tutte le persone attarantate (fuori di quelle che per qualche lor fine infingono d'esser tali) sono per lo piu donnicciuole,[1] dolce (come di suol dire) di sale, le quali entrando per qualche particolare indispositione in quel furor maniaconito di danno a credere secondo il commune e volgar prejudizio d'essere stati morsicati della tarantula. Et io mi ricordo d'havere osservate in Calabria donne che sopraprese de simili accidenti, sono state reputate per indemoniato: estendo in quella Provincia comune credenza che la maggior parte de' mal che travagliano il genere humano habbia origine da malie e spiriti cattivi. Ora mi sovviene d'un terribile male che assai sovente s'osserva in Calabria, e cola si chiama Coccio maligno. Egli nasce nella superficie cel corpo in forme d'una piccola macchia o lividura della grandezza d'un lupino. Questo arreca qualche dolore, et se indi a poco nato non s'infoca, pastorisce in picciolo spazio di tempo certissima morte. Credesi per comun sentimento di quei popoli che tal male avvenga solamente a coloro che si son pasciuti di carne d'animali spontaniamente morti. La quali opinione io posse per esperienza affermare d'essere falsi. Cosi frequentemente avviene che di molti effetti meravigliosi che cotidianamente si sperimentano, non sapendosi la vera cagione, se ne assegni tal'una fondata in qualche volgare pregiudizio. Et io tale stimo essere la volgar sentenza della cagione del male degli attarantati. Ma perche non vogliamo credere che cotesto male sia più tosto cagionato da disposizione interne simile a quella che in alcuni mogli[2] della Germania suol produrre quel male che chiamano Chorea di Santo Vito? Ma di cio io spero di potere appresto scrivere altre conghietture che saranno bastanti a confutare questa favola della Tarantola.

Il signore Oldenburg mi da raguaglio di molte belle cose pubblicate dai Signori della reale societa io confidato della benignità di VS Illustrissima prendo ardimento d'importunarla, supplicandola che si compiaccia procurarmi quei libri che di presto sono usciti alla luce, purche non siano scritti in Lingua Inglese. Scrivero costà al Signor Marchese fonseca[3] per lo ricapito di quelli si degnera VS Illustrissima d'inviar l'acclusa al Sr. Oldenburg. Et io in tanto ambiziossimo d'esecutarmi me comandi de VS Illustrissima le fo' profonda riverenze Napoli 5 di Marzo 1672 [N.S.] VS Illustrissima

Devotissima et obligatissima Servitore
Tomaso Cornelio

V. Residente

TRANSLATION, largely from *Phil. Trans.*, no. 83 (20 May 1672), 4066–67 [Most illustrious Sir, most dear Lord,

I am dilatory in my reply to your excellency's letter because the state of weakness in which my sickness has left me has not allowed me to apply my mind to writing until this very day.] Now the time approaches, that I may send you some Tarantulas. Mean while I shall not omit to impart unto you, what was related to me, a few daies since, by a judicious and unprejudicate person, which is; That being in the Country of Otranto [in Apulia] (where those Insects are in great numbers,) there was a [serving-]man, who thinking himself stung by a Tarantula, shew'd in his neck a small [puncture or wound], about which in a very short time there arose some pimples full of a serous humour, and that, in a few hours after, that poor man was sorely afflicted with very violent symptoms, as Syncope's, very great agitations, giddines of the head, and vomit; but that without any inclination at all to dance, and without all desire of having any musical instruments, he miserably dyed within two daies.

The same person affirm'd to me, that all those that think themselves bitten by Tarantula's, (except such, as for some ends [of their own] fain themselves to be so,) are for the most part [dim-witted women, not quite all there as they say][1] who by some particular indisposition falling into this melancholly madness, perswade themselves according to the vulgar prejudice, to have been stung by a Tarantula. And I remember to have observed in Calabria some women, who seised on by some such accidents were counted to be possess'd with the Divel; it being the common belief in that Province, that the greatest part of the evils, which afflict man-kind, proceeds from [enchantments and] evil Spirits.

This brings to my mind a terrible evil, which often enough is observ'd in Calabria, and is call'd in their language *Coccio maligno* [bad spot]. It ariseth on the surface of the body, in the form of a small [mark or bruise], of the bigness of a [corn]. It causeth some pain, and if it grow not soon red thereupon, in a very short time certainly kills. 'Tis the common opinion of those people that such a distemper befals those only, that have eaten flesh of Animals dead of themselves: which opinion I can from experience affirm to be false. So it frequently falls out, that of many strang effects, we daily meet with, the true cause not being known, such an one is assigned, which is grounded upon some vulgar prejudice. And of this kind

I esteem to be the vulgar belief of the cause of that distemper, which appears in those that think themselves stung by Tarantulas.

But why should not we rather think, that that distemper is caused by an inward disposition, like that which in some places[2] of Germany is wont to produce that evil, which they call *Chorea Sti Viti*, St. Vite's dance. But of this I hope I shall soon be able to write my thoughts more fully, which will, I think, be sufficient to refute that fable of the Tarantula.

[Mr. Oldenburg reports to me the many fine things published by the gentlemen of the Royal Society; trusting in your excellency's kindness I make so bold as to importune you, begging you to be pleased to obtain those books for me as soon as they have been published, provided they are not written in the English language. I shall write over there to the Signor Marchese Fonseca[3] for the repayment for them if your excellency will be so good as to send the enclosed to Mr. Oldenburg. And being most desirous of performing my commands from your excellency I make a profound salutation. Naples 5 March 1672 [N.S.]

Your excellency's most devoted and obliged servant,
Tommaso Cornelio

The Resident at Venice

NOTES

This letter together with the preceding one was forwarded by Dodington to London; Oldenburg read both to the Society on 24 April.
1 Oldenburg's translation, "young wanton girles," is incorrect.
2 Presumably "women" would be more exact.
3 Don Manuel da Fonseca was the Spanish consul in London; Naples was, of course, a Spanish possession at this time.

1912
Oldenburg to Dodington
26 February 1671/2
From the draft in Royal Society MS. O 2, no. 78

London Febr. 26. 1671/2

Sir,

'Tis no longer than Friday last (Febr. 23th) that I acknowledged yr favor in ye care of conveying Sigr Malpighi's Excellent Observations de Ovo unto us.[1] At yesame time, under a Cover to yrself, I return'd the R. Society's cordial thanks to yt worthy gentleman, and promised him wthall, yt, by ye first opportunity of a ship going hence for Venice, I would send him one of Dr. Grew's books, treating of Vegetation, and concurring wth him in his former discourse of the Anatome of Plants.[2] This I herewth performe; and he will find some Englishman at Bononia, yt may be capable of interpreting ye chief contents of this book to him; And I would intreat you, Sir, to Joyne wth me in exhorting and pressing Sigr Malpighi, so to finish his said Dissertation of Plants, both as to ye Discourse and the Iconismes, yt they may be printed as soon as is possible; ye care of wch, if he so please, we shall willingly undertake here, considering, that not only these two Author[s] confirme yesame thing, but Sigr Malpighi carrieth it further, and enriches ye subject wth ampler Observations.[3] This you will be pleased to intimate to him from Sir,

Yr faithful servant,
H. Oldenburg

I pray, Sir, take particular care yt this book may wth speed and safety goe to Bononia, according to the Direction.

For John Dodington Esquire.

NOTES

1 Letter 1909, now lost.
2 See Letter 1908.
3 Malpighi did not receive Grew's *Anatomy of Vegetables begun* until late September 1672; see Vol. IX. Adelmann was unaware of the date of the book's despatch. It was not until August 1674 that Malpighi sent to London the final text of *Anatome plantarum*, together with the illustrations, Part I of which was printed at London in the following year.

1913
Oldenburg to Lister
27 February 1671/2
From the original in Bodleian Library MS. Lister 34, ff. 18–19

Sir,

I cannot but signify to you, yt on Thursday last[1] I deliver'd to Sr W. Petty a transcript of Sr Malpighi's papers de Anatome Plantarum; addressed, as was desired, to Mr Brooks at York.[2] I hope it will, if it be not already, come safely to yr hands. I have since received from thesame Italian a very Industrious and curious piece about the *Cicatricula in Ovo*,[3] wherein he pretends to evince, that, as the cheif parts of the plant are actually in its seed, so the rudiments of ye animal or chick are actually in that cicatrix. 'Tis done by him, both in discourse and likenes, in the accuratest and politest manner, yt a philosopher and an artist can doe; as you will see, when printed; wch it will be shortly, according to ye orders of ye R. Society, to wch he hath dedicated this piece, as he did the former *De Bombyce* and *Plantis*.

Yr last about the Tarantula, is also safely come to hand; wch is likely to clear that argument. I doubt not but Dr Cornelio will doe his part in making narrower observations.

I shall not faile to take notice of yt unhappy fault, committed in yr excellent discourse about the veins in Plants.[4] The word *As*, wch you would rather have, *and*, is so in your letter, as 'tis printed; but it may be easily alter'd, together wth the other, wch is much more material.

My humble service, I pray, to Mr Brooks from Sir

Yr faithful servant
Oldenburg

London
Febr. 27. 71.

Ye *Erratum* of ye presse was an omission of ye words *not-wanting*, for wch is badly printed *wanting*, wch makes ye whole Paragraph non-sense.

ADDRESS

    To his honored friend
    Dr Martyn Lister at his
    house wthout Mickel-gate-barr
        at York

NOTES

Reply to Letter 1910.
1 February 22.
2 See Letter 1897; but it seems likely that a letter from Lister is missing. See below, note 4.
3 "the cicatrix in the egg." See Letter 1879.
4 No letter now survives in which Lister complains of errors in the printing of Letter 1863. Oldenburg listed the errata at the very end of *Phil. Trans.*, no. 80 (19 February 1671/2), after the index to Volume VI.

1914
Vernon to Oldenburg
27 February 1671/2

From the original in Royal Society MS. V, no. 23

Paris March 8th 1672 [N.S.]

Sr

I have received severall of yours & am really ashamed that I have soe long delayed my answer my Businesse hath crossed my good purposes. neither have I now time sufficiently to excuse my self. I saw Sigre Cassini once of Late hee saith hee will write butt to write to the whole body of the Royal Society hee scarce knowes in what manner or what style to addresse himself. butt thinkes only to write a little Compliment to them. & referre to you to propose it in forme. The Gentleman for whom I did desire the model of Sr William Pettys ship is Monsieur Tonarte[1] & you will oblidge mee extreamely to have it accurately done & the Charge will bee noe grudgeing to him.

    They have made a trumpett here as neere as they can to the measures & description of Sr Samuel Moreland & it hath succeeded very well & beene heard at the distance of 4000. Toyses. I heare For² England as if Mr Hooke had hopes of improving this, as well as of Mr Newton's invention: God send him good luck for nothing can bee more beneficiall then to have two of the usefullest of our senses our sight & our hearing soe advanced. They are seeing at the Royal Academie what innovations may bee made in Mr Newtons Telescope. They iudge that a reflecting mirroir may exceed an ordinary glasse in clearnesse & greatnesse 16 times. This Monsieur Cassini told mee about a fortnight agoe & since Abbe Mareotte hath discoursed wth mee to the same purpose hee tells mee that hee thinkes a parabolicall line will improve Sr Samuel Morelands Trumpet for soe Monsieur Regnault of Leoni³ had intimated to him in a letter & that hee had made some speculations concerning it. Butt now I have not time to discourse of more matters to you. now I must beg your pardon & Rest

Your most obliged servant
Francis Vernon

My humble Respects to the Bishop of Sarisbury. Dr Wallis. Mr Boyle & Mr Hooke

NOTES

1 Compare Letters 1877 (note 14) and 1900 (note 2).
2 *Sic*; read: "from."
3 Lyons; see Vol. VII, p. 500, note 24.

1915
Hevelius to Oldenburg
28 February 1671/2
From the original in Royal Society MS. H 2, no. 29

Vir Illustris

Nec ad Tuas binas, mihi multo gratissimas modo respondeo, nec silentium meum diuturnum excusare volo,¹ sed nova quaedam breviter vobis significare, quod novus Cometa a die 2 Martij² hic conspiciatur, quem autem, cum per aliquot dies peregre domo abfuerim, ante 6 Martij vesperi observare Instrumentis haud potui. Conspicitur tam tempore vespertino, quam matutino; exiguae est magnitudinis, caudam non nisi unius aut unius et dimidij grad. modo prae se fert; maiorem sine dubie exhiberet, si non circa crepusculum existeret, tum Luna abesset. Versatur nunc circa stellas in brachio dextro Andromedae supra scapulas; quantum ex una alterave observatione dijudicare adhuc possum, tendit Lucidam Cinguli circiter versus Andromedae, et quidem motu directo diurno duorum circiter graduum in suo tramite. Die 6 Martij vesperi hor. 7 40′ versebatur in 7 grad. Arietis sub latitudine Boreale 35 grad. quantum radiori minerva ex globo conjicere licet. Die 7 Martij mane Hor. 3.30′ Longitudo eius erat fere 8 grad. Arietis cum paullo minori Latitudine vesperi eiusdem diei Longitudo eius extitit 10 grad. Arietis et Latitudo 34 grad. fere. Die 8 Martij mane Hor. 4 Longitudo Cometae erat 12 grad. Arietis et Latitudo 33. grad., sed ruditer tantum, ut recte capias: observationes enim meas calculo adhuc subjicere nequeo. Vesperi deo favente me iterum illum observaturum spero, utut hodie mane ob caelum nubilum nihil vidimus. Specialiores observationes meas quas summa diligentia octante meo Orichalcico 9 fere pedum, quoties licet perago, proxima occasione Vobis transmittam. Quid Vos vel alij circa illum notastis magna desiderio exspectamus. De caetero scias me novam stellam sub capite Cygni[3] die 6 Martij mane denuo observasse, sed vix ac ne vix nudis oculis adhuc conspicitur. Vale a saluta totam Illustrissimam nostram Societatem quam officiose; brevis pluribus ad Tuas respondebo. Dabam raptim ut vides. Gedani Anno 1672, die 9 Martij [N.S.]. Tuus officiosa voluntate

J. Hevelius

Cometa
Anno 1672 die 6 Martii vesperi observatus
a
J. Hevelio

Caudam projiciebat eo tempora ad stellas in dextra manu Andromedae.

ADDRESS
    A Monsieur
Monsieur Grubendol
        A
    Londres
Franco Anwerpen

TRANSLATION, mostly from *Phil. Trans.*, no. 81 (25 March 1672), 4017–18

[Illustrious Sir,

I shall not now reply to your two letters, to me most welcome, nor seek to] excuse my long silence,[1] but acquaint you in brief [with the news that] there hath been seen here a New Comet from the 2d of March 1672,[2] which [, however,] I my self, being some daies absent from home and from my instruments, could not observe [with instruments] till March 6th in the evening. It is seen both mornings and evenings. It is but little [in magnitude], having at the present a train [tail] not above a degree or a degree and an half long: which would doubtless appear bigger, if it were not for the twy-light, and the Moon were absent. It is [moving] now about the Stars in the right Arm of Andromeda on her Shoulder-blade. As far as I can collect from one or two observations, it tends towards the [bright star] of Andromeda's girdle, and that with a direct diurnal motion of about two degrees in its course.

The 6th of March in the evening, h.7. 40.' it was [moving] in grad. 7 of Aries in the 35th deg. of Northern Latitude, as I guessed by the hasty inspection of a Globe.

March 7. in the morning h.3.30'. its Longitude was about 8. deg. Aries, with a somewhat lesser latitude than before: in the Evening of the same day its Longitude was 10. deg. Aries and Latitude [almost] 34 deg.

March 8. in the morning h.4. the Longitude was 12 deg. Aries and the Latitude 33. deg: Which yet I would not have taken precisely, because I cannot yet reduce my Observations to a calculus. This evening [with God's blessing], I hope, I shall see him again; although this morning we could see nothing by reason of the [cloudy sky].

I intend to send you by the next [opportunity] more particular and more accurate Observations, which I purpose to make carefully, as oft as I can, with my Brass Octant, which is about 9 feet long. And I long to hear, what you or other Nations have observed of this Phenomenon.

Besides, I cannot but advertise you, that I have observed again March 6. 1672. [in the morning], the New Star under the Head of the Constellation of the Swan:[3] but it can hardly be seen as yet with the naked Eye.

[Farewell. Greet the whole of our illustrious Society most dutifully. I shall shortly reply to yours upon many topics. Written in haste, as you see. Danzig, 9 March 1672 [N.S.]

Yours with dutiful goodwill,
J. Hevelius

A Comet
observed on 6 March 1672 [N.S.] in the evening by J. Hevelius

[*For the figure, see page 569*]

At that time the tail projected towards the stars in the right hand of Andromeda.

ADDRESS
To Mr. Grubendol
at London
Post-free to Antwerp]

NOTES

1 Presumably Letters 1723 and 1817. Hevelius had last written at the end of September 1671 (Letter 1792).
2 This and all subsequent dates are New Style. Oldenburg read this letter to the Royal Society on 21 March (having received it on the seventeenth); at that time the comet had not been seen in England.
3 See Vol. VII, *passim*.

1916
Oldenburg to Sluse
4 March 1671/2
From the draft in Royal Society MS. O 2, no. 79

Illustrissimo Viro
Domino Renato Francisco Slusio Canonico Leodiensi etc.
Henr. Oldenburg
Felicitatem

Distuli solito diutius responsionem meam ad novissimas tuas, 6 Cal. januar. ad me datas, quod Clarissimi Hugenii de secundis tuis circa Alhazeni Problema meditatis, plures ante septimanas ad ipsum transmissis, sensa exspectare volui.¹ At cum nimias ille in rescribendo moras nectat, diutius equidem officio deesse meo nolebam. Nostrates qui ea legerunt, impense, ut solent omnia tua, comprobant; laetabundi insuper, quod tua de Maximis et Minimis, deque Curvarum Tangentibus μελετήματα in lucem emittendi spem facis.

Diu est, quod Dominus Collinius, qui jugi Te studio colit, plurimamque Tibi salutem mittit Doctoris Wallisii tertiam de Motu et Mechanice partem, nec non Erasmi Bartholini Dioristicen, de Equationum limitibus tractantem, ad te curavit, libris illis cuidam Simoni Arc, Navarchae Belgico, traditis, et Elzevirio in tui usum concreditis.² Manu mea eidem Collinio utrumque librum a Te huc curatum, Mesolabum scilicet tuum et Laloveram de Cycloide, tradidi, qui pergrata mente insigne illud munus amplexabatur. Gestaremus equidem paria Tibi rependere, si vires suppeterent. Cum illae desint, ea non respues, quae a tenuitate nostra proficisci possunt. Matheseos in Academia Cantabrigiensi Professor doctissimus, Isaacus Newtonus, in Clarissimi Barrovii locum suffectus, novam pronuper Telescopii rationem, Cata-dioptricam scilicet R. Societati communicavit, qua Tubo-specilla longiora, citra effecti fraudem, insigniter contrahere novit.³ Praestat hoc ipsum bini Speculi Metallici, unius quidem concavi, alterius vero plani, nec non Lentis vitreae plano-convexae, beneficio. Prius Speculum Reflectens et fundo Tubi adhaerens (in illo quidem specimine, quod elaboravit Author ipse, et laudatae Societati examinandum transmisit) radium habet 13 dig. Anglicorum fere. Alterum vero, reflexos prioris radios recipiens, inque Lentem vitream denuo reverberans, ovali est figura, circuloque aeneo, intra Tubi cavitatem mobili, insertum. Lens haec vitrea $\frac{1}{12}$ digiti habet radium; Metallum quippe colligit Solis radios [ad distantiam $6\frac{1}{3}$ digitorum, et lens ocularis] ad $\frac{1}{6}$ digiti fere distantiam ab ejus vertice: quae quidem nobis exploratae sunt dimensiones ex vasis, in quibus fuere elaborata; speciatimque diametrum concavi hemi-sphaerici, in quo nita fuit Lens vitrea, dimensi, eam $\frac{1}{6}$ digiti esse deprehendimus. Caeterum speculi plani Centrum locatur in Axe Tubi, ita quidem ut in ipsum Perpendicularis, a centro Lentis demissa, cum Axe angulum rectum constituat, objectique species, a Speculo concavo in idem repercussa, versus Lentis focum reflectatur: jam vero conferendo distantias foci istius a verticibus Lentis et Speculi concavi, prodit ratio 1 ad 38; qua indicatur objecta 38 vicibus circiter in isto Tubulo ampliari.

In eo jam est Artifex, ut hujus generis Telescopium construat sexpedale, quod Tubo-specillam vulgare 50 pedes longum praestantia superaturum speramus, dummodo metallum nactus fuerit adeo compactum solidumque qui radios ut par est reflectat.⁴ Brevis forte rem totam una cum instrumenti Iconismo Adversariis meis Philosophicis inseram, ut hac ratione Virorum sagacium de ea Sententiam eo commodius liberiusque cognoscamus.⁵

Haud aegre feres, si Morelandi Equitis de sono articulato, ad. 1.2. vel 3. milliaria Anglica distincte et clare devehendo, Instrumentum adjiciam. Praestat illud ope Tubae, quam Stentoro-phonicam nuncupat, quae pedes quinque vel sex longa, uno sui extremo diametrum habet 21 pollicum, altero autem, quo admovetur ori, duorum; cujus quidem figura sensim ampliatur, orificiumque labris aptandum ita conformatur, ut aeris spiritusve ne quidquam intercidat, os tamen ipsum omnemoda se deducendi contrahendique libertate gaudeat. Res tota jam non Anglico duntaxat, sed et Gallico sermone est impressa, brevique sine dubio Gallia in oras vestras Exemplaria ejus transferentur.⁶ Quoad partem hujus Tubae demonstrativam, exactamque figuram ejus et dimensiones Physico-Mathematicis hoc Problema proponit Author; Quaenam scilicet sit Figura recti-linea, curvilinea, mixtave; quae ejusdem dimensiones exactae, quaeque sphaera activitatis ipsius, quae omnium optime et maxime Vocem humanam intendat diffundatque?

Liceat mihi jungere tertium, quod Societati nostrae examinandum ex Italia a Solertissimo Malpighio transmissum nuper fuit. Dum enim alii ab Ovo, animalium sollicite, exquirunt productionem, ille in Ovo ipso jam fere animal, etiam ante incubationem excitatum peraccuratis Observationibus et figuris ostendit. Dissertationem ipsam hactenus nonnisi manuscriptam luce publicae dignissimam cum memorata judicet Societas, eam Typographis Chalcographisque suis quantocyus edendam commisit.

Quid vero in eadem Italia fiat de 4. Musices voluminibus, a Mengole promissis; quid item de Gottignii dioptricis, Romae, ut ajunt sub praelo morantibus, hactenus nobis est incompertum. Ferunt, Baliani Opuscula Posthuma de Pendulis, inter alia, tractare; de quo argumento Clarissimus Hugenius integrum quoque librum Parisiis brevi edendum, adornavit. Lugduni Gallorum sub praelo laborare perhibent Milleti Cursum Mathematicum non vulgarem. Hic in Anglia nunc imprimuntur Horoxii scripta quae supersunt Astronomica, a Domino Wallisio digesta.⁷ Adhaec Barrovii in quatuor priores Apollonii libros Commentaria praelo destinata sunt; quibus Dominus Bernhardus Oxoniensis Astronomiae Professor, ex Arabicis Exemplaribus binis, Beni scilicet Musae, Eutocii notis illustratae, et Abdelmelechi, tres posteriores adjiciet.⁸ Spes insuper nos fovet, supramemoratum Dominum Newtonum Introductionem in Algebram, necnon Quadraturarum Analyticarum Methodum Generalem, Dioptricasque

Lectiones viginti, orbi litterato expositurum. Pellius quoque noster jam excudendam curat Quadratorum Tabulam, Canonemque laterum Triangulorum omnium rationalium rectangulorum, quorum Hypothenusa a 10000 deficit.⁹

Latere Te nequit, quendam Johannem Ott Helvetium in Tractatulo quodam, de Visione, Heidelbergae A. 1670 excuso, commemorare, se invenisse modum, quo longissimi quique Tubi in compendium redigi possint, laxa nequidquam eorum perfectione. Praeterea Instrumentum simplex se excogitasse quod commode moveatur hujus beneficio cujuscunque generis Hyperbolae, Ellipses, ac Parabolae describi queant, ut et Circuli Segmentum quodcunque. At hac de re felicem in praxi successum etiamnum desideramus.

In Adversariis meis sub. no. 75 de Domini Barrovii libris non ita dudum editis verba facientes ἐπιμετρον vice Theorema quoddam Accessorium de Cycloide addidimus; cui si mentem id subiisset Praestantissimi illius Authoris, adjecisset Theoremata sequentia:

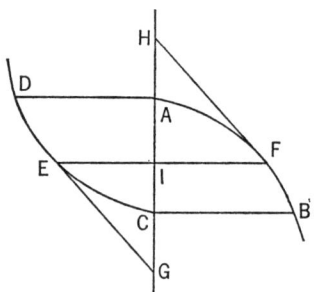

Si duae curvae, puta *AB*, *CD*, alternatim ductae fuerint circa eandem Axim *AC*, ordinata communis maxima est illa, cujus Tangentes *EG* et *FH* sunt parallelae.

Et maximum Rectangulum *EIF* illud est, quando Segmenta Axis producti (puta *CG*, *AH*) a Tangentibus secti, sunt aequalia.

Sed me cohibeo, ne graviora tua negotia taedio nimis molesto dispungam. Ignosce prolixitati, quaeso, et valetudinem tuam, reipublicae studiosae utilem, cura diligenter. Dabam Londini 4 Nonas Martii MDCLXXII.

TRANSLATION

Henry Oldenburg wishes happiness to the very illustrious Mr. René François de Sluse, Canon of Liège, etc.

I have deferred my reply to your most recent letter to me of 17 December more than usual because I wished to wait for the famous Huygens' opinion of your second thoughts about the problem of Alhazen, which were sent to him several weeks ago.[1] But as he takes too much time about making a reply I am reluctant to fail in my duty any longer. Our Fellows who have read them approve of them warmly, as they do all your work, rejoicing, moreover, because you give us some hope of the publication of your studies concerning maxima and minima and the tangents to curves.

It is a long while since Mr. Collins, who feels himself much obliged to you and sends you many greetings, took care to send you the third part of Dr. Wallis's *Mechanica, sive de motu*, and also Erasmus Bartholin's *Dioristice* (treating of the limits of equations), entrusting those books to a certain Dutch sailor, Simon Are, to be committed to Elzevir for your use.[2] With my own hands I delivered to the same Collins both of the books you sent here, that is, your *Mesolabum* and La Loubère's *De cycloide*, and he accepted this fine gift with much gratitude. We would have undertaken to repay you with the like gifts had it been in our power. As this cannot be done, do not spurn those that our feeble resources proffer. The very learned Professor of Mathematics in the University of Cambridge, Isaac Newton, who was promoted to the famous Barrow's post, has very recently communicated to the Royal Society a new kind of reflecto-refracting telescope, by which he can markedly shorten long telescopes without spoiling their effectiveness.[3] [*See pp. 507–8 for the remainder of this passage.*]

A craftsman is now engaged in making a telescope of this kind six feet long, which we hope will excel an ordinary telescope of fifty feet, if only a metal can be made so compact and solid that it will reflect the rays as it should.[4] I shall soon insert an account of the whole thing with a figure of the instrument in my *Philosophical Notebooks*, so that in this way we may the more easily and freely learn the opinion of those who are learned in such matters.[5]

You will hardly be displeased if I add Sir Samuel Morland's instrument for carrying clear and distinct articulate sound to a distance of one, two, or three English miles. He accomplishes this by means of a tube which he calls *stentorophonic*, which is five or six feet long and twenty-one inches in diameter at one end and two inches at the other, where the mouth is applied. The shape gradually widens out, and the orifice to which the lips are applied is so formed that no air or spirit is lost, while the mouth enjoys complete freedom of opening and shutting in every way. The whole thing has already been printed not in English alone but in French too, and no doubt copies of it will soon be transported from France to your part of the world.⁶ As for the theoretical aspect of this tube, its exact shape and dimensions, the author proposes this problem to mathematical physicists: What is that rectilinear, curvilinear, or mixed shape which, amongst all others, best intensifies and diffuses the human voice; what are its exact dimensions, and what is the range of its activity?

Let me in the third place annex what was lately sent from Italy by the most skilful Malpighi for the examination of our Society. For while others have diligently investigated the development of animals from the egg, he displays the animal within the egg itself in most accurate observations and figures, even before incubation has been begun. As the aforesaid Society judges that this dissertation which is hitherto extant in manuscript only is most worthy of being published, it is to be entrusted for printing to its engravers and printers as soon as possible.

We still do not know what has happened in Italy to those four volumes about music promised by Mengoli, nor to Gottignies's dioptrics, languishing, it is said, in a printer's shop in Rome. It is rumored that Baliani's opuscula treat among other things of pendulums, upon which subject the very celebrated Huygens also has completed a whole book, to be published at Paris shortly. They say that Millet [de Chales]'s by no means commonplace *Cursus mathematicus* is in press at Lyons. Here in England Horrox's extant writings on astronomy, compiled by Dr. Wallis, are being printed now.⁷ Moreover, Barrow's commentary on the first four books of Apollonius is intended for the press, to which Mr. Bernard, Professor of Astronomy at Oxford, will add the three latter books taken from two Arabic versions, that of the Beni Musa (illustrated with the notes of Eutocius) and that of Abdelmelech.⁸ We are also nourishing the hope that the above-mentioned Mr. Newton will give to the learned world an introduction to algebra together with a general method for the analytical quadrature of curves, and twenty lectures on dioptrics. Also, our Mr. Pell is seeing through the press a table of squares and a canon of the sides of all rational right-angled triangles whose hypotenuse is less than 10,000.⁹

You cannot be unaware that a certain Swiss, Johannes Ott, records in a certain little treatise on vision, printed at Heidelberg in 1670, that he has discovered a way by which the longest telescopes may be shortened without any loss of their perfection. Moreover, he has devised a simple instrument, easily moved, by means of which any kind of hyperbola, ellipse, and parabola may be described, and any segment of a circle too. But we still wish for [an account of] its practical success.

In my journal, no. 75, giving some account of Mr. Barrow's recently published books, we added something supplementary about the cycloid to which, if they had then come into that most excellent author's mind, he would have added the following theorems: [*for the translation, see above p. 546*].

But I must restrain myself lest I offer only a tedious weariness as a relief from your serious work. Ignore my verbosity, I beg you, and take good care of your health which is so useful to the world of the learned. London, 4 March 1672.

NOTES

Reply to Letter 1843.
1 See Letter 1899.
2 What follows is based on Letter 1906.
3 What follows is virtually identical with the account of Letter 1881.
4 See Letter 1899, note 3.
5 See *Phil. Trans.*, no. 81 (25 March 1672), 4004–10, which is an English version of Letter 1866a, followed by summaries of Letters 1871, 1883, 1886 (also in English), and 1928.
6 See Letter 1887, note 1.
7 See Letter 1906, note 3.
8 See Letter 1906, notes 4 and 5.
9 See Letter 1906, notes 6, 7, and 13.

1917
Malpighi to Oldenburg
5 March 1671/2

From the original in Royal Society Malpighi Letters, no. 13
Partially printed in *Opera omnia*, I, Appendix, p. 15

Illustrissimo Viro
Domino Henrico Oldenburg Regiae Societatis Anglicanae Secretario
Marcellus Malpighius S.P.

Iam Doctissimorum Virorum sensum, quibus placuit exercitatiunculam de plantis evolvere, tuis humanissimis mihi indicatum literis percepi. Parem in tam egregijs Viris agnosco cum sapientia humanitatem, qui licet Naturae abdita impenetrabilia sciant, indagantium tamen vel minimos non aspernantur conatus. Peravide expecto Praeclarissimi vestri Medici promissum de Plantarum Anatome librum, in quo propositam materiam tam docte, et dilucide examinatam me reperturum spero, ut meos omnino supervacaneos futuros putem labores. Interim tamen in languidi corporis, et animi solamen, observationes prosequar, pro ut mentis meae tenuitas permittet.

Alter iam excurrit mensis, quo tibi observationum actuariolum circa incubata ova transmisi,[1] ut Consociorum placitum circa rem tam obscuram exploratum haberem, quod tua intercedente humanitate me consequuturum non ambigo.

Binas, quas innuas, epistolas accepi; Harum prior Die 15 Martij altera vero 14 Decembris conscripta erat, quibus (ut debebat) responsum dedi, quod forte ad tuas non adhuc devenerit manus.[2] Circuli quadraturam italico sermone a Domino Mengolo editam quamprimum recipies,[3] una cum Excellentissimi Cassini epistola;[4] quam inscio Auctore, eiusque Amico, cui editio commissa fuit, furtim a Typographo recepi: Aliud insuper opsculum Gelatorum Academiae addidi;[5] quae omnia Serenissimi Regis Mandatarius apud Venetos, occasione Viri, brevi iter huc facturi, transmittenda spopondit. Me, ut soles, ama, diuque Vale. Dabam Bononiae die 15 Martij 1672 [N.S.].

ADDRESS

Illustrissimo Viro Domino Henrico Oldenburg
Regiae Societatis Anglicanae Secretario
                Londini

TRANSLATION

Marcello Malpighi sends many greetings to the very illustrious Mr. Henry Oldenburg, Secretary of the English Royal Society

I have now comprehended the opinion of those learned men to whom the consideration of my little essay on plants was entrusted, as indicated to me in your very kind letter. I acknowledge in such exceptional persons the combination of kindness with wisdom, since although they know how to disclose Nature's intimate secrets themselves, they do not despise the feeblest endeavors of others. I await very eagerly the promised book on the anatomy of plants by your distinguished physician, in which I hope to find the subject under discussion so learnedly and clearly examined that I may judge all future effort on my part superfluous. Meanwhile so far as my feeble abilities permit in weakness of body and spirit I am continuing my observations as a consolation.

A second month is now passing since I sent you a brief note of observations upon the incubated egg so that I might have the judgment of the Fellows upon so obscure a question, and I have no doubt that through your kind intercession I shall receive it.[1]

I have, as you suggest, received two letters. The first of these was written on 15 March and the second on 14 December and, as was fitting, I wrote answers to them which perhaps you have not yet received.[2] You will as soon as possible receive the *Quadrature of the Circle* published in Italian by Mr. Mengoli,[3] together with a letter by the excellent Cassini which, unknown to the writer and to the friend of his to whom the publication was entrusted, I have obtained secretly from the printer;4 I have added, moreover, another little work by the Accademia dei Gelati.5 His Majesty's envoy at Venice has promised to send all these things by a gentleman who happens to be making the journey from thence shortly. Continue to love me as you do and may you long fare well. Bologna, 15 March 1672 [N.S.]

ADDRESS

    To the very illustrious Mr. Henry Oldenburg
    Secretary of the English Royal Society,
                London

NOTES

Reply to Letters 1654 (Vol. VII), 1842, and 1875.

1 See Letter 1879, sent on 22 January.
2 See Letters 1705 and 1879.
3 Pietro Mengoli, *Circoli* (Bologna, 1672). Mengoli's quadrature is the same as Wallis's of 1657, that is, he states the ratio of the circle to the circumscribed square as that of two rational fractions converging to a limit; he seems to have been unaware of Wallis's prior work.
4 G. D. Cassini, *Lettera prima... terza sopra l'hipothesi solari e le refrazioni* [Bologna, 1672]. Oldenburg received the package of books in early May, and gave an account of these three letters—mainly on the calculation of atmospheric refraction—under an English title ("Three Letters... concerning his Hypothesis of the Suns motion and his doctrine of Refractions") in *Phil. Trans.*, no. 84 (17 June 1672), 5001–2. One at least of the letters was written in 1666; presumably all belonged to Cassini's Bologna period. It is possible that these letters are the apologia mentioned in Letter 1547 (Vol. VII, p. 244) and Letter 1705. Malpighi's words here—and in Letter 1805—suggest that though printed the letters were never published. The B.M. copies are in a volume pressmarked 532 k 15.
5 Probably this was the book mentioned in the postscript to Letter 1805 (and its notes 4 and 7). Oldenburg's review of it came out in *Phil. Trans.*, no. 89 (16 December 1672), 5125–28.

1918
Flamsteed to Oldenburg
8 March 1671/2
From the original in Royal Society MS. F 1, no. 82

Derby March 8. 1671/2

Mr Oldenburg
Sr

Yesterday, included in a letter to Mr Collins,[1] I sent yu an account of my observations of Jupiters transit by ye 24th star of virginis,[2] & the moons over ye Pleiades[3] both observed accurately & by methods more certeine then commonly used by which as I have there applyed them yu will find how much ye Celestiall tables are out of order & what need wee have of better observations to restore them: my way of observeing ye moons latitude by ye distances of ye fixed star from her illuminated cusps at theire occultations is so much ye better for yt it is independent on[4] ye selenography & lunar spots. The like I intended to have used in observeing ye latitudes of ye emergeing stars from ye moons center, but shee had no sooner coverd the last star e[5] but shee was receaved behind some houses so yt I could see her no more yt night. I request yu would impart these observations to Mr Hooke. & desire his if hee made any for mee. I promised Mr Collins to include in this a paper for him of those transits which Jove is like to make by fixed stars this yeare. I here send it. & desire yu present it to him wth my services.[6] after I had written Mr Collins letter I receaved one from a private freind intimateing yt Mr Hooke had presented a tube of but 12 inches which performes as well as ye best yt ever was, to ye R. Society I would gladly know ye truth of this relation from yu, & if yu have no tie of secrecy, ye manner of this wonderfull tube.[7] tis not yt I may onely satisfie my selfe wth ye knowledge but use of this secret which if either yu please to communicate to mee or procure from him I shall esteeme ye highest kindnesse yt can be conferd upon mee. & yu need not doubt but, if it bee injoynd, as secret in ye concealeing it, as any of ye Society to whom it is imparted & in lue of this favor besides my constant acknowledgments Yu shall command my accuratest observations.

Last night I waited for ye moons transit by ye star in Libra 11°. 34′8[8] & made some observations of it but not so accurate as I could wish, by reason yt I wanted a clock & an assistant; & ye moones altitude shee being neare ye meridian varied not so fast as that therefrom I dare pronounce ye times accurate besides Mr Townleys micrometer was not convenient for the observeing this transit by reason of ye shortnesse of his pointers; which in my owne intrument I have remidied, but cannot get it made yet, by reason our smith despaires of makeing mee such good screwes as Mr Townlys are. as soone as I can get leasure I shall give yu a draught of it, & if upon triall of my last nights observations I find any thinge worth ye knowledg, I shall hereafter impart it. I have receaved yr Hugenius,[9] & will be carefull of it. Yu make expect it back next terme desireing to heare what newes from yu at yr leasure I rest

      Yr most affectionate & obliged friend & servant
         John Flamsteed

ADDRESS
 To Henry Oldenburge
 Esqr at his house in ye middle
 of ye Pell mell neare St
  James's Wesminster
    these present
pd 3d

NOTES

1 Writing to Collins on 18 March 1671/2 (Royal Society MS. F 1, no. 83) Flamsteed acknowledges a letter from Collins dated the twelfth and informing him of the loss of this document which (Flamsteed said) had been delivered to the posthouse three days previously (9 March). "... in it [Flamsteed continues] I had included a paper to him [Oldenburg] conteining my observations of Jupiters transit by a star in Virginis 14°-08 on ye 16. 17. & 18 of Feb. last & account of ye moon's appulses in ye Pleiades ye 23 of ye same last month. this I have repeated here at large both as I observed it & what I deduced therefrom which is as materiall for ye correction of ye lunar Astronomy as any thinge can be. the observation of Jupiter's transit I have not now repeated because last Friday I began to observe a nearer transit of his to another star ye 38th of Leo which when I have finished I shall give you both togeather [*see Vol. IX, Letter 1945*]... I likewise certified you something of my opinion of Mr Newtons telescope yt if it be made of 4 or 5 foot long it will take in but a little... teare of this halfe sheet & deliver it with my services to Mr Oldenburg instead of yt which is lost..."

 No enclosure survives with this letter to Collins.

2 This close passage of Jupiter to a star in Virgo (the planet was to pass eleven minutes south of the star) was predicted by Flamsteed in a letter to Collins of 31 January 1671/2 (Rigaud, II, 127–28) as occurring on 13 February. He asked Collins to pass

the information on to Oldenburg and Hooke. In due course, Flamsteed sent his record of this observation with Letter 1945 (Vol. IX).
3 For Flamsteed's prediction of this event, see Letter 1849, and its note 1. The observation as made on 23 February and sent via Collins on 18 March 1671/2 was reported in *Phil. Trans.*, no. 86 (19 August 1672), 5034–36. It is perhaps worth remarking that Flamsteed was observing with a fourteen-foot telescope and a Towneley's micrometer given him by Jonas Moore.
4 Read: "of."
5 As shown in Flamsteed's prediction (see Letter 1849, note 1), it is the star 20 Pleiades.
6 The paper seems not to have survived; however, Flamsteed published another account of a close passage of Jupiter by a fixed star between 24 and 30 May, 1672 (*Phil. Trans.*, no. 86, 19 August 1672, 5037).
7 This report was incorrect.
8 This close passage is noted in *Phil. Trans.*, no. 77 (20 November 1671), 2297, 3000.
9 *Systema Saturnium.*

1919
Dodington to Oldenburg
8 March 1671/2

From the original in Royal Society MS. D 1, no. 26
Partly printed in *Phil. Trans.*, no. 83 (20 May 1672), 4067–68

Venice March 18: 1672 [N.S.]

Hond. Sr

In my last[1] I signifyed to you my observance of yr Commands in transmitting yrs[2] to doctor Cornelio at Naples & I hope ere the 10th of next month, I may have his answere to return, wch will doubtlesse be fuller & more satisfactorie.[3]

In ye natural observations & Historie possibly this may not bee unworthy yr notice.

Five miles from Padoa are the Waters or Baths called Aponensia from a Towne named Apponum,[4] both famous in Antiquitie, & frequently mention'd by T. Livie.[5] I find the word written both wayes viz wth a Single P. and with a double P.P. But I suppose ye single one more likely to be the Orthographie. especially if my conjecture be true that t'is derived from Απονον scil. a doloris vel laboris privatione.[6] Lucan & Claudian so write it, wth ye first Syllable allwayes short.[7] I will not doubt but Sr John Finch, &

doctor Baynes two worthy members of the R.S. & who lived long in Padoa, and whom I Honor with veneration for their singular parts & perticular Friendshipps towards me, have informed themselves most exactly of wt ever I shall be able to say on the present subject, yet in regard they may possibly, & with better Judgment then mine, think the matter it selfe trivial, I will give you but a short touch of wt I have to say. The Waters are actually very Hot. Secondly stinking, thridly they produce a great deale of very fine salt; of wch the natives serve themselves in their ordinary occasions. This Salt is ye Mark towards wch I levell my discourse. This Salt is gathered in this manner, the natives, after sun set, stirr peeces of wood in ye water & presently ye salt sticks to them, & comes off in small flakes, exceeding white, & very Salt. This never looseth it's savour. The Natives wth ye same water use to wash their walles to render them whiter then ordinary, wch it doth even whiter then lime such walles conserve their saltnesse some few dayes only, & then become insipid, even though the sayd walles swett forth a white excrescence in thinn & light flakes like Nitre, many yeares after. But that Salt, wch is collected from ye Stones, gravel, & Earth by which the Rivolets, descending from those Baths, doe run, is without any Taste of Salt, though there be no difference in the forme or Colour, from that wch is gathered wth ye woodden instruments by me mentiond. This is the sum of wt I have to say. If you think the matter tanti, & yr servant, par negotio,[8] I will send you a sheet or two in Latin or Eng[lish] on this subject wth my Thoughts, of it, as well as a more exact description of ye Scite & use of the place & waters. I crave yr excuse for this intrusion on your other Thoughts & Businesses.

 I must doe ye like for wt followes. In ye two yeares & halfe that I have binn yr Correspondent, I have expended some Eight pound or more in Bookes & Postage on yr Accompt, I doe not desire the monie, nor had I ever intention to demand it, or ye least thought of it, But an occasion offers itselfe, wch putts me on desiring in lieu thereof, a Book of you, wch is of greater price, vizt. Goltzius his workes, in 5 volumes I think, de Re nummaria, or de numismatibus.[9] I have a singulare use of this Book & you would doe me a great pleasure in sending it me, by ye first. Had not this binn out of ye Road, of my other acquaintance in London, I had never troubled you with it, & so once more making you my excuses for this Confidence, I shall ever Rest

Sr yr humble servant
John dodington

Mr Oldenburg

ADDRESS
> For my honoured friend
> Mr Hen: Oldenberg Secretary
> of the R.S.
>   In London

NOTES

1 Letter 1902 is the last surviving letter, and is too early; hence another letter from Dodington may be missing.
2 Letter 1893.
3 Letter 1911, which had not yet reached Venice.
4 Abano Terme. It had been visited by John Ray in 1663.
5 Titus Livius (59 B.C.–A.D. 17), the famous historian, was a native of Padua.
6 "Untroubled: that is, freedom from pain and care."
7 Marcus Annaeus Lucanus (39–65), grandson of Seneca, was author of a poem, *Bellum civile* or *Pharsalia*; Claudius Claudianus (late fourth century A.D.) was a Latin poet of the Imperial Court born in Egypt.
8 "worthwhile... equal to the business."
9 The *Opera omnia* of the painter and numismatist Hubrecht Goltzius were first published in five volumes at Antwerp in 1644.

1920
Oldenburg to Huygens
11 March 1671/2

From *Œuvres Complètes*, VII, 156
Original in the Huygens Collection at Leiden

A londres le 11me Mars 1672

Monsieur

Puisque vous le voulez ainsi, ie continue de vous envoier les Transactions. Dans cet inprimé[1] vous trouverez une theorie nouvelle de Monsieur Newton, (Inventeur du telescope Cata-dioptrique) touchant la lumiere et les couleurs: ou il maintient, que la lumiere n'est pas une chose similaire, mais un meslange de rayons refrangibles differemment et comme vous verrez amplement dans le Discours mesme. vous aurez la bonté de nous en dire vos pensees.

Monsieur de St. Hilaire,² qui est chez Monsieur l'Ambassadeur de France icy, fait estat, à ce qu'on m'a dit, d'envoier promptement à Paris un Telescope de la facon de Monsieur Newton: que vous examinerez à loisir. Peut estre que vous en trouverez la charge³ trop grande ou le petit verre objectif⁴ trop espais, pour des objects bien esloignez; en ce cas la vous vous servirez du remede, que vous conoissez.

J'espere, que vous aurez receu ma longue lettre du 12 Fevrier⁵ avec le Nombre 79 des Transactions. C'est pourquoy ie seray plus court à present, quoyque parfaitement Monsieur

       Vostre treshumble et tresobeissant serviteur
           Oldenburg

ADDRESS

A Monsieur
Monsieur Hugens de Zulechem
 dans la Bibliotheque du Roy
  a Paris

TRANSLATION

             London, 11 March 1671/2

Sir,

Since you so desire it, I continue to send you the *Transactions*. In this latest printed one[1] you will find a new theory of Mr. Newton (inventor of the catadioptric telescope) concerning light and colors: here he maintains that light is not a homogeneous substance but a mixture of differently refrangible rays, as you will see fully in the discourse itself. You will be so good as to tell us what you think about it.

Mr. de St Hilaire,[2] who resides with the French ambassador here, is, I am told, in process of sending a telescope of Mr. Newton's fashion to Paris soon, which you will be able to examine at leisure. Perhaps you will find the "charge"[3] too great or the small objective lens[4] too thick for very distant objects, but in that case you will make use of the remedy with which you are acquainted.

I hope you have received my long letter of 12 February[5] with no. 79 of the *Transactions*. This is the reason for my being brief on this occasion, although I am, Sir, absolutely

       Your very humble and obedient servant,
           Oldenburg

ADDRESS

Mr. Huygens of Zulichem
 The King's Library
  Paris

NOTES

1 *Phil. Trans.*, no. 80 (19 February 1671/2).
2 This person has often been mentioned in previous volumes.
3 This is the technical term always used in the seventeenth century, signifying the proportion of the magnification of the image by the eyepiece to the aperture of the instrument. Newton's eye lens was extremely small, with a correspondingly high magnification.
4 Read: "eye lens."
5 Letter 1899.

1921
Nehemiah Grew to Oldenburg
12 March 1671/2

From the original in Royal Society MS. G, no. 33
Partly printed in *Phil. Trans.*, no. 92 (25 March 1673) 5193-96

Coventry March 12—71

Sr,

About 3 weeks since I had from London yr Philosophical Transactions,[1] whereupon I wrote ye next day ye presentment of my many thanks to you,[2] finding therein how much I am obliged to you in giveing yourself ye trouble of so large & full an account of my booke. Wherefore, Sr, if ye first, wch were more early, have miscarryd, I hope these may yet have your acceptance. Yet am I not so immodest as to desire them understood a discharge, but only an acknowledgement, of my debts unto you; both upon ye account of this, & former favours.

Haveing so good an occasion for ye use of this paper, I will venture to fill up ye rest with ye following notes; wch I made sometime since, in part, but tooke occasion this Winter to refresh. The original I have not now by me; but as my thoughts at present shape themselves, you may be pleased to peruse them.

Some brief Observations
touching ye nature
of Snow

If those great Philosophers Aristotle & Cartesius, & others of their

Transcribers, who have wrote of Meteors, & amongst them of Snow, have not yet given us a full account hereof; it will not be needless to enquire yet farther of it.[3] He yt will do this, will do it best, not by ye pursuit of his phancy in a chaire, but with his eyes abroad. Where if we use ym well fixed, & with good caution, & this in a thin calme & still snow, we may by degrees observe.

First with Monsieur Des-Cartes, & Mr. Hook, yt many parts hereof are of a regular figure; for ye most part as it were so many little Rowels or Stars of 6. poynts; beeing perfect & transparent Ice, as any we see upon a poole or vessel of water. Upon each of these 6. poynts, are set other collateral poynts; & those always at ye same angles as are ye maine poynts themselves.

Next, amongst these regular figures, though many of them are large & faire; yet, from these takeing our first *Item*, many others, alike regular, but far less, may likewise be discovered.

Againe, amongst these not only regular, but entire parts of Snow, looking still more warily, we shall perceive, yt their are divers others, indeed irregular, yet chiefly but ye broken poynts parcels & fragments of ye regular ones.

Lastly, yt besides ye broken parts, there are some others wch seeme to have lost their regularity not so much in beeing broken, as, by various winds, first gently thawd, & then froze into little irregular clumpers againe.

From whence ye true notion & external nature of Snow seemeth to appeare; vizt, That not only some few parts of Snow, but, originally, ye whole body thereof, or of a snowy cloud, is an infinite mass of Icicles regularly figurd; not one particle thereof, I say originally, not one of so many millions, beeing indeterminate or irregular. That is to say, a cloud of Vapours beeing gatherd into Dropps, ye said drops forthwith descend; upon wch descent, meeting wth a soft freezing wind, or at least passing through a colder region of ayre, each drop is immediately froze into an Icicle shooting it self forth into serveral poynts or striae on each hand frorward its centre. But still continuing their descent, & meeting with some sprinkling & intermixed gales of warmer ayre, or in their continual motion & waftage too & fro touching upon each other; some are a little thawd blunted frosted clumped, others broken, but ye most hanked[4] & clung in several parcels together, wch we call flakes of snow.

It beeing known what Snow is, we understand, why though it seeme to be soft, yet tis truly hard; because true Ice, ye inseparable property whereof is, to be hard: seeming only to be soft, because upon ye first touch of ye finger upon any of its sharp edges or poynts, they instantly thaw; otherwise they would pierce our fingers as so many Lancets.

Why againe, though Snow be true Ice, & so an hard & dense body, yet very light; because of ye extreme thinnesse of each Icicle in comparison of its bredth. For so Gold, wch though of all bodys ye most ponderous, yet beeing beaten into Leaves, rides upon ye least breath of ayre; & so in all other bodyes, where there is but little matter conteined within large dimensions: & possibly in no other case.

Also how it is white. Not because hard; for yr are many soft bodys white; but because consistent of parts all of them singly transparent, but beeing mixed together, appear white: as ye parts of froth, glass, ice, & other transparent bodys, whether soft or hard.

Lastly why Anaxagoras would needs have it to be black: in yt in his country it might possibly be sometimes greater & thicker, & now & then give some glances of yt colour. For so transparent bodys, if they drink in ye rays of light somewhat deepe, at certaine positions oftentime appear black. so Diamonds even without ye Jewelers foyle, with yr sparkles often give their shades: & by Heraulds we know are put for Sable. Thus much for ye external nature of Snow, let us next a little enquire into its essential nature.

Now if we would make a judgment of this I think we may best do it by considering, what ye general figure of Snow is, & compareing ye same with such regular figures as we see in divers other bodys: in yt where we see ye like configurations, we may believe there is ye like subject therein, or ye like efficient whereby both those & these are made.

As for ye figure of Snow, 'tis generally one, scilicet yt wch is above described. Rarely of different ones, wch may be reduced chiefly to 2. generals, circulars & hexagonals, either simple, or compounded together. More rarely, either to be seen of more then 6. poynts but if so, then not of 8, or 10, but 12. Or in single shootes, as so many short slender cylinders, like those of Nitre. Or by one of these shoots as ye axletree, & touching upon ye centre of a paire of pointed Icicles, joyned together as ye two wheels. Or ye same hexagonal figure & of ye same usual bredth, but continued in thickness or profundity, like ye Stone wch, as I remember, Boetius calls Astroites.[5] Al these I say are rare, ye first described beeing ye general figure.

As for ye configurations of other bodys, we shall find, yt there are divers wch have some a less, others a more neere resemblance hereunto.

Nitre is formed, as is commonly known, into long cylindrical shoots: as also all Lixivial[6] Salts for ye most part; resembling, though not perfectly, ye several poynts of each starry Icicle of Snow. Salt of harts horn,[7] Sal Armoniac, & some other Volatile Salts, besides their maine & longer shoots, have other shorter branched out from them; resembling as those ye maine, so these ye collateral poynts of Snow. But ye Icicles of Urine are still more neere. For in Salt of Harts horn &c although ye collateral shoots stand at acute angles with ye maine, yet not by pairs at equal hight: & in Sal Armoniac, although they stand diametrically opposite or at equal hight, yet withal at right not acute angles: whereas in ye Icicles of Urine they stand at equal hight, & at acute angles both; in both like those of Snow. And it is observable, yt ye configuration of Feathers is likewise ye same. The reason whereof is, because Fowles haveing no Organs for evacuation of Urine; ye urinous parts of ye blood are evacuated by ye habit of skin, where they produce & nourish Feathers.

From hence it should seeme, That every a drop of Raine aforesaid, conteining in it self some more spirituous particles (as from ye hight to wch they are advanced, ye prolifique vertue of raine, & its easy tendency to putrefaction above other water, is argued they do) & meeting with others in their descent, of a Saline, & yt partly nitrous, but chiefly urinous, or of an acido-salinous nature; ye said spirituous parts are apprehended by them, & with those ye watery, & so ye whole drop is fixed; yet not into any indifferent & irregular shape, depriveing ye spirituous parts of their motion in an instant; but according to ye energy[8] of ye spirituous as ye pencil, & ye specifick nature or determinate passibility of ye saline parts as ye ruler, 'tis thus figurd into a little Starr. These things somewt farther considered & cleerd may add a little to yt great deal of light, wch ye Honourable Mr Boyle hath given to ye nature of Cold, ye Ayre, & ye Bodys yr in conteind, in his excellent Discourses hereof. Sr,

Your humble servant
Nehem. Grew.

I would gladly know how I might send directly & surely to you.

ADDRESS
   For
  Henry Oldenburge
    Esqr

NOTES

Nehemiah Grew (1641–1712) was the son of a Parliamentary divine; educated at Pembroke College, Cambridge (B.A. 1661) he began the study of plants in 1664. His first work he showed to his half brother, the physician Henry Sampson, in 1668; and this first book was read by Oldenburg and then by John Wilkins, in 1670. At some unknown date it was considered at a meeting of the Royal Society, and on 11 May 1671 the printing of the book, *The Anatomy of Vegetables begun*, by the Society's printer was authorized. During a rapid visit to Leiden Grew matriculated on 6 July 1671 and proceeded M.D. on the fourteenth. He practised for a time in Coventry, his native city, but later removed to London. Grew was elected F.R.S. on 30 November 1671 and the first copies of his book were available shortly thereafter. He published many more works, and succeeded to the Secretaryship of the Royal Society after Oldenburg's death in 1677. There is no doubt that Malpighi's work and Grew's, so close in time, were completely independent.

1 *Phil. Trans.*, no. 78 (18 December 1671), in which there is on pp. 3037–43 an adulatory account of Grew's recent book.
2 This letter (if it ever reached Oldenburg) is now lost.
3 Descartes had discussed snow in Chapter VI of *Les Météores* (published with *De la Méthode* at Paris in 1637); Robert Hooke (mentioned below) in *Micrographia* (London, 1665), p. 91; Grew seems to have been ignorant of Kepler's *Strena seu de nive sexangula* (Frankfurt-a-M., 1611).
4 Entangled.
5 The word *astroites* (from Greek) is used by Pliny to signify a star-shaped mineral.
6 Alkaline.
7 Ammonium carbonate.
8 That is, the *active power* of the spirituous, as contrasted with the *passive* contribution of the saline, component.

1922
Oldenburg to Newton
16 March 1671/2

This is answered by Newton in Letter 1928. Oldenburg evidently put forward some questions about the quality of the image seen in the telescope Newton had sent to London, and about its magnification.

1923
Newton to Oldenburg
16 March 1671/2

Printed in Newton, *Correspondence*, I, 120–21, from the original in Royal Society MS. N 1, no. 35

He thanks Oldenburg for an (unnamed) book, and briefly discusses the possibility that the telescope he had made and sent to the Royal Society had suffered from tarnishing. He also mentions a telescope in process of construction by a Fellow of Trinity College; it is just possible that the maker of this second (equally small) reflector was John Wickins, Newton's former "chamber-fellow."

1924
Oldenburg to Hevelius
18 March 1671/2

From the original in the Babson Institute

Per-Illustri Viro
Domino Johanni Hevelio, Gedan. Consuli Amplissimo
H. Oldenburg Salutem

En Tibi, Vir Clarissime, Acta Philosophica Anni 1671, una cum Clarissimi Wallisii munere, Tertia scilicet operis sui Mechanici parte; quos libros ut boni consulas, majorem in modum rogamus. Mitto hunc fasciculum per Secretarium Legationis nostrae in Daniam,[1] qui pollicitus est, se cum magna cura, quamprimum Hafnium advenerit, Dantiscum ad Te transmissurum.

Lubens scirem, quomodo placuerit Excellentissimo Domino Mareschallo Microscopium hic elaboratum, et praeterito autumno Tibi traditum;[2] lubentius vero quam sit colophoni proxima Machina Caelestis; quidque Te inter et Dominum Picardum, dum Huennae versaretur, in re Astronomica intercesserit? Paucissimas hic Observationes caelestes of[3] hyemem valde nebulosum habuimus; nec Parisienses instituisse multo plures existimamus.

Interim duo nobis subnata sunt nuper Inventa quae hic commemorare lubet. Unum est Samuelis Morelandi, Equitis, de sono Articulato ad duo vel tria milliaria Anglica, Tubae Stentorophonicae beneficio, distincte et clare devehendo. Alterum est, Matheseos in Acad. Cantabrigiensi Professorem, Isaacum Newtonum, communicasse novam Telescopii rationem Cata-dioptricam, qua scilicet Tubo-specilla longiora, citra effecti fraudem, insigniter contrahuntur. Praestat illud gemini speculi metallici, unius concavi, alterius plani, nec non Lentis Vitreae plano-convexae beneficio. Prius speculum reflectens, et fundo Tubi adhaerens (in illo specimine, quod Author ipse confecit.) radium habet 13. digitorum Anglic. fere. Alterum speculum, reflexeos radios prioris recipiens, et ad Lentem Vitream denuo repercutiens, est ovale, et circulo aeneo, intra Tubi cavitatem mobili, insertum. Lens Vitrea radium habet $\frac{1}{12}$ digiti; Metallum quippe colligit solis radios ad distantiam $6\frac{1}{3}$ digitorum, et Lens ocularis ad $\frac{1}{8}$ digitorum fere distantiam ab ejus vertice. Centrum speculi plani locatur in Axe Tubi, ita ut in ipsum perpendicularis, a centro lentis demissa, cum axe angulum rectum constituit, et objecti species a speculo concavo in idem repercussa versus lentis focum reflectatur. Conferendo distantias foci istius a verticibus Lentis et speculi concavi, prodit ratio 1. ad 38; qua indicatur, objecta 38. vicibus circiter in hoc Tubo ampliari.

Similem misi Domino Hugenio, Parisiis nunc degenti, descriptionem. Perplacere ipsi Inventum videtur.[4] Quaenam tua sit de eo sententia, lubenter cognosceremus.

Ne admodum fallor, jam ante Tibi hanc Telescopii novam rationem perscripsi: sed quia literas hac hyeme ad te datas intercidisse putem, cum nullas a Te responsorias obtinuerim, iccirco rem totam repetere paucis volui.[5] Rogo interim, ut properare responsum ne graveris ad Tui observantissimum Oldenburgium. Vale. Dabam Londini d. 18. Mart. 1672

Obsignato jam hoc fasciculo, accepi hoc. d. 18 Martij tuas gratissimas, 9 Martij datas. Necdum cuiquam Anglorum, quod sciam, Cometa ille novus, de quo loqueris, observatus vel visus fuit. De huic, a Te moniti illum observare studebimus.

ADDRESS
Per-Illustri Viro
Domino Johanni Hevelio
Gedanensium Consuli
Amplissimo etc.
Dantzick

TRANSLATION

H. Oldenburg greets the very illustrious Mr. Johannes Hevelius, most worthy Senator of Danzig

Here for you, famous Sir, are the *Philosophical Transactions* for the year 1671, together with a gift from the celebrated Wallis of the third part of his *Mechanica*. We beg you to look kindly on these volumes. I am sending this parcel through the secretary to our embassy to Denmark,[1] who has promised that as soon as he arrives at Copenhagen he will send them on to you at Danzig with the greatest care.

I would gladly know whether his excellency the Lord Marshal was satisfied with the microscope made here and sent to you last autumn,[2] and would be still more glad to learn how near the completion of your *Machina coelestis* may be and what happened as regards astronomy between Mr. Picard and yourself when he visited Hven. We have made very few observations of the heavens here because of a very cloudy winter, nor do we believe the Parisians to have performed many more.

However, two inventions have developed among us here which I am happy to record now. One has been made by Sir Samuel Morland, concerning the clear and distinct propagation of articulate sound to a distance of two or three English miles by means of a stentorophonic tube. [*For the remainder of this passage, see above, pp. 507–8.*]

I sent a similar account to Mr. Huygens, now living in Paris, The invention seems to please him very much.[4] We would be glad to know your opinion of it.

Unless I am much mistaken, I have already written you about this new kind of telescope, but because I suspect my letter addressed to you in the course of this winter may have gone astray, as I received no answer to it from yourself, I decided to repeat the whole briefly for that reason.[5] Meanwhile I beg you to be so good as to hasten your reply to your most devoted Oldenburg. Farewell. London, 18 March 1672.

The package was all sealed up when (on this eighteenth day of March) I received your welcome letter dated 9 March [N.S.]. No Englishman, so far as I know, has as yet seen or observed the comet of which you speak. We will be zealous in observing it after receiving your notice.

ADDRESS
  To the very illustrious
  Mr. Johannes Hevelius,
  Most worthy Senator of Danzig,
  Danzig.

NOTES

Reply to Letter 1915.
1 Thomas Henshaw; see Letter 1907 and its note 1.
2 See Vol. VII, p. 467, and in the present volume, Letters 1723 and 1817.
3 Read: "ob."
4 See Letter 1886.
5 It seems likely that Oldenburg misremembered. Letter 1817 was his last known to Hevelius. There is no indication that he had written since January, nor would it have been surprising (at this time of year) if a reply to a January letter had not yet been received.

1925
Oldenburg to Winthrop
18 March 1671/2

From the original in the Winthrop Papers, XVI, 40
Printed in MHS (1878), 248–49

London March 18. 1671/72

Sir,

Though I received yrs, dated at Hartford Nov. 28. 1671,¹ (wch I did not till March 1. 1671/72), yet I have not yet ye Indian dialogue and the sheet call'd ye Indian A. B. C;² nor doth the Master, yt brought ye letter, remember yt any such books were left wth him at Boston; though he adds, he will look for ym wth care. I cannot but thank you for the particulars contained in yr letter; for wch I have nothing to return at present, but the Transactions of ye last year.

I received yesterday news from Dantzick, written by Monsr Hevelius,³ importing, yt he had seen since March 6. (n.st.) a new Comete; wch had been observ'd there by others March 2. first of all. He intimates, yt he saw it from ye 6th to ye 9th of March (st.n.) (on wch day his letter was written) both mornings and evenings; and on ye 9th he found it, in *brachio dextro Andromedae*.⁴ If this Phaenomenon have appear'd to you also (wch it hath not yet done to us, yt I can learn,) I hope, you will impart to us yr observations by ye next.

There is also seen a new starr *sub capite Cygni*,⁵ wch was first observ'd ye last year, and is now observ'd again wch you will doe well to look after in yr parts. The Discourse of Mr Boyle concerning the Origine and Vertue of Gems is not yet printed off:[6] When it is, you shall not faile, God permitting, of a Copy of it sent you by ye first ship, yt shall goe for yr parts after its publication.

Yr noble friends here, MyLd Brereton, Mr Boyle, Sir Robert Moray etc. returne their affectionat services to you, and continue wth me their earnest request, that you would not delay to put in writing what you know of ye constitution and productions etc. of New England. Though it cannot be perfect, yet it will be very welcome, as much as can be said of it by you. What remains, and what shall be discover'd hereafter, will be the work of those, yt shall survive us. you will pardon this importunity to him, yt by his office must employ himself in constant sollicitations, and yt is somewhat impatient of all delays in matters of present utility; and who thinks also, he may presume to use a great degree of freedome wth a person, whom he knows to be both curious and able, and of a nature prone to pardon the tediousnesse of Sir

Yr faithful friend and servt
Oldenburg

ADDRESS
To his honor'd friend
John Winthrop esquire
Governour of Conectecut
  in New England

NOTES

1 Letter 1834, now missing.
2 John Eliot, *Indian Dialogues* (Cambridge, Mass., 1671) and either *Indian Primer* (Cambridge, Mass., 1669) or *Logick Primer* (Cambridge, Mass., 1672).
3 See Letter 1915.
4 "in the right arm of Andromeda."
5 "under the head of Cygnus."
6 This work (see Letter 1752, note 5) was presented to the Royal Society on 26 June 1672.

1926
Oldenburg to Kirkby
18 March 1671/2

This appears to be the date of a letter acknowledged by the recipient on 15 June 1672 "after a tedious passage." Perhaps it was a repetition of Letter 1864.

1927
Erich Mauritius to Oldenburg
19 March 1671/2
From the original in Royal Society MS. M 1, no. 68

Clarissime Vir,

Tanta voluptate, iam olim, cum in Academiis Tubingensi et Kiloniensi docerem, legi varia aetatis nostrae experimenta, quae Societatis vestrae vere Regiae indefessae diligentiae et Tui calami beneficio debet eruditus orbis, ut saepe doluerim deesse mihi occasionem, qua ostenderem reipsa, multa me, licet ignotum, vobis debere. Cum ne nunc quidem tam beato mihi esse liceat, affectus tamen mei et observantiae erga Illustrem huiusmodi consessum, & publico bono natas animas, testes esse volui has literas, quibus addo Schematismum observati nuper Argentorati Cometae. Eum ut ex Amicorum Argentoratensium literis intelligo, 12 mensis huius stil: vet:, primus, in ista urbe, observavit Julius Reichelt, Mathematum ibidem Professor.[1] Cum 16 Mensis huius die eius rei fama, epistolis aliquot comitata ad pervenisset, una cum ista quam mitto ex aere expressa delineatione, eum obscurae nubeculae instar, hora circiter octava, isto quem numeris et cruce signavi loco, visus sum mihi observare. Heri vero propius ad binas in pede Persei accessisse vidi. 15 Martii aspectum illius nubes prohibuisse Argentorato huc perscribitur. Hoc ipso momento, Excellentissimus Dominus Johan Adamas Schragh[2] S. Caes. Maj. et Imperii, modo ad quaedam supremi huius in Germania Judicis negotia examinanda, inter alios, Legatus amicus meus, mittit mihi legendas ipsius Reichelii literas,

Figur und stand desz Cometen/

Wie solcher den 12. 22. und 13. 23. Martij Anno 1672. nac der Sonnen Niedergang zu Straßburg observirt worden.

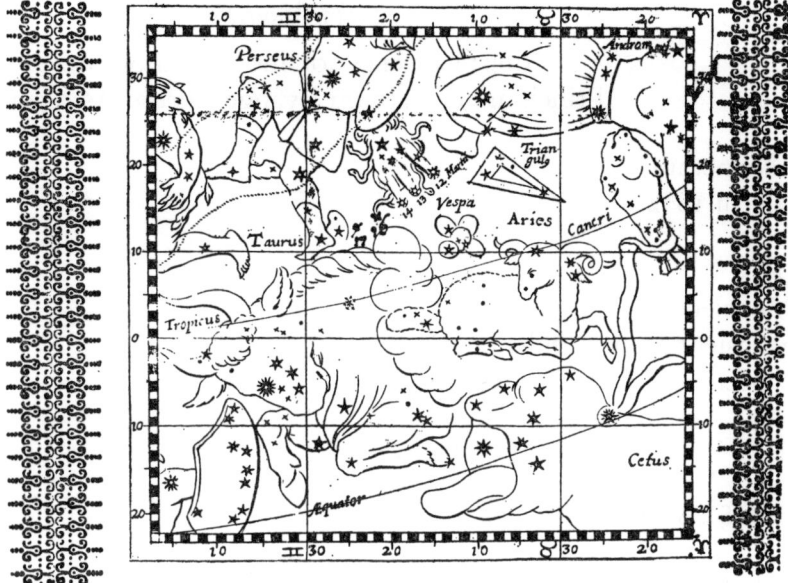

quibus commemorat, inaudisse se iam ante 14 dies ab aliis observatum eundem Cometam, viderique ortum esse in Andromeda. Inspexi illam heri Tubo (sed qui mediocritatem vix attingit, meliorem enim Hamburgo exspecto) ubi exiguae stellae speciem referre videbatur. Alius quidam ex domesticis Vitro perspicillari unico, Danielis de Pierre[3] politurae (qui nunc Augustae Vindelicorum, Weselii gener,[4] caeteris in Germanicis meliora Vitra parat, nisi quod nonnulli P. Anastalium antehac Capuccinum ei comparant)[5] sibi apparere veluti binas stellulas perhibebat, non tamen sine aliqua umbri specie. Sed visu ille alioquin est debili. Acta Collegii Vestri *(Philosophical Transactions)* curavi iam ab anno MDCLXV ut primum edi animadverti ex Anglia Hamburgum, inde Tubingam, primus, ni fallor, in has oras afferri, legique ad usque illa anni LXXI quae cum Augusto pagina 2238. desinunt. Caetera Hamburgo avide exspecto. Quod si in Germania imprimis vicinis huic loco regionibus eius, studiis vestris aliquid prodesse possim meam esse obsequi gloriam putabo. Acidulae in vicinia et thermae sunt multae, inter illas Swalbacenses & Deinacenses,[6] quae posteriores in Wurtembergico agro Lapidis Lazuli et auri aliquid habent, miraque in quartana delirio, morbisque aliis plurimis, praestant, cum noxae minus quam solent plerumque acidulae relinquant, et secure bibantur. Si fortassis aliquando aliquid eius argumenti tractare animus sit, lubens quae eo pertinent, et quae nolueritis alia perscribam. Interim Vale et Fave.

Cultore Tuo
Erico Mauritio

Imp: Camerae nomine Circuli Suevici
Principum et statuum Evangelicorum Assessori.

Spirae Nemetum
d. 19 Martij 1672

ADDRESS
   A Monsieur
      Monsieur Henry Oldenburgh
         Secretaire de la Societe Royale
            a
               Londen

TRANSLATION

Famous Sir,

Long ago when I was teaching at the Universities of Tübingen and Kiel I read with such great pleasure [the accounts of] the various experiments of our age which the world of learning owes to the tireless diligence of your truly Royal Society by means of your pen, that I often lamented my lack of an opportunity by which I might show how much I, a stranger, owe to you on that account. As I do not even yet find myself so happy, yet I wished this letter to testify to my regard and respect towards such an illustrious assembly of the kind this is, and to public-spirited persons; to it I add a sketch of the comet recently observed at Strasbourg. As I gather from the letters of friends there the comet was first seen in that city on the twelfth of this month (Old Style) by Julius Reichelt, Professor of Mathematics there.[1] When a rumor of this event had reached me with accompanying letters, together with the engraved picture of it that I send you, I seemed to observe it at about the eighth hour like a faint little cloud at that place which I have indicated with a cross and numbers. Yesterday I saw that it had approached

Diagram and configuration of the comet
as it was observed on 12/22 and 13/23 March 1672
after sunset in Strasbourg.

[*For the figure, see page 597*]

closer to the two [stars] in the foot of Perseus. Letters from Strasbourg indicate that clouds prohibited [examination of] its appearance on 15 March. At this very moment the very excellent Mr. Johann Adam Schrage, Legate of his Sacred and Imperial Majesty and my friend,[2] who is now (among other things) to investigate some concerns of this supreme judge in Germany, sends me a letter from that same Reichelt to read in which Reichelt records that in two weeks he has not heard of any one else's observing the same comet, and that it was seen to rise in Andromeda. Yesterday I examined it with a telescope—which hardly attained mediocrity, for I expect a better one from Hamburg—in which it seemed to look like a tiny star. Another person in the household, using a single perspective glass polished by Daniel de Pierre[3] (a relative of Wiesel,[4] who now makes at Augsburg the best glasses in Germany, except that some place in the same bracket with him Fr. Anastalius, who was formerly a Capucin),[5] asserted that it appeared to him like two little stars, not without some kind of shadow. But he is pretty dim-sighted. I have seen to it that the transactions of your Society (the *Philosophical Transactions*) from 1665 onwards, when I first came across their publication, are brought from England via Hamburg and thence to Tübingen, being the first in these parts to do so if I am not mistaken; and I have read them up to the year 1671, when from August [onwards] p. 2238 they are lacking. I am eagerly awaiting the rest from Hamburg. If I can furnish anything [relevant to] your studies from Germany and especially from the parts adjacent to this place I shall think myself covered in glory. There are many spas and hot springs in the neighborhood, among them those of Swabia and Deinach,[6] which latter ones (in the Württemberg district) have something of gold and lapis lazuli in them and work wonders in quartan fevers and many other complaints; they may be drunk without risk as they leave fewer harmful after effects than many spas do. If, perhaps, you would like something on this subject some time, I will gladly write what is relevant and you cannot have from elsewhere. Meanwhile, farewell and cherish

Your devoted
Erich Mauritius
Assessor of the Imperial Chamber, in the name of the
Princes and Spiritual States of the Swabian Circle

Speyer, 19 March 1672.

NOTES

This letter was not received until 15 April.

Erich Mauritius (1631–91; cf. Vol. VII, p. 170, note 1) took his doctorate at Tübingen in 1654 after studies at a number of German universities. He also traveled extensively otherwise. He settled down to teach public law at Heidelberg for a while, and was professor at the University of Kiel from 1665. In 1672 he went as Assessor to the Imperial Court at Speyer. He wrote voluminously on legal topics.

1 Julius Reichelt (1637–1719), a native of Strasbourg, became a teacher of mathematics there from 1667; he was also learned in ancient numismatics.
2 Johann Adam Schrage (?1617–87) was employed as a councilor and legal adviser by several heads of state in Germany, as well as the Free City of Strasbourg, and sent on a number of diplomatic missions.
3 Daniel de Pierre was an Augsburg optical-instrument maker, son-in-law to Johannes Wiesel. He was presumably still living. Some correspondence of his with Hevelius is extant. The reference to the instrument is obscure. What may be meant is that it had a single (inverting) eye lens instead of the multilens erecting eyepieces normal in Weisel/Schyrlaeus telescopes.
4 Johannes Wiesel (b. *c.* 1583 and alive in 1660 at the age of 77), Imperial Optician at Augsburg, was a famous glassworker. In association with Schyrlaeus he had made the first Keplerian telescopes.
5 The man who must be meant here is Anton Maria Schyrlaeus (1597–1660), called "da Rheita" after the Capucin house in Bohemia in which he served. He died at Ravenna, hence the Italian form of his name. He was effectively the originator of the Keplerian telescope (see *Oculus Enoch et Eliae*, Antwerp, 1645).
6 Deinach is a very small spa in the valley of the Ens, in the northern Black Forest west of Stuttgart.

1927a

The Comet of March 1671/2

? Enclosure with Letter 1927

From the original in Royal Society Letter Book V, 190–91

Observationes Cometae filares Argentorati habitae

Ao 1672 d. $\frac{12}{22}$ Martii prior extensio fili transibat lucidam Plejadum *a* Cometam et lucidam pedis australis Andromedae *b*.

posterior Cometam, Algol *c* et eductionem pedis sinistri Persei *d*.

Corpus Cometicum aequabat fixas quartae magnitudinis.

Cauda surgebat ad Gorgoneam secundam *e*.[1]

$\frac{13}{23}$ Martii in priori observatione eandem fere lineam rectam exhibebant lucida Plejadum *a* Cometa et lucida pedis australis Andromedae *b*. Cometae tamen recessus versus septentrionem oculis notari satis poterat.

In posteriori in eandem incidebant rectam Cometa, Algol *c* et Genib *f*.

Cauda ad Gorgoneam tertiam *g* defecerat.

$\frac{14}{24}$ Martii prius extensum filum ducebatur per lucidam pedis australis Andromedae *b* Cometam et Hyadem ad oculum bovum *h*.

secundo extensum pervadebat Cometam, Algol *c* et stellam in sinistro humero Persei *i*

Cauda et lumine et magnitudine aliquantum defecerat.

$\frac{15}{25}$ Martii propter nubes densiores et copiosas phaenomenon observari non poterat

$\frac{16}{26}$ Martii primum notabantur in eadem recta stella in imo pede dextro Persei sequens *k*, praecedens *l* et Cometa.

deinde recta occurrebant duarum in capite Erichthonii[2] australiae *m*, stella juxta dextrum genu Persei *n* et Cometa.

$\frac{17}{72}$ Martii prima vice filum extendebatur per haedorum[3] sequentem *o* stellam ad tibiam dextram Persei *p* et Cometam.

secunda vice extensum determinabat lucidam Plejadum *a* Cometam et stellam in latere dextro Persei *q*.

Cauda terminabatur ad stellam sextae magnitudinis *r*.

$\frac{18}{28}$ Martii Cometa adeo jungabatur stellae in imo pede dextro Persei praecedenti *l*, et in filari extensione distingui non posset. Erat autem illa et occidentalia cometa et meridionalia; Cauda dirigebatur per eandem *l*.

TRANSLATION

Thread observations of the Comet made at Strasbourg

[For star map, see page 600]

$\frac{12}{22}$ March 1672 On first stretching the thread it passed through *a*, the bright star in the Pleiades, the comet, and the bright star in the southern foot of Andromeda, *b*.

Secondly, the comet, the star *c* Algol, and the extension of the left foot of Perseus, *d*.

The body of the comet was equal to a star of the fourth magnitude; the tail pointed up to *e*, the second star of the Gorgon.[1]

$\frac{13}{23}$ March. At the first observation *a*, the bright star in the Pleiades, the comet, and *b* the bright star in the southern foot of Andromeda show almost the same straight line. Yet the comet's backward motion towards the north was pretty obvious to the eye.

In the later observation the comet, Algol *c*, and Genib *f* fell on the same straight line. The tail had moved towards *g*, the third star of the Gorgon.

$\frac{14}{24}$ March. The first line of the thread passed through *b*, the bright star in the southern foot of Andromeda, the comet, and *h* in the Hyades at the eye of Taurus. On a second stretching it passed through the comet, Algol *c*, and *i*, the star in the left shoulder of Perseus. The tail had lost a little in brilliance and size.

$\frac{15}{25}$ March. It was not possible to observe the phenomenon because of numerous thick clouds.

$\frac{16}{26}$ March. At first, the star *k* at the bottom of Perseus' right foot leading, followed by the star *l* and the comet, were observed in the same straight line.

Secondly, the line met the southern star of the two in the head of Erichthonius,[2] *m*, the star by Perseus' right knee *n*, and the comet.

$\frac{17}{27}$ March. The first time the thread was stretched it went through the star *o* of Haedus[3] to *p* in the right tibia of Perseus and the comet.

The second time it was stretched it marked out *a*, the bright star in the Pleiades, the comet, and *q* the star in the right side of Perseus.

The tail ended at the sixth-magnitude star *r*.

$\frac{18}{28}$ March. The comet was so close to the star by *l* at the bottom of Perseus' right foot that in stretching the thread it could not be distinguished from it. But the comet was west and south of the star; the tail was directed through the same star *l*.

NOTES

There are three printed star maps showing the positions of the comet associated with this letter. That bound with the original letter itself, showing printed positions for 12 and 13 March only, is clearly not that sent by Mauritius. Of the two maps in the Letter Book, one (reproduced above, in Letter 1927) bears Mauritius's inked-in positions for 16 and 17 March, as well as the printed positions for the previous days, presumably by Reichelt. The third map, reproduced above, is signed by Reichelt and has printed positions up to 17 March; this again is not the map mentioned by Mauritius.

However, we have inserted this third map here since, whatever its source, it has long been associated with this letter. The manuscript notes of observations probably come from Reichelt. There is a similar paper in the *Œuvres Complètes*, VII, p. 162, but its map is a hand-drawn copy.

The observations were made by stretching a thread—either between the fingers or on a simple support—so that when held before the eye it fell on the comet and two easily recognizable stars. By tracing two such lines, nearly at right angles, the comet's position was defined. To make the positions clearer we have redrawn them, using a modern atlas to plot the reference stars, in the figure below.

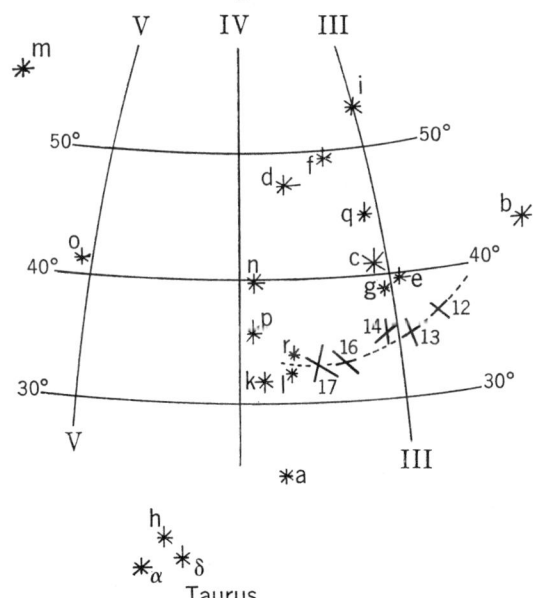

The Stars Denoted

a	=	η Tauri (Alcyone)	f = α Persei
b	=	γ Andromedae	g = ρν Persei
h	=	ε Tauri	i = γ Persei
m	=	δ Aurigae	k = ζ Persei
o	=	η Aurigae	l = ο Persei
			n = ε Persei
c	=	β Persei (Algol)	p = ξ Persei
d	=	δ Persei	q = κ Persei
e	=	π Persei	r = 40 Persei

The dotted line represents approximately the possible path of the comet; on this the intersections of the sighting strings with their respective dates are indicated. The position for 14/24 March was incorrectly designated; probably α Tauri (Aldebaran) or δ Tauri was chosen as the reference star, for the latter especially would put the comet back on the curve. Similarly, the vaguely defined position for 18/28 March causes an unlikely southward bend (which may be seen in the printed figures).

1 This old constellation is now included in Perseus.
2 This constellation was then more commonly and is now invariably known as Auriga (The Waggoner, or Charioteer).
3 Now included in Auriga.

1928

Newton to Oldenburg

19 March 1671/2

Printed in Newton, *Correspondence*, I, 121–22, from the original in Royal Society MS. N 1, no. 63

In this reply to Letter 1922 Newton comments upon the state of the metal mirror in the telescope sent to the Society, and also upon his method of calculating its magnification. He gives further details of the new telescope being constructed (see Letter 1923), which he authorizes Oldenburg to print; they appeared in *Phil. Trans.*, no 81 (25 March 1672), 4009–10. He warns Oldenburg that his "answer to Mr Hooks observations" will not be ready until at least the next month.

1929

Lister to Oldenburg

19 March 1671/2

From the original in Royal Society MS. L 5, no. 44

Sir,

According to your desire & my owne inclination I have perused ye Papers of Signore *Malpighi*, & indeed not without great satisfaction. I must needs say in general, yt I long to see this Peice published wth

Scheames, wch would undoubtedly render it more intelligible; it being very hard to comprehend some Notions without ym, especially if such Notions were taken by ye assistance of Glasses, as I am persuaded those of ye *Utriculj, perforatarum fibrarum fasciculi, spirales fistulae, sive Tracheae*[1] etc. were. but in detail, I am very glad to meet here, wth an ample Confirmation of those Vessells, wch I call ye Veines of Plants & this authour *peculiare vas lactiferum*.[2] About wch I agree wth him yt they are to be found in ye *Cortex & medulla* of plants. 2. yt this sort of vessell is in every *species* of plant. 3. I add, yt there are noe other Vessells (yt may properly be soe called) besides these Milky-Veines. 4. Again yt these Veines hold ye only vital juices of plants, wch I shall confirme by divers reasons & experiments. But more of this, when I shall endeavour to acquit my selfe of ye Commands of ye R. Society.

Before I conclude, I cannot but take notice yt our authour designes a particular discourse concerning Vegetable Excrescencies & yt he is dissatisfyed & doubtfull concerning *plantigenous* Animals, wch was Aristotle's opinion of old (v. lib. 1. de plantis)[3] & has lately been countenanced by ye promised Observations of Signore Redi.[4] The whole series of this authour's observations about this particular are very faithfull & tru.

This is a busie time wth me, & I can only add at present my hearty acknowledgement for this favour I am

Your most humble servant
Martin Lister

Yorke March 19th 1671
From my house in Stone-gate

ADDRESS
    These
For my very honourd friend
    Henry Oldenburg Esq
at his house in ye Palmal
        London

NOTES

Reply to Letter 1913.
1 "Little bags, bundles of perforated fibres, spiral tubes or trachea."
2 "a special vessel for milky fluid."
3 The *De plantis* is now held to have been written in the first century B.C. by Nicholas of Damascus. At 816a, line 22, there is a reference to animals "which grow from trees" (*quae ex arboribus crescant*).

4 See Malpighi, *Opera omnia*, p. 10: he believed that worms generated in galls, etc., did not arise from the host plant but from an insect-deposited egg. Redi's work on plant parasitism appears not to have been published.

1930
Dodington to Oldenburg
21 March 1671/2
From the copy in Royal Society MS. D 1, no. 27

Venice March ult. 1672 [N.S.]

Sr

Hee desires an accompt of the Trade which is driven between this Cittie and the adjoyning Countrys of Germany Viz. Havonia,[1] Croatia, Styria, Carynthia, Tyrol, Austria, Hongaria &c &c.

First as to the persons who manage this Trade, they are worthy Germans. The Italians concer[n]ing themselfes but little therein, or indeed in any Trade, only some few of them, I call them few, in respect of the great multitude of others, who are dispersed up and down all over Italy, whereas there are not many of these natives who either doe or desire to live out of their owne Country, and in it they are too vicious to be trusted, or too soft to sett themselfes a worke. They are then mostly High and Low Dutch who carry on this Trade.

Secondly as to [the] manner of it. The Conveiance or Transportation, is that, which is the great impediment to the Trade, were this cheaper, and securer, I assure you, t'would render it a very considerable Trade indeed. But the Carriage or Conveiance, is either by Horses and Mules, or by waggons: which are drawn by lusty German Horses, or by strong bigg-bon[e]d oxen. The wayes are rough, not very bad and dangerous, only somtimes the robbers meet them, somtimes Extreamitie of rayne, Frost or the like, all which contribute to encrease the Charge of Transportation, which in Truth is [the] mayn thing in all Commerce, and which all princes ought to make cheape and secure, that intend to incourage Trade. Thirdly the Commodities carried hence thither are as followeth, wax, well whited, for the use of Churches and great men's palaces, refin'd sugars, all Kind of druggs, wrought & Raw Silkes of all sorts. velvets, Tabbies, sattins, damasks, Broccadoes, some of wch at 50f.[2] sterling ye yard & more; There are also sent great store of Oyles, Almonds, Figgs. They also send hence some of our English fish as Pilchoords, salmon, Red & white herrings into Germany, & more would be sent, but the state deales most rigorously in Exacting a Custom on it, of wch. more towards the end of my letter.

Some Currants which with them are only imployed, in Apothecarries shopps; all sort of spice, which generally comes from England & Holland hither: silke stockens, Cottons wrought and Raw: what is besides these is of small moment, such as looking and drinking Glasses, some oringes, Raysins and the like in no great quantitie.

Lastly the Commodities which come thence are Principally linnen Cloth of all sorts, Course and fine: Thread, steele and Iron in Grosse and wrought, that is to say of this last sort, Lockes, Keyes, nayles, Hinges, Bitts, Edgetools, Casements & these are hence vended all over Italy, Sicily, Zant and the Levant. when Lead also beares as good price, (as now it is at 60 ducates) they can afford to bring it: They bring moreover From those Countries, all kinds of Mettalls, Brasse, Copper and quicksilver. They bring thence, Pitch, Tarr, Turpentine, Deal Boards, in abundance and all sorts of wood for building, but these come downe by Rivers, upon great Floods, in Huge Rafts compacted together, with a man or two to conduct each parcell, some parcells consisting of 20000 Boards & thirty or 40 of these parcells comeing together. These, there are oftentimes passengers, Travellers, nay Coaches which are Transported on these Rafts (here they call them Satyraes) and they goe at least 60 miles per diem & somtimes 70, 80 & 100, upon great Floods.

I must observe to you, In goeing hence to Vienna, there is a necessity of passing by Inspruch, which stands on a River, where there are good lusty Boats, and these serve to conveigh both goods and passengers from thither, but this to, is only in the spring and winter, for in the summer, the waters are too low and too slow.[3] There are no boates can passe at any time on ye Rivers of Germany which fall into this sea, untill they come within 50 miles or thereabouts of the sea, in regard of the frequent indeed continual precipices and Rocks, though loose wood for fuel, Cutts and lengths fo[r] buildings and the Rafts premised, venture securely, when the floods serve, else not. I have seene a River covered wth such wood some miles together, so as you could see no water, and there they stay expecting a good Tyde. The loose wood is all marked, so as every one knowes his owne, & it is mostly deale that is firr and Pine.

But to turne to Trad[e]s. most of the beefe they eat here comes from Hungary, and really it is not much inferior to our renowned English Beefe. But it is somthing dearer in regard of the great Excise it pays, howbeit it is allways sold at about threepence the pound, only wee have but 12 ounces to ye pound. The Prince takes a full moyety or more, as his duety, besides the Head and Hyde.

Germany also sends hither aboundance of Boxes, Rattles, Hobbyhorses and such like small wares, skins Raw and dressd, Furr viz squirrel skins, Fitchets, Vares,[4] and the like. These small wares are dispersed all over Italy, Sicilly, Smyrna Con[stantino]ple Aleppo &c.

To tell you which Trade hath the Ballance I dare not pretende to so much Exactnesse, But I guesse, by the great quantitie of Hongars which Pass here, that Venice sends more In Value, though of lesse Bulk, to Germany, than Germanie doth to Venice. Besides Venice without doubt makes notable advantages by this Trade, else they would never encourage it, as they doe, for the German merchant have a Kind of a style yard[5] here or house called the Fontica, where all goods are laden and unladen, that come or goe from or to Germany, and this house or Guild, enjoyes very considerable priviledges. I will name one, when a Ball of goods is made up to be exported, the Merchant goes to the Custome house, and enters them, then takes a wayfer and seales them, if now a sercher will seize and open such Pack, he may. But he must first deposite ye value of the Goods. if the Goods are according to the Entry, the sercher looseth his money, If they are not, the prince gaynes one halfe and the sercher ¼ the other ¼ goes to a certain Hospitale. But there are many other Franchises belonging to this house and the society of those Inland Traders, which I forbeare to mention. I will observe one thing more to you in the Trade of this Cyttie, The Port is a free port, as to all goods which are imported, Except Fish, which comes most if not all from England, so as no goods pay any Custome, which are brought in here, Except as before, But all pay a Custome going out.

I remember Ferrante Imperato in this 2d Edition fol. 681. mentions the Tarantula and his effects, but he only toucheth on it and pace tanti viri[6] somwhat contradictoraly to himselfe, for in the beginning of his Paragraph he saith[7] they have their phalangi sottera intanati; e nella boccadelle lor tane vi si vede intessimento di bianca e spessa tela; and six lines after, non tessono tele; which is quite contrary; but 'tis possible his meaning is, they make no netts to hunt or Ketch flyes as other spiders, but sure they make phalangia, by all observations, I referr the Elucidation of it to what Dr Cornelio will send you shortly from Naples, by my hand, which is ambitious to Contribute to the service of the R. Society in what ever remote degree.

I will ere long send you more Exact information of the Aponensian Bathes, when I have seen them a second time and so with all due observance I rest Honed. Sr.

your most humble servant
John Dodington

NOTES

The original of this letter was almost certainly sent to Joseph Williamson, who is presumably the "Hee" opening the copy, though we have not found the original among the State Papers. Dodington, as Resident at Venice, was much concerned with commercial matters on which, of course, he reported directly to the authorities; at the moment he was negotiating about the Zante currant trade.

1 Copyist's error for "Slavonia."
2 Florins.
3 What is meant is that goods went up the Trent valley, over the Brenner Pass, and from Innsbruck down the Inn and the Danube to Vienna.
4 Both words signify an animal of the weasel-stoat-polecat group—that is, possibly, ermine.
5 Like the Steelyard in London.
6 "with all respect to so great a man."
7 See Ferrante Imperato, *Historia naturale* (Venice, 1672), p. 681. Dodington is hardly fair to his author, who writes that the species of phalangids called Tarantula are named after the district of Taranto, that they are a kind of large spider and that (as quoted here) "they remain in a den underground; and thick, white webs may be seen woven at the mouths of their dens," in such a way as not to impede the creature's passage. The bite of the first species, he goes on, causes no pain nor harm; but there is another species, called *Solofizzi*, larger, black, and more poisonous, whose bite provokes a swelling; "they do not weave webs," but live in dens underground. Sufferers are cured by the fatigue and sweating caused by dancing "to a tune fitting to the emotion of the infection."
8 See Letter 1919.

1931
De Graaf to Oldenburg
21 March 1671/2
From the original in Royal Society MS. G, no. 9

Doctissime Oldenburgi,

Literis Tuis 16 Octob. ad me datis citius responsissem nisi tractatum meum de Mulierum organis etc.¹ cuius exemplar per D. Hallingk Legati nostri secretarium² ad Te mitto, meis adjungere voluissem. misissem quoque (nisi futuri belli rumor omnes transmittendi occasiones abstulisset)³ alterum exemplar pro D. D. Clarkio una cum vesiculis seminariis a me praeparatis, ex quibus motum seminis meae opinioni conformem luce clarius conspexisset et adhuc uti spero occasione data conspiciet. Causam cur tractatum meum de succo pancreatico⁴ non acceperis investigare non potui, sed iacturam illam parvifaciendam sentio dummodo ab alliis tractatum illum acceperis. quid de hoc tractatu meo senties avide expectabo; nec dubito quin quantum Kerckringius a meis dissentiat satis cognosces.⁵ Vale vir Doctissime et D. D. Clarkium meo nomine plurimum saluta atque conatus meos aequi bonique consule.

Vester Humillimus
R De Graaf

Raptim Delphis 31 martii 1672 [N.S.]

professor Diemerbroeck misit ante triduum ultraiecto ad me Anatomiam suam corporis humani in duo volumina reductam in 4to⁶

ADDRESS
  A Monsieur
  Monsieur Oldenburg
  A Londres

TRANSLATION

Most learned Oldenburg!

I should have replied more quickly to your letter of 16 October, except that I wished to add to my answer my treatise *De mulierum organis*, etc.,[1] of which I send you a copy by Mr. Hallingk, secretary to our Ambassador.[2] I should also have sent another copy for the learned Mr. Clarke, together with the seminal vesicles prepared by myself (from which it ought to appear clearer than daylight that the movement of the semen does conform to my opinion and, as I hope, when opportunity serves may yet appear [to him]), if the talk of a coming war had not obstructed all opportunities for sending them.[3] I could not investigate the reason for your not receiving my treatise on the pancreatic juice,[4] but I attach little importance to its loss so long as you obtain that treatise from others. I eagerly await your idea of this treatise of mine, and I don't doubt that you have pretty good knowledge of the extent to which Kerckring disagrees with my notions.[5] Farewell, learned Sir; greet the learned Mr. Clarke many times in my name, and think well of my endeavors.

Your very humble
R. De Graaf

Delft, in haste, 31 March 1672 [N.S.]

Three days ago Professor Diermerbroek sent me from Utrecht his *Anatomy of the Human Body* reduced to two quarto volumes.[6]

ADDRESS
To Mr. Oldenburg,
London

NOTES

Reply to Letter 1801 (which is lost).
1 This is his *De mulierum organis generationi inservientibus tractatus novus* (Leiden, 1672). Compare Letter 1729, note 1.
2 The family of Dordrecht spelled its name usually as "Hallincg" at this time. A "Mynheer Halling" was secretary to the Dutch Deputies to the English crown and elected to stay in England when the Deputies departed early in August, as a supporter of the Prince of Orange against the States General (*C.S.P.D.* 6 Aug. 1672, from an anonymous letter to Lord Arlington), but it is impossible to identify which member of the family this was.
3 On 12 March 1672 an English fleet under Sir Robert Holmes attacked a Dutch merchant convoy in the Channel; this was the opening of the Third Dutch War.
4 See Letter 1729.
5 In his *Anthropogeniae ichnographia*; see Letter 1694, note 5.

6 Isbrand de Diermerbroeck (1609–74) had been Professor of Anatomy and Medicine at Utrecht since 1649. His *Anatome corporis humanae* (Utrecht, 1672) proved an enormously popular work—it was rendered into English in 1689.

1932
Mauritius to Oldenburg
22 March 1671/2

Mentioned in Oldenburg's reply, Letter 1963.

1933
Oldenburg to Newton
23 March 1671/2

From the memorandum in Royal Society MS. N 1, no. 36
Printed in Newton, *Correspondence*, I, 123, note 7

Rec March. 20. 71.
Answ. March 23. comm. ye Comet and star sub cap. Cygni from Hevel.

NOTE

Reply to Letter 1928.

1934
Oldenburg to Vogel
23 March 1671/2
From the memorandum in Royal Society MS. F 1, no. 35

Acc. d. 28 Febr. 1671/2
Resp. d. 23 Mart...
Retuli Fogelio de tuba Stentorophonica, de Newtoni Telescopio Novo, de Morisono de Plantis. Petii, ut mittat Rawolfii Itinerarium,[1] et Photonomicam Tassii.[2] Promisi me scripturum ad viros illos doctos nominatos in hac epistola. Dixi, nos curare transcribi vitam Galilaei, nil nobis constare de scriptis Bot. Hovi, nec de notis Pocockii in G. ab Horto.

TRANSLATION

Received 28 February 1671/2.
Answered on 23 March...
I reported to Vogel on the stentorophonic trumpet, the new Newtonian telescope, on Morison's [book] on plants; I asked him to send Rauwolff's *Itinerary*[1] and the *Photonomics* of Tasse.[2] I promised that I would write to the learned men named in this letter. I said that we were taking steps to get the life of Galileo transcribed, that nothing was known to us of How's botanical writings nor of Pocock's notes on Garcia d'Orta.

NOTES

Reply to Letter 1885.
1 Leonhard Rauwolff, *Aigentliche Beschreibung der Raisz... in die Morgenlander* (Laugingen, 1582–83); this is the first complete edition, but there were many reprints of this account of botanical travels including one at Leipzig in 1659; an English version was published in 1683.
2 See Letter 1885, note 1.

1935
Oldenburg to Heinrich Sivers
23 March 1671/2

From the memorandum in Royal Society MS. F 1, no. 35

... Eodem tempore scripsi ad Siferum de deproperanda Phoronomica Jungii ...

TRANSLATION

... At the same time I wrote to Sivers about pressing on quickly with Jungius' *Phoranomica* ...

NOTE

This sentence is interposed in the memorandum composing Letter 1934. Sivers has often been mentioned in the correspondence between Oldenburg and Vogel as the assiduous editor of Jungius.

1936
Malpighi to Oldenburg
26 March 1672

From the original in Royal Society Malpighi Letters, no. 14
Printed in *Opera omnia*, II, *De formatione pulli in ovo*, pp. 15–16

Praeclarissimo et eruditissimo Viro
Domino Henrico Oldenburg Regiae Societatis Anglicanae Secretario
Marcellus Malpighius S.P.

Regiae Societatis humanitati tuisque officiis ita me obstrictum profiteor, ut quibus exponam non occurrat: desiderium enim meum Naturae misteria indagandi, transmissis dessertatiunculis exaratum, hilari animo adeo recepistis, et ulteriora meis studiis praesidia adeo parata voluistis, ut ad novos labores alacriter capescendos exciter. Nec miror diversas etiam calcantibus semitas eadem omnino occurrere; non leve tamen solamen esset si meditationes meae, et observata, aliorumque labores et inventa in idem concurrerent. Quamobrem plantarum indaginem ineuntis veris beneficio, iuxta infirmam mei corporis constitutionem, iterum assumam, ut inventa confirmem, et dubia (si licebit) dilucidiora reddam.[1] Icones pariter, pro ut mea fert ruditas, ad faciliorem intelligentiam paratas servabo; ut additis, quae ad breviorem singulorum historiam faciunt, non admodum dissimilem a transmissa epistola plantarum anatomicam exarationem compaginem, quae ad te transmissa, Regiae Societatis arbitrio luce fruetur. Ovorum pariter incubatorum observationes aestivo tempore iterum repetam, ut in re tam obscura minus dubie incedam, et allantoidis perquisitionem, cuius indicia in pullis columbinis et gallinaceis mihi visus sum deprehendisse, ulteriori disquisitione prosequi valeam;[2] Reliqua pariter, quae galli spermaticas partes et gallinarum uterum respiciunt, si opportuna censebuntur, adaucta dissertatione in historiolam congesta vestras iterum subibunt manus, ut vel suppressa iaceant, vel sub tanto praesidio vivant.

In detegendis Naturae arcanis compendiariam viam non omnibus, & mihi praesertim, opportunum esse censeo; difficilimum namque est immenso fere observationum penu Naturae misteria retexere, facilimum vero paucis observatis aequivoca, et falsa concludere. Non deero tamen, ea quae temporum opportunitas meaque patietur tenuitas, labore prosequi, ut vobis saltem, quibus propitia sorte mei arrident conatus, debitae servitutis officia perpetuo exhibeam. Vale, Vir Clarissime, et tui Sociorumque amorem mihi perpetuare ne desinas. Dabam Bononiae Die quinta Aprilis 1672

TRANSLATION

Marcello Malpighi sends many greetings to the very famous and learned Mr. Henry Oldenburg, Secretary of the English Royal Society

I find myself with such a deep obligation on account of the Royal Society's kindness and your own courtesies that I lack words in which to express it. For you have welcomed my desire to investigate nature's mysteries, expressed in the little treatises I sent to you, with such enthusiasm and intend to have such considerable further assistance ready for my studies that I am inspired to undertake new labors cheerfully. And I am not surprised that those who follow different paths should nevertheless come across exactly the same things, yet it would be no small recompense if my reflections and observations should end with the same results as the labors and discoveries of others. For that reason, when the beginning of spring and the infirm state of my body allow it, I shall again undertake the investigation of plants so that I may confirm my discoveries and (if I can) render the doubtful points clearer.¹ I shall likewise make drawings ready, as well as my rude skill will serve me, for easier understanding, so that with the added matter (which amounts to a brief account of particular details) I may compose a paper on the anatomy of plants not very dissimilar from the letter that was sent, which, when it has been submitted to you, may be published at the Royal Society's discretion. I shall likewise repeat the observations of incubated eggs in the summer so that I may proceed less doubtfully in a subject of such great obscurity, and be able to continue by a further inquiry the careful examination of the allantois, indications of which I seemed to have discovered in the chicks of doves and fowls.² Likewise I shall again place in your hands the remaining materials which are concerned with the spermatic parts of the cock and the uterus of the hen, if that shall be judged appropriate, for I have compressed an enlarged discussion into a brief account, so that they either remain suppressed or flourish under such high protection.

I believe that in the discovery of the secrets of nature short cuts are not suitable for everyone and not for myself in particular, for it is very difficult to unravel nature's mysteries from a vast stock of observations and very easy to come to misleading conclusions from a few. Yet I shall not be lacking in industry to follow up those matters which opportunity of time and my own feeble powers permit me [to tackle], so that I may at least continually present you, whom a propitious fate has caused to bless my endeavors, with the courtesies proper to obligation. Farewell, famous Sir, and do not cease to devote to me the affection of yourself and your Fellows.

Bologna, 5 April 1672 [N.S.]

NOTES

Reply to Letter 1908.
1 This further investigation led to the writing and illustration of *Anatome plantarum*; see Letter 1912, note 3.
2 *De ovo incubato observationes*, Malpighi's second embryological study, was published with the *Anatome plantarum*, Part I (London, 1675). The further researches mentioned here were not communicated to the Royal Society.

1937
Newton to Oldenburg
26 March 1672

Printed in Newton, *Correspondence*, I, 123–25, from the original in CUL MS. Add. 3976, no. 2

In reply to Letter 1933, Newton reports having seen the comet, mistaking it for a star. He reports on his comparison of the new reflector with a six-foot refractor, makes further suggestions for improvement, and gives a table of apertures and "charges, or diameters of the spheres on wch the convex superficies of the eye glasses are to be ground." The letter was printed in *Phil. Trans.*, no. 82 (22 April 1672) 4032–34.

1938
Jan Swammerdam to Oldenburg
26 March 1672

From the original in Royal Society MS. S 1, no. 116

A Amst. le 5 d'Avril 1672 [N.S.]

Monsieur,

Le soin que Vous prites de l'affaire dont Monsieur Witsen vous avoit parlé, m'a donné le coeur á me servir de la permission que vous m'avez donnée de vous escrire;[1] si est ce que je vous prie instamment de presenter cette feuille de ma part á la Societé Royalle; et de me vouloir aussi donner quelque adresse, pour vous envoyer en seureté l'admirable matrice, et les autres parties du corps humain, preparees, dont je parle dans la feuille.[2] Cependant que j'attens que vous me fassiez l'honneur de faire reponse, je me recommande tres ardamment dans vostre bonne grace, en vous priant encore une fois, de me recommander à la Societé R., de laquelle je demeure Monsieur

le treshumble serviteur
Johannes Swammerdam

Je demeure A Amsterdam
Op de Verwers Graht.

P.S.

Mons. Witsen m'a prié de vous faire scavoir que le vaisseau dans la quelle le livre des Indes fut envoyè vers vous ayant des ja este devant la Tamise s'en retournast à cause qu'il appercent le rumeur de la guerre. Apres donc que vous m'aurez fait l'Honneur d'escrire par quelle vois je vous dois envoyer les pieces anatomiques, il vous envoyera au mesme temps ce livre des Indes orientales, que vous desirez.

TRANSLATION

Amsterdam, 5 April 1672 [N.S.]

Sir,

The care which you took over the business about which Mr. Witsen had spoken to you has given me courage to avail myself of the permission you gave me to write to you.[1] This is to beg you earnestly to present this sheet to the Royal Society on my behalf, and also to be kind enough to give me an address for sending to you safely the human uterus and the other preparations of parts of the human body spoken of in this sheet.[2] While waiting until you honor me with a reply I commend myself warmly to your kind favor, begging you once more to commend me to the Royal Society, of which I remain, Sir,

the very humble servant
Johannes Swammerdam

I live in Amsterdam on the Verwers Gracht.

P.S. Mr. Witsen has asked me to let you know that the ship on board which the book on the Indies was sent to you, being already at the mouth of the Thames, turned back because they heard rumors of war. After, therefore, you have honored me by telling me the route by which to send the anatomical specimens he will at the same time send you this book on the East Indies that you wish for.

NOTES

Jan Swammerdam (1637–80) derived his name from a village on the Old Rhine; his father was an apothecary in Amsterdam. In 1661 he began the study of medicine at Leiden, where he met Steno and De Graaf. He was already a keen anatomist and skilled dissector. After two years he moved to Saumur, where he discovered the valves in the lymphatic vessels, and also spent some time in Paris where he was befriended by Thevenot. He returned to Amsterdam in 1665 and took his degree at Leiden in 1667, his thesis being the work on respiration mentioned before. Later in life he became obsessed with religion.

1 See Letter 1839; evidently correspondence has been lost.
2 This was the printed sheet: *Illustrissimae ... Regiae Societati Londini ... hoc anatomici*

sui studii specimen et futuri operis quendam quasi prodromum ... *dedicat* ... *J.S.* [n.p., n.d., B.M. pressmark 748 g 10(2)]. Oldenburg presented it to the Royal Society on 4 April. At some time in May 1672 Swammerdam also sent to the Royal Society to whom it was dedicated his book, *Miraculum naturae, sive uteri muliebris fabrica* (Leiden, 1672), which Oldenburg presented to the meeting of 12 June. The first two plates in this little volume are identical with those of the earlier sheet; the third and last plate had been issued about a year before with a dedication to the Dr. Tulp immortalized by Rembrandt (see the Introduction, p. xxvii). Finally, Swammerdam sent specimens injected and prepared in his special way (see Grew, *Musaeum*, p. 8), which were presented on 18 December 1672—these survived in the British Museum until at least 1785. Swammerdam was exceedingly anxious to assert his priority in these anatomical researches—begun with Johann van Horne (Vol. IV, p. 369, note 24) in 1667—over his friend De Graaf.

1939
Oldenburg to Newton
c. 26 March 1672

Newton's Letter 1941 is in reply to one by Oldenburg received since the writing of Letter 1937.

1940
Charas to Oldenburg
28 March 1672

From the original in Royal Society MS. C 1, no. 101

A paris Le 7e Avril 1672 [N.S.]

Monsieur

Dans l'incertitude où je suis si Vous aurez encore receu quelque Exemplaire de mon dernier Livre sur les Viperes,[1] n'ayant encore aucun avis de reception des Examplaires que j'ay envoyez par diverses Voyes. J'ay profité Volontiers de La bonne commodité de Monsieur Couck gentilhomme Anglois[2] & L'ay pris de Vous faire rendre Un Exemplaire nouveau que je Luy ay remie, afin que d'une façon ou dautre quelque Exemplaire Vous soit rendu. Cependant, Monsieur, Je Vous suis tres-redevable de la part que Vous avez cy devant prise à mes interests et Lhonneur que Vous avez procuré à mes escrits dans vostre celebre Compagnie Comme aussi, une tesmoignage particuliere et bienvueillance que Vous m'avez cy devant accordez fort obligeamment. Je prens la liberté, Monsieur, de Vous en demander la continuation, & de Vous prier de me Vouloir procurer la Suspension des Jugemens de Vostre Societé Royale sur le sujet de mon Livre, non seulement jusqu'à ce qu'on l'ait bien examiné, Mais jusqu'à ce que le Veritable journal des Savans quon fait de temps en temps à Paris Vous ait esté communiqué.[3] Ce n'est pas, Monsieur, que je pretends qu'on ait besoin parmj Vous de jugemmens estrangeres pour y fonder les Vostres, estant tres persuadé de la suffisance & de la netteté des Esprits qui composent Vostre illustre assemblée, Mais parce que je scay que les memoirs que Monsieur Denis a commencé de dresser & de publier ne manquent pas de Vous estre communiquer & ne trouvant pas dans celuy du premier de ce mois où il parle de mon Livre[4] ni toutes les Veritez ni toute l'exactitude, ni les justes reflexions que je pouvois esperer, j'ay sujet de desirer cette grace de Vostre Royale Societé & de Vous, Monsieur, en particulier, Et quoy que le temps me soit assez court, puis que le gentilhomme est prest à partir ce matin par le Messager de Calais, & quoy qu'il me seroit tresdifficile de Vous estaler toutes les raisons que j'ay de ne trouver pas dans ce memoire sujet de satisfaction, je Vous en toucheray pourtant un peu et mets quelque chose, à quoy Vous aurez s'il Vous plait la bonté de faire Vos affectueuses reflexions.

Les generalites de la generation & de la naissance des Vipereaux dont Monsr. Denis parle au commencement estoyent assez inutiles puis qu'un nombre infinj d'auteurs en ont parlé, Mais tout cela peut passer pour amuser ceux qui nont pas lus les Livres; Il pouvoit aussi abbreger Les Symptomes qui suivent la Morsure de la Vipere, puis qu'on les pouvoit assez Voir dans mon Livre de mesme que linnocence du fiel, dont mes sentimens se trouvent conformes à ceux de Monsieur Redj; Mais il a peu remplir deux pages de cette matiere. Ce que je trouve en premier lieu Un peu hors de propos & de la tache quil avoit prise de parler de mon Livre, c'est qu'il introduit Monsieur Redi comme sortant du dernier de quelque tapisserie, qu'apres luy avoir fait parler de la non existence des Vaisseaux pretendus pour porter le suc jaune du fiel de la Vipere aux gencives, dont je suis daccort avec luy, il Veut luy faire dire que le suc jaune Vient de quelques glandes ou Vesicules Voisinies quoy quil en ait tesmoigné au pleinement son doubt dans ses escrits & que je puisse me dire le premier inventeur des glandes & des Vaisseaux salivaires & que je sois le seul qui les ait bien descrites & depeints & qui en ait parlé avec certitude, Je ne mestendray pas sur ce quil en dit aprés ni sur tout ce qui est dans la page 76 en son memoire: Mais Venant a la 77e Je ne trouve pas que La conclusion quil m'impute, soit conforme à mes sens, Car quoy que dans limprobation de ce que Monsr. Redi a assigné le Venin de la Vipere au seul suc jaune, j'aye dit que le Venin n'est ni Visible ni papable & tesmoigné quil nest pas materiel, ce n'a esté qu'en comparaison du suc jaune qui est Un corps Visible, Ne doutant pas de ma part que les esprits irritez ne puissent & ne doivent estre appellez des corps, Mais ce sont des corps qui ne se peuvent Voir ni toucher comme fait le suc jaune, & qui aussi nont proprement aucun Lieu particulier dans le corps de la Vipere où lon puisse designer leur appartement & logement, quoy quon peut dire qu'estans eslevez & separez soit de la masse du sang soit si on Veut de toute l'habitude du corps, ils ont leur rendevous à la teste ayant esté excitez par la concussion & grande émotion que la Vipere recoit en tout son corps lors quelle est irrite, Ne doubtant pas quil ne faitte que lirritation ait esté precedée de quelque sujet & que la Vipere nait des sentimens du mal qu'on luy fait quelle n'en soit irritée & quelle nait deslors ljdée ou le desir de se vanger qui luy est commun avec plusieurs autres animaux, & que ce mesme desir aydé de la colere nexcite & ne serve à leslevation & à laction precipitée des esprits irritez, Ne pretendant pas selon luy que ces esprits n'ayent aucune place ni estendu, car ils ne sauroyent partir de la Vipere sans s'estre trouvez dans son corps, & sachant quils ne sauroyent entre dans le corps de l'animal mordu sans y estre & par consequent sans avoir de place & estendue, aussi bien que les choses materieles Visibles, & ne niant pas quils ne soyent Un effect de la colere & de limagination de vengeance de la Vipere, & quils ne soyent eslevez produites & poussez en Un moment. Ce quil dit aprés des Viperes mortes & de Leur incapacité de colere & de fournir ces Esprits irritez parle de soy mesme & aucune personne raisonnable n'en doutera.

Il Vient aprés à mes Usages des parties du corps de la Vipere & passant par dessus les reformations que j'ay faites aux preparations des anciens, il ne parle guere que de ce qui se peut faire dans Une Cuisine, & apres cela du Sal Volatile seulement. Il parle apres de mon experience de la teste du coeur & du foye de la Vipere & joint mon experience de Lhomme mordu dans mon dernier Traité à lhistoire de celuy qui fut mordu dans le premier. Cependant il ne dit que trois mots de mon dernier Livre, de crainte sans doute que les amis de Monsieur Redi ne le regardassent de travers sil sy estoit estendu.

Mais la Reflexion quil fait en suite ma encore plus surpris que tout le reste, Car il me veut faire dire que ce Venin n'a rien de materiel, n'ayant pas compris que ni sens ni mon intention ni mes escrits ne tendent aucunement a cela, & que ce que j'en ay dit n'a esté que pour marquer la difference de ces esprits davec le suc jaune qui se voit se touche & se gouste & bien que jasseure que ces esprits sont produite eslevez & poussez dans le moment de lirritation, je ne pretens pas leur aneantissement, dont je n'ay jamais parlé, & ne doute pas qu'ils nexistent aprés & quils ne cherchent leur place dans lair ou ailleurs lors que la Vipere n'a peu mordre & les introduire & mesler avec le sang de lanimal mordu. Les physiciens pourroyent avoir peine de comprendre sa doctrine qui nest pas la mienne & qui me fait juger qu'il n'a pas pris la peine de Lire mon Livre, ou quil a voulu ignorer ce que jen dis. Je m'estonne aussi quil mait voulu faire dire davoir fait avaller du sang de la Vipere, puis que je nen ay jamais parlé & n'ay fait avaller que du Suc jaune, des testes avec leur col des coeurs & des foyes, & ne me suis servi du sang que pour en frotter le lieu de la morsure. Jespere, Monsieur, que Vous jugerez equitablement de la chose & que ce peu de mots Vous servira dun esclaircissement suffisant de mes intentions, quoy quil soit fort à la haste & assez mal poly & que Vous ne douterez pas que je ne sois du meilleur de mon coeur Monsieur

Vostre treshumble & tresobeissant serviteur
Charas

ADDRESS
A Monsieur
Monsieur Oldenburg secretaire
de la Societé Royale
A Londres

TRANSLATION

Paris, 7 April 1672 [N.S.]

Sir,

Being uncertain if you have yet received any copy of my last book on vipers,[1] having not yet any news of the receipt of the copies which I sent by different routes, I have gladly taken advantage of the kind offices of Mr. Cook, an English gentleman,[2] and have begged him to have delivered to you a new copy which I gave him, so that one way or another some copy might reach you. However, Sir, I am very much indebted to you for the interest you have formerly taken in my affairs and the honor you have procured for my writings in your illustrious Society, as well as the particular testimony of benevolence which you formerly very obligingly granted to me. I take the liberty, Sir, of asking you for its continuation, and beg you to kindly procure for me a suspension of your Royal Society's judgment on the matter of my book, not only until it has been thoroughly examined, but until the genuine *Journal des Sçavans* published from time to time at Paris has reached you.[3] It is not, Sir, that I claim that you require the opinions of foreigners upon which to base your own, being very certain of the sufficiency and clarity of the minds of those who make up your illustrious society, but because I know that the *Mémoires* that Mr. Denis has begun to assemble and publish cannot fail to be sent to you. Now finding in that of the first of this month in which he mentions my book[4] neither all the truth nor all the exactness nor the just reflections which I could hope for, I have occasion to request this favor of your Royal Society and of you, Sir, in particular. And although time is pretty short, since the gentleman is ready to leave this morning by the Calais coach, and although it would be very difficult to set out to you all the reasons why I do not take any satisfaction from this *Mémoire*, I shall touch on them a little nevertheless and put down something on which, if you please, you will be so good as to reflect in friendly fashion.

    The generalities about the generation and birth of the viper kind of which Mr. Denis speaks at the beginning might seem pretty useless since an infinite number of authors have spoken thereon, but all this might pass as intended to amuse those who have not read books. He might also have cut short [his account of] the symptoms which result from viper bites, since they can be read in my book, as also the innocence of the venom, about which my sentiments are conformable to those of Mr. Redi. But he has been able to fill two pages with these matters. What I find first rather off the subject, and aside from the task he had undertaken of speaking about my book, is that he introduces Mr. Redi as though from behind the arras. After having made him speak of the nonexistence of the pretended vessels for carrying the yellow fluid of viper venom to the gums, on which I am in agreement with him, he wants to make him say that the yellow fluid comes from certain glands or neighboring vesicles, although he has plainly testified to his doubts in his writings and although I can proclaim myself the first discoverer of the glands and the salivary vessels and although I am the only one who has carefully described and depicted them and who has spoken of them with certainty. I shall not dwell upon what he has said after this, nor upon all that is set out on page 76 of his *Mémoire*, but coming to page 77, I do not find that the conclusion he imputes to me is in keeping with my meaning. For although in the disproof of Mr. Redi's assigning the venom of vipers only to the yellow fluid I said that the venom is neither visible nor palpable, and affirmed that it is not material, this was only by comparison with the yellow fluid which is a visible body. For my part I do not doubt that the irritated spirits could and should be denominated bodies; but they are bodies which cannot be seen nor touched as can the yellow fluid and they have properly speaking no specific place in the body of the viper which could be designated their abode and dwelling place, although it can be said that, being elevated and separated either from the mass of the blood or, if you like, from the whole habit of the body, they come together in the head after being excited by the concussion and the great emotion received by the viper in every part of its body when it is irritated. Nor do I doubt that it happens that the irritation is preceded by some reason, and that the viper has malicious feelings given to it by its being irritated, and that henceforward it has the idea or desire of avenging itself which it shares with many other animals, and that this same desire, assisted by anger, excites and serves for the elevation and precipitate action of the irritated spirits. Nor do I claim as he says that these spirits have neither place nor extension, for they would not be able to come forth from the viper without being located in its body and I know that they could not enter the body of the bitten animal without being there and consequently without having place and extension just as much as visible material bodies do, nor do I deny that they are a result of the anger and dream of vengeance of the viper and that they can be elevated, produced and impelled in an instant. What he says afterwards of dead vipers and their inability to feel anger and to produce these irritated spirits speaks for itself and no reasonable person could doubt it.

He next comes to my usage of the parts of vipers' bodies, and passing over the reforms which I have made in the preparations of the ancients he only speaks of what can be done in a kitchen, and after that only of sal volatile. He next speaks of my experiment with the head, heart, and liver of the viper, and joins together my experience of the bitten man in my latest treatise to the history of the man who was bitten in the first. However he says only three words of my latest book, for fear doubtless lest Mr. Redi's friends should look at him askance if he had continued.

But the reflection which he makes in conclusion surprised me more than all the rest. For he wants me to say that the venom is quite immaterial, not having understood that neither my meaning nor my intention nor my writings at all point to that, and that what I have said about that was only to stress the difference between these spirits and the yellow fluid which can be seen, touched, and tasted. And although I assert that these spirits are produced, elevated, and impelled at the moment of irritation, I do not at all claim their annihilation, about which I have never spoken and I do not doubt but that they exist afterwards and that they seek their place in the air or elsewhere when the viper has not been able to bite and so introduce them into and mix them with the blood of the bitten animal. Physicians will find difficulty in understanding his teaching, which is not mine, and which makes me judge that he has not taken the trouble to read my book, or that he deliberately avoids knowing what I have said about it. I am also surprised that he has wanted to make me say that I have had viper's blood swallowed, since I never spoke of it and have only had swallowed the yellow fluid, the heads with their necks, the hearts, and the livers and have only used blood for rubbing on the place bitten. I hope, Sir, that you will judge the matter fairly and that these few words will serve to enlighten you sufficiently about my intentions, although this is very much in haste and pretty poorly polished. I hope too that you will not doubt that I am, Sir, with all my heart,

Your very humble, obedient servant
Charas

ADDRESS
Mr. Oldenburg Secretary
  of the Royal Society
    London

NOTES

1 Moise Charas, *Suite des nouvelles Experiences sur la Vipère, avec une Dissertation sur son Vénin* (Paris, 1671), summarized in *Phil. Trans.*, no. 83 (20 May 1672), 4073–77.
2 As appears later, this was Miles Cook (*c.* 1630–1699), younger son of Sir Robert Cook of Highnam, Glos., who was called to the Bar (Middle Temple) in 1654 and became a Master in Chancery in 1673; he was knighted in the following year.
3 The *Journal des Sçavans* was published on the following [N.S.] dates: 29 February, 21 March, 11 April, 13 and 21 June. None of these mentions Charas's book.
4 Denis, *Sixième Mémoire*, is dated 1 April 1672 [N.S.]. The article is mostly devoted to the *Nouvelles Experiences sur la Vipère* (Paris, 1669) and Redi's criticism of it (see Vol. VII, p. 275, note 24). The *Suite* is (as Charas complains) only mentioned in one sentence at the end.

1941
Newton to Oldenburg
30 March 1672

Printed in Newton, *Correspondence*, I, 126–29, from the original in CUL MS. Add. 3976, no. 3

In this reply to Letter 1939 (now lost) Newton comments on Auzout's views upon the theory and practice of reflecting telescopes and answers queries raised by Denis about their construction. This letter was partly printed in *Phil. Trans.*, no. 82 (22 April 1672), 4034–35.

Auzout's and Denis's comments—probably arising from Letter 1866a, or the French version of it in the *Journal des Sçavans* of 29 February 1672 [N.S.], and Denis's *Troisième Mémoire* of 1 March—are unknown except as they may be inferred from Newton's rejoinders. Any letter, possibly sent via Justel, is now lost.

1942
Pardies to Oldenburg
30 March 1672

From the original in Royal Society MS. P 1, no. 76

Paris 9. Avril 1672 [N.S.]

Monsieur

Je vous ecris ce mot pour vous faire scavoir que je donnay il ya 8 jours un pacquet à M. Justel pour vous faire tenir par le moyen d'un gentilhomme qui devoit partir le lendemain c'est à dire le 2e d'Avril.[1] Ce sont deux exemplaires d'un *discours de la Connoissance des Bestes*[2] que je viens de faire. Comme vous m'avez fait la grace de m'en promettre un sur semblable sujet de M. Willis[3] vous m'obligerez de vouloir en presenter un de ma part à cet autheur, à moins que vous n'en vouliez disposer autrement, ce que vous pourrez faire comme il vous plairra, et je vous donne de tout mon coeur tous les deux exemplaires. J'y ay ajouté un livre qui n'a fait ici que paroitre et il a disparu incontinent. Il est escrit avec beaucoup d'erudition et de force contre les Cartesiens: ces messieurs voyant que ce livre ne se debitoit point ont fait courir le bruit qu'il estoit supprimé par ordre du Roy de peur qu'il ne fît du bruit. mais cela ne s'est past trouvé veritable. la cause de cette suppression est l'emprisonnement du libraire dont tous les magazins ont esté saisis, de sorte que ce livre s'est trouvé enveloppé parmy les autres et il faut attendre que la vente de ces magazins se fasse ce qui sera dit-on dans peu de jours, et alors on reverra paroitre ce livre. Je m'interesse un peu pour cela car celuy qui passe pour autheur est mon intime ami que je voudrois servir, qui est tres-intelligent dans ces matieres il enseigne la Philosophie à Poitiers et s'appelle le P. Rouchon.4

Je ne vous ay pas encore remercié des avis qu'il vous a plu me donner touchant mon dessein des Mechaniques. Je suis infiniment obligé entr'-autres à l'illustre M. Wallis. je n'ay garde de vouloir comparer mon dessein à celuy de ce grandhomme. Je ne traitteray que fort superficiellement et d'un façon qui rende seulement intelligibles, les choses qui sont traittées avec tant d'érudition dans son bel ouvrage. J'ay recu le discours de la trompette stentorée dont je vous suis bien obligé. Si je recevois de bonne heure quelque semblable sujet qui fust curieux, je prendrois plaisir de le traduire en françois.

Si vos libraires n'ont pas fait encore l'emplette que je demandois, je vous prie de ne pas vous en mettre en peine, parce que M. Jolly qui est parti depuis deux ou 3 jours nous a promis de nous envoyer tout ce que nous demandions. Je demeure vostre tres-humble tres-obeissant serviteur

Ignace

ADDRESS
A Monsieur
   Monsieur Grubendol
      A Londres

TRANSLATION

Paris, 9 April 1672 [N.S.]

Sir,

I am writing this word just to let you know that eight days ago I gave a packet to Mr. Justel to be delivered to you by a gentleman who should have left the next day, that is the second of April [N.S.].[1] It contains two copies of the book I have just finished, a *Discours de la Connoissance des Bestes*.[2] As you have been so kind as to promise me one on a similar subject by Mr. Willis,[3] you will oblige me if you graciously present one on my behalf to that author, at least if you do not want to dispose of it otherwise, which you may do as you please, and I wholeheartedly give you both copies. I have added a book which has only just appeared here and disappeared forthwith. It is written with considerable erudition and strength against the Cartesians; these gentlemen, seeing that it didn't sell, have spread the rumor that it was suppressed by order of the king for fear lest it make a stir. But this has not been found to be true. The cause of this suppression is the imprisonment of the bookseller, all of whose stocks have been seized, so that this book has found itself caught up with the others, and it will be necessary to wait until these stocks are sold, which, they say, will be in a few days, and then this book will reappear. I am a little concerned for this, because the reputed author is an intimate friend whom I should like to assist, who understands these things very well; he teaches philosophy at Poitiers and is called Père Rouchon.[4]

I have not yet thanked you for the comments you have kindly given me about my plan for mechanics. I am infinitely obliged to, among others, the celebrated Mr. Wallis. I have taken care not to compare my plan with that of this great man. What he has dealt with in so learned a manner in his fine work I have dealt with only superficially, in a fashion which just makes them intelligible, I have received the discourse about the stentorian trumpet, for which I am much obliged to you. If I received in good time any similar subject which was of interest, I should take pleasure in translating it into French.

If your booksellers have not yet made the purchase I asked for, I beg you not to bother about it because Mr. Jolly who left two or three days ago promised to send us everything we asked for. I remain your very humble, obedient servant,

Ignace

ADDRESS
   To Mr. Grubendol
      London

NOTES

Reply to Letter 1884.
1 There was apparently no letter with this.
2 See Letter 1859, note 11.
3 See Letter 1687, note 13.
4 This book is probably R. J., *Lettre d'un philosophe à un Cartésien de ses amis* (Paris, 1672); the copy in the BN has a manuscript note ascribing the work to either Pardies or "le P. Rochon." From this letter it appears that the latter is the true author. The bookseller's name is given on the title page as "T. Jolly"—which is curious in view of the final paragraph of this letter.

1943
Charas to Oldenburg
30 March 1672

From the original in Royal Society MS. C 1, no. 102

A Paris le 9 Avril 1672 [N.S.]

Monsieur

J'ay veu dépuis peu Une edition de vos Actes Philosophiques Royaux, translatée en Latin & imprimée a Amsterdam,[1] Et bien que j'aye esté averti que la traduction est fautive & qu'elle est mesme contraire à Vostre sens en plusieurs endroits, & que cela Vous ait obligé en Vous plaignant du traducteur, de travailler a Une plus pure & plus correcte, que je n'ay pas eu L'avantage de Voir, J'ay pourtant grand Sujet de Vous tesmoigner mes treshumbles reconnaissances & à toute Vostre Royale Societé, d'avoir parlé tresavantageusement de moy dans Vos escrits & d'avoir honoré mes petites ouvrages de Vostre approbation & de Vos louanges. Je le suis dautant plus, que le jugement que Vous en avez fait se trouve non seulement preceder celuy que Mons. Denis a entrepris de faire, au commencement de ce mois dans la Suite des memoires qu'il a commencés de publier cette année,[2] mais qu'il a esté sans doute mieux digeré que le Sien & avec toute autre examen du Livre, et qu'il passera sans doute par tout pour Une chose de grand poids & digne de Vostre trescelebre compagnie. Je ne doute pas, Monsieur, que ce dernier escrit de Monsieur Denis ne Vous ait esté communiqué de mesme que les precedents, & qu'il n'ait esté capable de Vous surprendre tant pour la difformité de son jugement, davec le Vostre que pour y avoir avancé des choses qui ne sont pas contenues dans mon livre & qui sont contre mon sens, m'avoir fait dire des choses à quoy je nay jamais pensé, avoir introduit Monsr. Redj dans son discours, Luy avoir fait dire ce qu'il n'a jamais dit, mais dont il na tesmoigné que toute incertitude, & qui n'a esté dit, avoués, asseurés & descrit que par moy, comme Vous me faitez lhonneur de le tesmoigner dans Vostre escrit, au sujet des glandes & des Vaisseaux salivaires de la Vipere & de l'origine de son suc jaune; & d'avoir entrepris demployer des fondemens supposez & controuvez et faire des reflexions qui ne sauroyent estre receues, et ceux qui auront leu & examiné mon livre & qui connoitront ce qu'il a mal à propos supposé. Il Vous sera tresaisé,

Monsieur, de juger par la Lecture de son escrit quil n'a pas eu le soin de lire ni d'examiner mon Livre, & qu'il a esté poussé par quelquun pour deguiser les Veritez qui y sont contenues, Ce qu'il tesmoigne assez, puis quil met sous le boisseau ma replique à Monsr. Redi, qui est mon dernier ouvrage & qui est celuy qui devroit fournir de principale matiere à son discours, Vous pourrez aussi remarquer qu'il a noircj inutilement le papier par des choses peu necessaires à l'Extrait dun Livre & quil a copiées de moy d'ailleurs, tant au commencement & à la suite de son discours, qu'a la fin de sa reflexion. Au reste, Monsieur, je suis dans Une inquiétude assez grande pour savoir si Vous aurez receu quelque Exemplaire de mon dernier ouvrage en ayant envoyé par deux fois plusieurs Exemplaires a Monsieur Dun Medicin Escossais[3] qui loge chez Monsr Kemp au Black frayer & l'ayant prié de Vous en faire part au plustost; il y a du moins cinq ou six semaines qu'il doit en avoir receu & il Vous en aura fait part sil a esté à Londres; J'avois aussi prié Monsr. Le fevre Apoticaire du Roy[4] de suppléer à son defaut & daller chez Luy & au cas quil fut absent, d'ouvrir luy mesme les paquets & de Vous en porter quelque Exemplaire. Cependant je nay aucun advis de quoy que ce soit, quoy que les paquets esté remis à des personnes de connoissance. Cela m'obligea à profiter jeudy dernier de la bonne commodité dé Monsieur Koock[5] gentilhomme Anglois qui partit par le Messager de Calais & de le prier de Vous rendre au plustost Un paquet que je luy remis contenant Un de mes Livres, & Un Exemplaire de mon dernier Livre relié en Veau, J'espere qu'il le fera avec Soin & que Vous y reconnoitrez le peu de fondement que [ledit?] Sieur Denis a d'escrire de la sorte. Jespere, Monsieur, que Vous prendrez Volontiers la peine de l'examiner & que si Vous trouvez qu'il vaille la peine d'occuper quelque place dans Vos journaux, Vous prendrez plaisir à me faire justice & à me defendre contre le tort qu'on a entrepris de me faire. Je me suis un peu expliqué quoy que fort en haste dans la Lettre qui est avec le Livre que Monsier Kouck Vous rendra, je ne Vous en diray pas icy grand chose, & me contenteray de Vous dire que le sujet de l'ecrit de Mons. Denis, a esté qu'il n'a pas compris que mon principal but ayant esté de publier l'innocence du suc jaune, je me suis efforcé de faire comprendre que le Venin de la Vipere estoit tout spirituel & qu'il n'estoit ni grossier ni touchable ni Visible. Mais je n'ay jamais pretendu de nier que ces Esprits itritez fussent des corps & les ay tousiours considerez & je les considere encore pour Une matiere spirituelle & par consequent fort differente du suc jaune & de toutes les parties de la Vipere qui se discernent par nos sens corporeles & grossieres et pour Une matiere dije si spirituelle qu'on n'en peut Voir ni la forme ni la couleur & qui ne peut estre connue que par nostre pensée. Je pretens encore moins, suivant que Mr. Denis a pretendu de moy, que ces esprits n'ayent ni place ni estendue. Car ils ne pourroyent sortir de la Vipere sans avoir esté dans son corps, non plus que passer le long & au travers de ses dents & entrer dans louverture qu'elle ont faite, se mesler avec le sang & y causer tous les effets funestes dont ils sont capables Sans avoir leur place & leur estendue & dans la Vipere & dans le corps de l'animal mordu. Ne pretendant pas pourtant que ces esprits ayant en tout temps Un Lieu particulier dans le corps de la Vipere pour y faire leur sejour, comme le suc jaune le fait dans les Vesicules. Mais estant persuadé quils sont excitez & separez de la Vipere par la concussion que la Vipere fait à toutes ses parties, lors quelle se met en colere, laquelle colere j'estime estre precedée de limagination & du desir de Vengeance de la Vipere lors quelle se sent mal traitée, Je ne pretens pas non plus que ces esprits s'aneantissent comme Mr. Denis a avancé, & qu'ils nexistent après la morsure, soit dans le corps de l'animal mordu soit en lair soit ailleurs & quils n'ayent telle place que les savans se peuvent imaginer. Je suis si persuadé, Monsieur, de Vostre bonté envers moy, que je ne doute point que Vous ne soyez facilement porté a expliquer en bien mes Veritables pensées & à les seconder des Vostres qui ne manqueront pas d'estre meilleure & plus relevées. Je n'ay pas pretendu d'escrire en Philosophe en faisant mon Livre, Mais de parler en Naturaliste & faire bien comprendre le Siege du Venin de la Vipere, en Laissant la faculté aux savans de donner aux Esprits irritez telle corps qu'ils trouvoyent à propos, me contentant de faire Voir linnocence du suc jaune & le droit que jay de l'exclurre du Venin de mesme que toutes les parties Visibles & grossieres de la Vipere. Je Vous demande bien pardon, de la liberté que je prens, & Vous supplie de me Vouloir honorer de Vos commandemens & me vouloir fournir des occasions où je Vous puisse tesmoigner comme à Vostre tresillustre assemblée que je suis fort sincerement & fort respectueusement Monsieur

       Vostre tres humble tresobeissant
       & tres obligé serviteur
       Charas

Monsieur Kooke qui s'est chargé de mon paquet arrivera suivant l'apparence à Londres Mercredy ou Jeudy prochaine son addresse est Monsr. Miles Kooke advocat chez Monsr. Miler à lenseigne du Cheval noir Viz à Viz Hind Court in fleet street, où a defaut chez sieur Peter Ball[6] demeurant au Temple en fleet street

ADDRESS
A Monsieur
Monsieur Oldemburg secretaire
   de la Societé Royale
      A Londres

TRANSLATION

Paris, 9 April 1672 [N.S.]

Sir,

I recently saw an edition of your *Royal Philosophical Transactions*, translated into Latin and printed at Amsterdam.[1] And although I have been warned that the translation is faulty and that it even goes against your meaning in many places and that this has forced you while complaining to the translator to work on a purer and more correct version which I have not had the advantage of seeing, I have nevertheless strong reason to testify to you and to the whole of your Royal Society my very humble gratitude for having spoken of me so very favorably in your writings and for having honored my little works with your approval and praise. I am the more grateful because the judgement you have there made not only precedes that which Mr. Denis has undertaken at the beginning of this month in the continuation of the *Memoires* which he began to publish this year,[2] but it is without doubt better considered than his, and with quite a different examination of the book, and it will doubtless pass everywhere as a matter of great weight, worthy of your very celebrated assembly. I do not doubt, Sir, that this last journal of Mr. Denis has been communicated to you just like the preceding ones, nor that it was able to surprise you as much for the disparity between his judgment and yours as for having there set forth things which are not contained in my book and are contrary to my meaning, having made me say things I had never thought. He has also introduced Mr. Redi into his discourse, making *him* say things he had never said, but about which he had only manifested uncertainty, and which were only said, avowed, asserted and described by myself, as you do me the honor to bear witness in your account, on the subject of the glands and the salivary vessels of the viper and the origin of its yellow fluid. He has also undertaken to employ suppositious and feigned premises and to make reflections which ought not to be accepted, and anyone who has read and examined my book will recognize what he has imagined which is not to the purpose. It will be very easy for you, Sir, to judge from reading his account that he has not taken the trouble to read or examine my book and that he has been pushed by someone into disguising the truths contained in it. This he sufficiently demonstrates since he hides under a bushel my reply to Mr. Redi, which is my latest work and that which ought to furnish the chief matter for his discourse. You can also notice that he has uselessly blackened the paper with things not really necessary in making an extract of a book, and that he has copied from me or others, both at the beginning and end of his discourse as well as at the conclusion of his reflections. For the rest, Sir, I am rather disquieted by not knowing whether you have received any copy of my last work, having sent twice several copies to Mr. Dun, a Scottish physician[3] who lives with Mr. Kemp in Blackfriars, and having begged him to share them with you as soon as possible. It is at least five or six weeks since he should have received them and he would have shared them with you if he had been in London. I also requested Mr. Le Fevre, the King's Apothecary,[4] to make good his failure and to go to his lodgings and in case he was absent to open the packages himself and to take you a copy. However I have had no word of what has happened, although these parcels were entrusted to knowledgeable people. This obliged me last Thursday to take advantage of the good offices of Mr. Cook,[5] an English gentleman who left by the Calais coach, and to beg him to deliver to you as soon as possible a parcel which I entrusted to him containing one of my books and a copy of my last book bound in calf. I hope that he will do so carefully and that you will recognize the slight foundation which [the said?] Mr. Denis has for writing in that fashion. I hope, Sir, that you will be willing to take the trouble of examining it and that if you think it worth the trouble of taking a place in your journals you will be pleased to do me justice and defend me against the wrong which some have undertaken to do me. I did explain myself a little, although very much in haste in the letter with the book which Mr. Cook will give you. I shall not say very much about it here and shall content myself with telling you that the reason for Mr. Denis's account was that he did not understand that my main aim having been to proclaim the innocence of the yellow fluid, I found myself constrained to make [the reader] understand that the viper's venom is wholly spirituous and neither coarse nor palpable nor visible. But I have never claimed to deny that the irritated spirits are bodies and I have always considered them and I consider them still to be a spirituous matter and consequently very different from the yellow fluid and from all the parts of the viper which are perceived by our corporeal and coarse senses—as, I say, a matter so spirituous that neither the form nor the color can be seen nor can they be known except by our minds. Still less do I claim, according to what Mr. Denis has claimed of me, that these spirits have neither place nor extension. For they could not issue from the viper without having been in his body nor passed the length and width of his teeth and entered into the hole these made, mixing with the blood and there causing all the fatal results of which they are capable, without having their place and extension both in the viper and in the body of the bitten animal. Not that I claim however that these spirits always have a particular place in the body of the viper where they reside, as the yellow fluid does in the vesicles. But I am convinced that they are excited and separated from the viper by the concussion which the viper effects in all its parts when it grows angry, which anger I regard as proceeding from the imagination and desire for vengeance of the viper when it feels itself ill treated. Hence I do not claim either that these spirits are annihilated as Mr. Denis proposed, and that they do not exist after the bite, either in the body of the bitten animal or in the air or elsewhere and that they have no such place as learned men may imagine. I am so well persuaded, Sir, of your kindness to me that I do not at all doubt that you will be easily led to explain properly my true thoughts and to assist them with your own which cannot fail to be better and more lofty. I have not claimed in writing my book to speak philosophically, but rather as a naturalist, and to make perfectly comprehensible the seat of the viper's venom. I have left the option to learned men of assigning to the irritated spirits whatever body they find suitable, contenting myself with demonstrating the innocence of the yellow fluid and the right which I have of excluding it from the venom as well as all the visible and gross parts of the viper. I beg your pardon for the freedom I take and beg you to be so good as to honor me with your commands and to furnish occasions upon which I can testify to you as also to your illustrious Society that I am very sincerely and respectfully,

Your very humble, obedient, and obliged servant
Charas

Mr. Cook who is burdened with my parcel is likely to arrive in London next Wednesday or Thursday; his address is Mr. Miles Cook, lawyer, at Mr. Miller's at the sign of the Black Horse opposite Hind Court in Fleet Street, or failing that at Mr. Peter Balle's,[6] who lives at the Temple in Fleet Street.

ADDRESS
    To Mr. Oldenburg Secretary
        of the Royal Society
            London

NOTES

1 This was the Sterpin translation of Volume IV (1669) of the *Philosophical Transactions*, published at Amsterdam in 1671, containing Oldenburg's notice of Charas's earlier book (see Vol. VI, p. 491, note 2).
2 Compare for what follows Letter 1940, and its notes 3 and 4.
3 Possibly Robert Dun (b. c. 1607), formerly of Marischal College, Aberdeen, of which he was a benefactor, who matriculated as a medical student at Leiden in 1632. Kemp is not identifiable.
4 Nicolas Lefevre (d. 1674); see Vols. I, p. 229, note 13, and II, p. 230, note 3. The date of his death, given earlier from the *Dictionary of National Biography*, is incorrect, as is evident from this reference.
5 See Letter 1940, note 2.
6 Peter Balle (d. 1675) was, like his brother William, the astronomer, F.R.S. Professionally he was a physician, elected Hon. F.C.P. in 1664. He was buried in the Temple Church.

1944
Huygens to Oldenburg
30 March 1672

From the original in Royal Society MS. H 1, no. 72
Printed in *Œuvres Complètes*, VII, 165–67

a Paris ce 9 Avril 1672 [N.S.]

Monsieur

Vos deux dernieres avec les Exemplaires des Transactions m'ont estè bien rendues, dont je vous remercie treshumblement et vous prie de vouloir continuer tousjours de me les envoier, afin que dorenavant la collection que j'en feray soit complete. Car pour ceux que vous avez donnez jusqu'icy j'ay priè Mr. Vernon de m'en faire venir tout le volume. J'ay estè bien aise de trouver dans les dernieres ce que Mr. Newton escrit touchant l'effect des verres et des miroirs en matiere de lunettes, ou je vois qu'il a remarquè comme moy le defaut de la refraction des verres convexes objectifs a cause de l'inclinaison de leurs 2 surfaces. Pour ce qui est de sa nouvelle theorie des couleurs, elle me paroit fort ingenieuse, mais il faudra veoir si elle est compatible avec toutes les experiences.

J'ay encore à vous rendre graces de ce que vous avez pris la peine de m'envoier de l'analyse de Mr. Sluse sur le Probleme d'Alhazen;[1] Laquelle est tresscavante et digne de luy, Et a estè cause en l'examinant ces jours passez que j'ay resvè de nouveau sur ce mesme probleme, pour tascher d'obtenir la construction la plus courte et la plus naturelle. En quoy je pense a la fin avoir reussi. Vous voudrez bien prendre la peine je m'assure de l'examiner c'est pourquoy je m'en vay la mettre icy, apres vous avoir dit l'abbregement que j'ay trouvè en mesme temps dans la premiere que je vous envoyay imprimee de la maniere que vous scavez.[2] qui est que tirant la ligne AT parallele à CB, et la divisant egalement en V, ce point est celuy par ou doit passer l'une des hyperboles opposees dont les asymptotes ont estè trouvees YM, MN.

Mais voicy la bonne construction et qui a lieu dans tous les cas imaginables. Soit le cercle donnè ED, dont le centre est A. Les points donnez B et C.

Ayant tirè les lignes AB, AC, soient faites proportionelles BA, le rayon du cercle, et FA. Et de mesme CA, le rayon du cercle, et GA.

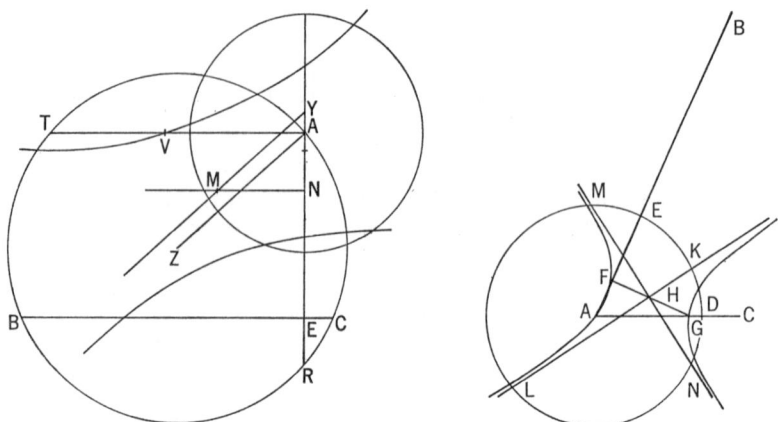

Joigney en suite FG, et divisez la par le milieu en H. Et par ce point minez les lignes LHK MHN se coupant a angles droits et dont LHK soit parallele a celle qui divise l'angle BAC par le milieu. Ce seront les 2 asymptotes des hyperboles, qu'il faut descrire par les points F et G, et dont l'une passera aussi par le centre A. les intersections des quelles avec la circonference du cercle marqueront les points de reflexion requis. Je suis Monsieur

Vostre treshumble et tresobeissant serviteur
Hugens de Zulichem

Il y a un de mes amis qui desire avoir les traitez de Kinchuijzen que je crois avoir estè traduits en latin chez vous.³ Je vous prie Monsieur d'avoir la bontè de dire à Mr. Collins a qui Mr. Vernon escrit pour mes livres qu'il y veuille joindre cet autre.

ADDRESS
    A Monsieur
  Monsieur de Grubendol
            à
        Londres

TRANSLATION

Paris, 9 April 1672 [N.S.]

Sir,

I have had safely delivered to me your last two letters with the copies of the *Transactions* for which I thank you most warmly, and I beg you to be so good as to continue to send them to me always, so that from now on the collection of them that I am making will be complete. For as to those which you have given me hitherto, I have requested Mr. Vernon to procure me [others to complete] the whole volume. I was very glad to find in the last [copies] what Mr. Newton writes about the effect of lenses and mirrors with respect to telescopes, where I see he has noticed as I have the defects in refraction of convex objective lenses, caused by the inclination of their two surfaces. As for his new theory of colors, it seems to me very ingenious, but it must be seen whether it is compatible with all experiments.

I have also to send you thanks for what you took the trouble to transmit to me about Mr. Sluse's analysis of Alhazen's problem.[1] It is very learned and worthy of him; it has caused me as I examined it these last days to cogitate again on this same problem to try to obtain the shortest and most natural construction. And in this I believe I have succeeded. I am sure you will take the trouble to examine it, and so I shall set it out here, after having told you of the short cut I found at the same time in the first [construction] which I sent to you printed after the fashion you know of.[2] Which is that drawing the line AT parallel to CB, and dividing it equally at V, this point is that through which should pass one of the opposed hyperbolas whose asymptotes were found to be YM, MN.

Here is the good construction which holds in all imaginable cases. Let the given circle be ED, whose center is A. And the given points B and C [see the figures, p. 636].

Having drawn the lines AB, AC, let BA, the radius of the circle, and FA be proportional. And similarly for CA, the radius of the circle, and GA. Then join FG and divide it in the middle at H. And trace through this point the lines LHK, MHN, cutting one another at right angles and let LHK be parallel to that dividing the angle BAC in half. These will be the two asymptotes of the hyperbolas, which must be described through the points F and G, of which one will also pass through the center A. The intersections of these with the circumference of the circle will mark the required points of reflection. I am, Sir,

Your very humble, obedient servant,
Huygens of Zulichem

One of my friends wishes to have the treatise by Kinckhuysen which I think has been translated into Latin in your country.[3] I beg you, Sir, please ask Mr. Collins, to whom Mr. Vernon wrote for my books, to be so good as to add this one.

ADDRESS
Mr. Grubendol
London

NOTES

Reply to Letters 1899 and 1920; a Latin translation of the mathematical portion was printed in *Phil. Trans.*, no. 98 (17 November 1673), 6140–41.
1 See Letter 1843.
2 See Vol. VI, p. 43, and Vol. VII, p. 191, notes 3 and 4.
3 See Vol. VII, pp. 159 and 160, note 4.

Index

Boldface figures indicate Letter numbers. Both originals and translations have been indexed.

Abano Terme, baths at, 582–84, 609
Abdelmelech ('Abd al-Malik al-Shīrāzī), 545, 573, 576
Abu Bakr ibn Al Tufail, Al Ishbili: *Philosophus autodidactus*, transl. by E. Pocock (London, 1671), 388, 392
Abulfeda (Abu-l-Fida Ismail ibn Ali, 1273–1331), 310, 312, 372, 388
Academia Curiosorum, xxi, 213, 253–55, 321–24
Académie Royale des Sciences, 168, 170, 384, 501, 519, 521, 523, 568; *Description anatomique d'un Cameleon* (Paris, 1669), 431; *Mémoires pour servir à l'histoire des plantes* (Paris, 1676), 116, 168, 170, 523; *Mémoires pour servir à l'histoire naturelle des animaux* (Paris, 1671), 392, 431–32, 523
An Academy or College.... See Chamberlayne, Edward
Accademia dei Gelati, 308, 309. See also Capponi, G. B.
Accademia dei Lincei, 174
Accademia del Cimento: experiments with organ, 414, 416, 452, 457, 509, 510; *Saggi di Naturali Esperienze* (Florence, 1667), 122, 282, 284
Acoustics, 282, 284, 467, 573, 576; in vacuo, 414, 415–16, 452, 457. See also Morland, Sir Samuel
Acta medica et philosophica.... See Bartholin, Thomas
Admirandorum fossilium... descriptio. See Lachmund, Friedrich
Aeloude en hendendaegsche Scheeps-bouw en bestier. See Witsen, Nicolaas
Aesop, 422 n5
Aglionby, William: *The Present State of the United Provinces of the Low-Countries* (London, 1669), 188

Agriculture, xix; in Huntingdonshire, 344–48; in Yorkshire, 74–75
Aigentliche Beschreibung. See Rauwolff, Leonhard
Aldrovandi, Ulyssi: *De animalibus insectis* (Bologna, 1602), 106; *Dendrologiae... libri duo... Montalbanus... opus colligit* (Bologna, 1668), 146, 148
Algebra. See Kinckhuysen, Gerard
Allin, Sir Thomas (1612–85), 139, 142 n13
Almagestum novum. See Riccioli, Giovanni Battista
Amber, 33–35, 394
Anatome corporis humanae. See Diermerbroeck, Isbrand de
Anatomes plantarum. See Malpighi, Marcello
Anatomia hepatis. See Glisson, Francis
Anatomy: abnormal, 37, 39; discoveries in, 500, 610, 611, 617, 618. See also Académie Royale des Sciences; Graaf, Regnier De; Ray, John; Swammerdam, Jan
Anatomy of Vegetables Begun. See Grew, Nehemiah
Anaxagoras, 588
Animals: Brazilian, 228–29, 242–43. See also Pereyra, Gomez
Anthropogeniae ichnographia. See Kerckring, Theodor
Anthropology, Brazilian, 229–30, 243–44
Antoniana margarita. See Pereyra, Gomez
Apollonius of Perga, 510, 511, 547 n5; edition of, by Isaac Barrow, 545, 547 n4, 573, 576; edition of, by Giovanni Alphonso Borelli, 42
Aquinas, St. Thomas, 151, 152
Archimedes, 453, 457; edition of, by Isaac Barrow, 545, 547 n4, 573, 576; edition of, by Giovanni Alphonso Borelli, 42, 546
Are, Simon, 545, 572, 575
Aristotle, 122, 151–53, 255, 587; *De anima*,

152, 153; *De generatione animalium*, 164; *De Plantis*, 605; *Natural History*, 261, 262, 319, 420, 421
Arithmeticae empiricae compendium. See Tasse, Johann Adolph
Ars de medicina statica. See Santorio, Santorio
Aston, Francis (*c*. 1645–*c*. 1715), 493
Astrology, 17, 20
Astronomia Britannica. See Wing, Vincent
Astronomia Carolina. See Streete, Thomas
Astronomia Philolaica. See Bouilliaud, Ismael
Astronomy: xix, 580–81; comets, xx, 122, 568–71, 592, 593, 594, 596–604, 612, 617; conjunctions, 45–47, 65, 97, 98, 356, 357, 424, 426; eclipses of moon, 140, 194, 207–8, 269, 276, 331, 333, 350–53, 356, 357, 424, 426, 428, 476, 477: in southern hemisphere, 220–21, 235; Japet, xx, 383–85, 386 n1, 398, 423–24, 425, 427, 439–442, 475, 476; Jupiter's satellites, 199, 200, 218, 219, 271, 273, 276, 331, 333, 356, 357, 362, 365–66, 524–25: lunar diameter, 362, 366; lunar distance, 140; lunar motions, 47; motion of earth, 122; motion of Saturn, 208, 362, 366–67, 439–42; new stars, 4, 7, 97, 98, 569, 570, 594–95, 612; occultations, 4, 6, 45, 66, 85, 86, 97, 98, 217, 219, 269, 271, 273, 331, 332–33, 362–91; refraction, 578, 579; Saturn's ring, xx, 97, 98, 194, 217, 218, 219, 272, 273, 314–16, 331, 333, 349, 351–52, 356, 357, 367, 369, 371, 383, 390, 424, 426, 476, 477, 519, 522, 533; selenography, 65, 87 nn2 and 3, 350–53; star positions, 362; sunspots, xx, 194, 199–201, 216–19, 314, 315, 330, 332, 333, 350, 351, 356, 357, 369, 371, 424, 425–26, 427; transits, 580; variable stars, 5, 7, 271–74, 308, 309, 385. *See also* Brahe, Tycho; Cassini, Giovanni Domenico; Flamsteed, John; Hevelius, Johannes; Hooke, Robert; Huygens, Constantijn; Picard, Jean
Atlases. *See* Ogilby, John; Pitt, Moses
Aulus Gellius, 493
Austin, Ralph (*d*. 1676), 187
Auzout, Adrien (1622–91), 122, 292, 296, 626
Avicenna, 151, 152

Babin, Jacques Paul, S.J., 95 n3, 285 n10
Bacon, Francis (1561–1626), 111, 141, 254; *De Paracevis*, 112; *De Praerogativis*, 112; *Novum organum* (London, 1621), 122, 124, 127—in *Opera omnia* (Frankfurt, 1665), 111–13
Baconianism, 122
Baines, Thomas (1622–80), 583
Baldaeus, Philippus: *Naauwkeurige beschryvinge van Malabar en Choromandel* . . . (Amsterdam, 1672), 396, 397 n1, 618
Baliani, Giovanni Battista: *De motu* (Genoa, 1638), 453, 458, 485, 488; *Opera diverse* (Genoa, 1666), 546, 573, 576
Balle, Peter (*d*. 1675), 631, 634
Barometers. *See* Instruments
Baron, Samuel, 189 n5
Barrow, Isaac (1630–77), xxiii, 17, 20, 123, 128 n8, 525, 572, 575; *Archemedis opera*; *Apollonii Pergae conicorum libri IV* . . . (London, 1675), 545, 547 n4, 573, 576; *Euclidis elementorum libri XV* (Cambridge, 1655), 282, 284; *Lectiones geometricae* (London, 1670), 67, 68, 509, 510, 546, 574, 576; *Lectiones opticae* (London, 1669), xxiv, 67, 68
Bart, Jean (1651–1702), 142 n20
BARTHOLIN, ERASMUS (1625–98): *Dioristice* (Copenhagen, 1663), 545, 572, 575; and Picard, 548, 549; and Tycho Brahe, 548, 550
— Letter to: 22 February 1671/2, **1907**, 548
Bartholin, Thomas (1616–80), 448, 450; *Acta medica et philosophica A. 1671 et 1672* (Copenhagen, 1672), 143 n25
"Basil Valentine," 13, 147, 149. *See also* Kerckring, Theodor
Baths, 582–84, 597, 599, 609
Bathurst, Ralph (1620–74), 253
Bayer, Johann: *Uranometria* (Augsberg, 1603), 384, 439, 441
BEALE, JOHN (?1603–83), 127; *Herefordshire Orchards a Pattern for all England* (London, 1657), 188; his xenophobia, 253
— Letters to: 20 June 1671, **1730**, 116; 27 June, **1734**, 126; 1 July 1671, **1737**, 132; 25 July 1671, **1756**, 176; 14 September 1671, **1788**, 265
— Letters from: 13 May 1671, **1700**, 52; *c*. 12 June 1671, **1722**, 92; *c*. 16 June 1671, **1728**, 111; 24 June 1671, **1733**, 119; 8 July 1671, **1743**, 139; 6 August 1671, **1764**, 186; 2 September 1671, **1784**, 253
BECHER, JOHANN JOACHIM (1635–82), 25, 29, 78, 80, 278, 279; *Experimentum chymicum novum* (Frankfurt, 1671), 29 n11; *Physica subterranea libri duo* (Frankfurt, 1669), 304

Index

— Letter from: 16 October 1671, **1802**, 303
Beguin, Jean: *Tyrocinium Chymicum* (Paris, 1610), 82 n11
BELL, PHINEAS
— Letter from: 3 June 1671, **1714**, 74
Beni Musa, 545, 573, 576
BERNARD, EDWARD (1638–96), 310, 312, 467; translations of mathematics, 545, 573, 576
— Letters to: 27 June 1671, **1735**, 126; 6 February 1671/2, **1890**, 527
— Letter from: 4 February 1671/2, **1887**, 523
Bernhardides, Dr., 513, 515
Berniz, Bernard von, 107, 109; *Catalogus plantarum* (Danzig, 1652), 111 n2
Billy, Jacques de: *Diophanti redivivi* (Lyons, 1670), 15, 18, 128 n7, 146, 148
Birch, Thomas, *History of the Royal Society* (London, 1756–57): omissions from, xxvii
Blaeu, Johannes (1650–1712), 173, 174
Blith, Walter: *The English Improver Improved* (London, 1652), 349 n10
Blount, Thomas: *Glossographia* (London, 1670?), 11, 12
Bobart, Jacob, the Younger, 57 n4
Boetius de Boodt, Anselm (1550–1632), 588
Bohun, Ralph: *A Discourse concerning the Origins and Properties of Wind &c* (Oxford, 1671), 326, 328, 370, 371, 430, 443, 530, 531, 548, 549—censoring of, 467, 483
Bonanus, Procopius: *De admirandis rebus Hungariae*, 254
Bond, Henry (*c.* 1600–78), 25, 28
Books: banning of, 17, 20, 467; difficulty in printing, 414, 416; Hevelius and, 67–68; Leibniz and, 102, 104; loans of, xix, 47, 65, 136, 398 n, 427, 532, 541, 581, 591; news of, 37–39, 61, 146–49, 170, 173–74, 326, 328, 368–71, 430, 451, 456, 546, 573, 576; purchases of, 11, 12, 16, 19, 172, 281, 284, 314, 316, 341, 413, 415, 430, 451–52, 456, 546, 562, 564, 583; sale of, 388
Borel, Pierre (*c.* 1620–71), 94, 119, 502 n13; *A summary ... of the life of ... Descartes* (London, 1670), 124 n3; *Vitae Renati Cartesii...* (Paris, 1656), 124 n3
BORELLI, GIOVANNI ALPHONSO (1608–79), 42; *De motionibus naturalibus a gravitate pendentibus liber* (Reggio, 1670), 61, 128, 337, 338; edition of Apollonius of Perga, 42; edition of Archimedes, 42, 546; *Historia et meteorologia incendii Aetnaei anni 1669* (Reggio Julio, 1670), 61, 331, 333, 337, 338, 357, 358; "Responsio ad censuras ... Honorati Fabri contra librum ... de vi percussionis" (in *Historia*), 61; *Theorica mediceorum planetarum a causis physicis deducta* (Florence 1666), 365, 367 n2
— Letter to: 2 November 1671, **1812**, 337
Borelly, Jacques (d. 1689), 501
Borri, Giuseppe Francesco (*c.* 1620–95): *Epistolae duae ad Thomam Bartholinum* (Copenhagen, 1669), 41 n17; on vision, 37, 39, 177, 213
Bosse, Abraham (1602–70), 117 n3
Botany. *See* Plants
Boulliaud, Ismael (1605–94), 207–8; *Astronomia Philolaica* (Paris, 1645), 97, 98, 207, 208 n1; and astronomy, 97, 98, 207, 208 n1, 269; correspondence of, 208 n; on eclipses, 209 n, 268, 356, 357; on occultation of sun and moon, 99 n4
Bourdelin, Claude (1621–99), 117 n3
Bourdelot, l'Abbé (Pierre Michon, 1610 or 1620–85), 108, 110; *Recherches & Observations sur Les Vipères* (Paris, 1671), 287
Boyle, Robert (1629–91), xxvi, 38, 39, 92, 127, 255, 282, 284, 295, 299, 310, 312, 355 n2, 364, 386, 393, 430, 451, 456, 486, 489, 501, 505; and airpump, 51; his baroscope, 125 n29; and Beale, 111, 122, 139ff, 253–55; chemical experiments of, 509–10; *Continuation of New Experiments Physico-Mechanical ...* (Oxford, 1669), 112, 120, 168, 170, 416 n5; *De cosmicis rerum qualitatibus* (Amsterdam and Hamburg, 1671), 11, 12, 135, 146, 149, 173, 332, 333; *De absoluta quieta* (in *De cosmicis rerum qualitatibu*, third Amsterdam issue, 1671), 173, 174, 293, 297; *Essay about the Origine and Virtues of Gems* (London, 1672), 168, 170, 530, 531, 548, 549, 595—Latin edition (London, 1673), 548, 549—; experiments on air, 369, 370, 406, 411, 509, 510; experiments on sound in vacuum, 414, 415–16, 452, 457; health of, 139, 140, 495, 496, 529, 530; and mechanical philosophy, 293, 297, 341, 342; and medicine, 14; *New Experiments and Observations touching Cold* (London, 1665), 31, 118, 589; *New Experiments Physico-Mechanicall touching the Spring of the Air* (Oxford, 1660), 416 n4; *Origo formarum et qualitatum* (Oxford, 1669), 17, 20, 67, 68, 337, 338; *Some Considerations touching the Usefulnesse of*

Experimental Naturall Philosophy (Oxford, 1663), 187—Tome II (Oxford, 1671), 139, 141, 168, 170, 314, 316—; and sunspots, 217, 218, 219; *Tractatus ... ubi mira aeris* (London, 1670, 1671), 11, 12, 17, 20, 60, 61, 62, 67, 68, 117, 134, 135, 168, 170, 337, 338, 529, 530; *Tracts ... containing New Experiments, touching the Relation betwixt Flame and Air* (London, 1672), 124 n5, 168, 170

Brahe, Tycho (1546-1601), 366, 423, 425; star catalogue, 439, 441; works of, 391, 548, 550. *See also* Picard, Jean

Brazil, queries on, xix, xxii, 155, 220-51, 544

Brereton, William, Baron (1631-80), 595

Brevis annotatio in systema Saturnium. *See* Fabri, Honoré

Brewer, Mr., 153, 154 n4, 157

Brooke, John (*c.* 1635-91), 301, 307, 534, 566

Brothais, F.: "A narrative of some Observations lately made by certain Missionaries in the Upper Egypt", 95 n3

Brouncker, William, Viscount (1620?-84), 204, 217, 218, 327, 329, 443, 486, 489; on anomalous suspension of mercury, 50-51, 88

Browne, Dr. Thomas, 56 n13

Butler, Mr., 144, 191, 192

Butler, John: χριστολογια (London, 1671), 17, 20

*C*ampanella Revived. *See* Stubbe, Henry

Campanella, Tommaso (1568-1639), 120, 122

Campani, Giuseppe, 424, 426

[Capponi, G. B., ed.]: *Memorie, imprese e ritratti de' Signore Accademici Gelati di Bologna* (Bologna, 1672), 310 n7; *Prose de' Signori Accademici Gelati di Bologna* (Bologna, 1671), 308, 309, 310 n7, 493, 578, 579

Carcavy, Pierre de (d. 1684), 469, 470

Cardianastrophe admiranda. *See* Hoffman, Friedrich

Caroline tables. *See* Streete, Thomas

Casaubon, Meric (1599-1671), 93; *A Letter ... to Peter du Moulin* (Cambridge, 1669), 96 n17

Cassianus Bassus, 334 n10

CASSINI, GIOVANNI DOMENICO (1625-1712), xix, xx, xxii, 97, 98, 272, 274, 350, 356, 357, 383, 392, 395, 568; his "Apology," 61, 579 n4; and conjunctions, 424, 426; discovery of Japet, 383-85, 386 n1, 423-25, 439-42, 475,

476; election to Royal Society, 501, 567; *Ephemerides mediceorum syderum* (Bologna, 1668), 180, 367; and Jupiter's satellites, 199, 200, 362, 365, 368 n4, 501, 524-25; *Lettera prima ... terza sopra l'hipothesi solari e le refrazioni* [Bologna, 1672], 578, 579; and lunar eclipse, 424, 426, 476, 477; *Nouvelles observations des taches du Soleil* (Paris, 1671), 194, 216, 218, 278, 279; and Saturn, 217, 218, 314, 315, 350, 352, 383, 424, 426, 443, 445, 476, 477; *Suite des observations des taches du Soleil* (Paris, 1671), 314, 315, 317 n1, 443, 445; and sunspots, 369, 371, 424, 425-26; unpublished papers by, 308, 309

— Letters to: 26 August 1671, **1779**, 216; 15 January 1671/2, **1868**, 475

— Letters from: 10 August 1671, **1769**, 193; 22 December 1671, **1848**, 423

Catalogus plantarum. *See* Berniz, Bernard von

Catalogus plantarum. *See* Ray, John

Catalogus plantarum Angliae. *See* Ray, John

Cazré, Pierre de, 453, 458; *Physica demonstratio ...* (Paris, 1645), 453, 458, 460 n5, 485, 488. *See also* La Loubère, Antoine de

Celsus, C. (2nd century A.D.), 212

Ceylon. *See* Baldaeus, Philippus

Chales, Claude François Milliet de: *Cursus seu mundus mathematicus* (Lyons, 1674), 546, 573, 576

Chamberlayne, Edward (1616-1703), 92, 95, 119, 123, 186, 255; *An Academy or College ...* (London, 1671), 95 n2

CHARAS, MOISE (1618-98), *Nouvelles Expériences sur la Vipère* (Paris, 1669), 287; *Suite des nouvelles Expériences* (Paris, 1617), 619, 622; and vipers, 620-25, 629-34

— Letters from: 28 March 1672, **1940**, 619; 30 March 1672, **1943**, 629

Charles II, King of England (1630-85), 204, 443, 448, 449

Charleton, Walter: *De scorbuto liber* (London, 1671), 326, 328, 371, 392, 407, 411

Chemistry, 37, 39; antimony, 17, 20, 77, 80, 146, 149-50, 368, 370; artificial iron, 25, 29, 78, 80, 278, 279; explosives, 25, 28, 77, 80, 278, 279; niter, 147, 149, 368, 370; salt of tartar, 38, 39; sal ammoniac, 407, 411-12

Childrey, Joshua: *Britannia Baconica* (London, 1660), 254, 513, 515

Chimia in artis formam redocta. *See* Rolfinck, Werner

Chronology. *See* Ravius, Christian
Cider and perry, 53–55, 187–8
Circoli. See Mengoli, Pietro
Clarke, Samuel (1625–69), 372, 388
Clarke, Timothy (d. 1672), 114, 115, 610, 611
Claudianus, Claudius, 582
Clavis mathematica. See Oughtred, William
Climate. *See* Weather Observations
Clocks. *See* Huygens, Christiaan, and longitude; Instruments
Cock, Christopher, 537 n3
Cock, Mr. (merchant), 97, 98, 271, 273
Cogitata physico-mathematica. See Mersenne, Marin
Cogitationes physico-mechanicae. See Ott, Johannes
Cohen, I. Bernard, 461 n8
Cold, 118
COLLINS, JOHN (1625–83), xxiii, 15, 18, 95 n3, 467, 511 n9; address of, 209 n7; and Borelli, 337, 338; and Flamsteed, 47, 136, 180, 363, 367, 390, 427, 526 nn 2 and 3, 533, 580; and Gregory, 22 n15, 128 n7, 136 n2, 171 nn2 and 8, 208; and Newton, 443, 467; and Sluse, 369, 371, 406, 411, 545, 572, 575; and Vernon, 438, 443, 501, 636, 637
— Letter from: *c.* 20 February 1671/2, **1906**, 545
Colonna, Fabio (*c.* 1567–1650), 213, 214
Colson, John: *The Method of Fluxions and Infinite Series*, 547 n6
Colwall, Daniel (d. 1690), 306 n, 428
Comenius, Johann Amos (1592–1671), 267
Commentarius in currum triumphalem. See Kerckring, Theodor
Commercium epistolicum. See Wallis, John
Comparaison de Platon et d'Aristote. See Rapin, René
Conférences sur les Sciences, xx
Considerations sur ... "Des passions ...." See Papin, Nicolas
Cook, Miles (*c.* 1630–99), 619, 622, 630, 631, 633, 634
Coral, tincture of, 60
Corcilli, Giuseppe, 61
CORNELIO, TOMMASO (1614–84?), xxii, 61, 62, 319, 493, 582; *Progymnasmata physica* (Venice 1663), 42, 494, 496; and Royal Society, 558–61; and tarantulas, 42, 307, 319, 494–97 529, 530, 534, 541, 555–57, 566, 609
— Letter to: 9 February 1671/2, **1893**, 529

— Letters from: 24 February 1671/2, **1911**, 558; to Dodington, 9 January 1671/2, **1876a**, 494; 24 February 1671/2, **1911a**, 561
Cosmicall Qualities. See Boyle, Robert
Cosmotheoria: *See* Fernel, Jean
Courbey, Mr., 4, 6
Court of the Gentiles. See Gale, Theophilus
Crabtree, William (1610?–44), 179, 180 n3
Cramoisy, André, 311, 313
Crew, Nathaniel (1633–1721), 341, 388
Croke, Richard (1623–83), 187
Croke, Unton, the Younger, 187
Cromwell, Oliver (1599–1658), 277, 279
Croone, William (1633–84), 554 n2
Crystallography, 586–89
Cursus mathematicus. See Chales, Claude François Milliet de
Curtius, Sir William, 24, 28

Dames (or Daems), Henry, 16, 19, 148, 150, 546
Daniel, Roger, printer, 188
De admirandis rebus Hungariae. See Bonanus, Procopius
De analysi. See Newton, Isaac
De anima brutorum. See Willis, Thomas
De animalibus insectis. See Aldrovandi, Ulyssi
"De antiguis mensuris," 282, 284
De ave Diomede. See Lachmund, Friedrich
De corpore. See Hobbes, Thomas
De cosmicis rerum qualitatibus. See Boyle, Robert
De cycloide. See La Loubère, Antoine de
De formatione pulli in ovo. See Malpighi, Marcello
De generatione animalium. See Aristotle; Harvey, William
De imaginatione. See Kisner, Johannes
De Indiae utriusque re naturali et medica libris XIV (Amsterdam, 1648). *See* Marggraf, Georg; Piso, Wilhelm
Dei summam honorem ... ex ... chronologia biblica. See Ravius, Christian
De jure manium. See Gouthieres, Jacques
De jure sensuum. See Stryk, Samuel
De lapide, 42
Delboe, Simon, 189 n5
De l'Education d'un Prince. See Nicole, Pierre
Dell' Istoria naturale. See Imperato, Ferrante
De magnete. See Gilbert, William
Democritean philosophy, 146, 148

De motionibus naturalibus a gravitate pendentibus liber. See Borelli, Giovanni Alphonso

De motu. See Baliani, Giovanni Battista

De mulierum organis. See Graaf, Regnier De

Dendrologiae . . . libri duo. See Aldrovandi, Ulyssi

Denis, Jean (d. 1704), 418, 419, 626; and Charas, 620–25, 629–34. See also *Conférences sur les Sciences*; *Mémoires concernant les Arts et les Sciences*

De piscibus marinis. See Rondelet, Guillaume

De Proportione qua gravia decidentia accelerantur. See Gassendi, Pierre

De resistentia solidorum. See Marchetti, Alessandro

Descartes, René (1596–1650), 95, 112, 122, 292, 295, 296, 299, 328, 329, 341, 342, 406, 411; letters of, 112, 144, 510; physiology of, 16, 19; *Principia philosophiae* (Amsterdam, 1644), 295, 299; on snow, 587; system of, 16, 20, 119–20, 146, 148, 293–94, 297–98, 326, 328

De scorbuto liber. See Charleton, Walter

Description anatomique . . . . See Académie Royale des Sciences

De sectionibus conicis. See Wallis, John

De solido intra solidum . . . dissertationis Prodromus. See Steno, Nicholas

De Son, Mr., 295, 298

De suffocatione hypochondriaca. See Kisner, Johannes

Deux machines propre à faire les quadrans. See Pardies, Ignace-Gaston

Diemerbroeck, Isbrand de: *Anatome corporis humanae* (Utrecht, 1672), 610, 611

Digby, Kenelm: *Experimenta medica* (Liège, 1671), 37, 39

Diophanti Alexandrini arithmeticorum. See Fermat, Samuel de

Diophanti redivivi. See Billy, Jacques de

Dioptrice. See Kepler, Johannes

Dioristice. See Bartholin, Erasmus

Diribitorium. See Helvetius, Jan Frederik

Discorsi matematiche. See Galilei, Galileo

Discours de la connoissance des bestes. See Pardies, Ignace-Gaston

Discours du mouvement local. See Pardies, Ignace-Gaston

Discourse concerning the Origins and Properties of Wind. See Bohun, Ralph

A Discourse of Local Motion. See Pardies, Ignace-Gaston

Discourse touching the Original of Human Literature. See Gale, Theophilus

Discours . . . sur l'anatomie du cerveau. See Steno, Nicholas

Discovery of Subterraneall Treasure. See Plattes, Gabriel

Disputatio de tarantula. See Senguerdius, Wolferdius

Dissertatio de origine catharri. See Lower, Richard

Dissertatio epistolico de bombyce. See Malpighi, Marcello

Dissertatio epistolica de formatione pulli in ovo. See Malpighi, Marcello

Dissertation de la philosophie en général. See Launay, Gilles de

Dissertationes duae medicae. See La Font, Charles de

Dissertatio physico-mathematica. See Screta, Heinrich

Divine History of Genesis of the World. See [Gott, Samuel]

Dodart, Denis (1634–1707), 117 n3: *Mémoires pour servir à l'histoire des plantes* (Paris, 1676), 116, 171 n3, 523

DODINGTON, JOHN (d. 1673), xxii, 61, 307, 529, 530; and Malpighi, xxii, 61, 62, 398, 400, 422, 490, 541, 555, 565, 579

— Letters to: 12 June 1671, **1725**, 105; 14 November 1671, **1822**, 358; 22 December 1671, **1847**, 422; 18 January 1671/2, **1874**, 490; 9 February 1671/2, **1894**, 532; 23 Febrary 1671/2, **1909**, 555; 26 February 1671/2 **1912**, 565

— Letters from: 12 May 1671, **1695**, 42; 25 May 1671, **1706**, 62; 5 January 1671/2, **1860**, 461; 19 January 1671/2, **1876**, 493; 16 February 1671/2, **1902**, 541; 8 March 1671/2, **1919**, 582; 21 March 1671/2, **1930**, 606

Donellan, John, 272, 274

Donzelli, Giuseppe: *Teatro farmaceutico* (Naples, 1661), 37, 39

Drebbel, Cornelius (1572–1634), 25, 28

Duclos, Samuel (d. 1715), 117 n3

Duke, Sir Edward (c. 1604–71), 133

Dun, Robert, (b. c. 1607), 630, 633

Dunkirk, fortification of, 140, 142 n20

Dupuy, Jacques (1586–1656) and Pierre (1582–1651), 540 n

Du Rietz, Grégoire-François (1607–82), 118

Dury, John (1596–1680), 267; *The Reformed Librarie-keeper* (London, 1650), 96 n16
Dyes: Lister's black, 43, 63, 302, 307, 354–55, 364; from worms, 37, 39, 69–70, 106, 137–38, 176, 178, 213

Earthquakes, 122
Eberhardt, Dr., 37, 39
Egypt, 92
Electricity, 147, 149, 151 n19, 294, 298
Elementa historiae. *See* Howell, William
Eliot, John: *Indian Dialogues* (Cambridge, Mass., 1671), 594; *Indian Primer* (Cambridge, Mass., 1669), 594; *Logick Primer* (Cambridge, Mass., 1672), 594
Elzevir, 545, 572, 575
Embryology. *See* Croone, William; Malpighi, Marcello
Enchiridion metaphysicum. *See* More, Henry
English Atlas: 77, 80, 82 n7
English Improver Improved. *See* Blith, Walter
English Pilot. *See* Seller, John
Ent, Sir George (1604–89), 83, 84
Entomology, 32, 289; ants, 301, 307; bees, 55, 153; capricorn beetle, 133, 156–57, 212, 301, 307; centipede, 153–54, 157, 212; *cimex*, 69–70, 79; glow worms, 79–80, 106, 139; ichneumon wasps, 154, 156, 209–11, 212, 258 n1, 263–64, 317–19; scale insects (kermes), 57–59, 63, 69–71, 89, 105–6, 137–38, 165, 302; silkworms, 154; viviparous flies, 43, 79, 211. *See also* Plants, excrescencies on
Eosander, Nils (1636–1705), 34, 35
Ephemerides mediceorum syderum. *See* Cassini, Giovanni Domenico
Ephemerides motuum coelestium. *See* Hecker, Johannes
Epicurean philosophy, 16–20, 120
Epistolae duae ad Thomam Bartholinum. *See* Borri, Giuseppe Francesco
Epistolam ... de scypho vitreo ... rupto. *See* Morhof, Daniel George
Epistolary Discourse concerning Phlebotomy. *See* Stubbe, Henry
Eratosthenes, 432
Eratosthenes Batavus: *See* Snel, Willberord
Erpenius (van Erpe), Thomas (1584–1624), 388
Escorial Library, 141

Esperienze intorno a diverse cose naturali. *See* Redi Francesco
Esperienze intorno alle generazione degl'insetti. *See* Redi, Francesco
Essay pour les Coniques. *See* Pascal, Blaise
Essay towards a Real Character. *See* Wilkins, John
Euclidis elementorum .... *See* Barrow, Isaac
Euripus. *See* Tides
Eutocios (*c*. 500), 545, 573, 576
Evangeliorum harmonia. *See* Toinard, Nicolas
Evelyn, John (1620–1706), 556; and Beale, 187
Exoticorum libri decem. *See* L'Ecluse, Charles de
Experimental Philosophy. *See* Power, Henry
Experimenta medica. *See* Digby, Kenelm
Experimenta nova ... Magdeburgica. *See* Guericke, Otto von
Experimentum chymicum novum. *See* Becher. Johann Joachim

Fabri, Honoré (*c*. 1607–88), 61, 120; on Archimedes, 546; *Brevis annotatio in systema Saturnium Christiani Eugenii* (Rome, 1660), 391 n5; *Synopsis optica* (Lyons, 1667), 390; *Tractatus physicus de motu locali* (Lyons, 1646), 453, 458, 460 n5, 485, 488
Fachs, Modestin: *Probier Büchlein* (Leipzig, 1595), 173, 174
Fairweather, Captain, 266, 305, 594
Fanoisius, Guido, 40 n10
Fasciculus 60. questionum. *See* Hannemann, Johann Ludwig
Fens, Hunts., 344–48
Ferdinandi, Epifanio (1569–1638), 535
Fermat, Pierre de (1601–65), 281, 283, 453, 458, 485, 488; *Oeuvres* (Paris, 1894), 460 n7
FERMAT, SAMUEL DE (1630–90), *Diophanti Alexandrini arithmeticorum libri sex* (Toulouse, 1670), 15, 18, 127, 134, 135, 146, 148
— Letters to: 7 August 1671, **1765**, 190; 25 January 1671/2, **1881**, 506
— Letters from: 4 July 1671, **1739**, 134; 22 December 1671, **1846**, 420
Fernel, Jean (1497–1558), 432, 437; *Cosmotheoria* (Paris, 1527), 438 n4, 500
Finch, Sir John (1626–82), 582
Fire, extinguishing of, 108, 110
Fish, Brazilian, 224–25, 238–39
FLAMSTEED, JOHN (1646–1719), xix, xx, xxvii, 140; and astronomical predictions, 45–47, 97, 98, 121, 207–8, 361–63, 391, 392, 427;

and Cassini, 362; and Collins, 47, 136, 180, 208, 363, 367, 390, 427, 526 nn2 and 3, 533, 580; and conjunctions, 45–47, 65; "De inaequalitate dierum naturalium," 136; and Hevelius, 65–66; and Jupiter's satellites, 362, 365–66, 524–25; and lenses, 390, 398 n, 427; and lunar diameter, 362, 366; and micrometer, 425, 581; and Newton, 525–26; and occultations, 45, 66, 362, 391, 580; and Saturn, 362, 366–67, 390; and Towneley, 362, 365, 367, 428, 581

— Letters to: 20 May 1671, **1702**, 57; 8 August 1671, **1766**, 190; 25 November 1671, **1831**, 387; 12 December 1671, **1841**, 398; 16 February 1671/2, **1901**, 541

— Letters from: 13 May 1671, **1697**, 45; 29 May 1671, **1708**, 65; 4 July 1671, **1740**, 136; 1 August 1671, **1760**, 179; 23 August 1671, **1776**, 207; late September 1671, **1791**, 268; 15 November 1671, **1824**, 361; 21 November 1671, **1826**, 365; 2 December 1671, **1835**, 390; 23 December 1671, **1849**, 427; 5 February 1617/2, **1888**, 524; 10 February 1671/2, **1895**, 532; 8 March 1671/2, **1918**, 580

Fonseca, Don Manuel da, 562, 564
Forro, Giovanni Maria, 542
Foss, Laurens (1637–1703), 37, 39
Fossils, 214–15
Framboisière, Nicholas Abraham de, 147, 149
Frederick II, Holy Roman Emperor and King of Sicily, 375, 380, 383 n1
Frejus, Roland: *Relation d'un Voyage fait dans la Mauritanie en 1666* (Paris, 1670), 93
Friderici, Johann Arnold (1637–72), 38, 40
Fuller, Thomas: *History of the Worthies of England* (London, 1662), 344
Fundamenta physices. See Le Roy, Henry
Further Discovery of M. Stubbe. See Glanvill, Joseph

Gale, Theophilus (1628–78), 111–12, 119, 122, 126–27, 255; *Court of the Gentiles* (London, 1669), 126; *Discourse touching the Original of Human Literature* (Oxford, 1669, 1671), 113 n2
Gale, Thomas (1635?–1702), xxiii
Galen, 151, 152
Galilei, Galileo (1564–1642), 112, 120, 122; *Discorsi matematiche* (Leiden, 1638), 453, 458, 460 nn4 and 8; life of, 173, 174, 331, 333, 356, 357, 484, 487, 513, 515, 613; *Sidereus nuncius* (Venice, 1610), 112
Gallois, Jean (1632–1707), 314, 316
Galls. See Plants, excrescencies on
Garden of Eden. See Platt, Sir Hugh
Garibal, Mr., 385
Garmers, Vincent, 512, 515
Garter, installation of Knights of the, 88
Gascoigne, William (1612?–44), 179, 180 n3
Gassendi, Pierre (1592–1655), 119, 453, 458; *De proportione qua gravia decidentia accelerantur epistolae tres* (Paris, 1646), 453, 458, 460 n6, 485, 488; *Institutio astronomica juxta hypotheseis tam veterum quam Copernici et Tychonis* (Paris, 1647, London 1653), 112; *The Mirrour of true Nobility and Gentility, being the life of . . . Peiresk* (London, 1657), 93, 121, 122, 127; *Opera omnia* (Lyons, 1658), 460 nn6 and 7
Generation, spontaneous. See Plants, excrescensies on
Geodesy. See Picard, Jean
Geographia et hydrographia reformata. See Riccioli, Giovanni Battista
Geoponica: 332, 334
Gezelius, Johannes (1647–1718), 173, 174, 198, 200
Gesner, Conrad (1516–65), 260, 262
Gilbert, William: *De magnete* (London, 1600), 25, 28, 111, 112, 122, 127
Giornale de' Letterati, xx, 62, 109, 110, 139, 141, 253, 493
Glanvill, Joseph (1636–80), 93; *A Further Discovery of M. Stubbe . . .* (London, 1671), 93; *Plus Ultra* (London, 1671), 11, 12; *A Praefatory Answer to Mr. Henry Stubbe* (London, 1671), 96 n17
Glisson, Francis: *Anatomia hepatis* (London, 1654), 448, 450, 450 n1
Globi coelestis in tabulas planas redacti descriptio. See Pardies, Ignace-Gaston
Glossographia. See Blount, Thomas
Goddard, Jonathan (1617–75), 401 n3
Godolphin, Sir William (1634?–96), 359, 360
Goltzius, Hubrecht: *Opera omnia* (Antwerp, 1644), 583
Gotha, Duke of. See Saxe-Gotha, Duke Ernest I of
[Gott, Samuel]: *The Divine History of Genesis of the World* (London, 1670), 120, 124 n10

Index

Gottignies, Gilles François de (1630–89): on *dioptrics*, 16, 19, 146, 148, 546, 573, 576

Gottorfische Kunst-Kammer. See Olearius, Adam

Gouthieres, Jacques: *De jure manium* (Paris, 1615), 146, 148, 182, 183

GRAAF, REGNIER DE (1614–73), xix, xxi, 619 n; *De mulierum organis generationi inservientibus* (Leiden, 1672), 610, 611; "De partibus genitalibus mulierum", 114, 115; *De succo pancreatico* (Leiden, 1671), 114, 115, 610, 611

— Letter to: 16 October 1671, **1801**, 303

— Letters from: 19 June 1671, **1729**, 114; 21 March 1671/2, **1931**, 610

Gramann, Mr., 33, 34, 126

Grammar, French. *See* Mauger, Claude

Grandami, Jacques: *Nova demonstratio immobilitatis terrae* (La Flèche, 1645), 25, 28, 77, 80, 277, 279, 295, 299, 300 n16

Greaves, Edward (1608–80), 372, 388

Greaves, John (1602–52), xxv, 372, 388

Greaves, Thomas (1612–76), 373 n6, 388

Greenland, queries on, 140, 514, 516

Gregory, James (1638–75), xxiv, 17, 20, 282, 284, 330 n6, 510; correspondence with Collins, 22 n15, 128 n7, 136 n2, 547 n and n9

Gregory, Mr., 327, 328

GREW, NEHEMIAH (1641–1712), xix, xxii, 89, 309 n3; identified, 590 n; *Anatomy of Vegetables Begun* (London, 1671), xxiii, 89, 91 n3, 106, 392, 399, 400, 429, 462, 463, 529, 531, 551, 553, 586, 590 n—sent to Malpighi, 399, 400, 491, 492, 565, 577, 578—; on snow, 586–89

— Letter from: 12 March 1671/2, **1921**, 586

Grey, Thomas (1654–1720), 386

Grimaldi, Francesco Maria (1618–63), 87 n2

Grisley, Gabriel, 199, 201

Gryling, Dr., 513, 515

Gude, Marquard (1635–89), 332, 334

Guericke, Otto von (1602–86), 294, 298; *Experimenta nova (ut vocantur) Magdeburgica* (Amsterdam, 1672), 300 n9

Gutherius, Jacobus. *See* Gouthieres, Jacques

Hadley, John (1682–1744), xxiv

Hale, John, 267 n, 389 n

Halley, Edmond (1656–1742), 128 n8

Hallincg (Hallinkg, Halling), Mr., 610, 611

HANNEMANN, JOHANN LUDWIG (*c.* 1640–1724), identified, 450 n; *Fasciculus 60. questionum ...* (Bremen, 1672), 449, 450, 451 n2

— Letter from: 3 January 1671/2, **1858**, 448

Harell, Mr., 38, 40

Hartlib, Samuel (d. 1662), 96 n16, 188; *The Reformed Commonwealth of Bees* (London, 1655), 55

Harvey, William (1578–1657), 127, 448, 450; *De generatione animalium* (London, 1651), 554 n4

Hecker, Johannes: *Ephemerides motuum coelestium ab anno 1666 ad annum 1680* (Danzig, 1662), 362, 366

Heer, Henricus ab: *Spadacrene* (Liège, 1614, and Leiden, 1645), 147, 149

HELMFELD, GUSTAVUS (1651–74)

— Letters from: 3 May 1671, **1691**, 33; 15 November 1671, **1823**, 359

Helmont, Francis Mercury van (1614–99), 182, 183

Helmont, Johann Baptist van (1577?–1648), 13, 14 n3

Helvetius, Jan Frederik: *Diribitorium* (Amsterdam, 1670), 37, 39

Henshaw, Nathaniel (1628–73), 32

Henshaw, Thomas (1618–1700), 548, 549, 591, 593

Herodotus, 261

Hesse, Ludwig VII, Landgrave of, 38, 40

Hesychius, 319

HEVELIUS, JOHANNES (1611–87), xix, xx, 331, 333, 394–95; on comets, 122, 568–71, 592, 593, 594; and eclipses, 207–8, 428; and the French, 199, 200, 201, 218, 219, 272, 274, 395; *Machina coelestis* (Danzig, 1673), xix, 136, 272, 274, 356, 357, 369, 371, 391, 591, 593; *Mercurius in sole visus* (Danzig, 1662), 208, 367; his micrometer, 3, 6, 272, 274, 351, 353; his microscope, 3, 6, 67, 68, 85, 86, 97, 98, 273, 278, 280, 349, 351, 591, 593; and moon, 269, 331, 332–33; observations of, 65, 97, 98, 208, 217, 218, 219, 271–76, 330–31, 332–33, 356, 357, 424, 426, 443, 445, 568–71; receives books, 67–68, 273; and Royal Society, 349, 351; *Selenographia* (Danzig, 1647), 47, 65, 87 n2, 136, 439, 441

— Letters to: 29 May 1671, **1709**, 67; 12 June 1671, **1723**, 97; 9 November 1671, **1817**, 349; 18 March 1671/2, **1924**, 591

— Letters from: 21 April 1671, **1683**, 3; 9 June 1671, **1718**, 85; 27 September 1671,

1792, 371; 28 February 1671/2, **1915**, 568
Hickes, George, 395 n7
Hickman, Spencer, 429
Hill, Abraham (1635–1722), xxii, 156 n
HILL, THOMAS, xxii, 220, 235; identified, 156 n
— Letter to: ?30 August 1671, **1780**, 220
— Letters from: 13 July 1671, **1747**, 155; 20 February 1671/2, **1905**, 544
Historia et meteorologia incendii Aetnaei. See Borelli, Giovanni Alphonso
Historia insectorum generalis. See Swammerdam, Jan
Historia naturalis Brasiliae (Leiden and Amsterdam, 1648). *See* Marggraf, Georg; Piso, Wilhelm
History of Japan. See Kaempfer, Engelbert
History of the Royal Society. See Birch, Thomas; Sprat, Thomas
History of the Worthies of England. See Fuller, Thomas
HJÄRNE, URBAN (1641–1724), xxi; identified, 382 n; and election to Royal Society, 373, 379
— Letter from: 23 November 1671, **1829**, 373
Hobbes, Thomas (1588–1679), xx; *Considerations upon the Answer of Dr. Wallis* (London, 1671), 179 n, 204, 205–6; *Elementorum philosophiae secto prima: De corpore* (London, 1655), 294, 297, 300 n7; *Rosetum geometricum* (London, 1671), 128–31, 169, 171, 181, 202–3; *To the Right Honourable ... the Members of the Royal Society* (London, 1671), 179 n, 181, 202–3, 204; works of, 282, 284
Hoffmann, Friedrich (1626–75), 448, 450; *Cardianastrophe admiranda* (Leiden, 1740), 37, 39, 451 n2
Holles, Denzil: *A True Relation of the Unjust Accusation of certain French Gentlemen* (London, 1671), 139, 142 n5
Holmes, Sir Robert (1622–92), 611 n3
Hooke, Robert (1635–1703), 57 n3, 74 n1, 188, 282, 284, 295, 299, 386, 391, 401, 501; and astronomy, 45, 47, 65, 97, 98, 350–53, 362, 369, 371, 424, 426, 580; *Micrographia* (London, 1665), xix, 455, 459, 486, 489, 556; and Newton, 543, 544, 604; and optics, 452, 457, 509, 510, 523, 537 nn3 and 4, 568, 580; on snow, 587; his thermometer, 30–32; his wheel barometer, 125 n29
Horace: *Ars poetica*, 422 n5, 556
Horne, Johann van (1621–70), 619 n

Horneck, Anthony (1641–97), 122, 125 n25
Horologium. See Huygens, Christiaan
Horologium oscillatorium. See Huygens, Christiaan
Horologium thaumanticum. See Pardies, Ignace-Gaston
Horrox, Jeremiah (1617?–44), 180 nn3 and 4; *Opera posthuma* (London, 1672), 545, 573, 576
Horst, Johann Daniel (1620–85), 37, 39
Horticultura. See Laurenberg, Peter Villumsen
How, William (1620–56), 332, 334, 613; *Phytologia Britannica* (London, 1650), 334 n12
Howard, Henry, Duke of Norfolk (1628–84), 93, 123
Howard, House of, 121
Howell, William, *Elementa historiae* (London, 1671), 17, 20
Hungary, queries on, 254
Hunt, Henry, 502 n14
HUYGENS, CHRISTIAAN (1629–95), 122, 125 n19, 191, 192, 386 n1, 401, 407, 467, 483; and Alhazen's Problem, xix, xxi, xxii, 15, 18, 146, 314, 316, 369, 370, 444, 446, 519, 521, 571, 575, 635–37; anagrams of, 511 n1; and anomalous suspension of mercury, 51, 467 n5; on cycloidal motion, 454, 459, 486, 489, 509, 510; "De motu corporum ...," 511 n1; health of, 167, 170, 443, 445, 501; *Horologium* (The Hague, 1658), 490 n4; *Horologium oscillatorium* (Paris, 1673), 461 n9, 486, 489, 501, 546, 573, 576; and longitude, 315, 316, 444, 446, 511 n1, 519, 521; and optics, 523; and Newton, 447, 461, 473 n, 476, 477, 507, 508, 517–18, 520–21, 544, 592, 593, 635, 637; on Saturn's ring, xx, 97, 98, 217, 218, 314–16, 350, 351–52, 356, 357, 369, 371, 390, 519, 522; *Systema Saturnium* (The Hague, 1659), 217, 218, 391 n5, 398 n, 427, 532, 541, 581; and Wallis's *Mechanica sive de motu*, 469, 470, 518, 521. *See also* Cassini, Giovanni Domenico, *Suite des observations des taches du Soleil*
— Letters to: 22 July 1671, **1752**, 167; 14 October 1671, **1798**, 291; 1 January 1671/2, **1856**, 443; 15 January 1671/2, **1866**, 468; 12 February 1671/2, **1899**, 536; 11 March 1671/2, **1920**, 584
— Letters from: 28 October 1671, **1807**, 313; 3 February 1671/2, **1886**, 517; 30 March 1672, **1944**, 635

Huygens, Constantijn (1596–1687), 314, 316
Hyde, Thomas: *Catalogus impressorum librorum Bibliothecae Bodlejanae* (Oxford, 1674), 93, 123; *Tabulae long. ac. lat. stellarum fixarum ex observatione Ulugh Beighi* (Oxford, 1665), 282, 284
Hydrologia chymica. *See* Simpson, William
Hydrostatics, 37, 39
Hypomnemata mathematica. *See* Snel, Willebrord
Hypothesis physica nova. *See* Leibniz, Gottfried Wilhelm

Iatrochemistry, 13–14
ibn Ishaq, Hunain, 547 n5
Iceland, xix, 158–63
Idea of Mathematicks. *See* Pell, John
Imperato, Ferrante: *Dell' Istoria naturale libri XXVIII* (Naples, 1599, and Venice, 1672), 42, 43 n6, 542, 608–9
Indian curiosities, 266–67, 305
Indian Dialogues. *See* Eliot, John
Indian Primer. *See* Eliot, John
Inquiries: for agriculture, 344–48, 318 n1; for Brazil, xix, xxii, 155, 220–51, 544; for Greenland, 140, 514, 516; for Hungary, 254; for Japan, 189 n5; for Moscow, 53 n1
Institutio astronomica. *See* Gassendi, Pierre
Instruments: barometers, 118, 123, 443, 527; clocks, 30 31, 315, 316, 444, 446, 519, 521, 546, 581; micrometers, 3, 6, 272, 274, 351, 353, 390–91, 428, 581, 582 n3; microscopes, 3, 6, 67, 68, 85, 86, 97, 98, 278, 280, 349, 351, 394; thermometers, 30–32, 294, 298; thermostat, 25, 28. *See also* Astronomy; Microscopy; Morland, Sir Samuel; Telescopes
Introduction to Algebra, *See* Rahn, J. H.
Inventions: air gun, 294, 298; communication of, 43–44; steel, 78, 81, 277, 279, 535; sundial, 452, 457; water-raising device, 374, 379. *See also* Instruments

Jamaica, 139–40
Japan: relations with, 186; queries on, 189 n5
Jesuits, xxii, 92, 120–23, 139, 140, 191, 192; in Brazil, 155, 220, 544
Jolly, T. (bookseller), 627, 628
Jones, Henry (c. 1642–95), 30
Jones, Richard, Viscount Ranelagh (1640/41–1712), 303, 304

Josephus: *Jewish Antiquities*, 93
Journal des Sçavans, xx, 77, 80, 620, 623, 626; Latin translation of, 108, 110; nonappearance of, 314, 316
Journal des Voyages. *See* Monconys, Balthazar de
Judaism, 527
Jungius, Joachim (1587–1657), 173, 174, 356, 357, 512, 514–15; *Phoranomica*, ed. H. Sivers, 199, 201, 512, 513, 514, 515, 614
Justel, Henri (1620–93), xxvii, 36, 38, 108, 110, 134, 135, 281, 283, 291 n1, 385, 386, 452, 456–57, 468, 470, 518, 521, 540 n, 626, 627

Kaempfer, Engelbert, *History of Japan* (London, 1727–28), 189 n5
Keeling, Lord Chief Justice, 139, 142 n5
Kepler, Johannes: *Tabulae Rudolphinae* (Ulm, 1627), 5, 6, 97, 98, 331, 333; *Dioptrice* (Augsburg, 1611), 112; *Strena seu de nive sexangula* (Frankfurt-am-Main, 1611), 590 n3
Kerckring, Theodor (1639 or 1640–93), xxi; *Anthropogeniae ichnographia* (Amsterdam, 1671), 37, 39, 53, 610, 611; *Commentarius in currum triumphalem antimonii Basilii Valentini* (Amsterdam, 1671), 37, 39, 146, 149
Kermes. *See* Entomology, scale insects
Kinckhuysen, Gerard: English translation of his *Algebra, ofte stel-Konst* (Haarlem, 1661), 547 n6, 573, 576; proposed Latin translation of his *Algebra*, 385, 392, 636, 637
Kircher, Athanasius (1602–80), 121, 322, 324, 452, 457, 535; *Magnes, sive de arte magnetica* (Rome, 1641), 29 n8; on magnetism, 25, 28, 77, 80
KIRKBY, CHRISTOPHER, 7 n2, 67, 68; and lenses, 394
— Letters to: 29 May 1671, **1710**, 69; 12 January 1671/2, **1864**, 466; 18 March 1671/2, **1926**, 596
—Letters from: 16 September 1671, **1790**, 268; 9 December 1671, **1838**, 393; 10 February 1671/2, **1898**, 535
Kerkby, Colonel, 395
KISNER, JOHANNES: identified, 40 n; *De imaginatione* (Jena, 1665), and *De suffocatione hypochondriaca* (Leiden, 1670), 37, 39, 40 n2
— Letter to: 24 July 1671, **1754**, 172
— Letter from: 12 May 1671, **1694**, 36
Kornmann, Dr., 37, 39, 172, 176, 178

Küffler, Johann Siberius (1595–1677), 25–28, 77, 80, 267, 277, 279

Lachmund, Friedrich: *Admirandorum fossilium ... descriptio* (Hildesheim, 1669), 173, 174; *De ave Diomede dissertatio* (Amsterdam, 1674), 513, 516
La Font, Charles de: *Dissertationes duae medicae de veneno pestilenti* (Amsterdam, 1671), 37, 39
La Loubère, Antoine de: *De cycloide* (Toulouse, 1660), 15, 19, 545, 572, 575; *Propositiones geometricae sex, quibus ostenditur ex cazraeianae hypothesi ...* [Toulouse, 1658], 453, 458, 460 n8, 485, 488
Lambecius, Petrus (1628–80), 322, 324
Lamphire, John (1614–88), 341
Lana, Francisco (1631–87), 140; *Prodromo ... all' Arte Maestra* (Brescia, 1670), 122
Launay, Gilles de, 146, 148; *Dissertation de la philosophie en général* (Paris, 1668), 16, 19
Laurenberg, Peter Villumsen: *Horticultura* (Frankfurt, 1631), 55
LE BOURGEOIS, ESSAIE, xxi; identified, 329 n
— Letter to: 11 November 1671, **1820**, 355
— Letter from: 31 October 1671, **1810**, 325
L'Ecluse, Charles de: *Exoticorum libri decem* (Antwerp, 1605), 466
Lectiones geometricae. See Barrow, Isaac
Lectiones opticae. See Barrow, Isaac; Newton, Isaac
Lee, Samuel, 67, 68, 394
Lefevre, Nicholas: *Traicté de la Chymie* (Paris, 1660), 13, 15 n4, 630, 633
Le Grand, Antoine: *Philosophia veterum e mente Renati Descartes, more scholastico breviter digesta* (London, 1671), 95, 122
LEIBNIZ, GOTTFRIED WILHELM (1646–1716), xxi, xxiv, 475 n; *Hypothesis physica nova* (Mainz, 1671), 10, 11, 22–28, 76, 79, 99–101, 103, 104, 182, 183, 256 n11, 277, 279, 337, 338—English edition (London, 1671), 102, 103, 191, 192—; on magnetism, 25, 28, 77, 80, 295, 299; on mechanical philosophy, 293, 297; *Notitia opticae promotae* (Frankfurt, 1671), 292, 296; *Theoria motus abstracti*, 10, 11, 73–74, 101–2, 103, 281, 283, 341–43, 388
— Letters to: 24 April 1671, **1685**, 10; 12 June 1671, **1724**, 99; 4 August 1671, **1762**, 182; 28 September 1671, **1793**, 277

— Letters from: 29 April 1671, **1688**, 22; 8 June 1671, **1716**, 76; 10 June 1671, **1721**, 91; 15 October 1671, **1799**, 292
Leijonberg, Johan (1625–91), 375, 380
Lenses. See Optics
Le Roy, Henri (1598–1679): *Fundamenta physices* (Amsterdam, 1646), 112
Lettera ... sopra alcune opposizione ... intorno alle vipere. See Redi, Francesco
Lettere. See Cassini, Giovanni Domenico
Lettre d'un philosophe. See R. J.
Ligon, Richard: *A true and exact history of Barbadoes* (London, 1650, 1657), 262
Lipstorp, Daniel: *Specimina philosophiae cartesianae* (Leiden, 1653), 112
LISTER, MARTIN (?1638–1712), xix, xxvii, 139, 262, 289; and anatomy of plants, 462–65, 505, 566, 604–5; and ants, 301, 307; his black resin, 43, 63, 302, 307, 354–55, 364, 429, 465, 505–6; on circulation of sap, 9; election to Royal Society, 43, 44, 63–64, 300, 306, 339, 354, 428; and fossil shells, 214–15; and glowworms, 106; health of, 137, 156; and ichneumon wasps, 154, 156, 209, 210, 212, 263–64, 317–19—why so called, 319—; and insect dyes, 213; on kermes, 57–59, 63, 105–6, 137–38, 165; and Ray, 71, 75, 90, 116, 132–33, 137, 154, 163, 213, 286, 364; and spiders, 210, 212, 340, 555–56; on vegetable colors, 44; and vegetable excrescences, 71–72, 116, 154, 156, 163–66, 176, 178, 215, 263–64, 317–19, 339, 605; and viviparous fly, 43, 211, 257
— Letters to: 27 May 1671, **1707**, 63; 10 June 1671, **1720**, 89; 24 June 1671, **1731**, 116; 13 July 1671, **1748**, 150; 27 July 1671, **1757**, 176; 4 September 1671, **1785**, 257; 12 October 1671, **1797**, 289; 21 October 1671, **1804**, 316; 4 November 1671, **1814**, 339; 18 November 1671, **1825**, 364; 23 December 1671, **1850**, 428; 24 January 1671/2, **1880**, 505; 10 February 1671/2, **1897**, 534; 27 February 1671/2, **1913**, 566
— Letters from: 28 April and 13 May 1671, **1696**, 43; 22 May 1671, **1703**, 57; 30 May 1671, **1711**, 69; 31 May 1671, **1712**, 71; 14 June 1671, **1726**, 105; 5 July 1671, **1741**, 137; 17 July 1671, **1751**, 163; 25 August 1671, **1778**, 212; 13 September 1671, **1787**, 263; 16 October 1671, **1800**, 300; 28 October 1671, **1808**, 317; 11 November 1671,

1819, 354; 10 January 1671/2, **1863**, 462; 24 February 1671/2, **1910**, 555; 19 March 1671/2, **1929**, 604

Livy, Titus Livius, 582

Locke, John (1632–1704), 540 n

Loft, John, 43, 70, 89

Logick Primer. See Eliot, John

Lohrman, Gustavus, 118

Longitude, determination of, 121, 315, 316, 444, 446, 511 n1, 519, 521

Lonicer, Adam: *Naturalis historiae opus novum* (Frankfurt-am-Main, 1551), 513, 515

Lord Bacons Relation of the Sweating Sickness. See Stubbe, Henry

Lower, Richard: *Dissertatio de origine catharri* (Amsterdam, 1671), 168, 170, 199, 201— (London, 1671), 201 n7—; *Tractatus de corde* (2nd ed., London, 1671), 168, 170, 282, 284

Lucan, Marcus Annaeus Lucanus, 582

Ludwig, Daniel (1625–80), 38, 39; *Dissertatio de volatilitate salis tartari* (Gotha, 1667), 41 n23

M*achina coelestis*. See Hevelius, Johannes

Magiae universalis. See Schott, Gaspar

Magnes. See Kircher, Athanasius

Magnetism: 25, 28, 121, 255, 295, 299

Mainz, Elector of. See Schönborn, Johann Philip von

MALPIGHI, MARCELLO (1628–94), xix, xxii, xxiii, 62, 493, 497 n, 541, 555, 590 n; *Anatome plantarum* (London, 1675), 309 n2, 565 n3, 615, 616; *Anatomes plantarum idea* (London, 1675), xxii, 308, 309, 392, 398–401, 429, 462, 503, 504, 505, 530, 531, 534, 551, 553, 555, 565, 566, 577, 578, 604–5, 615, 616; *De ovo incubato observationes* (London, 1675), 615, 616; *Dissertatio epistolica de bombyce* (London, 1669), 429, 566; *Dissertatito espistolica de formatione pulli in ovo* (London, 1673), xxii, 503–4, 551, 553, 565, 566, 573, 576, 577, 578; health of, 61, 308, 309, 577, 578, 615–16; and Royal Society, 503–4, 551–54, 565, 577, 578, 614, 615

— Letters to: 14 December 1671, **1842**, 398; 18 January 1671/2, **1875**, 491; 22 February 1671/2, **1908**, 551

— Letters from: 24 May 1671, **1705**, 60; 22 October 1671, **1805**, 308; 22 January 1671/2,

1879, 503; 5 March 1671/2, **1917**, 577; 26 March 1672, **1936**, 614

al-Mamun, Abdullah (786–833), 432

Mandelslo, Johann Albrecht (1616–44), 534

Marchand, Léon (d. *c*. 1682), 523

Marchetti, Alessandro: *De resistentia solidorum* (Florence, 1669), 15, 19, 127

Marggraf, Georg: *Historiae rerum naturalium Brasiliae libri VIII*, in *Historia naturalis Brasiliae* (Amsterdam, 1648), 220–51, 466, 483; *Tractatus topographicus & meteorologus Brasiliae*, in *De Indiae utriusque re naturali et medica libris XIV* (Amsterdam, 1648), 220–51, 466, 483

Mariotte, Edmé (*c*. 1620–84), 524 n5, 568

Marmora Arundelliana. See Selden, John

Marmora Oxoniensis (Oxford, 1676), 93, 96 n10

Martin, John, 11, 12, 102, 104, 104 n8, 417, 419

Mathematics, 15–21, 127–28; algebra, 545; Alhazen's Problem, xix, xxiii, 15, 18, 146, 168, 170, 314, 316, 369, 370, 401–6, 407–11, 444, 446, 519, 521, 536, 537, 635–37; conics, 510, 511, 545, 546, 574, 576; logarithms, 168, 170, 546; maxima and minima, 17–18, 20–21, 546; monachos, 406, 412 n4; printing of books on, 93; tangents, method of, 510

Matter, definition of, 341–43

Mattioli, Pietro Andrea (1501–77), 301

Mauger, Claude: *French Grammar*, 326, 328

MAURITIUS, ERICH (1631–91), xxi; identified, 599 n

— Letters from: 19 March 1671/2, **1927**, 596; 22 March 1671/2, **1932**, 612

Maurolyco, Francesco (1494–1575), 42

Mechanica, sive de motu. See Wallis, John

Mechanical philosophy, 255, 293, 297

Mechanics, 484–89, 509, 510, 627, 628; anomalous suspension of mercury, 50–51, 88; cycloidal motion, 459, 461 n9; falling bodies, 453, 458, 461 n8; laws of motion, 102, 103, 293–94, 297–98, 341–43; pendulum, 432; "theses on local motion", 282, 284, 413, 415. *See also* Leibniz, Gottfried Wilhelm; Pardies, Ignace-Gaston; Wallis, John; Werner, Georg Christoph

Medici, Leopold de' (1617–75), 108, 110

Medicine: baths, 14; chemical remedies, 13–14, 38, 39–40, 60, 109, 110, 256 n10, 301, 407, 411; correspondence, 172; pathological

evacuation, 418, 419; promotion of, 108, 110; resuscitation, 374–82; scurvy, 326, 328, 370, 371, 406–7, 411; tropical, 221–23, 236–37. *See also* Charleton, Walter; *Miscellanea curiosa*; Spas; Willis, Thomas
Meibom, Heinrich, the Younger (1638–1700), 513, 515
Mémoires concernant les Arts et les Sciences, xx, 524 n1, 620, 623, 626, 629, 632
Mémoires pour servir à l'histoire naturelle des animaux. *See* Académie Royale des Sciences
Mengoli, Pietro, 61; *Circoli* (Bologna, 1672), 578; *Speculazioni di Musica* (Bologna, 1670), 16, 19, 146, 148, 308, 309, 546, 573, 576
Mercator, Nicholas (fl. 1640–87), 295, 299; writings of, 168, 170, 171 n8, 282, 284
Mercurius Librarius, 11, 12
Merman, 286, 287, 289
Merret, Christopher (1614–95), 188, 254; *Pinax* (London, 1666), 256 n6, 538, 540
Mersenne, Marin: *Cogitata physico-mathematica* (Paris, 1644), 510, 511 n9
Mesure de la Terre. *See* Picard, Jean
Metrology, 311, 312, 434, 436
Meurisse, Mr., 317 n7
Mewe, William, 55
Mice, plague of, 420–22, 506, 507
Micrographia. *See* Hooke, Robert
Microscopy, xix, 605. *See also* Grew, Nehemiah; Hevelius, Johannes; Hooke, Robert; Malpighi, Marcello
Milliet de Chales, Claude François. *See* Chales, Claude François Milliet de
Mills, 347
Mining in Sweden, 173, 174
Miraculum naturae. *See* Swammerdam, Jan
Miscellanea curiosa, xx, 107, 109, 122, 153, 154 n3, 157, 253; account of second year, 321–24, 417, 418
Monconys, Balthazar de: *Journal des Voyages* (Lyons, 1665–66), 25, 28, 77, 80, 277, 279
Monmouth, James Scott, Duke of (1649–85), 327, 329
Montagu, Edward, Earl of Sandwich (1625–72), 30
Montalbani, Ovidio, 146, 148
Montanari, Geminiano (1632–87), 60, 61; *Speculazioni fisiche ... sopra gli effeti di que' vetri temprati ...* (Bologna, 1671), 37, 39; on sunspots, 308, 309; and variable stars, 308, 309, 385

Moore, Jonas (1617–79), xix, 137 n5, 180 and n4, 582 n3
Moray, Sir Robert (c. 1608–73), 443, 468, 469, 520, 522, 595
More, Henry (1614–87), 120, 168, 170, 282, 284; *Antidote against Atheism* (2nd ed., London, 1662), 124 n4; *Enchiridion metaphysicum* (London, 1671), 548, 549, 550 n3
Morgan, Henry (1635?–88), 142 n14
Morhof, Daniel George: *De cosmicis rerum qualitatibus* (Amsterdam and Hamburg, 1671), 332, 333; *Epistolam ... de scypho vitreo ... rupto* (Kiel, 1672), 513, 516
Morison, Robert (1620–83), 254, 372, 466, 483; *Plantarum umbelliferarum distributio nova* (Oxford, 1672), 56, 93, 94, 548, 549, 613; *Praeludia botanica* (London, 1669), 94
Morland, Sir Samuel: *Tuba stentoro-phonica* (London, 1671), 392, 417, 419, 429, 430, 443, 445, 446, 467, 468, 469, 493, 506, 507, 513, 516, 519, 521, 530, 531, 538, 540, 546, 573, 575–76, 592, 593, 613, 627, 628— French version, 523, 567–68, 573, 575
Moscow, queries on, 35 n1
Mouffet, Thomas: *Insectorum sive minimorum animalium theatrum* (London, 1634), 153, 157, 212

Naauwkeurige beschryvinge van Malabar en Choromandel. *See* Baldaeus, P.
Natural history: xix, 121, 267; anomalous, 107–8, 109; exotic, 220–51, 331, 333, 357, 358, 443, 446, 513, 515; in France, 359–61, 420–22, 538, 540; in Greenland, 514, 516; in Germany, 356, 357, 393–94, 513, 515; in Italy, 559, 561; in New England, 595. *See also* Inquiries
Naturalis historiae opus. *See* Lonicer, Adam
Nature of the drink Kauhi. *See* Pocock, Edward
Needham, Walter (d. 1691), 17, 20
Neile, William (1637–70), 73, 74, 102, 103, 341, 342
Nelson, Peter, 14 n1
New Experiments and Observations touching Cold. *See* Boyle, Robert
New Experiments, Physico-Mechanicall. *See* Boyle, Robert
NEWTON, ISAAC (1642–1727), xxi, xxiii, 300 n7, 443, 572, 575; and astronomy, 617; and cider, 190 n18; *De analysi*, 547 n6, 573, 576; *Lectiones opticae* (London, 1729), 545, 547 n6,

573, 576; and mathematics, 545; and optical theory, 523, 528, 533, 543, 544, 545, 585, 604; and Pardies, xxi; and Royal Society, 443, 447, 461, 502, 509; his telescope, 443, 444, 445–46, 447, 461, 466–67, 468–73, 476, 477, 501, 502, 507–8, 509, 517–18, 520–21, 525–26, 530, 531, 536, 537, 538, 540, 541, 544, 545, 549, 550, 568, 572–73, 575, 581 n1, 585, 590, 591, 592, 604, 613, 617, 626. *See also* Colson, John; Kinckhuysen, Gerard
— Letters to: 2 January 1671/2, **1857**, 447; 20 January 1671/2, **1878**, 502; 27 January 1671/2, **1882**, 508; 8 February 1671/2, **1892**, 528; 17 or 19 February 1671/2, **1903**, 543; 16 March 1671/2, **1922**, 590; 23 March 1671/2, **1933**, 612; *c.* 26 March 1672, **1939**, 619
— Letters from: 6 January 1671/2, **1861**, 461; 18 January 1671/2, **1871**, 482; 29 January 1671/2, **1883**, 509; 6 February 1671/2, **1891**, 528; 10 February 1671/2, **1896**, 533; 20 February 1671/2, **1904**, 544; 16 March 1671/2, **1923**, 591; 19 March 1671/2, **1928**, 604; 26 March 1672, **1937**, 617; 30 March 1672, **1941**, 626
Nicholas of Damascus, 605 n3
Nicole, Pierre, *De l'Education d'un Prince* (Paris, 1670), 523
Nitzsche, Fridericus (1645–1702), 108, 110
Notitia opticae promotae. See Leibniz, Gottfried Wilhelm
Nouvelles Expériences sur la Vipère. See Charas, Moise
Nouvelles observations. See Cassini, Giovanni Domenico
Nova de machinis philosophia. See Zucchi, Niccolo
Nova demonstratio immobilitatis terrae. See Grandami, Jacques
Novgorod, plan of, 396
Novum Organum. See Bacon, Francis
Nucleus historiae ecclesiasticae. See Sandius, Christopher
Nuland, Franz Wilhelm, Freiherr von, 48, 49, 122; *Elementa physica* (The Hague, 1669), 125 n19, 294, 298
Nunnes, Thomas, 428 n3
Nuns, Mr., 427

Observatory, Paris, xxii, 98, 186, 523
Oculus Enoch et Eliae. See Schyrlaeus, Anton Maria

Ogilby, John (1600–76), maps of (1670–75), 80, 82 n7
Oldenburg, Dora Katherina (1654–77), 141
OLDENBURG, HENRY (?1618–77), book deals of, 11, 12, 16, 19, 172, 281, 284, 341, 413, 415, 451–52, 456, 562, 564, 583; and Boyle, xxvi; correspondence with Germany, xxi; correspondence with Italy, 300; correspondence with Sweden, xxi; as editor, xx, 95, 119, 139; and Grew, 590 n; loan of books, xix, 47, 65, 136, 398 n, 427, 532, 541, 581, 591; as Secretary, xxi, 595; sends books to Hevelius, 67–68; sends books to Leibniz, 102, 104; as translator, 125 n23
LETTERS TO
— from Beale: 13 May 1671, **1700**, 52; *c.* 12 June 1671, **1722**, 92; *c.* 16 June 1671, **1728**, 111; 24 June 1671, **1733**, 119; 8 July 1671, **1743**, 139; 6 August 1671, **1764**, 186; 2 September 1671, **1784**, 253
— from Becher: 16 October 1671, **1802**, 303
— from Bell: 3 June 1671, **1714**, 74
— from Bernard: 4 February 1671/2, **1887**, 523
— from Cassini: 10 August 1671, **1769**, 193; 22 December 1671, **1848**, 423
— from Charas: 28 March 1672, **1940**, 619; 30 March 1672, **1943**, 629
— from Collins: *c.* 20 February 1671/2, **1906**, 545
— from Cornelio: 24 February 1671/2, **1911**, 558
— from Dodington: 12 May 1671, **1695**, 42; 25 May 1671, **1706**, 62; 5 January 1671/2, **1860**, 461; 19 January 1671/2, **1876**, 493; 16 February 1671/2, **1902**, 541; 8 March 1671/2, **1919**, 582; 21 March 1671/2, **1930**, 606
— from Fermat: 4 July 1671, **1739**, 134; 22 December 1671, **1846**, 420
— from Flamsteed: 13 May 1671, **1697**, 45; 29 May 1671, **1708**, 65; 4 July 1671, **1740**, 136; 1 August 1671, **1760**, 179; 23 August 1671, **1776**, 207; late September 1671, **1791**, 268; 15 November 1671, **1824**, 361; 21 November 1671, **1826**, 365; 2 December 1671, **1835**, 390; 23 December 1671, **1849**, 427; 5 February 1671/2, **1888**, 524; 10 February 1671/2, **1895**, 532; 8 March 1671/2, **1918**, 580
— from De Graaf: 19 June 1671, **1729**, 114; 21 March 1671/2, **1931**, 610

— from Grew: 12 March 1671/2, **1921**, 586
— from Hannemann: 3 January 1671/2, **1858**, 448
— from Helmfeld: 3 May 1671, **1691**, 33; 15 November 1671, **1823**, 359
— from Hevelius: 21 April 1671, **1683**, 3; 9 June 1671, **1718**, 85; 27 September 1671, **1792**, 271; 28 February 1671/2, **1915**, 568
— from Hill: 13 July 1671, **1747**, 155; 20 February 1671/2, **1905**, 544
— from Hjärne: 23 November 1671, **1829**, 373
— from Huygens: 28 October 1671, **1807**, 313; 3 February 1671/2, **1886**, 517; 30 March 1672, **1944**, 635
— from Kirkby: 16 September 1671, **1790**, 268; 9 December 1671, **1838**, 393; 10 February 1671/2, **1898**, 535
— from Kisner: 12 May 1671, **1694**, 36
— from Le Bourgeois: 31 October 1671, **1810**, 325
— from Leibniz: 29 April 1671, **1688**, 22; 8 June 1671, **1716**, 76; 10 June 1671, **1721**, 91; 15 October 1671, **1799**, 292
— from Lister: 28 April and 13 May 1671, **1696**, 43; 22 May 1671, **1703**, 57; 30 May 1671, **1711**, 69; 31 May 1671, **1712**, 71; 14 June 1671, **1726**, 105; 5 July 1671, **1741**, 137; 17 July 1671, **1751**, 163; 25 August 1671, **1778**, 212; 13 September 1671, **1787**, 263; 16 October 1671, **1800**, 300; 28 October 1671, **1808**, 317; 11 November 1671, **1819**, 354; 10 January 1671/2, **1863**, 462; 24 February 1671/2, **1910**, 555; 19 March 1671/2, **1929**, 604
— from Malpighi: 24 May 1671, **1705**, 60; 22 October 1671, **1805**, 308; 22 January 1671/2, **1879**, 503; 5 March 1671/2, **1917**, 577; 26 March 1672, **1936**, 614
— from Mauritius: 19 March 1671/2, **1927**, 596; 22 March 1671/2, **1932**, 612
— from Newton: 6 January 1671/2, **1861**, 461; 18 January 1671/2, **1871**, 482; 29 January 1671/2, **1883**, 509; 6 February 1671/2, **1891**, 528; 10 February 1671/2, **1896**, 533; 20 February 1671/2, **1904**, 544; 16 March 1671/2, **1923**, 591; 19 March 1671/2, **1928**, 604; 26 March 1672, **1937**, 617; 30 March 1672, **1941**, 626
— from Pall Björnsson: 13 July 1671, **1750**, 158
— from Pardies: 8 July 1671, **1744**, 143; 10 October 1671, **1794**, 281; 3 January 1671/2, **1859**, 451; 30 March 1672, **1942**, 626
— from Ray: 3 July 1671, **1738**, 132; 12 September 1671, **1786**, 258
— from Sachs: 16 June 1671, **1727**, 107; 29 October 1671, **1809**, 321
— from Selbie: 28 April 1671, **1686**, 13
— from Sluse: 8 July 1671, **1745**, 145; 17 December 1671, **1843**, 401
— from Swammerdam: 26 March 1672, **1938**, 617
— from Sylvius: 13 May 1671, **1698**, 48; 8 June 1671, **1717**, 83; 15 August 1671, **1774**, 205
— from Tenison: 7 November 1671, **1816**, 344
— from Thevenot: 28 October 1671, **1806**, 310
— from Vernon: 23 November 1671, **1830**, 383; 27 December 1671, **1853**, 431; 30 December 1671, **1854**, 431; 17 January 1671/2, **1870**, 478; 20 January 1671/2, **1877**, 497; 27 February 1671/2, **1914**, 567
— from Vogel: 25 July 1671, **1755**, 173; 11 August 1671, **1771**, 198; 1 November 1671, **1811**, 330; 31 January 1671/2, **1885**, 512
— from Wallis: 9 May 1671, **1692**, 36; 13 May 1671, **1699**, 50; 2 June 1671, **1713**, 72; 10 June 1671, **1719**, 88; 27 June 1671, **1736**, 128; 4 August 1671, **1761**, 181; 10 August 1671, **1770**, 195; 13 August 1671, **1772**, 202; 16 August 1671, **1775**, 205; 6 November 1671, **1815**, 341; 23 November 1671, **1828**, 372; 27 November 1671, **1833**, 387; 14 January 1671/2, **1865**, 466; 18 January 1671/2, **1872**, 482; **1873**, 484; 5 February 1671/2, **1889**, 527
— from Werden: 29 April 1671, **1689**, 30; 24 June 1671, **1732**, 117
— from Willughby: 21 April 1671, **1684**, 9; 10 July 1671, **1746**, 153; 24 August 1671, **1777**, 209
— from J. Winthrop: September 1671?, **1789**, 265; 28 November 1671, **1834**, 389
— from W. Winthrop: 17 October 1671, **1803**, 305
— from Witsen: 10 December 1671, **1839**, 396

LETTERS FROM
— to E. Bartholin: 22 February 1671/2, **1907**, 548
— to Beale: 20 June 1671, **1730**, 116; 27 June

1671, **1734**, 126; 1 July 1671, **1737**, 132; 25 July 1671, **1756**, 176; 14 September 1671, **1788**, 265
— to Bernard: 27 June 1671, **1735**, 126; 6 February 1671/2, **1890**, 527
— to Borelli: 2 November 1671, **1812**, 337
— to Cassini: 26 August 1671, **1779**, 216; 15 January 1671/2, **1868**, 475
— to Cornelio: 9 February 1671/2, **1893**, 529
— to Dodington: 12 June 1671, **1725**, 105; 14 November 1671, **1822**, 358; 22 December 1671, **1847**, 422; 18 January 1671/2, **1874**, 490; 9 February 1671/2, **1894**, 532; 23 February 1671/2, **1909**, 555; 26 February 1671/2, **1912**, 565
— to Fermat: 7 August 1671, **1765**, 190; 25 January 1671/2, **1881**, 506
— to Flamsteed: 20 May 1671, **1702**, 57; 8 August 1671, **1766**, 190; 25 November 1671, **1831**, 387; 12 December 1671, **1841**, 398; 16 February 1671/2, **1901**, 541
— to De Graaf: 16 October 1671, **1801**, 303
— to Hevelius: 29 May 1671, **1709**, 67; 12 June 1671, **1723**, 97; 9 November 1671, **1817**, 349; 18 March 1671/2, **1924**, 591
— to Hill: ?30 August 1671, **1780**, 220
— to Huygens: 22 July 1671, **1752**, 167; 14 October 1671, **1798**, 291; 1 January 1671/2, **1856**, 443; 15 January 1671/2, **1866**, 468; 12 February 1671/2, **1899**, 536; 11 March 1671/2, **1920**, 584
— to Kirkby: 29 May 1671, **1710**, 69; 12 January 1671/2, **1864**, 466; 18 March 1671/2, **1926**, 596
— to Kisner: 24 July 1671, **1754**, 172
— to Le Bourgeois: 11 November 1671, **1820**, 355
— to Leibniz: 24 April 1671, **1685**, 10; 12 June 1671, **1724**, 99; 5 August 1671, **1762**, 182; 28 September 1671, **1793**, 277
— to Lister: 27 May 1671, **1707**, 63; 10 June 1671, **1720**, 89; 24 June 1671, **1731**, 116; 13 July 1671, **1748**, 150; 27 July 1671, **1757**, 176; 4 September 1671, **1785**, 257; 12 October 1671, **1797**, 289; 21 October 1671, **1804**, 316; 4 November 1671, **1814**, 339; 18 November 1671, **1825**, 364; 23 December 1671, **1850**, 428; 24 January 1671/2, **1880**, 505; 10 February 1671/2, **1897**, 534; 27 February 1671/2, **1913**, 566
— to Malpighi: 14 December 1671, **1842**, 398;

18 January 1671/2, **1875**, 491; 22 February 1671/2, **1908**, 551
— to Newton: 2 January 1671/2, **1857**, 447; 20 January 1671/2, **1878**, 502; 27 January 1671/2, **1882**, 508; 8 February 1671/2, **1892**, 528; 17 or 19 February 1671/2, **1903**, 543; 16 March 1671/2, **1922**, 590; 23 March 1671/2, **1933**, 612; c. 26 March 1672, **1939**, 619
— to Ott: 15 January 1671/2, **1867**, 474
— to Pardies: 10 August 1671, **1767**, 191; 18 December 1671, **1844**, 412; 29 January 1671/2, **1884**, 509
— to Ray: 3 June 1671, **1715**, 75; 31 August 1671, **1781**, 251; 11 October 1671, **1795**, 286
— to Sachs: 22 December 1671, **1845**, 417
— to Selbie: 24 May 1671, **1704**, 60
— to Sivers: 23 March 1671/2, **1935**, 614
— to Sluse: 28 April 1671, **1687**, 15; 21 November 1671, **1827**, 368; 4 March 1671/2, **1916**, 571
— to Sylvius: 5 July 1671, **1742**, 138
— to Tenison: 23 December 1671, **1851**, 430
— to Toinard: 15 February 1671/2, **1900**, 538
— to Vernon: 4 December 1671, **1836**, 392; 11 December 1671, **1840**, 397
— to Vogel: 1 September 1671, **1783**, 252; 14 November 1671, **1821**, 356; 26 December 1671, **1852**, 430; 23 March 1671/2, **1934**, 613
— to Wallis: 9 May 1671, **1693**, 36; 1 August 1671, **1759**, 179; 5 August 1671, **1763**, 184; 10 August 1671, **1768**, 193; 15 August 1671, **1773**, 204; 4 November 1671, **1813**, 339; 11 November 1671, **1818**, 354; 26 November 1671, **1832**, 387; 5 December 1671, **1837**, 393; 30 December 1671, **1855**, 443; 9 January 1671/2, **1862**, 462; 16 January 1671/2, **1869**, 478
— to Werden: 24 July 1671, **1753**, 172
— to Willughby: 29 April 1671, **1690**, 32; 16 May 1671, **1701**, 56; 13 July 1671, **1749**, 158; 27 July 1671, **1758**, 178; 31 August 1671, **1782**, 252; 11 October 1671, **1796**, 288
— to J. Winthrop: 18 March 1671/2, **1925**, 594
Olearius, Adam: *Voyages and Travels ... of Ambassadors*, 355 n3; *Die Gottorfische Kunst-Kammer* (Schleswig, 1666), 375, 379, 383 n1
Omphalius, Mr., 303, 304
Opera diverse. See Baliani, Giovanni Battista

Opera mathematica. See Wallis, John
Opera omnia. See Gassendi, Pierre; Goltzius, Hubrecht
Optics: 16, 19, 295, 299; burning mirrors, 523; lens-grinding machines, 25, 28, 281, 283, 295, 298; luminescence, 327, 329; non-spherical lenses, 315, 316, 444, 446, 518, 521; refraction, 452, 457, 578, 579; wave motion, 455, 459. *See also* Huygens, Constantijn; Leibniz, Gottfried Wilhelm; Newton, Isaac; Ott, Johannes
Opuscula mathematica. See Tasse, Johann Adolph
Origen: *Contra Celsus*, 343 n3
Origo formarum et qualitatum. See Boyle, Robert
Orta, Garcia da (16th cent.), 331, 333, 613; *Coloquios dos simples e drogas* (Goa, 1563), 334 n7, 514, 516
Osservazioni intorno alle Vipere. See Redi, Francesco
Ott, Franz (1614–91), 475 n
OTT, JOHANNES (1639–1717), xxi, 25, 28, 292, 296; identified, 475 n; *Cogitationes physico-mechanicae de natura visionis* (Heidelberg, 1670), 29 n10, 474, 545–46, 574, 576
— Letter to: 15 January 1671/2, **1867**, 474
Oughtred, William: *Clavis mathematica* (London, 1631), 282, 284
Overbury, Sir Thomas, "Characters" of, 186
Oxford University, 123; history of, 93. *See also* Hyde, Thomas, *Catalogus . . .*
Oxhuwen (Oxehufvud), Mr., 377, 382

Paillet (or Palliot), Pierre (1608–98), 385, 386 n8
PÁLL BJÖRNSSON (1621–1706):
— Letter from: 13 July 1671, **1750**, 158
Palmer, John (1612–79), 140
Panama, 139
Papin, Nicolas: *Considerations sur le traité "Des passions de l'ame de Descartes"* (Paris, 1652), 112
PARDIES, GASTON-IGNACE (1636–73), xxi, 95 n3, 385, 523; identified, 145 n; address, 451, 456; *Deux machines propres à faire les quadrans* (Paris, 1673), 460 n2; *Discours de la connoissance des bestes* (Paris, 1672), 456, 460, 626, 627; *Discours du mouvement local* (Paris, 1670), 122, 125 n23, 143, 144, 145 n, 385; *A Discourse of Local Motion by A.M.* (London, 1670), 122, 125 n23, 191, 192, 385; *Elemens de Geometrie* (Paris, 1671), 144–45, 191, 192, 413, 415; *Globi coelestis in tabulas planas redacti descriptio* (Paris, 1674), 385, 386 n7, 392; *Horologium thaumanticum duplex* (Paris, 1662), 452, 457, 460 n2; on Leibniz, 281, 283; on mechanics, 385, 392, 413, 415, 452–56, 457–60; *Remarques sur une lettre de M. Descartes touchant la Lumiere* (n.p., n.d.), 144, 145 n1, 191, 192; *La Statique ou La Science des Forces Mouvantes* (Paris, 1673), 453, 458, 460 n4—summary of, 453–60, 478, 483, 484–89
— Letters to: 10 August 1671, **1767**, 191; 18 December 1671, **1844**, 412; 29 January 1671/2, **1884**, 509
— Letters from: 8 July 1671, **1744**, 143; 10 October 1671, **1794**, 281; 3 Janaury 1671/2, **1859**, 451; 30 March 1672, **1942**, 626
Parsons, William, third Earl of Rosse (1800–67), xxiv
Pascal, Blaise (1623–62): *Essay pour les Coniques* (Paris, 1650), 510
Pathologiae cerebri. See Willis, Thomas
Pears, 54
Pecquet, Jean (1622–74), xxvii, 448, 450, 500; and eye, 523, 524 n5
Peirce, Captain, 266
Peiresc, Nicolas Claude Fabri de (1580–1637), 93, 111, 121; his manuscripts, 94, 96 n22. *See also* Gassendi, Pierre
Pell, John (1611–85), 127; *Idea of Mathematicks* (London, 1650), 93; *Tabula numerorum quadratorum* (London, 1672), 546, 574, 576. *See also* Rahn, J. H.
Pendulum. *See* Mechanics
Pereyra, Gomez: *Antoniana margarita* (Medina del Campo, 1554), 16, 19, 146, 148, 151–53, 368, 370
Perrault, Claude (1613–88), 117 n3, 171 n3
Perry. *See* Cider and perry
Petit, Pierre (1594 or 1598–1677), 386 n9
Petty, Sir William (1623–87), 566; his double-bottom boats, 501, 539, 540—model of, 501, 539, 540, 567
Pharmacology, Brazilian, 220–48. *See also* Medicine
Philips, Henry (fl. 1648–77), 295, 299
Philosophia veterum. See Le Grand, Antoine
Philosophical Transactions, xx, xxv, 139, 143, 144, 199, 201, 253, 322, 324, 392; contents of, 92, 139, 147, 149, 153, 255, 429, 474, 477;

errors in, 93–94, 123, 154 n4, 302, 307; Latin translation of, xxi, 146, 148, 332, 334, 385, 392, 513, 515, 629, 632; printing in, 24, 28, 339–40, 443, 445; requests for, 6, 11, 12, 31, 118, 282, 284, 314, 316, 413, 415, 417, 419, 452, 456, 584–85, 635, 636
Philosophie tirée des anciens .... See Roure, Jacques du
Philosophus autodidactus. See Abu Bakr ibn Al Tufail
Phoranomica. See Jungius, Joachim
Photicae. See Tasse, Johann Adolph
Physica demonstratio. See Cazré, Pierre de
Physica subterranea. See Becher, Johan Joachim
Physiognomie, and Cheiromancie. See Saunders, Richard
Physiology: birds' feathers, 589; source of blood, 448, 450. See also Descartes, René; Plants; Reproduction, mammalian
Phytologia Britannica. See How, William
Picard, Jean (1620–83), xix, xx, 8 n9, 219, 272, 274, 331, 333, 548, 549; *Mesure de la Terre* (Paris, 1671), 171 n3, 199, 200, 392, 431, 478, 523, 548, 549—English summary of, xxii, 431–37, 478–81, 497–501—; and sunspots, 199–201, 218, 219, 350, 351, 369, 371; at Uraniburg, xix, 194, 198–201, 271, 273, 350, 351, 523, 548, 550, 591, 593; *Voyage d'Uranibourg* (Amsterdam, 1736), 195 n3
Pierre, Daniel de, 597, 599
Piso, Wilhelm: *De medicina Brasiliensis libri IV* (in *Historia naturalis Brasiliae*, Amsterdam, 1648), 220–51, 466; *Historiae naturalis & medicae Indiae occidentalis libri V* (in *De Indiae utriusque re naturali et medica libris XIV*, Amsterdam, 1648), 220–51, 466, 483
Pitt, Moses (fl. 1654–96), 82 n7, 171 n8, 429
Plantarum umbelliferarum distributio nova. See Morison, Robert
Plants, 199, 201; anatomy of, xxii–xxiii, 89, 462–65, 505; Brazilian, 222–48; circulation of sap, 9–10, 32, 52–53, 56, 63; excrescensies on, 63, 71–72, 90, 116, 132–33, 154, 156, 163–66, 176, 178, 215, 263–64, 317–19, 605. See also Grew, Nehemiah; Lister, Martin; Malpighi, Marcello
Platt, Sir Hugh (d. c. 1611), 254; *Garden of Eden* (London, 1675), 256 n8
Plattes, Gabriel: *A Discovery of Subterraneall Treasure* (London, 1639, 1653, 1679), 77, 80, 277, 279

Pliny, the Elder: *Natural History*, 261, 319, 420, 421, 462, 590 n5
Pliny, the Younger: *Epistles*, 261, 262
Plus Ultra. See Glanvill, Joseph
Pneumatics, 369, 370, 406, 411; Torricellian experiment, 139
Pocock, Edward (1604–91), 372, 387–88, 397, 514, 516, 613; *The Nature of the drink Kauhi or Coffee* (Oxford, 1659), 331, 333, 357, 358, 372, 387, 430, 513, 515. See also Abu Bakr ibn Al Tufail
Poisons, 223, 227, 231–34, 237, 241, 245–48, 394; Spanish arrow, 199, 201, 331, 333, 514, 516
Ponthon, Mr., 385
Porpoise, 133, 251, 258–62, 286
Posidonius, 432
Power, Henry (1623–68), 295, 299; *Experimental Philosophy* (London, 1664), 300 n16
Praefactory Answer to Mr. Henry Stubbe. See Glanvill, Joseph
Praeludia botanica. See Morison, Robert
Praxeos medicae. See Sylvius, Franciscus
Present State of the United Provinces. See Aglionby, William
Prince Rupert's drops, 321, 323
Probier Büchlein. See Fachs, Modestin; Schreittmann, Cyriac
Prodromus omnium fere scientiarum Italice, 37, 39
Propositiones geometricae sex. See La Loubère, Antoine de
Prose de' Signori Accademici Gelati di Bologna. See Capponi, G. B.
Pro veteri medicina. See Schuyl, F.
Ptolemy, 432
Pyrologia mimica. See Wittie, Robert

Quaestio triplex. See Seneschall, Michel
"Quantum in se est", 294, 300 n7

Rahn, J. H.: *Introduction to Algebra ... alter'd and augmented* by Dr. J. P[ell], trans. T. Branker (London, 1668), 282, 284
Ramlovious, Dr., 513, 515
Rancher, Mr., 291, 469, 470
Ranelagh, Lord. See Jones, Richard, Viscount Ranelagh
Rapin, René: *La comparaison de Platon et d'Aristote* (Paris, 1671), 282, 284, 413, 415

Rauwolff, Leonhard: *Aigentliche Beschreibung der Raisz . . . in die Morgenlander* (Laugingen, 1582–83), 613
Ravius (Rau), Christian (1603–77): *Dei summam honorem . . . ex . . . chronologia biblica* (Kiel, 1670), 174, 175
RAY, JOHN (1627–1705), xix, 156, 157, 188, 584 n4; *Catalogus plantarum Angliae* (London, 1670), 319, 556; *Catalogus plantarum circa Cantabrigium nascentium* (Cambridge, 1660), 165, 254; and entomology, 133, 156–57, 210–11, 212, 319; and Lister, 71, 75, 90, 116, 132–33, 137, 156, 163, 364; and natural history, 254; on porpoise, 133, 251, 258–62, 286; on snails, 213; on vegetable excrescencies, 154, 176, 178
— Letters to: 3 June 1671, **1715**, 75; 31 August 1671, **1781**, 251; 11 October 1671, **1795**, 286
— Letters from: 3 July 1671, **1738**, 132; 12 September 1671, **1786**, 258
Recherches & Observations sur les Vipères. See Bourdelot, l'Abbé
Redi, Francesco (1626–97), 213, 385, 605; and Charas, 620–25, 629, 632; *Esperienze intorno a diverse cose naturali* (Florence, 1671), 321, 323; *Esperienze intorno alle generazione degl'insetti* (Florence, 1668), 71, 132, 146, 149, 163, 165, 213; *Lettera . . . sopra alcune opposizione . . . intorno alle vipere* (Florence, 1670), 287; *Osservazioni intorno alle Vipere* (Florence, 1664), 321, 323
Reed, Richard, 52–55, 123
Reformed Commonwealth of Bees. See Hartlib, Samuel
Regius. See Le Roy, Henri
Regnauld, André de (d. ?1702), 568
Reichelt, Julius (1637–1719), 596, 598, 599, 603 n
Relation d'un Voyage fait dans la Mauritanie. See Frejus, Roland
Relatione dello Stato presente dell' Egypto. See Wansleben, Johann Michael
Remarques sur une Lettre de M. Descartes touchant la Lumiere. See Pardies, Gaston-Ignace
Renaldini, Carlo (1615–98), 424, 426
Reproduction, mammalian, xxi, 114, 115, 610, 611
Rhodagini, Ludovicus Coelius (1450?–1525), 493
Ribadeneira, Pedro (1527–1611), 121

Ricci, Michelangelo (1619–82), 406, 411
Riccioli, Giovanni Battista (1598–1671), 120; *Almagestum novum* (Bologna, 1651), 87 n2, 437; *Geographia et hydrographia reformata* (Bologna, 1661), 500
Richer, Jean (d. 1696), 317 n7
Richmond, Charles Stuart, Duke of (1639–72), 548, 549, 550 n1
R. J., *Lettre d'un philosophe à un Cartésien* (Paris, 1672), 626, 627
Robert, Nicolas (1610–84), 117 n3
Robinson, John (1575–1625), 121
Rohault, Jacques (1620–73), 92, 146, 148; *Traité de Physique* (Paris, 1671), 95 n5, 122, 146, 148
Rolfinck, Werner (1599–1673), 38, 40; *Chimia in artis formam redacta* (Jena, 1661; Geneva, 1671), 146, 148
Rondelet, Guillaume: *De piscibus marinis* (Lyons, 1554–55), 133, 258–62
Rosa Ursina. See Scheiner, Christoph
Rossini (author), 493
Rouchon, Père. See R. J.
Roure, Jacques du: *Philosophie tirée des anciens et des nouveaux auteurs* (Paris, 1652), 112
Royal Society: aims of, 253, 538–40; approval sought, 24, 28, 308, 309, 503–4; criticism of, xxv–xxvi, 119–20, 186, 483; fame of, xxi, 253, 448, 449, 558–561; method of, 398, 400; and priority, 447; repository of, 215, 257, 266, 502 n14; vacations of, 306, 326, 328, 502
Rudbeck, Olaus (1630–1702), xxi, 31, 117–18; inventions of, 30, 118
Rufine, James (c. 1649–93), 83, 84
Rupert, Prince (1619–82), 277, 279, 354, 355 n2, 364, 365 n1, 506
Russia, 33–35

SACHS, PHILIPP JACOB (1627–72), xx, 253, 255
— Letter to: 22 December 1671, **1845**, 417
— Letters from: 16 June 1671, **1727**, 107; 29 October 1671, **1809**, 321
Saggi di Naturali Esperienze. See Accademia del Cimento
St. Hilaire, M. de, 585
Salusbury, Thomas: biography of Galileo, 173, 174, 331, 333
Sampson, Henry (c. 1629–1700), 38, 40, 590 n

Sand, Christophe von den. *See* Sandius, Christopher

Sandius, Christopher (1644–80), 141; *Nucleus historiae ecclesiasticae* (Amsterdam, 1668), 141

Santorio, Santorio: *Ars de medicina statica* (Venice, 1614), 139

Sargeant, Mr. 179, 190 n, 207, 268, 363, 367, 390, 427, 532

Saunders, Richard, *Physiognomie, and Cheiromancie* (London, 1653), 326, 328

Saxe-Gotha, Duke Ernest I of (1601–75), 38, 40

Scaliger, Julius Caesar (1484–1558), 420, 421

Schacht, Lucas, 115 n1

Schaeffer, Sebastian (1631–86), 37, 39, 41 n22

Schaeffer, Wilhelm Ernst, 41 n22

Scheiner, Christoph (1575–1650), 406, 411; *Rosa Ursina* (Bracciano, 1630), 412 n4

Schenck, Johann Theodor (1619–71), 38, 40

Schneider, Conrad Victor (*c*. 1614–80), 38, 40

Schönborn, Johann Philip von, Elector of Mainz (1605–73), 78, 81, 295, 298

Schott, Gaspar, *Magiae universalis naturae et artis* (Würzburg, 1657–59), 77, 80

Schreittmann, Cyriac: *Probierbüchlein* (Frankfurt, 1578), 173, 174

Schulz, Gottfried, 11, 12, 102, 104, 173, 174, 277, 279, 321, 323, 332, 333, 334, 417, 419, 513, 515

Schuyl, F.: *Pro veteri medicina* (Leiden and Amsterdam, 1670), 37, 39

Schyrlaeus, Anton Maria (1597–1660), 597, 599, 600 n5; *Oculus Enoch et Eliae* (Antwerp, 1645), 600 n5

Screta, Heinrich: *Dessertatio physico-mathematica de causis ac natura auditionis* (Heidelberg, 1670), 292, 296

Sea Atlas. *See* Seller, John, *The Sea Atlas*

Seawater sweetened: 25, 28

SELBIE, ROBERT

— Letter to: 24 May 1671, **1845**, 417

— Letter from: 28 April 1671, **1686**, 13–14

Selden, John: *Marmora Arundelliana* (London, 1628), 93

Seller, John (fl. 1658–98), 139; *The English Pilot* (London, 1671), 142 n12; *The Sea Atlas* (London, 1671), 142 n12

Sendivogius, Michael (?1556–?1636), 78, 81

Seneca, 406, 411

Seneschall, Michel: *Quaestio triplex* (Liège, 1670), 17, 20

Senguerdius, Wolferdius: *Disputatio de tarantula* (Leiden, 1667), 535

Sharrock, Robert (1630–84), 187, 245; *History of the Propagation and Improvement of Vegetables* (2nd ed., Oxford, 1672), 254

Sheldonian Press, 93, 123

Shortgrave, Richard, 32 n3

Schrage, Johann Adam (?1617–87), 596, 599

Sidereus nuncius. *See* Galilei, Galileo

Simpson, William: *Hydrologia chymica* (London, 1669), 147, 149

SIVERS, HEINRICH (1626–91), xx; and Jungius, 199, 201, 512–13, 514–15, 614; and sunspots, 199, 200, 330, 332, 333, 335–36, 356, 357, 369, 371, 476, 477; and Tasse, 512, 514–15

— Letter to: 23 March 1671/2, **1935**, 614

Skippon, Philip (1641–91), 106

Skütt, Samuel, 272, 274

SLUSE, RENÉ FRANÇOIS DE (1622–85), xix; and Alhazen's problem, 146, 148, 168, 170, 314, 316, 370, 401–6, 407–11, 444, 446, 519, 521, 536, 537, 571, 575, 635, 637; and analysis, 406, 546; and books, 146–49, 545, 546, 572, 575; and chemistry, 17, 20, 146–47, 149, 368, 370, 407, 411–12; *De analysi* (in *Mesolabum*), 403, 408, 412 n1; *Mesolabum* (2nd. ed., Liège, 1668), 15, 19, 412 n1, 545, 572, 575

— Letters to: 28 April 1671, **1687**, 15; 15 November 1671, **1827**, 368; 4 March 1671/2, **1916**, 571

— Letters from: 8 July 1671, **1745**, 145; 17 December 1671, **1843**, 401

Smethwick, Francis, 317 n6, 444, 446, 518, 521, 536, 537

Smoking, 325, 328

Snel, Willebrord (1591–1626), 432, 437; *Eratosthenes Batavus* (Leiden, 1617), 438 n5, 500; *Hypomnemata mathematica* (Leiden, 1608), 490 n1

Society, customs of, 325–28

Some Considerations Touching the Usefulness of Experimental Naturall Philosophy. *See* Boyle, Robert

Southwell, Sir Robert (1635–1702), 538, 539, 540, 540 n2

Spadacrene. *See* Heer, Henricus ab

Spas, 147, 149, 597, 599

Spa water, artificial, 417, 418

Speaking trumpet. *See* Morland, Sir Samuel

Specimina philosophiae cartesianae. See Lipstorp, Daniel
Speculazioni di Musica. See Mengoli, Pietro
Speculazioni fisiche. See Montanari, Geminiano
Spiders, 72, 116, 210, 212, 264, 340, 555–56. *See also* Tarantulas
Spinoza, Benedict de (1632–77), 299 n3
Spontaneous generation. *See* Lister, Martin; Plants, excrescencies on; Ray, John; Redi, Francesco
Spragge, Sir Edward (d. 1673), 139
Sprat, Thomas: *History of the Royal Society* (London, 1667), 76, 79
Statique. See Pardies, Ignace-Gaston
Steel, new processes for making, 78, 81, 277, 279, 535
Steno, Nicholas (1638–86), 257, 396; *Discours ... sur l'anatomie du cerveau* (Paris, 1669), 40 n16—Latin translation (Leiden, 1671), 37, 39—; *De solido intra solidum naturaliter contento dissertationis Prodromus* (Florence, 1669), 37, 39, 214
Sterpin, John, 146, 148
Stevin, Simon: 'Van het Tauwicht,' in *Wisconstighe Ghedachtenissen* (Leiden, 1608), 485, 487, 490 n1
Stiernhelm, Georg, 31, 378, 382
Stochus, Dr., 513, 515
Stockholm, 30
Stoll, Mr. 25, 28
Streete, Thomas: *Astronomia Carolina* (London, 1661), 207, 208, 268, 362
Strena. See Kepler, Johannes
Strode, Sir William, 55
Stryk, Samuel: *De jure sensuum* (Frankfurt, 1665), 182, 183
Stubbe, Henry (1632–76), xxv, 93, 122, 140, 186, 188 n2, 254–55; *Campanella revived* (London, 1670), 256 n10; *Epistolary Discourse concerning Phlebotomy* (London, 1671), 256 n10; *The Lord Bacons Relation of the Sweating Sickness Examined* (London, 1671), 254
Suite des nouvelles Expériences. See Charas, Moise
Suite des observations. See Cassini, Giovanni Domenico
Summary ... of the Life of ... Descartes. See Borel, Pierre
SWAMMERDAM, JAN (1637–80), xix, xxi, 212–13; identified, 618 n; on anatomy, xxvii, 396, 617, 618; *Historia insectorum generalis* (Utrecht, 1669), 213; *Illustrissimae ... Regiae Societati ... hoc anatomici sui ... dedicat* (n.p., n.d.), 617, 618, 618–19 n; *Miraculum naturae* (Leiden, 1672), 619 n; on snails, 212–13
— Letter from: 26 March 1672, **1938**, 617
Sweden, mines in, 173, 174
Sylva Hercynia. See Thal, Johann
SYLVIUS, FRANCISCUS DE LE BOE (1614–72), 139; *Oratio de affectus epidemii* (Leiden, 1670), 83, 84; *Praxeos medicae idea nova* (Leiden, 1671), 37, 39, 83, 84, 94—(Frankfurt, 1671), 37, 39, 146, 149—; portrait of, 49
— Letter to: 5 July 1671, **1742**, 138
— Letters from: 13 May 1671, **1698**, 48; 8 June 1671, **1717**, 83; 15 August 1671, **1774**, 205
Synopsis optica. See Fabri, Honoré

T*abula numerorum. See* Pell, John
Tabulae long. ac lat. stellarum. See Hyde, Thomas
Tabulae Rudolphinae. See Kepler, Johannes
Tacke, Johann (c. 1618–75), 38, 40
Tangiers, 140
Tarantulas, 42, 301, 306–7, 340, 494–97, 529, 530, 534–35, 541, 555–57, 561–64, 566, 609
Tasse, Johann Adolph (1585–1654), 512, 514; *Arithmeticae empiricae compendium* (Hamburg, 1673), 512, 514; *Opuscula mathematicae* (Hamburg, 1699), 516 n1; *Photicae ... compendium* (Hamburg, 1678), 516 n1, 613
Teatro farmaceutico. See Donzelli, Giuseppe
Telescopes, 278, 280, 394, 501, 546, 568, 581 n3, 597, 599; Hooke's, 537, 568, 580; Leibniz's telescope, 292, 296; Newton's telescope, xxiii–xxiv, 443, 444, 445–46, 447, 461, 466–67, 468–73, 476, 477, 482, 501, 507–8, 509, 525–26, 530, 531, 536, 537, 538, 540, 541, 568, 581 n1, 585, 590, 591, 592, 593, 604, 613, 626—Huygens on, 507, 508, 592, 593
Temple, Sir William (1628–99), 31 n
Templer, John (d. 1678), 89, 91 n4
TENISON, THOMAS (1636–1715)
— Letter to: 23 December 1671, **1851**, 430
— Letter from: 7 November 1671, **1816**, 344
Terry, Edward: *A Voyage to East India* (London, 1655), 262
Thabit ibn Qurra, 547 n5
Thal, Johann: *Sylva Hercynia* (Frankfurt-am-Main, 1588), 513, 515

Theology, 123
Theorica medicearum planetarum. See Borelli, Giovanni Alphonso
THEVENOT, MELCHISÉDEC (*c.* 1620–92), 354, 373, 388, 392; *Relation de divers Voyages Curieux, IVe Partie* (Paris, 1672), 310–12, 313 n1
— Letter from: 28 October 1671, **1806**, 310
Third Dutch War, 330 n7, 610, 611, 618
Thomson, George (*c.* 1620–76), 254, 256 n10; Αιματιατις (London, 1670), 256 n10; Μιτοχυμιας ἐλεμχος (London, 1671), 256 n10
Tides, 92; in Brazil, 223, 238; in Euripus, 92, 282, 284, 450; in Iceland, 159, 161
Tobacco, 223, 227, 237, 241, 326, 328
TOINARD, NICOLAS (1629–1706), xxi, 501, 502 n14, 567; identified, 540 n; *Evangeliorum harmonia* (Paris, 1707), 540 n
— Letter to: 15 February 1671/2, **1900** 538
Torricelli, Evangelista (1608–47), 484, 487
Towneley, Christopher (1604–74), xix, 180 nn2 and 3
Towneley, Richard (1629–1707), xix, 179, 180 n2, 391, 428; and astronomy, 362, 365, 367, 390; his micrometer, 390, 581
Tractatus de corde. See Lower, Richard
Tractatus duo, prior de cycloide. See Wallis, John
Tractatus physicus. See Fabri, Honoré
Tractatus ... ubi mira acris. See Boyle, Robert
Tracts ... Touching ... Flame and Air. See Boyle, Robert
Trade and trade routes, 606–8
Traité de Physique. See Rohault, Jacques
Translation, importance of, 122
Travagino, Francisco, 62; *Super observationibus a se factis tempore ultimorum terrae-motuum ... disquisitio* (Leiden, 1669), 122, 125 n18
Trevor, Sir John (1626–72), 31
Troutbeck, John (d. 1684), 354, 364
True and exact history of Barbadoes. See Ligon, Richard
Tuba stentoro-phonica. See Morland, Sir Samuel
Tulp, Nicholas (1593–1674), xxvii, 619 n
Turini, Giulio, 424, 426
Tyrocinium Chymicum. See Beguin, Jean

Ulug Beg. See Hyde, Thomas
Upsala, 30–31
Uraniburg. *See* Picard, Jean

Uranometria. See Bayer, Johann
Usefulnesse of Experimental Naturall Philosophy. See Boyle, Robert

Vacuum, 293–99, 388, 414, 415–16, 452, 457
Vallet, Guillaume, 386 n7
Vallet, Jean Charles (1637–1713), 424, 426
Vauban, Sébastien le Prestre, Marquis de (1633–1707), 142 n20
VERNON, FRANCIS (?1637–77), xxii, xxvii, 171 n2, 372–73, 388, 412, 414, 483; and Cassini, 217, 218, 383–85, 398, 424, 425, 476, 477, 567, 568; and Collins, 438, 443; and Huygens, 167, 169, 315, 316, 445, 446, 467, 468, 469, 519, 521, 635, 637; and Picard, 431–37, 478–81, 497–501
— Letters to: 4 December 1671, **1836**, 392; 11 December 1671, **1840**, 397
— Letters from: 23 November 1671, **1830**, 383; 27 December 1671, **1853**, 431; 30 December 1671, **1854**, 431; 17 January 1671/2, **1870**, 478; 20 January 1671/2, **1877**, 497; 27 February 1671/2, **1914**, 567
Veterum geometria promota in septem de cycloide libris. See La Loubère, Antoine de, *De cycloide*
Vipers. See Bourdelot, l'Abbé; Charas, Moise; Lister, Martin; Redi, Francesco
Vision, restoration of, 37, 39, 177, 213–14
Vitae Renati Cartesii. See Borel, Pierre
Viviani, Vincenzo (1622–1703), 173, 174, 331, 333, 424, 426
VOGEL, MARTIN (1634–75), xx, 354, 371; and botany, 199, 201, 331, 333, 357, 358, 443, 512–16; history of the Lincei, 173, 174; life of Galileo, 173, 174, 331, 333, 513, 515; and sunspots, 199, 200, 218, 219, 330, 332
— Letters to: 1 September 1671, **1783**, 252; 14 November 1671, **1821**, 356; 26 December 1671, **1852**, 430; 23 March 1671/2, **1934**, 613
— Letters from: 25 July 1671, **1755**, 173; 11 August 1671, **1771**, 198; 1 November 1671, **1811**, 330; 31 January 1671/2, **1885**, 512
Voituret, Anthelme (*c.* 1618–83), 8 n9
Volcanoes in Iceland, 160, 162
Vossius, Gerard John (1577–1649), 319
Vossius, Isaac (1618–89), 140–41, 311, 313
Voyage d'Uranibourg. See Picard, Jean
Voyages: to Cayenne, 315, 316, 317 n7; to

Mauritania, 93. *See also* Thevenot, Melchisédec

Voyages and Travels. See Olearius. Adam

Voyage to East India. See Terry, Edward

WALLIS, JOHN (1616–1703), 93, 191, 192, 386, 527; *An Answer to three papers of Mr Hobbes* (London, 1671), 179 n; *Arithmetica infinitorum* (Oxford, 1655), 206, 281–84, 486, 489, *Commercium epistolicum* (Oxford, 1658), 282, 284, 285 n3; controversy with Hobbes, xx, 128–31, 169, 171, 179, 181, 195–97, 202–4, 205–6; *De sectionibus conicis* (in *Opera mathematica*), 281–84; health, 93, 168, 170, 181; *Hobbius Heauton-timorumenos* (Oxford, 1662), 206; and Horrox, 545, 547 n3, 573, 576; on Leibniz, 73–74, 99–103, 255, 277, 279, 292, 296, 341–43, 388; *Mechanica, sive de motu tractatus geometricus, pars prima* (London, 1670), 67, 68, 529, 530—*pars secunda* (London, 1670), 67, 68, 529, 530; *pars tertia* (London, 1671), 17, 20, 88, 168, 170, 278, 279, 281, 283, 291, 314, 316, 337, 338, 369, 371, 406, 411, 444, 446, 467, 469, 470, 483, 484–89, 518, 521, 529, 530, 545, 548, 549, 572, 575, 591, 593—; *Opera mathematica* (Oxford, 1656–57), 285 n2; and Pardies, 483–89, 509, 510, 627, 628; and tides, 92; *Tractatus duo, prior de cycloide* (Oxford, 1659), 281–84

— Letters to: 9 May 1671, **1693**, 36; 1 August 1671, **1759**, 179; 5 August 1671, **1763**, 184; 10 August 1671, **1768**; 193; 15 August 1671, **1773**, 204; 4 November 1671, **1813**, 339; 11 November 1671, **1818**, 354; 26 November 1671, **1832**, 387; 5 December 1671, **1837**, 393; 30 December 1671, **1855**, 443; 9 January 1671/2, **1862**, 462; 16 January 1671/2, **1869**, 478

— Letters from: 9 May 1671, **1692**, 36; 13 May 1671, **1699**, 50; 2 June 1671, **1713**, 72; 10 June 1671, **1719**, 88; 27 June 1671, **1736**, 128; 4 August 1671, **1761**, 181; 10 August 1671, **1770**, 195; 13 August 1671, **1772**, 202; 16 August 1671, **1775**, 205; 6 November 1671, **1815**, 341; 23 November 1671, **1828**, 372; 27 November 1671, **1833**, 387; 14 January 1671/2, **1865**, 466; 18 January 1671/2, **1872**, 482, **1873**, 484; 5 February 1671/2, **1889**, 527

Wallis, John, the Younger (b. 1651), 88

Wansleben, Johann Michael: *Relatione dello Stato presente dell' Egypto* (Paris, 1670), 95 n6

Ward, Seth (1617–89), xxiii, 127, 386, 501

Weather observations, 30–31, 118, 140, 443, 466, 483; in Brazil, 220–21, 235–36; in Iceland, 158, 161

Wedel, Georg Wolfgang (1645–1721), 38, 40

WERDEN, JOHN (1640–1716), xxi; identified, 31 n

— Letter to: 24 July 1671, **1753**, 172

— Letters from: 29 April 1671, **1689**, 30; 24 June 1671, **1732**, 117

Werden, Robert, 31

Werner, Georg Christoph, 25, 29, 76, 79

Whiteside, D. T., 412 n4, 547 n6

Whorwood, Brome (1615–84), 187

Wickins, John (?1644–1719), 591 n

Wiesel, Johannes (b. *c.* 1583), 597, 599

Wilkins, John (1614–72), 133, 590 n; *Essay towards a Real Character* (London, 1668), 24, 28

Williamson, Sir Joseph (1633–1701), 609 n

Willis, Thomas (1621–75), 38, 39 322, 324, 417, 418; *De anima brutorum* (Oxford, 1672), 17, 20, 21 n13, 168, 170, 326, 328, 370, 371, 392, 430, 509, 510, 529, 531, 548, 549, 626, 627; *Of Fermentation* (London, 1659), 109, 110, 111 n5; *Pathologiae cerebri et nervosi generis specimen: in quo agitur de morbis convulsis et scorbuto* (Oxford, 1667), 407, 411

Willisel, Thomas, 134 n8

WILLUGHBY, FRANCIS (1635–72), xix, 157, 258, 262, 286, 289, 301, 364; and entomology, 153–54, 209–11, 212–13, 257, 263–64, 301, 307; on vegetable excrescencies, 154, 176, 178, 215, 263–64

— Letters to: 29 April 1671, **1690**, 32; 16 May 1671, **1701**, 56; 13 July 1671, **1749**, 158; 27 July 1671, **1758**, 178; 31 August 1671, **1782**, 252; 11 October 1671, **1796**, 288

— Letters from: 21 April 1671, **1684**, 9; 10 July 1671, **1746**, 153; 24 August 1671, **1777**, 209

Wilson, Thomas, 136, 179

Wing, Vincent (1619–69), 208; *Astronomia Britannica* (London, 1669), 282, 284, 366

Winthrop, Adam (1647–1700), 266

WINTHROP, JOHN (1606–76): gifts to Royal Society, 266–67, 305

— Letter to: 18 March 1671/2, **1925**, 594

— Letters from: September 1671?, **1789**, 265;

28 November 1671, **1834**, 389

WINTHROP, WAIT (1641/2–1717): identified, 306 n
— Letter from: 17 October 1671, **1803**, 305

Wiscontighe Ghedactenissen. See Stevin. S.

Witchcraft, 326–27, 329

WITSEN, NICOLAAS, xxi, 617, 618; identified, 397 n; *Aeloude en Ledendaegsche Scheeps-bouw en Bestier* (Amsterdam, 1671), 392, 397 n; and Russia, 396
— Letter from: 10 December 1671, **1839**, 396

Wittie, Robert: *Pyrologia mimica* (London, 1669), 147, 149, 150 n15

Wood, Anthony à: *The History & Antiquities of the Colleges and Halls of the University of Oxford*, 93—Latin version, 96 n9

Wren, Christopher (1632–1723), 25, 28, 188, 191, 192, 281, 283, 386; his beehive, 56 n13; his drawing instrument, 123; his lens-grinding instrument, 281, 283, 295, 298; on mathematics, 281, 283, 509, 510

Wroth, Sir John (d. 1671), 127, 524 n9

Wroth, Sir John, the Younger, 523

Wroth, Sir Thomas (1584–1672), 523

Wurtz, Mr., 38, 40

Zachun, Martin, 349, 351

Zucchi, Niccolo: *Nova de machinis philosophia* (Rome, 1649), 77, 80

Zunner, Mr., 11, 12, 102, 104

Zwelfer, Johann (?1618–68), 13

FOGLER LIBRARY